Consuming Pleasures

THE ARTS AND INTELLECTUAL LIFE
IN MODERN AMERICA

Casey Nelson Blake, Series Editor

Volumes in the series explore questions at the intersection of the
history of expressive culture and the history of ideas in modern
America. The series is meant as a bold intervention in two fields
of cultural inquiry. It challenges scholars in American studies and
cultural studies to move beyond sociological categories of analysis
to consider the ideas that have informed and given form to artistic
expression—whether architecture and the visual arts or music,
dance, theater, and literature. The series also expands the domain of
intellectual history by examining how artistic works, and aesthetic
experience more generally, participate in the discussion of truth
and value, civic purpose and personal meaning that have engaged
scholars since the late nineteenth century.

CONSUMING PLEASURES

Intellectuals and Popular Culture
in the Postwar World

Daniel Horowitz

PENN

UNIVERSITY OF PENNSYLVANIA PRESS

PHILADELPHIA

#7482907900

Published by
University of Pennsylvania Press
Philadelphia, Pennsylvania 19104-4112
www.upenn.edu/pennpress

Printed in the United States of America on acid-free paper

10   9   8   7   6   5   4   3   2   1

Library of Congress Cataloging-in-Publication Data
Horowitz, Daniel, 1938–
    Consuming pleasures : intellectuals and popular culture in the postwar world / Daniel
Horowitz. — 1st ed.
        p. cm. — (The arts and intellectual life in modern America)
    Includes bibliographical references and index.
    ISBN 978-0-8122-4395-6 (hardcover : alk. paper)
    1. Popular culture—Economic aspects—United States—20th century. 2. Popular
culture—Economic aspects—Europe—20th century. 3. Consumption (Economics)—
United States—Psychological aspects—20th century. 4. Consumption (Economics)—
Europe—Psychological aspects—20th century. 5. Intellectuals—United States—
Attitudes—History—20th century. 6. Intellectuals—Europe—Attitudes—History—20th
century. I. Title. II. Series: Arts and intellectual life in modern America.
    E169.12.H675 2012
    306—dc23

                                                                            2011034159

To some of the colleagues and friends
who have sustained me over the years:
Bob Abzug, Ellen DuBois, Judy Smith, Char Miller,
Lynn Dumenil, Wendy Kline

And to Helen Horowitz
First, last, and always

Contents

Preface

As I neared completion of this book, I turned to Google to track down a quotation. Up on the screen came a 1937 article by Marion C. Sheridan titled "Rescuing Civilization through Motion Pictures." Right away I wondered if this was the Dr. Sheridan who taught me English in Hillhouse High School. Sure enough, the publication identified her as a teacher in my hometown, New Haven, at my high school, one that employed some teachers with Ph.D.s from Yale. She had earned hers in 1934, and perhaps a combination of sex discrimination, a desire to remain in New Haven, a genuine commitment to high school education, and the Great Depression persuaded her to teach in an urban public school that in the 1950s maintained some aspects of its elite character. The 1960s radical Andrew Kopkind, who preceded me in high school by several years, later described her as "the hated English teacher, Dr. Sheridan, Dr. Marion C. Sheridan, this big, right-wing Irish fascist." Memory plays funny tricks on us all. Accurately or not, I remember Andy Kopkind living in the only Republican household in our neighborhood and Dr. Sheridan as a slight and severe but not especially political woman, more bluestocking than "right-wing Irish fascist."[1]

What struck me when her 1937 article appeared on the screen is that almost three-quarters of a century before I completed this book, my high school English teacher had written on a subject central to *Consuming Pleasures*: how to deploy sophisticated literary theory, in her case that of the British critic I. A. Richards, to understand popular culture. "The way to rescue civilization, by way of the motion picture," Dr. Sheridan asserted in the year before I was born, "would be to sharpen in every possible way the perceptions of those who attend, so that they will be critical of what they see and cognizant of and responsive to the best when it was projected before them on the so-called 'silver-screen.'"[2]

Because in *Consuming Pleasures* I present a series of intellectual biographies through which I explore how writers from a wide range of vantage points found ways of seeing that broke through the prevailing understandings, I wish I could show that this book had its origins deep in my past, perhaps in a class where Dr. Sheridan taught me how to appreciate all those double feature B movies I saw at Saturday matinees. But honestly, I cannot. What I can do is appreciate

the continuities and contingencies of my life as a student. More salient to my
project is the subject I have been working on since the early 1970s, the story of
how intellectuals have responded to affluence and consumer culture. This book
thus continues an exploration I began with *The Morality of Spending: Attitudes
toward the Consumer Society in America, 1875–1940* and continued in *The Anxieties of Affluence: Critiques of American Consumer Culture, 1939–1979*. In those
books I traced shifts in moral stances toward consumer culture.[3]

In the United States, I argued, traditional moralism was the pervasive approach until the 1920s. Writers in this vein positively valued self-restraint and
criticized the supposed immorality of workers and their families, who, it was
assumed, relied on alcohol, gambling, and permissive sexual expression as they
pursued problematic pleasures. In the 1920s a different approach, the new moralism, developed among intellectuals. Owing much to a Protestant jeremiad
tradition, new moralists argued that consumer culture weakened the moral
fiber of citizens, tempting them to excess. They focused more on how capitalism generated consumer goods than on the reception of those goods by ordinary Americans. They relied on a sense of moral superiority, a belief that critics
of shopping were wiser than shoppers themselves. Intellectuals, they believed,
participated in a high culture that was more intriguing and enriching than the
debased low culture in which consumers indulged. Fears of declension, excess,
and pleasure suffused the writings of those who found mass culture problematically degrading. For many intellectuals, consumer culture raised questions
about authenticity and the political implications of defining American superiority in terms of the increased acquisition of consumer goods. Above all, they
believed, commercial culture threatened to undermine the stability, character,
and restraints necessary to sustain American values. This tradition culminated
beginning in the late 1930s, when New York intellectuals, influenced by the rise
of totalitarianism in Europe, set the terms of debate in ways that made it difficult for cultural observers in the immediate post–World War II period to talk
seriously and analytically, let alone appreciatively, about popular culture.

The new moralism was influential well into the 1960s, when the alternative that this book traces began to take hold. Postmoralism, not unrelated to
postmodernism, underwrote an embrace of pleasure and symbolic exchange,
often avoiding or transcending moral issues that bothered earlier generations
of intellectuals. With its arrival, American writers shifted their attention from
an emphasis on self-restraint to the achievement of satisfaction through commercial goods and experiences, a change this book explores.

Sometimes I think my timing is exquisitely off. *The Morality of Spending*
and *The Anxieties of Affluence*, explorations of the tradition of moralistic scorn,

appeared in the middle and at the height of the postwar boom in consumer culture. Work on this book, which explores the emergence of ideas about the pleasures of consumerism, began in 2004 as that boom reached it apogee and neared completion when, in response to the economic crises of the century's first decade, talk of a return in public discussions to thrift, prudence, and simple living reappeared. Perhaps Dr. Sheridan would have appreciated the ironies.

Introduction

Understanding Consumer Culture
in the Post–World War II World

In North America and Western Europe between 1950 and 1972, writers came to envision popular culture and consumer culture in fresh and provocative ways. Across national boundaries and in a series of major essays and books, they increasingly shifted attention from condemnation to critical appreciation, albeit almost always with hesitation or qualification. New perspectives on commercial culture emerged from multiple directions from outside the United States and from unexpected quarters of American intellectual and cultural life. Writers critiqued cultural hierarchies and moralistic approaches to commercial culture, instead emphasizing playfulness and pleasure. The symbolic processes by which individuals and groups communicate with each other about their identities were central to how these writers explored the power and richness of consumer culture. More and more, they pondered the sexual and gendered dynamics of commercial culture. They looked favorably on working-class culture and turned a more skeptical eye on elite sources of creativity. They reworked traditions—including the heritage of Marxism—in ways that took into account an increasingly wide range of social and cultural conditions.

Advocates of new ways of looking at consumer culture challenged the division between high and low that had long held sway, replacing hierarchical approaches with parallel ones. They shifted from an idealistic, elitist view of Culture with a capital "C" to an anthropological outlook on culture, with a lowercase "c." They reenvisioned the relationship between producers and consumers by making the exchanges between them more dynamic and, at times, the location of resistance. With writers and readers from the United States at the center, the story of these changes begins in Western Europe in the early 1950s and ends in the early 1970s when American intellectuals increasingly appreciated the rich inventiveness of popular culture. Yet as they moved to embrace consumer culture they generally did so equivocally, with a dialectical process that hardly moved in a simple direction.[1]

If the movement from hesitant to fuller appreciation of popular culture characterizes this book's principal trajectory, it also captures another significant shift. When the story begins critics were divided on whether to call what they witnessed "mass culture," a generally derogatory term suggesting tastelessness, degradation, and imposition, or "popular culture," which denoted something more positive precisely because it was a genuine expression of creativity that emerged from below. Over time, scholars and critics replaced these terms with the more capacious and more ambiguous notion of "consumer culture." The latter includes not only the intangibles of creative production but also the material objects and the institutions such as department stores and amusement parks that proffered commercial goods and experiences. The term "consumer movement" was coined in the 1920s; "consumerism" in the 1950s; and "consumer culture" in the 1960s. In order to avoid repetition this book sometimes uses key phrases—mass, popular, consumer, and commercial cultures among them—interchangeably. Moreover, there is about these terms a certain messiness and uncertainty. Yet one of the book's contributions is to show how over time writers shifted the terms of discussion from popular/mass culture to consumer culture.[2]

Changes in attitudes toward pleasure occurred in these years. Early twentieth-century observers had hardly denied the power of pleasurable experiences connected with commercialization but they linked them with what they considered lowly, corrupting, and escapist indulgences such as excessive drinking or illicit sex. As these moralistic attitudes waned, writers increasingly focused on pleasure, playfulness, and sexuality as key aspects of a more positive interpretation of commercial culture. They wrote of the way automobiles, clothing, the built environment, comics, advertisements, and movies enabled people to gain emotional enrichment from commercial goods and experiences. They argued for a positive, life-enhancing connection between consumer culture and pleasure, one in which playfulness and sexual passion were central. Many of the authors under consideration here—including Theodor Adorno, Max Horkheimer, Paddy Whannel, and Stuart Hall on the left and Marshall McLuhan on the right—decried how capitalism repressed pleasure rather than facilitated its genuine fulfillment. Radicals evoked a utopia, with capitalism overturned or harnessed, where pleasure would be more accessible. McLuhan adopted a variant on this argument, albeit with different emphases, especially with paradise in the Christian past rather than the postcapitalist future. Almost all writers worked to distinguish between authentic and false pleasures, between integrated and fragmented human experiences, but they no longer always linked the latter with popular culture. In the end what is striking is that although they explored the positive nature of new connections between pleasure, playfulness, commodities, and sexuality, they generally did so tentatively, ambiguously, skeptically, or quizzically.[3]

An extension and, in some ways, more profound transformation of this thinking about the links between pleasure and commercial culture came from those most committed to same-sex sexuality, including Roland Barthes, some of the pop artists, and Susan Sontag. "The anarchy of capitalism," one queer theorist has commented in discussing 1960s camp and 1970s disco, "throws up commodities that an oppressed group can take up and use to cobble together its own culture." "No other minority has depended so heavily on commercial enterprise to define itself," remarked the scholar and gay rights activist Dennis Altman, speaking mainly of male homosexuals. "One of the ironies of American capitalism," he continues, "is that it has been a major force in creating and maintaining a sense of identity among homosexuals." It is surely no accident that the two writers under consideration here who were respectively bisexual and homosexual, Sontag and Barthes, most fully connected performance with the sensuality of ordinary goods and experiences. Yet, as with others, so with Sontag: the connection between sex and commercialism was hardly straightforward or fully positive. Even when in her 1964 "Notes on 'Camp'" Sontag linked unconventional sexuality with unconventional albeit commercial goods and experiences, she both hid her own sexuality and kept her distance from mass culture.[4]

At the same time an understanding of consumer culture as a means of symbolic communication emerged. Writers saw popular culture as a way people conveyed to one another information about their individual identities and common experiences, and did so through the evocation of rich, complicated, and multiple meanings. Moreover, these writers increasingly believed that society came to understand itself through how commercial culture used symbolic markers to convey broader dimensions of social meaning. Again, earlier writers hardly denied the importance of symbolic exchanges. Moralists in the Progressive period objected to how working-class girls used stylish clothing. Cultural critics of the 1950s mocked extravagance in middle-class houses and automobiles as degrading symbolic renderings of identity. In contrast, from the 1950s until the early 1970s and beyond, intellectuals increasingly asserted that consumer culture was symbolically dense, complicated, and susceptible to illumination through careful, probing analyses. In other words, the consumer's experiences, communicated to a wider world, were as full of multiple meanings as were a wide variety of other, often more highly regarded cultural offerings, such as literary poems or novels. Over time, writers came to see symbolic communication as a source not of moral degradation but of possibilities that pointed toward how people used common, everyday objects to think about themselves and then communicate their understandings to others. We see this all around us, how the objects we purchase and experiences we have convey who we are, as individuals and as a society.

Over time challenges to the commitment to cultural hierarchy intensified. Before 1950 most critics, on both the left and the right, insisted on the ability to make critical judgments that ranked cultural productions from top (the Bible, Aristotle, Shakespeare) to bottom (folk tales, comic books, B movies). Moreover, well before midcentury, modernist artists such as James Joyce, T. S. Eliot, Pablo Picasso, and Gustav Mahler playfully explored the connections between popular and high cultures. Although most critics continued to insist on the ability to discriminate, increasingly after 1950 they called into question the clarity and persuasiveness of cultural hierarchies. More and more they came to develop a sense of the reciprocal relationships between levels, with creativity moving fluidly over once-fixed boundaries. Initially, as in the case of essays on popular culture by Umberto Eco written in the late 1950s, the central task remained using the elevated to probe the meanings embodied in the lowly. Yet even in the 1950s, there were hints of a more complicated position, one in which a creative and dynamic (but not unambiguous) tension existed between hierarchical and egalitarian modes of expression. As on other issues, a turning point came with the London-based Independent Group (IG). In the early to mid-1950s its members adopted the relativistic notion that it was important to judge every cultural field by standards appropriate to it, as they insisted on replacing a pyramid of cultural productions with a continuum. Even so, many of those who came after continued to develop yardsticks that separated the excellent from the mediocre.[5]

In time a fundamental transformation in the understanding of cultural hierarchies emerged as observers shifted from using high culture to explore ordinary objects to seeing the ordinary as a site of aesthetic innovation that in turn significantly shaped what was once considered transcendently high. Walter Benjamin articulated this position in the mid-1930s, and after 1950 others did so by emphasizing the rich inventiveness of contemporary commercial culture. Over time, writers placed high and low in parallel positions. Some went even farther. The New Journalist Tom Wolfe and with more reservations the sociologist Herbert Gans located creativity in the lower middle class and in the process appreciated nonelite forms of cultural expression that they found at least as worthy of admiration as their elite counterparts.

The shattering of cultural hierarchies, however, was never wholly unequivocal. Nonetheless, from the early 1950s on, the die was cast and nowhere more consequentially than in the shift from locating resistance in elite high culture, as Matthew Arnold and F. R. Leavis had done, to envisioning salvation from below. The elitist tradition remained powerful, presenting issues with which writers continued to struggle: Sontag reformulated the elite avant-garde tradition by making it powerfully adversarial and Robert Venturi saw creativity coming from above and below. However, already with David Riesman's *The Lonely Crowd* (1950) there were hints of a notion that innovation came not from the avant-garde but from the popular. From then on the trajectory was clear as major commentators connected creativity not with elite productions but with the ordinary artifacts, not wafting down from above but rising from below.

Cultural critics reconfigured ideas about hierarchy by shifting from literary criticism to anthropology and sociology. Robert S. Lynd and Helen M. Lynd in *Middletown: A Study in American Culture* (1929) had offered an evocative ethnography of how Americans lived amid a world of commercial goods and experiences. Still, well into the 1950s literary analysis reigned but its application to the texts of mass media led in different directions. In the 1950s American apostles of modernism were generally hostile to popular culture. In the same decade Eco and Barthes used sophisticated literary criticism to illuminate and at times appreciate popular culture. In Britain, the deployment of literary analysis to understand popular culture operated in a tradition that went back at least to Matthew Arnold and culminated in the work of Richard Hoggart, who at the same time shifted focus toward the anthropological.[6]

The difference between Hoggart's *The Uses of Literacy* (1957) and *The Popular Arts* (1964) by Stuart Hall and Paddy Whannel encapsulates many of the major changes this study charts. Those on the anti-Stalinist left, who had rejected what they felt politics and the popular contaminated, gave way to a post-Stalinist development of cultural Marxism that was more appreciative of democratic impulses. A native-born Briton was followed by a major postcolonial figure. From literary criticism emerged cultural studies. Focus shifted from working-class families to working-class youth. Attention moved from grave concern with new forms of media to a more or less full acceptance of new media. The cultural turn among intellectuals underwrote new understandings of popular culture. Writing in the early to mid-1960s, writers solidified the shift

from literary analysis to anthropology, although some who preceded and followed them would find ways of combining the two traditions.

Simultaneously writers transformed how they understood the relationships between producers and consumers of popular culture and commercially
produced commodities and experiences. This reconfiguration proceeded in a
number of directions, from a relatively limited notion of feedback, to a more
dynamic sense of reciprocity, and eventually to an emphasis on resistance. Reciprocity did not always involve democratic or popular sentiments. However,
some writers gave reciprocity a more democratic emphasis. Over time, writers ascribed greater and greater power to spectators whom they envisioned as
engaged in what came to be seen as dynamic exchange relationships. Analyzing new technologies increasingly played a key role in illuminating producer-
consumer dynamics, something seen early with Benjamin and then in the 1950s
with Eco, Jürgen Habermas, and members of the IG.[7]

Eventually these thinkers shifted from focusing on reciprocity to identifying the uses of cultural products as the means of resistance. As early as 1950,
David Riesman had tentatively hinted at what it meant to think of some elements of popular culture as potentially liberating. Similarly, in the 1950s others worked to transform audiences, once envisioned as passive, into active,
sophisticated, and even resisting interpreters. Hall and Whannel identified the
critical shift here, identifying postwar working-class youth as key players in a
change from a mass, seemingly passive, and undifferentiated audience of consumers to a society composed of insurgent social groups whose reactions were
potentially utopian. This is hardly to say that resistance was always connected
to popular impulses, for many writers conceptualized avant-garde resistance
with adversarial impulses, even as they saw that resistance emerging from the
lavishing of adoring but ironic attention on consumer goods and experiences.[8]

New, more positive attitudes to the popular and commercial played a central role in fostering these changes. Writers offered a broad range of alternatives: serious but critical consideration, ambivalence, hesitant or even adoring
fascination, equivocal endorsement, and finally, in some cases, full-throated acceptance. For decades many critics had written about popular culture without
stopping to analyze it or had taken popular culture seriously but concluded it
was problematic. As 1950s observers increasingly paid it serious attention, they
did so in ways that ranged from supposedly neutral social science analysis to
hesitant fascination, and even admiration. The story recounted here begins in
earnest with the reluctant engagement and then moves through a full range of
responses that rested on various intensities of endorsements combined with detachment, irony, skepticism, equivocation, and ambiguity. Indeed, many writ-

ers often held contradictory positions. Some melded moral disdain, a search for new cultural hierarchies, intense interest, and a critique of commodification in complicated mixtures. For still others discrimination remained critical as they mixed distance and fascination. Sometimes discrimination was something a cultured elite exercised; at other times, the emphasis was on its deployment by an adversarial elite.

Over time, uneven and often less than full understandings gave way to less ironic, less skeptical, and more hopeful appreciations. For some there were even hints of the utopian possibilities consumer culture opened up, a note that would develop more fully after 1972 but that was present earlier. Indeed with members of IG, some of whom eventually migrated to the United States, there emerged a vision that is closest to an unqualified endorsement of mass media, popular arts, and consumer culture. Yet even here complications are especially illuminating. Members of the IG had coined the term "pop art" to describe commercial products on which they lavished adoration. Yet the artists among their ranks, along with American pop artists, deployed irony and skepticism that usually kept full acceptance in check. From a 1950 essay by Herbert Gans on popular culture to Denise Scott Brown and Robert Venturi's *Learning from Las Vegas* slightly more than two decades later, unalloyed embrace was moderated by reservations based by commitments to discrimination and complexity.

Why Perspectives Changed

Charting change is one thing; explaining it, another. The shift from moral threat to symbolic promise, in full bloom by the 1970s and 1980s, rested on a series of changes both in consumer culture itself and in ways of understanding society. After more than a decade and a half of privation stretching from the onset of the Depression in 1929 to the end of World War II in 1945, the United States and Europe experienced a sustained period of economic growth. As one IG member, Lawrence Alloway, acknowledged in the 1950s, the growing prevalence of advertisements, household products, Hollywood movies, and popular music meant that some observers grew up experiencing new elements of commercial culture as part of their daily lives. This made it increasingly difficult for observers to deny or see as temporary or totally unacceptable the onrush of popular culture. Over time, the notions that it was important to prevent Americans from underconsuming or that commercial goods and experiences were either exciting or suppressing the masses became clichés. For more and more Americans and Western Europeans, production in factories and on farms was out of sight while consumption in department stores and shopping centers was all too visible. Changes in the economy made consumerism so prevalent that it was hard to ascribe the consumption of goods simply or primarily to moral weakness. This, in turn, undercut the explanatory power of familiar and increasingly shopworn jeremiads. Moreover, beginning in the late 1960s the collapse of the Fordist capitalism of the immediate postwar period (an unwritten agreement among corporations, government, and unions that steady incomes, ample benefits, and job security elevated millions into the middle class and made possible the spread of affluence) unleashed a series of cultural changes that helped underwrite new visions of consumer culture, which in turn emphasized the importance of individual subjectivity and the search for new, more fluid forms of cultural expression. In turn, all these changes shaped the very terms of influential discussions.

The larger forces at work—in the economy, society, and politics—powerfully prompted writers to rethink their approach. Television, along with suburbanization and family formation, shaped the 1950s in profound ways. Some responded with horror, intensifying their concerns about how mass media fostered conformity; others relied on more complex formulations. Some observers worked imaginatively to develop new and more accepting approaches. In the next decade, the war in Vietnam and movements for social justice, the civil rights movement especially, led many to challenge previously unchallenged authority. Popular insurgencies thus played a critical role in underwriting fresh perspectives, opening up space for an appreciation of the ordinary. The result was skepticism about the ways of understanding commercial culture an earlier generation of intellectuals had articulated. Significantly, it was in the 1970s, when in some quarters the energy crisis undercut confidence in the nation's future and fostered commitments to restraint, that one sees the development of a fuller welcoming of the pleasures of consumer culture. Deindustrialization and fears of national decline played a critical role in shifting attention from production to consumption.

However, if economic, social, political, and cultural changes fostered new and more positive understandings of commercial culture, shifts in attitudes, ideas, and approaches deserve at least equal attention. Indeed, in his 1990 discussion of postwar debates about mass culture Eugene Lunn goes so far as to say that what shaped the conversations was less "the expansion of the media when discretionary income and leisure time were growing in welfare-state societies" than the period's "shift in cultural outlook and political valence." The change from seeing commercial culture as a cause of moral decline to understanding it as a source of pleasure rested on a number of conceptual shifts. More and more, writers turned their attention from production to consumption, from a producerist approach to a consumerist one. Empirical studies of how people actually consumed culture revealed complications and resistance.[9]

Generational shifts played important roles, especially the waning of the memories of totalitarianism and of the prominence of writers for whom Stalinism and Nazism were central. An examination of Bernard Rosenberg and David Manning White's *Mass Culture: The Popular Arts in America* (1957), the locus classicus of its generation's most prominent writers on popular culture, makes clear the implications of the position of American intellectuals who came of age in the 1930s and 1940s. For many writers, the experiences of those decades connected disdain for the Popular Front's love affair with popular culture with concern about how Stalinists and Nazis had used mass media to come to and hold on to power. All of this had made highly problematic the serious, let alone sympathetic, consideration of the meaning of popular culture. Eventually as that generation of New York and émigré intellectuals lost its cultural authority, their works no longer had capacious explanatory power.[10]

It would be hard to overstate how important the anti-Stalinism of the late 1930s through the early 1950s was to the period's development of views of mass media. Debates for and against popular culture were part of the intellectual and political climate of the post-1945 world. In this context, it is notable that *Consuming Pleasures* focuses on only a few conservatives, McLuhan and Wolfe among them. More typically, the project of considering the meanings of commercial culture was a task of generations of the anti-Stalinist and then of the non- or post-Stalinist left. As the historian Paul Gorman has shown, many of the key debates over commercial culture took place within the left, debates that in the end involved changing attitudes to common people as one generation of writers gave way to another. In many cases, writers came to appreciate consumer culture because, suspicious of all fixed ideological systems including totalitarianism and rigid cultural elitism, they instead welcomed fluidity and complexity.[11]

A new set of imperatives emerged over time, in part as a result of how the waning or reconfiguration of Marxism underwrote these changes. Beginning in the 1950s, cultural Marxists and social democrats challenged the hold of what they saw as a more vulgar Marxism. Old understandings no longer seemed adequate. A broader and more cultural perspective made it possible for some to come to terms with postwar working-class culture in which the presence of mass media played a more important role than workplace exploitation. The result was a shift from how writers located resistance in elite culture, characteristic of anti-Stalinists, to finding it among workers and youth, typical of a generation for whom the fight over Stalinism was no longer salient. In turn, these shifts led to a questioning of the usefulness of drawing a sharp line between high and low culture.

Changes in attitudes toward race, class, gender, and sexuality played critical roles in underwriting fresh understandings. To my surprise, given the extraordinary importance of African American culture in creating a vital popular culture, race appears in these discussions as a minor and often contradictory theme. This is strikingly clear in the work of the two authors under consideration who had some African heritage, C. L. R. James and Stuart Hall. They are major postcolonial figures who ended up living in places that had much different racial configurations from those they experienced in their Caribbean homelands, something that goes part way to explaining how they did and did not engage issues of racial identity in United States and Britain. In uncharted territory, they were struggling with how to understand multiple forms of inequality and social analysis but in ways that provided no easy opening for the treatment of race. Moreover, how many of the writers under consideration avoided race and neglected or paid negative attention to jazz is especially striking in light of what Ralph Ellison and Amiri Baraka (LeRoi Jones) wrote in the period, as early, in Ellison's case, as 1946. Drawing on a rich combination of vernacular traditions and elite cultural criticism, in dialectical ways they appreciated how African American expressive culture, jazz especially, revealed the resilience and richness of that community's traditions and more generally provided a means of understanding American culture in suggestive ways.[12]

A shift in attitudes toward social class assumed considerable importance. Most New York intellectuals, who combined anti-Stalinism and literary modernism, distanced themselves from the expressive culture of the working class or lower middle class from which many of them came and instead admired elite or avant-garde culture. In contrast, the way Gans and Wolfe rethought issues of social class and cultural power reveals how critical was an emphasis on pleasure, symbolic communication, the leveling of hierarchies, and the emphasis on reciprocity. More broadly, other observers, having rejected the disdain of New York intellectuals for working-class and mass cultures, were able to develop fresh understandings of popular culture that relied on symbolic exchanges among ordinary people, rather than creativity among the few.

Gender and sexuality also helped transform discussions of the meaning of consumer culture. For most of the twentieth century, commentators saw mass culture as female (soft, passive, sentimental, artificial) as opposed to the masculine high culture (hard, active, and somehow more real). In much of the writing surveyed in this book we enter a highly gendered world. This is apparent Wolfe's world of tough men and absent women. In contrast, beginning in the late 1960s the work of a new generation of feminist writers favorably inclined to (or at least intrigued by) consumer culture countered the anticommercialism of those schooled in the Old Left like Betty Friedan. Feminists offered fresh perspectives and in the process, women, rather than being weak subjects or victims, became active agents in shaping and resisting commercial culture.[13]

All these changes in ideas, in the economy, among generations, and in attitudes underwrote what is one of the most fundamental shifts in American social thought in the last half of the twentieth century. In *Transcending Capitalism: Visions of a New Society in Modern American Social Thought* (2006), the historian Howard Brick writes of a crisis in the late 1960s that undermined long-standing patterns of social thought. This crisis provided an opening in which cultural analysis took the place of social thought based on an increasingly narrow view of economic issues. If understanding the new dynamics of capitalism commanded the attention of American intellectuals from the 1940s well into the 1960s, then coming to terms with the new dynamics of commercial culture was among the most compelling projects for intellectuals working in the last third of the century. In some ways, culture and style replaced politics and economics as the center of attention—or more precisely, a new vision combined politics and style.[14]

Rules of the Game

To explain these shifts in how writers understood consumer culture, this book focuses on a series of key texts and their creators that broke new ground and over time had a major impact. I do not see my task as making sharp and explicit judgments about writers. Rather, I work hard to get inside their minds, to see how they interacted, to understand the world as they understood it, and to play them off one against another. In each case, I explore how authors reached the point where, sometimes hesitatingly or unevenly, they made a conceptual breakthrough. I look at the relationship between biography, reading, and writing, for only an intensive examination of the lives of writers makes it possible to explore where ideas come from, how they develop, and what it means to write transformative works. Although some of what I say about individual books or authors is not especially new, I break fresh ground by juxtaposing one text with another in ways that dramatize a series of important themes. I demonstrate patterns and connections previously obscured by treating these texts and their authors in isolation. My consideration of an author typically ends at the point of a breakthrough book or article, even when the writer's later work might be germane to the topic under discussion. Looking at these authors as a group and carefully charting the development of their thought makes it possible to reveal the connections and play of ideas that so profoundly reshaped cultural criticism.

What I am describing had deep roots in American life, but the focus on the period since 1950 makes it possible to track the emergence of profoundly new ways of thinking about consumption that turned away from declension and toward appreciation. Writers after 1950 were hardly the first to be fascinated by and even embracing of popular culture. Beginning in the late seventeenth century, British authors explored the pleasures of commercial goods. At least as early as the antebellum period, a wide range of writers countered the narrative of the emergence of a consumer economy as the story of declension with a more complicated and even positive interpretation. In the late nineteenth and early twentieth centuries American novelists such as William Dean Howells and James Weldon Johnson, as well as social scientists such as Simon Patten, far from simply recoiling from mass culture, creatively engaged it in their work. In the early 1920s the cultural critic Gilbert Seldes and the novelist Anzia Yezierska wrote appreciatively about popular culture. Beginning in the mid-1920s cultural workers in major metropolitan areas developed responses to mass media that were neither procapitalist nor derogatory. In the middle third of the century, from within the Popular Front, cultural workers envisioned what Shannan Clark has called a social consumerism, a positive, social democratic vision of consumerism that stood in opposition to what members of the Frankfurt School would produce. Above all, in his pathbreaking discussion of the laboring of American culture during the middle third of the twentieth century, Michael Denning has recovered the modernist avant-garde that emerged from below. He shows how artists and intellectuals, often coming from humble backgrounds and working in a wide range of genres, produced symbolically rich written and visual material. Although not always fully realized, their writings nonetheless involved "a complex engagement with the popular and vernacular arts" that wrestled suggestively with the tension between capitalist production of mass culture and how ordinary people used popular culture as ways of negotiating modern life.[15]

Indeed, it is not too much to suggest that the story of how writers positively engaged consumer culture began at least in the late nineteenth century, was somewhat interrupted by the anti-Stalinists who dominated discussions from the late 1930s until the early 1960s, and then resumed with the writers under consideration here. Turning our eyes from what writers wrote to what advertisers promoted and at least some consumers actually enjoyed, we recognize that, as the historian Alexis McCrossen has noted, desire and pleasure were a "set of conditions that gained positive associations after the turn of the century," if not even earlier. In that sense, intellectuals came late to the table of consumer delights.[16]

Nor does the story I tell include all possible figures. I focus on academics who worked within disciplinary boundaries and those who crossed them; writers embedded in the academy and those without sustained institutional locations; artists and architects; cultural and social critics who were journalists, professors, independent public intellectuals. Yet coverage is selective, more intensive than inclusive. Readers will have their own suggestions of what I should have included. For example, in Europe there were theorists whose work has underwritten or even articulated a new vision that focused on the symbolic power of commercial culture, complicated cultural hierarchies, and emphasized the resilience of its consumers. One thinks of the work of Mikhail Bakhtin, Marcel Mauss, Henri Lefebvre, Guy Debord, Raymond Williams, and Jean Baudrillard. In the United States there were empirical studies of communications, especially those initiated by Paul Lazarsfeld and Elihu Katz. The cultural geographer J. B. Jackson remains an innovative thinker who early on imaginatively explored the new consumer landscape. In immensely influential books, Norman O. Brown, Herbert Marcuse, and Charles Reich explored the relationships between capacious sexual pleasure and other kinds of enjoyment. Among New York intellectuals, so many of whom decried popular culture as kitsch (the German word for mass culture), Robert Warshow and Leslie Fiedler remained intrigued by what others simply denounced. In addition there was Dwight Macdonald's role in creating film criticism, and the incorporation of popular iconography into photography by Walker Evans and Robert Frank. Over time and with some exceptions such as McLuhan and Daniel J. Boorstin, the shift among conservatives from an organicist, tradition-related ideology to a free-market one meant that those on the left dominated the discussion more than those on the right. In other words, a project such as this relies on choices that shape a book that is simultaneously selective, encompassing, and suggestive.[17]

The main focus here is on the consequences of the flow (or blockage) of people and ideas across national borders, what the historian Thomas Bender has called the result of "the permeability of the nation at boundaries, the zones of contact and exchange among people, money, knowledges, and things." This book has the intellectual history of the United States more or less at the center. In terms of consumer culture and in other ways, the immediate postwar period seemed like the American Century. In response, some key European observers developed an appreciation of American consumer culture without necessarily admiring American politics or foreign policy. At a time when

American cultural power seemed full of promise to war-weary peoples, Japanese and European imperialisms were still much in evidence and the most aggressive aspects of American foreign policy were not yet fully revealed. The nature of the debates led me to range across national borders because writers were simultaneously raising similar questions in different places. There is a considerable body of scholarship on the cultural, social, and economic aspects of global consumer culture, but remarkably little on its intellectual history. Writing intellectual history across national borders opens up a range of choices, not all of which I have taken. This book is not explicitly a comparative history that looks at the ways writers in different cultures approached mass media. Even so, there is abundant evidence in its pages about distinctive national traditions: the penchant among Continental Europeans for theoretical approaches, as well as their distancing from Anglo-American moralism; the British tradition that over the years shifted from literary criticism to cultural studies; and the emphasis in the United States on both trenchant essays and empirical investigation.[18]

The historian James Kloppenberg has spoken of "a transatlantic community of discourse." This sometimes exists for discussions of consumer culture; in other cases, there is discourse without community, as writers drew on or spoke to one another without being members of a community, even an imagined one. Although there are some exceptions to the patterns of geographical mobility, many of the writers under consideration moved from country to country. Several members of the IG changed residence from Britain to the United States after living in their home country, where America was the land of their imagination. Stuart Hall and C. L. R. James grew up on Caribbean islands but spent most of their lives elsewhere. Although Denise Scott Brown lived much of her adult life in the United States, she was born in a small mining town in Northern Rhodesia (now Zambia); grew up in South Africa; studied in London, where she encountered members of the IG; traveled in Europe for three years; moved to the United States in 1958; and with her husband and professional partner Robert Venturi designed the Sainsbury Wing of Britain's National Gallery. Ideas travel if people do not always do so. This book tracks how, at a time when consumer culture itself transcended geographical borders, ideas and imaginations moved across national boundaries. In instance after instance it is possible to see how observers from one nation responded to the ideas and cultural productions of another.[19]

If ideas moved easily across oceans, mountains, and national borders, imaginations traveled even more creatively. It should come as no surprise that at the center of a book on how intellectuals came to see consumer culture in new, more positive ways is the fascination authors on both sides of the Atlantic had with American popular culture. What has been surprising is how varied but rarely negative were the European reactions to the likes of Donald Duck, Li'l Abner, Mickey Spillane, Charlie Chaplin, and Ella Fitzgerald. In light of the expectation of pervasive hostility to American commercial culture signaled by the significant body of scholarship on the topic, it is surprising how many outside observers viewed American popular culture positively. With rapt admiration, important European writers made clear that American popular culture was worthy of serious attention and analysis. Moreover, they did so at a time when American imports—of ideas, money, movies, books, music, and cartoons—played such a dynamic role in the recovery of Europe from World War II in ways that prompted many other intellectuals to raise questions about cultural imperialism.[20]

Context is critical here. In 1945 the United States emerged relatively unscathed by World War II, while much of Europe lay in ruins. Well into the 1950s, daily life in Western Europe remained austere, as nations, faced with what Tony Judt called "the prospect of utter misery and desolation," rebuilt their economies. Initially governments focused not on discretionary consumer items but on basics in order to rebuild devastated infrastructures and provide essentials, aided by the Marshall Plan. Not until the mid-1950s did most Western Europeans shift their attention from the deprivations of the past to the possibilities of the future.[21]

By the late 1950s, with an economic boom under way, Europeans experienced dramatic growth of discretionary incomes. Cultural elites stood in opposition to American popular culture, while most Europeans eagerly watched American films, listened to American music, and found in American consumer goods the comfort and ease they longed for. Yet at the same moment certain key influential European intellectuals came to a growing appreciation for American popular culture precisely when high culture, often state-subsidized, was flourishing. Significantly, these appreciators came from outside the usual realms of intellectual, political, and cultural authority: the Roman Catholic Church, traditional cultural elites, Christian Democrats, and the Communist Party.

The complex history of these ideas as they were emerging will help explain later developments in cultural theory. This book and its narrative grew from the ground up, from the writings beginning in the early 1950s by those under consideration, rather from theory down, in terms of postmodernism or cultural studies that developed most clearly in the 1970s and beyond. Some readers will inevitably wonder why this book is not framed as an essential part of the history of postmodernism or of cultural studies. With ample justification, scholars have seen in the writings of virtually everyone under consideration here evidence of the origins or flourishing of these two approaches. Yet while some will see in this book a discussion of the origins of these two movements and will be able to mine it as such, in what follows this is not my primary concern.[22]

After an Introduction, in Chapter 1 I examine Rosenberg and White's *Mass Culture* in order to understand the dominant ways in which intellectuals in the 1940s and 1950s thought about commercial culture. This influential book of essays makes it possible to understand the powerful hold that arguments about what was seen as totalitarian uses of popular culture had on contemporary discussions. I then turn to writers who because they were working outside American traditions could begin to think about cultural productions in new ways. Chapter 2, "Lost in Translation," examines writers who did some of their most important work before or at the time of the publication of Rosenberg and White's book but whose work remained unknown in the United States: Habermas, whose early work became available in English only later or not at all; Barthes, whose *Mythologies* did not appear in English until 1972; and Eco, whose essays written in Italian between 1959 and 1965 similarly remained untranslated for some years. This theme of writers whose work Americans had no access to in the 1950s continues in Chapter 3 as attention shifts to Benjamin, whose works of the 1920s and 1930s were not available in America until decades later, and James, whose *American Civilization* (1950) circulated privately at the time but appeared in published form only in 1993. In Chapters 4 and 5 the focus moves to three influential books: Riesman's *The Lonely Crowd* (1950), McLuhan's *The Mechanical Bride* (1951), and Hoggart's *The Uses of Literacy* (1957), an examination of which enables us to see the ambivalent embrace of popular culture in the 1950s. With some hesitancy and ambiguity this trio offered pathbreaking and richly suggestive ways of understanding postwar mass media. Although artists in the Independent Group, discussed in Chapter 6, approached American popular culture with some irony, little such ambiguity appears in the essays written by members of this group, who considered appreciatively the wonders of iconic American commercial culture. It was no accident that Alloway, a member of the IG, in 1963 curated the first major museum exhibit in the United States of pop art.

In some ways the pivotal point in the story of increasing appreciation of consumer culture comes in Chapter 7 with Hall and Whannel's *The Popular Arts* (1964). Although scholars have paid relatively little attention to this book, one of its authors, Hall, is a much-heralded creator of cultural studies. Chapter 8 shifts attention to social class in the United States, with a discussion first of Wolfe's breakthrough book, *The Kandy-Kolored Tangerine-Flake Streamline*

Baby (1965), which celebrated the texture and flashiness of the car culture of the early 1960s. This focus on class in America continues with two books by the sociologist Gans—*The Urban Villagers* (1962) and *The Levittowners* (1967)—which revealed how consumers challenged, neglected, or transformed what producers generated. The discussion of Sontag's 1964 "Notes on 'Camp,'" the focus of Chapter 9, provides a lens through which to view the interplay between sexuality and a new sensibility toward material objects. The story this book narrates culminates in Chapter 10 with a discussion of Reyner Banham's *Los Angeles* (1971), along with Robert Venturi and Denise Scott Brown's *Learning from Las Vegas* (1972), two enthusiastic considerations of popular culture. Here there emerged a more or less full welcoming of consumer culture that in the hands of later writers would intensify.

Newly available sources make it possible to explore many of these writers in fresh ways. Some of the material, such as the mid-1950s untranslated articles by Habermas, early works by Eco, and essays of the IG, appeared in relatively hard-to-find publications generally unfamiliar to scholars. In addition, my archival research has revealed information from sources largely unexamined by historians—Gans's 1950 essay written in a class for Riesman; Sontag's only recently available diaries; correspondence and drafts of unpublished books from McLuhan's papers; reports on Hoggart's early years in adult education; Wolfe's senior honors paper and his articles from the late 1950s and early 1960s for the *Washington Post*; the early writings of Whannel; and material from the papers of Denise Scott Brown and Robert Venturi. All this makes it possible to see the work of these well-known writers from fresh perspectives.

Although drawing on the contributions of others, this book breaks fresh ground.[23] As a historian I ask questions not considered by most scholars in other fields, especially about causation and change. Although in important ways it remains rooted in the intellectual history of the United States, more than any previous work, this book is transnational in scope. By juxtaposing works often considered alone, it continually explores the conversations writers had (or did not have) with one another.[24] In wide ranging and inclusive ways, this book asks a series of new questions about a new vision of consumer society. In its answers it offers a new understanding of the transformative visions that emerged between 1950 and 1972.

Terms of Endearment?

Finally, an equivocation of my own regarding consumer culture. Because this book charts the movement from hesitation to admiration, some readers will think I have gone native, overboard in my own welcoming of the popular. Yet the art of fifteenth-century Sassetta compels me more than that of twentieth-century Warhol. I enjoy performances of baroque operas and Mozart symphonies more than those by contemporary musicians, whose concerts my students have on relatively rare occasions been able to cajole me to attend. I hardly think all standards are bad because they are elitist, just as I recognize that corporate capitalism is more powerfully elitist than were members of Ivy League English departments of the 1950s. Moreover, it is important to remember that the story I chronicle—of the shift from moral scorn to playful engagement—is not a Whiggish narrative of progress toward a wholly laudable triumph of consumer culture. Costs, challenges, and opportunities pervade all the responses I examine—the oppositional, skeptical, ambiguous, and embracing. The impediments to a richer understanding of commercial culture were formidable, but overcoming them involved both loss and gain. If moralistic condemnation is problematic because of its biases and blind spots, then celebratory acceptance is even more worrisome for a number of reasons, including its frequent inattention to the causes and costs of excess—environmental degradation, the growing gap in wealth and income between the rich and everyone else, and the erosion of standards. Some of those who celebrate consumer culture are in danger of helping consumers accommodate to commercial capitalism. My measuring writers by a yardstick hardly means I approve of the end point that they strove toward or failed to arrive at.[25]

Chapter 1

For and Against the American Grain

During the 1950s, American intellectuals participated in a spirited debate over the impact of mass culture. Although leading observers were by no means unanimous in their perspectives, a number of themes dominated what they wrote. They focused most of their attention on middle-class Americans who, in a rush to put the Depression and World War II behind them, chased after materialistic goals that critics believed were more tempting than genuinely satisfying. Most observers assumed that powerful corporations tricked passive consumers into paying for commercial goods and experiences that offered false satisfactions. Memories of European totalitarianism haunted them as they worried that Americans did not have the moral strength to resist a popular culture that might erode character and undermine democracy. In the midst of the Cold War, they countered the threat of Soviet collectivism and of 1930s Popular Front culture with paeans to what they saw as distinctive American individualism. They fiercely debated the tension between elite and popular commitments. They worried that a combination of excessive femininity and aberrant sexuality infused popular culture and in turn threatened national well-being. They feared that advertising, television, public relations campaigns, and suburban living eroded cultural standards, raising the prospect of the ascendancy of the lowest common denominator. A tone of disappointment undergirded much of the discussion. One observer's incantation about "the silliness of television, the childishness of the comic strips, the triviality of the press" only served to underscore how locked-in many intellectuals in the postwar generation were to familiar and increasingly trite formulations.[1]

In the immediate postwar years, the locus classicus of these debates was the 1957 book *Mass Culture: The Popular Arts in America*, edited by Bernard Rosenberg and David Manning White, professors respectively of sociology at City College of New York and journalism at Boston University. The book appeared at a time when the issues it raised were urgent. "Marxism apart," remarked the sociologist Daniel Bell soon after, the theory of mass society, which he went on to link to the spread of mass culture, "is probably the most influential social theory in the Western world today." The year of *Mass Culture*'s publication, the historian Michael Kammen has written, was "when the whole debate over mass culture reached a crescendo in terms of sheer volume." Indeed, as Theodor Adorno remarked in 1962, "outrage at the alleged mass era has become an article for mass consumption." An examination of *Mass Culture*—what it contained and what it omitted, where its authors agreed and disagreed, its dead ends and potential breakthrough—provides the contexts essential in understanding the even broader issues discussed in *Consuming Pleasures*.[2]

Authors and Essays

In geographical, sociological, and political terms, certain patterns in the book were striking. Of the over four dozen authors, two—Walt Whitman and Alexis de Tocqueville—wrote in the nineteenth century. José Ortega y Gasset, George Orwell, Adorno, and Marshall McLuhan were the only twentieth-century figures who lived most of their lives outside the United States—in Spain, Britain, Germany, and Canada respectively. Of all the authors, only one, the Canadian-born Japanese American linguist S. I. Hayakawa, was what a later generation would call a person of color, an ethnic designation he would doubtlessly have opposed had the phrase even existed at the time. Indeed, in an essay in a book that rarely discussed jazz, let alone did so in positive terms, he looked favorably on jazz, albeit in terms that denied any distinctive African American contribution or perspective. As best as can be determined, Whitman was the only homosexual among the essayists. The anthropologist Hortense Powdermaker was the only woman who was the sole author of a contribution; Martha Wolfenstein and Patricia J. Salter, the only other women among the writers, each coauthored her essay with a man. Émigrés from Europe to America, most of them Jews who had stayed at least one step ahead of the Nazis, were prominently represented, comprising at least a fifth of the authors. Of those contributors born in the United States, about half were Jewish, at least in background. Others were native born, and primarily Protestant. Most authors were on the anti-Stalinist or non-Stalinist left. Ernest van den Haag was the only clearly identifiable conservative contributor then living in the United States. Yet when Rosenberg linked positions on popular culture with larger ideologies, he unintentionally revealed how problematic political labels were. He made clear that both "radicals" (he named Dwight Macdonald, Clement Greenberg, and Irving Howe) and "arch-conservatives" (he listed Ortega y Gasset and T. S. Eliot), "for opposite reasons, are repelled by what they commonly regard as vulgar and manipulative." In contrast, "liberals" (he mentioned Gilbert Seldes, David Riesman, and Max Lerner) expressed greater appreciation for mass culture. Thus the authors were mostly male, liberal or left, citizens of the United States, in 1957 in their late thirties to late fifties, and as likely to be Jewish as Protestant.[3]

Not surprisingly given the times, the authors focused relatively little on race, ethnicity, or class—as later generations understood those terms. Yet powerfully formative in the book's tone and arguments was the influence of Jews—both native born and émigré. The connection between Jewish background or identity, on the one hand, and interest in mass culture, on the other, is important but complicated. German, middle European, and American Jews had significant relationships to the production and consumption of varied types of culture. Jews were among the most important creators of a wide range of culture, from the avant-garde (Arnold Schoenberg), to middle-brow (George Gershwin), to mass or popular (Samuel Goldwyn or Al Capp). Jews were also avid consumers of varieties of cultures—in Europe from which they emigrated and in America as both immigrants and natives. Jews crowded the boardwalk of Coney Island and went to the opera or listened to chamber music. Some Jewish writers opposed what entrepreneurial Jews created, as when Jewish advocates of elite culture attacked popular culture. In other cases they were calling for respect for ethnically inflected popular culture that many critics of Christian background—and many Jewish ones as well—scorned or avoided. Whatever the sociological origins of concerns among Jews about popular culture, it is hard to overestimate the impact on them of an awareness of how Hitler had used mass media to advance Nazism.[4]

Gender raises other issues. As James Gilbert has written perceptively, many of those who worried about mass culture in the 1950s saw the problem in highly gendered terms. They linked the feminine with popular culture as "submissive, soft, flighty, emotional, and consumerist" and the masculine with modernist high culture as "productive, inventive, creative, action-oriented, and tough-minded." Thus in his opening essay Bernard Rosenberg wrote of how in *Madame Bovary* Gustave Flaubert pictured Emma's search for satisfaction as involving "an osmotic process that has only in our day come into its own as full-blown mass culture." In their essay, Paul Lazarsfeld and Robert Merton, two of the nation's most prominent sociologists, were sure that "the women who are daily entranced for three or four hours by some twelve consecutive 'soap operas,' all cut to the same dismal pattern, exhibit an appalling lack of esthetic judgment."[5]

In contrast to a feminized mass culture stood a masculine, elite one. It is hardly surprising that most of the producers of high culture whom these cultural critics heralded—Schoenberg, Pablo Picasso, D. H. Lawrence, James Joyce—were men. More than that, critics of mass culture saw elite or avant-garde culture as tough: representing intellect rather than sentimentality, the disciplined mind rather than the too easily pleasured sensibilities. Only partly hidden in all this was a fear of male homosexuality. If popular culture was feminized and swept up gay men in its wake, then a tough masculine high culture would protect against both the feminization of American culture and what many contemporaries assumed was its corollary, the influence of effete, homosexual men. As Adorno wrote in his essay in the volume, without adopting the position he was describing, popular culture pictured the artist as "an 'aesthete,' a weakling, and a 'sissy.'" Media tended "to identify the artist with the homosexual and to respect the 'man of action' as a real, strong man."[6]

Popular or Mass Culture and Its Discontents

Rosenberg and White set the book up as a dialogue between those who were optimistic and those who were pessimistic about mass or popular culture. They probably reached a compromise on the book's name with the word "mass" in the title, which Rosenberg as the acerbic critic doubtlessly preferred, standing in opposition to the phrase "popular arts" in the subtitle, which White, a cautious advocate, perhaps defended. The pairings were often of opposites, with Whitman and Herbert Gans, for example, on one side, and Ortega y Gasset, de Tocqueville, Macdonald, and Adorno on the other. Though they tried to be even-handed in their choices, the editors acknowledged that "there have been far more excoriators of mass culture than defenders," an imbalance their selections reflected.[7]

Most of the contributors to the book worked within a widely accepted ideology that many American intellectuals relied on to understand commercial culture for much of the twentieth century, which I have elsewhere called the new or modern moralism, an outlook that saw middle-class culture as degrading. In addition, many, especially the detractors, were haunted by the specter of the Popular Front. As one of the contributors wrote, what he called "the New 'Popular Front'" could undermine an "open society" built on "the prominence and persistence of a body of persons who remain skeptical, critical, querulous and deeply hesitant about popular imagination and taste." Many of the authors, especially the pessimists, believed that the spread of mass culture involved a revival of the Popular Front's rejection of ambiguity and an embrace of totalitarianism—a term then in fashion that combined Nazi and Soviet horrors. Tellingly, when Rosenberg and White reprinted Greenberg's 1939 "Avant-

Garde and Kitsch," they omitted some key passages in the essay, not only those that referred to events of the 1930s but also Greenberg's espousal of social- ist politics that did not fit well with the celebration of democratic capitalism common in 1957. Most but not all of the contributors engaged, if they did not actually embrace, the mixture of modernism and Marxism offered by those connected with or influenced by *Partisan Review* beginning in the late 1930s. As the historian Paul Gorman has written, they considered "the people to be passive victims of commercial entertainments" and believed "that the only ef- fective cultural countermeasure was to cultivate the most difficult arts."[8]

Rosenberg led off the debate with a short essay in which he excoriated contemporary American mass culture. A series of words that would appear throughout the book dominated his essay: sameness, interchangeable, dehu- manized, deadened, bored, alienated, lonely, entrapped, anxious, manipulated, and vulgar. "Never before have the sacred and the profane, the genuine and the specious, the exalted and the debased," he asserted, "been so thoroughly mixed that they are all but indistinguishable." He singled out examples to drive home his point. "Shakespeare is dumped on the market along with Mickey Spillane," he wrote, "and publishers are rightly confident that their audience will not feel obliged to make any greater preparation for the master of world literature than for its latent lickspittle." He indicted "sleazy fiction, trashy films, and bathetic soap operas, in all their maddening forms." Anyone who justified "organized distraction," he insisted, had to understand that it exploited rather than fulfilled human needs. Whenever "*kitsch* pervades the atmosphere," it made virtually impossible "a genuine esthetic (or religious or love) experience." Rosenberg re- alized that his attitude toward "cultural pap and gruel" might be "dismissed as snobbery, an egghead affectation," but he defended his position as democratic, offering as it did an aspiration of all people for higher things than the "sub-art and pseudo-knowledge" of mass culture. Indeed Rosenberg made clear that his criticism came from the left not the right. Citing *White Collar* by C. Wright Mills and using a Marxist phrase, he described the United States as "an enor- mous salesroom devoted to the fetishism of commodities." Then he pulled back from the potential radicalism of his analysis. He blamed not capitalism but technology for mass culture, proof of which was that it flourished even more in the Soviet Union than in America.[9]

Rosenberg took special aim at the portrayal of excessive or non-normative sexuality in popular culture, and then went on to connect that to the totalitar- ian threat. He doubted that anyone could find "hidden virtue" in pin-up maga- zines with titles such as *Cover Girls, Whirl, Keyhole, Stag, Brief, Bare, Titter,* and *Flirt* whose names suggested nudity, excess, and homosexuality. He found especially distasteful the depiction of lesbians in popular fiction, "dressed in riding attire with spurs and whips, mercilessly flogging their victims." Then in the next sentence he talked with disgust of the juxtaposition in *U.S. Camera* of "an offer of lewd photographs" with that for Nazi "atrocity pictures." For Rosenberg, as for other authors included in the volume, especially powerful was the connection between degraded mass culture and what had happened in Europe in the 1930s and 1940s. Driving his point home, he wrote that "At its worst, mass culture threatens not merely to cretinize our taste, but to brutalize our senses while paving the way to totalitarianism."[10]

In his opening essay White responded cautiously to Rosenberg's attack on contemporary mass culture. By beginning with a quote from Socrates that denounced youth for their contempt for authority and love of luxury, White drove home his point that postwar complaints had abundant historical precedents. Thus he asserted that "xenophilic critics who discuss American culture as if they were holding dead vermin in their hands" incorrectly assumed that there was a golden age in the past when the people were creative lovers of beauty. White wrote that "masochism, sadism, sexual fantasies" were "as old as recorded history." While not denying the pervasiveness of mass culture in contemporary America, he criticized its critics for focusing on the worst examples. He insisted that to turn comics into the dragon "whose slaying . . . will eliminate children's tensions, [and] juvenile delinquency" was "neither scientifically defensible or reasonable."[11]

Instead White asserted that popular culture enriched America. Citing *Life* magazine's publication of Ernest Hemingway's *Old Man and the Sea*, children's television that communicated cultural values, paperbacks that made great literature accessible, concerts that offered serious music in hundreds of small towns, and a TV documentary on mental illness that featured Orson Welles and Dr. William Menninger, he argued that critics, by overlooking contributions to culture that the media made, encouraged "the very banality they purport to despise." He also called into question the elitism of mass culture critics, whose "mixture of noblesse oblige and polite contempt" for people who were not in universities or the avant-garde blinded them to the way the media offered an unprecedented "cultural richness" to average citizens.[12]

Compared to Rosenberg's confident assertiveness about what frightened him, White was defensive. This came through most clearly in the ground he conceded to Rosenberg and his like-minded critics. As with Rosenberg, the specter of totalitarianism haunted him, but White gave this concern a distinctive twist by arguing that German Nazis and Soviet Communists simultaneously embraced high culture and carried out heinous acts. Above all, what is striking is how much White sharply critiqued what he supposedly supported and often did so in language that resembled Rosenberg's. White deplored "the pathological quality of some" comic books and declared that he would not defend on "either on esthetic or moral grounds" aspects of popular culture he considered "banal, dehumanizing and downright ugly." One indication that Rosenberg and White shared more than they realized was that, missing the ambiguities of McLuhan's *The Mechanical Bride* (1951), the subject of a later chapter in this book, they assumed the Canadian author was unambiguously against popular culture. Neither White nor Rosenberg imagined the possibility of embracing commercial culture as a source of genuine pleasure, utopian possibilities, or symbolic communication, ideas that became more common in succeeding generations.[13]

The book's authors elaborated on the themes that its editors articulated in their opening essays. Some authors made clear that what stood in opposition to popular culture was high culture. As Leo Lowenthal, an émigré who was a core member of the Frankfurt School, put it in ways others echoed, there was an "unbridgeable difference between art and popular culture"—between what he called "a genuine experience as a step to greater individual fulfillment" and "spurious gratification." Pessimistic critics denounced mass culture for making elite art precarious at best. Ernest van den Haag wrote that "corruption of past high culture by popular culture" involved "direct adulteration," a category in which he included "Bach candied by Stokowski, Bizet coarsened by Rodgers and Hammerstein, the Bible discolored and smoothed down into academic prose, Shakespeare spiced and made into treacly musical comedy, Freud vulgarized into columns of newspaper correspondence advice." On the other hand, more optimistic essayists offered qualifications—pointing, as White had done, to historical precedents for mass society and current evidence of its benefits.[14]

Potential Breakthroughs in the Debate's Limitations

In some instances, contributors chafed against or broke through the constricting qualities of contemporary debates. Charles S. Rolo came close to suggesting what writers considered later in this book would accomplish more fully when he used a nonhierarchical approach to place popular fiction alongside works by John Milton, Sigmund Freud, and Immanuel Kant. Similarly, in "How to Read 'Li'l Abner' Intelligently," Arthur J. Brodbeck and White hailed Al Capp's comic strip as art, which they compared favorably to plays by William Congreve, Aeschylus, and Shakespeare. Capp's creations, they wrote, explored the differences between the perfect and the real, enabling the reader "simultaneously to laugh at the discrepancy, to see our human condition humbly but bravely." Then, driving home their point, they argued that the gulf between high and popular culture was not as wide as critics suggested and, they added, "some of the elements of 'good' art are present in Capp's comic-strip fantasies."[15]

Other essayists probed for new ways of thinking about contemporary media and culture. Riesman, the subject of a later chapter here and author of the immensely influential *The Lonely Crowd* (1950), countered critics of mass culture on several grounds. Like others, he chafed at the elitism of naysaying pessimists. "One can easily forget," he wrote, "that things that strike the sophisticated person as trash may open new vistas for the unsophisticated." He also questioned those who emphasized the power of producers to control the consciousness of consumers. Instead, he insisted, "the same or virtually the same popular cultural materials are used by audiences in radically different ways and for radically different purposes." Evoking a notion of the reciprocal relationship between producers and consumers, he argued that it was the audience that manipulated "the product (and hence the producer), no less than the other way around." Gans, a student of Riesman whose work is the subject of another chapter in this book, challenged the assumption that the relationships between producers and consumers of popular culture involved top-down, one-way invasions. Instead he used the idea of "feedback" to suggest a reciprocal relationship. Focusing on the ways movie makers developed images of their audiences, he emphasized "the active, although indirect interaction between the audience and the creators, and that both affect the makeup of the final product." In addition, working against the notion of a mass audience, he emphasized the variety and multiplicity of audiences for popular culture.[16]

Other writers provided promising critiques of pessimists. Henry Pachter offered one of the most biting attacks on elitists from the left and right who were "trying to outdo each other at deriding the 'mass.'" He said that some examples of popular culture "express a yearning for a different world and reflect a search for a different humanity" and even point to "pre-conscious states of rebellion." Using *Li'l Abner* as his example, he opened the possibility that a cartoon could project "the immolated image of humanity into crudely ironical utopias." Finally, in one of his essays in this volume McLuhan offered tantalizing suggestions of what it means to consider new media in fresh ways. At the time he was well along on the road from *The Mechanical Bride* of 1951, in which he was ambivalent about mass media, to *Understanding Media* of 1964, in which he embraced them. In a 1954 essay that the editors included he called for closing the gap between the culture and new media "of sight and sound" so that it would be possible to "see the new media as serious culture." He hailed "the magical, transforming power" of the movies. He saw Bob Hope, Marilyn Monroe, Donald Duck, and Li'l Abner as "types of collective life felt and perceived through a mass medium. . . . points of collective awareness and communication for an entire society."[17]

Finally, in any discussion of possible breakthroughs to fresh understandings, attention must be given to Gilbert Seldes, someone whose writings in the 1950s were more pessimistic about popular culture than what he had expressed in his pathbreaking 1924 book *The Seven Lively Arts*. The editors prominently featured two of Seldes's essays from the 1950s. Seldes was divided in his view, which underscores the limits to new perspectives common elsewhere as well. On the one hand, he hailed the "exceptional products" of the mass media as "prophetic of greatness." Moreover, like "the great arts" and folk arts, the popular ones satisfied "desires unfulfilled in our common life." Seldes pointed to Charlie Chaplin as a genius and more generally to popular artists who had the "power to communicate directly with everyone." He criticized moralists as Puritans who condemned "the pleasures of the people because they are not uplifting." He attacked "noncommunist radicals," such as James T. Farrell and Macdonald, for seeing the potential of mass culture corrupted by the forces of capitalist commercialism.[18]

Yet Seldes's reservations outweighed his praise. At times he seemed conflicted, criticizing elitist intellectuals who shied away from new media at the same time that he expressed near horror about the very same phenomenon. At other moments he was downright pessimistic, worrying that the combination of capitalism and mass media threatened both authentic popular culture and vigorous democracy. Popular arts, he asserted, excluded the exceptional, diverted attention from reality, conveyed "a flat and limited picture of life," and encouraged "people to limit the range of their emotions and interests." The net result was both a rising standard of living and a declining "standard of life." In addition, mass culture threatened to "outstrip or displace all other arts," with its contagious infection and its power to "go steadily to lower levels of general intelligence and emotional maturity." For Seldes the decline in the imaginativeness and power of Walt Disney's work was symptomatic, with his studio's 1950s *Cinderella* offering "a superficial prettiness without growing in range of imagination and warmth of heart." What Seldes had admired in 1924 was a combination of live performances and silent movies that were technically inventive without being highly polished. In contrast, what offended him in the 1950s was what he saw as the dramatically increased commercialization of American culture, represented by slick Hollywood movies, blaring and mediocre radio shows, and engulfing television.[19]

New York Intellectuals and Mass Culture

Seldes's concern about the impact of mass media was just one example of how the Rosenberg and White book, despite promising breakthroughs, gave readers a frightening overall impression. And nowhere was this clearer than in what were the most widely read essays in the book, both from leading New York intellectuals: the art critic Clement Greenberg's "Avant-Garde and Kitsch" (1939) and the cultural critic Dwight Macdonald's "The Theory of Mass Culture" (1953), a version of which later appeared in his *Against the American Grain* (1962). Anti-Stalinists who wrote for *Partisan Review*, Greenberg and Macdonald, like their peers, combined an adversarial politics and a modernist sensibility. These were the two authors with whose essays most American (and even some European) intellectuals had to contend from 1938 until the early 1970s. What they shared was an assertion of the importance of cultural hierarchy, with elite modernism in ascendancy over what they saw as a debased mass culture produced by a greedy culture industry and consumed by a passive and deluded public. Their writings, like those of many contributors to *Mass Culture*, marked the full emergence of critiques of mass culture, long the preserve of the right, among those on the left.[20]

Though they were not entirely in agreement, during the Cold War both Greenberg and Macdonald participated in the drive to contain what they saw as a problematic mass culture. Greenberg rejected both Soviet socialist realism and Nazi hatred of modern art and instead celebrated avant-garde modernism. He emphasized the distinction between elite creativity, such as a poem by T. S. Eliot or a painting by Georges Braque, and kitsch, which for him included "popular, commercial art and literature with their chromeotypes, magazine covers, illustrations, ads, slick and pulp fiction, comics, Tin Pan Alley music, tap dancing, Hollywood movies." This "ersatz culture" was suited to those who, moving to cities, had abandoned their folk traditions. With the rise of universal literacy, the mass of people were "insensible to the values of genuine culture" but "hungry nevertheless for the diversion that only" kitsch—formulaic, market driven, and offering false pleasures—could provide. This false culture used "for raw material the debased and academicized simulacra of genuine culture." Generating profits but few genuine satisfactions, it was mechanical and formulaic, resulting only in "vicarious experience and faked sensations."[21]

Macdonald focused his attention on a series of kinds of culture. He differ-

FIRST PICTURES—ATOM BLASTS
THROUGH EYES OF VICTIMS

TV'S BIGGEST, PRETTIEST NEW SHOW

20 CENTS

SEPTEMBER 29, 1952

Figure 1. *Life* magazine cover, September 9, 1952. This cover offers an illustrative contrast between dancing women and first-person reports of the devastation caused by the dropping of atomic bombs on Japan in 1945. In the early 1950s Dwight Macdonald critiqued mass cult and midcult, excoriating the Luce publication for its lack of discrimination about levels of culture. Leonard McCombe/Time & Life Pictures/Getty Images.

entiated between the vitality of a vanishing, spontaneous folk culture and an embattled elite one. In between was a pretentious midcult, a central element of mass culture that was "imposed from above," "fabricated by technicians hired by businessmen," and purchased by "passive consumers." The dangers of mass culture were many, including its absorption into and debasement of "High Culture" and its use by corporate capitalism to sustain its power by making the world seem a "harmonious commonwealth" rather than what it was, "an exploitative class society." Thus the principal kind of interaction between levels of culture Macdonald could imagine involved how middlebrow culture engulfed all other varieties, posing a special threat to high culture. Among the reasons mass culture was problematic was that it voided "both the deep realities (sex, death, failure, tragedy) and also the simple, spontaneous pleasures." The only hope in such a situation was the creativity of an avant-garde, represented for him by Arthur Rimbaud, Igor Stravinsky, and Pablo Picasso, which, though it avoided competition, was always in danger of being degraded by encroachments of mass culture. This resulted in what he called "a tepid, flaccid Middlebrow Culture that threatens to engulf everything in its spreading ooze" that he saw suffusing American life in the 1950s. "There seems to be a Gresham's Law in cultural as well as monetary circulation," he argued, in which inferior culture drove out superior arts, issues of *Life* magazine, Mickey Spillane's detective stories, or paintings by Norman Rockwell blocking audiences from appreciating not only Shakespeare, the cathedral at Chartres, and the detective stories of Edgar Allan Poe but folk culture as well. Macdonald considered the mass culture of both the United States and the USSR as reprehensible. Though his concern originated with what happened in Russia in the 1930s, in the 1950s he was deeply worried about conditions for creativity in America. There the porousness of class lines, the lack of an enduring cultural tradition, the absence of a strong intelligentsia, and the ample capacity for making and disseminating mass culture all combined to produce a frightening situation.[22]

The Frankfurt School and America

Members of the Frankfurt School played a prominent role in shaping responses to popular culture in the post–World War II period, on both sides of the Atlantic. Formally titled the Institute for Social Research, it was founded in 1923 in the German city named in its more informal title. Interdisciplinary in orientation, its members, although by no means unified in their approaches, worked to reshape Marxism in ways that made it possible to understand both the rise of Nazism and the twists and turns of twentieth-century capitalism. With The-

odor Adorno and Max Horkheimer as its leaders, the Institute fled Germany
soon after Hitler assumed power in 1933 and then after a brief period in Geneva relocated to New York. After the war, a number of its most prominent
members—Leo Lowenthal, Herbert Marcuse, and Erich Fromm—remained in
the United States, while Adorno and Horkheimer returned to Frankfurt to re-
establish the Institute. Walter Benjamin had died tragically as he tried to escape
the Nazis. And Jürgen Habermas was the most influential of the second generation of Frankfurt School–inspired writers.

Mass Culture offered several selections by its members. The editors included
Lowenthal's 1950 "Historical Perspectives of Popular Culture" but not his vastly
more intriguing and influential "Biographies in Popular Magazines" (1944),
which powerfully joined content analysis with critical theory. Also in the volume was the trenchant 1956 essay by Günther Anders, "The Phantom World
of TV." Here the cousin of Benjamin, the former husband of Hannah Arendt,
and someone whose work Adorno rejected, explored the relationships between
technology, mass culture, and the human condition. Anders wrote of how a
television viewer "pays for selling himself: he must purchase the very unfree-
dom he himself helps to produce."[23]

Among the book's contributors from the Frankfurt School, Theodor
Adorno was the one whose life works offered the most influential and generally
negative critiques of mass culture. Soon after he arrived in the United States,
he worked as a music critic in Lazarsfeld's Radio Research Project and moved
to Los Angeles in 1941. Then, feeling he was an exile, he returned to Germany
in 1949, where with Max Horkheimer he reopened the Institut für Sozialforschung soon after. Rosenberg and White included in *Mass Culture* Adorno's 1954
"Television and the Patterns of Mass Culture." In this essay, whose orientation was more philosophical than empirical, Adorno was highly critical of the
impact of mass media but mildly optimistic that their adverse effects could be
remedied. He focused on the "culture industry" and its power, as if, as Eugene
Lunn has noted, he was responding to the "'populist' defense of American capitalism" so prominent in the United States beginning in 1935.[24]

Adorno argued that what made mid-twentieth-century popular culture
different from its predecessors was that it had "developed into a system" and
"seized all media of artistic expression," in the process creating a "virtually
'closed' society." He continued by stating that "this rigid institutionalization
transformed modern mass culture into a medium of undreamed of psychological control," undermining the possibility of "individual resistance." It had
eroded the enclaves that were once outside its purview, especially people living
on farms and elites whose position relied on culture or intellect. Anyone who

questioned its role, he insisted, would be demeaned as an elitist or highbrow. Drawing on the work of Martha Wolfenstein and Nathan Leites, Adorno argued that modern times had seen reversal of long-standing patterns, so that now women were portrayed as "erotically aggressive" figures who had put men on the defensive.[25]

Aside from its emphasis on the almost overwhelming power of the culture industry, the main issue in the essay was the relationships among different levels of culture. As had others before him, Adorno often distinguished between autonomous art (his favorite example was the music of Schoenberg) and commodity or dependent art (with various levels in between). The difficulty most people had understanding autonomous art guaranteed its integrity; in contrast, dependent art, formally simplistic and corrupted by its popularity, was worthy of serious analysis only in terms of its damaging effects. In this essay, though at moments he did not posit a rigid dichotomy between high and mass arts, Adorno saw their relationship as problematic. Thus he wrote that "many of the cultural products bearing the anticommercial trademark 'art for art's sake'" showed "traces of commercialism in their appeal to the sensational or in the conspicuous display of material wealth and sensuous stimuli at the expense of the meaningfulness of the work."[26]

Like other pessimists in the volume, Adorno thus emphasized what he saw as the disastrous consequences of mass culture, exercised through social-psychological controls. Mass media produced results that were formulaic, drove standards to the lowest common denominator, emphasized adjustment and conformity, and elevated society into a position of power over the individual. Television, he asserted, resulted in "the very smugness, intellectual passivity, and gullibility that seem to fit in with totalitarian creeds even if the explicit surface message of the shows may be antitotalitarian." This referencing of totalitarianism—common in the volume but particularly powerful for someone like Adorno who had escaped from Nazi Germany but lost many dear to him to the Nazis—reverberated throughout his essay. Again and again he pointed to what he saw as authoritarian or totalitarian forces at work in contemporary America. Despite his many dire statements, at the beginning and end of the essay Adorno expressed some hope that it was possible to fight back against mass media. In the first paragraph he wrote that "exposing the socio-psychological implications and mechanisms of television" might sensitize the public "to the nefarious effect" of its methods. Then at the essay's end, he "knowingly" talked of how "to face psychological mechanisms operating on various levels in order not to become blind and passive victims." Adorno's essay, like so many of the contributions in *Mass Culture*, underscores the way

European events of the 1930s—the Comintern's creation of the Popular Front, the rise of German fascism, the spread of Soviet Communism, and the devastation wreaked by the Holocaust—hung over the book. Though the volume was focused very much on America, many of the essayists looked through the eyes of German and Eastern European writers.[27]

Left Out: Frankfurt School

What Rosenberg and White did not include in the collection speaks volumes about how circumscribed were the debates over popular culture in 1950s America. Several strands of investigation were notable for their absence: the even more radical and pessimistic writings from the Frankfurt School; American social science research; the British tradition of literary criticism that so profoundly shaped that nation's response to commercial culture from the 1920s well into the 1970s; and the diverse group of authors, mainly from Continental Europe, who, as the next two chapters will show, were in the 1950s and earlier developing trailblazing perspectives. Thus the collection included nothing from Erich Fromm, who had broken with his Frankfurt School colleagues. However, perhaps because it was too radical, the book did not include anything from Herbert Marcuse's 1955 *Eros and Civilization*. Here the émigré philosopher, who was to greatly influence cultural and political radicals in the 1960s, brought Sigmund Freud and Karl Marx together, although he mentioned the former and not the latter. Marcuse historicized the way civilization created sexual repression and in turn heralded a nonrepressive world where sexual expressiveness was fully possible.[28]

Similarly, when making the decision about which of Adorno's writings to include, although the editors had fewer choices of his work in English than would later be available, their selection of "Television and the Patterns of Mass Culture" was significant. In 1957, in book form there was little in print in English on mass culture by Adorno, the most notable exception being *The Authoritarian Personality*, written with others and published in 1950. Rosenberg and White could have authorized a translation of "The Culture Industry: Enlightenment as Mass Deception," from *Dialectic of Enlightenment*, which Adorno coauthored with Max Horkheimer. Adorno and Horkheimer had published this, the foundational text of Frankfurt School, in German in mimeographed form in 1944 and as a book in German in 1947, with the first English translation appearing in 1972. In using "The Culture Industry" as the title of their essay they were making clear their rejection of terms like "mass culture" or "popular culture," which they believed falsely conveyed a sense that culture came from below.[29]

More so than in Adorno's essay about television, "The Culture Industry" reveals how their experiences with Nazi Germany and corporate America helped convince Adorno and Horkheimer that within the Enlightenment was its opposite—forces of barbarism, irrationality, and reaction. They revealed that they were acutely aware of how the Nazis had used mass media to rise to power and, closer at hand physically if not emotionally, how Hollywood shaped culture and consciousness, two elemental situations that at times they elided. Thus even though Charlie Chaplin used his own funds to produce an important antifascist film in 1939 at a time when studios were unwilling to risk losing German markets, Adorno and Horkheimer wrote of how "the ears of corn blowing in the wind at the end of Chaplin's *The Great Dictator* give lie to the anti-fascist plea for freedom. They are like the blond hair of the German girl whose camp life is photographed by the Nazi film company in the summer breeze."[30]

Their analysis was bold and powerful—much more comprehensively so than in Adorno's essay on television. They argued that capitalism enervated workers in the sphere of production and then in turn dominated them in the realm of consumption. Workers sought escape from the oppression of mechanization which in turn "has such power over a man's leisure and happiness, and so profoundly determines the manufacture of amusement goods, that his experiences are inevitably after-images of the work process itself." Drawing on Benjamin's insights, they emphasized the processes of mechanical reproduction that produced only copies of reality that in turn eroded individualism, authenticity, and autonomy. They asserted that the culture industry had succeeded in shaping taste, as intermediary institutions such as the family had weakened. Capitalism powerfully shaped consumer culture, which in turn promoted a false consciousness among consumers, degrading their lives and lulling them into passivity.[31]

These processes were visible to them in contemporary movies, radio, magazines, and architecture. Cartoons, "once exponents of fantasy," now served only to confirm the triumph of technology and capitalism—seen so vividly in Disney cartoons and in actual lives where "the audience can learn to take their own punishment." The capitalist system also produced midcult, which in turn corrupted high culture, as when Benny Goodman performed with the Budapest String Quintet. Moreover, the culture industry continually cheated its consumers of what it perpetually promised, a process Adorno and Horkheimer understood as closely connected with sexual dynamics of the expectation of coitus that was never achieved. "The promissory note" offered more than it delivered, drawing as it did "on pleasure" that was "endlessly prolonged; . . . all it actually confirms is that the real point will never be reached." Far from being puritanical, Adorno and Horkheimer lamented the way capitalism repressed pleasure rather than promoted its fulfillment. For many who read "The Culture Industry," there seemed no way of escaping the dominating power of capitalism—and indeed there was plenty in the essay to support such a reading. Adorno and Horkheimer made clear that the problem was not with a moralistic puritanism but with the "necessity inherent in the system . . . not for a moment to allow" the customer "any suspicion that resistance is possible." Indeed, consumers were aware of how capitalism trapped them and of how they could do nothing to escape. "The triumph of advertising in the culture industry," they wrote, "is that consumers feel compelled to buy and use its products even though they see through them."[32]

Some observers have linked Adorno and Horkheimer to conservative critics of mass culture such as Eliot and Ortega y Gasset, but the situation is far more complex. Although Adorno and Horkheimer held out the possibility that culture, by which they most prominently meant avant-garde creativity, had a critical function in holding up an alternative version of reality, they saw elite culture as shot through with contradictions. If they emphasized what Martin Jay calls "the redemptive power of high culture," they also acknowledged that it too was subject to being, as Eugene Lunn has shown, "tainted by its inevitable complicity, in class societies, with forces of political domination and social oppression." Nor did they see as clear a line between high and mass culture as most observers usually assume they did. Autonomous works and Hollywood films, Adorno wrote to Benjamin in 1936, both "bear the stigmata of capitalism" and were "torn halves of an integral freedom." Good dialecticians that they were, Adorno and Horkheimer were never completely negative about the possibility of achieving happiness (even through mass culture) or resisting capitalism's power. For them culture was both the problem and the solution, for they believed that all levels of culture contained elements of regression and promise. "Candy-floss entertainment," they insisted as they focused on contemporary radio and film, "simultaneously instructs and stultifies mankind."[33]

Yet overall Adorno and Horkheimer held a deeply pessimistic view of mass culture, more pessimistic than that offered in Adorno's essay on television. Elsewhere before 1957, Adorno had written on jazz in ways that were analytic and problematic. Adorno "was unwilling," writes a scholar of German popular culture, "to recognize jazz as a valid cultural and artistic expression and portrayed African American jazz musicians and their fans as culturally inferior." Thus a number of things were missing from Adorno's essay in *Mass Culture* but were present elsewhere, especially in what he wrote in 1944 with Horkheimer. The essay on television gave little sense of Adorno's deep pessimism, full-blown critique of capitalism, embrace of avant-garde art as the one saving remnant, and sharp attack on elements of America's commercial culture such as movies, jazz, and comics. Yet the message of his 1957 essay was clear enough: mass culture played a critical role in bringing fascism to Germany in the 1930s and might bring totalitarianism to the United States in the 1950s.[34]

The Missing British Traditions

What Rosenberg and White's book contained and neglected of traditions from outside those of the United States was notable. The only French writer in the book was de Tocqueville. The editors did include a selection from the Spanish author Ortega y Gasset's *The Revolt of the Masses*, a conservative attack on mass culture that appeared in 1932 in English. There were two essays by the Canadian McLuhan, whose work commands attention in a later chapter of this book. The only Briton whose work appeared in the book was Orwell—whose widely read 1944 "Raffles and Miss Blandish" explored the decline in quality of pulp fiction from 1900 to 1939.[35]

Had the editors turned their attention more fully to British writers, their readers would have discovered an Anglo-American tradition that included Matthew Arnold, T. S. Eliot, I. A. Richards, F. R. Leavis, and Q. D. Leavis. This outlook profoundly shaped later commentators, most notably Richard Hoggart, Paddy Whannel, and Stuart Hall. There was a distinctly elitist and conservative cast to the writings of the early formulators of this perspective whose key works spanned the period from the late nineteenth century well into the post–World War II years. To varying degrees, and in some ways not unlike Adorno and Horkheimer, they worried that a combination of democracy, mass education, and rising industrialization threatened high culture and hastened the arrival of debased, homogenized society. To stem the tide, these Britons advocated various avenues to the sacralization of art in whose interpretation elites could take the lead by fostering close and discriminating readings. As Patrick Brantlinger has written, "Conservative theorists . . . tend to see mass culture as mechanical rather than organic, secular rather than sacred, commercial rather than free or unconditioned, plebian or bourgeois and vulgar rather than aristocratic and 'noble,' based on self-interest rather than on high ideals . . . cheap and shoddy rather than enduring, imitative rather than original, and urban, bureaucratic, and centralized rather than close to nature, communal and individualized."[36]

From its publication in 1869 until the 1960s, Matthew Arnold's *Culture and Anarchy: An Essay in Political and Social Criticism* wielded immense influence over British and American attitudes toward high and low culture. In one of the

book's most famous passages, Arnold wrote of culture as an "inward operation" which involved "a pursuit of our total perfection by means of getting to
know . . . the best which has been thought and said in the world." The finest
works of literature and art would help people fight against their base, bodily
instincts and instead grow spiritually so they could approach perfection. This
"harmonious perfection" brought together sweetness and light, beauty and intelligence. Culture, and its handmaiden religion, would redeem society, purging
all that was uncouth and brash. Leadership in such a vital effort would come
not from philistines who sought only material riches, or aristocrats to whom
true culture was only a superficial accoutrement, but from a cultivated elite. Its
task, Arnold wrote, as an education reformer and an opponent of both women's
suffrage and working-class social movements, was to fight against the anarchy
represented by social, political, and religious conflict and for the importance of
higher things as they spoke for the enlightened. Although Arnold spent relatively little time on what a later generation would call popular culture, the little
that he did say and the more general implications of his argument were clear—a
cultured elite provided the bulwark against all that was degraded and base.[37]

Despite his protests to the contrary, in critical ways Eliot carried on Arnold's work. Eliot's approach to popular culture was complicated. Seldes remarked that Eliot's "own early poetry indicates that he was once influenced
by, and perhaps even took pleasure in, one of the popular arts, in his use of
the rhythms of jazz to contrast with the stately phrases of the past." Moreover,
at key moments in his critical writings, Eliot offered a somewhat inclusive
definition of culture. Thus in *Notes towards the Definition of Culture* (1948) he
remarked that he continually had to remind himself that the term "culture"
capaciously included "the dog races, the pin table, the dart board, Wensley-
dale cheese, . . . nineteenth-century Gothic churches and the music of Elgar."
Yet the apparent capaciousness of Eliot's vision is deceptive. He embraced the
culture of lower orders only when imbedded and contained in a hierarchical
society. Moreover, his 1948 list of the leisure activities of ordinary folks is deeply
rooted in the pre-1914 world of Britain, displaying as it does no recognition of
the importance of radio or movies.[38]

Eliot advocated a conservative position, one sharply critical of the effects
of industrialism, democracy, and mass culture. In *After Strange Gods* (1934), he
worried that in a heterogeneous society cultures were likely to become adulter-
ated. What was still more important, he wrote just as Hitler was taking over
Germany, was that "unity of religious background; and reasons of race and
religion combine to make any large number of free-thinking Jews undesirable."
Tradition, he concluded, would be weakened by the arrival of "foreign popula-

tions." Then, in two long essays of 1939 and 1948, Eliot responded to Britain's appeasement of Nazi Germany by asking, "Was our society, which has always been so assured of its superiority and rectitude, . . . assembled round anything more permanent than a congeries of banks, insurance companies, and industries, and had it any beliefs more essential than a belief in compound interest and the maintenance of dividends?"[39]

If some words in this passage make the son of a successful St. Louis businessman sound like an anticapitalist, the words "permanent" and "essential" point elsewhere. Eliot relied on a powerful mixture of commitments to Anglo-Catholic Christianity, a hierarchical social order, and an elite "minority culture." Like Arnold, he believed in the importance of a cultured elite. Where he differed from Arnold was in his rejection of the soothing emphasis on sweetness and light, his insistence on the inextricable relationship of culture and religion, his seeing no hope for elevating the nonelect, and his embrace of an aristocratic elite that worked together with an intellectual one to form what he called a clerisy. In 1944 Eliot spoke of an elite clerisy that originated "the dominant ideas, and alter the sensibility, of their time." Thus he insisted that a Christian society "can only be realised when the great majority of the sheep belong to one fold." Moreover, a culture grounded in religion had to have "a positive set of values, and the dissentients must remain marginal." People "from the dominant class who compose the nucleus of the cultural élite," he continued, had an obligation "to transmit the culture which they have inherited" and "keep it from ossification." In this context, the function of education was to preserve an elite-based culture, rather than to build an organic society where education allowed people with native abilities to gain cultural power or legitimacy. Expansion of education inevitably lowered cultural standards, resulting in the substitution of cultivated elites with "élites of brains, or perhaps only of sharp wits."[40]

If such a statement made clear his hostility to sharp-witted, brainy groups that ascended educationally, more than likely a reference to smart and ambitious Jews, elsewhere he linked cultural disintegration to crude people who pursued pleasure through commerce. Unchecked industrialism and democracy resulted in the creation of "bodies of men and women—of all classes—detached from tradition, alienated from religion and susceptible to mass suggestion: in other words, a mob." This last quote makes clear some of what Eliot shared with many of the contributors to *Mass Culture*, especially an insistence of how high culture stood in opposition to the false pleasures of consumer culture. Indeed, in January 1944, Eliot acknowledged that he benefited from reading the 1944 version of Macdonald's attack on mass media. Yet it is not hard to figure out why the editors did not include any contribution from Eliot, especially from his *Notes Toward the Definition of Culture* (1948). Whether Eliot was anti-Semitic as some scholars have claimed, his ideology was problematic to the editors. After all he had spoken of "élites of brains, or only of sharp wits" and more generally relied on an inextricable linking of Christianity and hereditary social class—all of which was surely anathema to Jews like Rosenberg and White.[41]

I. A. Richards was another Anglo-American writer who shaped both literary criticism and responses to popular culture but whose social ideology was neither so apparent nor so central to his role as a cultural critic as was true of Arnold and Eliot. His 1929 *Practical Criticism: A Study in Literary Judgment* profoundly influenced literary studies in Britain and America. Richard's book was unprecedented in its reliance on empirical studies of how students actually read literary texts. Over several years, he gave hundreds of Cambridge University students poems to read, ranging from those by Shakespeare to those of an early twentieth-century woman poet known for her sentimental writings. Without providing any information on the authors or dates of composition, Richards asked students to write down their responses. What surprised him was the problematic nature of their readings. Students brought to poetry what Richards saw as a wide range of "irrelevant associations," "stock responses," and "sentimentality."[42]

Richards asserted that among the factors that influenced his students' responses was prior experience with mass media. He decried what made authentic experience elusive, including the ways movies and newspapers shaped "emotional responses" that, "judged by the standards of poetry," were "crude and vague rather than subtle or appropriate." This and other factors involved a tendency "towards standardization, towards a leveling down." "Mechanical inventions, . . . and a too sudden diffusion of indigestible ideas," he remarked, were influencing readers. Richards felt that "bad literature, bad art, the cinema" were having a deleterious effect on the reading public. Yet he also insisted that popular culture was "worthy of very close study." Literary critics should not ignore the best American advertisements, for example, because of their effectiveness in representing "literary ideals," the way market researchers carefully tested them, and the fact that they were "among the best indices available of what is happening to taste." Moreover he believed literary critics could illuminate "under what conditions popularity and possible high value are compatible."[43]

The solution for Richards was "poetry, the unique, linguistic instrument by which our minds have ordered their thoughts, emotions, desires." So he developed ways to cut through to the true meaning of poems and other literary texts,

in particular close readings based on sensibility and discrimination that would
enable the reader to experience the poem, and the poet's meaning, as directly as
possible. All this would, as Arnold had proposed but was only implicit in *Practical Criticism*, make literature serve as a means of reinvigorating culture that
stood in opposition to mass culture. Indeed, in 2004 Richard Hoggart summed
up Richards's message when he said that he made it possible for his own generation to "identify the bogus in thought and language, the sentimental, the
evasive, the sloppily ad hominem. 'Close reading' was the start" of Richards's
"honestly bracing message," Hoggart wrote, and "'stock responses' was one of
the key anathemas." If Richards, like Eliot, influenced American New Critics
by giving them the tools to analyze poetry without reference to biography or
history, he influenced other, more culturally oriented critics by using empirical
data to capture reader response, by exploring the relationships between text
and its consumers, and by taking seriously (albeit from an elitist perspective)
texts of a wide range of quality.[44]

As important as Eliot and Richards were among Britons who combined literary and cultural criticism, it was F. R. Leavis and his circle, including his
wife Q. D. Leavis and his colleague Denys Thompson, who wielded the greatest
influence in Britain on the teaching about the relationship between literature
and popular culture. From the early 1930s until well into the 1970s and beyond,
through teaching and writing Leavis and members of his circle influenced
thousands of teachers in secondary schools, adult education programs, and
universities who prodded their students to read novels and poems closely and
in a discriminating manner—and to apply these very tactics to the interpretation of popular culture.[45]

F. R. Leavis wanted to extend training in analysis and appreciation of literature beyond elite universities and into secondary schools and adult education,
even as he privileged canonical texts that he hoped would enhance people's
moral sensibilities and enable them to fend off the dangers of mass culture.
For Leavis and his circle the key to understanding literature was close reading of texts that emphasized discrimination. Leavisites stood in opposition to
a disparate group of opponents: modernist writers gathered in Bloomsbury;
traditionalists in English departments who had a narrow and antiquated view
of the scope of English literature; biographers and Marxists who emphasized
background and context; followers of the amateur belletristic tradition that
valued connoisseurship over critical analysis; and popularizers of English literature who relied on fast-paced surveys. The favorite terms of Leavisites were
"authentic," "concreteness," "energy," "tautness," "maturity"—qualities they
found in literature that enabled readers to understand the seriousness of both

life and literature, seen most clearly in the works of Shakespeare, George Eliot, and D. H. Lawrence.[46]

Leavis and his colleagues had a vision not only of literature but also of the role of literature and criticism in a broader social ideology. Leavis located a better, more organic world in preindustrial England that industrialization beginning in the seventeenth century had undermined. He offered a sentimentalized view of an earlier age, what he called in 1933 "the organic community with the living culture it embodied." Unalienated labor went hand-in-hand with meaningful leisure in a world where there was no split between popular culture and culture. Leavis insisted that the healthy relationship people once had to communal life no longer existed in modern Britain, having been torn asunder by industry, mass production, materialism, standardization, and mass media. The loss of that earlier world resulted in the promotion of the false values of progress and optimism, and in people seeking unsatisfying compensation in fantasy and leisure that the new technologies of cinema, modern music, and radio offered. He remained sharply critical of advertising: a byproduct of Americanization, it connected materialism and progress, degraded standards, promoted a shallow optimism, and substituted false amusements for genuine pleasure. Leavis found in *Middletown* (1929) by Helen M. Lynd and Robert S. Lynd evidence of how change had "radically affected religion, broken up the family, and revolutionized social custom." In the 1930s Leavis wrote about how advertising, radio, the popular press, but especially cinema validated Gresham's law of how the bad drove out the good. The lack of meaningful engagement with work meant that leisure involved meaningless "compensation in Substitute-Living." Movies, he wrote in 1930, "involve surrender, under conditions of hypnotic receptivity, to the cheapest emotional appeals." Popular culture, Leavis and Thompson insisted in 1933, fostered fantasy and distraction by discouraging "all but the most shallow and immediate interests, the most superficial, automatic and cheap mental and emotional responses."[47]

To solve the resulting spiritual crisis, Leavisites, drawing on the writings of Arnold, saw literary critics trained in universities as the saving remnant that would spread the benefits of a rigorous analysis of literature and thereby save society. Upon "a very small minority" Leavis wrote in 1930, as he sundered the connection between social class and an educated elite that Eliot emphasized, "depends our power of profiting by the finest human experience of the past; they keep alive the subtlest and most perishable parts of tradition." Teachers of literature would inculcate in their students the critical habits brought to both what they read and how they lived—in the process educating "positively for human living in accordance with some ideal of a civilized community."

The contrast between Eliot and the Leavisites helps us understand why Leavis and his circle provided such an important basis for later writers who took seriously the analysis of both popular culture and the culture of ordinary citizens. As Hall and Whannel wrote in their 1964 book *The Popular Arts*, Eliot saw democracy and mass education as the cause of cultural calamity. In contrast, Leavis saw industrialism as the villain but located the solution in "the study of literature as the core of liberal and human studies" which would make "the university a centre from which would come a minority dedicated to defending the highest standards against mass society."[48]

Among the things that helped amplify the influence of F. R. Leavis were the writings of his wife, Q. D. Leavis, and the publication of *Scrutiny*, the literary journal through which for twenty-one years beginning in 1932 the Leavises and others applied literary theory to popular culture. Q. D. Leavis's *Fiction and the Reading Public* (1932) provided a pathbreaking exploration of what it meant to consider the relationship of producers and consumers of literature. Following Richards's use of empirical methods, she sent questionnaires to writers as she searched for data on writing, publishing, and selling books. As was true with her husband, if Q. D. Leavis was innovative in her approach and if she took popular culture seriously, her attitude to what she studied was elitist and conservative. Inspired by Richards's call to study best-sellers, she took what she called an anthropological approach by doing empirical research on the relationship between authors, publishers, and readers. If Richards explored how readers developed multiple and often unpredictable meanings for poems, she examined how writers produced works in response to their reading publics, as she looked at the relationships between producers and consumers of texts from the perspective of the producers. She linked the rise of popular fiction and mass journalism to the threat to cultural standards represented by quality fiction. The literary marketplace, including reviewers and advertisers, she wrote, is "engaged in establishing undesirable attitudes" that stood in opposition to what truly great literature did. Against the "monstrous impersonality" of the "commercial and economic machinery" of book publishing she posed "resistance by an armed and conscious minority" of literary scholars who could redeem a world characterized by debased mass culture and degenerate elites. By understanding the reading public, an elite could direct educational efforts that would use great literature to counter the degradations wreaked by advertising, journalism, and movies. Moreover, Q. D. revealed that it was possible to be a conservative elitist and emphasize the importance of reciprocity between producers and consumers.[49]

In *Culture and Environment: The Training of Critical Awareness* (1933),

F. R. Leavis and Denys Thompson provided a full Leavisite discussion of what it meant to use literary analysis to interpret popular culture. Reproducing samples of popular culture drawn from advertisements, they told teachers how they could develop classroom strategies that used fieldwork with contemporary examples of mass media. They called for the kind of close, discriminating reading Richards had advocated in *Practical Criticism* to "be extended to the analysis of advertisements (the kind of appeal they make and their stylistic characteristics) followed up by comparison with representative passages of journalese and popular fiction." Using the same methods to analyze mass media and popular culture that he deployed in analysis of canonical literature, Leavis connected literary standards to cultural ones. The "debasement of language," Leavis and Thompson wrote about an advertisement, involved "a debasement of emotional life, and of the quality of living." What inferior popular culture and problematic literature shared was "crude emotional falsity," insincerity, sentimentality, and vulgarity. With D. H. Lawrence as their exemplar among modern writers, Leavis and Thompson attacked a whole range of writers whose "habit of cheerfulness" relied on a refusal "to see things as they are," which in turn involved "a habit of cowardice and irresponsibility taking itself for virtue, and so the more insidiously corrupting and debilitating." Through close readings of texts, a determination to separate the authentic from the meretricious, and a commitment to plumb the relationship between texts and cultural meanings, Leavisites brought a moral, albeit condescending seriousness to the examination of consumer culture, one in which the analysis of appeals to social class played a critical role.[50]

Despite their condescending attitudes to popular culture, as well as their preference for an earlier age, the Leavises and the *Scrutiny* group offered tools that in the hands of others would later build toward innovative analyses of popular culture, especially those who could overcome what the historian of the periodical called *Scrutiny*'s "general failure to make the practical connection between 'culture' and organized politics." Q. D. Leavis provided an exemplary if also problematic way of thinking about the dynamics of the relationships between producers and consumers. At a time when most literary critics displayed no interest in serious analysis of popular culture, the Leavisites showed what it meant to apply techniques of literary criticism to nonliterary texts. Although a later generation would find their analyses of mass media simple and condescending, in the context of the 1930s merely paying serious attention to advertisements and popular fiction constituted a significant breakthrough. Their commitment to inspiring teachers resulted, especially during the postwar period, in taking the serious study of literature and mass media well beyond the confines of elite universities. Finally, as Dennis Dworkin has written, the Leavisite "interest in the tangled relationship between community, culture, language, history, and tradition raised issues that could not be easily handled in existing disciplines." As we will see in the chapters on Hoggart, Hall, and Whannel, this led in the long run to a capacious, transformative, and interdisciplinary treatment of commercial culture. The Leavisite talk of social class, avaricious capitalists, alienated labor, and the devastation wrought by industrialization might make them sound like Marxists, but, lacking a specific political agenda, their political hopes rested with an educated cadre of literary critics and not with the working class, a labor movement, or insurgent youth.[51]

Toward What Was Lost in Translation

If *Mass Culture* neglected the British tradition that began with Arnold and culminated in the work of the Leavises, also missing were writers, many of them the focus of this book, who by 1957 had begun to contribute to new understandings. Some of their works were just being written, while others were not yet available in English or at all. The list of such writers whose works implicitly or explicitly illuminated consumer culture is long, many of them not discussed in this book: Henri Lefebvre, Marcel Mauss, Georg Simmel, Bertolt Brecht, Georges Bataille, Herbert Marcuse, and C. Wright Mills. The following two chapters focus on writers whose work *Mass Culture* neglected but who in interesting ways countered what the Rosenberg and White volume offered. All of which is another way of saying that by 1957, but more clearly in the ensuing two decades, the nature of the debate about popular culture, mass society, and consumerism would change in significantly important ways from what the essays in Rosenberg and White's *Mass Culture* offered.

Chapter 2

Lost in Translation

By the middle of the twentieth century new ways of looking at consumer culture emerged, ones that emphasized pleasure, symbolic communication, skepticism about moralistic judgments, and an exploration of the relationship between producers and consumers. Writers began to see popular culture as the locus of aesthetic creativity and rich meanings. They took consumer culture seriously without fully embracing it, as they mixed fascination, irony, criticism, and detachment. This happened in Continental Europe and from writers deeply learned in canonical literary and philosophical traditions. However, the most richly suggestive analyses, by Jürgen Habermas, Roland Barthes, Umberto Eco, Walter Benjamin, and C. L. R. James, were not available to American readers when Bernard Rosenberg and David Manning White published *Mass Culture: The Popular Arts in America* in 1957. As outsiders to America who experienced the dramatic contrast between wartime devastation and postwar recovery, these writers were in especially advantageous positions to understand the transformative power of consumer culture.

In the mid to late 1950s, Jürgen Habermas, the most prominent German intellectual from the second generation of the Frankfurt School, wrote essays that both worked within and mildly challenged the framework that his mentors Max Horkheimer and Theodor Adorno had offered in *Dialectic of Enlightenment* (1944). With *Mythologies* (1957) the Frenchman Roland Barthes explored the ways commercial performances and advertisements conveyed symbolic meanings. During the late 1950s and early 1960s, the Italian literary critic and philosopher Umberto Eco pondered the strengths and weaknesses of popular culture, much of it from the United States, as he, like Barthes, revealed what it meant to use sophisticated literary and philosophical approaches to understand mass media in new ways. Chapter 3 focuses on two more authors whose works, had they been available in America, Rosenberg and White might have drawn on. In the 1920s and 1930s Walter Benjamin developed perspectives that offered an alternative to the analysis developed later not only by the editors of *Mass*

Culture but also by his colleagues in the Frankfurt School. Most notably in his mid-1930s essay "Art in the Age of Mechanical Reproduction," Benjamin presented arguments that undermined the aura of high culture, challenged ways of understanding cultural expressions, and emphasized the role that expressiveness played in developing popular culture. In *American Civilization* (1950), C. L. R. James, born in Trinidad but living in the United States from 1938 to 1953, drew on Karl Marx and Georg Wilhelm Friedrich Hegel to present a view of popular culture that emphasized the reciprocal relationship between producers and consumers of movies, radio, and pulp magazines. All of the writers discussed in this chapter and the next were deeply steeped in European high culture, whose tools they used to understand popular culture.

However, in the 1950s the writings of Habermas, Barthes, Eco, Benjamin, and James were not available to American readers. Even now some of the relevant essays by Habermas remain publicly unavailable in English. Barthes's *Mythologies* was published in France in 1957 but not in English until fifteen years later, and then only in a somewhat abbreviated version. The relevant essays by Eco began to appear in translation in 1966, but some not until much later. The first translation of Benjamin's key essay from German into English came in 1968. With James's *American Civilization* the issue was not translation into English but the gap between a privately circulated manuscript and publicly available book—two versions separated by more than four decades.[1]

To lesser or greater degrees these authors went against the grain of the widely accepted framework within which many American intellectuals, including those whose essays appeared in *Mass Culture*, understood commercial culture. Implicitly or explicitly they challenged the moralistic approaches that dominated debates in the United States from at least the 1830s until well into the 1960s. They complicated the sharp separation of levels of culture—high, mid, low, and folk—that New York intellectuals such as Dwight Macdonald and Clement Greenberg had insisted upon. Moreover, they asked whether consumers were as passive as many cultural critics had suggested and instead advocated a somewhat more reciprocal relationship between producers and consumers. Finally, instead of seeing commercial culture causing moral degradation, they emphasized the possibility that it involved pleasurable expressiveness, rich meanings, and symbolic communication. To be sure, none of these writers took such positions unequivocally: it was precisely the complicated and rich nature of what they wrote that made their arguments so suggestive. Had their works been available in the 1950s they might have fostered more positive views by helping to undermine dominant approaches that emphasized the frightening power of consumer culture.

Post–World War II Germany

In the 1950s, when he was at the Institut für Sozialforschung, or Frankfurt School as it would later be called, Jürgen Habermas started to work his way hesitantly toward developing a theory of consumer society. He distanced himself from and eventually broke with his mentors. After the late 1950s, Habermas turned his attention away from a direct discussion of consumer society— although that topic helped shape his greatly influential treatment of lives in the public realm. Habermas drew on a long-standing German fascination with American popular culture. Beginning in the 1890s Karl May wrote novels about the American west, which he never visited; the novels sold tens of millions of copies. The fascination May and his audience had for American popular culture contrasted with powerful traditions of educated elites who well into the post–World War II period believed that Germany was culturally superior to the United States. In the 1920s and 1930s Germans intensely debated the virtues and vices of American mass culture. Many of those on both the left and right decried the decadence that they believed it promoted. Many influential writers on the left felt that under the capitalist system mass culture distracted the working class, a condition that would change under a new economic system that would turn popular culture into a liberatory force. Until that moment came, they worried that American commercial culture, as a product of capitalism, undercut the possibility of a radical working-class politics. If Adorno and Horkheimer would cast a critical eye on American mass culture, some from within the left in the 1920s, notably Bertolt Brecht and Kurt Weill, admired American jazz and westerns, hailing them as cultural forms that undermined the power of bourgeois culture. As Hans Siemsen wrote approvingly in 1921, jazz "knocks down every hint of dignity, correct posture, and starched collars."[2]

In postwar West Germany, the issue of America's economic and cultural impact had decidedly political ramifications, given the major role that the American government and corporations played in the nation's reconstruction. Ludwig Erhard was the most influential promoter of a modern consumer society who stood in opposition to the social democratic vision of egalitarian consumption and centralized planning. In the late 1920s he had worked for a market research firm. In 1949 he became minister for economic affairs in the newly established German Federal Republic and in the ensuing years he promoted a middle course between market capitalism and a planned economy. In 1957, six years before he became West Germany's chancellor, he published the widely read *Wohlstand für Alle*, translated into English not, following the German title, as *Prosperity for All* but characteristically as *Prosperity through Competition*. Answering the question "Does Prosperity Lead to Materialism?"

he insisted that economic growth helped people achieve nonmaterial goals. He attacked the connection critics made between increased prosperity and "a corrupting materialism" and argued that "the will to consume" was the engine of long-term, stable economic growth. As prosperity increased, people were "lifted from a purely primitive materialistic way of thinking." Attacking the elitist position that equated cultivation and class, he found it "pharisaical" that the well-off "complain about the pleasure-seeking and desires of those who basically have no other wish than to act like them." Why, he asked, would a radio or a vacuum cleaner be "an expression of civilization and culture" for the rich and yet provide "evidence of a materialistic attitude" for workers and their families. Having extolled a democracy of material goods in vague but familiar terms, Erhard envisioned a time when people, assured of material comfort and security, would "become free and ready for higher things."[3]

Erhard wrote at a time when West Germany was emerging from more than a third of a century of turmoil and devastation, experiencing rapid economic growth for which consumer culture was an essential component. As the historian Uta G. Poiger has shown, in the postwar period East and West Germans connected the impact of American popular culture to a wide range of issues surrounding national and personal identity. Until well into the 1960s, East Germans denounced American imports—first westerns, crime movies, and jazz and later rock and roll—as barbaric threats to German culture. In contrast, especially beginning in the late 1950s, West Germans increasingly embraced American popular culture and criticized their East German neighbors for feeling so threatened. Although the two Germanys looked critically at one another and developed different responses to American imports, what they shared was anguish over the meaning of Germanness. As they did so, they connected mass culture imported from America with adolescent sexuality, African American expressive culture, working-class values, the "oversexualization of women, and the feminization of men." Habermas strove to offer a critique of both the Christian Democratic Union's (CDU) emphasis on free markets and the Social Democratic Party's (SDP) vision of egalitarian abundance promoted by centralized planning.[4]

The Education of Jürgen Habermas

It was from Jürgen Habermas, the most prominent German intellectual of the last forty years of the twentieth century, that there came hints in the 1950s of a rethinking of the understanding of consumption and production. Born in Düsseldorf on June 18, 1929, and raised in a small town not far from Cologne,

Habermas grew up in a middle-class household that accommodated itself to the Nazi regime. His family, headed by a father who directed the local bureau of trade and industry, had made what Habermas later called a "bourgeois adaptation to a political environment with which one did not fully identify, but which one didn't seriously criticize either." As a teen near the end of World War II, Habermas joined the Hitler Youth. Soon after the war ended, listening to the Nuremberg Trials on radio and watching documentary films on the Holocaust awakened him to the horrors of the Nazi period and to his own complicity and that of others. "All at once," he later recalled of the immediate postwar year, "we saw that we had been living in a politically criminal system." In 1953 an article he wrote attacking Martin Heidegger for not renouncing, let alone acknowledging, his Nazi past caused considerable controversy. More generally, from the mid-1950s on, Habermas grew increasingly dissatisfied with the situation in Germany. Habermas, Tony Judt has remarked, saw West Germany as "a democracy without democrats" whose citizens had "had vaulted with shocking ease from Hitler to consumerism," in the process salving "their guilty memories by growing prosperous."[5]

Having studied economics, philosophy, history, and psychology at the universities in Göttingen, Zurich, and Bonn, Habermas obtained his doctorate in 1954 from Bonn and continued to come to terms with the writings of not only conservative cultural theorists but also the early Marx, the young Hegelians, Herbert Marcuse, Georg Lukács, Maurice Dobbs, Walter Benjamin, Sigmund Freud, Paul Baran, and Paul Sweezy. In addition, reading Horkheimer and Adorno's *Dialectic of Enlightenment*, he later remarked, "was a revelation: I suddenly realized that there were people who had been using Marx's theorems for their own systematic purposes, in the present." He married in 1955 and from 1956 to 1958 he worked as Adorno's research assistant at the Institute of Social Research, now reestablished in Frankfurt. At the time, Horkheimer hid from the younger generation at the Institute its prewar publications. Adorno, however, had a major impact on Habermas. Habermas later reported being shocked "when I met Adorno and saw how breathtakingly he spoke about commodity fetishism and applied this concept to cultural and everyday phenomena."[6]

More generally, being at the Institute helped connect Habermas with the tradition of German Jewish intellectual life that the Nazi era had obliterated from the universities and enabled him to break through the provincialism of postwar German intellectual life. Some of his work at the Institute, written in 1958 but not published until 1961 because of Horkheimer's objections, focused on the problem of political participation among German university students and called for a genuine, radical, and participatory democracy instead of a manipulative one operating through bureaucracies and interest groups in a welfare state. As was true of David Riesman in the late 1940s, a decade later the issue of political apathy compelled the attention of Habermas. In 1957–58, like Stuart Hall in Britain, Habermas participated in protests in the antinuclear movement, and in 1959 he joined the German social democratic student movement. Horkheimer, disturbed by Habermas's embrace of more radical aspects of Marxism, succeeded in getting him dismissed from the Institute. Habermas, Horkheimer wrote Adorno in 1958, might have "a good, or even brilliant career as a writer in front of him, but he would only cause the Institute immense damage," by which he meant jeopardize its financial and political support. Forced away from Frankfurt by Horkheimer, Habermas went to the University of Marburg in order to work under Wolfgang Abendroth, who was more sympathetic to his politics; he received his second thesis or *Habilitationsschrift* there in 1961 before going on to a professorship at Heidelberg. By now, Habermas was beginning to find German mentors—Abendroth and Hans-Georg Gadamer—who had not supported the Nazis. In 1964 he returned to the Institute at Frankfurt, as Horkheimer's successor.[7]

Habermas: Journalism and Social Philosophy

Beginning in 1952, Habermas worked as a freelance journalist, in the next half dozen years writing on a variety of subjects in articles published in newspapers. Only now have some of these essays by Habermas been translated into English, by people I worked with in the course of the writing of this book. Moreover, these essays are little if at all discussed in scholarship. Habermas was wrestling with issues Adorno and Horkheimer had raised, especially in their 1944 essay "The Culture Industry: Enlightenment as Mass Deception." There they had emphasized the inescapable power of capitalism to control people's lives not only in the realm of production, as more traditional Marxists had asserted, but also in the realm of consumption. Leisure, amusement, movies, and popular music, often thought of as sources of pleasure and play, turned out to be realms in which capitalism systematically oppressed as powerfully as it had done in factories. If there was any hope, they argued, it lay in avant-garde high culture.[8]

If what shaped Adorno and Horkheimer was what they had witnessed in Nazi Germany in the 1930s and in America, especially Hollywood, in the 1940s, what influenced Habermas was his engagement with new patterns of technology, production, and consumption whose implications he pondered in response to conferences he attended, industrial exhibits he saw, patterns of consumption he witnessed, and material he read. To a considerable extent, his journalistic essays, published in prominent German newspapers, reflected his agreement with the vision offered by Adorno and Horkheimer. He argued that what seemed to be the more free or democratic postwar system characterized by the rise of a new middle class in fact masked the powerful force of strengthened, administered systems of control by corporations and the state. He explored how consumption, now reliant on "amusement apparatuses," had become work. As he wrote in 1957, drawing on Riesman's discussion of play as work, a "false transfer of the work morale into the sphere of consumption" meant that aspects of "the work compulsion" were transformed "ironically into those of a consumption compulsion." He explored the differences between radio, television, and movies as technologies that shaped experience. He showed how contemporary technology intensified human alienation by disconnecting people from the physicality of industrial processes. Thus in 1953 he wrote of technology as Moloch, supported by the "bigotry of technological perfection and the pious subjugation" that resulted in humans losing an awareness of the ends in face of powerful means, in sacrificing their freedom, and in missing out on a sense of a world animated with meaningful things. Technology thus produced alienation in the realm of consumption, by underscoring the spread of factory rationality into it, for example, in the ways modern automobiles, with their emphasis on ease, perfection, and automation, eroded the chance for surprise and intense pleasure. Pointing forward to his later, more fully developed concerns about threats to public life, Habermas explored how the commercialization of leisure, seen in festivals and commemorations in contemporary West Germany, tried unsuccessfully "to recreate the rhythmic harmony of a joyful community."[9]

In contrast, Habermas found reason for cautious optimism about the relationships between culture and capitalism. He criticized those who demeaned the ability of the ordinary citizens. "Hitler saw the masses as a crowd inferior socially, intellectually and in terms of character. This notion is still rampant. It must finally be recognized as one of the most dangerous instruments of contempt for humanity," as he remarked in 1954, hinting at a connection between the 1930s and 1950s. He wondered whether new less hierarchical and more cooperative ways of organizing work could produce a somewhat more open society. He called for an embrace of authentic play, disassociated from the imperatives of production. Without giving specific examples, in one essay he celebrated how "the secret correlation between abundance and asceticism, discipline and intoxication is revealed: play as the superabundant *par excellence* is not in need of anything else; and the player attains free serene detachment through exertion." He hoped that innovative industrial design might encourage "fantasy and initiative" in people's relationships with what they purchased.

If he found little hope of liberation from television or movies, with radio it was otherwise. He located in contemporary, experimental radio plays, as he later would find in early modern public space, ways to counter the authority of capitalism and the state. What he called "the impersonal quality of the anonymous directive of the technological apparatus" that entered the home through the radio underscored the powerful impersonality of corporate and governmental bureaucracies. The way these plays juxtaposed "different realms of reality, real and unreal spaces" opened up room in which artists and listeners might operate with more freedom and imagination.[10]

To counter the power of alienating technology, Habermas emphasized the creativity of art: not just avant-garde modern art represented by Marc Chagall or Georges Braque but also that developed by industrial designers, cartoon animators, and modern architects. Bringing together art and technology would help recover the "thing character" of industrial processes and make people more aware of the objects in their daily lives, thus allowing consumers to use things for their own human ends rather than those prescribed by the sphere of production. If modern cars were problematically alienating, Habermas proposed two alternatives. One was the bumper cars he had witnessed at a carnival, for which driving involved "liberating breakthroughs, brazenness, cleverness, cunning, pedantry, and elegance." The other example was hot-rodders who drove in the American desert exhilarated by "fantasy, sensibility, individual willfulness, and desire to be a medium for mechanical excitations." These two alternatives point to how Habermas was trying to suggest what less alienated but hard-to-achieve driving might be like. When he talked of public celebrations, he mentioned the fluid "borders between spontaneous folk festival and manipulated hype." Moreover, he took some comfort from what he saw as "the mistrust of great stylizations, understatement, and the 'fractured attitude' towards celebratory pretension—as reactions to manipulated celebratory acts and emptied-out, late-bourgeois festival conventions." Here the young Habermas expressed a longing for authentic celebration and community not readily available under the more "fractured" conditions that obtained in the contemporary world.[11]

In these essays from the mid-1950s, it is possible to see Habermas coming to terms with the legacy of Horkheimer and Adorno much earlier than many scholars assume. He had turned away from their appreciation of elite, modernist art and instead emphasized how new patterns of work and leisure might counter the admittedly powerful forces of capitalism and the state. More so than in his later writings, there are hints in these essays of a young writer's existential worries about the impact of consumer culture. Yet what he accom-

plished was incomplete. Again and again, he hesitated, hiding through oblique-
ness his emphasis on optimistic possibilities. Perhaps it is unrealistic to expect
more from someone so young, living in such tumultuous times, and having to
contend with the crosscurrents of German intellectual life.[12]

Early Philosophical Essays by Habermas
on Production and Consumption

In scholarly essays, published in 1954 and 1958 but translated into English by
scholars who helped me in preparing this section of the book, Habermas began
to work out some of these ideas in more philosophical terms, as he offered hints
that he was trying to challenge the pessimism that Horkheimer and Adorno
had expressed in *Dialectic* about the impact of mass media on society in the
twentieth century. In 1954 Habermas published "The Dialectics of Rationalization: On Pauperization in Production and Consumption." Here he worked to
come to terms with a realization of the challenges that the increasing affluence
of the German working class and the growing middle class posed to traditional
Marxism, a project Richard Hoggart and others in Britain were focusing on at
the same time. He drew on writings of the Frankfurt School and on conservative German nationalists. Much of his essay was a dense, pessimistic discussion of what he called "pauperization," the ways in which in major industries
under modern capitalism used technology to make the situation of workers
worse at a time when their wages rose. Even experiments on labor morale, like
those carried out by Elton Mayo at Westinghouse's Hawthorne factory, were a
social therapy that served only to subject workers to technologically imposed
rationalization. Higher wages did not compensate for alienation. Further, the
ability of workers to use in their leisure time what they produced on the job,
rather than providing genuine enjoyment, served only to bind them even more
tightly to the economic system. The artificial mobilization of needs was more
or less a trick to encourage greater productivity. Consequently, mechanized
conditions of work and increased consumption only served to reinforce one
another. Continually referring to American conditions, Habermas emphasized
how accelerated consumption and affluence undermined the true value of objects of desire.[13]

Yet Habermas found reason for guarded optimism. He discussed experiments in which workers were given more control over their work: before World
War II at the Bata shoe factory in Moravia and during the war in an aircraft
plant in California. Studies of these examples by the émigré writer on management Peter Drucker and the French sociologist Georges Friedmann demon-

strated that workers were more productive if they had a major say in decisions about their working conditions. Giving workers more responsibility would enable them to understand how what they were doing fit into a larger process and see how they could "consciously contribute" to the creation of a product. All these changes, Habermas wrote, would result in less alienation. Indeed they could foster "enthusiasm for work" and greater performance and profitability. In addition, reductions in advertising would make responsible consumer choices and the proper enjoyment of goods more likely. Pointing to the sleek and innovative industrial designs by the American Raymond Loewy, who had emigrated from Paris in his mid-twenties, Habermas explored how entrepreneurs and designers could educate consumers to appreciate the unique properties of commercial goods. More effective industrial design could thus enhance the autonomy of consumers.[14]

In a second article, his 1958 "Sociological Notes Concerning the Relationship of Work and Leisure," Habermas again offered both pessimistic and slightly hopeful analyses. On the one hand, he asserted that under modern conditions, free time was an illusion because the dynamics of production controlled the nature of leisure. Capitalism and mechanization increasingly determined people's lives outside the sphere of production, in a situation in which leisure was ascendant over work. He worried that the pursuit of a higher standard of living might condemn workers "to a status of neobarbarians jollied along in the cage of consumer culture." Yet Habermas raised the possibility of pleasures outside the realm of work, hobbies as well as jobs in charitable, religious, and cultural organizations. But even there the imperatives of industrial activity, with its emphasis on organization and discipline, played a significant role. Moreover, he imagined that in the realm of leisure there was some hope. The enjoyment of real abundance would require a changed attitude regarding consumption in which self-restraint counteracted the tendency to equate leisure with materialism. This aestheticism, which was different from what would be obtained under conditions of poverty, would "give individuals back their freedom to acquire that which is respectively appropriate" and thus provide "the actual condition for satisfying real needs." Moreover, automation could mean that a shorter work week for laborers might reduce the prestige of work, open up more genuine free time, and thus enhance the value of cultural and political activities. Habermas held out the hope that truly free time could lead to "the conscious participation of the broad masses" in social life, through which people would regain control of their lives to fulfill "the promise that we can redeem that happiness which is possible here and now."[15]

In his writings of the late 1950s and early 1960s for both a general audience and a scholarly one, Habermas was trying to figure out what it meant to reaffirm and reformulate what Adorno and Horkheimer had written in an earlier and very different context. Like them, he saw modern capitalist production and consumption operating together to forcefully oppress human aspirations. Yet again and again, Habermas worked to avoid a position that, much more than that of his mentors, mediated between the extremes of apologetics and despair. His alternatives to the iron cage of producer and consumer capitalism were often not fully developed. Nonetheless, he was working toward an understanding of what other critics would emphasize more strongly in the 1950s and 1960s, not the liberation fostered by the avant-garde but the experimental reaches of the culture of ordinary people. He located this in animated comics, artists who experimented with popular culture, industrial designers, hot-rodders, and experiments in restoring the balance between work and leisure. To put it more broadly, Habermas was trying to figure out how it might be possible to overcome the alienation of consumers as workers by emphasizing passion, imagination, and citizenship.[16]

Structural Transformation of the Public Sphere (1962)

In late 1950s and early 1960s, at the same time that Habermas addressed issues of work and leisure, he began to turn his attention to questions about the public sphere. His first major work, a revision of his *Habilitationsschrift*, was *The Structural Transformation of the Public Sphere: An Inquiry into a Category of Bourgeois Society*, which appeared in German in 1962 but remained untranslated into English until 1989. Between 1956 and 1961, several events shaped his work, including German court decisions banning the Communist Party and rejecting an antinuclear plebiscite, the presence of former Nazis in the government and universities, the ascendancy of the Christian Democrats over the Social Democrats, NATO's decision to allow nuclear weapons on German soil, the resurgence of German nationalism and anti-Semitism, the shift of the Social Democrats away from their commitment as a workers' party, and the use by the Christian Democrats (under the leadership of Konrad Adenauer and Ludwig Erhard) of marketing techniques to mobilize voters to support their side. *Structural Transformation* was thus an exploration of the limits of German democracy in the immediate postwar period. All of these factors, as the historian Matthew Specter has shown, turned Habermas into both a theorist and activist vitally concerned with threats to the public sphere.[17]

In *Structural Transformation*, Habermas worked within the Frankfurt School tradition yet again pushed mildly against its pessimism. He focused on the modernization of the West and not the Americanization of Western Europe, even if he was acutely aware of American influence on German politics and culture. Without consistently equating mass media with Americanization, he highlighted the way many Americans such as William Randolph Hearst, Ivy Lee, and Edward Bernays had developed the innovations that undermined a genuine public sphere. With reservations and a suggestion of how to remedy the situation, he accepted the notion that modern mass media had helped to erode the importance of public space and to undermine both freedom and democracy. In the modern world the public sphere deteriorated by separating into "minorities of specialists who put their reason to use publicly," on the one hand, and "the great mass of consumers whose receptiveness is public but uncritical," on the other. In the eighteenth century, the press played a crucial role in supporting a public sphere; by the twentieth, mass media had undermined its vitality. From the eighteenth century to the twentieth, the transition was "from a public critically reflecting on its culture to one that merely consumes it." Drawing on David Riesman's *The Lonely Crowd* (1950) in a way that turned the American author's cautious optimism about consumer education into relatively bleak pessimism, Habermas wrote of how "the culture of harmony" subjected the public "to the soft compulsion of constant consumption training." To drive home his pessimistic points about the undermining of the public sphere, Habermas relied on, among other sources, observers of the American scene not all of whom would have agreed with his conclusions—Bernard Berelson, James Burnham, Alexis de Tocqueville, Peter Drucker, John Kenneth Galbraith, Paul Lazarsfeld, Rolf Meyersohn, C. Wright Mills, David Riesman, and William H. Whyte Jr.[18]

Not unlike Adorno and Horkheimer in their discussion of the power of the culture industry, Habermas argued that a whole range of forces came together by the middle of the twentieth century to form a powerful mixture, including advertising, public relations, publicity campaigns, public interest groups, political parties, public bureaucracies, the commodification of news ("a system of other-directed consumption habits" in the "so-called consumer culture"), the erosion of the distinction between public and private, the power of the social welfare state (which he opposed from the left), large labor unions, and oligopolistic industries. These forces made citizens increasingly passive and undermined the possibility of "rational-critical debate" in "the manufactured public sphere," with the commercialization of public space greatly weakening any prospect of participatory democracy. The expansion of modern media, he wrote pessimistically, gave "the masses in general access to the public sphere," but did so by depoliticizing that realm. Under these powerful conditions, the citizen became a consumer, experiencing a sense of self not through demo-cratic participation but by making purchases in an increasingly affluent society. In language considerably more abstract and dense than the similar and roughly contemporary writing of C. Wright Mills, Habermas wrote of "commodity ex-change" pervading the private fields of home and family. As a result, consump-tion increasingly replaced genuine public debates and, he concluded, "the web of public communication unraveled into acts of individualized reception, how-ever uniform in mode."[19]

At a few moments, offering what one scholar has called "a glimmer of hope," Habermas explored how a true public sphere might be reestablished. He looked forward to "a critical publicity" that would increase democratic decision making in large organizations and foster greater openness in the deliberations of the social welfare state, prospects, he argued, that could not be "disqualified as simply utopian." He wondered whether greater affluence might foster the "increasing plurality of interests," although at the same time he worried that nuclear war might bring "self-annihilation on a global scale." Habermas ended the book on a promising if somewhat vague and hedged note of optimism. In its final sentence, he wrote that real change was still possible in the bourgeois public sphere "whether the exercise of domination and power persists as a nega-tive constant, as it were, of history—or whether as a historical category itself, it is open to substantive change."[20]

The way in which Habermas emphasized the change of the citizen into consumer underscores the importance of the transformations that the histo-rian Lizabeth Cohen has suggested for postwar America. She charts the shift from the "citizen consumers" who during the New Deal and World War II "put the market power of the consumer to work politically"; to the "purchaser con-sumer" who at the same time "championed pursuit of self-interest in the mar-ketplace out of confidence in the ameliorative effects of aggregate purchasing power"; later to the "purchaser as citizen" who believed "satisfying personal material wants actually served the national interest" since recovery and then prosperity "depended on a dynamic mass consumption economy"; and fi-nally, beginning in the 1980s, to the "consumer/citizen/taxpayer/voter" in what Cohen calls a "Consumerized Republic, where self-interested citizens increas-ingly view government policies like other market transactions, judging them by how well served they feel personally." Although the American and German situations are not interchangeable, in important ways Habermas was recoiling against the way bourgeois citizens who participated in a public arena of the eighteenth century in the twentieth century had become consumers without any effective role as citizens.[21]

In the work of Habermas of the 1950s and early 1960s, as in Adorno and Horkheimer's *Dialectic*, pessimism about commercial culture's impact almost always trumped optimism. Yet there were differences between the teachers and their student. When he wrote an essay on Benjamin in 1972, Habermas noted that "on no other point did Adorno contradict Benjamin as vigorously" as on the commodification of art. Adorno, he noted, "regarded the mass art emerging with the new techniques and technologies of reproduction as a degeneration of art," where Benjamin and Habermas believed that under some circumstances (although they differed as to which) "it is to its commodity character that art owes its liberation in the first place." This disagreement with Adorno by Habermas shows one way in which the most prominent member of the second generation of the Frankfurt School worked against two of the most prominent members of the first, even while drawing on not only Marcuse but also Benjamin. In other ways, Habermas made more room than Adorno and Horkheimer for resistance and provided more sympathy for bourgeois democracy. Unlike Adorno and Horkheimer, Habermas did not believe that modern capitalism mobilized mass media to dominate consciousness in a totalizing manner. Moreover, if Adorno and Horkheimer's elitism came through in many ways, including their confidence in avant-garde high culture, Habermas located possibilities elsewhere, in the eighteenth century precisely at the heart of a vigorous public sphere in which then new media played such a role. He asserted that for a later period, if modern mass media had severely limited a vital public sphere, there was some hope that affluence might mitigate the worst effects of mass media and open up room for vital democracy. Yet Habermas's differences from his seniors, as significant as they were, should not blind us to the fact that, as we will see later, Benjamin pointed the way forward more forcefully and imaginatively, albeit ambiguously.[22]

Roland Barthes and the Symbolism of Everyday Life

In *Mythologies*, published in France in 1957 but not translated into English until 1972 (and in its full original version not until the appearance of *The Eiffel Tower* in 1979), the French critic Roland Barthes produced a pathbreaking book that helped its readers think about commercial culture. Drawing on the semiotics of the linguist Ferdinand de Saussure, on Marxist analysis, and on his sustained engagement with literary criticism, Barthes offered a compelling way to analyze everyday objects and phenomena. He presented penetrating analyses of advertisements and spectacles that connected consumer culture, race, class, and citizenship. He probed the meaning of the relationship of France with her colonies as filtered through consumption. He focused on the images themselves, albeit without neglecting to join their production and consumption. Behind the specifics of his case studies stood an argument that bourgeois society used commercial goods and experiences to turn the historical into the natural, in the process obfuscating the reality of power relations. Moreover, his approach, coming as it did from a critic steeped in a rich literary tradition, involved an exploration of the complexities of the relationships between high and low cultures. Like Habermas in Germany and Eco in Italy, Barthes used sophisticated ideas to understand apparently simple examples of popular culture.[23]

Well into the 1960s, Barthes led a life of tragedy, struggle, and relative obscurity. He was born on November 12, 1915, into a bourgeois, Protestant family in the port city of Cherbourg, Normandy. His father, a naval officer, was killed at sea before his son reached his first birthday. Then until he was eleven Barthes was raised by three women—his mother, aunt, and grandmother—in Bayonne, a small city in southwest France. In 1924 he moved with his mother to Paris, where they lived in genteel poverty on the Left Bank, although his maternal grandmother was well-to-do. By sixteen he was a socialist, a follower of the heritage of Jean Jaurès. Barthes studied at the Sorbonne from 1935 to 1939, earning his *licence* in classical letters and founding the Groupe de Théâtre Antique, which staged classical dramas. But the real drama of his twenties had begun when he was diagnosed with tuberculosis in 1934, a disease that interrupted his formal education, kept him out of military service, and absented him from many of the major events of World War II even as he remained a committed antifascist. Until the mid-1940s, his illness also required him to live in and out of sanatoriums, where, despite the company of other highly intellectual patients, he often felt isolated, lonely, and depressed. His confinement left him with abundant time to read works by Marx, as well as major books of history and literature, and to begin his career as a writer. Off and on from 1939 until 1960 he had increasingly solid but nonetheless less than ideal positions—in a series of lycées and at French cultural institutions in Bucharest (1948–49) and Alexandria, Egypt (1949–50). By 1950 he was back in Paris, continuing his education and employed in the cultural affairs section of the foreign office, and then as a researcher at Centre National de Recherche Scientifique, where he remained for seven years, a stint interrupted by employment as an editor. Despite his precarious situation, from 1946 on, Barthes started to make his way in the world of Parisian intellectuals.

When still in treatment in mountainous regions of France, Barthes began to publish: an essay on André Gide in 1942; one on literary criticism in 1947; his first book, *Writing Degree Zero*, in 1953; a book on the historian Jules Michelet in 1954; and a series of essays on figures such as Bertolt Brecht and Alain Robbe-Grillet. In the mid-1950s, Barthes wrestled with the implications of Marxism and existentialism. *Writing Degree Zero* drew on essays he had published in the influential left-wing Paris newspaper *Combat*, which had grown out of the Resistance and had published works by Jean-Paul Sartre, Albert Camus, Raymond Aron, and André Breton. This book, critical of Sartre, was a study of the relationship between literature, style, and the historical factors that shaped them. In the preface to the English translation in 1968, Susan Sontag named Barthes, along with Adorno and Kenneth Burke, as "distinguished examples of this rare breed of intellectual virtuoso." With that book, with the publication of *Mythologies* in 1957, and with his appointment in 1960 at the École Pratique des Hautes Études, Barthes began his ascent to the pinnacle of French academic and intellectual life, ending what he called the "instability" of his professional life that had lasted for more than fifteen years. Eventually he was chosen for a position of great national prestige—chair of sémiologie littéraire at the Collège de France in 1977—the same year as the death of his mother, with whom he had lived for decades. In February 1980, after leaving a lunch hosted by François Mitterand, Barthes was accidentally struck by a van on the streets of Paris and died a month later.[24]

Mythologies (1957)

Barthes divided *Mythologies* into two parts, the first a series of short essays and the second a more theoretical piece titled "Myth Today." In that latter section, the fruits of his interest in semiotics became clear. He explored how language worked to generate myths, what he called a "system of communication." Semiotics enabled Barthes to distinguish between denotation, the supposedly self-evident meaning, and connotation, the implied one. There were three key terms here: the signifier (a word or image, with Barthes's example being some roses), the signified (what roses mean—passion or romance), and the sign (the association of the signifier and signified—what he called "'passionified' roses"). Barthes's most intriguing example came from a cover of *Paris-Match*:

> A young Negro in a French uniform is saluting, with his eyes uplifted, probably fixed on a fold of the tricolour. All this is the *meaning* of the picture. But, whether naively or not, I see very well what it signifies to me: that France is a great Empire, that all her sons, without any colour discrimination, faithfully serve under her flag, and that there is no better answer to the detractors of an alleged colonialism than the zeal

shown by this Negro in serving his so-called oppressors. I am therefore faced with a greater semiological system: there is a signifier, itself already formed with a previous system (*a black soldier is giving the French salute*); there is a signified (it is here a purposeful mixture of Frenchness and militariness); finally, there is a presence of the signified through the signifier.

The power of this system lay in its ability to promote a process Barthes called "frozen speech," the way myth, through language, steals and neutralizes, in this instance how "the Negro's salute thickens, becomes vitrified, freezes into an eternal reference meant to *establish* French imperiality." As he remarked in the preface to the 1970 French edition, when he wrote *Mythologies*, he "had just read Saussure and as a result acquired the conviction that by treating 'collective representations' as sign-systems, one might hope to go further than the pious show of unmasking them and account *in detail* for the mystificaction which transforms petit-bourgeois culture into a universal nature."[25]

In the first section of *Mythologies*, Barthes offered short, intensive analyses of specific icons and a complicated unearthing of their aesthetically rich and larger meanings. Most of them originally published from 1954 to 1956 in a series called "Mythology of the Month" in *Les Lettres Nouvelles*, the essays ranged widely across the contemporary landscape, zeroing in on such phenomena as a court case, detergents, toys, movie stars, and food. By focusing on everyday life, Barthes's essays were part of an effort among French intellectuals to come to terms with the dramatic modernization that began in the mid to late 1950s. He interpreted commercial images and performances as texts, much as an anthropologist might read a ritual a tribe enacted. In economical and at times opaque prose, he linked high and low culture, demonstrating how philosophy and literature, for example, illuminated and paralleled the meanings of the mundane and commercial. Thus he connected "the function of grandiloquence" of the spectacle of wrestling with the power of classical theater to evoke themes of suffering or justice.[26]

He focused on how the excessive, flamboyant, and superficial enabled language to distort or steal meaning. He emphasized how artifice, the display of the body, sexuality, and sensuality were core features of much popular culture. He wrote of a travel writer as having "a good fleshly body" and of Garbo's image plunging "audiences into the deepest ecstasy, . . . when the face represented a kind of absolute state of the flesh." For him, professional wrestling, though superficially understood as a sport, was in fact a "spectacle of excess" filled with overflowing emotion.[27] Similarly, a striptease performed by a woman might in common-sense terms be about sexuality when, in fact, it was about precisely the opposite—the desexualization of the female body. The Parisian striptease, he wrote, was "a mystifying device which consists in inoculating the public with a touch of evil, the better to plunge it afterwards into a permanently immune Moral Good: a few particles of eroticism, highlighted by the very situation on which the show is based, are in fact absorbed in a reassuring ritual which negates the flesh as surely as the vaccine or the taboo circumscribe and control the illness of the crime." What seemed sexual ended with a naked body regaining "a perfectly chaste state of the flesh."[28]

For Barthes, the analysis of specific cultural artifacts and moments pointed to larger social meanings. Barthes wrote of new Citroëns as "the supreme creation of an era, conceived with passion by unknown artists, and consumed in image if not in usage by a whole population which appropriates them as a purely magical object." He made these observations at a time when, as we will see, members of London's Independent Group were oohing and aahing as they looked at American automobiles, but before Tom Wolfe would lavish his prose on custom cars. When turning his attention to an exhibition of new plastic products, Barthes wrote of people witnessing "the accomplishment of the magical operation par excellence: the transmutation of matter," produced by machines "watched over by an attendant in a cloth cap, half-god, half-robot" and the "stuff of alchemy," which, appropriately, has the "names of Greek shepherds" such as Polystyrene. Thus Barthes understood culture as comprising a series of dramatic, spectacular, and symbolic acts conveyed through texts people encountered in their daily lives. Attentive to the language, representations, symbolic meanings, and surface texture of images, he showed how the ordinary embodied myths that served as key components of a system of communication. As Dick Hebdige later remarked, Barthes "refers to the mystique of the object": the mysterious aspects of its appearance, its connection to "religious myths and archetypes," and how it involves "the transubstantiation of labor powers into things."[29]

Similarly, an advertisement for a laundry detergent or the cover of a popular magazine provided a window into how contradiction and dialectic revealed the fissures between appearances and social reality. Capitalism, imperialism, and the class system deployed symbolic systems to transform the physicality of objects and the ordinariness of the quotidian into powerful instruments of social control. Thus Barthes ended his analysis of laundry products by cautioning his readers not to forget that corporate power to shape the consumer's experience stood behind seemingly innocent images. The "euphoria" evoked by an advertisement that celebrated a soap's power, he wrote, "must not make us forget that there is one plane on which *Persil* and *Omo* are one and the same: the plane of the Anglo-Dutch trust *Unilever*." Significantly, Barthes focused on the European company Unilever and its two products during what the historian Victoria de Grazia has described as the "detergent wars," when the products of the European Unilever competed with those of American corporations, Procter and Gamble and Colgate-Palmolive. Barthes might have jumped on the anti-American bandwagon and held up Tide instead of Persil or Omo as the representative of a consumer culture that mystified capitalism's methods. Instead, he focused on a powerful Anglo-Dutch company and its products.[30]

Barthes was paying attention not to the United States but to the relationship between France and its colonies by connecting consumer culture with nationhood and citizenship. Exploring the nexus between the colonization of everyday life and the decolonization of North Africa, he linked the symbolic power of consumer items with what it meant for even nonwhites to belong to a nation when he wrote that for French people "to believe in wine is a coercive collective act," a universality that implied conformity. Writing at a time when the French were tightening their control over their increasingly restless colonies, Algeria especially, he identified the dynamics that connected consumer culture, nationalism, and imperialism. Central to the production of abundant wine, the "totem-drink" of France, was the way French capitalism in Algeria imposed "on the Muslims, on the very land of which they have been dispossessed, a crop of which they have no need, while they lack even bread." Similarly, the "young Negro in a French uniform," who appeared on the cover of *Paris-Match* saluting the French flag, made natural and thereby powerful the egalité and universal sense of Frenchness deployed in the defense of the French empire. Class also played a key role in giving symbols power. Symbolic systems enabled the bourgeoisie to identify itself with the nation, to gain compliance from the petite bourgeoisie whose "norms are the residue of bourgeois culture." Consequently, "the bourgeoisie is constantly absorbing into its ideology a whole section of humanity which does not have its basic status and cannot live up to it," he insisted, "except in imagination, that is, at the cost of an immobilization and an impoverishment of consciousness." The vehicles that carried the symbolic meaning of daily life such as newspapers, films, pulp stories, politics, and casual talk about weddings, meals, and clothes, were "dependent on the representation which the bourgeoisie *has and makes us have* of the relations of man and the world."[31]

Myths thus changed culture and history into nature, the factual into the transcendent, the particular into the universal and ideological, in the process shrouding the social order in a haze of mystification. As Barthes wrote in the preface to the 1957 edition, he "resented seeing Nature and History confused at every turn" and therefore "wanted to track down, in the decorative display of *what-goes-without-saying*, the ideological abuse which, in my view, is hidden there." In the book itself, among his most compelling examples of this process was the photographic exhibit, developed in the United States as *The Family of Man* but shown in Paris as *The Great Family of Man*. The exhibit's theme was that despite the distinctiveness of individual cultures, universality prevailed. "Man is born, works, laughs and dies everywhere in the same way," Barthes wrote as he cast a skeptical eye on its message. Then Barthes pointedly asked, "Why not ask the parents of Emmet Till, the young Negro assassinated by the Whites, what *they* think of *The Great Family of Man*?," as he referred to the killing in August 1955 of a fourteen-year-old African American in the Mississippi Delta, allegedly for whistling at a white woman. Again and again, Barthes drove home the point about history, nature, and mystification. When he wrote of Hachette's *Blue Guides*, he found in them the "disease of thinking in essences, which is at the bottom of every bourgeois mythology of man." At their best, myths were fluid, their meaning contingent, with Barthes likening them to a "constantly moving turnstile" through which traveled a series of continually shifting meanings.[32]

Forces were at work that turned myth into depoliticized or "frozen speech," making the symbolic systems that people encountered daily the means by which power in the society was organized and sustained. Reflecting the producerist ethic common to writers steeped in Marxism, Barthes used the "language of man as a producer" as the "one language that is not mythical." For Barthes, in these years on the non-Communist left, language was important to understand because it was the means by which corporations and the state maintained their power. His analysis extended not only to canonical texts but also to performances and advertisements, an examination of which revealed how symbols were connected to power relations. The lessons his exercises provided demonstrated (paralleling what McLuhan had written in *The Mechanical Bride* in 1951) how an active reader (so very much unlike the passive consumer) resisted by playfully interpreting mythologically encrusted commercial messages and thereby uncovered the social system's ideologies. Thus myth as stolen and depoliticized speech, driven by class dynamics, state imperatives, colonialism, and corporate power, emptied reality of all complexity, contradictions, tragedy, history, and politics. As Barthes wrote in 1953, an analysis of myths provided "the only effective way for an intellectual to take political action."[33]

Fascination and Critical Judgment

If *Mythologies* was a very political book, placing Barthes clearly on the left, he hardly engaged in the anti-Americanism typical in the 1950s of many of those on the left, especially Communists. Barthes wrote his book precisely at a time when the French left, Communists especially, opposed America's policies in the Cold War and America's exportation of its consumer culture, which many feared was eroding French cultural autonomy and replacing it with materialism, conformity, and corrosive popular culture. In contrast, in the mid-1950s French public opinion was strongly positive about the United States, especially the way it provided a model of a society that embraced the pursuit of a higher standard of living. In the book, Barthes, aware of France's imperial past and present when the war in Algeria was intensifying, hardly saw the killing of Emett Till as evidence of American racism in contrast to French innocence. Indeed, about the time of the book's publication, Barthes traveled to New York, and his initial response involved an appreciation of Manhattan's modernity, so much so that when he returned to Paris he tried to persuade his mother to buy a modern household appliance. A number of his essays focused on American cultural products, more prominently in the original French edition and its 1979 translation into English than in the 1972 English edition. At least three of the essays that did not appear in the 1972 version ("Billy Graham at the Vel' d' Hiv'"; "A Sympathetic Worker" on Elia Kazan's *On the Waterfront*; and "Buffet Finished Off New York") took on American subjects but did not emphasize that they represented a threat to bring to France an Americanized popular culture. Rather, the first two focused on the consequences of American anti-Communism. Barthes was working not against worries about an American invasion but on precisely the opposite, the tendency among French writers to assume that problems came from the outside.[34]

Moreover, the essay on Bernard Buffet's paintings of Manhattan involved a not unalloyed appreciation of America and a critique of France's provincial anti-Americanism. The artist's depiction of New York as "a petrified, infantile necropolis" would not, Barthes thought, "unsettle many prejudices"; rather it "confirms the Frenchman in the excellence of his habitat." To Barthes New York was a "marvelous city," alive and compelling. In contrast, Buffet's depictions followed "in the wake of our venerable moralists, for whom the refrigerator is antipathetic to the soul." For Barthes, Buffet's reaction to Manhattan evoked the notion that "we are bored when we are comfortable, in short, according to the most reactionary remark of human history, the alibi of all exploitations, that 'money doesn't make happiness.'"[35]

Barthes's response to consumer culture makes clear the consequences of his long encounter with genteel poverty. His financial situation improved in the spring of 1955 when the estate of his maternal grandmother was settled, leaving him with an inheritance. Yet his long experience living in straitened circumstances was one of the factors that made him criticize moralistic denunciations of consumer culture and in turn appreciate, if often critically, new elements of that culture. Writing about himself in the early 1970s, Barthes pointed to the *"endurable* privation" he experienced as a child and young man as possibly accounting "for a little philosophy of free compensation, of the overdetermination of pleasures." It is not stretching things too far to connect the straitened economic circumstances he experienced until just before his fortieth birthday with his fascination in *Mythologies* with the sensuousness, texture, display, and expressiveness commercial culture offered. In his memoir, Barthes wrote of himself that his "formative problem was doubtless money, not sex."[36]

Sexuality was indeed a factor that shaped his responses to consumer culture. Although sexual expressiveness was central to the vision Barthes offered in *Mythologies*, as a homosexual he himself remained very much in the closet during his lifetime. In his posthumously published *Roland Barthes*, he wrote elliptically but suggestively of his sexuality— remarking on both "the pleasure potential of a perversion," as he referred to both homosexuality and hashish, and on what it meant to see a young heterosexual couple wearing their *"sexuality and respectability"* like "the legion-of-honor ribbon in a buttonhole." The literary critic D. A. Miller has recently explored how "discreet" was the connection in Barthes's writing "with gay sexuality." Although he did not refer specifically to *Mythologies*, he writes that "Barthes's own emphasis on the body . . . belongs to the same gay male cultural project of resurrecting the flesh." It is possible to go even further in exploring the connection between Barthes's writings and his sexuality. Here his 1957 book can be fruitfully read next to Susan Sontag's 1964 "Notes on 'Camp,'" in a way that raises the question of whether *Mythologies* embodied some aspects of a gay aesthetic. In the preface to the English translation of Barthes's *Writing Degree Zero*, Sontag, herself then a closeted bisexual, hailed Barthes for "his talent for sensuous phenomenological description," made clear "in the brilliant essays-epiphanies" in *Mythologies*. Or as Habermas wrote in an essay on Benjamin but can be said of Barthes as well, "He insisted on both the most spiritual and the most sensuous happiness as a mass experience." An appreciation of the pleasures of consumer culture arose from many sources in the period after 1950, not the least among them from a linking of performance, sexuality (often queer sexuality), sensuousness, and pleasure. This is visible in Barthes's descriptions of men's bodies displayed in wrestling matches and of Garbo's face—and in a more elliptical way in his essay on striptease, where he emphasized the hazards of inauthentic sexual expression.[37]

With its brilliant and epigrammatic discussions of contemporary commercial culture and its unmasking of iconic meanings, Barthes's *Mythologies* had a significant impact. Its insights and mode of analysis gradually became a common way the French understood commercial culture. Barthes's approach made its way into films and cultural criticism. Nowhere was the book's influence clearer than in Georges Perec's bestselling and prize-winning novel *Les Choses* published in France in 1965 but not translated into English until 1990 as *Things: A Story of the Sixties*. Perec knew Barthes; in fact while he was finishing his book, Perec was taking a class in rhetoric from him. In the book Perec told the story of a petit-bourgeois couple in their twenties who worked in Paris as market researchers, carrying out interviews using the psychologically oriented Motivational Research made popular in the United States and Europe by the Ernest Dichter. The novel captured their world and their longings. Restless, they found few satisfactions in their work, except possibly as entry points into the desires of those they interviewed. So they turned to consumption, which was more pleasurable in Perec's descriptions than it was fulfilling in their lives. The acquisition and enjoyment of possessions stood at the center of their world. "Those were the years when they wandered endlessly around Paris," Perec wrote. "They would stop at every antique dealer's. They would go in to department stores and stay for hours on end, marveling and already scared but not daring to admit it to themselves, not daring to face squarely that particular type of despicable voracity which was to become their fate, their *raison d'etre*, their watchword, for they were still marveling at and almost drowning under the scale of their own needs, of the riches laid out before them, of the abundance on offer."[38]

Perec provided lavish descriptions of the world of commercial culture in which they were both voyeurs and consumers. Once they gave up dressing like students, "that is to say badly," he noted,

> they leapt ecstatically into fashionable English clothes. They discovered knitwear, silk blouses, skirts by Doucet, cotton voile ties, silk scarves, tweed, lambswool, cashmere, vicuna, leather and jerseywool, flax and, finally, the great staircase of footwear leading from Churches to Westons, from Westons to Buntings and from Buntings to Lobbs.

Bored and uncertain, and unsure they want to become junior executives, the couple eventually turn to a simpler life in Tunisia. Not long after, they return and at the end of the book we see them going to a provincial French town where they will be junior advertising executives. The easiest way to read *Things* is to see it as a critique of consumer culture written as the French were recovering from wartime austerity, as a story, not without its own angst, of young people pursuing the pleasures of goods whose fulfillments are always elusive. David Bellos, who translated the novel into English and wrote Perec's biography, offers a cautionary note, calling the novel "a masterpiece of detachment and ambiguity." Perec, he argued, was "reaching towards the kind of simultaneous passion and detachment characteristic of Flaubert."[39]

And, he might have added, characteristic of Barthes as well. For *Mythologies*, like Perec's novel, had that telling combination of a feel for the sensuous pleasures of consumer culture and penetrating, detached analysis of its meanings. Barthes's ambiguous and engaged encounter with commercial culture was clear in the early 1960s. In 1963 he wrote an essay for *Cahiers de la publicité*, the leading French publication for the advertising field, titled "La message publicitaire" (The Advertising Message) which appeared as "Rêve et poésie" (Dreams and Poetry). He offered a semiotic analysis of the function of advertising as a series of messages created by an agency. Barthes followed that up with an essay in 1964, published in *Communications*, in which he analyzed a poster promoting pasta. These articles attracted the attention of Georges Péninou, who as a student of philosophy had avidly studied Barthes, Gaston Bachelard, Roman Jakobson, and Claude Lévi-Strauss. At the time he was the head of research at Publicis, France's leading advertising agency. Péninou, convinced that the turn of advertising to psychoanalysis was a dead end, enrolled in a seminar Barthes taught. Setting out to write a Ph.D. dissertation on the semiotics of advertising, he captured the attention of his colleagues at Publicis. He invited Barthes to the company's offices, where Barthes gave a lecture to executives and eventually signed a contract with the agency, for a brief period applying semiotics to the promotion of Renault automobiles. As in *Mythologies*, Barthes thus displayed the striking combination of engaged, ambiguous fascination and critical judgment.[40]

Umberto Eco

In 1993, when Umberto Eco wrote the preface to his 1963 collection of essays *Diario minimo*, titled *Misreadings* in English, he remarked that "from the point of view of literary genre" his essays were like those in *Mythologies*. He went on to say that the similarity was a result of coincidence, since when he started writing the essays he had not yet come across the 1957 book by Barthes. Yet emblematic of the convergence of approaches across national boundaries, many of Eco's essays, short explorations of cultural texts, resembled what Barthes had offered. Indeed, like his French counterpart, Eco wrote an essay on a strip-tease show. In his 1959 piece, Eco, like Barthes, analyzed the show as a care-fully choreographed performance, in his words "a bored sexuality composed of indifference, here spiced by an expertise borne like a penance." To the men in the audience, the performing woman was not available for consumption even though a sexual tease without consummation was involved. Coming close to describing an orgasm, Eco wrote that the stripper offered the male viewer "the basic element that eludes him, the goal of ecstasy that he cannot achieve, the sense of triumph that is arrested in him." Mixing Freudian and Marxist lan-guage, Eco described the exchange between performer and audience as involv-ing sadomasochism whose frustration the spectator accepts, knowing "that the means of production are not in his possession." After the show, the spectator, "sustained by the fact that the command buttons of political life do not belong to him and that the pattern of his experiences is sanctioned by a realm of ideas he cannot alter," could "peacefully return to the responsibilities of every day, after the cathartic ritual has confirmed his position as a fixed and solid element in the existing order." In this brief essay, Eco offered an analysis that revealed so many key elements of his considerations of popular culture in the late 1950s and early 1960s: the commitment to analyze its texts seriously by using sophis-ticated literary and philosophical techniques rather than highly charged moral ones; an explication of the power of conventional forms; an exploration of the relationship between producers and consumers of contemporary media; an emphasis on sexuality and symbolic communication; and a complex combina-tion of appreciation, engagement, and ironic detachment.[41]

In the United States Eco is best known as the author of *The Name of the Rose* (1980; English edition, 1983) and *Foucault's Pendulum* (1988; English edition, 1989). Early in his career, however, he turned his attention to issues surrounding the interpretation of consumer culture. Born in 1932 into a middle-class family, he grew up in Alessandria, a provincial capital roughly equidistant from Turin, Milan, and Genoa and home to Borsalino, a manufacturer of stylish hats. He was educated at schools run by the Salesian Society, a Roman Catholic Order dedicated to helping the young, especially the disadvantaged, which he was not. Eco spent the war years living with his mother in a small village in the mountains, enabling him to escape the bombings but not wartime deprivations or fights between fascists and partisans. In his late teens and early twenties, he worked with Azione Cattolica, a conservative, anti-Communist organization. Eco earned his *laurea*, or doctorate, in philosophy from the University of Turin in 1954, with a thesis on Saint Thomas Aquinas; in 1961 he was awarded a *Libero Docente* in aesthetics. Eco continued to work on medieval studies but for our purposes among his most important works were *Opera aperta: Forma e indeterminazione nelle poetiche contemporanee* (1962), translated, partially, as two separate books, *The Open Work* in 1989 and *The Aesthetics of Chaosmos: The Middle Ages of James Joyce* in 1982; *Diario minimo* (1963), some of it translated as *Misreadings* in 1993; and *Apocalittici e integrati: Comunicazioni de massa e teorie della cultura de massa* (1964), partially translated, especially in *Apocalypse Postponed* in 1994.[42]

Between the completion of his thesis in 1954 and publication of a revised version two years later, a crisis of faith caused Eco to leave the Roman Catholic Church. He marked this with a change to the work's title in the book version, dropping the word "Saint" before the name Thomas Aquinas. Eco grew increasingly skeptical of Aquinas's fixed truths and more generally those of the Church, thus edging closer to an emphasis on historical context and multiple truths. As would be true of McLuhan, Eco's Catholicism made him aware of symbolic meaning embodied in visual culture; and throughout his life, Aquinas's scholasticism remained central to his method. As he noted in 1988, "Thomas Aquinas has returned through the medium of Marshall McLuhan, to haunt discussions of the mass media."[43]

Beginning in the mid-1950s, Eco pursued careers in both media and academic settings. From 1954 to 1959 he worked in Milan as an editor for cultural programs of RAI, the state-owned television station, placing him in an ideal position to participate in the development of new media. In 1956 he obtained his first academic position, at the University of Turin, and three years later he began a sixteen-year stint as a nonfiction editor for an Italian publisher. In the late 1950s, his circle of friends included artists and writers involved in the Italian avant-garde, many of whom would later form Gruppo 63. Beginning in 1959, he published a monthly column in the avant-garde publication *Il Verri*, brought together in 1963 in *Diario minimo*. In 1962 he married Renate Ramge, a German art teacher, with whom he had two children.

His publications of the late 1950s and early 1960s established Eco as a major figure in Italian intellectual life, initially in medieval studies and soon after in philosophy, literature, and media studies. By the early 1960s he was well on his way to a position as one of Italy's most influential writers, publishing widely in both academic and journalistic venues; he held a series of academic positions before ending up in 1971 as a professor of semiotics in Bologna. In the mid-1960s, he turned his attention increasingly to semiotics and later to structuralism. In 1980, with the publication of *The Name of the Rose*, a novel that combined his interests in medievalism and experimental writing, Eco achieved an audience, media attention, and notoriety outside both academia and Italy.

The Makings of a Consumer Society and of a Media Critic

Eco's writings on consumer culture appeared at a time, from the mid-1950s on, when Italy was experiencing dramatic economic growth. Recovering from the devastation of World War II, the Italian economy, especially in the north, boomed, with the years from 1958 to 1962 witnessing an especially dramatic spurt of growth that caused Italians to speak of "the economic miracle." GDP increased on average at a rate of 6 percent in the 1950s, almost doubling between 1951 and 1963. American investments, the lowering of protectionist barriers, and the increasing integration of Italy with Western Europe all fostered prosperity that was spread unevenly around the nation. Millions of people left farms and small towns and settled in cities. The manufacturing sector led the way in the transformation of the Italian economy, with automobiles, appliances, and office equipment finding markets at home and abroad. One significant result was the growth of a consumer culture, often identified as American and in some quarters stoking fears of Americanization.[44]

From his late teens until his early thirties, the years of his initial writings on popular culture, Eco lived in Turin and Milan, two major cities where consumer culture was most visible in the postwar period. Turin was the base for Fiat and Olivetti. Milan, where Eco worked beginning in 1954, was the epicenter of innovations that undergirded the new consumer culture. The city boomed in the late 1950s and early 1960s, the central point in Italy's postwar economic miracle. The nation's most modern city was home to advertising agencies (including branches of American ones), public relations firms, television stations, and publishing houses. In response to all these changes, many intellectuals warned that increased affluence would lead to the destruction of a distinct working-class culture, as well as to more general personal alienation and political apathy as new forms of pleasure and the anticipation of more affluent lives eroded a traditional social order based on a commitment to communal interests. Prominent in opposition to the new consumer society and its materialism in these debates were two groups of influential intellectuals, from the left and right, representing respectively the Communist Party and the Roman Catholic Church. They both arrived at the same anti-American conclusion from different positions: party members because the United States represented the capitalist enemy, and Catholics because an immoral American popular culture eroded the strength of families.[45]

Eco's probing and provocative writings of the late 1950s and early 1960s thus came at an important time in the history of Italian consumer culture. By the early 1960s, advertising agencies and the corporations that hired them promoted a new vision of the good life in Italy. In 1964 the sociologist and market researcher Francesco Alberoni published *Consumi e società* (*Consumption and Society*), in which he spelled out a new ethic of consumption as involving self-realization, women's liberation, sexual freedom, and pleasure. The advocacy by the Viennese-born American market researcher Ernest Dichter was also crucial in promoting this ethic of sexualized hedonism in Italy, as was, in the 1970s, advertisers' use of semiotics. In the 1970s Italian youth became the vanguard of this new ethic. By the 1980s the sociologist Gerardo Ragone hailed a new consumer ethic that relied not on a quest for social status but on a quest for "pure play, spectacle, enjoyment, pleasure." In all of this, Eco had paved the way. Like Habermas and Barthes, Eco was pondering the implications of the roles of affluence, consumer culture, and America in the rebuilding of postwar Europe.[46]

Eco's interest in commercial culture began early. In 1954, as a young man who wrote on detective stories in a Catholic youth publication, he showed evidence of taking popular culture seriously. This marked his dissent, at a remarkably early moment, from literary theories reigning in Italy that embraced high culture and refused to see popular expressions as worthy of serious consideration. Eco drew on the work of people who influenced him in Turin in the 1950s. These mentors and writers were rejecting the idealist literary approach of Benedetto Croce. They embraced the more experimental writing found among American authors, including Walt Whitman, Herman Melville, William Faulkner, and Sinclair Lewis. Beginning in 1954, when he started his job in Milan at RAI, Eco experienced the challenges of the new media as he worked on children's shows and historical reconstructions patterned after the American show *You Are There*. By the late 1950s, he was beginning to think through issues central to understanding popular culture. Eco's experience with Italian TV provided new and more fluid ways of examining texts and theories that made the relationship between texts and their consumers reciprocal.[47]

Eco's writings on popular culture began in earnest in 1959. From then until the mid-1960s he published a steady stream of essays on comics, television, and detective fiction. His essays appeared at a time when most cultural observers in Italy, especially Marxists, Crocean idealists, and Roman Catholics, decried an American invasion that they believed was destroying rich strands of Italian culture and replacing them with a standardized, degraded mass culture. Yet this was also a time when Italian poets and novelists, many of them in Eco's circle, were incorporating fragments of popular culture into their work.[48]

Finding His Way between Apocalyptic
and Integrated Intellectuals

Central to Eco's considerations was figuring out the relationship between intellectuals and the cultures they studied. His 1962 essay "Industry and Sexual Repression in a Po Valley Society" reveals his intellectual playfulness, his challenge to cultural hierarchies, and his parodying of works by Ruth Benedict and Margaret Mead. His position on the non-Communist left, similar to that of Barthes, Habermas, Hoggart, and members of the Independent Group, reminds us of the intellectual location from which fresh approaches to popular culture emerged in the 1950s. Here Eco wrote as if he were an anthropologist from a tribe in Tasmania. Adopting the stance of "cynical relativism," he parodied the way Italians participated in soccer matches as tribal rituals infused by racial tensions; worshipped the machine; engaged in acts of creative destruction; and danced in sexually repressed, ritualistic ways that were both obscene and chaste. At the end of the essay he contrasted the Church as a secular institution "intent on earthly rule" with industry, "a spiritual power, bent on winning souls, on propagating mysticism and askesis," a form of self-control used by religious groups. Eco-as-anthropologist described industrial workers as the "faithful" people who "live in gloomy conventlike buildings, where mechanical devices contribute to making the habitat more stark and inhuman."[49]

The leaders of industry participated in "ascetic retreats called 'board meetings,' during which they sit for many hours, in gray habits, . . . hollow-eyed from fasting, to debate disembodied problems connected with the mystical purpose of the association: the 'production' of objects as a kind of ongoing reenactment of divine creation." The theological basis of industry relied on rituals in which, "during frenzies of religious ecstasy," members of the priestly class "hasten to part with their 'merits,' diminishing their own value to make a gift of it to others, in an impressive crescendo of tension and hysterical *raptus.*" Eco concluded the essay with a discussion of scores of monks who lived in monasteries: "silent, shy men, who appear only occasionally" in public where they preached "obscure and prophetic crusades, accusing those who live in the world of being 'lackeys of neocapitalism' (an obscure expression, characteristic of their mystical speech)." Then they withdrew. "Protected by the spiritual power that governs them and the village, they are, to the scientist," the anthropological report concluded in the final sentence, "the only key to understanding this disturbing and savage mystery."[50]

If in this one essay Eco on the surface seemed to align himself with Marxist critics of contemporary capitalism, a year later he offered an essay critiquing the position of many of the authors in Rosenberg and White's *Mass Culture*, Marxists and ex-Marxists alike. Titled "The End Is at Hand," Eco's short essay was a scholarly spoof set in classical Athens on the eve of its Golden Age. Aristotle's *Rhetoric*, Eco wrote with tongue in cheek, "is nothing less than a catechism of marketing, a motivational inquiry into what appeals and what doesn't." Similarly Aristotle's *Poetics*, with its emphasis on mimesis, enabled readers to understand "mass-man" who, "enamored of his own appearance, . . . will be able to enjoy only what *appears* real" and "will take pleasure only in *imitation*." Eco told the story of triumph of "mass-man, citizen of democratic Athens, smug in his own cheap tastes," satisfied "with the noise in which he encloses himself like snail, the 'distraction' which he has raised to the level of a religion" and a creature of "the culture industry," who was "too content with its achievements to listen to the voice of wisdom." In contrast stood a philosopher "who knew that wisdom was too precious a treasure to be placed at everyone's disposal."[51]

As the reference to "culture industry" suggests, in his essays on how intellectuals approached popular culture, Eco had in mind a critique of Adorno and Horkheimer's *Dialectic of Enlightenment* (1944), which first appeared in Italian in 1962. In 1964 Eco published his more extended analysis of the relationships between intellectuals and popular culture, in an influential essay titled "Apocalyptic and Integrated Intellectuals: Mass Communications and Theories of Mass Culture." Although he was skeptical about such a dichotomous classification and in fact believed the two groups occupied complementary positions, Eco nonetheless distinguished between apocalyptic critics and integrated ones. Members of the second group, on whom Eco spent little time in his essay, worked in the media and offered optimistic paeans rather than theoretically informed critical analysis. He later identified McLuhan's 1964 *Understanding Media* as his prime example of the work of an integrated intellectual.[52]

In contrast, apocalyptic critics, on whom he focused much more fully, offered dramatic warnings that emphasized how threats to elite culture led to decadence. He singled out, among others, Adorno and Horkheimer. Like Habermas, but even more so, Eco was reading central texts of the Frankfurt School against the grain. Ironically, he made clear that he was indebted to apocalyptic writers "without whose unjust, biased, neurotic, desperate censure" he could not have developed most of his ideas. Without them, he insisted, "perhaps none of us would have realized that the question of mass culture is one in which we are all deeply involved." He accepted as givens many of their key insights. What motivated cultural producers, Eco acknowledged, was not "real opportunities for critical experience" but profitability. He also agreed that in a mass culture society "members of the working class consume bourgeois cultural models believing them to be the independent expression of their own class." Finally, he sided with those who knew that popular culture offered narratives that had "absolutely no connection with the situations actually experienced by its consumers but which, despite this, come to represent for them model situations."[53]

Yet if Eco credited apocalyptic intellectuals with important insights, his criticism of them was biting. They falsely assumed they were above but not in a world of mass media, with their books and essays "the most sophisticated product on offer for mass consumption." Turning the tables on them by continually using Marx against what he saw as "the pseudo-Marxist theories of the Frankfurt school," Eco asserted that their "indiscriminate use of a fetish concept such as 'the culture industry' basically implies an inability to accept" the historical transformations wrought since the invention of moveable type and, as a consequence of this changing technology, the possibility that humanity could alter the course of history. They offered their readers "*consolation*" by making it possible to "glimpse, against a background of catastrophe, a community of 'supermen' capable, if only by rejection, of rising above banal mediocrity." By their giving so much power to producers and so little to consumers of mass culture, as well as by contrasting "the lucidity of the intellectual in his solitude" with "the stupidity of mass man," they failed to see that "the only way the cultural operator can carry out his function is by entering into an active and conscious dialectical relationship with the conditionings of the cultural industry." Eco also cast a skeptical eye on the divisions apocalyptic intellectuals made between levels of culture, insisting that advocates of high culture saw mass culture as a subculture "without realizing that this mass culture still shares the same roots as 'high' culture." In addition, Eco pointed to positive aspects of popular culture. At a time when Herbert Gans was writing about how Italian Americans in Boston talked back to their television sets, Eco wrote how southern Italians did the same. Thus Eco commented on "the viewers' reaction" as having "a critical and active nature," how "the revelation of a world that is still a possibility rather than an actuality for them can provoke rebellion, realism." This led him to suggest that the production and reception of mass culture involved "unpredictable outcomes" that challenged the usual assumption about the relationships between producers and consumers as well as that between high and low cultures. Eco thus remained cautiously optimistic about mass culture, suggesting that as members of the working class became more active participants in public life, there occurred "the broadening of the social base of information consumption."[54]

Eco offered a penetrating analysis of the way apocalyptic intellectuals went about studying cultural texts, or more precisely not studying actual examples but decrying them nonetheless. They denounced the products of mass culture without carefully analyzing them or how consumers actually used them. These critics, he asserted, were "not interested in the message's content, its structural patterns, nor in the process of reception." Indeed, he remarked as he drove his points home, apocalyptic criticism "resembles the barely disguised manifestation of a frustrated passion, a love betrayed, or rather, the neurotic display of a repressed sensuality, similar to that of a moralist who, in the very act of denouncing the obscenity of an image, pauses at such length and with such voluptuousness to contemplate the loathsome object of his contempt that his true nature—that of a carnal, lustful animal—is betrayed." Instead he called for empirical examinations of media, their production, and their reception. He advocated an approach that defined both "the extent to which the form is determined by the objective conditions" of transmission and how reception varied with historic and sociological conditions.[55]

Although at times he sounded like an apocalyptic intellectual himself, Eco took a position between the two types. In 1961 he made clear his own identification as a man of culture, a person, he wrote, "aware of his surroundings, who knows how to discriminate within a hierarchy of values continually undergoing revision." His more extended presentation of his own position came in his 1962 essay "Form as Social Commitment." In order for an intellectual to understand commercial culture, he asserted, it was necessary to encounter it "as hostile and extraneous" but also to "implicate oneself in it. The object will thus be understood not as something that must be absolutely denied but rather as something that still bears the traces of the human purpose for which it was produced." Eco saw human engagement with the products of commercial culture, such as an automobile, as having an erotic dimension. "The extension of our body into the object we touch, the humanization of the object and the objectification of ourselves" was an inevitable and to-be-welcomed aspect of human history. As an example that evoked male fantasy, Eco mentioned a woman's relationship to her car: "driving barefoot, she feels its vibrations, in all her muscles, she knows it as one knows a lover, and she responds to its elasticity and its movements with her own body."[56]

The combination of distance and engagement that Eco insisted on in human relationships to mechanization and commercialism, not unlike what Barthes had articulated, was central, for it made possible a commitment to act in the world at the same time that it made people aware of the dangers of excessive integration. Formative in his mediating position was a recognition of human alienation, which would prompt people "to acquire new autonomy . . . and to devise new ways of being free." Avant-garde artists led the way in fashioning a stance toward popular culture that was neither apocalyptic nor integrated.

They delved into it and assumed a "critical condition from within, adopting, to describe it, the same alienated language in which it expressed itself." However, by describing rather than denouncing, they stripped popular culture "of its alienating aspects and allow us to demystify it." The artist thus dominated material by understanding it, avoiding becoming its "prisoner, no matter how severely he has judged it."[57]

Popular Culture as Open and Closed Works

In *The Open Work* (1962), but elsewhere as well, Eco shifted the terms of discussion about texts set by others, especially apocalyptic intellectuals. For him, the initial question was not whether a text belonged to high or low culture, or somewhere in between, or whether it represented good taste or bad. Rather, he wondered whether any texts, including those in the realm of popular culture, were closed or open. Representing a fixed and ordered cosmos, a closed work (music by Johann Sebastian Bach or Giuseppe Verdi, biblical exegesis by scholastic philosophers, medieval art, Dante's *Divine Comedy*, or contemporary mass media) was predictable, unambiguous (or when ambiguous, fixed by conventions), and univocal. The plots were repetitive, the formulas set, and the characters one-dimensional. Drawing on Norbert Wiener's contributions to information and communications theory, Eco explained that formulaic productions were wrapped "in a number of conventional reiterations" that ensured the constancy of their meanings.[58]

In contrast stood open works, key modernist texts such as the novels of Franz Kafka or James Joyce, the music of Karlheinz Stockhausen, paintings by Jackson Pollock, or the sculpture of Alexander Calder. As products of a cosmos in flux, these works placed the audience in a position different from that of those encountering closed works. Here artists in effect collaborated with the producer and consumer in creating works; in other words, these works placed the audience in an active position, capable of interpreting an ambiguous or unfinished text in multiple ways. Open works, by breaking with conventions, were indeterminate, ambiguous, and able to provide multiple meanings. They were open, Eco wrote, "to constantly shifting responses and interpretative stances." "The openness of a work of art," he insisted, "is the very condition of aesthetic pleasure." For Eco, the differences between open and closed texts had a vaguely spelled-out political dimension. In contemporary society, he wrote, most people, "unable to elude the systems of assumptions that are imposed" from the outside and lacking the shaping experience that came from "a direct exploration of reality," were part of a conformist mass society shaped by "a passive ac-

Figure 2. In this *Peanuts* cartoon of June 21, 1955, by Charles Schulz, Lucy
asks a question posed by cultural critics in the postwar period. Umberto
Eco responded in the affirmative to this question, to this cartoon series,
and to other aspects of American popular culture. He asserted that some
American cartoons and movies were artistically creative and capable of
liberating and transforming an audience. © 2010 Peanuts Worldwide LLC.,
dist. by UFS, Inc.

quisition" of ways of understanding the world that came from the acceptance of
conventional wisdom. In contrast, open texts could play a "liberating role" by
pointing people "toward the reconquest" of "lost autonomy at the level of both
perception and intelligence." Despite these differences, for Eco both open and
closed works of art could be good or bad, artful or artless.[59]

Charlie Brown, Television, Superman, James Bond

Although Eco considered most contemporary popular culture closed, at times
his judgments were more positive. Thus in 1963 he published an almost rhap-
sodic analysis of Charles Schulz's Charlie Brown comics. Eco acknowledged
that most comics were "bound by the iron rule of the industrial-commercial
circuit of production and consumption." Yet he also recognized that some artists, Schulz and Jules Feiffer, for example, "managed to alter profoundly their
consumers' way of feeling; and these artists, working within the system, performed a critical and liberating function." Thus he hailed Schulz as a poet
whose work had "the capacity of carrying tenderness, pity, wickedness to moments of extreme transparence, as if things passed through a light and there
were no telling any more what substance they are made of."[60]

Similarly, when he came to discuss television, the field in which he had
worked in the late 1950s, Eco saw closed, formulaic programs and considered
the possibility of more open, experimental ones, even in commercial venues.
At one end of the spectrum stood his ironic and scathing 1961 critique of Mike
Bongiorno (appropriately, "Have a Good Day"), the wildly popular American-
born Italian quiz show host. He had appeared on Italian TV in its earliest
days and beginning in 1955 he emceed a television program modeled on the

American show *The $64,000 Question*. The television ideal, Eco wrote, was the petit-bourgeois everyman. Bongiorno embodied this ideal, conveying in his conventional and utterly predictable persona "an absolute mediocrity" through whom the viewer "sees his own limitations glorified and supported by national authority."[61]

In contrast were live broadcasts, such as that of the 1956 wedding of Prince Rainier of Monaco and Grace Kelly, which were assembled by an editor from shots taken by multiple cameras and thus at their best were improvisational montages subject to chance and open to interpretation. In this they resembled artistic forms Eco appreciated for their open qualities, the jam sessions performed by jazz musicians and *cinéma verité*. Like these art forms, live TV offered examples of open "narrative structures and the possibility of reproducing life in all its multiplicity" with "its casual unfolding beside and beyond any pre-established plot." Eco was not entirely convinced that live television, subject to both commercial pressures and audience expectations, would necessarily fulfill its promise as an open text. But if it did so, following the experimental movies of Michelangelo Antonioni, "it could give the viewer the feeling, however vague, that life—that even he himself—is not confined to the story he so eagerly follows." By undermining the notion of a fixed plot, live television, along with jam sessions and experimental movies, could force an audience member "to judge, or at least to question, the persuasiveness of what he sees on the screen."[62]

Most of the popular culture Eco analyzed was closed, not open, like the striptease show in which, he wrote, the female performer would "faithfully follow a grand tradition now codified even in instruction manuals; and thus nothing is unexpected, nothing is seductive." More extensively his understanding of popular culture as closed came out in his analysis of the comic strip *Superman*. Eco wrote of how this superhero "must necessarily become immobilized in an emblematic and fixed nature which renders him easily recognizable." The comic strip's plot involved "recurrent stock situations," "the iterative scheme as a redundant message," and "the circular, static conveyance of a pedagogic message which is substantially immobilistic." Eco went on to connect the closed nature of the strip to its limited ideological reach. "The plot must be static and evade any development," he argued, "because Superman *must* make virtue consist of many little activities on a small scale, never achieving a total awareness," with evil involving attacks on private property and good equated with acts of local charity. These commitments in turn revealed the "concept of 'order' which pervades the cultural model in which the authors live," rather than, Eco seemed to mean without being explicit, a vision that involved utopian attempts to reconstruct the social order. Indeed, elsewhere he wrote of Superman as "a paragon of high moral standards untouched by political concerns." In other words, there was a relationship between the formulaic narrative structure and cautious ideology of *Superman* comics, as there was with most popular culture: its commitment to formulas was part and parcel of the way it reinforced conformity and undermined the possibility of historical change.[63]

Similarly, in his discussion of James Bond novels, beginning with *Casino Royale* in 1953, Eco viewed Ian Fleming's books as closed texts, in the sense that they were highly predictable. A Bond novel was like a carefully choreographed basketball game played by the Harlem Globe Trotters, with "ingenious deviations" reconfirming "the foregone conclusion." This made Bond's novels "typical of the escape machine geared for the entertainment of the masses." For Eco, the fault was not so much Fleming's politics (although he made clear he stood in opposition to Fleming's reactionary views) but the static nature of the devices he relied on. In the end, his judgment of Fleming's novels was close to what Horkheimer and Adorno might have written. When Fleming's novels provoked "elementary psychological reactions in which ironic detachment was absent," Eco wrote, this was "only a more subtle but not less mystifying operation of the industry of escape" and when they proffered "the thrill of poetic emotion," they were just another example of kitsch.[64]

Countering the Binaries of Producer/Consumer and High/Low

Eco also explored the relationships between producers and consumers of popular culture. For example, he explained how Fleming responded to both a mass and a sophisticated audience. Again and again Fleming drew on elements in storytelling that had proven their success with audiences, often adopting what Eco called a "racialist," conservative position to play on well-worn tropes of good/evil/ or white/black as he cynically devised "tales for general consumption." Yet Eco saw Fleming not offering a consistent ideology in his stories but over time tailoring his narrative "purely from reaction to popular demand," for example, no longer making Russians the enemy when public opinion saw the USSR as less menacing. At the same time that Fleming appealed to the masses by using elements from well-known fairy tales, he appealed to his more sophisticated readers by his clever translations of traditional modes and by his portrayal of "the cultured man, . . . naturally the most clever and broadminded." At the end of the essay on the Bond novels, Eco drove home his point about the importance of the audience. He insisted that a "message does not really end except in a concrete and local reception which qualifies it." The "definite verification" of a message took place not in the domain of the cultural product but "in that of the society that reads it." Likewise, in his essay on *Superman* comics, Eco explored why a hero with such abundant powers appealed to readers. Deprived of an ability to control the means of production, people needed a hero who embodied the power that "the average citizen nurtures but cannot satisfy." The comic book figure's dual identity, as Superman and Clark Kent, performed powerful "mythopoeic" functions. The reader could draw a sense of power from the figure of Superman. Through "self-identification" with the mild-mannered reporter, an accountant, Eco wrote (offering his father's profession as the example), "harassed by complexes and despised by his fellow men; . . . secretly feeds the hope that one day, from the slough of his actual personality, a superman can spring forth who is capable of redeeming years of mediocre existence."[65]

In ways that mixed playfulness and seriousness, Eco also explored the relationship between levels of culture, in the process challenging a simple dichotomy of high and low. As he wrote in 1986, "it is arguable whether" his work on medieval aesthetics was "more indebted" to leading French theologians who focused on key texts from the Middle Ages or to Beetle Bailey, a cartoon figure first offered in the fall of 1950. He added, "The Lord of Hosts bless them all." His most extended consideration of these relationships came in his 1964 essay "The Structure of Bad Taste." He opposed the elitism of Adorno, Croce, Macdonald, and Greenberg. "All these supercilious condemnations of mass taste," he argued, "in the name of an ideal community of readers involved solely in discovering the secret beauties of the cryptic messages produced by high art, neglect the average consumer (present in just about all of us)" who turns to popular media "in the hope that it may evoke a few basic reactions (laughter, fear, pleasure, sorrow, anger) and, through these, reestablish some balance in his or her physical or intellectual life." Their denunciation of mass culture and the people who consumed it "turns mass consumers into a generic fetish, . . . while totally ignoring the great variety of attitudes present at the level of mass consumption."[66]

Eco offered a rich and provocative analysis of avant-garde, high, low, and mid culture, not as separate and competing elements but operating reciprocally or dialectically with each other. "Not only does the avant-garde emerge as a reaction to the diffusion of Kitsch," he remarked, "but Kitsch keeps renewing itself and thriving on the very discoveries of the avant-garde." Similarly, producers of kitsch and midcult, such as comic books or knickknacks, "borrow new elements and unusual solutions" from high culture. Indeed, consumers of kitsch, far from being degraded, might "catch on to a . . . stylistic element" that maintained some of the "original's nobility" of what the low borrowed from the high. Nor did the transfer operate in only one direction, with borrowings by low from high. He noted that avant-garde culture, "reacting against the density and scope of mass culture," actually borrowed from it. For example, he wrote, pop art "chooses the most vulgar and pretentious graphic symbols of advertising and turns them into the objects of morbid and ironic attention by blowing them up out of all proportion and hanging them on the walls of a museum." As he often did, Eco ended his essay on a note that was both optimistic and ambiguous. The dialectic between different kinds of cultural products, he remarked, allowed "for the possibility of new procedural interventions," of which the final and "falsest" was "the restoration of an apparent adherence to the timeless value of Beauty, which is generally only a cover for the mercenary face of Kitsch."[67]

Eco paid the creators of comic strips the compliment of closely reading the texts they generated and of discussing the problem they faced in developing a narrative in a closed genre. He deployed the writings of Shakespeare and Aristotle, as well as of sophisticated literary criticism, to examine the creativity and meaning of popular texts. For example, he used the ideas of Jean-Paul Sartre, Edmund Husserl, Immanuel Kant, and Aristotle to explore how *Superman*'s creators offered suggestive solutions to the problems imposed by the constraints of commercial media, in the process using powerful philosophical concepts about the constraints imposed by time and the inevitably of death to understand narrative strategies. An evaluation of the "Superman stories reflects even though at a low level a series of diffuse persuasions in our culture about the problem of concepts of causality, temporality, and the irreversibility of events.". This was a relatively rare occasion when he suggested a hierarchy that placed the movie *Last Year at Marienbad* or James Joyce's *Finnegan's Wake* in a position superior to the popular comic strip. Again and again Eco used literary theory to analyze what others considered kitsch or trivial. When he analyzed Milt Caniff's comic strip *Steve Canyon*, he pointed to its "absolutely conventional symbology, magnifying the obvious ingredients of the character," but not involving us, he remarked, "in any discussion of its intrinsic merit." Yet Eco looked at the cartoon's iconography, plot structure, syntax, use of language, and character development with both seriousness and the techniques of someone exquisitely trained in literary and philosophical analysis. The comic strip, he insisted, "represents an autonomous literary sub-genre, possessing its own structural patterns, an original mode of communication with the reader and an interpretative code which the reader already shares and which the author refers to constantly in order to organize his message," a message that the critic could explicate by talking of metaphor, *"syntax of frame construction,"* framing devices, and *"montage rules."*[68]

Although he expressed it quietly and often indirectly, there was a politics (albeit a nonprogrammatic one) to Eco's analysis of the relationships between open/closed, producer/consumer, and high/low in popular culture. Open works, by breaking conventions and liberating the audience from fixed expectations, created the possibility of social change. Closed works, in contrast, fostered conformity and closed off possibilities of social change. With their reliance on formula and repetition, they were conservative in form. Connected to this was their espousal of conservative positions. Thus, when he talked of the vision *Steve Canyon* embodied, Eco pointed to "a substantial adherence to the values of an American way of life tinged with the Hollywood legend." Likewise, *Little Orphan Annie* "becomes for millions of readers the supporter of a nationalistic McCarthyism, a paleocapitalist classism, a petty bourgeois philistinism ready to celebrate the pomps of the John Birch Society." And as Peter Bondanella has noted of Eco's discussion of *Steve Canyon* and an untranslated essay on Al Capp's *Li'l Abner,* they offered a "belief in the possibility of reform and progress" combined "with an absolute faith in the American political and social system itself." In modern society, Eco himself remarked, faced with "a continuous load of information which proceeds by way of massive jolts" which under ideal conditions would cause members of the audience to continually reassess their situation, they instead relied on redundant stories "as an indulgent invitation to repose, the only occasion of true relaxation offered to the consumer."[69]

Eco in the Belly of the Beast?

Like other writers interested in consumer culture, including Barthes and McLuhan, Eco worked with corporations by connecting theories to the practical understanding of how consumer culture worked. Thus in 1969, along with market researchers, sociologists, and art critics, Eco contributed an essay to a volume, *La psicologia del vestire* (The Psychology of Clothing) sponsored by the textile corporation Gritti. Critics, especially from the Communist Party, looked askance at the way some Italian intellectuals, including Eco but not he alone, seemed to embrace consumer culture. Thus in 1981 the Communist-affiliated literary critic Romano Luperini, even though he did not name Eco specifically and in many ways was discussing writers of lesser note, accused cultural workers of having entered into the belly of the beast when they turned a favorable eye toward popular culture. Luperini asserted that in an earlier era a writer like Croce or Gramsci was a "custodian of taste," but an author now, in some rare cases with access to the higher levels of cultural productions in state television and major publishing houses, had become "a technician, a salaried worker in the service of the cultural apparatus for which he works." Indeed in 1968, more than a decade later than Barthes had done so, Eco turned his attention to advertisements. Looking at those for Camay soap, Volkswagen automobiles, Knorr soups, and swim suits and at antiwar propaganda, Eco explored how they could serve both positive and negative ideological functions, although in the end he emphasized the latter because ads revealed nothing new and had the conventional purpose of supporting consumer culture. Like Barthes and McLuhan, Eco paid commercial culture the compliment of seeing something positive in it and of using literary theory to uncover its meanings.[70]

This complaint that Eco and other intellectuals painted too positive a picture of capitalism's products was a common accusation. During the turmoil of the spring of 1968, critics leveled charges of complicity against Eco and his avant-garde comrades centered on Gruppo 63 and its short-lived publication *Quindici*. This collection of experimental artists collapsed in 1969 and Eco wrote its obituary in the same year. He noted that the original conception of *Quindici* was "as a lively magazine with lots of illustrations, halfway between a *Playboy* with a full-length pinup of Gertrude Stein as 'playmate of the month' plus the layout of the *New York Review of Books* and a *Sunday Times* weekend supplement specially for university heads of department." During its short life, lasting from 1963 to 1969, Gruppo 63 had been attacked from the right and left. On the one hand, "high priests" accused it "of being an Establishment itself, but one which wanted to destroy the existing Establishment with Establishmentarian methods." On the other hand, "official communists, those chorus-masters of socialist realism," attacked its members, with their commitment to formalist analysis, as "a secondary appendage of neo-capitalism" who "worked out their revolutionary impulses from inside the safe protection of the grant-dispensing industrial complex." Writing this way, Eco proved again that he could take as well as give sharp criticism.[71]

Conclusions

More so than Habermas, Barthes and Eco offered innovative analyses of popular culture, though compared with what Adorno and Horkheimer had written in 1944, even Habermas broke new ground. The French and Italian writers took seriously the craft, creativity, and ingenuity that went into the creation of mass media. They insisted on the importance of making discriminating distinctions and of engaging in careful analysis before jumping to judgments, especially highly charged moral ones. They relied on modernist high culture to probe what they saw as the complicated meanings of commercial culture. Above all, they shifted the terms of the debate: from high/low or elevating/degrading to a position in which serious analysis and playfulness combined to take the place of a sense of hierarchy. After all, traditional premodern works and most contemporary popular culture productions were both closed, even though the former belonged to high culture while the latter did not. This was precisely the kind of complicated and nuanced judgment through which Barthes and Eco offered a fresh and provocative interpretation that mixed appreciation and detachment. Eventually the writings of Habermas, Barthes, and Eco that fostered new understandings of consumer culture were no longer lost in translation. Much the same could be said of the writings of those considered in the next chapter: C. L. R. James and Walter Benjamin.

Chapter 3

Crossing Borders

If the writings of Jürgen Habermas, Roland Barthes, and Umberto Eco were not available to American readers in the 1950s and beyond, neither were those of Walter Benjamin and C. L. R. James, albeit for more complicated reasons. Benjamin and James spent their lives crossing borders: not only those between nations but also those between ways of explaining the world. Benjamin's writings were not available to American readers in part because only in the late 1960s and in some cases much later were they translated into English. The delayed availability of his letters, essays, and books also stemmed from his attempt to escape from the Nazis, which led him to leave behind pieces of his writings and ultimately his life itself. James's key text was delayed in appearing not because it remained untranslated but because of the nature of his border crossing. James finished *American Civilization* in 1950 and then circulated a few copies in manuscript form. However, forty years would pass before it was available to more than a handful of people. As he left France in 1940 en route to the United States, Benjamin took his own life because he doubted he could escape the Nazis. In ironic contrast, James wrote *American Civilization* when the United States government was trying to deport him. In 1940, Benjamin was a man without a country who had spent much of his life crossing national and intellectual borders. In 1950 James, whose visa had long expired, had likewise spent his life crossing literal and figurative borders. Habermas, Barthes, and Eco had spent almost all of their lives in the countries of their birth. Habermas focused his work in social and political philosophy, while Barthes and Eco, but Eco especially, ranged across disparate intellectual fields. In contrast, Benjamin and James traveled even more widely, geographically and intellectually. Like Barthes, Eco, and Habermas they explored what it meant to blur the lines between high and low culture, as well as between producers and consumers. More than they, Benjamin and James were marginal men whose works ranged as widely intellectually as did their lives geographically. Their marginality and border crossing helped them come to a fluid understanding of consumer culture.[1]

Walter Benjamin: The Life of a Border Crosser

If there was one text that emerged from the Frankfurt School that worked most imaginatively against Theodor Adorno and Max Horkheimer's negative view of popular culture, it was Walter Benjamin's "The Work of Art in the Age of Mechanical Reproduction."[2] This essay's history is as filled with complications and mysteries as was the life of its author. Benjamin wrote the first iteration in the fall of 1935 and then continued to develop different versions until 1939. Shortly before he fled Paris in June 1940, trying to keep one step ahead of the Nazis, he placed his manuscripts in safe keeping. Over the years the whereabouts of the drafts of this essay, and indeed most of Benjamin's unpublished writings, remained uncertain. Eventually they surfaced, in Adorno's papers and elsewhere. Thirty-two years separated the first appearance of this essay in print in May 1936, in French in *Zeitschrift für Sozialforschung*, and its first availability in English in 1968. So to call it an essay lost in translation evokes the literal translations into English, the development of different versions over a period of four years, and the ways in which unpublished versions came in and out of sight.[3]

Benjamin lived a peripatetic and tumultuous life, characteristics also of the content and fate of much of his writings. He was, Susan Sontag wrote of him in 1978, "melancholic," lost in a labyrinth, someone who, despite his many friendships, remarked of his childhood in Berlin that "solitude appeared to me as the only fit state of man." "With a precision suggesting a sleepwalker," Hannah Arendt remarked from firsthand knowledge of Benjamin's life, "his clumsiness invariably guided him to the very center of a misfortune, or wherever something of the sort might lurk." As a writer, especially in the English-speaking world, Benjamin achieved fame posthumously. In English much of his oeuvre, in print in his lifetime in French and German and translated from manuscripts well after he died, ended up in meticulously edited volumes published beginning in 1996. Yet his own life ended tragically in September of 1940, shrouded in mysteries around which debates still swirl.[4]

Born on July 15, 1892, Benjamin grew up in Berlin in a Jewish household headed by his father, a wealthy auctioneer, art dealer, and investor. Although Benjamin's family had roots in Orthodox Judaism, his parents were part of the generation that did not live long enough to realize that their secular embrace of Germany rested on a mistaken judgment that anti-Semitism had run its course

and that assimilation provided protection against its dangers. Sickly throughout his life, as a child and youth Benjamin received his education first from
private tutors and then, beginning at age twelve, at a gymnasium in Berlin,
interrupted by two years at a boarding school. As a youth, he played an important role in a radical German youth movement, served as president of a student
organization, and in 1910 published his first essays in a student journal. As a
young adult he studied philosophy at universities in Berlin, Freiburg, Munich,
and Bern. He escaped service in World War I through both real and feigned illnesses. In 1917 he married Dora Sophie Pollak, daughter of a prominent Zionist,
and in 1918 she gave birth to Stefan, Benjamin's only child. During the years in
and around World War I, he met the poet Rainer Maria Rilke, the philosopher
Ernst Bloch, and the scholar of Jewish mysticism Gershom Scholem. Benjamin
earned his Ph.D. at Bern in 1919. Unable to support himself, in 1920 he moved
with his wife and son back to Berlin to live with his parents in their villa located
next to the royal hunting fields.

Founded in 1923, the Institute for Social Research that came to be known
as the Frankfurt School sporadically provided Benjamin with an intellectual
home. It also connected him to Adorno, whom he met in that same year, and
who served variously as Benjamin's student, opponent, friend, and benefac-
tor. As Habermas later said, Adorno was "Benjamin's heir, critical partner,
and forerunner all in one." Adorno realized how brilliant Benjamin was and
worried when Benjamin strayed from Adorno's orthodoxy. The fate of Benjamin's other relationships was also complicated. The departure of his close
friend Scholem for Palestine in 1923 made it necessary for Benjamin to rely
on correspondence and reading rather than personal contact. Benjamin had
been active in the Zionist movement as a youth but turned down his friend's
persistent pleadings that he follow him to Palestine. Benjamin's Zionism was
more cultural than political: he envisioned Jews like himself as members of an
antibourgeois elite that would provide spiritual and intellectual leadership in
Western Europe. Benjamin turned increasingly away from Zionism and toward
surrealism and Marxism. He came close to joining the Communist Party but
ultimately never did. In his turn toward Marxism, among those who influenced
him was the Marxist literary critic and philosopher Georg Lukács. Also important was his romantic and intellectual relationship, beginning in 1924, with the
Latvian Bolshevik Asja Lacis, a woman who lived in Moscow and who in turn
introduced Benjamin to the Marxist playwright Bertolt Brecht in 1929. Over
the long term Brecht's positive view of technology and popular culture, which
stood in opposition to the beliefs of Adorno and Horkheimer, significantly influenced Benjamin's outlook.[5]

Through much of his life Benjamin remained in occupational, financial, and familial limbo. The German hyperinflation of the early 1920s undermined his father's ability to support Benjamin financially, something that father and son often fought over and that ended once and for all when his parents passed away—his father in 1926 and his mother four years later. Because his prose was opaque at best and because he made the mistake of attacking Germany's leading Goethe scholar, Benjamin did not earn his *Habilitation* at Frankfurt in 1925. Completion of the degree would have helped convince his father that he was worthy of support. It would also have made it possible for him to pursue a successful academic career, one newly open to an unbaptized Jew in the Weimar Republic, but also one about which Benjamin himself was ambivalent at best. As he wrote to Scholem, teaching students "would make murderous assaults on my time." Instead, he hoped to carve out for himself a career as an intellectual and man of letters. Benjamin separated from his wife in 1928 and they divorced two years later. In the 1920s, Benjamin seemed in continual motion, based principally in Berlin, but spending time in Moscow, Paris, Naples, San Remo, and Capri. Although he earned some money as a writer, throughout his life he was financially dependent on benefactors, among them his parents, his ex-wife and her family, Adorno and members of his family, and Brecht.[6]

As Hitler and the Nazis ascended to power, Benjamin considered what options he had, as a Jew and a radical. He thought about suicide, something he had contemplated at least as early as 1931. He considered moving to Ibiza and to Nice; to the town in Denmark where Brecht lived; and to San Remo where his ex-wife and son resided, before settling in Paris in the spring of 1933, not long after the Reichstag fire of February 27, 1933. In Paris he was in the world of exiles, Hannah Arendt, Hermann Hesse, and Kurt Weill among them. Also important to him was the French writer Georges Bataille. In the mid-1930s Benjamin garnered some financial support from the Institute, which had moved to Geneva in 1933 and soon after to New York. Moreover, Horkheimer helped secure the publication of "The Work of Art in the Age of Mechanical Reproduction" in the Institute's *Zeitschrift für Sozialforschung* in 1936. Yet Germany's stripping Jews of their citizenship left Benjamin stateless, and the French interned him for three months in late 1939.

Released, he returned to Paris in early 1940, but he fled one day after the Germans, having conquered the Netherlands and Belgium, entered the city. He worked his way through France in an attempt to enter Spain and reach the neutral nation of Portugal from which he could have sailed to the United States on a visa Horkheimer had helped secure. The journey toward safety was perilous. He could reasonably assume that as a radical and a Jew he might well be a prime target of the Nazis; after all, in 1933 the Nazis had arrested his brother (a Communist, Berlin official, and medical doctor) and then sentenced him to forced labor in 1938 before murdering him in 1942. Traveling with Henny Gurland (later the wife of Erich Fromm), Benjamin got as far as Port Bou, a Spanish town near the eastern border between France and Spain. The police detained him and the Jewish refugees with whom he was traveling as stateless people who were without the documents needed to complete the journey. Physically exhausted by the arduous journey and by his poor heart, fearing that the Gestapo might return him to Germany, ripped away from his library and manuscripts, and not looking forward to living in the United States because he felt it lacked culture and tradition, Benjamin took a powerful dose of morphine on the night of September 25, 1940, and died the next day. Soon after, the others with whom he was traveling were allowed to go on and safely reached Lisbon a few days later. At his death, Benjamin was carrying a suitcase filled with manuscripts for what he spoke of as his most important work, material that was never recovered. When Benjamin died, most of the key members of the Frankfurt School were in the United States, with some still to follow. Herbert Marcuse arrived in 1933; Horkheimer and Erich Fromm in 1934; Adorno in 1938; and Arendt, whose first husband was Benjamin's cousin, in 1941 when she completed the route that Benjamin had embarked upon but failed to finish.

Writer without Borders

"Instead of a theoretical synthesis," the historian Eugene Lunn has written, "Benjamin's writings reveal an explosive cross-fertilizing of intellectual currents and historical experiences which were registered as though on a seismograph." What Benjamin wrote about and the genres he wrote in make his work hard to characterize, though these very qualities meant that the impact of his work was widespread across disciplinary boundaries. By the early 1920s, Benjamin was beginning to publish important works. In rebellion against the expectations his parents held for him, he aspired to remain a critic who kept "aloof from both the state and society," except that, as Arendt remarked, "the very notion of thus becoming a useful member of society would have repelled him." Yet write he did, some of what he composed published in his life time and some posthumously: on Goethe, violence, German mourning plays, surrealism, photography, the history of Paris, his Berlin childhood filled with sensuous objects, and his experimentation with drugs that began in 1927, as well as translations of Charles Baudelaire and Marcel Proust (the latter published in 1927) and newspaper articles. If Eco's early work for a television station helped him understand the dynamics of mass media, Benjamin had somewhat parallel experiences. From 1927 to 1933 he developed pioneering radio programs in which he used a nonauthoritarian approach to teach his audience, of adults from modest backgrounds and children alike, how to understand events, literary texts, and city landscapes in fresh ways. He continued to write until shortly before his death, although during his lifetime much of what he wrote remained unpublished or partially published, often fragments on scraps of papers. In 1927 Benjamin started work on the project that compelled his passionate interest and that of scholars subsequently, *Das Passagen-Werk*. *The Arcades Project*, as it is called in English, finally appeared in German in 1982 and in English seventeen years later.[7]

The dramatic events between World War I and his death, his identity as a Jew, his residence in Berlin for so much of his adult life, and his friendships profoundly shaped Benjamin's life and his writings. Benjamin was twenty-two when World War I broke out in August 1914; twenty-five when the Bolsheviks seized power in Russia in October 1917; twenty-eight when hyperinflation started in Germany in the spring of 1921; and forty when Hitler assumed power in January 1933. For Benjamin, as a Jew and a radical, and for others, these dramatic events undermined any sense of an ordered, predictable, and benign world.

Living in Berlin from 1920 to 1933, and especially within the avant-garde circles in which he moved, enabled Benjamin to participate in and come to terms with the city's vibrant, experimental culture. In the 1920s Berlin was one of the most economically advanced and cosmopolitan cities in Western Europe. Benjamin and his friends could watch experimental films such as Fritz Lang's *Metropolis* (1927) and Sergei Eisenstein's *The Battleship Potemkin* (1925) or *October* (1927) or see Marlene Dietrich in *The Blue Angel* (1930). They saw performances of Bertolt Brecht and Kurt Weill's *The Threepenny Opera* (1930) with Lotte Lenya in her breakthrough role and looked at the caricatures of George Grosz and the multimedia work of László Moholy-Nagy. Farther afield, they surely knew of the transformative work in religion of Paul Tillich and others and in physics of Albert Einstein, who from 1914 to 1933 directed Berlin's Kaiser Wilhelm Institute for Physics. All this, plus experiments with fashion, drugs, sexuality, and the occult, provided a rich cultural tapestry for Benjamin to witness and to savor and for the Nazis to attack as decadent and then to destroy or drive away beginning in 1933.

Paris and *The Arcades Project*

If Berlin was where Benjamin resided much of the time until 1933, it was Paris, where he had often visited as early as 1913 and where he lived from 1933 until 1940, that inspired *The Arcades Project*, on which he began work in 1927, stopped three years later, resumed in 1934, and continued to almost the end of his life. However, it was not the Paris of the 1930s but of the nineteenth century that inspired this work. Nineteenth-century Parisian arcades compelled Benjamin's attention, as symbols of the destructive and redemptive powers of new technologies. Their cast iron skeletons symbolized the functionality of a new architecture. Their combination of marble, glass, mirrors, and light (both artificial and natural) provided the phantasmagoric setting for displays of commercial goods that powerfully evoked people's desires. Here Benjamin, emphasizing the pleasures of material objects, built on Marx's notion of the sensuous property of commodities. Benjamin called arcades the "temples of commodity capital," with advertisements serving as "the ruse by which the dream forces itself on industry."[8]

However, Benjamin's descriptive phrases capture only one side of his vision: if technology brought abundance, the danger was that commercial capitalism would hijack its possibilities that were fully realized only under revolutionary, working-class socialism. As Susan Buck-Morss has written, Benjamin focused on arcades "because they were the precise material replica of the internal consciousness, or rather, the *unconscious* of the dreaming collective. All of the errors of bourgeois consciousness could be found there (commodity fetishism, reification, the world as 'inwardness'), as well as (in fashion, prostitution, gambling) all of its utopian dreams." As would be true of Marshall McLuhan, for Benjamin the task of the cultural critic was to teach readers not to dwell in dreams but to analyze them. "Humanity, rubbing its eyes" might awaken and recognize a dream state for what it was. "It is at this moment," Benjamin continued as he acknowledged the usefulness of Sigmund Freud to social criticism, "that the historian takes up . . . the task of dream interpretation."[9]

In this project, as in others, Benjamin synthesized the writings of Marx and Marxists, Freud, Scholem, Adorno, Brecht, the surrealism of Charles Baudelaire, Louis Aragon, and André Breton, and the work on mass culture by Siegfried Kracauer. "The trouble with everything Benjamin wrote," remarked Arendt in 1968, "was that it always turned out to be *sui generis*," and nothing more so, one might add, than his work on *The Arcades Project*. This was his life's passion, what in a 1930 letter he called "the theater of all my struggles and all my ideas." He carried out a historical excavation by walking and by reading and writing at the Bibliothèque Nationale in Paris. What he left behind was a

Figure 3. Walter Benjamin highlighted nineteenth-century commercial arcades, such as this Passage de l'Opéra in Paris, as locations that combined glass, marble, mirrors, and light to provide a dreamlike setting that helped evoke people's passions for commercial goods. © Musée Carnavalet/Roger-Viollet/The Image Works.

series of "Convolutes" or sheaves of notes, grouped by topic and each containing a mixture of quotes from archival and published materials, lists of objects to explore, and illustrations, as well as his comments on them all. This project thus resulted in a sprawling collection of quotes and comments, exotic shards of history, through which Benjamin focused on the history of Paris in the nineteenth century—the figures of the prostitute, the collector, and the flâneur, who like himself delighted in being a spectator, in observing and wandering, with an apparent aimlessness. As Benjamin wrote in 1939, the flâneur "abandons himself to the phantasmagorias of the marketplace," a process by which goods, ripped from their producers, took on emotional meanings not inherent in the object and that thus stood in opposition to their use or exchange values.[10]

If ever there was what Eco later called an open work, this was it. "Method of this project: literary montage," Benjamin wrote about *The Arcades Project*. "I needn't *say* anything. Merely show. . . . the rags, the refuse—these I will not inventory but allow, in the only way possible, to come into their own: by making use of them." Benjamin worked to recapture the physicality and sensuousness of the material world. His identity as a Jew and his interest in surrealism shaped how he assembled his collection. As Margaret Cohen wrote, referring to the Jewish practice of repairing the world by a series of small acts, "Benjamin fused *tikkun* with the Surrealist notion that liberation would come through releasing repressed collective material." The political, cultural, economic, and social upheavals of nineteenth-century Paris reverberated in the worlds he occupied in the 1920s and 1930s. It was important to focus on "the fate of art in the nineteenth century," he noted, "because it is contained in the ticking of a clockwork whose hourly chiming has first penetrated into *our* ears." As Benjamin famously wrote in January 1940 as the Germans were sweeping across Europe but before they reached Paris, and in a way that both stood against his notion of *tikkun* as repair and expressed the contradictory ways he understood the world, "There is no document of culture that is not at the same time a document of barbarism."[11]

As he explored the possibilities of both degradation and utopia that nineteenth-century Paris opened up and evoked the dreams commodities conveyed, Benjamin worked to find the meaning of history in the scraps and fragments left behind, and in the connections between them. He conveyed a sense that the visual world he was excavating opened up collective aspirations and dreams that involved possibilities for both improvement and disaster. "What all other cities seem to permit only reluctantly to the dregs of society—strolling, idling, *flânerie*," Arendt wrote as she tried to explain why the French city so compelled Benjamin, "Paris streets actually invite everyone to do." Benjamin was also a collector, a figure who, as he remarked, "dreams his way not only into a remote or bygone world, but at the same time into a better one in which, to be sure, people are not provided with what they need any more than they are in the everyday world." This meant, he insisted in a powerful phrase that underscored the transformative power of collecting, that "things are liberated from the drudgery of usefulness."[12]

The result was that much of what Benjamin wrote resembled a dream-like surrealist montage. Sontag, who wrote her essay on Benjamin when his work on *The Arcades Project* was not publicly available, remarked that his "Surrealist-inspired eye for the treasures of meaning in the ephemeral, discredited, and neglected worked in tandem with his loyalty to the traditional canon of learned taste." Indebted to Marcel Proust, Benjamin worked to recover historical memory. He lavished his attention on the commercial culture found in the streets and shop windows, in novels and magazines, and in advertisements. As the historian Vanessa Schwartz has written, *The Arcades Project* offered "a history of capitalism, with an emphasis on the transformation from a culture of production to one of consumption." Relying on the work of Sigfried Giedion and others, Benjamin explored the meaning of the architecture of arcades, department stores, and railroad stations. He loved to dwell on the sensuousness of material goods and the spaces that contained them. "The creations and lifestyles that were mainly conditioned by commodity production and which we owe to the previous century," he wrote, were "sensuously transfigured in their immediate presence." He applied a Marxist notion of commodity fetishism to nineteenth-century urban life, which he found expressed most vividly in fashion, panoramas, and international exhibitions.[13]

However, if Benjamin was indebted to Marx, and to the version of Marxism that Adorno and Horkheimer promoted at the Institute, in crucial ways he challenged their approach. His combination of Marxism and surrealism, among other elements, made him focus hardly at all on the economic base. Rather, with much affection he concentrated mainly on the cultural superstructure, on the display, surface, gloss, and erotic qualities of commodities. Thus, like others connecting consumption, sexuality, and femininity, he wrote of a woman's hat as an "article of dress that can give expression to such divergent erotic tendencies," going on to suggest that the turning down of the bonnet's brim demonstrated "how the crinoline must be turned up in order to make sexual access to the woman easier for the man."[14]

Benjamin's analysis relied for its power on a joining of surrealism and neo-Marxism. From the former, he took an emphasis on the pleasure of ordinary objects, including kitsch. Not surprisingly, the section in *The Arcades Project*

on Baudelaire, at 160 pages, is the longest in the book. Benjamin pointed to
"Baudelaire's 'religious intoxication of great cities': the department stores are
temples to this intoxication." Rather than seeing consumer culture as resulting
in false consciousness, Benjamin conveyed a sense of magic about it, making
clear that what he found was both promising and frightening. "He maintained
a vision of how capitalism would not simply provide its own undoing but would
actually create opportunities for liberation and transformation," Schwartz has
noted, going on to add that "he was particularly interested in the way modern
cities and the nascent forms of mass culture created a potential for democratization and eventual social transformation." Moreover, he countered the
traditional Marxist view of the relationship between base and superstructure. As Benjamin himself said, he was studying "not the economic origins
of culture . . . but the expression of the economy in its culture"—a statement
that reflected his emphasis on the dialogic relationship between base and superstructure. As Buck-Morss asked of Benjamin's work on the project, "Could
the metropolis of consumption, the high ground of bourgeois capitalist culture, be transformed from a world of mystifying enchantment into one of both
metaphysical and political illumination?" However, if for Benjamin history and
technology opened up liberatory prospects, he also underscored the destructive, chaotic heritage of the nineteenth century. Messianic possibilities were
both threatening and redemptive.[15]

In addition to surrealism and Marxism, Judaism also shaped Benjamin's
outlook. Jewish mysticism, especially the esoteric Kabbalah to which Scholem
introduced him, was central to Benjamin's vision. He wrote, "I have never been
able to do research and think in a way other than, if I may so put it, in a theological sense—namely, in accordance with the Talmudic teaching of the forty-nine
levels of meaning in every passage in the Torah." Yet Benjamin's engagement
as a Jew took place in specific, troubling circumstances. A 1912 essay by Moritz
Goldstein captured an aspect of Benjamin's Jewishness different from his engagement with mysticism, the dilemma he and his generation of young Jewish
intellectuals encountered. Goldstein had written, "Our relationship to Germany is one of unrequited love." For Benjamin and other Jewish writers of his
generation what was problematic was not German anti-Semitism but what Arendt called "the lying denial of the very existence of widespread anti-Semitism,
of the isolation from reality staged with all the devices of self-deception by the
Jewish bourgeoisie." Jews in Germany faced the challenge of "administering
the spiritual property of a nation," Goldstein wrote, "which denies our right
and ability to do so." In these circumstances, Benjamin found it impossible
to accept the path of his parents' generation: both the assumption that there

was no tension between being a German and being a Jew and the adoption of a rational, secular Judaism stripped of all mystery. Benjamin considered two alternatives to his parents' choices—a full commitment to Zionism and to Communism— both of which seriously tempted him but which he could not fully accept. Instead, Benjamin embraced what the historian Anson Rabinbach calls "modern German Jewish Messianism," a utopian, redemptive, apocalyptic vision. In the end, Benjamin's position, Rabinbach has written, "represented the antinomies of Messianic politics: on the one side the rejection of the world and violence in an apocalyptic vision, on the other a radical affirmation of the new and creative destruction of the old order in what [Ernst] Bloch called 'a colorful explosion of forms.'"[16]

"The Work of Art in the Age of Mechanical Reproduction" (1936)

In *The Arcades Project* Benjamin worked to recover the commercial culture of nineteenth-century Paris. With "The Work of Art in the Age of Mechanical Reproduction" he focused on mass media of the 1920s and 1930s. Both projects involved approaches central to a fresh understanding of modern culture. They offered complicated and varying mixtures of materialist explanations, a focus on new technologies, an exploration of the texture and possibilities of commercial culture, a consideration of the meaning of visual culture, and expressions of despair and hope. Involvement with media played a critical role in shaping new understandings. If Eco's work on newspapers and television beginning in the 1950s revealed to him the transformative potential of mass media, so Benjamin's work on radio programs in late 1920s and early 1930s, and more generally his experience with the experimental cultural productions of Berlin, prompted him to think through how new technologies and media transformed the relationship between producers and consumers of culture. He understood his work as countering "the limitless spread of a consumer mentality" and prompting audience members to develop greater and more effective autonomy. Radio promised a dialogic means that would "overcome the separation between broadcaster and public," in the end providing a model for an innovative "people's art." Like Brecht, Benjamin held out hope that new entertainment media could serve as a means of sophisticated education.[17]

In his essay Benjamin concentrated on the consequences of the fact that modern technology such as lithography, photography, phonographs, and above all motion pictures had dramatically increased the possibilities of making art reproducible, a process that had enormous consequences for its reception,

meaning, and impact. Primary among the consequences was the way modern reproduction undermined the authenticity, the "aura," Benjamin called
it, of works of art. Benjamin's concept of the aura challenged Soviet Socialist
Realism but especially Nazi exaltation of heroic leaders encased in a charis-
matic haze. Benjamin saw both threat and promise in the way reproduction
undermined aura. He used phrases like "devalue the here and now of the art-
work" and "decay of the aura" and wrote of how the undermining of authenticity "touches on a highly sensitive core" and how its "historical testimony" was
"jeopardized by reproduction."[18]

Yet technology, including that which made reproduction possible, by fragmenting reality encouraged utopian dreams and opened up new possibilities of
representing and shaping consciousness. That art was no longer fixed in time
and space had tremendous and often positive consequences for the relationships between producers, objects, and audiences. The origins of an object's
aura lay deep in history, in the process by which cults and rituals fetishized objects. In more modern times, when faced with photographs, critics continued
this ennobling of art by what Benjamin called the "negative theology" of pure
art. Instead, Benjamin underscored the way reproducibility undermined art's
transcendent beauty, its autonomy, and its authenticity and in turn opened up
the possibility of art connected to a radical politics. If the strength of the aura
placed the spectator in a subservient position, then technology, as he put it so
suggestively, enabled "the original to meet the recipient halfway." An art lover
could now appreciate the cathedral in a studio and an orchestral work in the
home. "*Replicating the work many times over,*" Benjamin wrote, "*substitutes a
mass existence for a unique*" one.[19]

Benjamin believed film was especially revolutionary in its potential. He explored the implications of a film actor performing not in front of a live audience
but facing cameras and experts such as a director and a cinematographer, who
like a surgeon skillfully cut through surface realities and "dispelled" the aura
of both the actor and the figure portrayed. This process underscored the way
the actor's self-alienation represented human alienation in the modern world.
What made film so powerful was its promotion of multiple perspectives. As an
example of the meaning of cinematic technology, Benjamin explored the possibilities opened up when Charlie Chaplin, in *A Woman in Paris* (1923), used
montage to transform 125,000 meters of unedited film into a final cut 3,000
meters long. Benjamin linked the creativity involved in such a process to film's
"*radical renunciation of eternal value.*" More broadly, film's function, he wrote,
was "*to train human beings in the apperceptions and reactions needed to deal
with a vast apparatus whose role in their lives is expanding almost daily.*" Even-

tually they would learn to free themselves "from their enslavement" to capital-ism's powers. As modern productive powers increasingly released people from "drudgery," the power of modern technology, including modern media, would help make the achievement of "utopian" goals possible, bringing about a world in which "the individual suddenly sees his scope for play."[20]

For a range of media, Benjamin chronicled the transformation of the rela-tionship between creators and consumers of culture, made possible by letters to the editor, the proliferation of publications, and the availability of new cine-matic forms. As a result, readers became writers, skilled workers became expert observers, and in experimental Russian movies ordinary people became film actors. All this made more likely the utopian possibility that ordinary people could find ways of communicating their dreams and experiences. Especially if freed from the constraints of capitalist cultural production, which with movies relied on the star system and elaborate public relation schemes, the reproduc-ibility of art, by destroying the aura, could make art available to the masses. It thus turned spectatorship from a passive, individual act into an active, collec-tive one.[21]

Central to this transformation was that "the distinction between author and public" was "about to lose its axiomatic character." The reaction of the "masses" to a Chaplin movie, as opposed to a Picasso painting, was "*highly progres-sive* . . . characterized by an immediate, intimate fusion of pleasure—pleasure in seeing and experiencing—with an attitude of expert appraisal." Watching a film made possible, as seeing a painting could not, not only a playfulness but also "simultaneous collective reception." If Adorno had insisted that members of an audience concentrate on a work of art, Benjamin accepted distraction, what he called "casual noticing, rather than attentive observation," as an appro-priate response. In addition, he wrote, "film furthers insight into the necessities governing our lives by its use of close-ups, by the accentuation of hidden details in familiar objects, and by its exploration of commonplace milieux through the ingenious guidance of the camera" at the same time that it expanded the audience's sense of space. Before film, city spaces such as streets, factories, and railroad stations made the world seem closed in. With the movie came an ex-plosion of "this prison-world with its dynamite of the split second," making it possible to explore modern landscapes with a sense of adventure and through a promotion of the "optical unconscious."[22]

Given the world he lived in, Benjamin well understood that new media could involve a politics of art connected to fascism but he also imagined an alternative. Benjamin was hardly naive about the way capitalism curtailed the utopian possibilities that new technology, cinema especially, offered. "Until film

has liberated itself from the fetters of capitalist exploitation," the utopian possibility of cinema was limited. Fascism in Germany revealed the implications
of cinema used for evil purposes. The film industry, like the Nazis, stimulated
"the involvement of the masses through illusionary displays and ambiguous
speculations" drawing on "an immense publicity machine" and beauty con-
tests. Fascism relied on display without politics. In contrast, Communism connected media with collective, progressive political action.[23]

Benjamin's major concern was thus not so much the general proposition
that reproductions undermined tradition and authenticity but that, in the
hands of the Nazis, they had great destructive power. Reproductions, by creating a mass culture and making objects actualized for individuals, produced in
modern films (and here he was surely thinking of Hitler's use of the spectacle
and film) "destructive, cathartic" power. In the hands of reactionaries, film
promoted a "cult of the audience" which in turn reinforced "the corruption
by which fascism is seeking to supplant the class consciousness of the masses"
with something dangerous rather than liberatory. Benjamin linked the control
of new media by capitalists with its exploitation by fascists: they both "clandes-
tinely exploited" new opportunities for social change and made urgent "the ex-
propriation of film capital . . . an urgent demand for the proletariat." For him,
although he did not say it quite this way, the process by which modern media
caused "the liquidation of the value of tradition in the cultural heritage" rang
true for someone steeped in German literary and philosophical culture who
was witnessing the way the Führer offered a different version of Germany's cultural tradition, one that seemed heroic but was actually vicious.[24]

Although at the essay's very beginning Benjamin acknowledged the importance of Marx's discussion of the relationship of modes of production and consumption, the base and the superstructure, his political purpose lay elsewhere.
Urgently so for a Jew and radical in the fall of 1935, what was on his mind was
not the future of capitalism but the presence of fascism. Consequently, it was
essential to "neutralize" ideas about "creativity and genius, eternal value and
mystery" in art and more generally in culture, concepts central to Hitler's National Socialism. An alternative view of culture, he asserted, was *useful for the
formulation of revolutionary demands in the politics of art*" that, without saying
so explicitly, he considered critical in the overthrow not of capitalism but of fascism. The fact that fascism deployed new media to give the masses a superficial
sense of possibility, without actually changing property relations, should not
blind readers to the positive potential of new media technologies. Benjamin
was not a member of the Communist Party, but until the Nazi-Soviet Pact of
late August 1939, with considerable reservations, he supported the USSR as the

leader of a world working-class revolution. On this and other issues he aligned himself with Brecht but differed with Adorno. Unlike members of the Institute, who worried that mass art in the hands of the fascists served ill-gotten ends, Benjamin recognized the problem but hoped for a technologically based mass culture that was both collectivized and politically progressive.[25]

Thus Benjamin offered a mixed but in vital ways ultimately optimistic judgment about cinema's (and by extension modern mass media's) potential. On the one hand, in Hitler's Germany the new technology fostered dangerous, even psychotic tendencies among the masses. However, Benjamin insisted that the fact that cinematic innovations first appeared to have such terrible results should not blind the critic to the new technology's possibilities and encourage an emphasis on the way the masses sought escape. The very technological forces that were so dangerous in Nazi Germany, he argued, had *created the possibility of psychic immunization against such mass psychoses.* They did so in a number of ways. The ability of film to shock, which it accomplished by montage that underscored the discontinuous nature of experience, opened up the possibility that ordinary people could master technology. The movie star, though susceptible to being used by studios to reinforce power relationships in a capitalist system, could also provide a model for the triumph over technology. Most people living in modern cities, Benjamin wrote, in the factories and offices where they worked during the day "have to relinquish their humanity in the face of an apparatus." Yet when they went to movies in the evening, they witnessed "the film actor taking revenge on their behalf not only by asserting *his* humanity (or what appears to them as such) against the apparatus, but by placing that apparatus in the service of his triumph."[26]

There were additional dimensions to the transformative power of movies. Some movies, which Benjamin did not name but connected to early dadaist experiments, by their very use of the power of "*sadistic fantasies or masochistic delusions,*" might prevent the "natural and dangerous maturation in the masses." In addition, "collective laughter" involved a "healing outbreak of mass psychosis." From the United States came slapstick comedies, Disney productions, and the eccentric figure of Chaplin, who with his fights against technology could trigger a healthy "therapeutic release of unconscious energies" and thereby serve as a safety valve for tensions of the capitalist system. Thus, despite what was happening in Europe, "The Work of Art in the Age of Mechanical Reproduction" has about it a hopeful, even utopian note. Remember that before he offered his own words in the essay, Benjamin reproduced those of the early nineteenth-century novelist and salonnière Madame Claire de Duras: "The true is what he can; the false is what he wants." In this context, Benjamin's embrace of popular cinema and more generally of modern mass media involved skepticism about the values of high art, even if avant-garde, for progressive purposes. On this question he stood in opposition to Adorno and Horkheimer, who in the 1930s and 1940s embraced modernist art and rejected popular culture. "At no point in time, no matter how utopian," Benjamin remarked in *The Arcades Project*, "will anyone win the masses over to a higher art," including "the avant-garde of the bourgeoisie." Rather, what would work for the masses was an art "nearer to them." The danger was that such an art, within "the circle of consumer items," would involve passionate "hatred" that "burns or sears without providing the 'heart's ease' which qualified art for consumption." The solution could be found in kitsch, the best example of which was films, not abstract ones but ones such as American slapstick comedies. This was a version of kitsch which had "a 100 percent, absolute and instantaneous availability for consumption." Reiterating a dialectic perspective, Benjamin wrote that popular film had within itself "something stirring, useful, ultimately heartening— . . . while yet surmounting the kitsch." Thus film, if freed from fascism's auratic qualities or the avant-garde's pretension, provided a collective experience that would help the masses use technology productively.[27]

The reaction of Adorno and Horkheimer to drafts of the essay underscored the differences between the Institute's leaders and Benjamin, as well as the need they felt to avoid political trouble in United States. Over the years, Adorno and Horkheimer criticized Benjamin on a number of grounds: for the lack of clarity in his writings, for evidence of the vulgar Marxism with which they believed Brecht had infected him, for what they saw as his insufficient acceptance of dialectical materialism, and for his embrace of surrealism and mysticism. With "The Work of Art in the Age of Mechanical Reproduction" they forcefully insisted that Benjamin make specific changes. Benjamin had offered one ending: "Such is the aestheticizing of politics, as practiced by fascism. This is the situation of politics which Fascism is rendering aesthetic. Communism replies by politicizing art." When the essay appeared in the Institute's publication *Zeitschrift*, however, at Horkheimer's insistence "the totalitarian doctrine" had replaced "Fascism" and "the constructive forces of mankind" stood in for "Communism." These changes, Martin Jay has written, were "a reflection of the Aesopian language the *Zeitschrift* frequently used, to protect itself from political harassment." Throughout his career, but especially in *The Arcades Project* and in "The Work of Art in the Age of Mechanical Reproduction," Benjamin accepted elements of Adorno and Horkheimer's analysis in "The Culture Industry." Yet he also ventured forth on more utopian paths, ones that opened up new perspectives that relied on multiple meanings, contested cultural borders, and emphasized the dynamics of the relationships of producers and audiences. More than anyone else Benjamin envisioned how new modes of cultural production based on new technologies could, in a revolutionary order beyond capitalism, produce a truly democratic and socialist culture.[28]

C. L. R. James, *American Civilization* (1950)

In exile, members of the Frankfurt School, who were under FBI surveillance, had good reason to worry about speaking their minds. C. L. R. James had even more reason to worry. After all, in the late 1940s and early 1950s he was an Afro-Caribbean, living in the United States without a valid visa, and far more radical than most prominent German émigrés. Threatened with deportation, James pulled up stakes again and left America in 1953. *Beyond a Boundary*, the title of the book James wrote on cricket ten years later, which remains one of the best ever written on sports, underscores key aspects of his life. In a literal sense, the word "boundary" in the title referred to the markers on a cricket field that separate the areas where the cricket ball is in or out of play. However, on the more figurative level, the word "boundary," especially when linked with the word "beyond," evoked for James, as it might have for Benjamin, the national and disciplinary boundaries he crossed in his life. James moved not only between memoir, novel, biography, history, sports journalism, pamphlets, political theory, and cultural criticism but also between Trinidad, England, Africa, and the United States. His border crossing vividly represents the shift from "roots" to "routes" that Paul Gilroy identified as so critical to diasporic or postcolonial black intellectuals.[29]

James was an activist, artist, and radical who focused in his long and productive writing career on cricket, Pan-Africanism, anti-imperialism, Marxism, culture, race, popular culture, and revolution.[30] In *American Civilization*, at the time also titled "The Struggle for Happiness," drafted by 1950 but not published until 1993, he offered a richly suggestive consideration of American popular culture. He wrote the manuscript at the height of the Cold War, when he was facing deportation because of his politics and his lack of a proper visa. Here, as he did throughout his life, James grappled with the issue of how to bring together high and low. This issue emerged early in his own life in Trinidad as he both avidly watched cricket matches and read classics of Western literature. Later, having read key Marxist and Hegelian texts, he found in the concept of the dialectic a way of thinking about high and low cultures, their creators and consumers.[31]

James's experiences as a child and young adult sharpened his skills as a border-crossing observer caught between conflicting realms: the fairness of cricket and the unfairness of the racism he encountered; black and white and all shades in between; intellectual discussions and activist engagement; the quests for personal happiness and radical social change; West Indian, American, British, and Pan-African identities; Marxism and the classics of ancient Greece, Britain, and nineteenth-century United States; and popular culture that ranged from cricket to mass media. From the moment when, at age six, he watched cricket matches from the window of his parents' home, what fascinated him was the role that a mass audience had in creating cultural productions. Compelled by the relationship between the experiences of ordinary people and the nature of high art, between the intellectuals and masses, he tried to bring together what others kept apart. Reciprocity was central to his work: the dynamics of the relationships between intellectuals and ordinary people, between culture and politics, between high culture and low culture, between those who had power and those who did not. He worked hard to understand how ordinary people— the crowds at cricket matches, participants in revolutionary movements, and members of the audience for Shakespeare's plays and American movies— inspired those who excelled in politics, sports, cinema, theater, and literature. His upbringing and education put him in a position to explore, as Barthes, Eco, and Benjamin had done from their own distinct perspectives, the relationship between the high culture of the West and the popular culture he saw around him. His experiences had made him aware of the role women, African Americans, and young people played in social movements.

A Life of Border Crossings

Born in 1901, James spent his first thirty-one years on the West Indian island of Trinidad, a British colony that achieved independence in 1958. A member of the island's "brown" middle class, he was, one commentator later remarked, "suspended between the resentful African-American and East Indian poor and the dominant white colonial and Creole elites." He grew up in a small town, in a household that had both a working-class past and a tenuous middle-class present. His father was a schoolteacher and his mother was an avid reader of literature. Cricket and reading were his twin passions, both of which sustained his perspective as an observer. From a window in the house in which he grew up he could watch cricket matches. If the British introduced cricket to civilize the island natives, the Trinidadians themselves used it as a way of beating the colonial masters at their own game, of achieving social mobility on fair playing fields, and of creating a realm that gave them the crucial skills and perspectives so useful in the fight for national pride and self-government. James played, followed, and wrote about cricket, the scene of contested spectacles of identity in Trinidad in which race, manliness, agency, and empire came together. Throughout much of his career as a writer he explored cricket both in his journalistic pieces—first in Trinidad in his twenties; later in articles for the *Manchester Guardian* when he lived in Britain—and then in *Beyond a Boundary*. In his book, he wrote compellingly about how the choice of which team to join (Shannon, the team of the black lower middle class, or Maple, which he did join, of the brown middle class) reflected the tensions over class, race, ideology, and social location that he faced as long as he remained on the island, and after.[32]

In addition to cricket, books were central to James's life in Trinidad. He read and reread classical drama and philosophy: Matthew Arnold's robust defense of high culture in *Culture and Anarchy*; key texts in Western philosophy; and British literature from Shakespeare to James Joyce, with William Makepeace Thackeray's *Vanity Fair* as his favorite. After winning honors as a student at a young age, beginning in 1911 and on a scholarship James attended the prestigious, British-oriented, and elite Queen's Royal College. "He was educated," Stuart Hall later remarked of James, "in a sort of mimickry of an English public school." In his twenties in Trinidad, James later wrote, he "lived according to the tenets of Matthew Arnold, spreading sweetness and light and the best that has been thought and said in the world." Arnold also conveyed to him a puritanical sense of the ethics of fair play. Yet eventually James took the fair play ethics of the educated elite and turned them into support for fair play for the disenfranchised. Cricket and calypso distracted him from the kind of academic performance his father hoped he would achieve and that would have provided entry into the local professional classes. Soon after finishing his formal education in 1918, he started out as a schoolteacher.[33]

While still in Trinidad, James published short stories and worked on projects that placed him close to the center of the island's artistic and intellectual world. In the late 1920s, he completed *Minty Alley*, a novel published in 1936 that later achieved a reputation as an early classic in Caribbean literature. In his twenties and early thirties in Trinidad, neither his race consciousness nor his politics, which involved a fascination with the island's masses and a commitment to West Indian self-rule, were prominent or fully formed in his mind, despite his publication in 1932 of *The Life of Captain Cipriani*, the biography of a local leader in both labor and nationalist movements.[34]

Determined to succeed as a writer, James departed for Britain in 1932, leaving behind his first wife, the first of four women he would marry and then split from. In England he began a serious study of Marxist theory: first while living in an industrial town in Lancashire, where he joined the household of a famous black cricketer from Trinidad and where working-class militancy was evident, and then, beginning in 1933, in London. Coming to a mostly white England made him conscious of his color and of British racism. Earning a living as the cricket correspondent for the *Manchester Guardian* enabled him, as a man of color from the colonies, to immerse himself in British popular culture; to recapture one of the ways people sustained themselves in a gritty, depressed, urban and industrial world; and to contemplate the relationship between performers and spectators. At the same time, he began work on his *The Black Jacobins: Toussaint L'Ouverture and the San Domingo Revolution* (1938), a history of the only successful slave revolt in modern times and one in which he explored the relationship between Toussaint and the masses who made the revolution possible. A leader of the Pan-African movement in Britain and a member of the Trotskyist Independent Labour Party, he worked on thinking through what it meant to connect Trotskyism and anti-imperialism. Russia's support for Italy in the crisis in Abyssinia (now Ethiopia), as well as the British labor movement's equivocal stance on colonialism, enabled him to stand in opposition to the USSR, the Communist Party of Great Britain, and the British Labour Party.[35]

James in American Civilization, 1938–53

James moved again, in 1938, this time to the United States. Under Trotskyist auspices and free to move about on a temporary visa, he spoke across the nation on race and the war. "In the Trotskyist movement," he remarked in an interview with Stuart Hall, "I was the Third World complete. There was nobody else." After trying to organize African American sharecroppers in southeast Missouri, he moved in 1942 to Manhattan. His visa having expired, in the 1940s he lived underground in the United States as he worked on writing and organizing with small groups of radicals in and around the Socialist Workers Party, then in the spring of 1940 in the Workers Party before rejoining the Socialist Workers Party in 1947. In Manhattan James moved in cosmopolitan circles, coming to know not only Richard Wright and Ralph Ellison but also European émigrés and leading white radicals, including Dwight Macdonald. James and Macdonald were both active in Max Shachtman's Workers Party though they parted ways, with James in 1940 calling Macdonald a "counterrevolutionary songbird."[36]

However, the group that most commanded his attention for more than a decade beginning in 1941 was the Johnson-Forest Tendency, a tiny cluster of radicals dedicated to rethinking Marxism and one which initially existed within the Shachtmanite Workers Party. Two women were prominent in the Tendency and worked closely with James. One was the Russian-born Raya Dunayevskaya, Trotsky's secretary for a brief period in the late 1930s. The other was the Asian American Grace Lee, who in 1940 earned a Ph.D. in philosophy from Bryn Mawr and played a role in bringing Marx's *Economic and Philosophical Manuscripts* to light in 1947. For twenty years beginning in the early 1930s, like other radicals James had struggled to come to terms with the implications of the Bolshevik Revolution, the creation of the Soviet Union, and the applicability of Marxist-Leninist theory to domestic and international events. Gradually, along with his colleagues in the Tendency, he worked to break from the narrow confines of Marxist debates and of concern for European culture. Like his colleagues in the Tendency, James emphasized the role of organized but relatively spontaneous mobilization from the ground up, independent of labor or radical parties and responsive to the relation between popular culture and political insurgency. James and others rejected the notion that the Communist Party represented the vanguard of the revolution. His break with Trotskyism was long in the making, beginning around 1941 and becoming firm in the early 1950s. He remained an anti-Stalinist, anti–Popular Front radical who professed his commitment to Marxism-Leninism even as he reinterpreted many of its core commitments. Despite fragile health and finances, James was active as a pamphleteer, writer, and speaker. He stood in opposition to Stalinism, the USSR, and the Communist Party because he believed that the Soviet Union, in adopting a form of state capitalism, had betrayed the revolution by suppressing insurgencies from below and by abandoning the cause of world revolution as it consolidated its power at home and aligned itself with imperialist powers abroad.[37]

For James the vanguard of revolution was not the Party; rather, he believed that social movements of the masses, with African Americans playing a special role, would lead on the path toward a better world. With his arrival in the United States James became effectively engaged in issues surrounding racism and in 1948 published a pamphlet titled "The Revolutionary Answer to the Negro Problem in the USA." There he talked of "the independent Negro struggle" as able "to exercise a powerful influence upon the revolutionary proletariat," together playing a key role in bringing socialism to the United States. Drawing on his experience as a speaker, writer, and organizer, he had come to see the quest of African Americans for social justice, at times independent of the ranks of organized labor and Marxist parties, as something that would provide the critical force carrying America (and colonial peoples around the world) to socialism. Underscoring African American social protests as genuinely American, he saw them originating from many focal points, including churches, community newspapers, and neighborhood associations.[38]

In the 1940s, as he had done at other times in his life, James strove to connect revolutionary politics and artistic creations, a project closely connected to his relationship with Constance Webb, a young actress and model whom he met soon after his arrival in the United States, whom he married in 1946, with whom he had his only child, and from whom he split by the early 1950s. During his fifteen years in the United States, he immersed himself in American popular culture, reading detective novels, watching popular films, and listening to jazz in Harlem. His ability to remain in the United States was uncertain, given his activity as a radical and the expiration of his visa. The federal government interned him on Ellis Island in 1952 and deported him in 1953 after federal officials examined his writing. All this happened at the height of the Cold War when the left experienced repression and schisms. In the ensuing decades, James spent time in England, the United States, Trinidad, and Africa. He continued to write and speak on race, Pan-Africanism, Pan-Caribbeanism, revolution, cricket, and culture.[39]

On the Road to *American Civilization*

These issues came together compellingly in *American Civilization*, published in 1993 but originally written in the late 1940s as a fragmented and incomplete manuscript. Coming to America had a profound effect on James, as someone prepared to appreciate the United States as a counter to the British imperialism he experienced in Trinidad. Not long after he arrived in 1938, he developed a determination to comprehend the nation as a civilization. Stuart Hall talked of James's refusal "simply to read off cultural things against the economic base" and his development instead of "a notion of collective and creative totality." Soon after his arrival, James avidly and voraciously consumed popular culture. Writing in 1953, he spoke of his experiences during the early 1940s when, struck by insomnia, he watched movies at a theater for three hours beginning at midnight, after which he caught some sleep at home and, after he awoke, listened to soap operas. What his watching, reading, discussions, and experiences impelled him toward was what the editor of his writings, Anna Grimshaw, later called "his recognition of the creative energies of ordinary men and women and their critical place in modern history as the force for humanity."[40]

With *American Civilization*, James struggled to break free of the confines of European bourgeois civilization. America to James seemed open to fresh possibilities and filled with opportunity for individualistic expression, which he wanted to understand and explain in a holistic manner. Just before his deportation, when he was trying to convince federal authorities that he appreciated his host nation, he commented in a 1953 letter to Daniel Bell on "the great power of the American people" in the creation of popular arts, as something "due to the size of the country, to the high development of technology and, above all, what so many people abuse the American masses for, to the absence of traditional culture." As Grimshaw has written, James was "open to the distinctiveness of the United States—its sheer size, its geographical expanse and variation, its revolutionary history and break with Europe, the vitality and independence of its people." He did not want to fall into the trap of fitting "America into 'old world' categories, dismissing it as a brash, new society, a cultural wasteland deficient in all those features of social life which they identified with civilization." Indeed, among the most striking, if somewhat problematic aspects of *American Civilization* was James's celebration of the United States as a culture that had achieved unprecedented degrees of social integration, given a capacious meaning to citizenship, and fostered expressions of individualism and creativity. As early as 1944, responding to the poetry of Walt Whitman, he spoke of the United States as a culture "*without the European roots* and more democratic in its social life than any European society."⁴¹

In his correspondence with Webb in the 1940s, James first articulated what would emerge more fully in *American Civilization*. He was working out his ideas about the relationship between movies and their audiences at the very moment when Adorno and Horkheimer were doing so but coming to different conclusions. In 1943 James remarked that westerns were so popular among American youth because they compensated for the conditions they encountered in their work in factories. Writing to Webb, James suggested that "even the most absurd Hollywood" movies were "an expression of life, and being made for people who pay their money, they express what the people *need*—that is, what the people miss in their own lives." Thus movies were "not merely a reflection, but an extension of the actual—an extension along the lines which people feel are lacking and possible in the actual. That, my dear, is the complete secret of Hegelian dialectic." In another letter in the same year, linking technological progress, work, and consumption, he wrote Webb that "the more technical discoveries of capitalism bring culture to the masses, the more they resent the degradation and humiliation of their role in *production*."⁴²

American Civilization and the Popular Arts

In *American Civilization*, James framed his discussion of popular arts, a term he preferred to mass or popular culture, in the United States within a larger argument about the nation's past and destiny. Nowhere more than in the United States, he commented, "has happiness been pursued with such uninhibited energy and zest." He argued that until 1876, in ways that posited a golden age, the United States was distinctly different from Europe. Here, his remarks anticipated what Daniel J. Boorstin would write about more generally in *The Genius of American Politics* (1953) and Louis Hartz in *The Liberal Tradition in America* (1955)—though James offered a radical analysis that they avoided, even though they both had radical pasts. Without feudalism or an aristocracy, for a century beginning around the time of the American Revolution, the nation presented, James asserted in a way that underscored his avoidance of the enslavement of millions of African Americans, "a spectacle of economic and social equality unknown in history" with bourgeois individualism—"freedom, initiative, adventure, self-expression"—laying the basis for the formation of American national character.[43]

James explored how American writers wrestled with the question of how to reconcile democracy with individualism. James found the poetry of Walt Whitman and prose of Herman Melville especially illuminating. Whitman, James believed, expressed an individualism that, relying on social longing without social contact, turned in on itself and in the end resulted in a rebellious loneliness rather than a social movement, something he saw as parallel to the embrace of existentialism and psychoanalysis by later generations of writers. Yet in the process Whitman revealed the yearning that remained for James so central to the lives of most Americans: how to reconcile free expression and social connectedness. Though he admired his poetry, James insisted that Whitman's celebration of freedom was all too easily co-opted, so that rulers of America linked individualism and democracy with free enterprise during the Cold War. In contrast, Melville recognized the dangers of excessive individualism in *Moby Dick*, so visible in the figure of Captain Ahab gone mad, a figure who stood for James as a precursor of both American industrialists and Adolf Hitler. James celebrated Melville, identifying him as the artist who came closest to realizing the heights he so admired in the best of ancient Greek civilization, in the philosophy of Aristotle and the plays of Aeschylus. James insisted that Melville understood the social connectedness of the multiracial group of men on the *Pequod*; his attention to the social dynamics of their relationships revealed that he fully grasped the tension between individualism and authority. Finally, although James's language of exceptionalism minimized the importance of the enslavement of African Americans and the genocide of Native Americans, for him the abolitionists were thinkers whose "creativity was the expression of precise social forces," something that enabled them to form and lead a social movement.[44]

For James, 1876 marked a major turning point in the nation's history. The growth of industry and large-scale organizations prompted modern Americans to believe that the language of individualism and freedom provided the framework for understanding their society. More than half a century later, the New Deal further eroded genuine freedom by emphasizing not a renewal of authentic individualism but security. Promises of jobs, of increased consumption, and of greater leisure reduced "mankind to the level of horses and cows with an instinct for exercise." James attacked the combination of industrial capitalism and the welfare state, seeing as a corrupt bargain what later historians would characterize as the Keynesian synthesis of government intervention, higher wages, and more ample consumption. As James noted in *State Capitalism and World Revolution* (1950), the bureaucracy replaced a struggle over production with one "over consumption, higher wages, pensions, education." This meant that if laborers sought satisfaction in work, the economic system instead provided it through consumer goods and experiences. Consequently, the bureaucracy brought "a new social program in the realm of consumption because it cannot attack capitalism at the point of production without destroying capitalism itself." Critical of the cooptation he believed the Congress of Industrial Organizations had accepted by the late 1940s, James wrote that the economic system had converted labor insurgency "into a weapon of struggle against the proletariat" as it celebrated a rising standard of living for workers in ways that ensured the persistence of "capitalist production." Thus from a radical Marxist perspective James offered a powerful and bitter critique of the post–World War II consensus. "The babblers who think that all the American workers want is 'full employment,'" he wrote in 1947, "are in for a rude awakening. That capitalism increases the use-values (radio, education, books, etc)" only intensified the hostility of workers. Eventually, he predicted, "bourgeois society" would collapse and workers would rebel as "resentment against the whole system explodes with terrible power."[45]

Americans and the Pursuit of Happiness

All these forces, but especially the alienation fostered by modern conditions of production and consumption, prevented Americans from pursuing happiness, the ability to bring together the needs for individual expression and social commitment that James struggled to achieve in his own life as well. To James, what was missing in America was unalientated work achieved through workers' control of modern industrial processes. The result was that mechanization and the state had undermined the nation's powerful tradition of freedom, in the process crushing "the very individuality which tradition nourishes and the abundance of mass-produced goods encourages." Following Alexis de Tocqueville, whom he considered his intellectual ancestor, and drawing on Marx's 1844 *Economic and Philosophical Manuscripts*, which he had a role in recovering in 1947, James emphasized the power of association to balance traditional American individualism and contemporary alienation.[46]

Other forces prevented the realization of happiness in mid-twentieth-century America. In addition to his criticism of complicit labor unions, James leveled some of his strongest attacks against intellectuals, who he felt either lent their weight to organized society or retreated to privatized concerns through existentialism and psychoanalysis. He included on his list writers such as Arthur M. Schlesinger Jr., Lewis Mumford, Robert Lynd, Norman Mailer, and John Dewey. "The majority of intellectuals drift along," James remarked rather carelessly, "knocking from pillar to post and finding themselves in the strangest places. They can tell no one anything, for they have no coherent ideas on anything." Anticipating later discussions of a new class of technical and administrative elites in a bureaucracy, James called "the outstanding change in the social structure" the "centralization, the bureaucratization, the incorporation of the great mass of *intelligentsia* into the unit which governs, manages, instructs, organizes the great undifferentiated mass."[47]

African Americans and women were for James the saving remnant that might over time transform the nation into a society where the pursuit of happiness and genuine individualism triumphed over the forces that had made America an industrialized and bureaucratized nation. The fate of those he called Negroes was the touchstone as to whether the issue of race would be solved in the United States and the world. He understood the situation of African Americans in both transnational and national terms. He emphasized the reservoir of organizational skills of members and leaders of black churches. Segregated, they were nonetheless integral to American life. Their situation revealed "the intolerable strains and stresses to which the whole nation is subjected." Relying on a notion of the dialectic, James wrote that "*the key to the Marxist analysis of the Negro question*" was that the more African Americans were integrated into the nation's production, the more they became conscious of their "*exclusion* from democratic privileges as a separate group in the community."[48] Social movements led by African Americans, James wrote at a time when the basis was being laid for the civil rights movement, would herald the "advance notice of the whole nation in movement."[49]

What James wrote about middle-class women was equally prophetic. Though to James they seemed to have an equality unprecedented in world history, on closer examination "the thing that tears them to pieces is that when they examine their equality, they find that it is a spurious thing." James wrote tellingly of the way media turned women into objects. "Women, their legs and their breasts," he observed in terms analogous to those used by Marshall McLuhan in *The Mechanical Bride* (1951), "are called into service to sell everything from insecticides to aeroplanes." For James the solution was a "revolution in the home" that rested "upon a revolution outside of it," a remark he made at a time when Popular Front labor union feminists like the young Betty Friedan were saying much the same thing. A fundamental transformation in relationships between men and women would occur when equality between the sexes extended to housework, dress, and sports and when society no longer considered men the principal breadwinners.[50]

Within the larger framework of his argument, especially in a section titled "Popular Arts and Modern Society," James developed his analysis of commercial culture. Over the years since 1876, powerful forces had eroded individualism and freedom. Harking back to another golden age, he asserted that the popular culture of the 1920s, jazz, as well as films by Charlie Chaplin and Walt Disney, involved an unusual combination of social criticism and artistic creativity, comparable in power and imagination to classical Greek drama and the novels of Melville. Some of this creativity continued into the 1930s in films by Disney and the Marx Brothers. The depression of the 1930s and the worldwide crisis of World War II had made popular culture less artistic and more formulaic but provided a window into the aspirations of ordinary Americans. The yearnings of Americans for happiness and freedom were too great to destroy, since the nation's citizens had developed a "consuming rage with the social and psychological problems of society."[51]

Underneath the political conservatism of workers and others lay explosive, unresolved tensions and aspirations, revealed through an examination of popular culture that relied on a Hegelian dialectic. To James, high culture (represented for him by the works of James Joyce, T. S. Eliot, Ernest Hemingway, and even John Ford) did not help in understanding what was on the mind of ordinary Americans, even though he admitted that it was highly artistic and had the power to move him. They "express so much of the modern world," he remarked but continued to say that they did so only partially. He focused instead on popular films, widely read newspapers (like New York's *Daily News*),

Figure 4. This still from the silent film *City Lights* (1931) features the writer, actor, and director Charlie Chaplin. Walter Benjamin, C.L. R. James, members of the Independent Group, Paddy Whannel, and Stuart Hall were among the international observers who hailed Chaplin's artistic creativity and social commentary and noted how effectively his work illustrated what it meant to complicate cultural hierarchies. Courtesy of Photofest.

comic strips, jazz, popular novels (like those of Frank Yerby), and magazines with large circulations (such as *Time* and *Life*). He scorned much of what he studied on aesthetic grounds, calling novels by Yerby "as bad, as writing, as they can possibly be." Yet serious study of these texts, he argued, provided "the clearest ideological expression of the sentiments and deepest feelings of the American people and a great window into the future of America and the modern world." In important ways, James remained compelled by the standards and commitment to fine literature that his mother had inspired in him, even as he acknowledged what serious examination of more popular modes of expression said about their consumers.[52]

What the study of major strands of popular culture revealed was "the bitterness, the violence, the brutality, the sadism simmering in the population, the desire to revenge themselves with their own hands, to get some release for what society had done to them." If James understood that popular magazines and movies were democratic in form, he also asserted that their content was not, that indeed it contained seeds of a totalitarianism that he saw fully expressed in Hitler's Germany and Stalin's Soviet Union. As Andrew Ross has pointed out, here James adopted a dialectic, arguing that "entertainment is actually the dialectical opposite of what its mass audience truly wants," control over production that would encourage both collectivism and individualism. In the meantime, the comic strip *Dick Tracy*, gangster films such as *Public Enemy* (1931) with James Cagney and *High Sierra* (1941) with Humphrey Bogart, or the detective stories by Dashiell Hammett and Raymond Chandler expressed the rage that disenfranchised Americans felt as well as their suspicion of the state's ability to keep public order. Moreover, the heroes of these stories had their female counterparts, seen most vividly in films starring Bette Davis or Joan Crawford, who portrayed evil women living violent lives. Thus, for James, Rita Hayworth was no "mere creation of predatory industrialists for stupid masses" but an expression of the primitive realism that satisfied American audiences.[53]

If much of what James found revealed through a study of popular culture was violent and threatening, other aspects provided more hope. James highlighted a different tendency, one he located in the comic strips *Gasoline Alley* and *Blondie*, in radio soap operas, and magazines like *True Confessions*. What they offered the audience was the dramatic representation of "the everyday commonplace inconsequential actions of life." Though he considered much of them vulgar and trivial, he nonetheless insisted that they revealed how closely art captured the humdrum experiences of millions of Americans, something he found powerfully expressed in the films and radio shows during World War II that provided literal renderings of the experiences of women on the home front, burdened by children and household duties, and men abroad fighting, facing danger and temptation.[54]

In addition, the popular arts provided "an esthetic compensation in the contemplation of free individuals who go out into the world and settle their problems by free activity and individualistic methods." They re-invoked the heroism, bravery, and determination that for workers or farmers, whose jobs were humdrum, derisively symbolized the tension between ideal and reality. They offered audiences "a sense of active living" and release from anger in a world where their lives were "ordered and restricted at every turn, where there is no certainty of employment, far less of being able to rise by energy and ability." In other words, mechanization could not kill "the passionate individualistic American temperament" so deeply rooted in the nation's life. Popular culture remained the vehicle through which the masses, among whom he included the working class, the lower middle class, and those who dwelled in small towns and on farms in remote areas of America, could experience this tradition. Movie stars, supported by a publicity apparatus worthy of analysis in terms set by Adorno and Horkheimer's notion of a culture industry, enabled Americans to live vicariously by experiencing the "free individuality which is the dominant need of the vast mass today." Modern society simultaneously built up "all sorts of possibilities and vistas for individual personality" and confined those personalities "to a narrow routinized existence with mechanical means." In response, people needed to "realize the thwarted possibilities . . . through some symbolic personality." What post-1929 popular culture provided was "a new type of symbolism, a symbolism that goes to the very heart of the modern age, its denial of personality to the mass and the determination of the mass to realize some form of individuality in however vicarious a form."[55]

In developing his argument, James had to rethink the question of the relationship between producers and consumers of popular culture. Readily aware of the commonly held belief that the entertainment industry worked to distract the masses from serious social problems, he insisted that critics had to focus on why a particular kind of cultural expression became popular at specific moments. Moreover, he pointed to a tacit agreement on both sides, "a sort of armed neutrality" he called it, to avoid controversial political and social issues. Owners of major movie studios, for example, could have developed anti-union or anti-socialist films but they realized this would not work at the box office. In addition, he worked against the notion of active producer/passive consumer. "To believe that the great masses of people are merely passive recipients of what purveyors of popular art give to them," he insisted, "is in reality to see people as dumb slaves." Rather, he saw reciprocity operating: cultural producers spending time and money on figuring out what would sell, and readers and spectators actively deciding what they would purchase and doing so in ways that shaped what entrepreneurs decided to create. He emphasized the "organic relation between the creative imagination of an artist, the receptivity of a public and the connection between them." Consequently, within the framework of a common understanding of what potential controversy kept off bounds, popular cultural products represented the deepest longings of their audiences, a way they communicated to themselves and others. Moreover, the popular arts gave ample evidence of how ripe the nation was for "drastic social transformations," which in Germany had led to Hitler, and which he feared might lead to totalitarianism in the United States even though he held out the possibility of progressive social change.[56]

On the Road Again

Coming to terms with *American Civilization* as a historical document is no easy task. James wrote under less than ideal circumstances, resulting in a manuscript that was fragmentary, incomplete, and unresolved. He composed it in 1949–50, when his recent marriage and the birth of his son put him under more than usual financial pressure. He hoped he could earn a sizeable advance for an accessible and significant book. Juxtaposing it with much of James's other writings raises the issue of whether, with the federal government investigating him and under threat of deportation, he compromised his positions much more than he would have done under more favorable conditions. At some level, he was determined to demonstrate that he understood the United States as a civilization and to convince federal authorities of his loyalty so he could avoid deportation. These factors go part of the way to explain his embrace of iconic American concepts such as individualism and happiness, although he gave them distinctive, radical treatment. Yet his assertions of American exceptionalism and his celebrations of American virtues were striking. Though he handled them in his distinctive ways, at times what he wrote was eerily reminiscent of mainstream Cold War hosannas. Americans, he remarked, enjoyed "an immense preponderance over the rest of the world" in a whole range of consumer items, removing "the United States qualitatively from all previous civilizations. To this can be added," he continued, "a freedom of social intercourse and a sense of equality also unparalleled in any previous or contemporary society." Such a statement is surprising given both his commitment to internationalism and his own perpetual marginality from the mainstreams in Trinidad, Britain, and the United States. In addition, far from emphasizing the imperial ambitions of the American government, corporations, and culture producers, an approach consonant with the anticolonialism he expressed before and after 1950, he saw American commercial culture as transnational in a different way. Products of American mass media, he wrote in 1953, are "received with immense popularity all over the world."[57] Indeed, among the intriguing things about *American Civilization* was how James avoided bringing into the book any discussion of creolization or boundary crossing from his earlier works, on cricket especially. In this instance, compartmentalizing the various parts of his career resulted in making this book less rich and provocative than it might have been.

In other ways, what he wrote in *American Civilization* was problematic. Outside of the section on African Americans, he paid remarkably little attention to race, notably in his neglect of Latinos and Native Americans, to say nothing of his inattention to the problematic relationship between popular culture and race. Indeed, in 1953 James hailed D. W. Griffith's *The Birth of a Nation*, which he acknowledged he was in favor of picketing, as the finest movie he knew, an aesthetically acceptable position that also made clear his political objections. What compelled James was that Griffith was "a supreme master" who displayed "the epic breadth and the historical imagination" comparable to Leo Tolstoy's *War and Peace* and Homer's *Iliad*. Perhaps the insurgency by African Americans, women, and labor unions in the immediate postwar period made him more optimistic than was justifiable in retrospect, and even by 1949, when the tide had begun to turn as the Cold War intensified. Yet problems with the book remain. He simultaneously made race an issue and paid far too little attention to it, especially avoiding recognition that antebellum slavery spoiled his pre-1876 American Eden.[58]

Yet to his credit, unlike more vulgar Marxists, James saw base and superstructure in reciprocal relations and emphasized that the popular arts emerged not as a result of top-down control but of cultural contestation or insurgency. Thus among the important contributions of the book was that he was developing a position on popular culture that stood in sharp contrast to that of New York intellectuals and the Frankfurt School. He dismissed modernist culture as out of touch with American life and focused instead on popular arts, which he appreciated for their creativity. Though he admired the aesthetic qualities of high culture, he took seriously the popular arts, which, in a dialectical relationship with the labor of mass production, he saw as an ideal window into the consciousness of ordinary Americans. James was taking a clear stand against what one critic has called the "left-intellectual creed of vanguard modernism" of ex-Trotskyists in the *Partisan Review* crowd, with whom he often tangled, and against members of the Frankfurt School, with whose writings he was far less if at all familiar. Although he saw much to admire in high art, he gave no ground to those who were trying to wed anti-Stalinism to the canonization of great literature. James envisioned reconciliation of the popular and the aesthetic—which he located in the plays of Aeschylus and Shakespeare, the novels of Melville, and then saw achieved by Chaplin before 1929—to be possible in the future America where revolutionary change would overturn capitalism and bourgeois society.[59]

Much of this became clear in a letter he wrote to Daniel Bell in 1953 and a talk he delivered in Paris a year later. He wrote to Bell, who had seen his book manuscript and believed that James was speaking ironically when he expressed admiration for comic strips. James reiterated his understanding of the relationship between creators and audiences as reciprocal. He spoke of how jazz, by which he meant big band music performed by whites and African Americans (including Louis Armstrong as "the greatest of them all"), depended "entirely upon popular support." Making clear how fully grounded he was in the classics of Western civilization, doubtless with the *Partisan Review* crowd in mind, he told Bell how much he opposed "that considerable body of American intellectuals who believe that they are defenders of the culture of Europe against the masses of the American people." He went on to assert that the aesthetic quality of cultural products did not matter to him, even as he found equally compelling, artful, and creative the best of American popular culture and canonical works by Aeschylus and Shakespeare, both of which he saw as taking their inspiration from and appealing to mass, largely working-class audiences. "That is why I look with an interest that grows with the years at the immense vitality and the new forms by which the American *mass*, using modern technology, interests and amuses itself." He made clear how much he admired American comics (*Dick Tracy* especially), *Keystone* comedies, western and gangster movies, detective novels, jazz, and soap operas. For example, he cited the work of television comedians like Jackie Gleason and Sid Caesar, whom he much preferred to the tonier television plays the *Omnibus* series offered.[60]

Less than a year later, in March 1954, James continued his defense of the popular arts in a talk in Paris sponsored by the Congress of Cultural Freedom but not published until 1989. The world of modern man, he insisted, "is one of constantly increasing multiplicity of relations between himself, immense mechanical constructions and social organizations of world-wide scope." Representation of this world, he continued in ways that echoed what Benjamin had written in the 1920s and 1930s, demands new forms such as the panorama, flashback, cross-cutting, and a highly mobile camera. Here James accomplished what he set out to do in *American Civilization* and elsewhere: using analyses drawn from classics of Western culture to understand new cultural forms, in the process placing Aeschylus, Shakespeare, and Chaplin on the same level. Deploying his command of Shakespeare's plays and Aristotle's philosophy, he explored how the films of Griffith and Chaplin represented true artistic quality and developed in ways shaped by the artists, the audience, and the corporations. In Chaplin's best work and in an ideal society, the combination of the high and low, Thackeray and cricket, would resolve the tension between the aesthetic and the popular.[61]

Conclusions

In very different contexts and from different perspectives, Benjamin and James analyzed popular culture in somewhat parallel ways. Both of them deeply steeped in traditional high Culture, they nonetheless stripped it of its aura and then honored, however equivocally, popular modes of expression. In suggestive ways, they explored the relationship between new technologies and cultural productions. They emphasized the abilities of new cultural forms to produce disjunctive consciousness. Both used high culture to understand the popular. Like Adorno, Benjamin and James recognized how popular culture was a product of corporate efforts that resulted in commodification. Unlike Adorno, they did not see the avant-garde as art independent of society or as a savior of an overconsumed society. For Adorno, art was separate from life; for Benjamin and James, inseparable. Using the dialectic and themselves ambivalent about new forms, Benjamin and James offered suggestive and complicated ways of understanding the relationship of producers and their audiences. Above all, both of them crossed borders in multiple ways, in their own lives across national boundaries to begin with. As writers, they moved between genres even as they explored the complicated relationships between producer and consumer, levels of culture, and technology and culture.[62]

The relationships of Benjamin and James, as well as Habermas, Barthes, and Eco, to American popular culture were far from straightforward. None of these men evinced strong or persistent antipathy to the products of American mass media. On the contrary, they often found American popular culture appealing and richly inventive and, when they did not, they refused to link their distaste to a broader argument about American cultural imperialism. Like others, such as members of London's Independent Group, Stuart Hall, and Paddy Whannel, they remained fascinated, if not always enamored, with American popular culture. Immersed in both Culture and popular culture, Barthes, Benjamin, Eco, and James used the techniques of high culture to explore the popular.

Indeed Barthes, Eco, and James used canonical theater to understand wrestling, cricket, and contemporary mass media. Along with others, they worked to erode the borders between high/low and producer/consumer, trying with varying degrees of success to make such relationships more reciprocal or egalitarian. Turning away from moral condemnation, to varying degrees they instead emphasized pleasure and symbolic communication, finding in stretches of popular culture evidence of creativity and sensuousness. Yet if many of them took consumer culture seriously and moved away from moral denunciations, they still relied heavily on a Marxist critique of commodification. Benjamin, with his insistence on multiple meanings and utopian possibilities went further, though Barthes and Eco hinted at such possibilities as well.

One can only speculate about what difference it would have made to American discussions of popular culture had the works of Barthes, Benjamin, Eco, Habermas, and James been available in the immediate postwar period. Not much is the best guess. Early on, the terms of debate in the United States were too well entrenched, only to be upended by generational change and the events of the late 1960s. The antitotalitarianism of New York intellectuals, who wielded such considerable intellectual influence for thirty years beginning in the late 1930s, made them fear that the spread of a debased popular culture in America might underwrite something like a repetition of what happened in Nazi Germany and Soviet Russia. In contrast, the fact that all five of the non-American writers stood in opposition to Stalinism (and Barthes and Eco to the Catholicism that dominated their nations) undergirded their antipathy to what they saw as authoritarianism. In turn these commitments made it possible for them to wonder playfully about the creative possibilities of consumer culture, to imagine that in movies, comics, and spectacles people might find the ludic possibilities not available in the Party or the Church.

With David Riesman's *The Lonely Crowd* (1950) and Marshall McLuhan's *The Mechanical Bride* (1951) we come upon two works that were not lost in translation but that remind us that in their response to consumer culture two influential North American writers in the early 1950s were fascinated, but reluctantly so.

Chapter 4

Reluctant Fascination

In the 1950s two North American writers wrestled with how to think about consumer culture—and did so in a manner that broke new ground in important but hesitant ways. In *The Lonely Crowd* (1950) the American David Riesman presented a probing interpretation of the emergence of new styles of affluent living among cosmopolitan members of the white middle and upper-middle classes. A year later, the Canadian Marshall McLuhan offered a suggestive but unresolved analysis in *The Mechanical Bride* (1951), in this case of the visual imagery of mass media. McLuhan would emerge in the mid-1960s as an influential writer for members of the counterculture, offering a much more celebratory understanding of consumer culture and one that contrasted with the ambivalences he revealed in 1951. Like the works discussed in the two previous chapters, but for different reasons, *The Mechanical Bride* failed to reach much of an audience. In contrast, *The Lonely Crowd* attracted a wide and rapt readership. Both McLuhan and Riesman were struggling to understand newly emerging aspects of popular culture by deploying their remarkably capacious commitments to interdisciplinary perspectives. If by the end of the 1950s, new understandings of consumer culture had developed on both sides of the Atlantic, ones that relied on notions of pleasure and symbolic communication, Riesman was exceptional in his location within the main currents of American intellectual life.

David Riesman: Far from the Lonely Crowd

In 1950, University of Chicago professor David Riesman published *The Lonely Crowd: A Study of the Changing American Character*. The book quickly became the nation's most influential and widely read midcentury work of social and cultural criticism. It even catapulted its author to the cover of *Time* magazine in 1954, one of the first social scientists so honored. With *The Lonely Crowd* Riesman offered a nuanced and complicated portrait of the nation's middle and upper-middle classes. This book is a key text in what the historian Howard Brick has called the "displacement" of the economy and economics in the social sciences and social criticism at midcentury. Drawing on (and transforming) the work of émigré intellectuals, Riesman pictured a nation in the midst of a shift from a society based on production to one fundamentally shaped by consumption. He explored how people used commercial goods to communicate with one another. He criticized, mostly in an implicit manner, the observers who celebrated high culture and denigrated the popular. In addition, he embraced playfulness as a way people could achieve autonomy.[1]

Riesman came to write *The Lonely Crowd* by a circuitous route, a result of an almost two-decade-long search for a vocation.[2] Born into a prosperous, cosmopolitan, and assimilated German Jewish family, he grew up in a household that was, he later said, "Jewish by birth but without a trace of religious connection . . . [or] ethnic sentiment." His father was a prominent Philadelphia physician who had migrated from Germany before making his mark as a doctor, teacher, and writer. His cultivated, Bryn Mawr–educated mother, Riesman later wrote, "was an aesthete . . . who looked down on people who did the day-to-day work of the world." As a child, he wrote McLuhan in 1959, Riesman read detective stories, which he understood as having no respectability. Explaining his favorable attitude toward popular modes of expression, Riesman noted that "the culture of an earlier, more aggressively highbrow generation of Americans—my parents' generation—was thin and donnish" lacking as it did "a strenuous dialectic vis-à-vis lowbrow and middlebrow culture" that "made the possession of correct taste too easy and complacent a matter." His early life was sheltered and privileged. Until he entered college, he had not known any "Democrats, let alone Socialists or Communists." He and his familial world remained unscathed by the Depression, with his friends as young adults still having "their boats, their debutante parties, their parents' summer places."[3]

After graduating from Harvard in 1931 with a degree in biochemistry, Riesman had a series of experiences that enabled him to hammer out his vision of a vocation as he struggled, in the historian Wilfred McClay's words, "to break out of the psychological imprisonment of his upbringing." He earned his degree from Harvard Law School in 1934, clerked for Supreme Court Justice Louis D. Brandeis, practiced law at a Boston firm, and, having married Evelyn Thompson in 1936, from 1937 to 1941 taught law at the University of Buffalo. After a year's fellowship at Columbia Law School, he worked briefly in the office of the attorney general of New York and from 1943 to 1946 for Sperry Gyroscope Company. Beginning in 1946, he taught on the social science faculty at the University of Chicago, a campus brimming with talent, including scholars who focused on the relationships between culture, society, and personality. In 1947 he took a leave from Chicago to focus on a project at Yale, which sponsored the work that led to *The Lonely Crowd*. In 1958, he left Chicago for a position as University Professor at Harvard, where he remained for the rest of his teaching career.[4]

By the time he wrote *The Lonely Crowd*, Riesman had encountered the works of German émigrés. In the 1940s, he read the essays of Leo Lowenthal, one of the Frankfurt School's experts on the sociology of mass culture. Lowenthal's influential scholarship on the depiction of heroes in magazines revealed a major transition for American culture that he located in the mid-1920s, from heroes who were "idols of production" to those that were "idols of consumption." As a result, Lowenthal suggested, leisure and celebrity replaced hard work as the focal point of cultural expression. Articles in *Collier's* and the *Saturday Evening Post* revealed that people increasingly faced adjustment to the world "by exhibiting amiable and sociable qualities." Leisure time was "the new social riddle." Complex and controversial issues, Lowenthal wrote, referring to the hold celebrities had on the popular imagination, "are submerged in the experience of being at one with the lofty and great in the sphere of consumption."[5]

Of the émigrés Riesman encountered, it was Erich Fromm who most influenced him. Fromm was among the founders of the Frankfurt School, though in the late 1930s he distanced himself from the positions of many of its most influential members. After migrating to the United States, during the 1940s and 1950s Fromm was an immensely popular writer, bringing together and making easily accessible the insights of Karl Marx and Sigmund Freud. Fromm served as Riesman's psychoanalyst in the early 1940s, an encounter that, Riesman later said, inaccurately, was more like a tutorial than traditional therapy. Two of Fromm's books influenced Riesman, *Escape from Freedom* (1941) and *Man for Himself* (1947). In the first work Fromm drew lessons from his experience with Nazi totalitarianism to explore whether freedom and individualism could survive in the modern world. He identified at least three alternatives people faced as they met the challenges modernization posed: escape into totalitarianism; the achievement of *"positive freedom,"* which *"consists in the spontaneous activity of the total, integrated personality"*; and the "compulsive conforming" he believed characterized American life. In *Man for Himself*, Fromm continued his exploration of the relationship between personality, character, and social structure. He highlighted a "marketing orientation" as one characteristic of a "nonproductive" character type in the urban middle class. This outlook fostered in an individual "the experience of oneself as a commodity," as exchange rather than as use value. As a result, personalities became saleable commodities with the media acting as the vehicle of instruction. Man found the "conviction of identity not in reference to himself and his powers but in the opinion of others about him. His prestige, status, and success," Fromm concluded, "are a substitute for the genuine feeling of identity." Although Fromm applauded the way market orientation fostered a receptivity to change, overall his conclusion was pessimistic. The modern, market-oriented person was insecure, alienated, and superficial. In contrast, healthy individuals developed a "productive orientation," using their abilities to realize their full potential through self-reliance and spontaneity.[6]

Riesman both absorbed and transformed what he learned from Fromm and other émigrés. He combined European critical theory with American traditions of social criticism based on empirical social science research. Like those he read, he mistrusted centralized power and feared the way mass culture fostered conformity and undermined individualism. Yet his writings lacked the declarative and radical dimensions of European critical theory. He replaced them with a tentative, careful musing on what he saw around him. He turned the pessimism of some members of the Frankfurt School into an anti-Stalinist and qualified endorsement of postwar American society. He responded to the Keynesian consensus that growing consumption was central to national prosperity. Considering the importance of the increasing separation of work and leisure, the entry of the working class into the mainstream, and early evidence of the explosive power of postwar abundance, Riesman offered a liberal, pluralist exploration of consumer culture in capitalist democracy.[7]

The Lonely Crowd (1950)

A discussion of Riesman's biography, including an acknowledgment of the sources on which he drew, cannot capture the range of qualities that undergirded *The Lonely Crowd* and made it such a compelling book. Riesman pioneered in the development of the genre of sociology as literature. He had an omnivorous curiosity, a capacious temperament that made him open to a broad spectrum of cultural experiences. He drew on observations of a wide range of material including children's books, movies, novels, interviews, and social science data. He offered a book that readers read in myriad ways, as an invitation to understand their own lives, as a subject of dinner party conversations, and as a contribution to scholarship and cultural criticism. Supple, nuanced, complicated, playful, and lucid, his mind sought imaginative connections between disparate phenomena. Riesman's tendency to see issues from multiple perspectives pervaded the book, which was accessible but complex and even enigmatic.

As his friend Eric Larrabee noted, *The Lonely Crowd* was "a witty, garrulous, shrewd, wandering, and intermittently brilliant set of notes that read as though brutal blue-penciling might someday make a book of them."[8]

Riesman's accomplishments were all the more remarkable given some of the circumstances under which he worked. He researched and wrote the book in less than three years. He did so at a time, 1947–50, when the abundance of postwar America was, at best, only on the horizon for most Americans and when contrasting visions of the future, Popular Front and Democratic Capitalist among them, competed for dominance. Although *The Lonely Crowd* was his generation's most suggestive guide to the new world of suburban affluence, Riesman wrote it from the social location of university communities in urban America.

If these qualities meant that the book opened itself to misunderstandings, the historian Eugene Lunn convincingly suggests that *The Lonely Crowd* moved the debate over popular culture to new ground, rather than, as many at the time and since have supposed, repeating old laments about deleterious effects of mass society. "Riesman," Lunn observes, "never tired of championing the virtues of playful leisure and consumer abundance freed from an ascetic 'scarcity-psychology,' which had previously forced humanity to mold the human personality for work, and which intellectuals continued in their disparaging reactions to mass entertainment and recreation." As Riesman wrote the historian Cushing Strout in 1964, "You understand so well what so few readers have grasped . . . the idea that other-direction is not simply external conformity seems almost impossible to get across." Still, as Lunn and McClay admit, the book was filled with irony, ambivalence, and bet-hedging. Again and again, Riesman made statements and then contradicted or qualified them, leaving readers unsure of what he meant. McClay suggests that Riesman's ambiguities captured contemporary anxieties and ambivalences.[9]

In the book, Riesman explored how a society influences its citizens by inculcating in them forms of social and psychological conformity. In the first stage, that of traditional or premodern society, the individual had a clearly defined place, shaped by expectations fostered through family, kin, and community networks. In the inner-directed stage, the age of production characteristic of Western bourgeois societies from the Renaissance to the late nineteenth century, parents emphasized character as they taught children to internalize authority. The result was self-reliant, driven, and highly individualistic entrepreneurs. What guided them, in Riesman's memorable analogy that drew on his job at Sperry, was the gyroscope, an internalized mechanism that kept individuals focused on work in a production-oriented economy.

In the twentieth century, the age of consumption, the other-directed personality was the dominant psychosocial type, one most fully developed in the urban, upper middle class. Meditating on Fromm's notion of the market-oriented person finely attuned to signals others sent, Riesman switched to radar as his metaphor, enabling him to describe the process of socialization by media and peers that made people acutely sensitive to clues from outside. Executives in the bureaucratic world of the organization man succumbed to the tyranny of peer groups which emphasized adjustment rather than rebellion or autonomy. In politics, people operated as consumers in a world characterized by the pluralism of competing interest groups. Inside dopesters turned politically aware citizens into consumers of gossip rather than producers of moral judgments. Flexibility in all areas of life replaced a strict moralism. Other-directed people, shaped now by personality not character, anxiously searched new frontiers of a consumer society and struggled against the pressures to conform. Indeed, for Riesman "one prime psychological lever of the other-directed person is a diffuse *anxiety*" about work, child-rearing, and sex. The other-directed person's sense of self was fluid and uncertain. Drawing on Fromm's emphasis on the productive personality, Riesman ended the book with a long discussion of autonomy. He explored the ways in which it could emerge among tradition-, inner-, and other-directed people.[10]

Despite what Riesman said at key moments, contemporaries commonly assumed that he preferred the inner-directed person in whom autonomy and inner-direction were closely linked.[11] People read him as one of a host of 1950s critics who worried about how mass media threatened individualism by promoting conformity. Yet he saw promise in the other-directed personality's flexibility and openness. As McClay notes, Riesman offered "a celebration of the possibilities presented by consumption unfettered by the constraints of moralism or scarcity." Indeed, Riesman provided a penetrating, suggestive exploration of how modern consumer culture opened up new possibilities for prosperous Americans. What he found problematic was not the consumption of a post-scarcity, abundant world but the pressures that peers and the media deployed to foster socialized and often compulsive pleasure. In fact, at key moments Riesman celebrated the play and leisure of the emerging consumer culture that had rejected "scarcity psychology." Under ideal conditions, he wrote, modernization would liberate, not trap the individual. Leisure counselors would educate Americans about how to consume in a discriminating manner, and market researchers would uncover unmet consumer desires. If we might see these strategies as problematic, Riesman believed they were potentially utopian. He understood the individualizing (as opposed to conformity-inducing) potential of mass media, which he believed would provide a source of resistance to the pressure of the peer group. Though the world of the other-directed contained pressures for conformity, it also promised flexibility and self-expression. The mass media "exert a constant pressure on the accepted peer-groups and suggest new modes of escape from them . . . autonomy, building on an exploration of a tension between peers and media, must take advantage of both sides of the tension." Thus he found that "many movies, in many conventionally unexpected ways, are liberating agents."[12]

Riesman criticized the critics of popular culture, especially those on the left, for assuming an all-powerful, capitalist-driven mass media and passive audiences. "I know that there is much snobbery and asceticism behind current criticism, including socialist criticism, of mass leisure," he remarked as he drew on his awareness of his parents' elitism and on what he had learned from members of the Frankfurt School as well as from contemporary social critics, which involved "a view of the potentialities of leisure and abundance to which both the glad hand and the search for self- and group-adjusting lessons in popular culture are themselves often poignant testimonials." His criticism of popular culture's critics rested in turn on a skepticism about highly moralistic attitudes, which he labeled "ascetic or self-righteous." From Veblen to Freud and on into contemporary cultural criticism, he saw the persistence of anti-hedonistic aestheticism. Writing in 1950 on Freud's handling of issues of work and play, he celebrated fun and leisure that were "spontaneous, amiable, frivolous, or tender," "surreptitious—even sinful." Abundance and consumer culture undermined a world governed by scarcity, moralism, and compulsive exercise of the work ethic. In their place, Riesman, although himself both playful and a workaholic, emphasized pleasure and play exercised by autonomous people in an abundant society.[13]

Central to Riesman's understanding of popular culture were his efforts to complicate the division among levels of culture that contemporary critics relied upon. He thought the distinction between high and low overlooked "ambiguities on both sides." In contrast to those, like Theodor Adorno and T. S. Eliot, who enshrined an elite avant-garde culture, Riesman celebrated "nonpopular avant-garde culture" that he found in jazz and bebop. Moreover, he envisioned American consumers engaged in a constant process of "taste-exchanging," continually discarding "earlier affections and affectations for later, high-brow, and more sophisticated ones." With *The Lonely Crowd*, Riesman provided an example of what it meant to integrate, or blur the lines between high and low. The book's power rested on an interweaving of sources, to no one of which

Riesman assigned a privileged position: readings of Leo Tolstoy and Honoré de Balzac, European social theory, folklore, children's books, popular success manuals, dime novels, cookbooks, radio shows, and widely circulated magazines from *Ladies' Home Journal* to *Hot Rod*.[14]

To Riesman, critics not only failed to realize how good were "American movies, popular novels, and magazines" but also "how energetic and understanding are some of the comments of the amateur taste exchangers who seem at first glance to be part of a very passive, uncreative audience." What critics overlooked was that peers, mediators between the individual and the media, were more powerful than media in shaping people's choices. More than that, Riesman pictured ordinary, middle- and upper-middle-class consumers as active agents. He described a complicated process in which individuals, peers, business groups, and media shaped systems of symbolic communication through popular culture, with influence moving in all directions. He took from Veblen an understanding of how communication through consumption provided society with its social dynamic. However, if for Veblen the wealthy leisure class played the key role in this process, for Riesman it was the middle-class peer group, and from an early age on. "Children and adolescents," he wrote, "far more sophisticated than the old people, form a consumers' union; indeed each child in the middle class is automatically a consumer trainee before he can walk." "The consumer today," he observed, "has most of his potential individuality trained out of him by his membership in the consumers' union. He is kept within his consumption limits not by goal-directed but by other-directed guidance, kept from splurging too much by fear of others' envy, and from consuming too little by his own envy of the others." For other-directed people of all ages, consumer culture served less as an avenue of escape than as a means of education and communication, language and experiences through which people learned about politics, social dynamics, and their relationships with one another.[15]

In the world of the other-directed, play and sexuality became key instruments for achieving autonomy. Riesman underscored how lessened emphasis on work might open up more opportunity for play and fantasy, which he linked primarily to consumership. As a result, individualism would flourish based on an ability to consume without pressure from peers or media. "Play may prove to be the sphere in which there is still some room left for the would-be autonomous man," he commented, "to reclaim his individual character from the pervasive demands of his social character." Riesman went on to connect play with sexuality through the notion of "liberated fantasy" or "fantasy and spontaneous playfulness." Sexual experience "is perhaps the last frontier of consumption, an area of mystery in which" other-directed people anxiously test "the power to attract others and to have 'experience.'"[16]

In a short but suggestive section titled "Sex: The Last Frontier" and elsewhere, Riesman spelled out what sex meant for the other-directed. With work providing less and less satisfaction and with the increase in opportunities that abundance afforded, for the modern leisure-oriented consumer sex "permeates the daytime as well as the playtime consciousness." For men and women, he wrote, "the game of sex . . . provides a kind of defense against the threat of total apathy" that the routines of work and domesticity underwrote. Because consumer goods in a mass society were only slightly differentiated, the other-directed individual, he wrote, "can scarcely conceive of a consumption good that can maintain for any length of time undisputed dominance over his imagination," then he added, "except perhaps sex." Sexual partners differed from even expensive automobiles, for they were more mysterious. Sexual expression became "an area of competition and a locus of the search, never completely suppressed, for meaning and emotional response in life." In the sexual arena for the other-directed, gender dynamics played a key role. Men followed their vision of what their male ancestors had done: "having chaste and modest women," they could "maintain the initiative" sexually. They might "also feel compelled to compete with the Kinsey athletes" among their peers.[17]

The situations women faced were more complicated. Technology freed them from much of the drudgery of household responsibilities and gave them "many 'aids to romance.'" This enabled millions of women to "become pioneers, with men, on the frontier of sex. . . . The very ability of women to respond in a way that only courtesans were supposed to in an earlier age means, moreover, that qualitative differences of sex experience—the impenetrable mystery—can be sought for night after night, and not only in periodic visits to a mistress or brothel." The new society of consumers allowed women to "act as nonpecuniary pirates" on the sexual frontier, "as if to punish men for the previous privatizations of women." Again and again, married, nonstraying women had to wonder anxiously whether they should take the initiative sexually. Autonomous women among the other-directed had to decide whether to "foster aggressiveness or simulate modesty." The situation married career women faced was even trickier, for they had to wonder whether their sexual lives detracted from or added to their professional ones. Riesman's reference to mistresses and prostitutes pointed back to earlier, problematic roles for women. Yet his emphasis on fantasy, partnership, the relationship between sex and careers, along with his exploration of the frontiers of sexual experience, pointed forward to the sexual revolution that in 1950 was more than a decade away. If in much of *The Lonely Crowd* Riesman seemed to assume that men were its members, at least for the autonomous among the other-directed, his married women were experimental sexually. Interestingly enough, Riesman paid relatively little attention to women in his book but when he did so in this instance he focused on their sexual friskiness.[18]

Toward a New View of Consumer Culture

In *The Lonely Crowd*, given his engagement with popular culture and his suggestion of its connection to play and sex, Riesman distanced himself from the reigning attitudes toward these matters. Yet he gave no explicit sense of his relationship to the critique of mass culture offered by New York intellectuals and émigrés from Europe. In other writings in the early 1950s, however, he explored his disagreements with their positions. Nowhere was this clearer than in his brief contribution to *Partisan Review*'s 1952 symposium "Our Country and Our Culture," a key moment when American intellectuals talked of their relationship to the nation. To begin with, Riesman provided a penetrating sociological analysis, without naming names, of how the position of intellectuals in Cold War America shaped their attitude to mass culture. Calling on his peers to enjoy popular culture more, he saw avant-garde writers, "subtly frightened by the huge malleability of America," responding formulaically to what they saw as mass culture in ways that intensified their alienation from the society. Moving beyond their "novitiate of emotional expatriation," he cautioned, if they stopped fearing popularization and the middlebrow they might no longer be "afraid of liking people and cultural objects which do not fit some momentary critical canon." Riesman went on to contrast his own background in an assimilated and prosperous household with the life trajectory of many of the New York intellectuals who were born into poor, observant Jewish families in New York's outer boroughs and then went to City College of New York and not Harvard College. Noting how many critics of mass culture established their bona fides by being "contemptuous" of what popular audiences embraced, he wondered out loud "how soon can the descendants of immigrants again eat garlic and other savory foods after a bland, self-inhibited period of 'Americanization.'" As more children and grandchildren of intellectuals arrived on the scene, he wrote prophetically, the problem of the writers' encounter with popular culture would become "less intense" and by implication more accepting.[19]

Having distanced himself from purveyors of mass culture critiques, in his writings after *The Lonely Crowd* Riesman went on to put forth his own vision.

He offered a major breakthrough toward a pluralistic vision when he took issue with those who emphasized the homogeneity of a mass audience, asserting instead that the nation contained "a series of audiences, stratified by taste and class, each (even that of *Partisan Review* devotees) large enough to constitute, in psychological terms, a 'mass.'" Nor were these consumers as passive as critics imagined. They had "more critical judgment, at more of these levels, than is generally realized" and were "not so manipulated as often supposed: they fight back by refusing to 'understand,' by selective interpretation, by apathy." He warned against interpreting culture by examining its products as he insisted that it was important to understand "how individuals actually *interpret* the commodities and endow them with meanings." Consequently, here and elsewhere in the early 1950s, rather than seeing declension, Riesman saw variety. He emphasized how small groups of cosmopolitan adults resisted mass media by embracing noncommercial productions and, pointing to the youthfulness of moviegoers, asserted that they responded to the material of popular culture "in radically different ways and for radically different purposes." For example, they used a movie theater "to get warm, to sleep, to neck, to learn new styles, to expand one's imaginative understanding of people and places."[20]

In a similar vein, at one point in a 1950 article, "Listening to Popular Music," which Bernard Rosenberg and David Manning White reprinted in *Mass Culture*, Riesman listed the types of intellectuals who denigrated popular culture: "gifted Europeans" disgusted by the vulgar taste supposedly spurred by industrialization; those who drew on Veblen and Marx to see mass media "as an antirevolutionary narcotic"; and "high-brows who fear poaching on their preserves" by those who celebrated the middlebrow. One person who fit all these categories and whose work Riesman challenged in this article was Adorno, whose early 1940s writings on radio music Riesman knew well. In a 1945 article, "A Social Critique of Radio Music," the German émigré asked questions that interested Riesman. Monopoly capitalism, Adorno asserted, created standardization and false needs, with radio listening by mass audiences resembling "the ideal of Aunt Jemima's ready-mix for pancakes extended to the field of music" resulting in "pseudo-individualism" that undermined any possibility of effective social criticism. In contrast, Riesman understood that popular culture provided a means of symbolic exchange, a process by which people communicated aspects of their identity to peers. He remained skeptical about drawing sharp lines between high and low and explored the reciprocal relationship between producers and consumers, with each party manipulating the other.[21]

Rereading what Riesman wrote in the early 1950s raises a number of issues. Even though he had gathered extensive material on racial, ethnic, and class dimensions of postwar America, in *The Lonely Crowd* he was describing the world of the white, urban and suburban, middle- and upper-middle class men. Indeed in *Faces in the Crowd: Individual Studies in Character and Politics* (1952), where he presented and analyzed many of the interviews on which he relied in *The Lonely Crowd*, Riesman explored the racial, ethnic, and religious dimensions of this three-pronged typology. He discussed extensively the worlds of African Americans in Harlem and of working-class Roman Catholic ethnics in Bridgeport. Despite the messiness of the evidence, he lumped these two groups together among the tradition-directed. In contrast, in *The Lonely Crowd* when he listed members of that category, he did not consistently refer to those two groups. Yet despite the reputation of his 1950 book and other major postwar works of social criticism for focusing exclusively on the nation's white middle and upper-middle class, in *Faces in the Crowd* Riesman revealed his engagement with issues of race and class, as well as an awareness of the problems in applying categories developed for the middle-class to others.[22] In this respect, Riesman was no different from other public intellectuals of his generation who assumed that middle-class suburbanites, whom they saw as the quintessential modern Americans, faced more challenging situations than did less privileged social groups. Betty Friedan, who had extensive knowledge of the lives of working-class, African American, and professional women, instead focused *The Feminine Mystique* (1963) on white, suburban stay-at-home mothers. John Kenneth Galbraith set out to write about poverty but instead wrote *The Affluent Society* (1958).[23]

Riesman focused more on gender than on race or class. As his treatment of sex reveals, he discussed the ways that the shift to other-direction posed challenges and opportunities for women. Writing along lines that Betty Friedan would explore more than a dozen years later, in 1950 he worried that many middle-class women among the other-directed were veering away from the opportunities that autonomy, sexual liberation, and profession offered. "In a futile effort to recapture the older and seemingly more secure patterns," he observed, some women gave into "a diffuse image of male expectations, female peer-group jealousies, and reactionary counseling dressed up as the psychoanalytic inside story." He knew that the pressures for women to conform to less liberated models were abundant. Calculations of the GNP, Riesman noted, did not include the work of housewives, even though they produced real economic value. Insult was added to injury when housewives were "exhausted at the end of the day without feeling any right to be." Riesman also worried about efforts "to reprivatize women by redefining their role in some comfortably domestic and traditional way." He explored the pressures of "enforced privatization" that kept men and women from associating with each other on equal terms, at work and play. This took a considerable toll on suburban women, whose isolation made them "psychological prisoners even when the physical and economic handicaps to their mobility are removed." When relatively autonomous women sought satisfaction through volunteer work, they often found themselves shut out because of the professionalization of tasks such as caring for others or raising money. The son and husband of cultivated, educated women who did not have sustained professional commitments that brought money into the household, Riesman in 1950 understood some of the underlying conditions that would later drive women's liberation.[24]

Yet Riesman's handling of issues of gender was, in critical ways, puzzling. In *The Feminine Mystique*, Friedan characterized Riesman somewhat incompletely when she attributed to him the preference that women, rather than seeking autonomy by working outside the home, "might better help their husbands hold on to theirs, through play." Twenty years later, Barbara Ehrenreich in *The Hearts of Men* correctly noted that Riesman's inner-directed people had traits usually identified as masculine: tough, ambitious, instrumental, self-contained, better with things than with people. In contrast, his other-directed people had traits often associated with the feminine: sensitive to feelings, aware of the needs and opinions of others, expressive, and better with people than with objects. "Today it is the 'softness' of men rather than the 'hardness' of material," Riesman had written, "that calls on talent and opens new channels of social mobility." Usually, Riesman did not explicitly gender his typologies, using "man" or "person" when he meant men, assuming human was equivalent to male, and implicitly proceeding on the basis that men were the principal objects of study.[25]

Some scholars have taken Riesman's contrast between hard, focused masculine inner-directed individuals and soft, uncertain other-directed individuals as signaling a crisis in masculinity in which emasculated, conforming, and feminized men were at sea in a world of suburban homes, consumer goods, and conformity. In the 1950s, the argument goes, middle-class organization men, unlike their entrepreneurial predecessors, no longer derived satisfaction from work. In the 1950s, their entrance into an other-directed world made them problematically feminized: at sea in the world of suburban domesticity and consumer culture, both traditionally women's worlds. Such a characterization assumed that Riesman in important ways preferred the confident inner-directed man to the unsure other-directed one. However, if we acknowledge that Riesman was either ambivalent about the shift from one character type to another or even preferred the challenges the other-directed men had (especially the autonomous among them), then the story was not for Riesman one of masculinity in crisis or decline. Rather, if Riesman indeed saw the possibilities that other-direction opened for affluent men, then the story was ambiguous at worst, promising at best.[26]

As much as any category other than class, it was youth that captured Riesman's imagination. Mainly through his collaborator Reuel Denney, in working on the book, Riesman, who was forty-one in 1950, engaged himself with the popular culture of children and young adults: reading children's books, poring over the pages of *Hot Rod* magazine, and carefully relying on students to track contemporary music, including jazz and bebop, that had a youthful audience. "Children," he wrote, "live at the wave front of the successive population phases and are the partially plastic receivers of the social character of the future." Riesman saw young adults as sophisticated interpreters of popular culture. "Groups of young hot-jazz fans," he noted appreciatively, "have highly elaborate standards for evaluating popular music, standards of almost pedantic precision." It was precisely the seriousness of Riesman's engagement with youth—his hipness, a later generation might have said—that generated the disapproval of Elizabeth Hardwick. Writing in *Partisan Review* in 1954, she remarked that "perhaps the trouble is that Riesman is going with too young a crowd" and then went on to note that, in comparison with "his sheer contemporaneity, his briskly marching in the forward ranks— . . . many a younger man appears a bit sallow and run-down by the world of comics, television, pop tunes, 'crazy' teen-agers, all the raw diet Riesman thrives upon."[27]

Riesman's political positions also deserve note. Written when the Cold War was taking hold, *The Lonely Crowd* is especially striking in its ambiguous political messages. Throughout his life, Riesman's politics were those of an internationalist and a pluralist skeptic, leery of fixed ideological positions, of commitments to utopian dreams, of fervent nationalism, and of allegiance to authority. A trip to the Soviet Union in the spring of 1931 had solidified his antipathy to American Communists and fellow travelers who naively worshiped the USSR and denigrated key aspects of life in the United States. From early on, he opposed war (though with some reluctance he supported American entry into World War II) and centralized government. In the late 1940s and throughout the 1950s, he remained a social democrat who rejected the virulent expressions of anti-Communism and embraced liberal commitment to social betterment. His principal concern, from the dropping of the atomic bombs on Japan in 1945 until the end of his life, rested on fear of the consequences of nuclear war.[28]

Observers on the right and left took issue with Riesman's politics. From the right in 1956 came Russell Kirk, whose *The Conservative Mind* had recently appeared. Kirk saw Riesman as a nondoctrinaire liberal with "a number of conservative elements." Riesman's achievement, he continued (though he might also have had in mind Reinhold Niebuhr or Arthur Schlesinger Jr.) was that he offered a "chastened" liberalism. Kirk saw Riesman as lacking any transcendent moral or religious vision, left with only the chastised view that "all man can hope for is a round of small pleasures." From the left came equally sharp critiques. Writing in *Dissent* in 1954, its first year of publication, like Kirk but from a different perspective, Norman Mailer found Riesman too much of a centrist liberal, someone more content with what is than dreaming of what might be. He accused Riesman of seeing corporations as too benign, power as too dissipated, media as too diffuse in influence, and affluence as too soporific. Even more antagonistic was the critique that the historian and Communist Party intellectual Herbert Aptheker offered in a 1955 essay titled "The Cadillac Credo of David Riesman." What Riesman wrote, Aptheker asserted with more drama than accuracy, was indistinguishable from the propaganda turned out by the National Association of Manufacturers and the Chamber of Commerce: celebration of the "glories of the bourgeoisie and the aggressiveness of his Babbitry," denial of the existence of a ruling class, assertions of the irrelevance of Marxism, and an assumption that America had solved fundamental social problems by assuring abundance and equality.[29]

Kirk, Mailer, and Aptheker, in their desire to pigeonhole Riesman politically, missed more than they captured. To be sure, the emphasis Mailer and Aptheker placed on dreams and fantasies captured important elements of Riesman's approach. Yet to talk of "immanent hopes of lotus-land," soporific affluence, and the "glories of the bourgeoisie and the aggressiveness of his Babbitry" missed the mark. Riesman was moving into uncharted territory. As he drew on the writings of the Frankfurt School, he nonetheless challenged their emphasis on top-down control with an exploration of consumer culture that was too subtle for these reviewers and indeed most readers to understand. Thoughtfully avoiding simple answers, Riesman remained both fascinated by what he observed and reluctant to embrace it without hesitation.

Marshall McLuhan

In 1951, a year after the publication of *Lonely Crowd*, the Canadian and Roman Catholic Marshall McLuhan wrote in the preface to *The Mechanical Bride*, "I wish to acknowledge the advantage I have enjoyed in reading unpublished views of Professor David Riesman on the consumer mentality." His 1951 book was one step on the long road he took in his consideration of the impact of media on society. More than a dozen years later, McLuhan became a favorite among advocates of the counterculture with his evocation of a world united by new electronic technologies that encouraged communal and sensuous expressiveness in the global village. Years before he reached a wide audience with *The Gutenberg Galaxy* (1962), *Understanding Media* (1964), and *The Medium Is the Massage* (1967), McLuhan offered fresh though often hesitant ways of understanding mass culture. After a decade and a half as a literary critic, McLuhan's halting breakthrough as a media analyst came with *The Mechanical Bride*. With this book, he cast a skeptical and ambivalent eye on moralistic critiques of consumer culture, hoped to educate consumers in how to understand (and thereby resist) commercialism's calls, used literary analysis to explore popular culture, and suggested that the medium was as significant as the message. He understood advertisements as part of a system of symbolic communication rich in aesthetic innovation and yet emphasized the importance of an authentic sexuality unpolluted by commercialism. From the mid-1960s on, McLuhan was one of the most cited writers in the trans-Atlantic world. Indeed, in a 1978 article on Roland Barthes titled "Meet France's Marshall McLuhan," the author noted that the French even used the term "macluhanisme" to stand for broad-ranging strategies for understanding popular culture.[30]

Moving Around and Settling Down

McLuhan grew up in Edmonton and Winnipeg, son of a businessman father and a mother who was an actress, theater director, and drama teacher. In the 1920s, his parents increasingly lived separate lives, with his father largely responsible for raising Marshall and his brother, while his mother was away from the family for long stretches of time. In 1928 McLuhan entered the University of Manitoba, before long switching from engineering to English literature. He was already developing the idea that, as his biographer Philip Marchand notes, literature "was a noble protest of the human soul against the mechanical and the commercial, against the vulgarities of modern life." McLuhan received his B.A. in 1933 and his M.A. a year later.[31]

In 1934, he began two years at Cambridge University, where he learned from I.A. Richards and F. R. Leavis. Equally important to him intellectually while he was in Cambridge were two other British writers, G. K. Chesterton and Wyndham Lewis. In addition, reading the Swiss historian of architecture and technology Siegfried Giedion taught McLuhan how to analyze material artifacts as cultural expressions. While in Cambridge, he also avidly watched American

films, confiding to his diary in 1935 that he "could not help but admire . . . the
open declaration and conduct of sex-war" by Mae West. Returning to North
America, he taught at the University of Wisconsin at Madison in 1936–37. During his year there, he converted to Catholicism, having over a long time moved
away from the Protestantism and spiritualism of his parents. From the fall of
1937 on, he taught at Catholic institutions: St. Louis University from 1937 to
1944 (spending 1939–40 back at Cambridge, from which he earned his Ph.D.
in 1943 with a thesis on Thomas Nashe); Assumption College in Windsor, On-
tario, 1944–46, which was a men's college until 1953; and then at St. Michael's
College at the University of Toronto beginning in 1946, with a all-male student
body until 1952. In 1939, he married the Texan Corinne Lewis and they had six
children, born between 1942 and 1952.[32]

In 1939, as he was courting Corinne, an Episcopalian and Southerner who
feared that her suitor lacked worldly ambition, McLuhan wrote a letter that reveals much about his outlook. In the United States, he noted, "where the main
currents of life are profoundly anti-Catholic, the average Catholic is too timid,
too over-awed by the surrounding material 'splendor,' to feel able to be anything but an 'interior' Catholic. As the 'splendor' rapidly becomes ludicrous
and stupid the Church will press forward in America," something he believed
was already happening. Then he went on to discuss his aspirations in highly
gendered and religious terms. He reassured Corinne that he was "prepared to
do all I can to achieve a reasonable 'standard of living.'" He then contrasted material and nonmaterial ways of living. "My trouble, of course, is that I now enjoy
such a high standard of *living*." He affirmed that he intended to spend little
money on himself and had "never been able to understand why a man earning
a fixed dollar stipend should concern himself about money. My 'instinct' is to
turn *all* of it over to the other partner in the enterprise!," a process which he
identified as the "traditional European method." "Isn't it queer, at first glance,"
he continued, "that in America of all places, where women are ostensibly the
only object of 'money-making' that men should 'budget' them?" This provided
additional "evidence that the American male has an *essential* contempt for, as
well as a fear of women." As a husband and father, McLuhan avoided luxuries
and minimized the presence of media in the lives of his children. In the 1950s,
when television became available in Toronto, his household was among the last
in the neighborhood to have a set. He struggled to make do on an academic sal-
ary with a stay-at-home wife and six children. He dreamt up schemes for escaping a life of academic penury, including proposals for what in retrospect seem
like crassly commercial projects such as serving as a consultant to the Luce
publications, even though he scorned them. Being a provider for such a large

family had implications for his aspirations and his writing. Also influential in the development of his ideas was his identity as a Canadian and even more so as a conservative Roman Catholic. It was not Catholicism per se that so shaped McLuhan's vision but his particular set of commitments as a culturally conservative and Thomist Catholic. [33]

The Making of a Conservative

In the 1930s and 1940s McLuhan embraced quite conservative positions, core beliefs from which he never fully moved as he struggled on a personal level with the relationship between family and academic life. As the historian Daniel Czitrom has remarked, "McLuhan expressed a personal variant of the Tory, neo-Catholic, antimodern tradition flourishing on both sides of the Atlantic." In 1934, while still in Manitoba, he celebrated the wholeness of medieval civilization and lamented the way modern industrialism undermined human integrity and sexuality. He turned not to Marxism, which from early on he deplored for its godlessness and materialism, but to fascism. As his biographer noted of McLuhan's youthful response, "The Fascists, in urging a return to heroic enterprises, in rejecting the dull, 'emasculating' utopias of socialism as well as the rapacious appetites of capitalism, seemed to him to be on the right track." In 1938 he again articulated his belief that a potent combination of Marxism, big business, and advertising threatened the traditional family.[34]

Evidence of his outlook was clear in much of what he wrote. In the first scholarly piece he published, in 1936, McLuhan praised Chesterton for his commitment "to re-establish agriculture and small property" as the only basis of a free civilization. Chesterton, an influential Roman Catholic intellectual, was a polemical opponent of imperialism and feminism and the leader of the Distributist League, a conservative and agrarian-oriented organization McLuhan joined while in Cambridge. In 1932, reading Chesterton's *What's Wrong with the World* (1910) had confirmed his inclination to believe in the sacredness of the family and the power of Christian civilization in Europe to oppose socialism and capitalism. As was true of Umberto Eco, reading Catholic theology was important to McLuhan, especially the writings of St. Thomas Aquinas. In 1943, he extolled the "moral and intellectual discipline" of St. Thomas, which stood in opposition to "the barbarism of comfort and ease and slackness." St. Thomas's approach was especially needed, he noted, "when a triumphant technology croons the sickly boasts of the advertising men, when the great vaults and vistas of the human soul are obscured by images of silken glamor [*sic*], and when it is plain that man lives not by bread alone but by toothpaste also." In the mid- to late 1940s, he was able to bring into print, in conservative and scholarly publications, a series of articles in which he contrasted the agrarian, aristocratic South with the utilitarian, materialistic North. In 1947 he celebrated traditional values of elite whites in the South for their "passionate and tragic sense of life," "cult of feminine beauty and elegance," and "profound acceptance of the destiny of one's blood and kin."[35]

Gender and sexuality were central to McLuhan's deep and fundamental conservatism. Already in his late teens he had developed views of women that were retrograde even for the time, inspired in part by his intense ambivalence about his mother, a woman who was both absent and forceful. While in college, his first serious romantic experience, with a woman training to be a medical doctor, made him lament that some women pursued careers. During World War II, when millions of women entered the workforce and Rosie the Riveter rose to prominence, McLuhan became fascinated with Dagwood Bumstead, a meek husband ruled by a powerful wife. In 1944 he published an article on Dagwood in the widely circulated magazine of the Catholic fraternal organization, the Knights of Columbus. In this, his first published work on popular culture, McLuhan wrote that "Blondie and her children own America, control American business and entertainment, run hog-wild in spreading materialism." Following Aquinas and Leavis, McLuhan argued that the only solution to the problems Western civilization faced was "the detached use of autonomous reason for the critical appraisal of life." In 1946, as North Americans battled over the role of women in the postwar world, he proposed to *Esquire* that he write an article that would link feminism, homosexuals, and commerce as forces undermining the monogamous family. This confirms Barbara Ehrenreich's judgment that the postwar revolt of men preceded women's liberation. All of this was happening, as McLuhan's biographer has noted, at precisely the time that McLuhan, though no Dagwood Bumstead, was losing the battle of the sexes at home. By the mid-1940s, Marchand notes, "the man who resolutely opposed the feminization of America knew for certain . . . that the gods had rewarded him for his opposition by granting him a household," with a strong wife, four daughters, and two sons, "that would become a female preserve." In contrast Assumption and St. Michael's colleges remained male bastions where faculty did not have to deal with women among their colleagues or students.[36]

With an eye on the success of Philip Wylie's attack on "momism" in *Generation of Vipers* (1942), McLuhan hoped to expand "Dagwood's America," proposing it to *Esquire* as the basis for a book. He worked on this larger project for at least seven years before both abandoning it and making it the basis of *The Mechanical Bride* in 1951. At first he produced a manuscript titled "New

American Vortex" (which referred to Wyndham Lewis' 1914 project on English Vorticism) and then one called "Typhon in America" (whose title, he wrote, drew on the classical myth of "mama-boy with the Oedipus complex"). He worked on this project in the context of educational reform, pursuing a strategy that turned away from University of Chicago's emphasis on canonical texts and instead took up what he considered the more urgent task of developing an education that fostered an understanding of mass media. Both manuscripts, sprawling, rambling, arcane, and dense, focused more on discussing philosophy and literature than on examining examples of popular culture. Gradually McLuhan began to experiment more with highlighting material drawn from newspapers and magazines, with examples of this approach making their way from these two manuscripts into his 1951 book. At some point after 1947, relying on the technique he developed in slide shows on advertisements he presented to nonacademic audiences, he realized that in a book he had to submerge (or make implicit) his philosophical and literary discussions and concentrate instead on presenting and explicating examples drawn from commercial culture. [37]

Yet his two unpublished manuscripts contained the ideas that would drive his 1951 book, even though he did not fully spell them out there. Moreover, they reveal many of the themes that would make McLuhan so popular in the 1960s with the counterculture: the antagonism to commercialism and technology, as well as the embrace of community. The American use of the atomic bomb, he wrote, had laid bare the irresponsibility and arrogance of intellectuals and politicians, in contrast to which stood what McLuhan considered Southern values of an opposition to technology and a commitment to personal responsibility. During the preceding decade or so, he insisted, the United States had seen a fundamental transformation. He labeled the principal villain as American "Know-How," the belief that technology solved all problems. As a result, the increasing power of technology and commerce isolated "the individual physically and psychologically," at both work and play, "in the rigid little routine-boxes which promise jet propulsion towards the pot of gold." The implication of these changes, seen most vividly in newspapers, comics, and advertisements, were ominous. Commerce had robbed sexual relations of any genuine possibility for love. Women in modern America were masculinized. Men were feminized, in danger of becoming homosexual or sexually ambiguous. Having lost the possibility of meaningful work and with women in control of the marriage and family, men no longer had the capacity to reason. [38]

In the end, the American embrace of rationalization was highly problematic. "Society has used reason to subvert reason" by deploying "Know-How in order to suppress *what* should be known to men concerned with the perpetual living and recreation of a civilized community." Turning away from Know-How, McLuhan urged, would mean embracing true reason or what he called "purely speculative and disinterested pursuits." This would enable the transformation of "the zombies of the adman's making . . . into alert and confident persons aware of their power and autonomy as rational beings." McLuhan located the solution in an education that applied reason to media. Most intellectuals refused to take popular culture seriously, he wrote at a time when he was reading *Partisan Review* and trying to get *Commentary* to publish his essays on media analysis. The goal was not to make students more savvy shoppers but to use the classroom to immunize them against what they faced when they listened to radio, read magazines, and saw advertisements. This involved giving sustained and disciplined attention to mass media, as Leavis had done in Britain but was not an established tradition among cultural critics in the United States.[39]

Literary Criticism and Popular Culture

If McLuhan's work that led to *The Mechanical Bride* relied on projects he both discarded and built on, in the longer term his inspiration lay elsewhere. Like Barthes, Leavis, and Eco, McLuhan developed his approach to commercial culture through a grounding in the study of traditional literary texts. His interest in decoding advertisements began early. In 1930, when he was an undergraduate, he wrote in his diary that readers might be more interested in an analysis of advertisements than of literature. He reported that he had heard "an illuminating lecture on the development and technique of modern advertising . . . the appeal is always to some powerful feeling in man: fear, pride, sex, wealth, ambition." Then he continued by noting that "fifty years hence, if they have not proceeded to more absurd extremes, a volume of 1930s slogans and advertising tricks would make more interesting reading than anything that has appeared in this generation."[40] When he began teaching at Wisconsin in 1936, he recalled, he "confronted classes of freshmen and I suddenly realized that I was incapable of understanding them. I felt an urgent need to study their popular culture: advertising, games, movies. . . . To meet them on their grounds was my strategy in pedagogy: the world of pop culture. Advertising was a very convenient form of approach."[41]

Above all, it was his education at Cambridge that provided McLuhan with the tools to analyze popular culture. Carefully reading T. S. Eliot, Ezra Pound, and James Joyce for the first time, he marveled at the way they incorporated popular culture into their art. At Cambridge in the mid-1930s, he encountered Q. D. Leavis and F. R. Leavis and their work. He read Q. D.'s book on the reading public as well as *Culture and Environment* by F. R. Leavis and Denys Thompson. The work of Leavisites offered McLuhan a number of ways to think about literature and culture, especially the importance of an organic community and a cultural minority as bulwarks against mass culture; the dynamics of the interactions of producers and consumers; and instructions on how to read advertisements seriously and critically.[42]

In Cambridge the works by Wyndham Lewis also fueled his interest in developing a cultural critique of advertising. Lewis's analysis of popular and industrial cultures attracted young McLuhan's attention, not only his dissection of advertisements but also what McLuhan later called his "his painterly analysis of our industrial environment." For almost a decade beginning in the early 1930s, Lewis wrote sympathetically about Hitler, fascism, and National Socialism. However, though McLuhan drew on Lewis's antipathy to homosexuals and strong women (and even on his anti-Semitism), what most interested McLuhan was Lewis's way of seeing commercial culture. In the mid-1930s, as he read Lewis's *Time and Western Man* (1928), McLuhan absorbed his critique of advertising. Ads, Lewis asserted when the 1920s were proceeding at their most roaring pace, were romantic, unreal, "the apotheosis of the marvelous and the unusual," like the "the trance or dream-world of the hypnotist." Advertisements were momentary and depthless, appealing to a "submissive, hypnotized public"; they were the product of "the competitive frenzy of finance."[43]

The impact of Lewis on McLuhan continued when he encountered *The Doom of Youth* (1932). Lewis's remarks about homosexuals interested McLuhan, at a time when he was repulsed by the prevalence of male homosexuals among Cambridge undergraduates, many of them doubly unacceptable because of their embrace of Communism. Lewis asserted that homosexuals, produced by feminist mothers, threatened family life. Male Jewish movie stars, he noted at a time just before Hitler came to power, were "less 'manly' than the Nordic Blond, and the women never so chocolate-boxily 'feminine' as their anglo-saxon sisters." Lewis saw much of commercial culture as feminine, "low-grade, second-rate, child-minded, mesmerically-receptive, dependent." *The Doom of Youth*, McLuhan wrote later, "is an elaborately documented analysis of all aspects of 'feminism,' and of its twin—homosexuality." Lewis also provided a model of how to analyze the products of commercial culture. Blocked by copyright laws from reproducing advertisements visually, he offered scores of examples of screaming headlines and the written copy that followed them.[44]

In 1944, when he was beginning a friendship with Lewis that over time became problematic, McLuhan wrote an article that made clear the ways in which the British author influenced him. He hailed Lewis for what McLuhan called highlighting "the dehumanization of life by means of centralized methods of 'communication,' and by the lethal abstractionizing of the machine controlled by abstract greed." In opposition to "the dionysiac ecstasies of advertisement and high-finance," McLuhan wrote, Lewis asserted the power of human intelligence. This implied, McLuhan said of Lewis but meant of himself as well, that skepticism could counter "the vulgarization of the first-rate into the shoddy and the sensual by a swarm of dilettante competitors who relay their degraded product to ever lower levels of drab sensuality." Fed such debased culture by the media, McLuhan noted, the public "turns not in wrath but with envy towards its tormentors." One result was an attack on the family. The entry of women into the labor market drove down the wages and authority of men. The glorification of sex, children, and motherhood had destroyed family life, caused a flight from adulthood, and obliterated the distinctions between masculine and feminine.[45]

The Mechanical Bride

McLuhan began to think about writing The Mechanical Bride in the mid-1940s. Following the lead of I. A. Richards and F. R. Leavis, at St. Louis University he taught courses in practical criticism in which he used literary analysis to examine advertisements. In the spring of 1944 he proposed offering a course at Assumption titled "Culture and Environment," the title of a book by Leavis and Thompson. His course would focus, he wrote, on "an analysis of the present scene. Advertisements, newspapers, best-sellers[,] detective fiction[,] movies etc. contrasted with a true pattern of homogeneous culture, rationally ordered. This contrast made in concrete detail by an analysis say of a section of sixteenth century society—its architecture, literature, music, economics, etc." Yet as early as 1944, McLuhan made clear that he found Leavis's approach limiting, noting that "his passion for important work forbids him to look for the sun in the egg-tarnished spoons of the daily table." Before World War II ended, McLuhan began clipping thousands of items from magazines, relying on them to develop slide shows in which he taught audiences to read texts that combined printed words and visual material. Thus as was true with F. R. Leavis, Richard Hoggart, Paddy Whannel, and Stuart Hall, McLuhan's engagement with popular culture grew out of pedagogical challenges. Beginning to turn his slide shows into a book in 1946, in the summer of 1948 he wrote to Ezra Pound that the book would appear at the end of the year. However, his publisher hesitated in bringing it out because McLuhan, the editors of his letters noted, had resisted "their efforts to convert the original deliberately outrageous satirical text into the more 'linear' and restrained" one they preferred. As he wrote Pound just before the book came out, the publisher had been "castrating and textbookizing a job which originally was sprightly and not unworthy of Wyndham Lewis to whom it owes so much. Publishers offices now are crammed with homosexuals who have a horror of any writing with balls to it."[46]

In the book McLuhan took up the challenges that Lewis, the Leavisites, and others had thrown down. Following a brief preface, he offered a series of short, disjoined, and self-consciously nonlinear essays on what appeared in mass media, mostly in print. With each of his fifty-nine case studies, he reproduced a page from a magazine or newspaper; highlighted a handful of skeptical questions about the text; and wrote an essay several hundred to several thousand words in length. Among the texts on which he focused were advertisements for a burial vault, a pulp crime magazine, a feminine hygiene product, and the National Association for Manufacturers. His essays included an analysis of the iconography and text and an application of the insights offered by fiction writers, philosophers, and cultural critics such as Joyce, Kenneth Burke, Giedion, and Friedrich Nietzsche. He composed these essays in a way that relied on a series of probing questions rather than conclusive answers. They were simultaneously unfocused and flashily brilliant. As Susan Sontag noted of McLuhan's later books but could have said of *The Mechanical Bride* as well, despite his "magnitude of intellectual appetite and ambition," his work "suggests the risks of radical unevenness of quality and judgment." His approach, he himself insisted, involved a series of scattered strategies for taking "visual imagery" and "dislocating it into meaning by inspection."[47]

The nature of McLuhan's analysis was abundantly clear in his essay on Gotham Gold Stripe hosiery. He ranged widely in his discussion of the ad, which pictured a pair of women's legs covered with stockings and placed atop a classical pedestal. He connected what he wrote with discussions of texts such as a film by Charlie Chaplin, Samuel Butler's *Erewhon*, Marcel Duchamp's *Nude Descending a Staircase*, and a *Life* magazine story about a woman committing suicide. He brought all of this together in an argument critical of the ways modern print media fragmented and exploited human bodies, especially those of women. McLuhan linked an analysis of sex and technology as he excoriated purveyors of women's fashions for turning sensuous, integrated bodies into a series of fragmented, desexualized body parts whose problems beauty products and items of clothing promised to solve. This resulted in a woman seeing legs and breasts as "power points she has been taught to tailor" and "parts of the success kit rather than erotically or sensuously." Body parts resembled "display objects like the grill work on a car . . . date-baited power levers for the man-

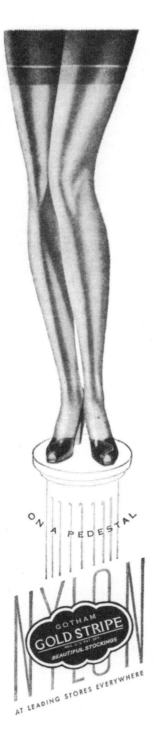

Figure 5. In *The Mechanical Bride* (1951) Marshall McLuhan offered this image to illustrate how advertisers disassembled and exploited women's human bodies. More generally, he was using such visual material to teach readers how to critically analyze popular culture.

agement of the male audience." To McLuhan, "the brittle, self-conscious pose of the mannequin suggests the activities of competitive display rather than spontaneous sensuality." In contrast, McLuhan preferred sexuality that was connected to authentic selfhood, drew on the "unity of the body," embraced sensuousness, and affirmed the relationship between pleasure, reproduction, marriage, and heterosexuality.[48]

As McLuhan saw it, his task was to help make his readers conscious of the ways commercial culture tried to shape their dreams. He would reveal the "intelligible meaning" of advertisements, using an interdisciplinary approach that combined literature, art history, social psychology, and anthropology to suggest how the mass media appropriated desires. He provided readers with ways of understanding the dreams advertisements offered so that they could resist them. He worked to get the tone right, remarking in 1949 that it was important to "let up on moral earnestness without loss of intellectual point." Referring to Edgar Allan Poe's "A Descent into the Maelstrom," he noted that the short story writer's "sailor saved himself by studying the action of the whirlpool and by co-operating with it." Therefore, McLuhan admitted, he would make "few attempts to attack the considerable currents and pressures" the mass media created. Like Poe's figure, McLuhan (and by implication his reader) would get out of the labyrinth by "this amusement born of his rational detachment as a spectator of his own situation." He insisted that "a whirling phantasmagoria can be grasped only when arrested for contemplation." Yet it would be wrong, he concluded, to "mistake this amusement for mere indifference." As he noted in an article titled "American Advertising" published in 1947, the intellectual "arms himself today against the impact of the stereotypes of commercialized culture by keenness of recognition and engages in a perpetual guerilla activity." Here McLuhan could not resist taking a swipe at unnamed cultural critics who felt it was beneath them to take advertising seriously, though he could have had Clement Greenberg, Dwight Macdonald, or even Theodor Adorno in mind. "That the highbrows have been content merely to cock a snook," he wrote, using an obscure phrase that meant a gesture of derision, "at the flora and fauna of popular commercial culture is sufficient testimony to the superficiality" of their outlook. Indeed, in a 1948 letter to McLuhan, a friend hailed a *Commentary* essay by Harold Rosenberg as "a magnificent side-swipe at *Partisan Review* and at anti-mass culture mass culture!"[49]

At a time when prominent cultural critics such as Greenberg and Macdonald called for a sharp separation of high culture from its lowly or mass counterparts, McLuhan both privileged high over low and explored what it meant to use the canonical texts to explore the meaning of commercial culture. For example, in his analysis of an ad for Lord Calvert whiskey's "Men of Distinc-tion Series," he pointed to how James Joyce was "a real high-brow, a man of real distinction; . . . who took an intelligent interest in everybody and everything" by writing *Ulysses* and drawing on "the ads, the comics, the pulps, and popular speech." The "alert and detached mind," he insisted in his discussion of popular treatments of high-, middle-, and lowbrow culture, "ignores such categories." In a somewhat similar move, he celebrated how the cartoonist responsible for the *Orphan Annie* series, by exploring generational tensions, provided evidence "of popular entertainment keeping in play a major psychological tension in America to which the sophisticated writers are often blind."[50]

In *The Mechanical Bride*, McLuhan offered sharp critiques of the Cold War consensus and kept his conservatism largely out of sight. In a series of commentaries on corporate advertisements, he poked fun at celebrations in the United States of commitments to individualism and freedom. Responding to an RCA advertisement titled "Freedom to LISTEN—Freedom to LOOK," McLuhan remarked that it was "not listening-freedom to be able to turn on or turn off the unweaned whimperings of hit-parade crooning." He showed how corporations managed consent by connecting traditional values with capital-istic practices that made monopolies or oligopolies possible. "As the industrial market extends its power and control over thoughts and earnings alike," he wrote, "it swathes itself increasingly in the archaic garments of pre-industrial man." He abhorred concentrated power, which he located especially in the way the media dominated "the superhighways of thought and feeling." He empha-sized how hollow and limited were freedoms in a nation controlled by media conglomerates, with mass media "shepherding their flocks along the paths of comfort and thrills." The abundance available in postwar society, he insisted, meant that the United States had taken on "the character of the kept woman whose role is expected to be submission and luxurious passivity." He chastised the Luce publications for using "the arts of communication and control . . . to tease, soothe, and flatter a mass public."[51]

He criticized American capitalism for equating wealth with happiness and opted instead for simpler living. The capitalist spirit of rivalry, he noted in response to an advertisement from the Oil Industry Information Commit-tee, resulted in the "psychological misery of millions whose budgets can never compass a fraction of the items considered indispensable if a family is to hold up its head," thus promoting "conformity" as the "sign and reward of success." He concluded by emphasizing the "corrosive spirit" promoted by competition, wondering if "there is anything left for this corrosive to destroy." Looking at a picture of a prosperous family on a picnic sponsored by Quaker State Motor

Oil, McLuhan raised a series of questions prompted by its title: "Freedom—American Style." He asked if Henry Thoreau was un-American, wondering, "is it not freedom and not American to have less money and fewer possessions?" This pursuit of freedom equated with abundance, he suggested, isolated the family and undermined a sense of community.[52]

As he examined the products of commercial culture, McLuhan both reiterated and critiqued a narrowly moralistic position. Though he called his stance one that combined "amusement" and "rational detachment," he might also have characterized what he offered as blistering, morally charged critiques both of advertisements and of modern capitalism itself. He disdained popular culture yet admired those who shaped it for their skill in understanding people's anxieties, and he insisted that the critic had an important role in subjecting it to rational analysis. He set out to "assist the public to observe consciously the drama which is intended to operate upon it unconsciously." He saw advertisements as the result of how those who skillfully probed the American mind "tried to keep everybody in the helpless state engendered by prolonged mental rutting." In modern societies, with their consolidation of state power, he insisted, with both European totalitarianism and contemporary America in mind and in ways reminiscent of the analysis of C. L. R. James, "the tyrant rules not by club or fist, but, disguised as a market researcher, he shepherds his flocks in the ways of utility and comfort." He laced his discussion with phrases that captured the disdain he felt: references to a *Time* magazine "full of predigested pap" and engaged in "irresponsible manipulation"; how RCA attempted to produce a nation of "supine consumers of processed goods"; and the "poisonous bilge" of pulp fiction novels. The "nihilistic dreams," such as the one coming from an ad agency that used the movie star Betty Grable to sell copies of *Modern Screen*, reached "a somnambulist public that accepts them uncritically," leading to an "absence of reaction in the name of the human dignity which they destroy."[53]

What was distinctive about McLuhan's cultural criticism, especially juxtaposed to that of Greenberg and Macdonald, was his recognition that those who shaped mass media were sophisticated students of dreams and desires who brilliantly captured people's deepest longings. To McLuhan, writers of the nineteenth and early twentieth centuries, especially Poe, Stéphane Mallarmé, and Joyce, appreciated the dreams that popular culture embodied, something contemporary writers of advertising copy pursued further. Where other critics were resigned or enraged, McLuhan could have some optimism because he distinguished between the content of advertisements, which he found wanting, and their form and structure, for which he saw parallels in avant-garde arts. For example, he talked of how newspapers, especially ones given to sensationalism, used "the visual technique of a Picasso, the literary technique of James Joyce." He discussed how the juxtaposition of stories from around the world helped "enforce a deep sense of human solidarity." Mass media was filled with "rich human symbolism" of which he wanted to make his audience more conscious. Scattered throughout his book, often in the final sentences of his essays, McLuhan held out the hope that informed consumers of popular culture would find ways of understanding and resisting media messages. Calling on the power of "rational self-awareness and reasonable programs of self-restraint," he hoped his study of the folklore that ads embodied would provide "the clue to understanding and guiding our world in more reasonable courses." Invoking the ability of the Ulysses of classical mythology "to withstand the siren onslaught," in his analysis of ads for women's girdles and Ivory soap McLuhan warned that "without the mirror of the mind, nobody can live a human life in the face of our present mechanized dream."[54]

Figuring out McLuhan's tone is no easy task, especially given the tension between the depth of his conservatism and the intensity of his interest in mass media. Although his criticism was sharp, McLuhan, like Riesman, also believed that commercial culture was filled with what he called "promises of rich new developments to which moral indignation is a very poor guide." Indeed, reviewers were divided about the nature and effectiveness of his tone. David L. Cohn, writing in the New York Times, remarked that McLuhan's abuse of "righteous anger" and "moralist" indignation was "nearly always as solemn as Nazi propagandists who told Germans that we were a decadent people." Yet a Catholic educator exclaimed, "How refreshing to see a critique of a period and its morals avoiding moral indignation!"[55]

Although much of what McLuhan wrote might make him sound like a left-wing critic, perhaps even a socialist feminist who decried the way capitalism disembodied women's bodies, he was nothing of the sort. Threaded through these antimodernist critiques were hints of the alternative McLuhan preferred, critiques easier for the historian to reconstruct retrospectively than for most contemporary readers to penetrate. Like Eco, he lamented the way business and technology had become the new religion. He looked askance at feminism and working mothers. Finally getting Dagwood and Blondie into a book, he spoke of the "model mother saddled with a sad sack and a dope. We are confronted," he wrote, "on a large scale with what Wyndham Lewis has described as mothering-wedlock." He had what one critic called a "rather Victorian attitude toward corsets, brief skirts, and high heels." He appreciated preindustrial cultures that relied on "a state of harmonious equilibrium with the soil and the seasons" and an authentic sense of community. He longed for a world in which God was omnipresent, not merely "outside the machine of the universe, to which he had merely given an initial push." He preferred, he wrote, a "vision of human integrity based on a noncommercial way of life." He hoped to restore cultural standards determined by experts who had good judgment. Since there were "no accepted standards of submission or resistance to commercially sponsored appeals," he commented, "it is urgent to foster habits of inspection until workable standards of securely civilized judgment emerge from those habits." He wished that American corporations would replace empty hosannas to freedom with a commitment to raising the cultural standards in the nation. As the historian Howard Brick has noted, McLuhan's "thinly disguised antimodernism heralded a new world, to be brought about by a great leap forward into the distant past."[56]

Conservative, Roman Catholic, Canadian

An examination of McLuhan's writings raises the question of the ways his identity as a conservative, Catholic, and Canadian influenced his outspoken and politically charged critiques of American capitalism at the height of Senator Joseph McCarthy's power. Part of the answer goes back to how opaque and scattered were expressions of McLuhan's politics. Many contemporaries would have found it difficult to understand let alone accept someone who critiqued commercial culture from such an antimodernist position. Given the prejudices of a consensus-bound culture, had he spoken his mind more clearly and directly, he would probably not have found a hearing among those readers skeptical of the work of a Roman Catholic and conservative intellectual. As someone who preferred the Middle Ages to the twentieth century, McLuhan found what he saw around him (technology, bureaucracy, capitalism, and mass media) both profane and capable of transformation. As his former student, the Jesuit Walter J. Ong, wrote in a review of *The Mechanical Bride*, McLuhan lamented "the complete reorientation of the symbolic world today," with advertising threatening the rich system of Catholic symbolism. McLuhan, he remarked, "leaves open a hundred doors here into every area of Catholic life," pointing toward the restoration of a social organism by means of more authoritative "orchestration." It is also possible that as a Canadian whose audience was largely in the United States, McLuhan was reluctant to express the hostility many living north of the border felt about the postwar invasion of commercial culture. Moreover, in 1951 McLuhan was still working his way out of the positions he had adopted from

F. R. Leavis and developing stances that enabled him simultaneously to articulate his conservatism and reach a significant audience in a secular society. In the meantime, his mixture of detachment and moral outrage would suffice. [57]

Rare would have been the person who, knowing nothing of McLuhan, could have easily figured out from any but an exceptionally careful reading of *The Mechanical Bride* anything of his nationality, religion, and, to a lesser extent, politics. In some ways it is useful to think that what shaped his approach to commercial culture was the political conundrum that the Cold War imposed on people with strong political convictions, in his case conservative ones undergirded by his Catholicism. He developed what the art historian Moira Roth has called the "aesthetics of indifference" as she pointed to *The Mechanical Bride* as "an early announcement" of such an approach. She has argued that many artists and critics of the 1950s responded to McCarthyism by avoiding moral outrage that might have been politically dangerous and instead adopted stances that were cool and at first glance amused. Roth's ideas help explain what Neil Compton called the "paradox" of Marshall McLuhan: how he became a progenitor of and hero for advocates of cultural radicalism even though he was a conservative Roman Catholic, a superbly trained literary critic, and a person whose ideal was Europe in the twelfth century. As Brick has noted, McLuhan had learned to "convey conservative values in an inhospitable environment." Relying on seeming indifference, or balancing it with outrage, made McLuhan's stance, not unlike Riesman's, opaque and complicated, open to ambiguous and uncertain interpretation.[58]

Yet McLuhan's politics, religion, and less clearly his nationality shaped the book. In 1944, writing in a Catholic publication with a small circulation, McLuhan acknowledged that Catholic minorities in the United States "crave to be regarded as 'hundred per-centers'" and "seek the security of complete social conformity." Early on when he began to address secular audiences, he consciously hid his Catholicism, out of a fear that revealing his religious commitments would prevent him from having a wide audience, let alone one that would take his ideas seriously. In private, McLuhan was more forthcoming. Writing to Ong in 1945, he remarked that it was important to "confront the secular in its most confident manifestations, . . . to shock it into awareness of its confusion, its illiteracy, and the terrifying drift of its logic." There was no necessity, he continued, "to mention Christianity. It is enough that it be known that the operator is a Christian." He then he went on to insist that "this job must be conducted on every front—every phrase of the press, book-rackets, music, cinema, education, economics." As the historian John McGreevy has shown, in the postwar period Catholic professors faced difficulty in gaining acceptance at elite institutions of higher education in the United States. Had McLuhan revealed more of his beliefs he would have confirmed the worst suspicions about Catholics: that they were hostile to modernity and inclined to authoritarianism. Indeed, throughout his life, McLuhan publicly revealed little about himself as a Catholic, while in private he experienced the religion with the intensity of a convert.[59]

Catholicism was central to McLuhan's outlook as a cultural critic. Steeped in the theology of St. Thomas Aquinas and the writings of Chesterton, he believed that people could use reason to work their way out of doubt and confusion. Through reason and a detached intelligence, individuals redeemed themselves as they encountered and battled popular culture. By the late 1940s, McLuhan drew on his engagement with the broader rethinking of Catholic theology during the 1930s and 1940s to understand the dynamics of even the most humdrum aspects of popular culture. In a wonderfully rich analysis of the impact of McLuhan's Catholicism on his view of popular culture, the Canadian writer Jeet Heer has remarked that from his work in the late 1940s and early 1950s to his later writings, "McLuhan moved from offering a critique of modernity and mass culture based on Catholic values to a more positive view of modernity and mass culture based on Catholic values." In working out his ideas in *The Mechanical Bride*, McLuhan drew on neo-Thomists such as Jacques Maritain and Etienne Gilson, along with the more experimental Pierre Teilhard de Chardin, all of whom who were trying to reconcile Catholicism and modernity. For McLuhan and others, the issue was how Catholics could use aspects of modernity such as popular culture for religious purposes. Thus in 1946 Hugh Kenner wrote to his mentor McLuhan that he was thinking about how to explore "the liturgical possibilities of electric signs." Similarly, Ong had explored how to "find things in the industrial world today capable of liturgical transposition and transformation." For McLuhan, Catholic faith and theology inspired a holistic critique and examination of the relationships between technology, art, and religion that might help heal the world. *The Mechanical Bride* was one result. As he said in the book, it was "out of the extreme discontinuity of modern existence, with its mingling of many cultures and periods, that there is being born today the vision of a rich and complex harmony."[60]

McLuhan's identity as a Canadian, a critical outsider in a perfect position to rely on firsthand observation, also shaped his response to the popular culture of the United States. Context and history are important here. Although we today consider Vancouver and Toronto as modern as San Francisco and New York, during McLuhan's years in America (1936–44) the situations in the two countries were quite different. At the time, innovative popular culture was much more pervasive in the United States than in Canada. McLuhan lived in the United States in his late twenties, during a severe economic depression and a world war, to be sure, but in a world that surely seemed more prosperous— and more committed to consumer culture—than what was familiar to him from his years in Edmonton, Winnipeg, and Cambridge. St. Louis, especially after 1938 when its factories began to play such an important role in supplying the Allies with war material, was then a prosperous Midwestern city. As Canadian-born John Kenneth Galbraith said of the wartime experience of his adopted country, "never before had there been so much talk of sacrifice with so little actual want."[61]

Once he was settled in Canada after 1944, what McLuhan had experienced south of the border must have seemed a harbinger of what Canada would soon face, which McLuhan doubtless considered a tragedy in the making. If Americans linked consumer goods with display and progress, their Canadian counterparts were more practical and somber. Even as consumer culture spread in Canada in the 1950s and after, the reactions of its citizens were "characteristically more subdued" than elsewhere, write two scholars. Living in Canada in the postwar period meant that McLuhan knew of the long-standing and rapidly intensifying debates in his homeland about the impact of the United States on Canada, debates that revealed that Canadians had an ambivalent relationship to popular culture south of the border, simultaneously jealous about and eager for it.[62]

English-speaking Canadian thinkers continually negotiated between what they saw in the United States and what they derived from their British origins, between a commitment to progress, on the one hand, and to history and tradition, on the other. Students of popular culture in Canada fully realized the power of dominant cultural expressions imported from the United States at the same time that they did not believe movies or advertisements from the United States adequately reflected Canadian values.[63] For members of the Conservative Party, the United States embodied individualism, the pursuit of happiness, a messianic commitment to transform the world, while Canada embraced the orderliness of an organic society and the national independence of a peaceful one. The ascendancy of the United States to imperial status coincided with the weakening of the British imperial position and was inextricably linked with the increased flow of cultural productions north across the border. In the 1940s and 1950s, Canadians, Conservatives especially, feared that the weakening of ties to Britain would throw Canada into the arms of the United States politically, economically, diplomatically, and culturally. When McLuhan was working on *The Mechanical Bride* in the 1940s, for Conservative intellectuals these beliefs, which did not fully emerge until after 1957, were not that far below the surface.[64] Indeed, in 1951 a government commission issued a report that decried the "American invasion by film, radio and periodicals" and advocated "resistance to the absorption of Canada into the general cultural pattern of the United States."[65]

McLuhan was surely aware of and sympathetic to these Conservative positions. Indeed the contrast McLuhan drew for the United States between the agricultural, traditional South and an industrial North committed to progress at any cost was an indirect (and politically safer) way of talking about Canada and United States. Writing in 1957 in *Shenandoah Review*, a Washington and Lee University publication that Tom Wolfe had helped found and where works by Pound and Southern Agrarians also appeared, McLuhan remarked that "merely as a Canadian I have something to say about the North-South clash that no American has said. Canada stands to the Yankee world very much in the same relation as did the Confederacy." Canada and the South, he went on to note, were both staple economies that had long resisted urbanization. Citizens of both (and here he was speaking of the English in Canada, but not the French; presumably of whites in the South but not African Americans) partook of "clan feeling, romantic nostalgia, personal loyalties, and sentiment for the past," as well as being "profoundly distrustful of bigness, bureaucracy, and central power." Eager to be taken seriously in the United States and not to make his argument narrowly nationalistic, he avoided stating the obvious: that as a Canadian conservative he had questions about America's imperial ambitions and its popular culture as well.[66]

After *The Mechanical Bride*

In the trajectory of McLuhan's career, *The Mechanical Bride* occupies an important place. Never again would he offer a critique of capitalism and popular culture. As he remarked in a 1969 interview in *Playboy*, beginning (albeit partially) with *The Mechanical Bride*, he no longer held "an extremely moralistic approach" that "equated mass media with the Fall." Even then, he acknowledged, "some of my old literate 'point of view' bias crept in." By the early 1950s he realized that television and new electronic technologies had made his focus on print media in his first book irrelevant. *The Mechanical Bride* appeared in 1951, the year in which *I Love Lucy* began its five-year run. In 1950, there were eight million television sets in the United States; in 1956 alone, Americans purchased over seven million. However, more was at work in changing his perspective than new technologies. Not unrelated to his development of a more positive approach to consumer culture, by the mid-1950s he would solve his household's economic situation. The failure of *The Mechanical Bride* to reach an audience of any consequence helped impel McLuhan into projects and perspectives for which he developed a more positive view of consumer culture. Now he would, as his biographer concluded, become an "explorer, the relentless seeker of insights unhindered by the striking of moral attitudes." *The Mechanical Bride* was, Marchand writes, McLuhan's "mordant farewell to Machine Age civilization," his final effort of opposition to it. Albeit implicitly or unevenly expressed, what became fully formed in his writings of the 1960s was present in *The Mechanical Bride*: a focus on the medium as the message, an understanding of the symbolic richness of print and visual culture, the power of the medium over the message, a joining of levels of culture, and a desire to find new ways of understanding consumer culture.[67]

Thus, after the early 1950s McLuhan was on his way to a fuller and less ambivalent and less moralistic development of the themes that would mark his highly influential books of the 1960s. What he read in the meantime (especially the work of Harold Innis, whose writings he did not encounter early enough to influence *The Mechanical Bride*) gave him the language to develop his ideas more explicitly and elaborately, but just as elliptically, in later works. Changes in the electronic media, in computer technology, and in the automated production line influenced what McLuhan presented in three books: *The Gutenberg Galaxy* (1962), *Understanding Media* (1964), and *The Medium Is the Massage* (1967). Relying on the assumption that changes in technology fundamentally shaped culture, he emphasized the momentous consequences of the shift from an expressive oral culture of the twelfth century to what he saw as the fragmenting and depressing consequences of Gutenberg's typographical revolution. Print culture centralized power in the nation-state, fragmented consciousness, undermined sensory expression, and made consumers passive.[68]

The situation began to change in the late nineteenth and early twentieth centuries, when a third era, driven by modern media, arrived. Reflecting his earlier appreciation for less developed parts of the Western world, McLuhan ascribed to artists "from backward oral areas," like the Southerner William Faulkner or the Irish James Joyce, a power to break through the constraints of print culture.[69] These artists drew on the power of new forms of mass communication to create "a mosaic of the postures of the collective consciousness." Joyce realized that "the new electronic technology, with its profound organic character," began to undermine the constraints of the closed system imposed by centuries of the dominance of Gutenberg's galaxy. By the middle of the twentieth century, the new media, best represented by television and electronic circuitry, created "electric conditions of simultaneous information movement and total human interdependence." New art forms, McLuhan wrote in 1962, invited the consumer to participate "in the method process itself." Yet for him in many ways the stage of modern media harkened back to a priestly, medieval world before print culture was hegemonic. Like its predecessor but on a different scale, the new era was characterized by the creativity, sensory engagement and intensity, communal involvement, organic integration, and new consciousness possible in the global village.[70]

McLuhan's 1960s vision reverberated with what he had written in *The Mechanical Bride*. He linked what he saw as the strengths of the medieval world and the electronic age. He asserted that consumers were empowered. He moved easily between high and low cultures. He insisted that the medium was more important than the message. Now, however, he had erased almost all traces of hesitancy about consumer culture. There was, however, at least one cautionary note. Toward the end of *The Medium Is the Massage*, which like *The Mechanical Bride* combined dramatic visual statements with elliptical written ones, McLuhan returned to where he began in his 1951 book. On one page of a two-page spread that pictured a middle-aged man on a surfboard, dressed in a suit and holding on to a briefcase with one hand and his hat with another, appeared a statement about Poe's story with which he had opened his earlier book. He wrote of how Poe's mariner in "The Descent into the Maelstrom" used "amusement born of his rational detachment as a spectator of his own situation," to stave off disaster by "understanding the action of the whirlpool." This strategy, McLuhan insisted, might make it possible for his own contemporaries to understand "our predicament, our electrically-configured whirl." Such an approach seems at odds with the embrace of the new that filled McLuhan's books of the 1960s, to say nothing of the enthusiasm with which youthful members of the counterculture embraced what he had to say. In the 1960s as in 1951, there was still "amusement" that sprang from "rational detachment." The British cultural critic Richard Hoggart, writing in 1964, said that "reading McLuhan is like being on a big-dipper operated by an imaginative but scatty intellectual." Yet Hoggart realized that something important had changed from *The Mechanical Bride* to *Understanding Media*. In his earlier book, Hoggart noted, McLuhan had written that "freedom, like taste, is an *activity of perception and judgment* based on a great range of particular acts and experience. Whatever fosters mere *passivity and submission* is the enemy of this vital activity." "That slightly Arnoldian note," Hoggart continued "is not heard now; indeed it is specifically disowned."[71]

McLuhan's move, well after the publication of *The Mechanical Bride*, to a less equivocal acceptance of modern culture helped transform him into a well-paid consultant to major corporations. Beginning in the early 1950s and increasingly so in the next decades, he participated in a variety of schemes that made commercial use of his ideas. In the mid-1950s with friends he formed Idea Consultants, which proposed new ways of increasing beer sales (including allowing corporate sponsors of announcements of upcoming stops on public transportation), and advised aides of Richard M. Nixon on how to use the media in his presidential campaigns. This effort was short lived and unsuccessful, but the same was not true of McLuhan's other attempt to make commercial hay of his media-savvy mind. Beginning in 1959, he lectured and led seminars for General Electric executives. In 1965, he worked with two American businessmen, skilled in the ways of Madison Avenue, to find way of promoting McLuhan and his ideas. In 1966, he was named senior creative consultant for a leading Canadian advertising agency. The height of his self-commercialization came in 1968 when he agreed to participate in a venture that promoted his ideas through a newsletter to which several thousand people subscribed. Toward such endeavors, important to the financial well-being of his large family, McLuhan's attitude ranged from fascination to contempt. Indeed, in *The Mechanical Bride* he had spoken of himself, unpersuasively, as "the reformer" who had "a sure method of diagnosis and therapeutic suggestion. It permits the reformer to co-operate with the same forces that have produced the disease, in order to point the way to health."[72]

In 1965 Tom Wolfe offered a vivid portrait of a McLuhan as a writer who appealed to both corporations and the counterculture. Using a familiar flourish, he characterized McLuhan as "Delphic! Cryptic! Metaphorical! Epigrammatic!" Wolfe told of how, by the mid-1960s, professors and then their students created happenings that drew on what McLuhan had recently written. One, in British Columbia, featured a sound and light show that highlighted his celebration of the aural and tactile. "Dancers flipped around through the crowds," Wolfe wrote, "and behind a stretch fabric wall . . . there was a girl, pressed against the stretched fabric wall, like a whole wall made of stretch pants, and *undulating* and humping around back there. Everybody was supposed to come up and *feel it*—the girl up against the stretch fabric—to understand this 'tactile communication' McLuhan talks about."[73]

Wolfe went on to explore how McLuhan served as an oracle to corporate executives interested in using his ideas to enhance their bottom lines. Aided by two San Francisco advertising executives, McLuhan earned handsome fees, talking to people in the business world who worried that they would miss something if the Canadian writer turned out to be "the most important thinker since Newton, Darwin, Freud, Einstein, and Pavlov." And so they sat in conference rooms, "with the day's first bloody mary squirting through their capillaries," listening to this rumpled professor "who just got through grading *papers*, for godsake," telling them "in an *of-course* voice and with I'm being-*patient* eyes, that, in effect, politely, they all know exactly ... nothing ... about the real business they're in." In the case of General Electric, executives assumed they were manufacturing light bulbs, an understanding for which McLuhan offered an alternative. "Swell!" they asked themselves, Wolfe wrote with his characteristic style. "But where did *this* guy come from? What is this—these cryptic, Delphian sayings: The *electric light is pure information*."[74]

Near the end of his article, Wolfe told a story that unintentionally reinvoked the image of the women in the Gotham hosiery ad that McLuhan dissected in *The Mechanical Bride*. McLuhan's handlers had taken him to a San Francisco restaurant where the men at McLuhan's table were served by women "walking around wearing nothing but high-heel shoes and bikini underpants." Embarrassed and not knowing what to say, one of the men with McLuhan commented on how good-looking one of the waitresses was. "Good looking," McLuhan responded. "That's a visual orientation. ... this is meant as a *tactile* experience." If Wolfe's tone was ironic but appreciative, Czitrom's judgment is harsher and more accurate. McLuhan's consulting with corporations, he notes, "made it hard to swallow his continual public stance that he *personally* abhorred the changes he described."[75]

Although it is highly unlikely that Barthes or Eco had read *The Mechanical Bride*, the similarities between McLuhan's book and their work of the late 1950s are striking. They were all coming to terms with the spread and growing sophistication of commercial culture in the postwar trans-Atlantic world. They offered intensive, relatively short analyses of the iconography of commercial culture. Though McLuhan did so more explicitly, they were trying to transform passive consumers into sophisticated, active, and even resisting interpreters: McLuhan through the slide shows out of which *The Mechanical Bride* grew, Barthes through the essays he brought together in *Mythologies*, and Eco through the essays that ended up in *Misreadings*. They shared a commitment to use literary analysis to decode commercial culture, in the process joining high and low culture but often on terms set by literary theory and texts. They saw mass media as systems of symbolic exchange through which a culture defined itself. What Marianne DeKoven said of Barthes applies to McLuhan as well: he "loathes the objects of his demythologizing study even as he legitimates them intellectually." In his short pieces, she has written of Barthes, "he is just as much ventriloquizing as he is occupying the position of the infatuated consumer, in order to understand, demystify, and repudiate that position."[76]

Yet in the 1950s the differences between the three authors' books are equally striking. If McLuhan mixed attacks on moralism with moral outrage, what Susan Sontag called Barthes's "temperamental dislike for the moralistic" was stronger and applied to Eco as well. If McLuhan was a Thomist, conservative Catholic living in a Protestant part of Canada, then Barthes was a Protestant living in a Catholic nation and Eco a lapsed Thomist living in another Catholic country, all of which goes to prove that there were multiple relationships between Catholicism and new views of commercial culture. Moreover, even though McLuhan was moving toward an emphasis on the medium as the message, Barthes and Eco were shifting from author to text more so than McLuhan. Though their essays, especially those of McLuhan and Barthes, were opaque, those of Barthes and Eco were more artfully constructed, less a mélange of quotes and quips than focused and tightly structured pieces. Their analysis rested, as McLuhan's did not, on sophisticated semiotics. For Barthes and McLuhan sexuality was central. Barthes, who posthumously revealed his homosexuality, celebrated artifice and sexual expression. McLuhan, whose homophobia was deep-seated, lamented these qualities. Above all, if McLuhan's politics were conservative and half-hidden, Barthes's were radical, coherent, and encompassing. To him, but not to McLuhan, race, class, and imperialism had central positions in an ideology that explored the relationship between mass media, citizenship, and power in a capitalist system. Though McLuhan had the material to do so, it was Barthes and Eco who suggestively understood culture as a series of performative texts rich in symbolic meaning.[77]

In the end the issue with McLuhan remains highlighting the complicated changes and contradictions in his positions. In 1968 Bernard Rosenberg remarked that by the mid-1960s McLuhan had "managed to swallow the nausea" he had earlier felt, now celebrating what used to sicken him. He "married the Mechanical Bride whose every gesture used to repel him," writing "in a psychedelic delirium comparable only to that of Timothy Leary." McLuhan went from the reluctant fascination with consumer culture so evident in *The Mechanical Bride* to an apparently full embrace in the 1960s. He flirted with fascism in the 1930s and remained a conservative Roman Catholic throughout his life yet became a guru for members of a counterculture immersed in ways of living that presumably were anathema to McLuhan. In 1951 he lamented the way popular culture disembodied women's bodies but later consented to an interview with *Playboy*. In part these changes have to do with the way his fertile imagination and drive as a good provider combined to impel him to seek the main chance, even if that meant merchandising himself for the very kind of corporate skullduggery he had denounced in *The Mechanical Bride*. Yet such an explanation gets us only so far. As Thomas C. Frank has made clear in his *The Conquest of Cool: Business Culture, Counterculture, and the Rise of Hip Consumerism*, the revolt against 1950s conformity came from many sources, including from within the belly of the beast of the advertising and fashion industries. And, one might do well to add, from a fundamentally conservative Canadian writer who wrote an elusive but suggestive book in 1951, and in the 1960s became a guru for the counterculture.[78]

In the 1954 essay that Rosenberg and White reprinted in *Mass Culture*, McLuhan remarked that when he wrote *The Mechanical Bride* he had not realized he was trying to defend "book-culture against the new media." Three years later, he could understand that what he was trying to do was "bring some of the critical awareness fostered by literary training to bear on the new media of light and sound." That approach, he now recognized, was wrong, because his "obsession with literary values blinded" him "to much that was actually happening for good or ill." In the end, he now acknowledged, the task was not to defend "the values developed in any particular culture or by any one mode of communication" but to ground the defense of human values "in analytical awareness of the nature of the creative process involved in human cognition." McLuhan had learned that the new media were so powerful that it was necessary to bring to bear a wide range of analytic tools, not just literary analysis grounded in the reading of Wyndham Lewis, I. A. Richards, and F. R. Leavis. For McLuhan "analytical awareness" was based on Thomist theology and on a longing for the organic society he believed existed in the monastic Middle Ages. By the mid-1950s he was coming to realize that modern media were good because they challenged the Gutenberg regime, which in turn had overturned the medieval one. What he celebrated in his transformative books of the 1960s was the way the new media helped recreate the conditions for a return to an earlier age.[79]

Riesman, McLuhan, and Beyond

In many ways, Riesman and McLuhan were significantly different in outlook. Riesman was a secular man of Jewish ancestry, an anti-Stalinist liberal, and author of a wildly popular 1950 book. McLuhan was a devout Roman Catholic, a deeply conservative man, and author of a 1951 book that made a splash only in limited circles who became a celebrity in the mid-1960s, when Riesman was growing more conservative in response to the very cultural forces McLuhan seemed to be speaking for. With hints of a future in which anthropology loomed large, Riesman was looking forward to new ways in which commercial culture was shaping culture and personality. Relying on high literary theory to understand popular culture, McLuhan was looking backward in this way and others in an effort to come to terms with the consequences of new media. Much more so than McLuhan, Riesman cast a skeptical eye on hierarchical ways of approaching cultural realms. Yet they shared a good deal. In the late 1940s, both Riesman and McLuhan were trying to figure out how to think about commercial culture sweeping across North America. They were both fascinated by what they observed but reluctant either to embrace or criticize it forcefully. They were carving out positions both related and in opposition to those of New York intellectuals. Rejecting the moralism of critics and at times adopting an anthropological stance, they emphasized playfulness as they explored how a rich and inventive commercial culture, one that opened up the possibility of multiple meanings, provided ways in which people communicated with each other through symbolic systems. They explored how ordinary citizens could simultaneously understand and resist commercial culture.

The focus now shifts to Britain, where in the 1950s the crosscurrents about popular culture were fully visible. In the early 1950s, the artists and critics in the Independent Group began to meet in London, where they pored over American advertisements with fascination that was not at all reluctant. Later in the decade, Hoggart in *The Uses of Literacy: Aspects of Working-Class Life* (1957) used a Leavisite approach to celebrate the popular culture of the interwar working class in Britain and to criticize the impact of American popular culture on British youth in the postwar period. If members of the Independent Group were enthusiastic, Hoggart, like Riesman and McLuhan but for different reasons, was compelled by the popular culture of a threatened working class but critical of what was replacing it.

Chapter 5

Literary Ethnography of Working-Class Life

In 1957 Richard Hoggart published *The Uses of Literacy: Aspects of Working-Class Life*, which explored the impact of commercialism on the British working class in the years before and after World War II. The appearance of this immensely influential book placed Hoggart on a path to play a key role in the development of cultural studies as it emerged out of British adult education programs beginning in the 1960s. Like Marshall McLuhan, Hoggart focused on print culture and analyzed it with the techniques of a literary critic. Yet Hoggart, however tentatively, broke fresh ground in significant ways. More so than McLuhan and like Roland Barthes, Hoggart treated a wide range of choices as cultural texts, including home decorations, speech patterns, and vacations. He remained poised between a hierarchal view of types of culture and a more parallel, egalitarian one. At a time when North American cultural critics focused on the middle class, he concentrated on the working class and in the process substantially addressed the issue of Americanization, something McLuhan and Barthes did not focus on even though the had abundant evidence to do so. Moreover, Hoggart ventured (however uneasily) into aspects of popular culture that McLuhan and Barthes (but not David Riesman) had generally avoided, both its expression in music and its role in the emergence of a distinctive youth culture. Above all, what makes Hoggart's 1957 book so pathbreaking was that with considerable equivocation it showed how an academic steeped in the study of canonical literature used an anthropological approach to emphasize resistance to and richness of popular culture.[1]

The British Background to Hoggart's Writing

Several factors, many of which obtained for British but not American observers, shaped Hoggart's approach. Unlike what was true in the United States, in Britain an elitist, Arnoldian critique remained strong and entrenched. Nowhere was this clearer than in the writings of America-born T. S. Eliot and his fellow British citizens, F. R. Leavis and Q. D. Leavis. In addition, British class politics, especially the issue of the dynamics of working-class life, shaped Hoggart's response, which was not the case in the United States, where the principal focus in discussions of popular culture was on the middle class and where African Americans often played the role that workers did in British social thought. Indeed, while the subtitle of the British edition indicated that the book was about "working-class life," the American subtitle announced its focus on "English mass culture."[2]

Political battles, economic change, and cultural attitudes also shaped Hoggart's book. The Labour Party won a stunning victory in 1945, enabling it to strengthen the welfare state. Some party members linked recovery with an austerity based on restrained consumption. In contrast, when they returned to power in 1951, Conservatives hailed the ways that the new affluence of the working class was weakening and even eliminating class allegiances. Rationing ended in 1954 and the mid-1950s witnessed dramatic economic growth, with one historian remarking that "rampant consumerism" arrived in the middle of the decade as people used increasing amounts of debt to buy appliances, home furnishings, cars—and went to supermarkets and cinemas, often in newly developed suburbs. Britons debated the now intensified impact of American culture. Some writers, mostly younger intellectuals, connected the United States with things modern, egalitarian, and fashionable. In contrast, cultural conservatives linked Americanization, materialism, feminization, family breakdown, and youthful rebellion to degradation and cultural leveling. Just when Hoggart was finishing his book, many on both the left and right despaired over the decline in Britain's role as a cultural and world power, especially in contrast to America's increasing hegemony.[3]

This all happened when official policy, most notably that of the BBC, tried to contain American commercial culture, rock and roll especially. Younger, less educated, and working-class Britons were more likely than others to embrace American materialism. Indeed, as Herbert Gans realized at the time, the condescending attitude of advocates of culture (and their control over what was offered through radio, television, and movies) helped impel ordinary Britons toward American popular culture. These changes had a particular impact on the British working classes. Against the appeal of a notion of *embourgeoisement,* working-class intellectuals like Hoggart insisted on the distinctive nature of class dynamics in Britain and on the importance of developing a left-wing critique of those who celebrated the arrival of mass culture in postwar Britain.[4]

The year before the publication of Hoggart's breakthrough book—1956— was a critical one in Britain's postwar history. It saw the publication of John

Osborne's *Look Back in Anger*, heralding the arrival of a generation of Angry Young Men. Commercial television became fully available. More immediately, dramatic events of that year—Khrushchev's denunciation of Stalin's brutality, the Soviet invasion of Hungary, and the takeover of the Suez Canal from Egypt by the French and British—profoundly shaped the outlook of the British. These events prompted many grounded in the Old Left (as Hoggart was not) to leave the Communist Party and/or to reconfigure their Marxism. At the time, two people were also working on landmark books in cultural and social history: Raymond Williams, a Party member briefly in the late 1930s and early 1940s who remained a sympathetic nonmember well into the 1950s, and E. P. Thompson, who left the Party in 1956. Williams and Thompson increasingly turned away from stark Marxist determinism that emphasized the power of the economic base to shape the cultural superstructure, an approach that relegated literature, religion, and education to positions where they lacked power or authenticity. Hoggart, like Thompson and Williams, embraced the cultural turn, although that was hardly a term they or others would have used at the time. As a result they created a new awareness of the relationships between culture and class. In his book, Hoggart emphasized the lived community, the vitally experiential, and structures of feeling understood through an anthropological approach to culture as a range of texts, from canonical novels to popular songs and stories.[5]

Coming of Age in the Working Class

With *The Uses of Literacy*, Hoggart produced a wonderfully evocative literary ethnography of working-class culture that drew on his own experiences. He grew up in Hunslet, a working-class area of Leeds, an industrial city in Yorkshire two hundred miles north of London. His immediate family's hold on middle-class life ended with his father's death when Hoggart was less than two years old, leaving his mother in dire straits, with three children in a household now dependent on public assistance. His mother died several years later, leaving Hoggart an orphan at a young age. He was then separated from his siblings and moved to what he later characterized as an "overwhelmingly domestic, internal, home and woman-centered" world of extended kin: a grandmother, two maiden aunts, a bachelor uncle, and an unmarried female cousin.[6]

His roots were deep in the respectable working class of Britain: ranging from family members who were unemployed, to a grandfather who was a skilled worker, and to those a generation ahead of him who in the 1930s had a tenuous grasp on the lower middle class through jobs in sales and shop keeping. The household of his youth, he wrote in his memoir as he described the center of his privatized world, was not "a gimcrack home but, at their best, its furniture and fittings were such as respectable working-class people would buy, objects produced in quantity but meant to last, to give good service; democratic American-style objects." Inspired by a grandmother who respected learning, and repelled as well by the verbal and physical violence in his family, he turned to books and school. Strong performance on a competitive exam gained him entrance into Cockburn High School where he was among a small number of students from the working class. "Brains plus tenacity," he later wrote, plus encouragement from teachers, he would surely add, carried him forward. By age fifteen he was moving toward a politics that he later described as "a Tawney-esque democratic socialism which stressed fraternity as the ground for equality." Early on, he developed a love of British literature. In an essay he wrote at the age of sixteen about Thomas Hardy, he first explored "received notions about 'culture' and 'cultivation'" as he responded to the novels by this author from a nonelite background who had written about the impact of industrialization on rural England.[7]

Lack of money and the forbidding reputation of Oxbridge kept him from applying; instead in the fall 1936 at age eighteen he entered Leeds University to study English. Leaving Hunslet for the local university, and by implication leaving a working-class world for the middle-class life of a scholar-teacher, he later remarked, meant that he could never again be "an integral part" of the world he left. "You have bitten the fruit," he later remarked of himself. In his first year, he met Mary France, a young woman from a middle-class family, whom he married in 1942 and with whom he had three children.[8]

At Leeds Hoggart focused on socialist politics, English poetry (T. S. Eliot and W. H. Auden especially), and newly emerging documentary forms (one example was the Depression-era films of John Grierson). Also important to Hoggart were the investigations of Mass-Observation, an interdisciplinary experiment begun in 1937 that charted the lives of members of the working class. For example, *The Pub and the People: A Worktown Study* (1943) and *Puzzled People: A Study in Popular Attitudes to Religion, Ethics, Progress and Politics in a London Borough* (1947) combined interviews, descriptions of the physical environment, statistics, and ethnographies into a jargon-free, vivid portrayal of the lives of workers and their families. In early published essays, Hoggart distanced himself from Communism but played with the potential of Christian radicalism and the connection between the university and a local working men's club. The teacher who most influenced Hoggart at Leeds was Bonamy Dobrée, a cosmopolitan literary figure who was a close friend of the art critic

Herbert Read. Dobrée offered Hoggart choices that were distinctly non-Leavisite. As one scholar noted, he represented "the anti-Puritanism of the cavalier, in its best sense, style—replete with disregard for disciplinary boundaries, formal niceties, appropriate tone and relishing the social reference which the modern defenders of the faith so dislike and call dilettantism." Hoggart graduated in 1939 with first class honors, entitling him to a two-year graduate fellowship, which, were it not for World War II, he would have most likely taken at Cambridge. On his graduation day Hoggart met T. S. Eliot, a friend of his mentor, who was at Leeds to receive an honorary degree.[9]

Soon after graduation, Hoggart left Leeds for good when he entered military service in 1940. After training in Britain, he served as an officer in the Royal Artillery, first in North Africa and then in Italy, but rarely on or near the front lines. He spent 1943 to 1946 in Naples after its liberation. There, he remarked much later, most Americans, with access to Coke and Lucky Strikes at their PX stores, "preferred to be cocooned in their creaturely signs and symbols they had come to associate with their own superior nationhood." In the last years of the war and the first of peace, while in Naples he played a major role in the Three Arts Club, which held readings, published poetry and stories, and developed art exhibitions. While in the service, Hoggart also participated in the efforts of the Army Bureau of Current Affairs (ABCA), educating the troops about politics, literature, and the futures they would face in postwar Britain. The classes sponsored by the ABCA, established in 1942 as an effort to enhance troop morale, focused mainly on the relationships between the war and citizenship. The ABCA was controversial, its reputation for left-wing politics prompting Conservatives to blame it for the 1945 victory of the Labour Party. Contemporaries feared or hoped that the education ABCA offered would help transform postwar Britain into a more open, egalitarian society. ABCA spurred soldiers, especially those from modest backgrounds, to think about a postwar Britain less class- and tradition-bound than the one they left. In London and in the military, there were fierce battles over the mission of the ABCA that centered on British imperialism, the tension between an authoritarian military and a democratic education, the involvement of left-wing tutors, and the response to a pamphlet on the 1942 Beveridge Report, which Prime Minister Winston Churchill ordered withdrawn.[10]

Reading the ABCA's pamphlets on social policy in postwar Britain made Hoggart realize, he reported retrospectively, that rank-and-file service men had never benefited from enjoying the works of Thomas Hardy, Jane Austen, or George Eliot. The tragedy was not that they were blocked from "access to some socially-defined . . . High Culture" but they had been denied "entry to one of

the most important of all liberating experiences—the opportunity to recognise
that it is possible to try disinterestedly to look at and give some sort of meaning to your life." His experience with ABCA as an education officer trying to
answer his students' questions about their lives helped him realize that people
like himself could teach in situations that would enable their students to understand that literature and ideas mattered. From Naples after V-E Day, he wrote
letters to people involved in the Workers' Educational Association (WEA) in
Britain. After a visit with his wife in Britain, he was back in Naples, teaching
English literature to Italians and Britons. Soon after the war's end, he began to
write; among his early published works were an essay in *Poetry Review* in 1947
and his first book, on W. H. Auden, in 1951.[11]

Teaching Adult Education

In 1946 Hoggart, now a civilian, returned to Britain, to his wife, to his first
child, and to a job at the University of Hull. Now began thirteen years when he
taught adults on the university level in adult education programs. Employed
by the University of Hull, for three years beginning in 1946 he taught a hundred miles to its north, living mostly in Redcar (a modest seaside resort and
"a dreary little town," he later called it) and Marske ("a tiny straggly village")
but circuit riding to other places, including the gritty city of Middlesbrough.
This was a region on the northeast coast of England, north of York and south
of Newcastle-upon-Tyne, known for its shipbuilding, chemicals, coal, iron, and
steel. Hoggart taught at night, isolated from the libraries and colleagues that his
presence in a more traditional higher educational setting would have afforded.[12]
   Students in his classes varied in background and abilities. There were many
middle-class housewives, as well as men from the upper reaches of the working
class and lower reaches of the white-collar class who were benefiting from the
spread of education and relative affluence in postwar Britain. Early on he reported how much they varied: "black-coated workers" in Middlesbrough; steel-
workers and their wives in Brotton; housewives in Dormanstown; and "solid
and respectable bourgeois" in Scarborough who read "pseudo-literature" that
made their "hackles rear at too overt attacks on their lares." In 1948 he described his best students as "an elementary-school-trained boy in a steelworks
office, an honours graduate in English with a research M.A., a forty-odd year
old village-school-educated farmer's wife, and a sub-editor on a provincial
paper who went to a minor public school." Indeed, in 1947 Hoggart moved beyond a traditional class analysis of his students when he observed that they
were "dispossessed": people who had suffered cultural loss and were "re-acting

deep down against the vile mass culture of our day," the "*homo vulgaris North-cliffi.*" Teaching adults of varying abilities constantly challenged him. In March 1948 he reported that in a class in Marske students "often blackout on me or retire behind a screen of final prejudices . . . after battering my way back to the point where a poem may connect *legitimately* with them I am ragged." Of another group, this one in Scarborough, Hoggart remarked that "they cling very grimly to their ideological passport into literature."[13]

In 1949 Hoggart and his growing family moved to Hull, where he continued his work in adult education. He now lived near the university, teaching adult education courses there and in Goole and Selby, twenty-eight and forty miles west of Hull, and Scarborough, a seaside resort town forty-two miles north of the city. At and from Hull, Hoggart normally taught two kinds of classes: tutorials from October to May, usually with enrollment from the high single digits to the mid-teens, offered in two dozen evening sessions, and teachers' classes designed for pre-university teachers but participated in by others as well, with enrollment as high as forty. Most of his students were in their thirties and early forties (with some as young as their early twenties and as old as their mid-sixties); more likely female than male; and typically more middle class than working class. Some of his peers, teaching adults elsewhere, lamented what they saw as the excessive presence of middle-class housewives in literature classes. Although there is no evidence Hoggart shared such strongly misogynist views, in 1954 he remarked that "we always needed more men" and with one class noted that "women outnumbered men by five to one, which is a pity." Moreover, the students he mentioned in his annual reports as exceptionally talented were usually men.[14]

Most of his students were middle class: teachers, housewives, and those he called "in clerical or professional work." At times, he taught some more highly trained professionals, such as a chemist or an engineer. On relatively rare occasions, he taught working-class men. One class during 1954–55 contained both "men, manual workers with little previous educational background, and the more highly trained among the women students." Initially Hoggart worried about how the differences, shaped by class, age, education, and gender, would play out. In the end, he noted, "this difficulty scarcely arose." Moreover, he remarked with satisfaction that some working-class men were among his best students. Teaching in Selby in 1952–53, he singled out "one student, a shy, 19 year-old elementary-school trained motor mechanic's apprentice" who "showed himself possessed of an enviable sensitivity in response and was always carefully attended to by others whenever he felt ready to speak." In contrast but equally satisfying was a situation in Scarborough in 1954–55. "The only problem, a slight and pleasant one," Hoggart commented at the end of the academic year, "was to keep one of the men—a motor mechanic with an unusual capacity for reading and discussing his reading seriously—from overawing almost everyone else."[15]

Mostly, Hoggart taught courses that focused on novels, poems, sermons, and plays by British, American, French, and Russian writers. In 2004, he wrote of trying to help his students "cast a critical eye on much of the received wisdom of their social group, a group much manipulated by the increasingly powerful media of mass communication." When he discussed his broad educational goals in his annual reports, which he did on occasion and usually in somewhat vague terms, he talked of "increasing appreciation of and judgement on the texture of prose" and of focusing on "literary discrimination." At times, Hoggart expressed his frustrations about the difficulty of achieving his goals. In the annual reports he often worried that there were too few students genuinely interested in the serious study of literature. Again and again, he wrote of having to persuade students to read, write, and discuss in engaged and disciplined ways. "I have had to play the policeman rather more than I like this year," he noted of a class in Goole in 1953–54. Rarer was the kind of comment he made of a class there in 1955–56: "Most of the time I was having to meet—in the most radical way—embattled prejudice from several students; blank incomprehension would perhaps have been easier to deal with." Yet Hoggart usually reported a high level of satisfaction. For example, for a course in Selby in 1954–55, he said that "although some members are not intellectually well-equipped and lack background all are hard-working, and I have no doubt that the class is valuable to them." Occasionally, he told of exceptionally good experiences. In one instance, he mentioned that the high quality of discussions was "largely a product of the class's unusual sense of unity which itself arises from mutual respect and an unsentimental and uncompromising readiness to get down to joint examination." In another instance, he remarked that he "had that splendid feeling of conducting a good orchestra."[16]

Despite the ups and downs of teaching, as well as the travel and isolation, teaching in an adult education program had its compensations. For better or worse, Hoggart lacked the captive students of traditional university age whose lives were geared to exams, degrees, and social life. Instead, challenged by his adult students to think through key issues of pedagogy and literary theory, he had to learn how to connect the lives of those students to canonical literature. This made him more aware of the challenges of reaching a wider public, something that stood him in good stead at a number of points, including the writing of his 1957 book. He had weekday mornings, long summers, and weekends to be with his family and to see movies, especially art films such as *Kind Hearts and Coronets* (1949), *The Lavender Hill Mob* (1951), *Bitter Rice* (1949), *Bicycle Thief* (1948), and *Orphée* (1950). Above all, he had time to read and write. And read he did: absorbing what the Leavises, Lionel Trilling, Arthur Koestler, Graham Greene, T. S. Eliot, C. S. Lewis, Arnold Toynbee, and George Orwell had to say. He contributed essays on adult education, finished his book on Auden, and by 1952 began what would become *The Uses of Literacy*.[17]

The Challenges of Adult Education

In the postwar period, adult education in Britain, much of it university-based but affiliated with the WEA, was a vital and controversial arena, which turned out to be the seedbed of cultural studies. There is nothing comparable in the United States to British adult education, neither in terms of institutions nor of its role in intellectual life. In its long and distinguished history, key figures in British intellectual life participated in the effort, including R. H. Tawney, G. D. H. Cole, Karl Polanyi, E. P. Thompson, Raymond Williams, and, most pertinently, Hoggart. In the late 1940s and early 1950s, intense debates took place about adult education: over whether Marxists, Communists, or Roman Catholics should be permitted to teach; over the tension between a commitment to workers' education and to a broader popular education; over the relationship between adult education and mainline university education; and over the role of objectivity in teaching. These debates were played out in publications which Hoggart read and to which he contributed: *Adult Education*, *Tutors' Bulletin*, and the WEA's *Highway*.[18]

In the immediate postwar period, adult education provided a space where a generation of academics and intellectuals, mainly on the left, developed interdisciplinary approaches to the study of the culture that emphasized the relationships between class dynamics, social history, and popular modes of expression. Many of them remained indebted to the approach to literature and to key elements of the larger vision of F. R. Leavis and those involved with *Scrutiny*. Leavis had impressed upon teachers the importance of teaching nontraditional students by focusing on close examination of a limited number of texts. The Leavisites, a scholar has noted, taught adult education tutors to emphasize "close reading of texts, a moral stance, contextual relevance" and to "scorn . . . dilettante literary history and biographical detail."[19]

In his memoir Hoggart talked about how his experiences in adult education shaped his later work. He credited his work teaching a wide range of subjects to adults with making it possible for him to write *The Uses of Literacy*. Especially in his first five years of teaching adults after World War II, he remarked, he learned gradually but "inescapably to move out from the study of literature as it is academically defined to work on many other aspects of contemporary culture." He realized that "the methods of literary criticism" would help him understand "all levels of writing and much else in popular culture," as well as how audiences reacted to them. Reading Orwell and C. S. Lewis made him question what readers might make of diverse materials, especially popular texts, "by the thought that obviously poor writing might appeal to good instincts, that the mind of a reader is not a *tabula rasa* but has been nurtured within a social setting which provides its own forms and filters for judgments and resistances, that one had to know very much more about how people used much of the stuff which to us might seem merely dismissible trash, before one could speak confidently about the effects it might have." In the process he came to understand "the appeal of, and the response to, all forms of popular literature and art."[20]

In a series of articles he wrote in the late 1940s and early 1950s, Hoggart participated in the debates over the nature, scope, and politics of adult education. He spoke movingly about the challenges he and his peers faced, especially what in 1948 he called "the strain of isolation from professional colleagues and the weight of constant and peculiarly intimate relations with so many who are promising or lonely or unhappy." Several other issues commanded his attention: developing a pedagogy; articulating just why literature was so important; finding a position among competing visions of adult education; wrestling with the tension between elitist and democratic commitments; and coming to terms with the relationships between teacher and students. In the end, drawing on the work of F. R. Leavis and others, Hoggart took relatively moderate to conservative positions in the debates among adult educators. Moreover, he did so in ways that both shaped what he would write in *The Uses of Literacy* and underscored the limitations of some of what he offered there.[21]

In the late 1940s and well into the 1950s, Hoggart and others involved in adult education continued a long-standing debate between "culturalists" who emphasized the integrity of the literary text and reconciliation of social classes and "workerists" who insisted on the social relevance of literature and class conflict. The culturalists stood in opposition to those members of the Communist Party who advocated a more politically radical position. Hoggart aligned himself with the culturalists, defending the centrality of the humanities against those who wanted to focus on the social sciences and the social relevance of literature. He cast his lot with those who were skeptical about whether Marxists or Communists could separate their politics from their teaching. He felt that the focus on workers' education was constricting; rather, he wanted to appeal to "the serious-minded who are also educationally under-privileged, which is not," he noted, "entirely synonymous with 'the working class.'" He emphasized the importance of education that had a "spiritual character" and whose central purpose was "wisdom," not "'social emancipation.'" Reacting against Popular Front notions of the political job of the writer but doing so in vague but coded language, he used anti-Stalinist language when he said a workerist approach would "push our society one step nearer the point where individual freedom and responsibility are finally denied by the authoritarian idea." Thus for him, an education, for workers and nonworkers alike, was what he called an "indivisible *activity*" that involved "a common seriousness and intensity of effort" when approaching canonical texts.[22]

Like many of his peers, Hoggart developed a pedagogy that, following the writings of Leavis and others, focused on intense, patient, and sustained readings of canonical literary texts, moving away from what Hoggart in 1948 called "the happy valley of the surface approach" or a year earlier "the static, carpet-slipper-and-pipe attitude." He wrote compellingly about the processes of teaching, emphasizing the intimate relationship between students and teacher, the importance of fostering a community of learners, and the necessity to avoid letting a lecture substitute for the student's direct encounter with the text. Instead, he understood the relationship between teacher and student as reciprocal, with discussions emerging from close encounters with texts. Reacting against the tradition of offering a fast-paced survey of a century or more of British literature, he often spent four to six weeks on one novel and even more time on a Shakespeare tragedy. Though it was acceptable for the teacher to provide literary and historical background, for Hoggart the emphasis remained on disciplined and intense encounters with canonical texts. As Raymond Williams, whom Hoggart did not meet until 1959, said in a 1948 response to what Hoggart had written in *Adult Education*, "I feel certain that Mr Hoggart will not need convincing that the discipline of reading—with no other end in view than that of the adequate response to an important text—needs no reservations educationally."[23]

In developing his position, Hoggart combined the approaches of Eliot, I. A. Richards, and even more centrally the Leavisites. Again and again, he talked of sensibility, discrimination, honest judgments, sincerity, morality, as he focused on the spiritual, metaphysical, and moral dimensions of studying literature. Consequently, he made clear that the proper basis for condemning the quality of "advertisements, newspaper leaders, public speeches" was to rely on "'literary judgments'—on the way words work, on the flatness of images, the second-hand quality of the phrasing." Like other Leavisites, he also wrestled with the tension between an elitist and a democratic approach to adult education. He articulated a position that aligned him with much of Leavis's elitism and placed him in clear opposition to advocates of a workerist stance. Hoggart felt that adult education had swung too much in a democratic direction and should instead focus on teaching a "saving remnant" or what Toynbee had called "internal proletariat," students defined not by social status but by outlook. Yet Hoggart's pedagogy also differed from that of Leavis, who at Cambridge taught mostly students with abundant cultural capital. Hoggart's engagement with his students was more intense, intimate, and individualized than was true of many of his peers at Oxbridge.[24]

In practice, Hoggart worked to resolve the tension between his hopes and his students' expectations. The issue was not generational: in 1948 Hoggart was thirty, an age not far from that of many of his students. Rather, at stake were expectations about culture, class, and education. When he discussed those he taught, it should come as no surprise that he revealed how teacher and students had disparate expectations. In 1948 he mentioned a class in which he "debunked" a passage written by "a bad author," leaving the students "hurt because they were aware that something which they cherished had been mocked and derided without their understanding why." Similarly, in 1951 he talked of many of his students as feeling "morally and politically confused" and "dissatisfied with the terms" of their lives at a time when he was farther along in knowing what he was doing. Students expressed a desire to study the relationship between literature and social reform, while as a tutor Hoggart wanted to pursue close readings. A sustained, disciplined reading would also counter the charge that teaching adults literature involved a feminized softness. Working-class male students, along with some of the more radical teachers, saw classes on literature, poetry especially, as a luxury women might indulge in but men should avoid.[25]

Nor was there much evidence in what Hoggart published before *The Uses of Literacy* of his commitment to analyzing popular culture. In *Changing Places* (1975) David Lodge, a colleague of Hoggart's at Birmingham, says of Philip Swallow, the British professor in his novel, that "he was as happy with Beowulf as with Virginia Woolf" but occasionally "read attentively the backs of cornflakes packets, the small print of railway tickets and the advertising matter in books of stamps." Perhaps while commuting Hoggart did carefully read such texts, but as a scholar he considered such material not worthy of much attention. In Hoggart's essays on teaching, there were few hints of a commitment to make popular culture texts anywhere near central to his teaching, to subject them, as Leavis had done, to practical criticism.[26]

In sum, compared with some of his peers involved in adult education, especially some members of the Communist Party and others whose socialism was
more Marxist than Hoggart's, Hoggart occupied a moderate position on many
key issues. He avoided openly or directly engaging many of the nonliterary
battles so prominent at the time, especially issues of the relationship of Britain
to the Soviet Union and the role of trade unions in the reconstruction of postwar Britain. Though during the late 1940s and into the 1950s he may have kept
his political positions somewhat to himself, he rejected or distanced himself
from both Marxists and Communists and from what in 1948 he called "the
anti-Communist witch-hunt." To be sure, from his teen years on, Hoggart was
a socialist, but his was a mild or not well-formed socialism and hardly Marxist
to boot, lacking as it did much sense of class conflict or of the way economic
forces shaped culture. Hoggart, Tom Steele writes, was "more concerned with
reading the signs of the times, which he saw as a logical extension of Leavis's
work, than with Williams's work of cultural materialism or Thompson's theo-
rized social history."[27]

Hoggart on W. H. Auden

Hoggart's commitment to a strand of literary analysis unlike what he adopted
in *The Uses of Literacy* but similar to what he used as a teacher was evident in
his first book, one published in 1951 on the poet W.H. Auden. This was a meditation on what it means to be a writer who combines political and literary interests. Hoggart, only thirty-three at the time, audaciously took on one of Britain's
most admired poets, albeit one whose poetry Leavis and his colleagues at *Scrutiny* held in low regard. In contrast to those in Britain who felt that Auden's
move to New York in 1939 caused a decline in the quality of his poetry, Hoggart
showed that continuity marked Auden's work. Indeed, Hoggart saw the United
States as a place that enhanced Auden's creativity. The rootlessness of American
life that intensified in New York, where Auden lived, Hoggart noted, "makes it
impossible to ignore those spiritual problems," such as alienation, "which such
technologically competent societies aggravate."[28]

Hoggart's analysis of Auden's poetry combined exploration of the authors
whose ideas influenced Auden, consideration of his political outlook, and
analysis of the technical problems his poems sought to resolve. He made clear
that to read Auden's poetry did not require any special literary training. Like
Leavisites, Hoggart embraced the task of offering critical evaluations, making
forceful distinctions about the quality of different poems: "brilliant diagnosis,"
he noted, "succeeded by the slapstick of a buffoon, controlled exposition con-

trasting with slipshod chatter." He provided close readings of Auden's poems, urging readers to understand how "poetry puts us into contact . . . with a sensitive personality exploring, and trying to put in order, its experience." He connected poetry to the poet's biography, historical circumstances, and political commitments, more so than would an American New Critic but less so than would a British Marxist. In Hoggart's analysis, Auden focused not only on the technical aspects of poems but also on what poetry revealed about profound issues of human experience, love, loneliness, artistic expression, but above all on the relationships between artistic creativity and political commitment. If in his analysis Hoggart drew on Richards's emphasis on formal elements, he also relied on F. R. Leavis's notion that a poem provides a manifestation of the mind and personality the reader gets to know.[29]

Politically Auden and Hoggart had much in common but their lives were different. Auden, a homosexual from the upper middle class, differed from Hoggart in sexual orientation and social experience. Yet they shared a commitment to monogamous marriage, something Hoggart was able to realize but for Auden remained elusive, and not only because marriage, a term Auden used to describe his aspirations, was then illegal for a gay man. Although Hoggart focused on love as a theme in Auden's poetry, typical of literary critics of the time he did not explore the relationship between Auden's sexuality and his poetry. Yet if class and sexual orientation separated them, Hoggart nonetheless found in Auden's work much to admire in ways that reflected his own situation. He said of Auden, but could just as well be talking of himself, that the poet "was not in the orthodox sense a Marxist." To be sure, Hoggart bristled at what he saw as Auden's condescending attitude to the working class, critiquing Auden's "stiff-collared" approach to workers in one of his poems and his naiveté in producing "the bourgeois idealisation of working-class life."[30]

Still, there was much that compelled Hoggart in Auden's work. He understood how Auden struggled to reach a wide audience. He identified with Auden's loneliness. Writing a year after the appearance of Riesman's *The Lonely Crowd* and at a time when Hoggart, as a circuit rider in adult education, lived outside the world of colleagues available within the walls of a university, he said of Auden's life in exile in America, "He is alone in a crowd." Though occasionally mentioning but hardly exploring the relationship between Auden's homosexuality and his poetry, Hoggart nonetheless related his own situation as a working-class scholarship boy now in a middle-class situation to Auden's exile and isolation. Hoggart also noted Auden's weaving of high and popular culture, with "echoes from Anglo-Saxon and the Icelandic sagas . . . placed alongside snippets from the popular Press and the music-hall; odd items from scientific textbooks or from musical analysis are mixed with debts to Eliot" and others. Here Hoggart talked of Auden's work, even from the 1930s, in ways that would echo in his discussion in *The Uses of Literacy* of postwar working-class life. Though in the book on Auden there was none of the romanticism of life in 1930s Britain that it was possible to see in his 1957 book, already in 1951 Hoggart was standing against the popular culture of postwar Britain. "The phenomena of modern life—the super-cinemas, the barnyard press and all the rest—are known to everyone," he wrote early in the book on Auden. "To a writer who is also a moralist they have a significance—as symptoms of a profound disease— which he must strive to make clear to his audience, an audience which is itself implicated in the cancerous state of affairs."[31]

Toward *The Uses of Literacy*

In the late 1940s Hoggart first started to think about the book that became *The Uses of Literacy*. In an October 1948 essay, using phrases and sentences that would reappear in his 1957 book, he described the racy publications that a traveler like himself would encounter in a bookseller's stall. "These books are heavy with sex and violence," he remarked, "with prolonged arm-twistings, long-drawn-out beatings from rubber tubes." Hoggart acknowledged that there had earlier been "on a small and esoteric scale, a literature of sadism and mas-ochism." As he would in his book, he drove home his point by comparing the sexual violence in William Faulkner's *Sanctuary* (1931) and in contemporary pulp fiction. Faulkner, he wrote, "sees beyond the rape: by implication he mea-sures it against larger issues, greater values, and the evil stands condemned." With gangster fiction, he continued, using the exact words that would appear in *The Uses of Literacy*, "we are in and of the world of the fierce alleyway as-sault; the stale disordered bed, the closed killer-car, the riverside-warehouse knifing . . . and there is no way out. There is nothing else: the sky never opens upwards; the world, consciousness, man's ends, are this . . . this tight, con-stricted, over-heated horror."[32]

In a March 1950 review of a memoir of someone from his own social back-ground, Hoggart made clear what kind of book he was beginning to think about. He worried about the "sentimental idealization of the simple urban citi-zen." Although he appreciated the author's documentary style, Hoggart called for developing forms of expression that were complex and creative. He missed "the compactness of poetry, and the architecture of the novel," as he referred specifically to D. H. Lawrence's *Sons and Lovers* (1913). Hoggart advocated "a closely integrated and complicated form, . . . because what is to be explored is intricate, subtle, constantly developing." In the end, Hoggart remarked that he only presumed "to offer this advice" to an author because his "own three-years-nibbled-at notes for just such a book confront me, notes revealing" none of the author's "powers but the same faults."[33]

As early as 1948 Hoggart had begun to contemplate the dangers American popular culture posed. Writing an essay in *Highway* in response to advertisements in *Life* magazine, he gave a foretaste of the way in *The Uses of Literacy* he would denounce how postwar American imports helped create the "candy floss world" of the British working class, its youth especially. He looked askance at the "glossy prosperity" its pages conveyed. He offered a powerful, negative, and gendered analysis. *Life*, he asserted, pictured women partaking in "joyrides in the old flivver, cokes at the corner drugstore, and bulgingly pneumatic sweaters." For him, men subscribed "to those herd customs which qualify a boy for the good-fellow-ticket later" of a world that evoked what Sinclair Lewis had described in *Babbitt* (1922). As "essentially *social* phenomena" the advertisements stood in marked contrast to the fact that many Americans lived in poverty and not "on the de-luxe car-refrigerator level." What the advertisements thus represented was not reality but "the communal wish, the euphoric dream which is rooted in creature worship," the American emphasis on competitive spending rather than communal values, the "herd fame" that chased after celebrities, the pressure to conform, and the childlike fantasy that commercialism provided genuine satisfaction. Hoggart ended the essay with an ominous question he posed to Britons still in the grip of postwar austerity: "How far is it true to say that there, but for the grace of present poverty, go we?"[34]

What *The Uses of Literacy* Relied on and Accomplished

The Uses of Literacy appeared in 1957, when those on the left were thinking through the implications of their own rejection of Stalinism and of the ways affluence, the welfare state, and Americanization threatened to erode working-class culture and to turn Britain into a classless society. Hoggart produced a book that was both timely and of lasting value. He offered a vivid, nuanced ethnography of the world he had grown up in, a working-class neighborhood in an industrial city during the 1920s and 1930s. He pondered the nature of class in a changing British world. He presented and analyzed a wide range of cultural texts and did so in ways that made dynamic the relationships between working-class, popular, and high cultures. And he offered a sustained and complicated consideration of fundamental changes in British cultural and social life. He emphasized the ability of the working classes, especially in the prewar period, to resist the power of mass media even as he worried that in the postwar period commercial culture was undermining the integrity of a genuine working-class world. Hoggart, like McLuhan, F. R. Leavis, and Denys Thompson before him and Stuart Hall and Paddy Whannel after him, thought of such a project as "a sort of guide or textbook to aspects of popular culture: newspapers, magazines, romantic or violent paperbacks, popular songs." He had an additional task, simultaneously drawing on the work of the Leavises and correcting what he saw as the mistakes they, but especially Q. D., made. He distanced himself from her condescending attitude to society's lower orders. Teaching adults had given him a "sense of the special social importance of our day-to-day work, a belief in the need for developed minds and imaginations—especially in wide-open, commercial, pyramidal societies—a sense of the many and major injustices in the lives of working people and so a deep suspicion of the power of class in Britain."[35]

At the heart of the book was Hoggart's analysis of working-class culture, illuminated by both an ethnographic approach and the application of the techniques of literary criticism to a wide range of cultural texts. He saw in the folkways of the working class sources of resistance. He focused on lived experience, insisting that culture involved the intricate connection between texts and actual experience. "In describing a working-class living room or a working-class woman's seaside outing," one reviewer noted, Hoggart's words were "as lovingly vivid as Dickens." The issue for Hoggart was not, as it was for many leading American intellectuals, how a middle-class nation confronted commercial culture in suburbs but how the working class came to terms with it in factory towns and gritty urban areas.[36]

The Uses of Literacy was thus an intensely personal book, one that drew on a wide range of sources to provide a compelling, vivid literary ethnography of working-class life both before and after World War II. In the preface Hoggart remarked that the "book is based to a larger extent on personal experience" and that it did not "purport to have the scientifically-tested character of a sociological survey." He placed members of his family and their histories at the center of the pre–World War II section and did so movingly. He spoke of his grandmother's life story as recapitulating the history of Britons who moved from country to city. "In every line of her body," he wrote, "and in many of her attitudes her country background spoke." He gave as an example how she "retained in the vitality of her spirit, in the vigour of her language, in the occasional peasant quality of her humour, a strength which her children had not and towards which they had at times something of a sophisticated and urbanized 'neshness' (soft squeamishness)." In a classic section that combined autobiography and cultural analysis, Hoggart wrote about the "Scholarship Boy" as an example of people made anxious by social change. "With them the sense of loss is increased," he wrote, "precisely because they are emotionally uprooted from their class, often under the stimulus of a stronger critical intelligence or imagination, qualities which can lead them into an unusual self-consciousness before their own situation." This discussion, and others, reflected the dynamics of his own life and that of his peers whom World War II and postwar education had transformed.[37]

Hoggart's use of the personal countered the notion of objective social science. At a time when most scholars avoided drawing openly on their own experiences as evidence, he discussed his own life. His work stood in opposition to the dry, academic sociology of the period and in some ways was a precursor of several genres that rose to prominence in the 1960s: the New Journalism and intensely personal social science of writers like Oscar Lewis. At the time, E. P Thompson criticized Hoggart's book for relying too heavily on "subjective impressions, largely based on childhood memories, and unchecked by historical referents." It is more useful to understand Hoggart's approach as one that, with its emphasis on subjectivity and the performative self, prefigured the contributions of postmodern writers.[38]

In addition to his own life experiences and those of members of his family, Hoggart relied on an analysis of oral tradition, classical studies of the working class by B. Seebohm Roundtree and J. L. and Barbara Hammonds, folk tales, speech patterns, widely shared myths, as well as the physical and cultural landscapes of homes, streets, and neighborhoods. His examination of such varied texts was especially true for the 1920s and 1930s. For both the pre- and postwar periods, he paid focused, extensive attention to what magazines offered, especially to members of the British working class. Because his publisher warned him of the possibility of intellectual property lawsuits, he simply made up extensive amounts of material that such publications might have offered, in the process showing just how fully and imaginatively he understood their content and emotional power. Tellingly, if for the prewar period Hoggart's attention was on both ethnography and analysis of print culture, for the postwar period he focused even more on popular magazines and gave no evidence of having direct let alone empathetic ethnographic readings of what he described.

Again and again in the book Hoggart drew on canonical writers, most often to use their insights to illuminate the lives of ordinary people. He began the second section of the book, on the postwar world, with a quote from Alexis de Tocqueville. In the 1950s, American social critics used the insights of the French writer to critique the emptiness of middle-class culture. In contrast, Hoggart used Tocqueville's warning about "a virtuous materialism" that might "enervate the soul, and noiselessly unbend its spring of action" to underscore his belief that materialism was enervating the souls of Britain's working class. Most of the canonical sources Hoggart drew on were novels and literary criticism. He wrote of how his grandmother's talk "had something of the elemental quality of Anglo-Saxon poetry." He frequently drew on the works on T. S. Eliot, in one instance to illuminate the lives of "the partly stoic, partly take-life-as-it-comes 'lower orders.'" Again and again he called on Matthew Arnold, for example offering as an epigraph to the chapter on the postwar "Candy-Floss World" Arnold's statement that people "will try to give to the masses, as they call them, an intellectual food prepared and adapted in the way they think proper." He continually showed how novelists help us understand the world, quoting at length George Eliot's description of a village parson. He compared gangster novels with Faulkner's *Sanctuary*, seeing the former as narrow and banal and the latter evidencing "a gifted, varied and complex perception." This deployment of the high to illuminate the low simultaneously privileged the high and suggested one way of bringing together the high and low by juxtaposing them in parallel ways.[39]

The most complicated and significant debt Hoggart discharged in *The Uses of Literacy* was to F. R. Leavis. Like McLuhan (whose *The Mechanical Bride* he listed among his sources and which he had read while at Hull), Hoggart took up the challenge of applying Leavisite literary analysis to popular culture.[40] Unlike Leavis and McLuhan, Hoggart did not look back to a preindustrial utopia. Although he was intensely aware of the danger of romanticizing the culture of the industrial working class, he appreciated its organic wholeness. Committed like Leavis to a hierarchical view of culture, he nonetheless made distinctions between commercial culture that was good, because its authenticity rested on its connection to the working class, and that which was not, because it was imposed by capitalism, a division he saw emerging around 1945. Hoggart also assumed that consumers of popular literature were not passive and he rejected a simple equation of standardization with evil. For Hoggart, both the popular culture of his youth in a working-class neighborhood and the high culture he studied (and later taught) at university provided ways of opposing postwar mass culture. However qualified was Hoggart's adoption of Leavis, he shared with Leavis (and with Roland Barthes and McLuhan) a hostility to capitalism, a preference for the power and quality of high culture, and a skepticism about the values of commercial culture. In fundamental ways, the Leavisite commitment to high culture and opposition to the depredations of mass culture fundamentally shaped Hoggart's response to commercial culture, especially for the postwar period.[41]

Transformation of British Culture
from the Interwar Years to the Postwar Ones

Hoggart drew a dramatic and depressing contrast between a vibrant British pre-1940 working-class culture and one threatened after World War II. In the first half of the book, an exploration of working-class culture during his own youth in the 1920s and 1930s, Hoggart emphasized how the persistence of class and family traditions, as well as selective adaptation, enabled the English working class to resist the inroads of mass culture. He focused on genuine, deeply held folk traditions, something most American cultural analysts had neglected since the late 1930s. He revealed how members of the working class found pleasure in commercial culture. He recreated a home- and neighborhood-centered world suffused by the values of tolerance, community, fatalism, concreteness, and class consciousness. He evoked the specificity and palpability of the world in which he had grown up. "A good 'living room,'" he wrote, describing what he called "the warm heart of the family," had to "provide three principal things: gregariousness, warmth and plenty of good food." He wrote movingly about pleasure, of "a mild hedonism, one informed by a more deeply-rooted sense— that the big and long-distance rewards are not for them." He captured the richness of working-class life. "Their energy in insisting on a place for, and in enjoying, their traditional kinds of amusement and recreation" in music halls and at pubs pointed to "a sprawling, highly-ornamental, rococo extravagance." Hoggart did not find the quest for happiness through commercial culture immoral or corrupting. "In all these acts," he wrote after describing raucous parties or excursions, "one is 'aving a go,' a fling, making a splash. It is a short-lived splash," he insisted, "but a good one, because most of the rest of life is humdrum and regulated." The pursuit of what might appear to be materialistic pleasures was "less an expression of a desire for a heavily material and possession-laden life than an elementary, allegorical and brief statement of a better, a fuller life."[42]

In contrast to Hoggart's picture of a vibrant, gritty prewar working class stood his presentation of the postwar "candy-floss world" of the working class so visible in print media and in music. After World War II, Hoggart insisted, "mass publicists," whose work appeared in cheap magazines, made their appeals "more insistently, effectively and in a more comprehensive form today than they were earlier." At the heart of Hoggart's analysis was a sophisticated sense of how social processes transformed culture. He showed the changes in what he called aspects of the "mental climate" but later generations would call *mentalities*. If in the interwar period the working classes used freedom, equality, and progress to build gritty lives in which materialism was enjoyed but circumscribed, now mass publicists took these values and gave them new meanings.

As a consequence, the older idea reconciling pleasure and struggle opened "the way to a soft mass-hedonism." The older sense of loyalty to one's social group "turned into an arrogant and slick conformity." Older notions of progress now fed a sense of an endless progress in which materialism was central.[43]

Although members of the working class did not totally abandon earlier commitments, the messages offered by mass publicists now tempted "a physically and materially emancipated working-class" to embrace materialism, kinds of self-gratification that he characterized as hedonistic. Drawing on D. H. Lawrence's notion of an "'anti-life,'" Hoggart saw a postwar working-class world "full of a corrupt brightness, of improper appeals and moral evasions." Progress, equality, and freedom, once vital values, were corrupted. The first was now linked with materialism; the second, with "a moral leveling"; and the third with "endless irresponsible pleasure." The assault by mass media on the working class threatened to trivialize, fragment, and personalize their lives. Relative affluence had made them freer, but this was a "freedom of a vast Vanity Fair of shouting indulgences."[44]

If in the first half of the book Hoggart used literary analysis to understand a wide range of aspects of working-class culture, in the second half he focused on showing how an appreciation of high culture underscored how poor in quality was what mass publicists had to offer. He pointed to George Eliot's description of an Anglican village parson as "evidence of the richness of texture which a very good writer will give to an apparently simple description of character." In contrast, his analysis of popular magazines revealed their moral and stylistic vacuity. Postwar popular writing gave no indication "of the fibre of life," opened no possibility of active enjoyment. It demanded nothing of the reader. "We are," Hoggart wrote as he drove home his point with charged language, "in a pallid half-light of the emotions." The result was "only the constant trickle of tinned-milk-and-water which staves off the pangs of a positive hunger and denies the satisfactions of a solidly-filling meal." Yet as depressing as his judgment was, Hoggart rejected the notion of false consciousness, "some sort of plot by 'the authorities', a clever way of keeping the working-classes quietly doped." Rather, he saw the writers of this vacuous prose, often from the very class that now read what they wrote, as having a relationship with their readers that was reciprocal. Writers and readers shared "fantasy worlds," with authors acting "as picture-makers for what is behind the readers' daydreams" but which the readers could not express in prose.[45]

Hoggart insisted that he did not assume for the earlier period an authentic working-class culture on which the media had made no inroads. However, he did think the change after World War II was significant. "We are moving towards the creation of a mass culture," Hoggart wrote. "The remnants of what was at least in part an urban culture 'of the people' are being destroyed; and . . . the new mass culture is in some important ways less healthy than the often rather crude culture it is replacing."[46]

Class, Culture, and Sex in Interwar and Postwar Britain

Hoggart's contrast between interwar and postwar Britain enabled him to intervene in the post-1945 debate in Britain about the future of the working class in an increasingly affluent nation as he resisted the omnipresent ideology of classlessness. Indeed, he opened the book by casting a somewhat skeptical eye on the notion that "there are no working-classes in England now, that a 'bloodless revolution' has taken place which has so reduced social differences that already most of us inhabit an almost flat plain, the plain of the lower middle- to middle-classes." He did not believe in class conflict in the ways Marxists did and he opposed a notion of the working class as a fixed entity. Moreover, in his book he intentionally avoided focusing on the members of the working class who led trade unions and radical organizations. Yet he strongly opposed the view that economic growth and spreading education had transformed Britain's working class into a middle class. Hoggart's discussion of sex and sexuality in the pre– and post–World War II periods provides a vivid example of how he envisioned changes in the worlds the working classes inhabited. For its time, his discussion was unusually frank, direct, and earthy. He wrote of how his grandmother had discussed, "with rough amusement," how "irregular intercourse behind the pulpit at chapel became popular." He openly mentioned methods of contraception, telling of a cheap "sheath" bursting, perhaps when a husband made "demands awkwardly after a night at the club." Attentive to the gendered nature of sexual experiences, he noted that girls more than boys escaped from "bitty, promiscuous sexual experience." For boys sexual talk and experience were common. From their early teens onward, "working-class boys' talk, then, is very often of sex adventures, of how easy such and such a girl is to 'feel' or to 'get down.'" In contrast, for married adult men and women, Hoggart described a situation where "sexual matters do seem nearer the surface" yet embarrassment was common. For the working class there was thus both sexual earthiness and "a great shyness about some aspects of sex—about discussing it 'sensibly', about being seen naked, or even about undressing for the act of sex." If for the 1920s and 1930s Hoggart focused on the vivid sexual experience of working-class people, for the postwar period his eyes were on representations of sexuality that the media offered, especially for working-class audiences. Like

McLuhan, Hoggart wrote of how the mass media fragmented women's bodies. Like many New York intellectuals, he feared, as he wrote a year after the book's publication, that Britain was "moving towards a sort of cultural classlessness." As evidence he pointed to television producing what American observers called "Blandness."[47]

From Vital Workers to Dangerous Youth

Hoggart's picture of postwar youth culture brought together his concerns about how popular culture and Americanization were corrupting young Britons in ways that undermined the interwar working-class world his book so powerfully evoked. If to American observers by the mid-1950s television was the source of danger, for Hoggart the threat came from popular music. This was partly because television came more slowly to Britain than to the United States; in fact, Hoggart later reported that only after the book's publication did his family purchase a TV set. Hoggart located the problematic new media in the world of teenage males, many of them from the working class in British cities, whom he called "Juke-Box Boys." They stood in contrast to the uprooted "Scholarship Boys," like himself, whom he treated so sympathetically. Reflecting the emergence of a generation gap, when he discussed working-class youth Hoggart struck a highly moralistic note, reminiscent of how his American counterparts discussed juvenile delinquency. Disappointed that working-class youth chose the popular rather than the elevated, Hoggart displayed little of his anti-elitist and ethnographic tone that suffused so much of the book. Even sharper was the contrast between Hoggart's stance and the writings on working-class young men that his successors at Birmingham, Stuart Hall and Dick Hebdige most notably, would later articulate. Moreover, Hoggart's literary training left him ill-equipped to think analytically, let alone sympathetically, about new cultural forms. He did not have "the critical equipment," he announced in 1957, to come to terms with contemporary popular music.[48]

What made British youth culture so problematic for Hoggart was its connection to Americanization, race, and sexuality. He was writing at a time when, as Tony Judt notes, "for the first time in European history, young people started buying things themselves," with sartorial and musical choices as the clear markers of a new generation. The most popular tunes in Britain in the mid-1950s to which the jukebox boys were surely listening were by Bill Haley and the Comets (who toured Britain in the fall of 1956), Elvis Presley, Carl Perkins, Buddy Holly, Little Richard, and Chuck Berry. This was music by African Americans and by white Americans who were so profoundly shaped by their own encounters with African Americans. The jukebox boys, Hoggart intoned in language that resembled Leavis's response to the unwashed masses but not Hoggart's to the interwar working class, "waggle one shoulder or stare, as desperately as Humphrey Bogart, across the tubular chairs." Listening to this music, Hoggart wrote, involved "a peculiarly thin and pallid form of dissipation, a sort of spiritual dry-rot amid the odour of boiled milk." He found these boys members of a "depressing group . . . more exposed than others to the debilitating mass-trends of the day." Hoggart did not have at his disposal the critical equipment to understand British youth partly because class was his main category of social analysis. In contemporary American terms whose racial implications Hoggart probably did not understand, they were lazy, teenage juvenile delinquents or, worse yet, shiftless African Americans. Hoggart appreciated boys, like himself, who were within family and kin networks but bristled at those who seemed outside family, part of an autonomous, dangerous, and potentially classless youth culture. If C. L. R. James could see American culture as an alternative to imperial and class-bound Britain, Hoggart understood Americanization as something destroying an authentic British working class.[49]

For Hoggart the American cultural invasion threatened the working class. Without acknowledging the racial aspects of his language, he talked of an importation from America of "the mythology of the teenage 'gang,' fond of jive and boogie-woogie." What he called "this kind of shiny barbarism" induced youth to adopt "the band-waggon [sic] mentality" that "abrogated personal responsibility for choice." Teenage boys, "with drape-suits, picture ties and an American slouch," listened to American phonograph records, something he later reported he had witnessed while in Goole. Here Hoggart was solidifying stock responses that linked Americanization, youth, mass culture, class dynamics, and Britain's future. "The hedonistic but passive barbarian who rides in a fifty-horse-power bus for threepence to see a five-million-dollar film for one-and-eightpence," he wrote ominously, "is not simply a social oddity; he is a portent." Hoggart was thus reasserting the integrity of the working class precisely when in Britain the definition of class generally and of working class specifically were being transformed.[50]

Hoggart's evaluations of postwar popular culture, including its treatment of sex, rested on a hierarchy of cultures and on sharp judgments. Compared with the artful and profound creations of Eliot or Henry James, what popular prose offered was "a region where nothing real ever happens, a twilight of half-responses automatically given," and a world of "sensation without commitment." Evoking what Lawrence had written, Hoggart said the mass media were corrupt and morally evasive, providing as they did the basis for "endless irresponsible pleasure." Hoggart saw mass entertainments as dangerous not so much because they debased taste as because "they over-excite it, eventually dull it, and finally kill it." He began the conclusion to this book with a discussion of "Resilience" but ended with the statement that "the great new classless class" would under the best of circumstances "regard themselves as free and be told that they were free." He objected "to the more trivial popular entertainments" not because they prevented their audiences from embracing the highbrow but because "they make it harder for people without an intellectual bent to become wise in their own way."[51]

The contrasting attitudes in the book's two sections are both striking and noteworthy. When discussing the response of the working class to commercial culture in interwar England, Hoggart saw resilience and pleasure. However, when he turned his attention to the situation in postwar Britain, he emphasized the threat that American popular culture posed to the integrity of the working class. What had come to replace homes characterized by vibrancy was a youth culture, influenced by an American invasion that threatened to undermine the wholeness of a once-proud working class, turning it into a potentially vacuous middle class that at its peril was abandoning its roots. The question then is why, if Hoggart's evaluation of the prewar working class was so perceptive, even if possibly naive, when it came to the postwar period did he change his evaluation into what David Fowler called "a diatribe more suited to a nineteenth-century Presbyterian pulpit than to a detached work of social and cultural criticism."[52]

To some extent, the difference derived from his and his generation's experience with a whole range of historical changes: the decline of the British Empire and the rise of American hegemony; the weakening of British culture in the immediate postwar period; and the arrival in Britain of a powerful, glossy American popular culture. If in his time abroad during World War II he had experienced Americans "cocooned in their creaturely signs and symbols they had come to associate with their own superior nationhood," the implication for postwar Britain was clear. Feminization, the loss of empire, and American comics, pulp magazines, and movies came together to threaten British culture, that of the working class especially.

There was another issue at work here, the continuing hold of the work of F. R. Leavis on Hoggart's outlook, something that is difficult to overestimate. Drawing on his own experiences in a working-class community in the late 1920s and 1930s, Hoggart was able to use Leavisite methods to picture the vitality of the early twentieth-century working class that Leavis himself would not have accepted. Then when he turned his attention to the postwar world, he aligned himself with Leavis's hostility to modern popular culture. This made it impossible for Hoggart to push forward to a fresh analysis of popular culture. As Stuart Hall later remarked, although Hoggart and others in his generation worked to free themselves from a Leavisite position, "they were doomed to repeat it." Like E. P. Thompson and Williams, Hoggart held to a left Leavisite position that drew on the critique by F. R. Leavis of modern industrialization and modern leisure and emphasized the importance of a community of a saving remnant that would go into the schools and adult education to rescue the people. Also at issue were the dynamics of his relationships to his adult students. Hoggart later wrote of the way literature tutors in adult education, committed to the Leavisite tradition, were interested in how students "learned about 'classical' literature in almost the Leavisite sense, but they *lived* in another world; . . . in the world of newspapers and magazines and radio . . . and pop song."[53]

Reactions to *The Uses of Literacy*

As happened with Roland Barthes, Umberto Eco, and Marshall McLuhan, so with Hoggart: an advertising agency wished to take advantage of his knowledge of patterns of consumption, in one case, to market Mars candy to aspiring working-class consumers. "They asked me to help them plan the publicity campaign for a new cocktail savoury 'aimed at the aspirant lower middle classes,'" he reported in 1960 of an incident that happened a few months after the publication of his book. After he said no to a secretary, he reported, "a bland male executive who bandied names like Riesman, Whyte and Packard, implicitly invited me to join his club of knowing operators who'd read all the best books— and still worked the market." To his credit, Hoggart, unlike his French, Italian, and Canadian counterparts, turned down such offers. He understood that there was a clear line between his work and that of corporate advertisers, between corporate culture and popular culture.[54]

The reviews of Hoggart's book were largely favorable and several deserve special mention. In the pages of *Encounter*, Dwight Macdonald found it compelling and authentic in contrast to Bernard Rosenberg and David M. White's *Mass Culture*, most of whose essays he saw as highly problematic. Writing in the *New Statesman and Nation*, the social historian J. F. C. Harrison hailed the book as showing "us a new and fruitful way forward" within "a field where it is all too easy to fall into the errors of middle-class Marxist romanticism or retreat into fashionable Lucky Jimmery," the latter a reference to *Lucky Jim*, Kingsley Amis's 1954 novel that spoofed the lives of professors at a provincial university. Referring to *Culture and Environment* by F. R. Leavis and Denys Thompson, Harrison remarked that Hoggart used the 1933 book as his "starting-point" to "modify a too-exclusively middle-class intellectual outlook on popular reading habits." Leavis responded to the review sarcastically. Bristling at being accused as having a "'middle-class outlook,'" he noted that his wife's book was precisely what Harrison credited Hoggart's work with being, "'a socio-literary study'" that "'broke new ground'" and "a pioneering inquiry into the old working-class culture of which the new processes of civilization were eliminating the traces."[55]

The review by Raymond Williams was mixed and probing. There was much in *The Uses of Literacy* that Williams admired. It was, he wrote, "a natural successor and complement" to Q. D. Leavis's *Fiction and the Reading Public*. If in the earlier book the public was "really only present in the title," Hoggart actually saw members of the audience as people. He congratulated Hoggart for avoiding "the older formula" of "enlightened minority, degraded mass" because, unlike conservative critics, Hoggart, recognizing in himself "the ties that still bind," understood that the masses were his own people. Unlike Orwell, Williams commented, Hoggart wrote "not as a visitor, but as a native." At its best moments, he credited Hoggart's book with having created an amalgam of the personal and observational that was "almost comparable with successful imaginative creation in its own right." Williams concluded his review with the assertion that Hoggart's was "a voice to listen to and to welcome." Yet Williams believed that Hoggart had encountered but left unresolved major interpretative problems. In trying to mix the personal and sociological, at times he failed to distinguish among forms as well as between the generalizeable and the individually idiosyncratic. He had been unable to free himself from either Arnoldian commitments or from sentimental ideas about the good old days among the working class. Moreover, for Williams, Hoggart too easily elided working-class and popular culture, the latter of which was, for Williams "instituted, financed and operated by the commercial *bourgeoisie*" and not by the working classes who were a minority of its consumers.[56]

At the time and especially in ensuing decades, critics took issue with Hoggart on a number of issues. They have insisted that he underestimated the attractiveness American popular culture had for the British working class in much of the twentieth century, but especially in the period after World War II. Indeed, what Hoggart said in the 1990s of Q. D. Leavis's response to working-class culture could just as well be said of his 1957 reaction to youth culture: "There was a kind of separation from the material she was writing about which didn't allow her to understand as well as she might have done what it really meant to people." Critics have also noticed the ways in which Hoggart's emphasis on the home and family as the centers of working-class life ensured a depoliticized view, one which minimized or even neglected the importance of working-class and trade union commitments. They pointed out that Hoggart's emphasis on the home and neighborhood led him to neglect the world of production. They explored how Hoggart's focus on a woman-centered home prompted him to offer a feminized but hardly feminist picture. Scholars have noted that Hoggart presented a homogenized picture of the British working class, one that focused mainly on its more respectable elements. In the process, among the groups in Hunslet and areas like it whom he neglected to include (or passed over without pausing) were the Irish Roman Catholics, Jews, more recent immigrants from South Asia and the Caribbean, and people with unconventional sexualities. Critics have demonstrated that the very jukebox boys and young men whom Hoggart critiqued for their empty embrace of what he saw as a vapid, candy floss popular culture were envisioned differently by Hall and Hebdige. Unlike Hoggart, they saw Teddy Boys, who emerged in Britain in the early 1950s, as teens who shaped a vital youth culture by using new forms of cultural expression, music and dress especially, as ways of heroically resisting and transforming forces that threatened to overwhelm them. Thus, Hoggart was not ready, as those he inspired would be, to see in postwar working-class youth signs of resistance through popular culture.[57]

The Uses of Literacy: An Assessment

Hoggart's analysis of the impact of commercial culture was forceful and problematic. He understood the deep and sustained traditions that enabled workers and their families to resist (or assimilate on their own terms) the inroads of the powerful force of popularization. He offered a sophisticated analysis of the relationship of producer and audience, exploring the way popular writers acted as "picture-makers for what is behind the readers' daydreams." He was persistently skeptical about whether the act of purchasing provided conclusive evidence of impact. At key moments, he treated commercial culture as a series of texts to be read not for evidence of moral weakness but as ways to understand the symbolic dimensions of people's lives. The "rococo extravagance" of the prewar working class, he wrote, did not involve a chase after materialism but a pursuit of a better life. His emphasis on the allegorical and nonmaterial qualities of popular expression, which he normally located in the interwar period, underscored the way he understood how commercial culture fostered symbolic communication. Ultimately, Hoggart resisted the notion of a conspiracy to keep the working class in a soporific state. For the postwar period he believed that those who controlled the media tempted a "materially emancipated working-class to have a largely material outlook" by transforming its earlier commitment to tolerance into hedonism and indulgence. He found the older values of loyalty, openness, and commitment to family and neighbors more healthy than the "commercial values—pride, ambition, outdoing your acquaintances, show for its own sake, conspicuous consumption." In the final reckoning, however, he insisted on the importance of the heroic agency the working class relied on in its encounters with popular culture.[58]

With *The Uses of Literacy*, Hoggart provided a powerful, nuanced consideration of class and culture. If in the second half he could not always contain the harshness of his moral judgments about youth culture and mass media, in much of the book he provided a subtle and compelling model of how to understand the ways in which cultural transmission took place between the working class and mass culture. Especially in the first half, he treated the relationship between high, low, and mass culture in dynamic ways. He legitimized the serious, academic study of popular culture. Distancing himself from parts of the Leavisite tradition, he did not see members of the working class as passive recipients of mass culture, incapable of developing a means of resistance based on the strength of their heritage. The people among whom he grew up, and by implication millions of others from a wide variety of social backgrounds, were active audience members capable of shaping and creating culture from their own resources. He worked hard to suggest how to reconcile what others kept separate, the high culture of canonical writers and the anthropological culture of ordinary people; the humanities and the social sciences; literary analysis and social criticism. He saw the working out of profound moral questions in both the writings of great novelists and the lives of the people among whom he had grown up. He avoided grand narratives of progress or immiseration and instead focused in an exemplary manner on the dailiness and specificity of the people whose lives he explored. What marked his vision, especially when he came to understand the culture of young men living in cities and listening to American music, was the way he adapted the Leavisite vision by seeing an organic society not in preindustrial rural England but in the British urban working class of the interwar period. Still, his achievement was considerable, pointing forward as it did to new understandings of issues of cultural hierarchy and moral judgment when applied to the working class.[59]

Yet with all its limitations and possibilities, *The Uses of Literacy* helped transform British cultural studies. Its publication also transformed its author's life. In 1959 Hoggart moved to the University of Leicester, not to an extramural program but to an English department; and in 1962 to the University of Birmingham, where he founded and served as the first director of its Center for Contemporary Cultural Studies, which opened in the fall of 1964. His 1957 book put him on a path toward a distinguished career: he had an important role in shaping British cultural institutions and intellectual life and through his work at UNESCO that of Western Europe as well.[60]

Hoggart stood on the cusp of major changes in the ways writers responded to consumer culture. He pointed back when he attacked British youth in highly moralistic terms. He was a precursor of future responses when he used an anthropological approach to appreciate the engagement of the British working class with popular culture in the interwar period. Meanwhile, while Hoggart was in provincial Britain working on *The Uses of Literacy*, members of the Independent Group were meeting in London and responding much more positively than Hoggart to popular culture, including its American expressions.

Interlude

David Riesman, Marshall McLuhan, and Richard Hoggart all made major strides toward new understandings of commercial culture. They questioned the certainty with which others, such as Clement Greenberg and Dwight Macdonald, divided high from mass or popular culture, and in the process they moved from a hierarchical toward horizontal or parallel rankings of cultural productions. They worked against seeing consumers as passive. Riesman, and to a lesser extent McLuhan, understood the exchange between producers and consumers as dynamic. All three questioned the persuasiveness of moralistic approaches to commercial culture and instead emphasized playfulness and pleasure. They also explored what it might mean to think of commercial culture as involving symbolic communication. They were all interested in the mediation of structures of feeling by commercial culture, the looming triumph of market mentality, the pressures in the postwar world on people to adhere to group standards, and the importance of the search for authenticity.

Gender and class played quite different roles in their analysis. McLuhan fully expressed a sense of crisis in the relationships between the sexes, with the male-headed family coming out on the short end of a dynamic driven by homosexuals and women. In contrast, the other two tentatively offered a more nuanced view: Hoggart with his presentation of a woman-centered household for the interwar period and Riesman, despite his focus on men, with his tentative exploration of new choices for women. Class also had quite varied roles in their analyses. Without acknowledging that it was so, McLuhan was describing a new middle class in America and Canada. Riesman had the material for a capacious analysis that included African Americans and members of the working class but chose instead to focus his attention on the white middle and upper middle classes. Hoggart's attention was on the working class, at a time when postwar prosperity was profoundly reshaping the meaning of class and gender in Britain.

Their attitudes to emerging forms of popular culture, especially American ones, varied widely. Particularly when it came to postwar youth culture, Hoggart, though celebrating earlier forms of expression, mixed horror and lack of comprehension about teen culture and its music, cultural expressions that came from America and influenced young Britons. In contrast, reluctant fascination characterized the response of Riesman and McLuhan. McLuhan used his detachment to control his outrage. Like Riesman, he ended up with an ambivalent position, albeit for different reasons. Indeed, uncertainty wove in and out of the reactions of all of them. Eugene Lunn, writing of Hoggart and Riesman, points to the "multiple and ambiguous structures" of their approaches. Riesman, McLuhan, and Hoggart wrote in ways that left them open, as Lunn would say, to being seen as joining those who decried the arrival of mass society, when they were actually offering a more complicated intervention into that debate. What is striking and significant historically is that new ways of understanding popular culture were emerging in the early 1950s from such disparate sources, Riesman's blend of Frankfurt School theory and American empirical sociology, McLuhan's combination of elite literary theory and conservative Catholicism, and Hoggart's mixture of the Leavisite and working-class traditions.[1]

Their politics, not always clear, were varied: McLuhan's Tory radicalism, Hoggart's blend of socialism and elitism, Riesman's combination of pluralism with his emphasis on sources of autonomy in a conforming society and his opposition to American foreign policy. Their analyses did not allow for a full explanation of the relationship between popular culture and capitalism. As a result, it is important not to overstate the gains they made toward new understandings of popular culture. To begin with, there is the question of the extent of their impact during the 1950s. McLuhan's *The Mechanical Bride* had little resonance outside small circles of readers. Although Hoggart's impact was extensive, in the 1950s it remained confined to Britain. Riesman is the great exception, but it is notable how commonly he was misread, as someone who did not offer new ways of understanding popular culture but instead participated in the usual debates and on familiar terms.

In other ways, their contributions involved hesitant steps forward. Take the issue of sexuality, one so central to the development of a view of commercial culture in which pleasure was central. In *The Mechanical Bride*, McLuhan lamented the way advertisements transformed human bodies into a series of mechanical parts more geared to commercial than erotic pleasure, even as he embraced heterosexuality as normative. After the mid-1960s his ideas about the relationship between technology and emotions fostered sensuousness in the counterculture, even though he remained committed to monogamy and heterosexuality. Yet at least from his days in Cambridge in the mid-1930s, he worried about how feminism spurred homosexuality and how homosexuals threatened to dominate cosmopolitan culture. Sexuality was not central to Hoggart's vision: though he offered a frank sense of working-class sexual experiences, he was recoiling from the more open sexuality of contemporary youth culture and its link to commercial culture. Riesman was struggling to reconceptualize relationships between men and women and to give heterosexual sexuality a more prominent and positive cast in cultural criticism.

Nor were their contributions to new ways of understanding consumer culture complete in other ways. Their toppling of cultural hierarchies was hardly unalloyed. McLuhan and Hoggart, exquisitely trained in literature, remained committed to an exalted position for modernist culture, however much they used it to appreciate the creativity of popular culture. Although the writings of all three men tentatively suggested the ways ordinary people might use popular culture as a vehicle for resistance, for them, resistance or creativity remained largely the bailiwick of intellectuals or some version of the avant-garde. Similarly tentative was their shift toward understanding consumer culture as involving symbolic communication. Hoggart embraced this possibility for the working-class families he knew in his youth but not the youth he witnessed in his adulthood. McLuhan remained torn between seeing commercial culture as morally reprehensible and as creative symbolically. Nor did he (or Hoggart when it came to the postwar youth culture) develop a full sense of the dynamic relationship between producer and consumer. On the issue of symbolic communication and the reciprocity between producers and audience, it was Riesman who made important yet tentative steps in new directions. In the 1960s, others would move beyond the hesitancy with which Riesman, McLuhan, and Hoggart approached new understandings of popular culture.

The 1960s changed the terms for understanding commercial culture. What had seemed in the 1950s a vast chasm between avant-garde or high culture and popular or middlebrow culture narrowed or even closed dramatically in the 1960s. The music of the Beatles, the paintings of Andy Warhol, even the irony-laden Batman series, in suggesting that popular culture could be experimental, called into question the ability to make a clear distinction between levels of culture. Unlike an earlier generation that had declared folk culture dead, writers and performers in the 1960s drew on minority subcultures that had hardly disappeared in the 1950s, African American, homosexual, and working class among them. Distancing themselves from the stances of Macdonald and Greenberg, intellectuals offered serious considerations of emerging—and widely appreciated—forms of culture. As John Cawelti observed in 1968, the decade had witnessed the coming of age of the "first intellectual generation which has really grown up with mass culture" and as a consequence was more interested in accepting, understanding, and playing with it than rejecting it or moralizing about it. These cultural transformations helped undercut the distinction between high and low cultures. Social protests and new technologies dramatically shortened the physical and psychic distance between experts and consumers, producers and audiences. The way protesters used popular culture underscored how social change came not as some critics claimed from the avant-garde but from insurgent social groups, including African Americans, women, and young people. The music of performers such as Bob Dylan, the Beatles, and Nina Simone placed popular culture in a central position in the struggles for social change and social justice. Musicians, mime troops, and street performers promoted a culture that was experimental and expressive even as it was deeply implicated in commercial culture from which it both borrowed and dissented.[2]

Yet already in the early 1950s new perspectives on popular culture were emerging and not just in the writings of Jürgen Habermas, Roland Barthes, Umberto Eco, Walter Benjamin, and C. L. R. James. As the next chapter will reveal, beginning in the early 1950s the artists and cultural critics among London's Independent Group relied on and moved past some of their predecessors, including McLuhan and Riesman. They offered fresh and celebratory appreciations of American popular culture that contrasted with Hoggart's analysis and even with those of two of their sources, McLuhan and Riesman. They replaced hierarchy with a continuum of cultural texts, as they insisted that creativity came not from a small elite but from many sources. They continued the shift from literary theory to anthropology that Riesman had begun to make. They emphasized reciprocity and even resistance as they explored the relationships between producers and audiences. They found in commercial culture more than a modicum of playfulness and pleasure. The writers among the Independent Group, more so than the artists among them or the American pop artists, embraced popular culture naively and with hardly a touch of irony.

The major transition to new understandings came in the 1960s, though the Independent Group had paved the way. By 1964 writers on both sides of the Atlantic had offered new interpretations of commercial culture that emphasized ways in which it enabled pleasurable and symbolically laden exchanges. Stuart Hall and Paddy Whannel's *The Popular Arts* (1964), though indebted to Hoggart's *The Uses of Literacy*, broke fresh ground in its focus on new media and youth culture and its shift from literary theory to anthropology. Tom Wolfe's *The Kandy-Kolored Tangerine-Flake Streamline Baby* (1965) and two books by Herbert Gans, *The Urban Villagers: Group and Class in the Life of Italian-*

Americans (1962) and *The Levittowners: Ways of Life and Politics in a New Suburban Community* (1967), revealed how an appreciation of the worlds of the working and lower-middle classes could take the place of an elitist disdain for popular culture. Susan Sontag's "Notes on 'Camp'" (1964) made clear that an embrace of sexuality, especially sexual expressions that diverged from heterosexual norms, played a key role in connecting commerce and pleasure. Then in the early 1970s Reyner Banham's *Los Angeles: The Architecture of the Four Ecologies* (1971) and Robert Venturi and Denise Scott Brown's *Learning from Las Vegas* (1972) made clear, as Wolfe had already done, how critical to new understandings of consumer culture was an appreciation of the cultural expressiveness of cities far from London and New York.

Chapter 6

Pop Art from Britain to America

In contrast to Richard Hoggart's emphasis on working-class culture and the dangers of Americanization stood the arguments of a handful of British critics, members of the Independent Group (IG). In 2007 the novelist David Lodge commented on the work of Hoggart, once his colleague in Birmingham, but he could have been talking about the IG as well. The author of *The Uses of Literacy*, he wrote, represented the "displacement of a literary establishment that was constituted of ageing remnants of pre-war modernism, Bloomsbury, and bohemianism, that was predominantly middle to upper-middle class, public-school, and Oxbridge-educated, domiciled in central London or the country, and enamoured of Abroad," meaning Continental Europe. Now a new generation, those involved in workers' education (including Hoggart), the Angry Young Men, and members of the IG, displaced older traditions of cultural criticism. A number of factors came together to shape the IG's view of commercial culture: social class, Britain's postwar experiences, the attitudes its citizens had about America's popular culture, and intellectual traditions. Mostly from the working class or marginally in the middle class, having taken advantage of the 1944 Education Act to go to university as few if any members of their families had done, they developed new stances toward commercial culture. The IG differed from Hoggart in important ways, most clearly in their attitudes toward postwar popular culture and Americanization and their perspectives on social class. With their focus on working-class and lower middle-class commercial culture, they played key roles in understanding American popular culture, and in naming pop art in the 1950s and curating it in the 1960s. Moreover, from the IG there emerged in the early 1970s in the writings of Reyner Banham and Denise Scott Brown two of the most intriguingly positive assessments of American commercial culture.[1]

The IG met in London from 1952 to 1955 at the Institute of Contemporary Arts (ICA) and discussed the relationships between art, technology, and popular culture.[2] With their ideas reaching audiences outside their small circle only late in the decade, beginning in the early 1950s and well into the 1970s these British critics and artists offered richly suggestive reflections on the relationship between art and consumer culture. Weary of moralism, they emphasized how mass media involved a process of symbolic communication or, as Lawrence Alloway put it in 1959, the conveying of "the drama of possessions." They coined the phrase "pop art" in the mid-1950s, defining it not as what Andy Warhol and others would soon produce but as the products of mass media. "Pop Art is," Richard Hamilton wrote, "Popular (designed for a mass audience)/Transient (short-term solution)/Expendable (easily forgotten)/Low cost/Mass produced/ Young (aimed at youth)/Witty/Sexy/Gimmicky/Glamorous/Big business."[3]

This epigrammatic statement captures many of the essential elements of the outlook of the IG: the fascination with mass media and commercial culture, the emphasis on youth and the erotic, and the focus on the expendable. What Clement Greenberg in 1962 said of Alloway was true of others as well: he was "an equally ardent, practically a sectarian champion of most things American." In addition, IG members revealed as dynamic the relationship between producers and consumers of objects of desire. Skeptical of hierarchy, they called for a transformation of the relationship between high art and popular culture. In 1966 Alloway captured what they had in common. They shared, he remarked, "a vernacular culture." They focused their attention on "mass-produced urban culture: movies, advertising, science fiction, Pop music." They did not feel "the dislike of commercial culture standard among many intellectuals, but accepted it as a fact, discussed it in detail, and consumed it enthusiastically." The result was that they "took Pop culture out of the realm of 'escapism,' 'sheer entertainment,' 'relaxation,'" and instead treated "it with the seriousness of art. These interests put" them "in opposition both to the supporters of indigenous folk art and to anti-American opinion in Britain," and, he might have added, both Marxist notions of how popular culture fostered false consciousness and elitist ideas of culture's transcendence.[4]

One observer has recently remarked, with only some exaggeration and in ways that are truer for the writers than the artists among them, that the IG "embraced contemporary American popular culture . . . with the whole-hearted enthusiasm of consumers." Members of the IG hardly agreed on everything. To a considerable extent the artists among them (for example, Eduardo Paolozzi and Nigel Henderson, and to a lesser extent John McHale) were more interested in technique, while content, especially the products of American popular culture, compelled the writers, such as Banham and Alloway, whom one artist in 1956 called "these effing word men." Characteristically, those most interested in technique were more likely to remain in Britain while those most compelled by American popular culture (Alloway, Banham, and McHale) moved to the United States.[5]

Pop Art in Postwar Britain

In Britain, the theory and practice of pop art emerged in particular cultural and historical contexts. During World War II American soldiers had exposed Britons to new trends in consumer culture, something that repulsed Hoggart but that others found attractive. In the postwar period, many in Britain, their lives shaped by the privations of the Depression, war, and postwar recovery (with rationing not fully ending until 1954 but with the worst over just as the IG first emerged), looked across the Atlantic at a more affluent United States, a nation some Brits saw as having a flourishing and attractive commercial culture. As Lodge noted in 1975, for a British academic the legacy of war and postwar rationing, American movies, and mass magazines created "a deep psychic link between American English and the goodies of which he was deprived by rationing." Similarly, as IG member Banham recalled, for his generation, having spent its formative years "surviving the horrors and deprivations" of World War II, "the fruits of peace had to be tangible." They could not find this in what one critic later called "the austere visual and cultural context" of postwar Britain. Rather, they discovered pleasure and playfulness as they looked at glossy American magazines and lavished their attention, as Banham wrote, on "the graphics and the colour-work in adverts for appliances that were almost inconceivable in power-short Britain, and food ads so luscious you wanted to eat them."[6]

Among discussants in the IG, the engagement with American commercial culture involved a criticism of the hostility to Americanization on the part of some elite and working-class intellectuals. In a more parochial sense, they were rejecting several British traditions. Henderson reported in 1947 that on a visit to France, Paolozzi was "busy reacting violently against anything 'English.'"[7] After all, Paolozzi was the son of Italian émigré parents, his father killed during his transportation as an enemy alien. Though not all IG members took such a strong position, they nonetheless opposed much of their homeland's elite cultural tradition. They stood against the art criticism of Roger Fry and his commitment to "disinterested contemplation." They especially opposed Herbert Read, the influential British critic and a major figure at the ICA, who celebrated European modernist fine art, such as the sculpture of Henry Moore, based on the capacity of artistic geniuses to transcend the mundane. They rejected the traditional iconography so evident at the Festival of Britain exhibition in London in 1951. They opposed what David Riesman in 1952 had identified as how the traditional middle-class and school officials in England saw Hollywood "as a source of disruptive leisure patterns, of vulgarity, spendthrift living, and false values." Above all they rejected Hoggart's fear of the impact of Americanization on British and especially working-class and youth cultures.[8]

Independent Group: Composition and Inspirations

Among the most prominent of the IG's members were the art critic Lawrence Alloway, the architectural critic Reyner Banham, the artist and critic Richard Hamilton, the photographer Nigel Henderson, the artist and critic John McHale, the sculptor Eduardo Paolozzi, the architects Alison and Peter Smithson, and the sculptor and film maker William Turnbull. Some of them came from the middle class. At least one of them, Nigel Henderson, had close connections to the Bloomsbury circle. Born in London, he attended public schools and from 1934 to 1936 studied biology at Chelsea Polytechnic, followed by three years as an assistant to a curator at the National Gallery. After serving in the Royal Air Force during World War II, he took courses at the Slade School of Fine Art for several years beginning in 1946. He soon turned his attention to photography, experimenting with composition and techniques. Beginning in 1948 he took photographs of the storefronts in London's working-class East End that captured their commercial bricolage. Peter Smithson was born into a middle-class family in a market town in northeast England. Before and after service in World War II, he attended King's College School of Architecture in Newcastle-upon-Tyne and then spent 1948–49 at the Royal Academy School. Alison (neé Gill) Smithson was born in Sheffield, the daughter of a father who was an artist and school principal and a mother who was a weaver. She met her husband while she was studying at King's College School of Architecture and they married in 1949, together going on to develop an architectural practice.[9]

Others came from more humble origins, benefiting even more from the expansion of higher education in postwar Britain. The parents of Paolozzi were immigrants from Italy who ran a small shop in Edinburgh, and their son spent World War II interned as an enemy alien. Banham had grown up during the 1930s in a working-class household in Norwich, although members of his family, involved in the Labour Party and in religious nonconformism, had entered the middle class. Banham's teachers at a local public school tried to persuade him to go to Cambridge but a long-standing interest in technology impelled him instead to train as an engineer with an airplane company during World War II. He went on to the Courtauld Institute of Art in London, earning a B.A.

in 1952. He then began to work on his doctorate, under the direction of Nikolaus Pevsner, with *Theory and Design in the First Machine Age* (1960) as the published version of his thesis. In the mid-1950s, Banham served as an editor and
writer for *Architectural Review*, where he emerged as a keen observer of contemporary design and architecture. Richard Hamilton grew up in a working-class
family in London. Of all members of the IG, his education was the most varied
but hardly atypical: at age twelve illegally attending a London Country Council
adult education class in art; a brief stint at a technical college in London in 1936;
training at the Royal Academy Schools before and after the war; during the
war, work on commercial art in the Design Unit and the recording company
EMI; three years at the Slade School of Fine Art (1948–51). Next came teaching
at Central School of Arts and Crafts (1952–53) and, beginning in 1953, at King's
College in Newcastle, then part of Durham University. As a biographer noted,
these varied experiences "prepared the ground for his subsequent exploration
of the means by which received boundaries between 'high' and 'low' art could
be eliminated." In 1955 Hamilton organized an exhibition that explored how
the design of automobiles spoke to issues of power, social status, and sexuality,
in much the same way that Continental writers such as Roland Barthes, Umberto Eco, and Jean Baudrillard were addressing those issues in their writing.[10]

Of the IG members, Alloway was the most important art critic. The son of
lower-middle-class parents, he grew up in Wimbledon, outside London. Confined to bed by tuberculosis as an adolescent, he voraciously read comic books,
continuing his education in popular culture later as an avid fan of American
western movies. Although he never completed his formal education, beginning
at seventeen he took four years of art history evening courses at the University
of London and at the same time began writing reviews of exhibitions for various British publications. From the late 1940s until he left for America in 1961,
he taught art history at London's National Gallery, the Tate Gallery, Courtauld
Institute of Art, the Arts Council of Great Britain, and the Workers' Education
Association. He worked as an administrator at the ICA beginning in 1954 before losing his position in 1957 because his positive attitude toward the United
States and popular culture clashed with the outlook of the ICA's leaders, Read
especially. Later on he credited his lack of formal education at the university
level for enabling him to think in new ways about popular culture.[11]

If their social origins were varied, by and large members of the Independent Group were from families on the fringes of the middle class. They were
educated by way of what Banham called climbing the educational ladder "hand
over hand," developed an early interest in the United States, and shared involvement with London's leading art institutions. Years later, Alloway sug-

gested the connection between their biographies and their outlooks. Noting
that they lacked formal educations at mainline universities, those involved in
the IG "were somewhat outside the traditional system." They had "grown up
with the mass media," he wrote; "we accepted it, and when we were at that
point in our lives when we might have gone to universities and become predis-
posed towards high culture, we didn't, so we were left free to keep our relish of
the mass media." Thus IG members stood outside the most obvious sources of
social and cultural power in mid-century Britain: the working class that Hoggart both came from and focused on; the academic world, especially as shaped
by Oxford and Cambridge; the upper class; and bohemian literary circles in
London. Insisting on knowledgeable and professional standards as artists and
critics, they found problematic the amateurism of both dilettantes and the in-
dependently wealthy in the British art world.[12]

IG members drew their inspiration from a number of sources. They looked
back to both the playfulness of dadaists earlier in the century and the vorticism
of Wyndham Lewis, the writer and artist who influenced Marshall McLuhan.
Lewis's early paintings captured the dynamism of industrial technology but his
negative reputation as a Nazi sympathizer was hardly rehabilitated with a later
exhibition of his work. Early in their careers, many of them worked directly
with technology and the mass media, developing an interest in commercial
art and in the United States. They relished the vibrancy and heterogeneity of
urban settings. As they pondered the implications of new technology, such as
the transistor, they came to understand the idea of communications as a flow
of information or images even before McLuhan did. They admired the work
of the American designers Buckminster Fuller, Raymond Loewy, and Charles
and Ray Eames. From the writings of Ernst Gombrich they learned to approach
visual culture as what Banham called "symbolic iconography." They took from
Norbert Wiener's *Cybernetics* (1948) a way of thinking about the relationship
between technology and consciousness. The work at the Communication Research Center, established in 1953 at London's University College, offered them
new ways of understanding communication processes. André Malraux's *Museum without Walls* (1952) helped them explore the display of visual materials
in nontraditional settings. Siegfried Giedion's 1948 *Mechanization Takes Command* taught them to understand the relationship between technology, culture,
and art with a special focus on vernacular forms. From Riesman's *The Lonely
Crowd* (1950) and A. C. Spectorsky's *The Exurbanites* (1955) they adopted the
notion that what helped improve mass culture was the feedback sophisticated
consumers gave to designers and manufacturers. This enabled members of the
IG to see the consumer as active rather than passive. As Alloway noted, Ries-

man emphasized how "the mass media give perpetual lessons in assimilation, instruction in role-taking, the use of new objects." McLuhan's *The Mechanical Bride* (1951) also inspired them, a book that had, Banham noted, "semi-legendary" importance to them and that an art historian said was "the chief resource for the IG's analyses of ads." McLuhan's book strengthened their commitment to a postmoralist attitude to consumer culture and to ways of reading it that emphasized the relationship between technology and sexuality.[13]

Visions of (American) Popular Culture
Dancing in Their Heads

Members of the IG approached popular culture from an anthropologist's perspective, less as arbiters of taste and more as interpreters interested in every aspect of the contemporary scene. They often focused on the spectacle and cacophony of visual, commercial culture. The key moment occurred in April 1952 when in his legendary "Bunk" lecture Paolozzi threw on a screen a series of images: in a manner not unlike McLuhan's in the mid-1940s with slide shows, but this time involving not individual images but simultaneous ones, postcards, advertisements, and movie posters. Years later, Henderson could still hear the response of members of the audience, Banham especially, "as a certain amount of embarrassment all around (at such an indecorous non-doctrinaire display) tried to take the mould of levity." Paolozzi's dazzling presentation inspired them to create scrapbooks which they filled playfully with snippets of visual culture. Henderson, for example, developed a series of them beginning in 1952. Taking a bound volume of a traditional publication, such as the *Magazine of Art*, on a seemingly random basis he pasted onto its pages his own drawings, as well as pictures he clipped from popular magazines—of natural scenes, sports events, circus posters, advertisements for American cars, television sets, and neon signs.[14]

Members of the IG saw America as a nation with a social system more open than England's and with a tradition of vernacular art that stood apart from both European modernism and British traditionalism. They preferred the temporal to the supposedly eternal. "Sensitiveness to the variables of our life and economy," Alloway wrote, enables "the mass arts to accompany the changes in our life far more closely than the fine arts which are a repository of time-binding values." They considered it important to judge each cultural field by standards appropriate to it rather than by universal or transcendent criteria. They embraced what in 1955 they labeled an "aesthetics of expendability," something underwritten by changes in consumer demands and technology. When

Banham described the exuberant American automobile designs of the mid-1950s, he remarked that "a good job of body styling should come across like a good musical—no fussing after big, timeless abstract virtues, but maximum glitter and maximum impact." Although apparently unaware of the writings of Walter Benjamin, they understood what Benjamin had explored as the consequences of art in an age of mechanical reproduction. On the one hand, new media, television especially, made it possible for people to give only "marginal attention" while they did other things. On the other hand, new media spurred, Alloway remarked, "intense participation" which involved "a careful discrimination of nuances in the action."[15]

The discussions of the Independent Group at the ICA focused on the relationships between art, urbanism, technology, and mass culture. As Umberto Eco and C. L. R. James were doing at the same time, IG members developed a fascination with science fiction and westerns in print and film. They lavished their attention on American vernacular phenomena that they found promising: not soap operas or romance novels but popular music and clippings from mass magazines that contained advertisements for automobiles, appliances, and household products. They labeled these illustrations "popular art," a term that in its shortened form, "pop art," originally referred to the mass culture products of commercial artists, and not until later to the work of painters or sculptors who turned representations of commercial items into self-consciously fashioned art exhibited in galleries and museums. They focused on how new media fostered sexualized fantasy, with Hollywood stars such as Kim Novak, science fiction, and the novels of Mickey Spillane providing both "datable fashion" and "timeless lust." Similarly, Banham could wax lyrical about the erotic possibility of contemporary American auto design. Leading "body stylists," he wrote in 1955 in "Vehicles of Desire," impart to "their creations qualities of apparent speed, power, brutalism, luxury, snob-appeal, exoticism, and plain common-or-garden sex." If elitist art critics saw auto designs as "a farrago of meaningless ornament," Banham and his colleagues instead believed they were "a means of saying something of breathless, but unverbalizable, consequence to the live culture of the Technological Century."[16]

They thus distanced themselves from the moral, political, and aesthetic position they saw Hoggart representing. In 1962 Banham talked of "sentimental Hoggartry" and noted that Hoggart was among "intelligent socialists" who apparently shared "the opinions of an 'Establishment' that they despise." Years later, Alloway wrote that the pleasures of urban life impelled members of the IG to separate themselves "from the working-class bias" of Hoggart. As Hamilton noted, the author of *The Uses of Literacy* was playing an all-too-familiar and depressing tune: "the end of the world is upon us unless we purge ourselves of the evils of soft living and reject the drive for social and economic advantages." Members of the IG opposed Hoggart's disdain for contemporary commercial culture, especially items that represented the threat of Americanization to postwar Britain. They differed from Hoggart in social location, temperament, orientation, and training. Most of them were less imbedded and identified with the working class; as young adults they lived in London, not in provincial cities and towns.[17]

IG writers also rejected more openly elitist defenses of culture, on both the left and the right. They opposed the tradition that went back to Matthew Arnold and found contemporary expression in the work of T. S. Eliot, F. R. Leavis, Herbert Read, Clement Greenberg, and Dwight Macdonald. Alloway contrasted "mass art" that was "urban and democratic" with elite art associated with "pastoral and upperclass ideas." They emphasized the importance of a shift from print to visual culture: the former encouraging elitism, hierarchy, and heritage; the latter, pluralism and democratic expression. Indeed, in a trenchant 1964 essay, Banham critiqued British adult education for its commitment to create "a nation of Shakespeare lovers" rather than citizens with a capacious range of interpretative skills with which they could understand "an unclassed and largely unclassifiable cultural phenomenon," such as science fiction and commercial art. Both a student and a teacher in adult education programs, Banham found troubling the power of a left, especially within the WEA, "culturally still in the grip of traditional conservative institutions such as universities and above all, Eng. Lit." To Banham and others, popular culture was neither an "opium of the people" nor "compensation for some social deprivation"; rather it was something "so largely consumed and with such enthusiasm and such passion" that critics had to take it seriously. Rather than spending time with "Morris dancing and reed thatching," cultural analysts should appreciate the popular culture enjoyed by Britons, including members of the working class.[18]

IG writers also turned against the idea that art, as a product of superior genius, obtained elevated standing in a cultural hierarchy. Instead they insisted on its connections with the relationships between science, technology, and creativity. This placed them in opposition to those who insisted on the purity and transcendence of design. "Where the mass media depart from the moralists," Hamilton wrote in 1960, "is in their refusal to accept the dogma of permanent values and in their efforts to welcome and promote the machine age with humour and affection." They understood that fine art was "a repository of time-binding values," but they called into question Greenberg's notion of a hierarchy of artistic expression. As Alloway wrote, Greenberg was "fatally prejudiced when he leaves modern fine art." In contrast, they preferred to cross the line between fine and commercial, replacing what Alloway called "frozen layers in a pyramid" with "a continuum." When it came to cultural choices, they preferred both/and to either/or. "Sensitiveness to the variables of our life and economy," Alloway wrote in ways that even placed the popular above the fine, "enable the mass arts to accompany the changes in our life far more closely than the fine arts which are a repository of time-binding values." Taking on the hierarchical notions Macdonald embraced in his 1953 article "A Theory of Mass Culture," McHale explored how high and popular culture enriched each other. Referring to the fine arts, he avowed that "we went off the Cultural Gold Standard decades ago, and have long been in a period of convertible currencies." Consequently, he continued, "there is no inherent 'value' contradiction in enjoying both a comic strip and a symphony." For him "an aura of 'canonized' communication, . . . is now broadcast among a plurality of messages, couched in different cultural vocabularies."[19]

"We grew up with the mass media," Alloway wrote in 1957, which "were established as a natural environment by the time we could see them." Members of the IG were, he noted, "born too late to be adopted into the system of taste that gave aesthetic certainty" to their elders. Consequently, "the pressure of the mass media and the failure of traditional aesthetics combined to unsettle fixed opinion and hint at new pleasures." Banham made clear that his working-class culture was thoroughly Americanized, something he relished rather than rejected. "The live culture, the culture in which we were involved," he wrote in 1964 of his childhood, "was American pulps, things like *Mechanix Illustrated*," *Betty Boop* comic books, and the movies of Charlie Chaplin and Buster Keaton. The result, Alloway remembered, was that IG members developed a yardstick that focused on symbols people relied upon in their lives, turning the art critic into "the spectator or consumer, free to move in a society defined by symbols." As Banham put it, popular culture "has become the language, musical, visual and (increasingly) literary, by which members of the mechanized urban culture" of the developed nations "can communicate with one another in the most direct, lively and meaningful manner." Thus members of the IG believed that commercial culture involved signs through which consumers communicated social meaning.[20]

In working on issues surrounding commercial design, IG members saw the relationship between producers, designers, and consumers in reciprocal terms, in the process imputing to ordinary consumers the power and insight McLuhan had hoped to inspire in them. Hamilton noted that the mass arts sprang not from the masses but from designers, "a professional group with a highly

developed cultural sensibility." IG members understood consumers as sophisticated, diverse interpreters of symbolic images rather than what Alloway called
"one drugged faceless consumer." They did not see consumers manipulated by
a system-driven desire for compensation for the pains inflicted by capitalism.
Like Riesman, they believed commercial culture offered education in what
Alloway called "entries in a descriptive account of a society's communication
system" that served as "a guide to life defined in terms of possessions and relationships." Their job, they believed, was not to judge but to decode the symbols
of mass culture. As Banham said in 1955, the automobile was "a vehicle of popular desire and a dream that money can just about buy." They preferred what
Alloway called "an aesthetics of plenty" that embraced and engaged playfully
with contemporary commercial culture. For them, commercial culture was
both varied and democratic: varied because, unlike what critics of mass culture
feared, it was not homogenous; and democratic because it spoke genuinely of
and to people's aspirations. As Alloway noted in 1959, "a mass audience" was
"a fiction," "numerically dense but highly diversified," with "consumer choice"
increasing as the market was enlarged.[21]

Independent Group: Its Members and Their Art

The art that members of the Independent Group produced amply reflects their
attitude to contemporary commercial culture as a system of symbolic communication, an approach that challenged notions of cultural hierarchies. Members
of the IG did not always agree with one another when it came to how they saw
American consumer culture. In their writings they were more favorably dis-
posed to what they saw coming from across the Atlantic than they were in their
art. In some instances, in their art, they offered what the art historian David
Mellor, describing *"Tory Futurism,"* has called "the apocalyptic sublime, the
ruination of the utopian disciplines of technicism, at the very moment of their
apogee." Yet in their writings and in some of their art, it is possible to see not
only their "conflicted ambivalence" toward popular culture but their conflicted
embrace.[22]

Their most memorable show, This Is Tomorrow, appeared for a month beginning in early September 1956 at the Whitechapel Art Gallery, a year after the
IG had stopped meeting. There they offered a varied series of twelve separate
exhibits, each designed by a three-person team that included young members
from different fields and typically a painter, architect, and sculptor. The overall
effect was to give viewers a sense of what it meant to experience competing,
often disruptive visual environments. The first thing visitors saw as they en-

tered was a space organized like a house of mirrors, one that included a series of dramatic images drawn from contemporary popular culture: Robby the Robot from MGM's science fiction film *Forbidden Planet*, a picture of Marilyn Monroe, a variety of optical illusions, a shiny jukebox playing rock and roll, a huge beer bottle, and a wall covered by movie posters. Recently, the art historian and curator Brian Wallis had written that the funhouse as spectacle at the entrance to This Is Tomorrow "impudently asserted the impermanent, the pleasurable, and the sensorily jarring." At the time, Alloway was chiefly responsible for promotional materials. Writing in *Art News and Review*, he commented that "at the disposal of pulp magazine artists, comic book staff, film studios, their publicity departments, toy manufacturers" were the iconographies of the popular arts, tools "of amazing flexibility and strength." In one of a series of press releases, he referred to the exhibit as "a playground of modern Art."[23]

The show drew what Alloway called record-breaking crowds and exposed the fault lines in British culture. "Where highbrow art makes lowbrow fun," read the headline of a provincial paper. "Perhaps the secret of the exhibition's popularity," remarked an article in the *East London Advertiser*, "is that it has successfully cut across barriers of high-brow and low-brow taste." Others noted the considerable impact the exhibition made on ordinary people. "Children from the working-class neighborhood came in off the street to hang out by the jukebox," a scholar noted later. In contrast, the exhibit offered what one observer called "an easy target for the conservative sniper." Thus, a review in *Apollo*, a leading British arts and antiques magazine, reveals how skeptically, sarcastically, traditionally at least one critic responded. The anonymous author remarked that the installation, as well as the explanations the artists offered for it, provided examples "of undergraduate obscenity and blasphemy." Entire walls, the reviewer noted, "are covered with bits and pieces of magazines, newspapers and cinema posters stuck on haphazard and with lots of bits of naked girls among them." In sum, the author concluded the show was "an untidy mess with a slight nasty-mindedness about it. . . . pretentious bunk." Then in the final paragraph, similar to Hoggart's evocation of jukebox boys, the reviewer noted that at the show "a juke-box . . . screams the poorest kind of popular contemporary music, punctuated by barbaric yawps and squeals." Somewhat similarly, in the *Spectator* the art historian Basil Taylor asserted that "the romanticism of these exhibits finds its promised land in the United States where conditions" were so remote from contemporary Britain. The heroes of those who worked on the exhibit "are the mass-media and advertising experts, the pulp-magazine writers and Professor Wiener." Likewise, another review remarked on how shocking was the "display of today's vulgarity, its film stars, popular music, TV, sex, and science fiction."[24]

The catalog, like the exhibit, was unconventional. As one hostile observer remarked, "typographically [it was] based entirely on the principle of being different, however silly that difference is" and was "completely unintelligible in the highfalutin style." Highfalutin or not, the catalog indeed pointed more toward the future than to the past. Bound with spiral plastic coils, it included essays, poems, biographies, photographs, drawings, snippets of popular culture, and pages with words (in print and script) scattered along with photographs. Several items deserve special note. In a brief statement McHale remarked that the artists set out to present "a complex of sense experience which is so organised, or disorganised, as to provoke acute awareness of our sensory function in an environmental situation." In the introductory essay, Alloway undercut any notion that the show made it possible to provide an integration of the arts. Rather, he asserted that what it put forth was "a lesson in spectatorship, which cuts across the learned responses of conventional perception." Rather than being "manifestations of universal laws," he wrote, "the competing messages" would prompt the viewer to understand "the responsibility of the spectator in the reception and communication of the many messages in the communications network of the whole exhibition." Then, near the end, three of the contributors, including Alloway, offered a brief statement of the theory of communications that stood behind their work. Anticipating Stuart Hall's 1980 essay "Encoding/ Decoding," they offered a diagram which on the left began with the "source" of a symbol, moved to an "encoder," then to a "signal" between one "field of experience" and another, and then on the right to a "decoder" and then finally to a "destination."[25]

The most influential work of the exhibition was the collage by Hamilton, originally designed as a poster for the exhibit and titled *Just what is it that makes today's home so different, so appealing?* Drawing on clippings of symbols from the mass media that McHale had brought back from America, this collage contained images of a muscle man holding a Tootsie Pop, a woman with her bare breasts emphasized, three modern appliances (a tape recorder, a television set, and a vacuum cleaner), an emblem from a Ford automobile, a cover of *Young Romance* placed on a wall next to a traditional portrait of a man, a large can of ham, and a theater marquee that featured Al Jolson in *The Jazz Singer*. Reflecting what it meant for Britain to enter an affluent world after the deprivations of war and rationing, the collage was playful, filled with visual humor. The images of Charles Atlas and the nude women highlighted the com-

Figure 6. Richard Hamilton's *Just what is it that makes today's homes so different, so appealing?* served as the poster for the 1956 exhibition This Is Tomorrow in London, a show in which members of the Independent Group played a significant role. Using iconic images, Hamilton mixed fascination and irony to evoke the rich possibilities of how popular culture conveyed symbolic meanings. © 2011 Artists Rights Society (ARS), New York/DACS, London. Photo courtesy of the Kunsthalle Tübingen Museum.

plex relationships between sexuality and commerce. The ham sitting on the coffee table evoked Wynd*ham*, Ban*ham*, and *Ham*ilton. The image of a woman cleaning the stairs with a Hoover vacuum, developed by the legendary industrial designer Henry Dreyfuss, evoked McLuhan's mechanical bride along with Giedion's space and time in architecture. Playing on Marcel Duchamp's *Nude Descending a Staircase*, the collage displayed a fully clothed housewife ascending a staircase. Jack Warner, of the Warner Brothers referenced in the theater marquee, died on Yom Kippur, the sacred holiday Al Jolson was performing on in the movie. Gender played a central role in the image. The collage offers varied, contrasting images of women in the 1950s: the housewife on the stairs, the nude women highlighting her naked breasts, the performer on the television screen, and the woman in the prewar romance magazine. The muscle man is holding a tennis racquet that is both a phallic symbol and a reference to popular culture.[26]

Although in their art members of the IG did not have a unified or consistent view of popular culture, in many ways they both playfully celebrated and ironically commented on commercial culture, especially American imports. Henderson's *Newsagent, East London* (1949–52), captures the assemblage that made up the front of a newsstand, a traditional wood frame surrounding (and visually dominated by) advertisements, including one for a Roy Rogers *Wonder Comic*. In *Transistor* (1954), McHale wove fragments from print media into a collage dominated by the lyrical fluidity of the new electronic technology. With *Real Gold* (1949), Paolozzi assembled the kinds of images that fascinated McLuhan in the same years, ones that explored the relationships between sexuality, technology, and commercial design. Hamilton's *Hommage à Chrysler Corp.* (1957) explored similar themes in a more abstract manner. In their proposal for *Golden Lane* (1952), the Smithsons, the chief exponents of Britain's New Brutalism, wove an architectural tapestry with snatches of nature, a self-portrait, and a complex landscape that included a bombed-out district, older buildings, and plans for newer, modern ones—and nostalgia for the pre–World War II working-class life that Hoggart captured so effectively five years later.[27]

Hot Art, Cold War

The affectionate and at times ironic embrace of American culture by the members of the IG placed them in a difficult situation, given the pressures of the Cold War. The 1956 show appeared the same year as the first major exhibit in London of the work of American abstract expressionists, an approach to art that some in the United States hailed as proving the vitality of the nation's creativity and individualism. Closer to home, 1956 was the year in which events abroad forced the left to reconsider the nature of its political commitments. Some on the left accused IG members of being capitalist dupes or fascists. Writing in 1960 in the *New Left Review*, one commentator remarked that Banham appeared "to lend support to that group of fashionable young architects who glory in the age of the ad-man, who profess an admiration for the vulgar forms

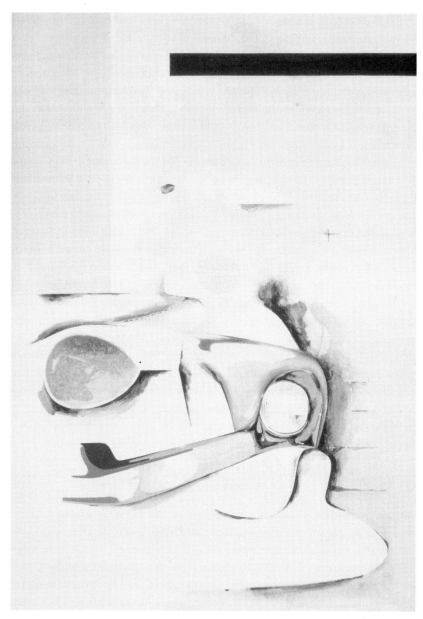

Figure 7. Richard Hamilton's 1957 *Hommage à Chrysler Corp.* vividly illustrates how members of London's Independent Group drew on advertisements to imaginatively explore the relationship between technology, sexuality, and American commercial culture. © 2011 Artists Rights Society (ARS), New York/DACS, London. Photo © Tate, London, 2011.

of American motor cars and juke-boxes." Accused of being too American-ized, Alloway responded that he doubted that he had "lost more by my taste for the American mass media (which are better than anyone else's) than have those older writers who look to the Mediterranean as the 'cradle of civiliza-tion.'" Using a highly charged Cold War phrase that Winston Churchill had introduced, Alloway noted that IG members had freed themselves "from the iron curtain of traditional aesthetics which separated absolutely art from non art." Banham captured their dilemma even more cogently. They had, he noted, "a curious set of divided loyalties." On the one hand, they loved "pop which is acceptance-culture, capitalistic." On the other hand, as the Cold War took hold in the late 1940s, this admiration stood in conflict with their left-wing politics that led them to oppose American policies. Consequently, Banham could write in 1964 about how he, unlike Macdonald and his elitist British counterparts, did not connect the acceptance and enjoyment of "the products of pop, the products of the entertainment of industry, Detroit-styling" with betrayal of "one's political position."[28]

The complicated relationship between the IG and Cold War culture under-scores the complex attitudes embodied in the art IG artists produced. If their writings were often overly enthusiastic, even naive, about American popular culture, in their art they mixed engagement and fascination with suggestions of irony. Although Banham addressed this in 1964 and acknowledged their left politics, the IG's critical writings, more than their art, echoed American cel-ebrations of democratic capitalism and consensus ideology that linked democ-racy and capitalism and that celebrated choice, freedom, innovation, progress, and obsolescence.

Pop Art: From Britain to the United States

In Britain, members of the IG labeled American commercial culture "pop art," although the artists among them also produced a British variant. But in the United States, the artistic movement known as pop art both intersected with and differed from what the IG wrote about in their criticism and created in their art. Significantly, IG member Alloway curated the first exhibition of pop art at a major American museum in a 1963 show at the Guggenheim Museum in Manhattan. His move from London to New York emphasized the trans-Atlantic nature of cultural flows. It also underscored the meanings of the shift in focus from London discussions of pop art in popular magazines to Manhat-tan showings of pop art in galleries and museums. Though the IG played a crucial role in discussions of the relationship of art and commerce and even produced some important art works that explored such connections, it was American artists who over time were most identified with pop art. Together with the British critics (some of them artists as well), the American artists offered important ways of understanding the connections between art and consumer culture. The Guggenheim show and the reactions of critics to it reveal the nature of discussions about the relationship between high art and popular culture, the symbolic nature of consumer culture, and the transactions that took place between producers and consumers of objects of desire. Barthes well understood what was involved. Pop art, the French critic remarked in 1980, had two voices that made up a fugue. "One says 'This is not Art'; the other says, at the same time: 'I am Art.'"[29]

Alloway as Art Critic

By 1961, when he left Britain for the United States, Alloway had emerged as a major presence in the art world, as an organizer of exhibits and as a prolific art critic.[30] To understand his work on the 1963 show at the Guggenheim, it is useful to learn how before 1963 he approached art criticism in general and pop art specifically. Like other members of the IG, Alloway challenged transcendent, unified, and hierarchical notions of culture. He wrote movingly of how early on he overcame his aesthetic snobbishness and developed a more capacious and egalitarian approach. He well understood that generations of artists, dadaists, surrealists, and postimpressionists among them, had incorporated in their works everyday, mass-produced objects. He excoriated elite custodians of culture who prized the fine arts for their formal qualities or supposedly eternal qualities. Reflecting class antagonism toward people who separated themselves from the ordinariness of the lives of common people, he attacked "trigger-happy aesthetes and arm-chair educationalists" who focused on fine art and neglected the popular. In 1958 Alloway singled out Clement Greenberg's classic 1939 article in *Partisan Review*, "Avant-Garde and Kitsch," as a notable example of how poorly a critic of fine art understood mass media. In place of elitist, transcendent yardsticks, Alloway offered several alternatives. He focused on the multiple and contradictory natures of artistic expression. For example, he argued that it was possible to understand Disney movies as drawing on "collective folkloristic elements" that involved themes such as malice, violence, omnipotence, and exaggeration. Alloway advocated an anthropological, anti-hierarchical approach to cultural productions, as he insisted on judging every cultural production by standards appropriate to its qualities. On this he agreed with Banham. Rejecting those who envisioned a pyramid, "with Picasso on the top and Elvis at the bottom," he preferred a continuum. Then "the spectator can go to the National Gallery by day and the London Pavilion by night, without getting smeared up and down the pyramid." Each cultural production was a "form of communication."[31]

The fact that for Alloway art offered complicated and often contradictory messages meant that the audience had to be active, even playful. Like Riesman before him, he understood the public reaction to visual materials as part of what he called "transmitter-audience feedback which is," he noted, "the secret of mass media." Moreover, Alloway challenged the very notion of a mass audience itself, arguing that it was divided by membership in all sorts of social and cultural groups. For Alloway the fluidity of the spectator's experience, the ability to reshape what producers of culture offered, was critical. As viewers worked to respond to the multiple signs that artists offered, they had the responsibility to absorb and interpret "the many messages in the communication network" a cluster of art objects offered. Here Alloway followed Riesman's emphasis on other-directed types as participants in a socially constituted world shaped by how people communicated through mass media.[32]

Alloway embraced popular culture as a means of symbolic exchange in a sprawling system of mass communication. This perspective emerged clearly in his response to the This Is Tomorrow exhibit, a show that involved "supporters of the popular arts who are interested in communication systems, the play of symbols, . . . [and] organizing feats performed by the spectator." The concern of critics "with traditionally defined reading habits and . . . snobbish assumptions about art," he believed, hid from view the vitality and symbolic power of commercial culture. Alloway was thus determined to take seriously the beauty, power, creativity, and symbolic functions of commercial culture. Countering critics who saw the principal task of advertisements as selling goods, sponsored by "monster capitalists milking a rabble public," he wanted to go beyond the analysis he thought such clichés offered. He insisted on seeing commercial culture as providing "some of the symbols by which we organise the environment we live in." The variety and profusion of commercial art provided members of a heterogeneous society with myriad signs to read.[33]

Alloway also emphasized the relationship between popular culture, sexual expression, and urbanism. He understood the power of popular culture to evoke fantasy and sexuality. He was especially interested in way in which the depiction of women on the covers of science fiction books, "channels open to erotic art in our half-censored urban culture," offered images that evoked "riotous fantasy" and "sadofetishistic" dreams. Alloway's celebration of popular arts also involved a city-centered vision, one in which pop art suffused the urban visual environment. When he wrote about his 1958 State Department–sponsored visit to a dozen cities in the United States, he explored the forces that made a city visually more complicated than architectural critics allowed. He embraced the contradictions of cities as visual spaces, what he called "a messy configuration" existing "in the dimensions of patched-up, expendable, and developing forms." He explored the ways in which popular culture, movies, pulp magazines, and spectacles, shaped the urban experience. He celebrated how popular music extended the sounds of radio and TV out of the home and into commercial establishments and he loved the "neon spectacle" of the American city. Thus for Alloway cities in the United States provided an example of the complex, jumbly communications systems of modern technology, with the "compound of traffic signals and ads" as "characteristic of the symbol-thick environment of American cities and highways." Well before Reyner Banham, Denise Scott Brown, and Robert Venturi explored the messiness and visual vitality of places like Los Angeles and Las Vegas, Alloway was thinking through how a world of freeways and neon-lit strips challenged widely accepted notions of urban space as problematically chaotic and ugly.[34]

Already by 1957 Alloway was so embracing of America that British critics began to accuse him of being Americanized, thus turning him into a "decadent islander, half-way between two cultures." He wrote from the United States in 1958 of his "wonderful feeling to be in Hollywood at last," in ways that reflected his enthusiasm for things American. He remarked that he had "only seen one movie actor but I feel so at home . . . Hospitable feeling, trees, low houses, swimming pools, drinks, lemon trees around the pool. I am absolutely sold on LA." Then in a momentous move in 1961 he and his wife, the artist Sylvia Sleigh, lit out for the territories, soon settling in Manhattan. In 1962 he began to work as a curator at the Guggenheim, a position he held until 1966. Writing in a British publication in 1962, he began to clear the way toward the 1963 exhibit by looking back. As a warning to those who saw pop art as a mainly or purely American product, he reminded his readers that at least since 1949 British artists, including members of the Independent Group, had been developing a variant of art that drew imaginatively on commercial culture. Certainly his 1958 trip to the United States was enchanting. He deepened his appreciation for American popular culture, art, and urban landscapes. Publishers, gallery owners, leading artists, and critics (including Harold Rosenberg and Clement Greenberg) wined and dined him. He now had even more chances to listen to jazz and watch American movies. One moment captures the irony of a European about to be in exile. When he first arrived in the United States in 1958 and early on went to the Phillips Collection in the nation's capital, he reported, referring to the artistic productions of two other émigrés, that he "sat in a Mies van der Rohe chair + looked at a Rothko. I really felt I was in the US, then."[35]

Pop Art at the Guggenheim

Because this show was a major challenge to the art establishment, Alloway had to move carefully. At the Guggenheim Museum in 1963 Alloway curated the exhibition Six Painters and the Object. The show included five paintings each by Jim Dine, James Rosenquist, and Andy Warhol and six each by Jasper Johns, Roy Lichtenstein, and Robert Rauschenberg. Many of them had prior experience as commercial artists, and all of them incorporated commercial culture into their works. Everything shown in the exhibition was a painting, a fact that helps explain the absence of any work by Claes Oldenburg and of any three-dimensional works by artists whom the show did include. Dine's *The Plant Becomes a Fan* (1961–63) was a charcoal drawing of an animate object becoming an industrial one. Johns's *Three Flags* (1958) revealed a series of American flags, one imposed on the other but all of them dramatically presented as icons of a contested nationalism. From Lichtenstein the show contained a much larger-than-life *Ice Cream Soda* (1962) that boldly and ironically captured its subject, overflowing with whipped cream. Also in the show was his *I Can See the Whole Room and There's No One in It* (1962), which pictured, in a cartoonlike rendition, a man lifting the cover of a peep hole with his finger and peering into the room where the viewer is situated. Several of the works by Rauschenberg were collages—including *Migration* (1959), composed of elements such as a clock with no hands and photographs from newspaper. From Rosenquist was his *Four 1949 Guys* (1962), offering four bold takes on masculinity. For Warhol, the pictures included several that we now recognize as characteristic of his work in the period, a 1960 *Dick Tracy* that portrays the detective (and a sidekick) as well as a 1962 multiple of Marilyn Monroe.[36]

In so many ways, it is clear that the 1963 show represented a considerable narrowing of Alloway's scope, leading the art historian Barbara Rose to remark how the paintings appear "almost to be seeking sanctuary on the Guggenheim's hallowed ground from the sensational press which pursues them." Alloway's caution comes into clearer focus when we bear in mind the avoidance of artists and works available from the same period that were more outré and that more fully represented an embrace of commercial culture. To begin with, missing were some of the bolder works by artists otherwise represented: from Lichtenstein, any that played on a legendary cartoon figure such as Popeye or Mickey Mouse or even his *Washington Crossing the Delaware* (1951); from Rosenquist,

Figure 8. In 1963, Lawrence Alloway, a member of the Independent Group who had recently moved to the United States, curated an exhibition of pop art at the Guggenheim Museum. Among the works he included was Roy Lichtenstein's 1962 *Live Ammo (Ha! Ha! Ha!)*, which illustrates the fascination both pop artists and members of the Independent Group expressed for commercial culture and technology. Roy Lichtenstein, *Live Ammo (Ha! Ha! Ha!)*, *1962*, gift of Walter P. Chrysler, Jr. Chrysler Museum of Art, Norfolk, Va. 71.676. © Estate of Roy Lichtenstein.

his big, bold renditions of commercial culture, such as *Marilyn Monroe I* (1961) or *I Love You with My Ford* (1961); from Warhol, his *Triple Elvis* (1962) and some of his now legendary multiples of Campbell Soup cans or Liz Taylor.[37]

The taming involved also becomes clear from a comparison between Alloway's August 1962 proposal for the show and what the Guggenheim actually exhibited a little over a year later. Alloway had originally envisioned a bold, encompassing display. He had proposed showing about forty-four works by up to twenty artists from both the East and West coasts, as compared with the exhibited thirty-three done by six artists, all of them from the East Coast. Among the California artists he hoped to include were Mel Ramos and Ed Ruscha. He hoped to display works other than two-dimensional painting, including what he called "Fully 3–D Objects" by Rauschenberg and Oldenburg and "Objects and Flat Paintings" such as "Anonymous artifacts" by Dine and "Paintings cut into figurative shapes" by Gene Beery. His preference was for bold representations of commercial objects, including Warhol's Campbell Soup cans, lusty and commercialized female nudes by Alan D'Arcangelo, and bold signs by Ruscha, Lichtenstein, Robert Indiana, and D'Arcangelo. While the proposal balanced paintings and objects, even though it leaned to the former, the catalog focused on these artists as painters of objects, not object makers. What happened between proposal and concrete plans is not clear but it is hard to believe that gallery owners, collectors, and artists would not have willingly lent whatever the Guggenheim wanted to display. What is likely is that the director at the Guggenheim curtailed Alloway's ambitions and his vision. Thus, the objects displayed did not reflect Alloway's more bold and capacious writings on the relationship of commercial culture, art, technology, sexuality, and urbanism.[38]

Moreover, Alloway's caution was readily apparent in the text he wrote for the catalog, especially when compared with the excitement he conveyed as a member of the Independent Group. In the catalog, Alloway anticipated the charges his superiors at the Guggenheim and critics might offer to demean the show as embracing commercial culture, which abstract expressionists had by and large avoided incorporating into their work. One of the strategies Alloway used was to reassure his audience that pop art stood in a time-honored tradition in the long sweep of the history of art. When discussing Lichtenstein's incorporation of popular material, he offered a quote from Sir Joshua Reynolds that "no man need be ashamed of copying the ancients: their works are considered as a magazine of common property, always open to the public, whence every man has a right to take what material he pleased." Alloway then insisted, not very convincingly, that "popular art has replaced classical art as 'common property', but the point of such borrowings has not changed much." He also reminded readers that since the eighteenth century "the use of popular art by artists has been widespread." Pop artists such as Warhol thus gained legitimacy through the connection of their work to a long line of artists, including Gustave Courbet, Paul Gauguin, Georges Seurat, and the dadaists, who had incorporated "mass-produced and popular" artifacts into their work.[39]

The words "object" and "painters" in the title of the show underscored other strategies Alloway used to defend the exhibition. Again and again, he insisted that the artists were individualistic and creative painters, rather than merely "object-makers, like the producers of happenings . . . [who] work toward the dissolution of formal boundaries and sponsor paradoxical cross-overs between art and nature." Rather, he asserted, the exhibition featured painters who were "committed to the surface" of their canvases "and to the process of translating objects into signs," items of popular culture into art. He noted, for example, that Johns assimilated "objects to a rigorous and delicate painting standard." What Dine depicted, he remarked as he used an ambiguous comparison to go against the grain of what he appreciated in the mid-1950s, were not "conspicuously new" objects, "smart and up-to-date like a slick magazine or an LP record-sleeve," but "timeless like a hardware store, or a Sears-Roebuck catalogue." He described Rauschenberg's images of radar equipment and baseball players as "so elaborately processed, by overlapping and corroding of contours and planes, that their topicality is opposed, though not cancelled, in a timeless blur." What these artists did was to transform objects into art rather than merely reproduce them.[40]

A comparison of what appeared in the Guggenheim show and less than six months earlier in the New Realists show at Sidney Janis Gallery also underscores the caution that underlay the museum exhibition. More international that the Guggenheim exhibition, New Realists included works from European artists. Not confining itself to painting, the show featured three-dimensional objects, such as Claes Oldenburg's *The Stove* (1962), George Segal's *The Bus Driver* (1962), and Jim Dine's *The Lawnmower* (1961). It also contained some paintings that more fully depicted the commercial, such as Tom Wesselmann's *Still Life # 17* (1962), which showed a housewife standing over a table filled with packages of name-brand products; Lichtenstein's *Blam* (1962), which depicted a fighter jet hit mid-air; Wayne Thiebaud's *Salads, Sandwiches, & Desserts* (1962), a display of food offered at a cafeteria; and Robert Indiana's *Black Diamond American Dream # 2* (1962), which revealed logos screaming "EAT," "JACK," "JUKE," and "THE AMERICAN DREAM." Moreover, the copy in the Janis catalog was hardly defensive. The American poet and critic John Ashbery hailed artists who were "at an advanced stage of the struggle to determine the real nature of reality." The catalog reproduced a quote from the French art critic Pierre Restany celebrating the way "contemporary nature is mechanical, industrial and flooded with advertisements . . . Born under the twin signs of standardization and efficiency, extroversion is the rule of the new world." Gallery director Janis hailed those whose works were on exhibition as trendsetters, as Alloway had not, urban folk artists who offered "highly intensified visual experience" because they were "intrigued and stimulated—even delighted—by the environment" from which they "enthusiastically created fresh and vigorous works of art."[41]

Messing with Messer

Why Alloway was so cautious or circumscribed begins to become clearer when looking at what *Newsweek* called the "gingerly preface" to the catalog by Thomas M. Messer, the Guggenheim's director and someone neither familiar nor comfortable with pop art. Messer announced that he found the "relationship between the *good* and the *new* in contemporary art" both "intriguing" and "baffling." Although he acknowledged that art was inventive, he also underscored "the suspicion of eccentricity" and the lack of any necessary connection between newness and "artistic validity." Introducing the curator, he invited the reader to focus on how Alloway would provide "an historical background to the profile of the new."[42]

What stood behind Messer's caution (and Alloway's defensiveness) was his unease, and that of the chair of Guggenheim's board of trustees, with contemporary American art in general and pop art specifically, sentiments deeply imbedded in the Guggenheim's history. The German baroness and artist Hilla Rebay had helped Solomon Guggenheim shape his collection, which first opened in 1939 as the Museum of Non-Objective Painting and featured works by Marc Chagall, Wassily Kandinsky, and Piet Mondrian. In 1939 Rebay conveyed her sense of the otherworldly importance of non-objective art, whose masterpieces, she wrote, "are alive with spiritual rhythm and organic with the cosmic order which rules the universe." Over time, the scope of the collection broadened, to include figurative works by artists such as Amedeo Modigliani and Fernand Léger.[43]

Yet the museum remained committed to European art, at least in what it collected. Messer became director not long after the Guggenheim opened on Fifth Avenue in 1959 in the building Frank Lloyd Wright designed. The startlingly modern nature of the new building was not the only reason Messer had reason to remain conservative. A cultured, diplomatic European gentleman, Messer grew up during the interwar years in Prague and came to the United States in 1939, where he trained as an art historian after World War II. Messer arrived at the Guggenheim, serving as its director beginning in 1961 following a period of poor relationship between the trustees and a series of directors. The Guggenheim board was small and familial, presided over by its founder's nephew Harry Guggenheim with a combination of tact and force. Messer quickly learned what Harry Guggenheim wanted. Messer remarked that his boss "would not say, 'You cannot do this or you cannot do that' but he did express—yes —he did express greater or lesser degrees of enthusiasm with my general orientation."[44]

Although the board was not much involved in the content of temporary exhibitions, Messer knew how to proceed, maneuvering carefully between a chairman with traditional tastes and the need to generate revenue with exhibitions that attracted considerable numbers of visitors. Alloway was the first curator Messer hired, because of his knowledge, Messer remarked much later, of the "avant garde, which was his passion more than mine." Messer commented that as director he "opposed a trendiness," implying that Alloway was one of those trendsetters. As time went on, he noted, "the curatorial staff, with some of its very gifted people, wanted a larger share in programming which I had to concede." With both the Whitney Museum of American Art and the Museum of Modern Art to compete with, Messer had to be especially careful about the tension between abstract expressionism and pop art. "The philistine reaction for years, or the philistine intention for years," he commented in an interview about a later show of the works of Lichtenstein, "had been somehow to get back from Abstract Expression into figurative stride. And then when Pop came upon the scene, they said, 'Yes, but not that. [laughs] That's not what we had in mind.'"[45]

If Messer's remarks in the catalog and in the interview reveal the sources of tensions over the 1963 show, the end of Alloway's tenure at the Guggenheim in 1966 underscores the problems he faced from the start. Writing under the headline "Not Exactly Trying to Please," the *New York Times* art critic Grace Glueck told the story of Alloway's departure. In June 1966 he resigned his post after he and Messer clashed over the planning of an exhibition at the Venice Biennale. Yet this all-too-public controversy brought long-standing issues to light. Glueck reported:

Alloway has not exactly been the sort of museum man that dealers dote on and rich old ladies invite for afternoon tea. Brisk, sometimes brusque, brilliant off and on, he is an unmistakable *vedette* [the French word for a movie star or celebrity] in an art scene where the cult of the curator is strong. Not unreasonably, the term "controversial" is often applied to him. . . . [At] London's Institute of Contemporary Arts . . . he earned a reputation as a *wunderkind* for his far-out, well-put together shows and knowledgeable critiques; as an *enfant terrible* for his cocky manner and often arbitrary opinions. . . . Alloway's maverick, unpredictable tastes disturb those who like to follow a developed line of thought. He has been criticized as brash, opportunistic, a hopper on bandwagons. But even the harshest Alloway-knockers have to admit that much of his critical writing is lively and provocative, and that he keeps diligently *au courant* with the bustling U.S. art scene.

Taking advantage of Glueck's interview, Alloway offered a parting shot at Messer and the Guggenheim. He attacked new museums for neglecting American art. At the Guggenheim, he noted, the shows he curated "were generally the relics of more ambitious proposals," tamed by the institution's culture. In sum, he insisted, his term at the museum had been "fairly frustrating." Though Alloway himself did not mention his 1963 show, the implication was clear enough: what he was able to display was one example of "relics of more ambitious proposals."[46]

Debating Pop Art

The ensuing debate over pop art, that on display at the Guggenheim and what was on view more generally in the early 1960s, makes even clearer why the catalog was so cautious and illuminates key issues at stake. An exploration of the reactions to pop art reveals how fluid were the way critics interpreted it. Moreover, focusing on the shifting meanings of pop art underscores how enthusiastically naive Alloway and members of the IG were about various iterations of pop art.[47]

Although we know what a tremendous and lasting impact pop art had, at the time it was not clear whether it was a "new movement or only a momentary revolt," as a reviewer for the *St. Louis Post-Dispatch* put it in 1961. To a broader public, pop art emerged quite suddenly and the response was impassioned, with the media stoking the flames by giving extensive coverage that celebrated its novelty and by hyping its investment value, which in turn commodified depictions of commodification. Supporters and detractors alike had a difficult time with several issues. They struggled to understand what pop art said about the division between high and low or commercial art, in the process revealing just how problematic was the attempt to draw impermeable boundaries. Supporters and detractors pondered the challenges these exhibitions represented, often built as they were on happenings that involved a dissolution of the lines between actors and audience, high art and the ordinary. Inaccurately characterized as entirely improvised, happenings were nonetheless performances that used plotless scenarios and appealed to multiple senses to engage the audience more directly and dramatically than more traditional theater pieces.[48]

Moreover, contemporaries puzzled over the attitude of pop artists to American consumer culture, unsure what combination of mockery, appreciation, celebration, criticism, irony, and ambivalence they offered. They wondered whether artists were corrupted by a commercial culture they embraced too uncritically or if through their art they were lodging a vigorous social protest against mass culture. "It is obviously impossible to declare," the art historian Leo Steinberg remarked in 1962, "whether pop art represents conformity with middle-class values, social satire, effective or otherwise, or again a completely asocial exploration of new, or newly intriguing, formal means." As another observer noted, the artists themselves made interpretation problematic because they remained "silent, or, worse, perversely" they made "public statements feeding the fury of the party they consider more absurd."[49]

Detractors were certain they knew how problematic pop art was. By and large well-established as critics who had earlier heralded abstract expressionism, they wrote from a combination of a commitment to a formalist perspective and a hostility to popular culture. Even though some abstract expressionists had incorporated popular culture into their work and some pop artists could skillfully handle stylistic techniques, critics saw the two styles as distinctly different. To them, pop art was too timid and lacked originality in developing formal elements. In 1962 Clement Greenberg remarked that "novelty, as distinct from originality, has no staying power." Two years later he asserted that pop art did not "really challenge taste on more than a superficial level." Similarly, Harold Rosenberg in 1965 decried how in the contemporary art world money, gossip, and anxiety transformed the "mediocre talent" that some pop artists displayed into "the ultimate phase in the evolution of world art." As modernists, critics saw pop art as outside the mainstream of the Western tradition, not sanctioned by an elite that could judge what to include in the canon. As against novelty and representations of the common, these critics preferred transcendence that was the product of individual genius. Artists, they asserted, should remain remote from life rather than embrace it, a judgment that relied on the certainty they felt that they could draw a clear line between fine and commercial art.[50]

To some critics, pop art lazily embraced the commercial. "Instead of cultivating the good, the true, the beautiful or the socially significant in understandable terms," wrote John Canaday, art critic for the *New York Times*, in 1964, it "has tied its wagon to a curious star, indeed—the bad, the false, the ugly and the socially deplorable." In *Partisan Review* Peter Selz, curator of painting at the Museum of Modern Art, echoed this judgment. "Far from protesting the banal . . . of our popular culture," he asserted, "the Pop painters positively wallow in them." "Instead of rejecting the incredible proliferation of *kitsch* which provides the visual environment and probably most of the esthetic experience of 99% of Americans," remarked Alan Solomon, director of the Jewish Museum in Manhattan, in ways that reflected his condescending attitude to kitsch, "these new artists have turned with relish and excitement to what those of us who know better regard as the wasteland of television commercials, comic strips, hot dog stands, billboards, junk yards, hamburger joints, used car lots, juke boxes, slot machines, and supermarkets." Critics were also horrified by how pop art, as an art that was too accessible, attracted people who had no taste: shamelessly hawking gallery owners, overeager publicists, and nouveau riche collectors. Max Kozloff, art critic for the *Nation* and for *Art International*, displayed his elitist disdain in an article titled "Pop Culture, Metaphysical Disgust and the New Vulgarians," lamenting that art galleries "were being invaded by the pin-headed and contemptible style of gum chewers, bobby soxers, and worse, delinquents." Herbert Read, the distinguished British critic whose perspective members of the IG had rejected, offered an extreme judgment when he remarked in 1963 that pop art was a "retrograde movement" that led "to a dulling of the sensibilities, to a relaxation of the consciousness of form" and in the end was "a present threat to our civilization."[51]

Supporters were generally younger than critics and, with Alloway as the most notable exception, relatively new to their roles. In the catalog for Six Painters, Alloway had echoed or anticipated themes others offered in support of pop art: it belonged in the mainstream of art history and it transformed rather than merely replicated the commercial. Although some praised its command of and innovation with formalist qualities, they opposed notions of transcendent beauty. They welcomed pop art as a rebellion against the art establishment, one that critiqued the pretentiousness of the art world itself. They saw in pop art an eagerness to cast a skeptical eye on the notion of originality, creativity, and the exalted nature of artist's role. They believed pop art thoughtfully explored the relationships between industrialization and commercialism. They welcomed the way the new approaches broke down barriers between commercial and fine arts, in the process embracing the ordinary and making art accessible to a wider audience. If opponents lamented the ways pop art gained an unsophisticated, money-mad clientele, then supporters welcomed the way the artists playfully engaged the audience. Thomas Hess, executive editor at *Artnews* whose early appreciation of abstract expressionism was waning, noted that the "artists were trying to reach out from their works to give the spectator's hand a good shake or nudge him in the ribs." "Why," asked the curator Henry Geldzahler as he questioned a central component of modernist ideology that equated quality with inaccessibility, "are we mistrustful of an art *because* it is readily acceptable?" Most supporters commended the artists for their stance toward commercial culture. Writing in the *New York Times*, Brian O'Doherty praised those whose works were shown at Janis for offering an ironic and satiric critique of mass culture that involved "an artful attempt to enrich spiritual poverty." The artists, he concluded, make "use of the standard ploys of an educated minority against a majority they indulgently despise—wit, satire, irony, parody."[52]

Also germane to the reception of pop art and more generally commercial culture was the reaction of Susan Sontag, who recognized the kinship between pop art and happenings. She commented on pop art at several points in *Against Interpretation* (1966), a collection of essays she had written beginning in 1961. Although in her opening essay she remarked that pop art, by "using a content so blatant, so 'what it is,' it, too, ends by being uninterpretable," elsewhere she found it more understandable. She recognized that it was one step along the road to a happening, as she pointed to work done by Rauschenberg in the mid- to late 1950s that was "a hybrid of painting, collage, and sculpture, using a sardonic variety of materials, mainly in the state of debris, including license plates, newspaper clippings, pieces of glass, machine parts, and the artist's socks." And in contrast to what Alloway selected for the Guggenheim show, she focused on more outré examples of pop art. Discussing the ways "in which people are employed . . . in the discovery or the impassioned, repetitive use of materials for their sensuous properties," she offered as one example Dine's *Car Crash* (1960), which culminated with "a man smashing and grinding pieces of colored chalk into a blackboard." Then, in "Notes on 'Camp,'" she commented that pop art "embodies an attitude that is related, but still very different" from camp. "Pop Art," she noted, "is more flat and more dry, more serious, more detached, ultimately nihilistic."[53]

In *Against Interpretation*, Sontag's more extensive discussion of pop art appeared as part of a longer essay on another subject entirely, Jack Smith's film *Flaming Creatures* with its "close-ups of limp penises and bouncing breasts, the shots of masturbation and oral sexuality." Sontag asserted that the film "has the sloppiness, the arbitrariness, the looseness of pop art," but also "pop art's gaiety, its ingenuousness, its exhilarating freedom from moralism." She appreciated pop art for "the way it blasts through the old imperative about taking a *position* toward one's subject matter." She believed it was imperative to have a position on some issues, but that "there are some elements of life—above all, sexual pleasure—about which it isn't necessary to have a position." She hailed "the best works among those that are called pop art" for their intention "that we abandon the old task of always either approving or disapproving of what is depicted in art—or, by extension, experienced in life." It was for this reason that she believed unnamed people were "obtuse" when they dismissed "pop art as a symptom of a new conformism, a cult of acceptance of the artifacts of mass civilization." She applauded pop art for the way it let in "wonderful and new mixtures of attitude, which before have seemed contradictions."[54]

Pop art, that which was included and excluded from the Guggenheim show, does indeed raise questions about the attitude of these artists to the commercial culture they dramatized. Pop artists, reacting to the severity and seriousness of abstract expressionism, emphasized playfulness, focused on symbolic qualities of commercial culture, and blurred the lines between fine and popular by offering icons of mass culture portrayed in a medium of high culture. Still, it remains difficult to determine their stance toward what they portrayed, a subject on which later commentators differed. When they wrote in the early 1960s about what they were doing, pop artists offered a wide range of responses. In 1962 and 1963, *ArtNews* published a series of interviews with prominent pop artists who served up a combination of put on, sarcasm, and social criticism, much of it more provocative than clear and all of it more strongly ironic than the writings of IG members. Dine dismissed the question about the social purpose of his work by saying that "if it's art, who cares if it's a comment." Lichtenstein noted that "the one thing everyone hated was commercial art," adding that "apparently they didn't hate that enough either." Pop art, he remarked, involved "the most brazen and threatening characteristics of our culture, things we hate, but which are also powerful in their impingement on us." He found in commercial art elements that were "usable, forceful and vital" but denied artists were "really advocating stupidity, international teenagerism and terrorism."[55]

Others were similarly provocative, suggestive, and elliptical. Warhol opened his interview by noting that under Communism everyone was thinking alike, something accomplished in the United States without government control. When asked why he painted soup cans, he responded with typical irreverence and evasiveness: "because I used to drink it." On the one hand, Rosenquist said that popular images were not the subject of his work, but he also talked about his "relations to the power of commercial advertising which is in turn related to our free society, the visual inspiration which accompanies the money that produces box tops and space cadets." Like many artists who insisted on their individuality, Johns claimed, "I'm not a Pop artist!" and then went on to emphasize technique over content. When pressed by the interviewer on whether his painting of a beer can involved social commentary, he responded in the negative, going on to say that "basically artists work out of rather stupid kinds of impulses."[56]

In the 1970s thoughtful critics accused pop artists of complicity with the worst impulses of consumer culture, though more recently the debate has complicated the distinction between complicity and criticism. Writing in 1970, Jean Baudrillard noted that pop art's "smile epitomizes its whole ambiguity: it is not the critical distance, it is the smile of *collusion*." In 1973 the art critic Max Kozloff juxtaposed events of the Cold War with presentations of pop art. He asserted that though many of the most prominent pop artists in the 1960s supported protests for peace and civil rights, with their art they claimed they took a stand that was morally neutral, one that offered "only an objectivity that seemed a mask for the celebration of what everyone, even the artists themselves, admitted to be the most abrasive images in the American urbanscape." In 1976 the critic and art historian Donald Kuspit echoed and intensified this judgment in an article titled "Pop Art: A Reactionary Realism." In the end, he asserted, it evaded "the social responsibility it at first glance seems to show," in the process placing "an artistic stamp of approval on the American status quo." Under the umbrella "The Aesthetics of Indifference," in 1977 the art historian Moira Roth linked McLuhan, camp, and pop art. She noted that while the abstract expressionists had combined political engagement with machismo, the pop artists embraced homosexuality and bisexuality even as they separated art from an older version of politics. Spurred on by the way McCarthyism made it necessary for liberals to hide their politics and gays their sexuality, they offered amusement rather than outrage. The aesthetics of indifference, she wrote, "advocated neutrality of feeling and denial of commitment in a period that otherwise might have produced an art of passion and commitment."[57]

Later and in contrast, Dick Hebdige, a British sociologist involved with the Birmingham Center, emphasized the importance of adversarial politics as he insisted on connecting the work of the IG and American pop artists. In 1983 he worked to recover the sense of insurgency pop art involved. He noted "the ease with which Pop art techniques have been incorporated into the persuasive strategies deployed by the advertising industry." Yet he reminded his readers that pop artists worked to erode the separation of the serious, the artistic, and the political, on the one hand, and the transitory, commercial, and pleasurable, on the other. Relying on the writings of Pierre Bourdieu, Hebdige recovered the shock of the work of both the IG members and pop artists, all of whom he saw working to cross lines between artists and audience, high and low, commercial and fine. "Pop reaches out to close those gaps," he insisted, "in order to produce not 'politics' as opposed to 'pleasure' but rather something new: a politics of pleasure." Other critics have reminded us that despite the marks of apolitical indifference, American pop arts offered trenchant, albeit often ambiguous, critiques of American patriotism and mass culture.[58]

In the vast literature on pop art, the issues of gender, sexuality, and class have recently attracted attention in ways that enable us to see the relationships between these artists and consumer culture. The art historian Kenneth Silver has explored issues of gay identity in early pop art. From the mid-1950s on, Johns (who was Rauschenberg's lover) and Warhol explored gay themes, but in ways that most viewers at the time were unlikely to decipher. Silver pondered how pop artists were reacting against the cult of masculinity in which abstract expressionists indulged. This is apparent in some of Warhol's early works, not widely circulated at the time, such as his *Untitled Boy with USN Tattoo* (1957) and *Strong Arms and Broads* (1960). In the *Target with Plaster Casts* (1955), *Painting with Two Balls* (1960), and *In Memory of My Feelings—Frank O'Hara* (1961), Johns explored gay themes, in the last of these three ventriloquizing his homosexuality by paying homage to a gay poet. Silver reveals how Warhol's 1962 depictions of Campbell soup cans and Marilyn Monroe brought together Warhol's "class origins and his sexual preferences . . . on the common ground of 'camp'" Silver also suggests that Warhol's multiples of celebrities and of commercial packaging recreated his own mother's world of working-class consumption at the same time that they brought wealthy men and women into galleries to shop for consumer items, something they thus did at galleries run by Sidney Janis or Leo Castelli but would not deign to do at supermarkets by Gristedes. This linking of gender, sexuality, class, and consumer culture, Silver suggests, came together in the style of camp, which Susan Sontag made famous in her 1964 essay.[59]

Another art historian, Cécile Whiting, has explored what she calls "Pop's intimate liaison with a consumer culture coded as feminine," often inflected by class as a way of challenging hierarchies. Kozloff's description of "the new vulgarians" captures some of the ways that class, embodied in the new audience and collectors pop art attracted, played a key role in the hostile reaction to pop art. Whiting also notes that words like "commercial," "banal," and "vulgar" involved a contrast between the male realm of high art and the lesser, female world of the domestic and ordinary. Thus in 1962 Greenberg referred to what he called the "'homeless representation'" of the abstract expressionists, implicitly in contrast to pop art's focus on domestic spaces. Oldenburg, Wesselmann, and Warhol turned items found in supermarkets into subjects of their art, in the process playfully complicating issues of class and taste. Wesselmann painted

pictures of domestic interiors: in *Great American Nude # 6* (1961) he placed a
sprawling female nude in front of a portrait by Modigliani, thereby mixing a
modernist icon with a figure of a woman that could have appeared, in different form, on a calendar hanging in an auto body shop. In his scenes that drew
on comic-book renderings Lichtenstein portrayed heroic men and anxious
women: see the contrast, for example, between two 1963 works, *Whaam* and
Drowning Girl. In all of this, the gaze by gay men at the female body and the
female gaze at commercial products were crucial. Pop artists thus appropriated
key aspects of consumer culture associated with the feminine. In the process
they undermined the possibility of drawing clear boundaries between high art
and mass culture and suggested the complicated pleasures of the commercial
goods they offered up.[60]

Alloway after the Guggenheim Show

After 1963 Alloway offered a series of presentations and discussions of pop art,
many of which recovered more dazzling examples than what he could display
at the Guggenheim. In 1974 he organized an exhibit on pop art for the Whitney Museum that displayed more outré examples of pre-1963 art than did the
earlier Guggenheim show. For example, it included Allan D'Archangelo's *Marilyn* (1962) with its paper doll assemblage; Tom Wesselmann's evocative *Great
American Nude 26* (1962); fuller, more playful explorations of comics, such as
Lichtenstein's *Look Mickey* (1961) and Warhol's *Popeye* (1961); and Mel Ramos's
Batmobile (1962); mixed media items such as Rauschenberg's *Odalisque* (1955–
56); Oldenburg's *The Street* (1960); and Wesselmann's *Still Life, 20* (1962).[61]

Nor was Alloway's post-1963 writing as defensive as what he authored for
the Guggenheim catalog. Indeed, in a 1968 article that explored the changing
meanings of the term "pop art," he implicitly made clear that the show he curated in 1963 appeared at a time when its range was at its narrowest. He began
by reminding readers of the origin of the phrase "pop art" "as a description of
mass communications." In Britain in the 1950s, it "was an expansionist esthet-
ics, aimed at relating art to the man-made environment" and encompassing
advertising, movies, television, and automobiles. Then from 1961 to 1964, he
noted of a second phase, "the compression of the term facilitated its rapid diffusion" precisely at the time of its greatest impact as an art movement. It was
then, he remarked, only by implication explaining what had happened at the
Guggenheim, that critics restricted its earlier "expansionist" thrust and embraced "the formalities of abstract art." This involved the "resistance, within

the art world, to using a nonhierarchic definition of art." Consequently the second period involved "an interruption of the anthropological view of art; though the mass media is iconographically present, the art is a consolidation of formal procedures that are largely traditional." Alloway identified a third, broadening period that began in 1965. One example he provided came from Robert Venturi's 1966 *Complexity and Contradiction in Architecture*. Drawing on a passage where Venturi accepted "honky-tonk elements in our architecture and townscape," Alloway quoted the architect's statement that "Pop art has demonstrated that these commonplace elements are often the main source of the occasional variety and vitality of our cities." Venturi, Alloway wrote, was here using pop art "to defend the kind of lively man-made environment which had originally contributed to the formation of the term in the first place," before 1961. And so after 1965 Alloway saw critics returning to the original expansive meaning, the one cut short in the early 1960s, precisely at the moment when he curated the first major exhibit of pop art in an American museum.[62]

A number of observers have argued that American pop art, and Alloway's writings on it, played a crucial role in the coming of postmodernism beginning in the 1950s but even more fully in the 1960s. One cultural historian has written that the arrival of pop art, along with beat literature, signaled a transformative reaction against the modernism of abstract expressionism, an element in "a version of modernism which had become domesticated during the 1950s." Beginning in the mid-1950s, Alloway's activity as an essayist and exhibition organizer played a key role in Britain and the United States in challenging the dominance of abstract expressionism and welcoming multiple, divergent new visual expressions. Thus Sylvia Harrison explores how the criticism that Alloway and others offered beginning in the mid-1950s reveals an understanding of pop art as an expression of postmodernism. The evidence for Alloway's contribution to seeing pop art as postmodern is considerable. He stressed diversity, indeterminacy, multiplicity, and contingency. He emphasized that popular culture and fine art belonged on a horizontal continuum not a hierarchical ladder. He challenged the essentialism and formalism of Greenberg. He understood that members of the audience for art and for mass culture were consumers, situated in distinctive ways. Finally, he saw pop art as part of a system of communications, a series of signs and sign systems. Alloway, Harrison notes, was among those who set out to explore "the deconstructive effect of key technological and economic characteristics of post-war Western urban society: mass communications and capitalist consumerism."[63]

Conclusions

With the Independent Group, pop art emerged in the early 1950s as a term that a small band of critics and artists used to show their admiration for American commercialism in a Britain where austerity and traditional design still ruled. Alloway was a key figure in the transit of pop art in London as commercial images drawn from magazines into pop art in New York as transformed images in paintings. The British members of the IG and the American pop artists differed on a number of issues, not least the political meaning of what they described and represented, and what mixture of appreciation and irony they evoked. Ideas and people moved across national borders in transformative ways. The relationships between technology, culture, sexuality, urbanism, and commercial culture fascinated IG members. They challenged the divisions between mass culture and high culture. They explored the reciprocal relationships between producers and consumers of everyday objects. In short, though their commitments were not unproblematic, they made it clear how certain people saw outside the ruling consensus, in the process breaking the barriers of hierarchy and helping mark the development from moralistic attacks to a more pleasure-filled acceptance of what commercial culture offered.

Chapter 7

From Workers and Literature
to Youth and Popular Culture

The role that members of Britain's Independent Group played in generating new understandings of consumer culture through their promotion of pop art was matched if not exceeded by the contributions toward a similar goal by leading figures at the Birmingham Center for Contemporary Cultural Studies, established in 1964 with Richard Hoggart as its first director. Over the next decades the Center came to exercise a commanding role in the field of cultural studies, shaping analysis of popular culture not only in Britain but also in the United States.[1] In 1964 Stuart Hall joined Hoggart at the Center. The same year saw the publication of *The Popular Arts* (1964), coauthored by Hall and Paddy Whannel. Hall's interests, though dovetailing to a considerable extent with Hoggart's, eventually led the Center, and more generally the understanding of popular culture, in new directions. In the meantime *The Popular Arts* stood as a landmark book on mass media, albeit one to which scholars have paid relatively little attention.[2]

In their books of 1957 and 1964, Hoggart, Hall, and Whannel had worked out some of the principal dimensions of new understandings of commercial culture, understandings that would eventually undergird cultural studies. In addition, *The Popular Arts* reminds us of the origins of cultural studies in the attempt to teach teens how to think seriously about media, of the continuing importance of a left-Leavisite position, and of the significance of the shift from views of culture that relied on literary criticism to those informed by anthropology and sociology. Although Hoggart saw postwar youth as corrupted by popular music, he lodged resistance to popular culture in the interwar working class. In contrast, Hall and Whannel emphasized how young men from working-class backgrounds developed forms of cultural expression that enabled them to resist commercial culture. Their emphasis on anthropology, new media, and youth marked a major step toward new understandings. As the

scholar Grant Farred has noted, *The Popular Arts* betrayed "a conceptual ambivalence," poised as it was between cultural studies in the future and both the
early New Left and long-standing traditions of literary studies, much of them
conservative and elitist, in the past.[3]

A series of political, social, economic, and cultural changes in the postwar
world shaped the consciousness of Hall and Whannel's generation: the promise and limitations of the social welfare system, the return of Conservatives to
power, the narrowing of Labour's vision and constituency, the opening up of
educational opportunities, and growing affluence all promised or threatened
to transform the lives of Britons, especially members of the working class. Although immigration from the British empire, especially Africa, the Caribbean,
and South Asia, was beginning to turn Britain into a more diverse and less
white nation, if what they wrote publicly is any indication, this was less on the
minds of most members of the Hall and Whannel's cohort than were issues
surrounding the dynamic of class and youth in a relatively prosperous society.

Paddy Whannel

Paddy Whannel was born Atholl Douglas Whannel in Pitlochry, Perthshire,
Scotland, a small Victorian resort town surrounded by mountains, seventy
miles north of Edinburgh. After finishing at the local schools in 1937 at age
fourteen, for four years he acquired an extensive education in film as projec-
tionist at the Royal Theater in his hometown. Following service in the British
Royal Navy from 1942 to 1945, he studied at Alnwick College of Education in
a small town just south of the eastern edge of the Scottish border. Having received his teaching diploma in 1948, he moved to London, where he studied at
University of London until 1953, earning a diploma in art history. Beginning in
1948 he taught media, film, and social studies at two London secondary schools.
Then in 1957 he went to the British Film Institute (BFI), where he served as its
film appreciation officer, a position soon retitled education officer. As much as
anyone else, Whannel was responsible for establishing film studies in Britain.
Under the BFI's auspices he lectured on film around Britain, turned the BFI
into a center for the emerging fields of film criticism and theory, developed
programs for educating secondary school teachers about film, and helped establish Britain's first university-based film studies program. He shifted focus
away from art films and toward American popular and commercial ones.
Then he resigned his position at the BFI in 1971 and soon moved to the United
States, where he took a full-time position at Northwestern University, teaching

courses in film and helping to organize the curriculum in the department of radio, television, and film.[4]

In the late 1950s and early 1960s Whannel was emerging as a major figure in media criticism. His work appeared in pamphlets, in the *Universities and Left Review* and the *New Left Review*, and most frequently in the *Teacher*. Using a pseudonym, from 1962 to 1966 he published scores of articles in this weekly publication of the National Union of Teachers (NUT), under the title "Albert Casey's Entertainment Guide." As a former schoolteacher and now as education director of the BFI, he was in a perfect position to talk to schoolteachers about crucial issues involved in teaching mass media. In what he wrote before the publication of *The Popular Arts* in 1964, he addressed topics that informed the book he wrote with Hall, especially the role of media education in secondary schools. He also participated in the debates over competing approaches to the study of popular culture.[5]

In his Albert Casey essays and elsewhere Whannel extensively discussed how to understand the popular arts. In an essay on the book he wrote with Hall, without acknowledging that the author of the review and the coauthor of the book were the same person, Whannel explored the traditions that informed debates over popular culture. He began with T. S. Eliot's *Notes Towards a Definition of Culture* and F. R. Leavis and Denys Thompson's *Culture and Environment*, asserting that these books relied on a "yardstick of the past to judge the cultural decline of the present." He went on to explore the similarities between their positions and that of Dwight Macdonald, who, he noted, had "a great love for the English class system" and whose solution was to let a cultured minority enjoy authentic art and the vast majority to experience only banal cultural productions. Then he turned to Richard Hoggart and Raymond Williams as representatives of what he called "the radical wing" of the tradition of cultural criticism that went back at least to Eliot and Leavis. Elsewhere he found only hints of how to proceed when discussing visual media, including in the work of, among others, Reyner Banham, David Riesman, and Marshall McLuhan. *The Mechanical Bride*, he wrote, was "full of bizarre but intriguing observations," while McLuhan's writings had given way in the 1960s to "grand theorising."[6]

Social class was central to Whannel's writings on popular culture. In the late 1950s he bristled when members of the British establishment condemned "the popular simply because it is popular" and instead wanted to impose "'aristocratic or middle-class standards on working-class children.'" Such responses, Whannel wrote, were challenged by the working-class world that Hoggart described in the first half of *The Uses of Literacy* or in Raymond Williams's writings on the strength of working-class institutions. The alternative to imposing culture on workers was to understand the longings that lay behind working-class embrace of mass culture. Whannel found in the trite, such as the saccharine songs of Frankie Laine, evidence of "a genuine aspiration for the poetic." He hoped for more, asserting that what popular culture reflected back of ordinary people's desires "bears only a very oblique relationship" to what he called their "'real selves.'" Teachers had to avoid tempting students to higher cultural aspirations and instead find ways, through new media, of connecting them with life.[7]

Whannel made use of and moved beyond the Leavisite tradition, remarking in 1959 that "what the cinema needs is a Leavis," a position he was in the process of fulfilling. As he did so he drew on his reading not only of Leavis but also of David Riesman, Vance Packard, Richard Hoggart, Raymond Williams, George Orwell, and *Mass Culture* by Bernard Rosenberg and David Manning White. Industrialization had destroyed folk art, Whannel asserted, and there was no sense in yearning for a return of what was gone forever. Moreover, far from lamenting the impact of technology on culture, Whannel embraced the inventiveness and creativity of artists who used new technologies. Thus he hailed tape recorders and modern cinematic techniques as "new media of communication." Although here Whannel seemed to consign Leavis to the dustbin of history, elsewhere he made clear his debt to the Leavisites. The task for left-Leavisites, including Whannel, was to separate Leavis's conservatism and longing for an idyllic, preindustrial past from his commitment to analyze cultural products in a disciplined, rigorous manner. Moreover, Whannel shied away from a full embrace of a strict Marxist position. He rejected an analysis that focused on false consciousness fostered by greedy capitalists. Thus Whannel asserted that uninformed "moral indignation," whether from the right or left, was "a very bad guide to an understanding of the cinema and the other modern media." Writing in *New Left Review* in 1960, Whannel wondered whether it was "true that when you scratch a New Leftist you reveal the old puritan?"[8]

When Whannel assessed commercial media, he made clear how he balanced a Leavisite approach with other stances. Writing in the introduction to a 1964 BFI pamphlet, *Film Teaching*, he recognized that contemporary media posed problems of critical analysis different from literature, making it necessary to develop "a language that will enable us to deal with its sounds, imagery and rhythm as a whole." Yet Whannel insisted that "the best films can be studied with the kind of thoroughness and attention that we bring to literature and the other arts." Central to Whannel's articles in the *Teacher* was that the same standards of judgment or criticism were relevant to all cultural expressions,

from classical music to jazz, from classical theater to television dramas. Therefore, drawing on the Leavisites, he insisted on the ability to discriminate, to
develop informed and disciplined judgments that neither rejected pop culture
outright nor embraced it indiscriminately. There was for Whannel no "unified
mass culture" but many levels that he worked to distinguish among. At top
were movies (by Jean Renoir, Akira Kurosawa, or Luis Buñuel) whose creators
were "comparable in terms of seriousness and integrity to those working in
any other medium." Next were "more modest but honest achievements" like
the television documentaries of Denis Mitchell. Then came "pure entertainment," which might be easy to dismiss out of hand as "escapism," though he
acknowledged that the best of escapist entertainment brought people "back to
life refreshed."[9]

Again and again, Whannel stated his preference for widely available art
forms that wrestled with moral dilemmas, relied on complex treatment, developed organically, and conveyed their force and subtlety through powerful
images. In contrast, he criticized cultural products that were trite, contrived,
and formulaic. As Hoggart had done in his discussions of teaching literature to
adults, so Whannel made clear his opposition to popular fiction and films that
were overly ideological, even as he recognized that in some ways every genre
also had to be judged on its own terms. Rather, Whannel wanted to bring the
social and aesthetic together. What was at issue was an approach to morality
and politics that was personal and experiential. "It is not the moral line a play
or film offers that is important," he wrote, "but the quality of experience it gives
us." However, it is important not to exaggerate the clarity of Whannel's hierarchies before the publication of *The Popular Arts*. He wanted to break down the
notion of a unified mass culture and distinguish among levels, but his distinctions were not terribly clear or firm.[10]

Nonetheless, Whannel's commitment to discriminate was clear, for example, when he wrote about detective stories and the movies based on them. He
objected to novels by Mickey Spillane, whose poorly written books contained
"sickening treatment of sex and violence." He faulted Ian Fleming novels for the
same reason, as well as for their "unpleasant layer of social snobbery." Although
he did not think Raymond Chandler was very good as a storyteller, he admired
the American writer for his ability to create characters, develop dialogue, evoke
an atmosphere, and suggest how to handle violence in a popular art form. Were
he a teacher of English who discovered that his students were reading Spillane
or Fleming, he concluded, "I think I would regard it as an achievement if I
shifted them on to Raymond Chandler." What was at stake in such a judgment
was Whannel's insistence that it was possible to judge every genre both on its

own terms and by some more rigorous yardstick as well. When he turned his
attention to films, Whannel articulated the same commitment to discrimination and judgment. He distinguished between formulaic films, art films made
for a very small audience, and "the film of quality produced within a popular
form" available to a sizeable audience. Working to blur the lines between art
and formula films, he made clear his admiration for Hollywood productions,
such as musicals, gangster films, and especially westerns, listing those by Howard Hawks, John Ford, and Frank Capra as capable of exploring tragedy, morality, and heroism.[11]

Whannel also insisted on making careful judgments about radio and television programs rather than simply dismissing them outright. With television,
for example, he admired the 1964 production *The Long Journey*, in which the
director ingeniously used the tape recorder to convey the richness of working-
class life. For the communities it portrayed, the film conveyed "a spontaneity,
a way of speaking which very directly expresses the feelings, qualities which
are withered by the conventions of middle-class life."[12] Similarly with radio,
he singled out the creativity of a BBC program *Radio Ballads*, which he saw as
reminiscent of the work of John Grierson and Mass-Observation. Weaving together songs and interviews into a "poetry of the oral tradition which has been
submerged in the age of print," the producers of the radio show developed "a
distinctive art form" that imaginatively recreated people's lives. The series was,
Whannel remarked, "one of the few attempts to begin mending our broken
culture, to make out of the new media a genuine popular art."[13]

Likewise, Whannel called on teachers to help their students analyze advertising. Again, rather than issue blanket condemnations, as highbrow critics
usually did, he pressed for discrimination and analysis. His primary concern
with this medium was how it threatened moral values. He pointed to the appeal
to people's "worst instincts," for example judging one another by the cutlery
they used. In addition, he lamented the way advertisers, although not responsible for inventing "greed, fear, snobbery and envy," nonetheless exploited
them. Above all what angered him was the way ads corrupted language, making it difficult for poets and filmmakers to convey the power and authenticity
of concepts such as love or beauty. Consequently, much as McLuhan had done
in *The Mechanical Bride*, Whannel called on teachers to help students analyze
advertising so that they would bring "to the surface its hidden assumptions as
a safeguard against the danger that we might import these unconsciously into
our thinking."[14]

For Whannel, jazz, along with cinema, was the art form most deserving of
respect. In his discussion of jazz, he mentioned but did not extensively develop

the role that race played. When movies incorporated jazz, he noted, they almost always focused on white performers and "show the Negro originators of jazz as simple and lovable folk playing uncomplicated music." In contrast, in 1964 he hailed the work of Duke Ellington, whose music was familiar to sophisticated British audiences, and Jimmy Witherspoon, a blues and R&B performer who was less well known. He also hailed the talents of Billie Holiday as "an urban jazz singer who sang of urban experiences using the pop song as her raw material." Yet despite this evidence of Whannel's appreciation of music by African Americans, it is striking how little he discussed the culture of people of color in Britain in the early 1960s, a category that included those who had migrated from the West Indies. This is pertinent in light of both increased consciousness of racial diversity and strife in Britain in the late 1950s and early 1960s and of the ways writers from the Birmingham Center later engaged with race.[15]

There were hints in Whannel's essays of how mass media might bring pleasure. This was evident in his embrace of some escapism as refreshing. It was even clearer in his persistent emphasis on the connection between popular culture and personal experience. In his introduction to *Film Teaching*, he noted that a movie was not only "a form of mass communication having important social effects but is also a vehicle for personal expression." Similarly, writing in the *Teacher* about how to evaluate movies, he remarked, "Let us have more anecdotes, more subjectivity. The best and richest evidence is within ourselves." Working against notions of scholarly expertise and audience passivity, positions that would become more common among critics as the 1960s progressed, he remarked that teachers should encourage students to explore their own responses to movies and TV programs. For him, the relationship between creators of popular culture and audiences was reciprocal. As he remarked in 1961, in ways that resembled what Walter Benjamin and C. L. R. James had written earlier, "A film is an act of collaboration with the viewer."[16]

In his discussion of teen culture, which Hoggart abhorred, Whannel emphasized both resistance and pleasure. With teens especially, he stressed how ordinary people fought against and transformed what mass media offered. "The response to the surly aggressiveness of Presley," he noted perceptively, "contains within itself valuable sources of non-conformism." Teen consumers could "size up the world they are dealing with, because it is not the only world they know. The teenage culture," he remarked as he took a swipe at Hoggart's analysis in *The Uses of Literacy*, "does not only consist of coffee bars and juke boxes." Similarly, when looking at how critics reacted to the movie *Lucky Jim* (1957), Whannel wrote of how embarrassed they were "when human relationships are shown to involve the passions and interests of men and women" and instead treated them like "cheese-cake and peep-show sex." Responding to the 1963 Newsom Report on school reform, he talked of healthy conversations about sex, love, and feelings that a classroom discussion of a movie such as *Saturday Night and Sunday Morning* (1960) would make possible. Whannel found problematic the usual "picture of 'pop dancing' as 'hypnotic' and 'brutalizing.'" Where emerging cultural forms of quality were concerned, he wrote, evoking a notion of hip, it was better for the teacher "to be with it than without it."[17]

Yet if at moments Whannel focused appreciatively on teen culture, he did not do so as extensively or as sympathetically as writers connected with the Birmingham Center would later do. Indeed, just as Hoggart noted conflicts in adult education between teachers and their students, so too Whannel hinted at the problematic nature of the relationship between teachers and their teenage students. He mentioned the tension between the "traditional training of the classroom and the glittering attractions of the world of commercialized leisure." On occasion Whannel seemed skeptical about teen engagement with popular culture, in the vein of Hoggart's criticism of jukebox boys. This was apparent in his discussion of the movie *A Hard Day's Night* (1964) when he noted how easy it was to be "slightly sour about" the Beatles. He preferred the soothing music of his own generation to the insurgent songs his students listened to. This came through in his favorable response in 1963 to Ella Fitzgerald's singing Rogers and Hart, performances he preferred to her more vibrant and improvisational songs. Such a comment was in line with Whannel's appreciation for popular culture that was more comforting than adversarial. "Kelly dancing in the rain and Sinatra singing Hoagy Carmichael," he wrote in 1960, "nourish our ideals, open out our responses and help us to live together." In sum, in his writing in the *Teacher* about new strands of popular music, at moments Whannel was closer to Hoggart's opposition than to the celebration Center members would soon discover.[18]

Stuart Hall

The life of Stuart Hall was very different from Whannel's, although he shared with his coauthor the status of someone outside the locations of social and cultural power in Britain, an early commitment to understanding new media, and experience in teaching diverse students in London's secondary schools. Hall grew up in Kingston, Jamaica, in a household riven by tensions over class and color. His ancestry included Asian Indians, Black Africans, Portuguese Jews, and white Brits. His upwardly mobile, brown-skinned father was from a respectable lower-middle-class family in a small village. A scholarship boy who benefited by being continually selected to break racial, cultural, and occupational barriers, Hall's father rose to be chief accountant of the island's major employer, the United States–owned United Fruit Company, which ran its plantations in a neofeudal manner. Hall's mother, with some white or nearly white ancestors, as a child had more class than money. That situation changed when a well-to-do, Anglophilic uncle adopted her and she lived in a large house where she took on "peculiar airs and graces as the adopted daughter of a landowner." Living in a society that made exquisite distinctions along the color line, members of his family and some people in the larger Jamaican society thought of Hall as black, although that was a term he later recalled that he never heard in Jamaica. In the gradations of color and class in Jamaica it would be more accurate to call him a brown, middle-class person whose parents, in opposition to independence, strongly identified with Britain.[19]

Given the tensions already apparent before Hall left Jamaica, between his family's complicated relations to class, color, and power, on the one hand, and his emerging, adversarial politics, on the other, his long-time concern with hybridity and complicated identities is understandable. His family's "aspirations were oriented toward England," he later recalled. "My mother felt she was all but white. We were to aspire upwards, and have little to do with brown—or certainly black—Jamaicans." Race shaped his family's history in deeply tragic ways. After Hall's parents prevented his sister from dating a middle-class black Barbadian medical student, she had a nervous breakdown which was treated with electrical shock; she never dated again and instead stayed at home to take care of her blind brother and her parents. Hall himself grew up, he later recalled, "in a lower-middle-class family that was trying to be a middle-class Jamaican family trying to be an upper-middle-class Jamaican family trying to be an English Victorian family."[20]

Politics, race, and culture stood at the center of his young adulthood. In Jamaica, Hall's politics, he later recalled were "anti-imperialist," shaped by the tensions over race and class in his household and by how whites patronized his father. He had been influenced by Karl Marx but did not consider himself a Marxist, because, he later said, orthodox Marxism failed to come to terms with colonialism, race, and ethnicity. Popular culture was also important to him in Jamaica: it is possible that watching American movies, melodramas as well as films starring Humphrey Bogart and Bette Davis, provided a counterweight to British influence. In retrospect, he thought about himself as a student of literature who tracked the debates between Leavisites and Marxists, but in the end, because of its moral seriousness, he had to "acknowledge that *Scrutiny* won.'" In Jamaica he criticized the Leavisite publication's conservatism and elitism but, lacking access to the works of modern theorists, found Marxist literary criticism "far too mechanical and reductive." In 1951 Hall graduated from Jamaica College, a private, prestigious all-boys boarding school modeled on the elite English schools. Issues of social status, class, nationality, and race at Jamaica College reinforced the even more intense complications of these issues he experienced at home.[21]

Hall left Jamaica for good in 1951, going to Merton College, Oxford, on a Rhodes scholarship. He studied English for six years, during which time he participated in the struggle for his homeland's independence and in the reconfiguration of left politics in Britain. Now he was not a brown man but, in a racially bipolar world, a black one, and an immigrant to boot. He was a member of the Windrush generation, named after the British troopship *Empire Windrush* whose arrival in England in 1948 marked the beginning of major immigration from the West Indies. At Oxford, Hall was trying to figure out what the connections between his politics and his multiple identities meant, though the concepts that might have clarified such considerations were not readily available. He performed as a jazz pianist, playing with Jamaican bus conductors and drivers. He joined the West Indian Students Union, where with his fellow émigrés he debated the relationship between the Cold War, colonialism, imperialism, and West Indian independence.

Reading English as an undergraduate and graduate student at a university where literary studies were mired in tradition and dilettantism, Hall turned for inspiration to sources outside the mainline curriculum. He took a seminar with the socialist, historian, and political theorist G. D. H. Cole. He met Raymond Williams in the Oxford Socialist Club and in a literature class, one that intensified his interest in F. R. Leavis. These experiences provided him with alternatives to the narrow traditionalism of literary studies at Oxford. As a left-Leavisite, someone who embraced Leavis's approach to texts but rejected his elitism, Hall took "literature seriously, as a *deadly serious issue*." Hall focused on questions about language and culture that F. R. Leavis probed and about popular fiction and its audiences that Q. D. Leavis offered. The Leavisite approach compelled him because it provided an alternative to what he saw as the dead ends of both vulgar Marxism and ossified literary studies. Oxford in the early and mid-1950s, Hall later recalled, was difficult for him, dominated as it was by upper-class students, those he called "'Hooray Henries,'" who created a "relentlessly masculine" atmosphere as they attempted "to relive *Brideshead Revisited*." Hall described an "intellectual minority culture" that represented a wider range of types than was then available in most American universities: outsiders from abroad like himself, trade unionists at Ruskin College, "scholar-

ship boys" whom Hoggart had described so movingly, women of varied backgrounds and affiliations, and internal exiles such as Jews.[22]

Beginning around 1954, especially in Cole's seminar and in the conversations that grew out of it, Hall and his friends explored the consequences of a
thaw in the Cold War political and intellectual climate. Slowly and hesitatingly,
they tried to think their way through issues that the Cold War made hard to
understand as anything other than an either/or choice. They wondered about
the impact on British culture of Americanization, with its more pervasive liberalism, greater fluidity of class lines, and more advanced forms of consumer
culture. They pondered the implications for the Labour Party of the revival
of the Conservative Party, which beginning in 1951 won a series of electoral
victories. They focused on the implications of the growth of affluence and the
welfare state on both class and culture, wondering how the more widespread
availability of consumer goods and services, from automobiles to televisions to
education, transformed the political and social connections between culture
and politics. After all, Hall had arrived in Britain when rationing was still in
effect and then experienced its lifting and the gradual, but dramatic, spread of
consumer culture. "Whether we knew it or not," he later wrote about the period
of change in the two years before the crises in Suez and Hungary, he and others were "trying to find a language in which to map an emergent 'new world'
and its cultural transformations, which defied analysis within the conventional
terms of the left while at the same time deeply undermining them." In the summer of 1956, absorbing the meaning of Khrushchev's criticisms of Stalin, he
and a friend considered writing a book tentatively titled "Contemporary Capitalism." Away from Oxford, they read *Culture and Environment* (1933), several
chapters of the manuscript of Raymond Williams's soon to appear *Culture and
Society* (1958), Anthony Crosland's *Future of Socialism* (1956), and some of the
recent books from the angry young men, including John Osborne's *Look Back
in Anger* (1957).[23]

Stuart Hall and the British New Left

The events of 1956—in late February the denunciation of Stalin by Nikita
Khrushchev and then in the fall the takeover of Suez by the French and British and the Soviet suppression of a rebellion in Hungary—sent shock waves
through Britain's left. Khrushchev's speech further eroded whatever faith some
on the left still had in the USSR, something that the violent suppression of the
Hungarian uprising reinforced. The British action in Suez made clear to those
on the left that Britain was not easily giving up its imperial position. Members

of the New Left were also responding to what was happening in Britain, trying to figure out how well-worn Marxism and socialism explained, or failed to
explain, contemporary society and politics.[24]

At Oxford, the events of 1956 intensified Hall's search for a new cultural
politics, this time as a leading figure in the British New Left: first as de facto
editor of *Universities and Left Review*, launched in the spring of 1957, and then
as the founding editor of *New Left Review*, which first appeared in 1960. Taking
on these editorial challenges meant that Hall gave up work on his Ph.D. thesis
on Henry James. It is not hard to imagine what interested him about James,
an expatriate who, though he had a very different background and sensibility,
possessed a keen sense of the nature of power, representation, and social conventions. After all, like James, Hall was compelled by questions about what it
meant to live in Britain but be from the colonies, literally and metaphorically.[25]

Hall's editorial work put him into close relationships with an older generation of left intellectuals, including Hoggart, E. P. Thompson, and Williams.
Hall's strongest connections, however, were with members of his own generation. The editorial board of *Universities and Left Review* was composed of two
former members of Great Britain's Communist Party (Gabriel Pearson and Raphael Samuel, both of them Jews who left the Party after Hungary) and two "In-
dependents" (Hall and the Canadian philosopher Charles Taylor). In December
1959 the older and younger generations came together when *New Left Review*
was formed as a result of a merger between *Universities and Left Review* with
The New Reasoner, founded in 1956 by E. P. Thompson and John Saville, two
Marxist historians who had left the Communist Party that year. Hall served as
editor of *New Left Review* in 1960 and 1961.[26]

In response to events at home and abroad, in the late 1950s and early 1960s
members of the New Left distanced themselves from the Communist and Labour parties, both of which Hall and most of his generation in the New Left saw
as going toward dead ends. As the editors of *Universities and Left Review*, Hall
among them, said in the editorial in the first issue, they were working against
dichotomies: between fellow-traveler and Keynesian liberal, between allegiance
to the USSR and to the welfare state. The New Left worked to broaden the definition of politics to include cultural and social dimensions of British life. They
struggled to reformulate Marxism to take new information into account, in the
process creating what the historian Dennis Dworkin has called cultural Marxism and what they themselves (along with their older counterparts) called socialist humanism. They wrestled with how to think about working-class lives,
consumer culture, and new media. Unlike most members of the Frankfurt
School, who emphasized the passivity of consumers and the debasement of

products of what Max Horkheimer and Theodor Adorno called the culture industry, Hall and members of his cohort offered a more positive view of modern commercial culture. Long-term cultural changes took prominence over short-term political considerations. Theirs was a movement seeking not tangible political power but intangible, albeit transformative, understandings.[27]

From Oxford to London

When he left Oxford in 1957, Hall moved to London, where he edited the *Universities and Left Review* and taught adults in Oxford's extramural department and working-class natives and West Indian immigrants in a secondary school. He served a two-year stint, 1957–59, as a substitute teacher at a secondary modern school in Brixton, a neighborhood in south London where native-born whites lived alongside colored immigrants from the British empire. Many of the teachers he knew, he commented soon after, suffered from threats to their morale and status, as parvenu scholarship boys who lived in the suburbs but taught urban students for whose backgrounds and abilities they had little respect. Many of these teachers also inverted "their affronted sense of status into an attack upon" people like Hall, substitute teachers many of whom had migrated from the colonies. In August 1958, right in the middle of his two years of secondary school teaching, riots broke out in at Notting Hill, when young white men, many of them Teddy Boys, attacked the Swedish wife of a West Indian man and then went on a rampage against other West Indians in the vicinity. In the wake of the riots, hostility to immigrants intensified among conservatives. An even broader swath of the British population realized that the nation was no longer so white and homogenous as once imagined. In 1967 Hall recalled that several of the young men in his class had been in the mob and had expressed irreconcilable views. On the one hand, they saw the West Indians as "savages flooding the country, taking jobs, filling up classrooms, stealing women." On the other hand, toward Hall and their West Indian classmates they expressed only positive, friendly views.[28]

Soon after the riots, an unsigned essay in *Universities and Left Review,* in which Hall surely had a hand as the lead editor and an émigré from the West Indies, focused on the events at Notting Hill. Accompanying the essay were the angry words of several fifteen-year-old white girls from West London describing what they saw as the migrants' uncivilized savagery and their taking the women, housing, and jobs of white male Britons. The essay itself noted the prominent role the British Union of Fascists played in the attacks on immigrants. Their leader appeared "on the advertising billboards—right next door," the authors noted, to a sign reading "'Advertising Brings You the Good Things of Life.'" These reactionaries, the essay continued, surely "acted as a trigger," but, quoting the prime minister of Jamaica, the authors asked, "'Who Loaded the Gun?'" This observation thus brought together Hall's Jamaican heritage with his interest in the false promises of commercial culture. What ensued in the essay was an analysis of the abject social conditions in London's slums and the Conservative attacks on an already limited social welfare system that offered little help to poor whites. The article also laid blame for the racist riots on the past and present of British colonial policy. Finally, the authors focused on the riots as an expression of the alienation of white working-class adolescents. "A generation with more to spend but nothing to spend it on" was cast adrift in "the conformist class culture" that surrounded them. They discovered in "song and skiffle, rock and roll, drain-pipe jeans, Tony Curtis haircuts— rhythm, colour, and *violence*" what their confined lives had drained from them. Their action represented "not wilful, violence of the organized minority, but the floating violence of the many."[29]

Along with the events of 1956 and the race riot in Notting Hill, the formation of the Campaign for Nuclear Disarmament (CND) in 1958 was for Hall and those around him a transforming movement. The CND called on Britain to acknowledge that, no longer a world power, it should give up nuclear weapons and not allow the United States to have nuclear military installations on the nation's soil. As Hall wrote in an editorial in the last issue of *Universities and Left Review*, people involved in CND were fed up with "the 'Two Camps' cast of mind, terrified by what C. Wright Mills calls the 'drift and thrust' to World War III." Hall wrote in retrospect that the CND was one of the first of a new type of social movement in the postwar period, like civil rights or environmentalism: a broad-based, radical effort that had appeal across class and organizational lines. While on a march at Aldermaston, Hall met Catherine Barrett, a woman from Northamptonshire who was thirteen years his junior. They married in 1964. As Catherine Hall, his wife emerged as a historian who wrote on the histories of race, class, gender, and colonization in Britain during the long nineteenth century.[30]

After teaching high school, Hall served as editor of *New Left Review* for two years. Then in 1961 he joined the faculty at Chelsea College of Advanced Technology, teaching film and media studies on a full-time basis to students who were preparing for careers in science and technology. For such students education in the media was somewhere between a pleasant distraction and an unscientific pursuit. The position enabled Hall to read sociology and anthropology for the first time, subjects that provided the bridge between Leavisite discussions of culture and broader considerations that his encounters with books by Hoggart and Williams had earlier begun. In the early 1960s he traveled extensively in Britain, teaching some classes in adult education and helping to organize clubs for the New Left. While at Chelsea College he also lectured on westerns at a London prison. Then he worked at the BFI on the project that led to *The Popular Arts*.[31]

Hall as New Left Editor and Essayist

In the late 1950s and early 1960s Hall spelled out his view of Britain's situation, an analysis through which it is possible to see what lay behind his contribution to *The Popular Arts*. The exposure of Britain's imperial ambitions in the Suez crisis and the nation's commitment to an alliance with the United States inspired him to criticize what he saw as retrogressive Cold War policies. In 1961, aligning himself with the nonaligned nations, he argued that the social revolutions in developing nations were not part of the Cold War but revolutions "against the old structure of imperialism and therefore, profoundly hostile to capitalism as an economic system." Following what Mills had written in *Listen, Yankee: The Revolution in Cuba* (1960), Hall defended the Cuban revolution as one continually in process, as he combined a celebration of the Cuban leadership's "improvisational flair" with worry about the possibility that "totalitarian abuse" in the future might limit the possibility of socialist revolutions elsewhere. Soon after, writing on the strengthening of the Common Market, Hall reiterated his concerns with Cold War international relations, American foreign policy, and the well-being of developing nations. This time he connected these issues to the future of left politics in Britain and on the Continent. Hall dreamed of a "radical alternative" that involved increasingly neutral nations in the developing world and in Western Europe along with "a determined reshaping of our own economic structure" that would simultaneously strengthen the British left and enable Britain to stand aside from "the new menacing homogeneity of the Western Alliance."[32]

Domestically, Hall worried about a number of issues. He regretted the consolidation of the Labour Party's welfare state and the return to power of the Conservative Party in 1951. He was also concerned with the growth, albeit uneven, in the affluence of members of the lower middle class and middle class, many of whom were working class in origin who now held jobs in private industry and the service sector. All these forces were helping to create vested interests that stood in opposition to an expanded welfare state based on increased taxation. Hall stood in opposition to those, free-market Conservatives as well as

Labourites like Crosland, whom he considered "champions of 'me-too' advance into the calm waters of an 'American' future." Characteristically for this period, Hall did not mention the Britain's disenfranchised Africans, West Indians, or South Asians. Rather, he focused on the "inarticulate needs" of members of the skilled working class, unmarked in terms of race but presumably white. Hall refused to see them, as he claimed many Labour leaders did, as embodying "the crass, debased image of telly-glued, car-raving mindless *consumers*." Treating them as citizens for whom community was more important than individualism, Hall instead called for dramatic expansion of social welfare programs.[33]

Hall found left politics struggling to give voice and meaning to emerging social realities, which meant that talk of dramatic changes in the experience of social class, as well as what Americans called democratic capitalism, hid deep social and cultural fissures. In the editorial of the first issue of *New Left Review*, Hall, convinced that a narrow conception of politics had caused youth to reject socialism, called on the British left to build "a genuinely popular socialist movement." To do so, it was necessary to focus not just on the political and economic but also on the cultural and social. Concentration on popular culture was essential, for it was "directly relevant to the imaginative resistances of people who have to live within capitalism—the growing points of social discontent, the projections of deeply-felt needs." Of note here is the way Hall linked youth culture, resistance, and feelings as part of an effort to insist that socialists had to accept popular culture as a given and enter the fray over its meanings.[34]

In the late 1950s and early 1960s Hall built his analysis of contemporary capitalism, in which consumption was central, from a wide range of sources. He drew on the works of Hoggart and more fully of Williams, on rereadings of Marx, especially the newly available *Economic and Philosophical Manuscripts*, and on the works of widely read American social critics, including C. Wright Mills's *The Power Elite* (1956), John Kenneth Galbraith's *The Affluent Society* (1958), and David Riesman's *The Lonely Crowd* (1950). In postwar Britain, the growth of corporations, the increasing separation of ownership and control, and the rise of a managerial class that included in its ranks people recruited from the working class meant that ownership had become harder to locate and responsibility more difficult to assign. At the same time, the growth of the service sector and of industries shaped by new technologies and by automation had increasingly replaced the physically exhausting work in coal mines and steel factories with work that required more brains than brawn, as well as some tolerance of boredom. Drawing on the work of Riesman, Hall heralded "a shift 'from the hardness of materials to the softness of men.'" Hall saw this happening in working-class urban districts, but especially in new suburban towns where there were "subtle modes of status differentiation and striving, a new kind of individualism which enters working class lives" through home furnishings and popular magazines. In contrast, when Hall wrote these words in 1958, Gans was already undertaking the research in Boston and Levittown that enabled him to argue that in new suburban towns and old urban neighborhoods there was more community and resilience than individualism and submission. More germane, Riesman's concept of the other-directed person, sensitive to the experience of others, gave Hall the language to describe a status-driven population.[35]

As a rising standard of living had begun to change consciousness, turning workers into consumers, what compelled Hall's attention was how cultural forces enhanced the power of persuasion. What was critical here was advertising and personnel management, aided by the extension of credit through hire-purchase, which was the British term for installment plans. Capitalism promoted the fantasies and dreams that newly or more widely available consumer goods and services might make possible. Central to all these changes was what Hall called "a sense of classlessness." It was not that Britain was becoming a less class-bound society but that new kinds of capitalism had given the *appearance* of classlessness, to the working class but especially to working-class youth. Ultimately, consumer capitalism involved a situation in which working people not only "genuinely began to savour the joys of personal display and status through the possession of goods" but also experienced "more muted, more confusing" patterns of partial satisfactions and unfulfilled longings. Rather than creating a utopian society, consumer capitalism "gave us a definition of the Good Life."[36]

Central to Hall's analysis was an exploration of new methods of persuasion, advertising especially. Here and elsewhere Hall seemed to adopt the stance that Hoggart had offered in the second half of *The Uses of Literacy*, where, in Hall's own words (and ones somewhat more up to date than those of Hoggart), he cast a skeptical eye on "the *way of life* based on telly and the glossy magazines." Alienation had surpassed what Marx predicted, with goods accumulating "a *social value*," in the process becoming "insignias of class and status" through whose possession working-class families could "*realise* themselves" even as they aspired to live like the wealthy. Thus in both production and consumption "the working class is gradually becoming factors in its own permanent alienation." Hall also recognized the sexualization of consumer dreams, writing in 1960 of the role that "the figures of sexual sensation" played "in the general montage of 'Success,' seducing our consciousness, undermining and corrupting moral standards, encouraging a weak, flaccid, self-indulgence at odds with adult, critical standards demanded by life." Only in dreams, fostered by sex "as the universal salesman of prosperity" and by the promotion of a false sense of social status, was the gap between rich and poor closeable. The mass media "continually feed and nourish these fantasies, eagerly opening the windows of the Dorchester set, giving little glimpses of the Success Heroes lolling on the beaches in Jamaica." Here Hall implicitly contrasted a tourist version of Jamaica with the more workaday island he had known. This was one of the rare times in the main body of his social and economic analysis that Hall mentioned (and even so only in passing) his original homeland. Moreover, he did so without acknowledging the presence of West Indians in Britain.[37]

The results of all these changes were momentous. Although Hall understood that much had remained the same, the thrust of his argument was that there had occurred a shift in focus from production to consumption that heralded a new consumer capitalism. "Because of increased purchasing power," Hall wrote in 1958, "the commodities which the worker as *producer* makes at the factory, he purchases back as a *consumer* in the shops." These changes threatened to replace the communal or cooperative nature of working-class life that Hoggart had portrayed in the first half of *The Uses of Literacy* and that Williams had written on extensively. What took their place was what Hall described as "the bourgeois notion of society as a stage upon which each individual tries to 'realise' himself through personal effort and competitiveness." Again and again he drew a dismal picture of the impact of commercial culture. He envisioned "a bland, half-thing of a man, peering nervously at the frontiers of consumption and taste," whom consumer capitalism offered the promise of freedom even as it made its reality impossible. New consumers were anxious, apathetic, unsuccessfully striving, and confused, with many members of the working class among them having lost their commitment to a communal way of life. With communal solidarity giving way to a series of lifestyles, the processes of anxious individual striving took hold, with alienation more than exploitation as the result. At times skeptical as to whether modern capitalism had successfully captured the consciousness of Britons of modest means, Hall was far from assuming that citizen-consumers were puritanical. He distinguished between the "natural aspiration of ordinary people to improve their material circumstances" and the way media encouraged them to develop "social envy and status seeking."[38]

This new kind of capitalism, with the promise of consumer choices and pleasures at its center but its results more mixed, set clear limits to the possibilities of progressive social and political change. Here Hall drew on the writing of Mills, who had argued, as Hall reported, that the "'mass' has been, if you like, 'proletarianized'—not, as Marx thought *downwards* towards minimum wage levels, but *upwards* toward roughly middle-class styles of living." In addition, relying on the work of Galbraith, Hall emphasized the gap between the abundance of private goods and the stinginess of public ones. However, more so than Galbraith, the Canadian economist who lived in the United States, Hall saw the contradiction as the source of "*structural* faults and weaknesses" of the capitalist system rather than, as Galbraith had suggested, one remediable by changes in tax policy.[39]

In working all this out, Hall had to recast the traditional Marxist distinction between an all-powerful economic base and a mostly reflective superstructure. He wanted to reformulate the left's view of working-class culture and politics, blurring or expanding the sense of class dynamics and placing popular culture in a more central position. What concerned him were the ways that the old left had refused to take mass culture seriously because they considered it a mere epiphenomenon. If he placed culture in a key position, he did so not because he did not take politics seriously but because for him culture was political. As Williams was doing at the same time, Hall was revising the base-superstructure model, where culture, once thought of as peripheral and a product of the base, was now central and a key element in the base. "We want to break with the view that cultural or family life is an entertaining sideshow," the editors of *Universities and Left Review* wrote in the summer of 1958. Insisting on the importance of both the cultural and the economic, they asserted that "literature and art as well as the machine can be made the groundwork of a fuller life for the human person and the community." Similarly, writing in "A Sense of Classlessness" in 1958, Hall called for a "much freer play in our interpretation between 'base' and 'superstructure'" than that offered in "vulgar-Marxist interpretations." Forms of communication, he insisted, were an integral part of the productive system. He went on to assert that "they were not peripheral to the 'economic base': they are part of it."[40]

Youth played an important role in Hall's analysis, even earlier than C. Wright Mills's "Letter to the New Left," which first appeared in *New Left Review* in the fall of 1960 before being published in the United States a year later. Mills argued that the left had to turn away from what he called "the labor metaphysic" and realize that it was the "young intelligentsia" who might provide "a possible, immediate, radical agency of change." If Mills emphasized both "young" and "intelligentsia," Hall and his colleagues, who fit both categories, emphasized the young more than the intelligentsia even as they made clear that they found the category of "working class" too restrictive. How important youth was to Hall became clear when he reviewed a series of books on secondary modern schools, which he saw as a cauldron of cultural and social conflict in the modern but class-segregated British welfare state. Hall pictured the kind of students he taught as full of talent and potential. However, they were dragged down by the educational and social system that, not willing to offer them what Pierre Bourdieu would later call cultural capital, was pegging them in a low-status social slot. In their early teens, they entered the orbit of peer culture and "the heady atmosphere of the mass entertainments." As they began to face the prospect of dead-end jobs when they finished school, "the aimless frenzy of their leisure life" became "a displacement of the energies and aspirations which have been trained or drained out of them by school and work." Connecting racialization and alienation, Hall insisted that what inspired acting out against "'niggers' or 'paddies' or 'yids'" came from "a deeper level of social frustration against the society and the adult world."[41]

In thinking about the relationship between class and education, Hall was beginning to develop the categories of cultural analysis that he and Whannel would elaborate in *The Popular Arts*. The patterns of education in these schools provided him, he remarked in 1959, with clues to explain "the increasing gap between 'high' and 'popular' culture, and for the degeneration of 'popular' culture into 'mass culture,'" distinctions central to the 1964 book. The "cultural gap between the 'haves' and the 'have-nots'" provided "the conditions within which the purveyors of mass culture operate." Without such deep social divisions, he argued, a common culture, available to everyone but transformed by the experiences of divergent social groups, would ensure "a genuinely democratic society." Youth remained emotionally attached "to its commodities: whilst 'high culture' is increasingly taken over by dilettantism, precocity, and narrowness, and marked by that thinness of response and lack of social relevance which characterizes so much minority art." Similarly, schools rejected the youth culture based on leisure as teachers struggled unsuccessfully with their students' boredom and confusion. Over time schools and families lost the battle for the emotional lives of youth, as "the quarrel between the generations becomes a vast, deadly silence of incomprehension." Postwar prosperity had thus raised the expectations nonelite youth had for their futures without allowing them genuine satisfaction.[42]

At the end of his long essay on youth culture, Hall turned more optimistic as he shifted his attention from working-class teens, who benefited from the spread of affluence but remained trapped socially, to more socially mobile university students, who were the harbingers of a more politicized response. "The sophisticated advance guard of the teenage revolution"—which is how he described students at universities, technical colleges, and art schools, as well as those in advanced apprentice programs—were "articulate in their protest about social issues," the atomic bomb, and South Africa. "If the cool young men of today were to become the social conscience of tomorrow," he concluded, this would not be the "first Utopia" that "came out of social deprivation."[43]

Usually without being explicit, Hall's focus on youth culture was highly gendered. He paid special attention to unmarried males from the working class who were benefiting from the rise of their discretionary incomes so they could purchase commercial goods and experiences inspired by what American capitalism produced for its own burgeoning youth market. In his analysis of postwar British capitalism, Hall was among those in the British New Left who were connecting youth, masculinity, and self-expression with what he called "the power and capacity to feel" and feel intensely. Here he drew on Williams's notion of structures of feeling, which Williams first discussed in a 1954 book on film. As Susan Brook has argued, Hall, along with his contemporaries, saw feeling as a key element "in the vitality and energy of postwar youth culture," offering "an alternative to Britain's moribund, hidebound hierarchies" of a postwar world that was not changing fast enough.[44]

Unlike Hoggart, who connected postwar youth culture with danger, Hall reformulated ideas about the sources of frustration and transformation in the popular culture and everyday life of British youth. Moreover, he based resistance on an assertion of feelings associated with pleasure. For Hall, the danger was not the expressiveness of youth culture but the lack of expressiveness in British politics and society. Thus in 1959 he wrote that British "politics has no emotional resonance, and no humanity: it is stiff, and dry and colourless and conciliatory." He called for "new ways of speaking together about the deep, immobilizing contradictions of our culture," which appeared most clearly, not in traditional politics but "in our ways of feeling and response, in the manners and postures of our moral life." If the language of ordinary politics could not provide the necessary combination of feeling and morality, then the language of exceptional literature could. "What we need above all, as Leavis once remarked of the nineteenth century novel," Hall wrote as he talked about socialist humanism, "'is a vital capacity for experience, a kind of reverent openness before life, and a marked moral intensity.'"[45]

Thus, unlike Hoggart or Leavis, Hall located the source of resistance and hope in youth culture, especially among male working-class youth. Writing about groups such as Teddy Boys and in some ways paralleling what Norman Mailer had written in "The White Negro" (1957) about "cool" as an attitude among white, marginalized hipsters, Hall spoke of how when adolescents danced, "the absence of feeling in their faces and eyes betrays the depth of

Figure 9. This July 1955 photograph shows a group of Teddy Boys hanging out in South London. In *The Uses of Literacy* (1957) Richard Hoggart had denounced these working-class youths as "Juke-Box Boys" for their embrace of a "candy floss world." In contrast, a year later, Stuart Hall looked at this working-class, teen subculture, some of whose members had attacked immigrants of color in the Notting Hill riots, as exemplifying vital, new forms of cultural expression. Popperfoto/Getty Images.

feeling they have," something they evidenced in "an expressive language of their own: a language of rhythm, in jazz and skiffle, a language of movement in jive . . . a language of colour and variety in their dress." Here Hall used key words that evoked a world of pleasure expressed through youth culture, words like "feeling," "experience," "movement," "expressive," "color." Tellingly, when he discussed working-class and middle-class adults as consumers, Hall took the familiar, moralistic line that they participated in a consumer capitalism that was bored, bland, and anxious. Yet when he came to discuss youths as participants in consumer capitalism, he saw them as feeling, pleasure-seeking people. He thus reversed the positions Hoggart held, that working-class adults sought pleasure in ordinary commercial goods and experience but that youth immorally succumbed to popular culture.[46]

As the reference to Leavis just above suggests, literature played a key role in Hall's analysis. Using Leavisite language, in 1958 Hall remarked that restoring literature to its proper place in social analysis meant it was "the centre which we need now, to give our lives—and our culture—meaning." Three years later, he made clear his preference for culture over politics, literature over Marxist analysis. D. H. Lawrence's novel *Women in Love*, he wrote in *New Left Review* in summer of 1961, "deals more creatively with the theme of human alienation than most Marxist treatises." Moreover, when he turned his attention to the relationship between different levels of cultural expression, Hall made clear his opposition to separating high from popular. Even if one acknowledged such a split, he wrote in the summer of 1958, this division "represents the depth of man's alienation from himself and his creations," in the process revealing "the solidarities of class-life in the Opportunity State," the name given to Conservative Party prime minister Harold Macmillan's vision.[47]

Hall's analysis did not go unchallenged, nowhere more forcefully than by E. P. Thompson, a towering figure at this stage in the development of cultural Marxism. Writing in response to Hall's 1958 "A Sense of Classlessness," Thompson offered a biting critique of Hall specifically and culturalism more generally. "The ULR types," he wrote, were passionate in their cultural commitments but avoided commitment when it came to power and politics. They were more angry "about ugly architecture than they are about the ugly poverty of old-age pensioners, angrier about the 'materialism' of the Labour Movement than about the rapacity of financiers." Their insensitivity to issues the working class faced came through in their wearing "upon their sleeves a tender sensibility" and in their being "more at ease discussing alienation than exploitation." They had excessive admiration for Matthew Arnold and F. R. Leavis but insufficient concern with the plight of workers. As solutions to social problems they offered "only education and cultural therapy . . . too pure-at-heart to immerse themselves" in the demanding messiness of political action. "The whole lot may be dismissed by the communal socialist as the last intellectual waifs and strays in the long romantic grouse against industrialism, striking in Soho the final futile attitudes of protest in the face of the inexorable approach of the nuclear age."[48]

I quote Thompson at length because his position was so clear and his tone so passionate. Whenever Hall spoke in public debates, his arguments seemed nuanced, tentative, and self-reflexive. However, more than tone was at issue in the disagreement. Thompson articulated some generational differences among those on the left. He valued workers more than youth, politics as much as culture, discipline more than feeling, social theory more than literary analysis, class struggle more than cultural conflict, and presence in a union hall more than at a coffee bar. Hall responded to the critiques of Thompson and others, saying he was glad to "take the opportunity to pick up one or two of the bricks and heave them back." He then went on to clarify his position, asserting that socialists had to develop fresh understandings in order to come to terms with the power and newness of postwar consumer capitalism. Not surprisingly by 1962, the coalitions that undergirded the *New Left Review*, which originally brought together the generations that Thompson and Hall represented, were breaking apart, over issues involving the place of history, theory, and activism in the left. With the appointment of Perry Anderson as editor of *New Left Review* in 1962, Hall, living in London, turned his attention away from editorial work and increasingly toward the serious study of popular culture. Collaborating with Whannel, at least implicitly he responded more fully to Thompson's critique in *The Popular Arts*, something especially important given Thompson's considerable influence on New Left discussions.[49]

"Popular Culture and Personal Responsibility"

For both Whannel and Hall, *The Popular Arts* emerged out of a combination of left politics, epochal social and cultural changes, and secondary school teaching. In 1959 the Crowther Report had warned about the ways mass media threatened the nation's youth. Three years later the Pilkington Report warned of the dangers of commercial television. A more immediate impetus to Whannel and Hall to write *The Popular Arts* was a three-day conference in October 1960, "Popular Culture and Personal Responsibility," sponsored by the National Union of Teachers (NUT). This brought together teachers, parents, government officials, local authorities, university leaders, and representatives of media, women's groups, labor unions, cultural institutions, religious bodies, and youth organizations. Over three hundred people attended, most notably for our purposes Hoggart, Hall, Williams, Whannel, and Richard Hamilton. As he opened the conference, the president of the NUT, reflecting the persistence of an older cultural order, threw down the gauntlet to those like Hall and Whannel who would treat popular culture sympathetically. He stood in opposition to "the cheap, the meretricious and the nasty" as forces that worked against values he wished to inculcate in the classroom.[50]

When it came time for Whannel to talk, he began by showing a seventeen-minute documentary film, *Next Time*, produced in 1957 and sponsored by a grant from the BFI. With no narration, the film revealed crowds of people in Piccadilly on weekends, focusing on how they experienced flirtation, prostitution, and commercial culture. This screening underscored how central to Whannel and to Hall were documentaries, especially those that emerged from the Free Cinema movement. In his comments, Whannel focused on how to offer an authentic treatment of violence and sex in movies. He talked movingly about sex and love, exploring how a couple went to a movie, hoping to have their feelings "given some meaning and form in the picture," but would come away from a bad movie with "a stereotyped way of thinking which does not enrich your contact one with the other." Finally, he focused on an issue he explored in the *Teacher*, how instructors in secondary schools should approach media analytically. Education did not involve passive spectatorship "of a processed culture, nor should it be the patronized handmaiden of a technological society or a training of an elite whose culture is dried up at the roots because it is cut off from life." Rather, education should "really transform our society and create a future which is rich for us all because it has a culture shared by all." Using Leavisite language, Whannel called for "a programme of the teaching of discrimination in relation to film and television and other media," distinguishing between good and bad in popular culture "by recognizing there is a difference between jazz and rock-and-roll and between Ella Fitzgerald and Frankie Laine." Avoid teaching popular culture as a way to something higher, he cautioned teachers, for that would be "rather like the vicar having skiffle," a British improvisational folk music, "in the crypt to help teach religion—for they know this is only a stepping stone to something they will really not enjoy much."[51]

Hall used Leavisite language at the conference to echo what Whannel had said. He found among teachers either "a sort of philistine disdain" that left them unwilling to work imaginatively to teach their students about popular culture or "the attitude of the high cultural elite, which says—there is no point in talking to children of this kind about television, you have to lead them to an appreciation of higher things." Like Whannel, he urged teachers "to help children discriminate as regards mass media" by developing "a very sharp critical response to the media themselves, increasing critical, discriminating sense of what was good and what was bad." He wanted to emphasize "a general extension of quality over the whole field," rather than to distinguish between high and popular.[52]

The impression one gets from what Hall and Whannel said at the conference was that they were fighting a lonely battle against philistines and elitists. Yet had they listened carefully to a speech by Richard Hamilton, an artist and critic who had been an important member of the Independent Group but whose politics were not theirs, they would have heard a position that was much more accepting of commercial culture than theirs, less discriminating. "The mass media," Hamilton remarked, "cannot project a moral philosophy of form but they can, and do, go some way to set examples of what is smart, enviable, and worth attaining," which he found in Bauhaus design, in the covers of *Harper's Bazaar*, in glossy magazines, in Hollywood sets, and in American automobile design. The creators of mass media differed from the moralists in "their refusal to accept the dogma of permanent values and in their efforts to welcome and promote the machine age with humour and affection." He called on teachers to develop an approach to education that embodied "a positive sense towards a complete understanding of the techniques of the mass media, whose products they already know and appreciate." In important ways Hamilton went beyond Whannel and Hall. He evoked popular culture as bricolage, suggesting that every classroom have a bulletin board on which students could put up "bits that they tore out of magazines or horror comics." He called for teachers to embrace "the new sensibilities of younger people." And he endorsed an ethic of pleasurable enjoyment, remarking that teachers should figure out what the younger generation enjoyed. "If we can go with them rather than against them," he concluded, "the battle is going to be very much easier." Yet the conference provided an important impetus for Hall and Whannel to write *The Popular Arts*. They bristled at how speakers had used the language of how media debased standards and how teachers, in return, had to elevate the taste of their students. They well understood the tension "between the values inculcated in the classroom and those encountered by young people in the world outside."[53]

The Popular Arts (1964)

The Popular Arts appeared at a time when there was remarkably little focused scholarship on popular culture, even in America, where Riesman was among the few respected intellectuals to take it seriously rather than simply denounce it. Hall and Whannel ranged widely in their discussion of popular culture, focusing on newspapers, advertising, romance novels, detective stories, radio, television, documentaries, and musical genres including rock and roll, jazz, and the blues. They were determined to reject the approach to popular culture that focused on its effects and instead consider its content critically. They relied on a number of writers, their own colleagues in the New Left, as well as Williams, Hoggart, McLuhan, Eliot, and the Leavises. Like F. R. Leavis, they extended the social reach of education in textual analysis and used literary criticism to analyze a wide range of texts. Especially in *Education and the University*, they asserted, he had "argued convincingly that criticism, with its attention to a whole response and its concern for the life of the mind and the tone of civilization, is a creative activity in the true sense," a series of commitments they wished to apply and extend. As F. R. Leavis and Denys Thompson had done in *Culture and Environment*, Hall and Whannel offered school teachers practical guidance on the teaching of popular culture, providing as they did material for instruction in classes. At the end of the book Hall and Whannel recommended projects for teachers to follow, as well as long lists of books to read, records to listen to, film and television to watch, and organizations to call on.[54]

They wrote with an awareness of the tension between teachers who wanted to persuade their students to oppose popular culture and students who embraced an unthinking indulgence. In the book's opening paragraph they remarked that like other teachers in secondary modern schools they were "acutely aware of the conflict between the norms and expectations of formal education and the complexities of the real world which children and young people inhabit." Some teachers, they claimed later in the book, saw "a uniform mass culture standing in bleak hostility to the traditional virtues," while others wanted to use the study of popular culture as a teaser to elevate taste of students who loved living in the worlds of popular culture. In response, most teachers treated mass media either as entertainment or as the object of moral censure. Others, more sympathetic to their students, saw classes on popular music or jazz as "stepping- stones in a hierarchy of taste" eventually leading students to appreciate Shakespeare or Mozart.[55]

For Hall and Whannel discrimination was the central activity of the critic. Quoting McLuhan's *The Mechanical Bride*, they underscored the importance of the "*activity of perception and judgment*" when examining "a great range of particular acts and experiences." Like Q. D. Leavis and Hoggart, the authors of *The Popular Arts* were interested in the dynamics of the relationships between producers and consumers of culture, as well as between high, literary culture and popular culture. They adopted from Arnold and F. R. Leavis a commitment to use discrimination and judgment in order to analyze popular culture. However, they differed from them in several important respects. In their hands, discrimination was not, as it was for Leavisites, a tool to criticize debased popular culture but rather to challenge the widely accepted binaries of high/low and good/bad that dominated the discussion of culture. They insisted that all culture be judged on terms particular to its own genre and purpose, arguing that "jazz music and the movies have their own special virtues but it is doubtful if these can be revealed when they are regarded only as stepping-stones in a hierarchy of taste." With Hannah Arendt in mind, they distanced themselves from the way many from the Frankfurt School celebrated high art as permanent but demeaned mass or folk art as ephemeral. "Is there, in fact," they asked rhetorically about new media as art, "a body of cultural work which can be discussed and judged in creative terms, but which does not 'resist' time in quite the way she suggests."[56]

Hall and Whannel separated themselves from Leavis even further than Hoggart had. Like other left-Leavisites, they were more democratic and less elitist than either of their predecessors, displaying remarkably little evidence of what they called in their book the "language of moral censure" others had used to castigate popular cultural expressions. Turning against what they called "cultural nostalgia," they did not look back to better times, neither to Leavis's Britain before the Industrial Revolution nor to Hoggart's working class in the interwar years. Nor did they want what Q. D. Leavis had called "resistance by an armed and conscious minority" to contemporary culture; rather, they sought to find "the points of growth" especially among youth "within the society that now exists." They also differed from Leavis and in many ways from Hoggart because they wished to use discrimination not to condemn popular culture but to study it. More so than Hoggart, Hall and Whannel complicated the simple division between a worthy high culture and a debased popular one. Allowing themselves more wiggle room than a strict Leavisite position but not entirely abandoning its premises, they separated popular and mass arts, something neither Hoggart nor the members of the Independent Group did clearly if at all. They held in high esteem popular arts, which they believed folk culture had influenced. They admired the blues, which they connected to "the experience of the negro folk." They credited jazz with "much of the expressive intensity of folk art." Moreover, in a way that made clear the political valence of popular culture, they hailed the way contemporary jazz musicians returned "to the blues and to 'soul'" in ways that "directly connected" music "with the new urgency with which negro minorities in America are seeking their identity and their freedom within the American community." They believed that in contrast to most commercial popular music, produced under conditions not unlike what obtained on the assembly line, "commercial jazz seems capable of inner growth and change." They asserted that some of the products of contemporary culture, such as the movies of Charlie Chaplin and John Ford

Figure 10. In *The Popular Arts* (1964) Stuart Hall and Paddy Whannel
prominently featured this still from the 1946 movie *My Darling Clementine*,
directed by John Ford and starring Henry Fonda (pictured here as
Wyatt Earp). Hall and Whannel joined others, including members of the
Independent Group and C. L. R. James, who admired American westerns
for how they revealed the creativity of popular culture and challenged
hierarchal understandings of cultural productions. Courtesy of Photofest.

or the jazz of Miles Davis, took their inspiration from folk traditions. For example, they lauded Ford's depiction of a Sunday morning in Tombstone City in *My Darling Clementine* (1946) for its "evocation of mood, the creation of a sense of community" and for Henry Fonda's playing Wyatt Earp "with extraordinary delicacy."[57]

For them, popular arts represented authentic, challenging, creative, and from-the-bottom-up expressions of the experiences of urban Britons. Because of the connection of the popular to both high and folk, it was worthy of respect and serious analysis rather than simplified condemnation. When popular arts used conventions, they did so to surprise and delight, not to pander. Popular art, Hall and Whannel insisted, "persuades by the depths and intensity of its feelings and values." It relies on a dynamic relationship between performer and audience, "improvised," they wrote, "out of the common experiences which audience and performer share," experiences that were "deepened when re-enacted." Drawing on "the force and imprint of his personal style" and re-establishing a rapport with the audience that the folk artist had, the popular artist used "familiar conventions and compression and stylization" to intensify communally shared qualities. In contrast, Hall and Whannel relied on the familiar tropes of critics of mass culture when they identified the formulaic top-down, escapist mass arts that corrupted popular arts, such as the performances of Liberace, movies like *The Ten Commandments* (1956), and the detective novels of Mickey Spillane. They found these cultural products manipulative and formulaic expressions of lesser quality shaped by commercial forces and lacking respect for those they tried to reach. If members of the Independent Group earlier had embraced a wide range of mass culture, for Hall and Whannel mass culture became a corrupt form of the popular, a distinction so central to their analysis.[58]

The result was that Hall and Whannel were considerably more successful and capacious than most contemporary cultural critics in their exploration of what an analysis of the tone, style, and content of texts (those of high literature and popular culture in distinct realms but with equal seriousness) would reveal about a community's structures of feeling. Elsewhere, Hall wrote of film teaching as offering "an education of the feelings," "a deepening of existing pleasures," and, quoting Williams without naming him, "the 'structure of feeling.'" Again and again in their book, they connected feelings with spontaneity, pleasure, and intensity. Drawing on the writings of D. H. Lawrence when they focused on romance novels, Hall and Whannel called on educators to connect discussions of media treatments of love and sexuality with an education of feelings. Related was their emphasis on a healthy sexuality, which they defined as

connected to love and "permanent" relationships. They insisted on the difference between the faked sex offered by mass culture and the authentic version
proffered by popular arts.[59]

Although they paid little attention to television, in their discussions of
music, movies, and advertising, Hall and Whannel vividly conveyed what it
meant to realize that literary texts were not the only kinds of imaginative works
it was possible to analyze and understand. The distinctions between serious
and popular culture made by those holding "conventional ethical attitudes,"
they insisted, offered "a false framework for reference and judgement." They
explored a series of advertisements that relied on "*sophisticated* style." They
explored how in ads "hidden psychological feelings are being explored, subtle
associations are made, strange, dream-like transformations enacted." They argued that the conflict between the good and the "debased" was "not a struggle
against the modern forms of communication, but a conflict *within* these media."
They believed the cultural critic should pay "attention to style and form—the
way the communication is made, and its internal and implied rhythms and emphases." To illustrate this they pointed to *A Generation* by the Polish filmmaker
Andrzej Wajda, which they insisted should be examined as both a literary and
a visual text, one with both an aesthetics and a politics.[60]

These commitments led Hall and Whannel to analyze artifacts of commercial culture in rich and symbolic ways that underscore how they were moving toward a Marxist-inflected symbolic analysis of consumption. In a chapter
whose title, "The Big Bazaar," came from *White Collar* (1951) by Mills, they explored what such symbolic analysis would reveal as they gave close and imaginative readings of the words and images contained in advertisements. Here
they also drew on a 1960 article by Williams in *New Left Review* on advertising as "The Magic System." Using a quote from his article, they asserted that
objects "must be validated, if only in fantasy, by association with social and
personal meanings," how the "magic system" suggested ways of "negotiating
problems of death, loneliness, frustration, the need for respect and identity."
Hall and Whannel, like Williams, did not treat advertisements as free-floating
symbolic expressions. Exploring the dynamic and complex relationships between base and superstructure, they connected the cultural and economic as
they suffused their discussion with references to privatization of needs as well
as to mystification and control of markets. They made careful distinctions between advertisements of varying quality, noting that while some were crude
and all were manipulative and of dubious social usefulness, others were "skil-
ful, witty, beautifully composed, with an excellent use of colour, line, typogra-
phy, and illustration."[61]

Hall and Whannel went on to speak of commercial images as "a kind of visual metaphor: a symbol of the total appeal" brought together by design, pictures, and words. They illustrated this by pointing to an advertisement for Vaseline Liquid Shampoo, which they analyzed in terms of how the picture and words involved language and argument that they analyzed as if it were a literary text. In a way reminiscent of what McLuhan had done in *The Mechanical Bride*, which they had read, or what Roland Barthes achieved in *Mythologies* or Umberto Eco in *Misreadings*, neither of which they had seen, they examined advertisements as texts, examples of "a kind of bastard art, whose purpose is to mobilize human aspirations and values, . . . specifically to attach them by sleight-of-hand to the sphere of consumption." They explored how ads for shampoo, cutlery, shoes, and perfume, when critically and imaginatively read, conveyed the meaning of security, love, gender, excitement, and nationalism. Advertising, they noted, was "teaching society new ways of feeling and thinking, and new ways of giving expression to human values in its imaginative work."[62]

While they understood ads as having aspects of a playful visual culture, more so than with any other cultural form they drew on their New Left commitments to offer a biting critique. There was no rapport here between producers and consumers, for they saw advertising as "a one-way transmission" that alienated work from consumption. Advertising, with its appeal to the individual, was antisocial and anticommunal. Thus in the end, though they recognized the artfulness of much advertising, in most cases, they had to acknowledge that the fact that "social attitudes are being used for the purpose of selling goods and the artistic skill involved only makes the process of manipulation more effective—and, by the same token, socially more damaging." Tellingly, what followed the chapter on advertising was one titled "The Institutions" in which they explored the economic base of media cultures. Marxists would have placed such a discussion at the book's beginning; instead, Hall and Whannel chose to place it near the end in a way that followed up on their analysis of advertising as the form of socially deleterious mass media.[63]

One of the most striking differences between *The Uses of Literacy* and *The Popular Arts* involved the shift in focus from the working class to urban youth as the object of analysis and the repository of hopes. Scholars have recognized that the work of Hoggart, Thompson, and Williams grew out of their experiences in worker education. Less well understood is that the writings of Hall and Whannel emerged from their jobs as secondary school teachers. Teaching high school in urban settings, Hall and Whannel wanted

The Popular Arts to be pedagogical in purpose, written with an eye to how teachers could educate students shaped by popular culture. This fundamentally informed their outlook: not only did youth replace class as the reigning social category but musical and visual media replaced what were for Hoggart characteristically printed texts. *The Popular Arts* appeared at a time when economic, social, and political changes in Britain were eroding the solidity of the working class and heightening the outlines of a new youth culture. Thus Hall and Whannel playfully but romantically conveyed what it was like to be inside contemporary youth culture. In political engagement, sexual experimentation, and popular culture, they found evidence of the "ways the younger generation have acted as a creative minority, pioneering ahead of the puritan restraints so deeply built into English bourgeois morality, towards a code of behaviour . . . more humane and civilized." Moreover, they did not think youth were victims of false consciousness promoted by mass media. Rather, they envisioned a dynamic tension between "the authentic and the manufactured," between "the use actually made by the audience" and that "intended by the provider," which "never wholly coincide, and frequently conflict." For Hall and Whannel the "fantasies and reveries" of popular culture offered "an important way of coming to terms with emotional problems not involved in our waking lives."[64]

The task Hall and Whannel set for themselves was not to "wean teenagers away from the juke-box heroes, but to alert them to the severe limitations and the ephemeral quality of music" that commercial imperatives shaped. In light of such pressures, the job of the critic was, they wrote in language that drew on the writings of Williams, the "widening of sensibility and emotional range . . . an extension of tastes which might lead to an extension of pleasure." Aware of how British youth both absorbed and resisted commercial culture, they also articulated a more complicated understanding of mass media than Hoggart. The "symbolic fictions" that commercial culture offered was "the folklore by means of which the teenager, in part, shapes and composes his mental picture of the world." As they pointed to how young Britons adopted and played with commercialized versions of the Twist, they wrote that teen culture "is a contradictory mixture of the authentic and the manufactured: it is an area of self-expression for the young and a lush grazing pasture for the commercial providers." As illustration, they pointed to two contrasting cinematic depictions of teen culture: the picture of "relaxed and informal" teens from Karel Reisz's *The Lambeth Boys* (1959) and "a rather frenzied and orgiastic" rendering from Basil Dearden's *Violent Playground* (1958).[65]

The Popular Arts in Perspective

The Popular Arts was not without problems. When they wrote the book, Hall and Whannel were in the process of making the shift from the literary analysis of Leavis/Hoggart to an approach based on sociology and anthropology, but that process was incomplete. They remained worried about the relativism and functional analysis of the social sciences. The anthropological approach, they wrote, "invites a slack relativism, whereby pop music of any kind is excused because it plays a functional role in the teenage world." Rather, they remained wedded to the critical apparatus that literary studies provided. Moreover, central to their book was the problematic distinction between popular and mass, which replaced the binary of high/low with a tripartite division of high/popular/mass.[66]

Race was also a problematic topic. Hall and Whannel were more committed than Hoggart to discuss its role in popular culture, best seen in their treatment of jazz and the blues. However, although they praised jazz for its authenticity, they cast a less-than-appreciative eye on rock and roll musicians such as Fats Domino and Ray Charles who were so deeply enmeshed in African American traditions. They found rock music overcommercialized and engineered by managers and record producers, "the creation of artificial wants in the field of commercial culture," and dominated by "American trends and tastes." The difficulty that Hall and Whannel had with rock music became clear in their response to Elvis and the Beatles. Presley, they wrote, "has managed to stay at the top by the dint of superb commercial management and judicious modification of his image." And they demeaned the Beatles by calling them "provincialized," a harsh judgment by Londoners of performers from Liverpool. In a book that was in press in the summer or fall of 1964, Hall and Whannel missed what observers later focused on: with Elvis the reliance on African American music and the way his early songs sparked rebellion among youths, and with the Beatles, playfulness and inventiveness. Contradicting their emphasis on provincialism, they failed to notice the transnational exchanges between, among others, Elvis and the Beatles.[67]

There is plenty of irony in this split judgment of Hall and Whannel, their appreciation of the sophisticated jazz whose roots in the African American community they did not fully explore and their distance from the more recent and insurgent rock and roll, with its roots deep in a more religious and rural African American tradition. Leaving unnoticed the history and cultural productions of West Indians in the Caribbean or in Britain, they appreciated the blues and presented a long treatment of the history of African Americans, going on to connect music to the civil rights movement.[68]

Realizing how little Hall and Whannel focused on race and on colonial immigrants in Britain points to a comparison of the life and work of Hall with
those of C. L. R. James. Although Hall did not come to appreciate the work
of James until relatively late in his life, they shared much in common. Hall
and James were both from the Caribbean, where they attended British-oriented
schools. They were middle-class black Caribbeans who were engaged in movements for independence of colonial nations, including their own. From an early
age, both wanted to be writers. They lived in Britain and shared an engagement
with anti-Stalinist and independent socialist strands of Marxism. Hall spoke
eloquently of how he drew on James, who was, he remarked, "a model of what
it might be to be a black intellectual." Hall connected his interest in reciprocity
to the fact that he and James were from the Caribbean and had what Hall called
a "marginal position of double insights, double voices, double consciousness."
All of this gave a special cast, Hall thought, to their understanding of culture
and politics, an interest in capturing the lives of ordinary people and placing
them in larger contexts.[69]

Yet despite the similarities there were important differences. Born thirty-
one years apart, they were members of different generations, something that
in part explains why workers remained central for James and youth for Hall.
James spent more time in Trinidad than Hall did in Jamaica. James was more
involved in struggles involving labor, anti-imperialism, and transnational race.
At least in his writing James focused on race earlier and more consistently than
did Hall, something that changed for Hall well after 1964. The history of slavery played a critical role in James's vision, but not in Hall's. Unlike Hall, who
feared Americanization, James spent more time in the United States, was more
powerfully engaged in American radical politics, and more compelled by its
popular culture. Much more so than Hall, James was steeped in and committed to Marxism, although hardly a conventional version. They both followed
contemporary trends in consumer culture, something to which James gave a
greater valence, as he also did to organized radical politics and the creative
power of the masses. At least until 1964, much more so than James throughout
his life, Hall was more elitist, an approach that came in part from his early
commitment to approach popular culture through literary analysis.[70]

Indeed, what infused the analysis of Hall and Whannel was their commitment to the Leavisite tradition with its emphasis on discrimination in the
reading of literary texts. Thus only five lines separated these two contradictory statements: that "modern media like the cinema, . . . have this potential
for undermining the established hierarchies of culture" and that "the best
cinema—like the most advanced jazz—seems to push towards high art." The

role of gender in the Leavisite tradition is also notable in its impact on Hall and Whannel. In hindsight, we can understand that the emphasis Leavis and, later, left-Leavisites like Hall and Whannel placed on rigor and discipline was a masculinized reaction to a feminized, belletristic tradition of literary analysis that they associated with class elitism. Moreover, the political implications of their analysis remained unclear. Like many works of social criticism of the early 1960s, what they wrote was fuller on analysis than on solutions, unless, as they probably did, one assumes that teaching working-class teens in secondary modern schools was political action. Yet Hall and Whannel too often analyzed popular culture without connecting it to the social and political contexts through which it arose. As Dworkin has noted, "The relationship between popular culture and social struggle was precisely what *The Popular Arts* never considered."[71]

With *The Popular Arts*, Hall and Whannel made significant contributions to the study of commercial culture. Unlike what one reviewer called McLuhan's "rejection of moralistic nattering," they were willing to make careful value-laden judgments. They challenged the binaries of high/low and good/bad. Their notion of "rapport" provided a useful tool for thinking about the relationship between performers and their audiences. They broke in important ways from the Leavisite tradition when, John Storey has noted, they advocated "a training in critical awareness, not as a means of defence *against* popular culture, but as a means to discriminate between what is good and what is bad *within*." The shifts they made from Hoggart's positions were momentous, representing as they did a change in focus from working class to youth, from print media and a privileged position for fine literature to the visual and aural forms of communication, from a residual moralism to judgments that were more egalitarian and less censorious, from literary analysis to an anthropological one. If Hoggart's work points to an origin of cultural studies in postwar adult education, then that of Hall and Whannel underscores another origin, in teaching nonelite secondary school students how to analyze media. More so than Hoggart but not as much as was true of members of the Independent Group, they focused on and appreciated newer forms of commercial culture. Unlike Arnold, the Leavises, and even Hoggart, they lacked nostalgia and a commitment to the centrality of literature and thus focused on the present and on contemporary movies and music.[72]

Chapter 8

Class and Consumption

Changes in the ways writers dealt with social class were key to the emergence of new views of consumer culture. Whatever their own social origins, many critics from the left and right who disdained popular culture articulated an elitist position. They embraced high culture as designated by those who possessed some combination of social and cultural capital. And they looked down on what they considered lesser cultural traditions, especially when they believed they had lost their authenticity. Greater appreciation of nonelite forms of cultural expression, and for the people who both created and enjoyed them, made way for a greater appreciation of mass culture. We have already seen how members of the Independent Group, Richard Hoggart, Stuart Hall, and Paddy Whannel rested their embrace of popular arts on relatively capacious social sympathies. In the 1960s the New Journalist Tom Wolfe and the sociologist Herbert Gans wrote books in which they connected an acknowledgment of the importance of popular culture with commitments to understand how members of the working class and lower middle class produced and consumed new elements of consumer culture. Though the markers of class were inextricably bound up with masculinity for Wolfe and ethnicity for Gans, social class remained their dominant focus. Their appreciation of the connection between social class and commercial culture was essential in developing new attitudes to consumption as a source of pleasure and symbolic communication and locating creativity among nonelites.

Tom Wolfe, the Kandy-Kolored Kamp of Konsumer Kulture

Tom Wolfe once noted that he was to writing what pop art was to painting, with *Time* magazine calling him "America's foremost pop journalist." Beginning in 1963, the then largely unknown Wolfe published in the Sunday supplement of the *New York Herald Tribune*, *Esquire*, and *Harper's Bazaar* a series of essays that offered an American version of what Hall and Whannel would describe in *The Popular Arts*, as well as a somewhat different take on camp from the one Susan Sontag would chronicle in 1964. As a writer Wolfe drew on what he learned growing up in Richmond, Virginia, studying as an undergraduate at Washington and Lee University and then as a graduate student at Yale. Over his long and productive career he explored the intersection of social status, commerce, the arts, and emerging forms of expressive culture. His breakthrough from journalist to cultural observer came in 1965 with the publication of *The Kandy-Kolored Tangerine-Flake Streamline Baby*, a collection of essays in which he explored modes of expression that were upsetting traditional hierarchies of class, taste, and writing.[1]

Thomas Kennerly Wolfe Jr.

Born in Richmond, Virginia in March of 1931, Thomas Kennerly Wolfe Jr. grew up in a family that honored reading and writing. His mother encouraged his interest in books and art. His father was an agronomist who had earned a Ph.D. at Cornell, taught at Virginia Polytechnic Institute, and then moved to Richmond, where during his son's childhood he edited *Southern Planter*, a publication that combined good writing and news of regional agriculture. At a young age as he watched his father transform writing into print, Tom developed the habits of a voracious reader. He dreamed of being a novelist, inspired by Jack London, L. Frank Baum, James T. Farrell, and Thomas Wolfe, with whom he shared a name but no bloodlines. He read publications such as *True Detective* that engrossed him as a boy. He was also learning to listen and write with a Southern patois he absorbed from the world around him. He grew up in an in-town neighborhood of gracious homes and lush landscaping and went to an Episcopal day school for boys, where he edited and wrote for the school paper, already experimenting with prose styles.

Wolfe benefited from his privileged position. He later characterized his childhood as serene, commenting that he "was not conscious of the Depression." In the material on his years in Richmond, written by him and about him, there is virtually no mention of race. Yet with African Americans taking care of him and his family, he experienced firsthand key aspects of Southern racial dynamics. More broadly, race was central to life in Richmond during World War II and the immediate postwar period. As the former capital of the Confederacy, the locus of the political machine of the conservative senator Harry Byrd, and the home of newspaper editor and staunch segregationist James Kilpatrick, Richmond was where whites remained firmly in control of a system of segregated schools and public facilities and limited the political participation of African Americans. To be sure, there were among whites some racial moderates such as the local journalist Virginius Dabney, although moderation had its limits. Yet in the 1940s Richmond whites, priding themselves on living in a New South city, did not experience the racial turmoil that roiled other cities. By supporting the local African American elite, Richmond's white elite made concessions without undermining the forces that maintained strong patterns of segregation and privilege.[2]

T. K. or Tekay Wolfe, B.A.

In 1947, Wolfe went to college at Washington and Lee University, which had an all-male undergraduate student body of less than a thousand and whose two names reflected the benefaction of the nation's first president and the appointment to the college's presidency of the defeated Confederate general. W&L, with its college and law school, was in Lexington, Virginia, a town of four thousand in the Shenandoah Valley of western Virginia that it dominated along with its neighboring Virginia Military Institute. Many of its undergraduates were members of the Southern elite, with about a fifth of the students coming from elsewhere, the Northeast and Midwest especially. The student body was hardly diverse, though there were a good number of Jewish students, including some who played prominent roles in campus life. With dates imported from nearby women's colleges, the social life at W&L revolved around a series of parties during long weekends. Though the region was dominated by Appalachian whites, there was a well-established African American community in Lexington in late 1940s and early 1950s, with black-owned stores prominent in the central business district adjacent to the campus. There were no African Americans among the students, faculty, or administrators. However, in Wolfe's fraternity African American women cleaned students' rooms and made their beds; and African American butlers waited on students at meals.[3]

As an undergraduate, Wolfe (known variously as T. K. and Tekay) was active as writer and editor. Wolfe, a classmate recalled, "had from the very first a real sense of the absurd." He wrote extensively for student publications on sports, displaying a stylistic flair. For example, in the fall of his junior year he began a story of a football game by noting that "a pair of center halfbacks with steel stamina were the cynosures of all onlookers yesterday" and then went on to remark that the end of the game took place "in a drizzling rain attended by a dismal semi-darkness which leagued with the unsure footing to make speed a memory of drier days and precision a mere word on paper." In his junior year Wolfe helped found and then served as one of the editors of the university's

Shenandoah Review, a literary magazine that at the time published work by e.e. cummings, John Dos Passos, and the Southern agrarian Donald Davidson.[4]

In the spring and summer of 1950 Wolfe published two short stories in the review that reveal his skills as a writer and his concerns with what he saw as the trials of masculinity. One concerned a football player injured in the season's first game and the other focused on a chance meeting on a bus that culminates in the young man dreaming of romance while the young woman wonders if this was the moment when she would begin her life as a prostitute. Wolfe was skillful in creating vivid characters, setting a scene, and conveying the drama of a young man's dashed hopes. These stories reveal a young Southern writer focused not on race but on class, masculinity, and style.[5]

Wolfe majored in English, but the faculty member who most influenced him was Marshall Fishwick, who arrived between Wolfe's sophomore and junior years, fresh from the completion of his doctorate in American studies at Yale. Fishwick introduced Wolfe to the integrated study of the American experience, including popular culture, a field in which Fishwick emerged as a major figure in the 1960s. In a class with Fishwick during the spring of his senior year at W&L, Wolfe wrote a term paper titled "A Zoo Full of Zebras: Anti-Intellectualism in the United States." This essay reveals a college senior who made broad, even extravagant claims, wrote with stylistic flair in a distinctly nonacademic manner, and offered a bleak view of the world. Combining sophomoric observations with wide-ranging reading and a penchant for comprehensive synthesis, he posed as a provocative contrarian. American capitalism, he asserted, had produced "abortions of human nature" so evident in pulp magazines and a political system that furthered "threadbare idealism offering sentimental inanities." Wolfe found that democracy's "pristine ideals are parodied by racial prejudice and a whole conglomeration of social taboos." Writing not long after the emergence of Senator Joseph R. McCarthy onto the American stage, Wolfe believed that Americans' embrace of conformity led to a problematic and anti-intellectual fear of Communism. In contrast he asserted that Communism was the only "significant spiritual movement" in contemporary America. He seemed to admire those who flirted with and then ultimately rejected Communism. With his characteristic penchant for the provocative, Wolfe went on to suggest that that a commitment to what he called "animal materialism" and a hostility to individualism meant that Americans had "a communion not only with Communism but with something even more abhorrent to our national consciousness—Nazism."[6]

Wolfe worried that conformity in a mass society sharply undermined the role of the intellectual. The United States, he asserted, was "preeminently a nation of Goodguys, of mediocre people bound forever to the scared oath of non-excellence." Moreover, American intellectuals, "too prone to become hypnotized by their own delightful enterprises," tended to "make a fetish of unintelligibility" and "spray favorite expressions about as a substitute for erudition." Yet in the end he hoped that elite intellectuals would provide the means to overcome the nation's conformity and materialism. He ended the paper on a confident note. "This, then, is the real American crisis," he argued, "to find her intellectual conscience, not her animal superiority over an animal foe, to beat animalism, not Communism, to be winners in a race for her own humanity." Fishwick responded to this conclusion by noting, "Bravo! A clear statement of a worthy conclusion—ON TO YALE!"[7]

Thomas Kennerly Wolfe Jr., Ph.D.

After graduating from W&L 1951, Wolfe entered graduate school at Yale. At the time Yale's American studies program offered an imaginative, interdisciplinary curriculum. It had benefited from a substantial gift from William Robertson Coe in 1950 to support a program that would serve, as Coe wrote to Yale's president, "as a safeguard against Communism, Socialism, Totalitarianism, and for the preservation of our System of Free Enterprise." Other factors shaped Wolfe's Yale education. One professor who influenced him was Norman Holmes Pearson, author of a 1952 essay on the impact of the Nazi-Soviet pact on American writers, a specialist in American literature, a powerful force in shaping American studies at Yale consonant with Cold War imperatives, and someone with a storied past as an Office of Strategic Services (OSS) operative and an important present as an intermediary between Yale and the OSS's successor, the CIA. Ironic, aristocratic, mysterious, and "cagy," as Wolfe described him at the time, Pearson was a compelling role model. Also critical to Wolfe's graduate education was his introduction to sociology's concept of social status, an idea so central to his later work as a writer. Wolfe earned his Ph.D. in American studies with a dissertation on the Communist Party's League of American Writers from 1929 until 1942.[8]

Wolfe focused not on what the League authors wrote but on the manipulative techniques the American Communist Party, following the instructions from the USSR, used to mobilize support of American writers for the Soviet Union. The dissertation reflected Wolfe's lifelong fascination with status hierarchies, which he now applied to the world of New York writers in the 1920s and 1930s whom he saw pursuing "literary prestige" more than royalties. Living in a hierarchical status system, members of the elite looked down on popular writers who wrote to increase their incomes. For its cohesion and prestige, the elite community of authors in the 1920s relied on an informal round of invitational cocktail parties and personal relationships, which in the 1930s the Communist Party worked to transform through the League, formed in 1935 as part of the Party's Popular Front effort to organize writers, into a cohesive organization that would support the USSR. Wolfe asserted that the Party achieved its goals by 1939 when the Nazi-Soviet pact in August of that year undermined its efforts.[9]

Drawing on Max Weber, Wolfe asserted that the Party engaged in an effort to integrate writers "into the industrial structures with which they were involved commercially," overcoming their social isolation and independence. Especially after 1935 the Party employed literary prestige, "status competition," social gatherings that were politically manipulative, and networks of writers to rationalize social relationships in the literary community. At some point during cocktail parties, "most of the guests, steeped in alcoholic spirits and entertainment, would be in precisely the state which Communist organizers found most advantageous, a half-chemical, half-psychological state in which the conventional cocktail party symbols of literary status would be indistinguishable from the political symbols and ideology embodied in the cause." The Party's control of communication systems enabled it to exploit the literary community for its own political purposes. It worked to integrate organizationally elite literati with more commercially oriented writers who worked in radio and movies. By the late 1930s, this enabled commercial writers to counter the image of them as producing "merely slick, cheap, escapist entertainment" by claiming the mantle of creators of "a genuine popular culture that would demand the very best creative talents in the development and protection of the democratic heritage." In the process, according to Wolfe, the Party narrowed the gap between elite and commercial, high and low.[10]

In writing his thesis, Wolfe was pondering what it meant to be a creative writer who pursued a nonacademic career and who might find his way between elite and popular forms of expression. He was wondering about the relationships between creativity and popularity, between new forms of expression and commercialization. Given his claim that the Communist Party tried to narrow boundaries disingenuously between high and low, it is ironic that over time he himself emerged as a writer who was both creative and commercially successful. At the time, he was wondering how ideological and bureaucratic forces squelched the creativity of writers who went against the conforming grain, experimental writers in the USSR in the 1920s, James T. Farrell in the case of the United States in the 1930s, and himself in 1950s America.[11]

The anti-Communism of Wolfe's thesis stood in sharp contrast with what he had naively written as an undergraduate. He relied heavily on hearings before the House Special Committee on Un-American Activities. He saw proletarian novels as too expensive for workers to buy. Instead, he claimed that their real audience was elite members of the New York literary community. He emphasized the strength of Soviet control of the American Communist Party and by extension of the nation's literary life, thus countering those who thought the Popular Front was a spontaneous social movement largely independent of the USSR. He paid almost no attention to the prevalence of poverty and unemployment at home or to the rise of Nazism and anti-Semitism abroad. Instead he used the word "alleged" to describe "social evils" or the "worldwide fascist threat to culture." The more sympathetic ways in which others, including Pearson, have seen the League and more generally the story of the literary left in the 1930s highlights the particularity of Wolfe's perspective. Compared with Wolfe, most scholars have paid less attention to the ways that the USSR and the Communist Party controlled Popular Front writers. They have explored the relationship between a small cadre of Party faithful and the vast majority of members who carved out positions independent of the dictates of the Comintern or the Party. Rather than seeing writers as a monolithic group, they have carefully differentiated among the factions and have explored the tension among radical writers between a commitment to proletarian novels and to modernism, between radicalism and liberalism. They have located the debates among members of the League in the context of the Depression of the 1930s and the rise of Nazism. Above all, they have not focused as Wolfe did on organizational dynamics and strategies but on the ideological, cultural, and literary dimensions of what contemporaries actually wrote.[12]

What remains surprising is that as someone so deeply interested in writing, Wolfe in his thesis paid so little attention to the creative work of League members. Indeed Wolfe's thesis provided an extended lamentation on the way the Soviet Union marginalized and persecuted experimental, avant-garde artists. Among the many books Wolfe admired as a graduate student was Eugene Zamyatin's *We* (1921), an influential anti-utopian satire by an author who began as a Bolshevik and ended his life as a critic of Stalinism in exile in Paris. Zamyatin combined a revolt against group think with an experimental style. An article in 1923 in which he explained his style, amply reflected in his novel, suggests how he influenced Wolfe. He talked of every word having to be "supercharged, high-voltage"; syntax becoming "elliptic, volatile"; and images as "sharp, synthetic, with a single salient feature—the one feature you will glimpse from a speeding car." Wolfe learned from Zamyatin how to develop a style that was nonnarrative, bold, personal, experimental, and ironic. Moreover, Zamyatin's attack on Stalinism, utopianism, and collectivism dovetailed with the political perspective Wolfe offered in his dissertation.[13]

Thomas Wolfe, Journalist

With his Ph.D. completed, Wolfe was headed for a career not as a professor but as a writer. In 1956, even before he handed in his dissertation, he had already begun to work as a professional journalist, beginning at the Springfield, Massachusetts, *Union* as a general assignment reporter who on short notice covered whatever story the editors asked him to write up. Then, from early July 1959 until late March 1962, he wrote for the *Washington Post*, a newspaper then only partly transformed from a minor regional outlet into a significant force in the nation's capital and beyond. To the task at hand Wolfe brought a number of skills, not the least among them experience with varied styles of writing, knowledge of a broad range of American life, tremendous ambition, and familiarity with the historic relationships between the United States and the Communist world. Sarcastic and innovative, his political conservatism and his fascination with the markings of status already apparent, Wolfe pushed at the boundaries of acceptable journalistic style, often working to turn routine crime stories into more dramatic features. One story, signed Thomas Wolfe like the others, gives evidence of his flourishes. In early May 1961 he wrote about a parade in the District of Columbia, which he described as "twenty-six thousand cart-wheeling, cancanning, cloud-kicking, cadence-counting, kilt-flipping, skirt-flouncing, show-boating, baton-twirling, tall-strutting, crowd-ticking" people parading. Then he remarked, "Take a breather here. We've got 10 Blocks to go." In this and other articles, Wolfe made evident a number of qualities that would come to characterize his writing and, more generally, the New Journalism of the 1960s: the stylistic breakthroughs that challenged staid journalistic conventions, the focus on dramatic elements in ordinary life, and the insertion of the author into the story.[14]

Wolfe began as a staff reporter on the city desk whose byline at one point included a self-description as a "partially reconstructed rebel from Richmond." He covered conventions meeting in the nation's capital; fires, murders, stray animals, and robberies; animal antics at the National Zoo; victims of mental and physical illnesses who were objects of local charities; talks by visiting poets and novelists; controversies over local ordinances, evictions, and schools. Stories of restiveness in the Soviet Bloc enabled him to connect his Yale dissertation with current events.[15]

His break came in late April 1960 when, for seven months, writing from Washington and Latin America, he covered the Cuban Revolution, eventually winning an award from the Washington Newspaper Guild. From the start he was skeptical about the revolution. On the front page, in the first article in a major series, dated June 29, 1960, he called Che Guevara the "Charles Addams-ish Rasputin of the Revolution" and "an international Communist agent" who was masterminding the creation of an authoritarian government that was using a "backstage organization apparatus," taking control of every aspect of Cuban society, suppressing dissent, and mobilizing the masses. There followed articles that connected with other themes of his Yale dissertation: the role of writers covering a Communist revolution, the betrayal of initial hopes, the naiveté of those blind to its crimes, the suppression of dissent, the attack on bourgeois values, the celebration of workers and peasants, and the violent, disciplined determination of its leaders. Wolfe was especially hard on American intellectuals who supported Castro's regime. In November 1960 he counted forty-four-year old C. Wright Mills as among many "aging left wing American intellectuals" for whom the revolution was like a "massive dose of Geritol" and who had "mounted Fidel Castro's podium primarily to get a few things about the United States off his own chest."[16]

Early on and then throughout his stint at the *Washington Post*, Wolfe focused on topics that would later capture his attention as a New Journalist: shifts in patterns of consumer culture such as those on view at auto shows; the curiosities of folk cultures; and the foibles of the rich. In March 1960 he reported on the poet Stanley Kunitz talking about how "sales-crazy hucksters are overrunning the arts" thereby "converting culture into a 'commodity.'" In April 1960 he wrote an article in which he connected women with the symbolism of consumer culture, at the same time that he belittled the struggle for women's equality. The amendment that gave women the vote, he remarked, contained "not one word, not even a hint of the come-hither look, the old chills-and-fever stuff, love's tender wiles, or, for that matter, perfume," the subject of the story. In February 1961, he reported on the British author Denis Brogan's call for a return to snobbery toward popular culture in America. In March 1962 he wrote vividly of how women dressed when they went to supermarkets and shopping centers. He referred to the "Suburban Bohemian" and the "Supermarket Siren," the latter fashionably and suggestively dressed, but whose "only liaison, however, is likely to be a rather businesslike tete-a-tete with the checkout clerk." Still, despite his breakthrough with the stories on Cuba, his testing of new styles, and his colorful features, the *Post*'s editors did not know how to deal with Wolfe, and so at age thirty-two he departed, "frustrated like a leashed animal."[17]

In the spring of 1962, Wolfe left Washington for Manhattan, where he worked for the *New York Herald-Tribune*, beginning as a writer of both general assignment and feature articles but increasingly making the shift to feature writing for both the paper and for magazines. The *Trib*, trying to survive in a competitive New York marketplace, was home to some of the best editors and nonfiction writers. Clay Felker and Jimmy Breslin were hired in 1963, and along with Wolfe they transformed its Sunday supplement, which emerged as a section of the paper titled *New York* and then as a separate magazine two years after the *Trib* folded in 1966. Wolfe also kept a keen eye on the work of Gay Talese at the *New York Times*, whose 1962 piece on the boxer Joe Louis was among the factors that helped inspire Wolfe to imagine a new style of nonfiction writing that resembled fiction based on reporting.[18]

Tom Wolfe, New Journalist

Wolfe's break came during a newspaper strike in 1963 with the publication in *Esquire* of "There Goes [Varoom! Varoom!] That Kandy-Kolored Tangerine-Flake Streamline Baby." He then brought together essays from *Harper's Bazaar*, *New York*, and *Esquire* in his first book, *The Kandy-Kolored Tangerine-Flake Streamline Baby* (1965). The first of a string of bestsellers, this book established Wolfe as a leading practitioner of the New Journalism and an astute observer of American scene. As he later recalled, by 1963 he was discovering that "it was possible in non-fiction, in journalism, to use any literary device . . . to excite the reader both intellectually and emotionally." Covering the Hot Rod and Custom Car Show at New York's Coliseum for the *Trib*, Wolfe had found himself writing the kind of story usually expected of him, one that would portray "a side-show, a panopticon, for creeps and kooks" including "lower class creeps and nutballs with dermatitic skin and ratty hair," which nonetheless reassuringly told readers "don't worry, these people are nothing." Trapped within the formulaic approach was the story he wanted to write: on how those who designed custom cars "had been living like the *complete artist* for years," a starving artist who created cars "which more than 99 per cent of the American people would consider ridiculous, vulgar and lower-class awful beyond comment almost." Sensing he had a powerful story to tell, he convinced his editors at *Esquire* to send him to Los Angeles, the center of custom car culture. Yet when he returned to Manhattan to write the story, he was blocked. Under the pressure of a deadline, between 8 p.m. and 6:15 a.m., listening to rock and roll and "typing like a maniac," he wrote up his notes from his trip in the form of a memo, which the next day his editor accepted as the article.[19]

Kandy-Kolored contained a series of essays about the odd, the new, the hip, and the curious. Here, as Wolfe heaped praise on California car culture, he was unknowingly following Jürgen Habermas, who had written in 1954 that "the latest auto shows have become more important than the museums displaying the latest art." What Wolfe discovered in Los Angeles was not unlike what Sontag found in lower Manhattan's happenings in the early 1960s: the emergence of free form, expressive cultural productions. The book ranged widely, but Wolfe was especially fascinated by the emergence of new trends in popular culture among Americans, especially male, white, nonelite ones in their teens and twenties. He recalled that what inspired him was what he learned at a teen fair in Burbank, California. "Here," he remarked, "was this incredible combination of form plus money in a place nobody ever thought about finding it, namely, among teenagers." Earlier monuments considered high culture—Versailles or Egyptian pyramids, for example—had come from aristocratic culture. In contrast, World War II infused massive amounts of money into American society, including into the hands of "classes of people whose styles of life had been practically invisible" but who had the resources "to build monuments to their own styles" that now transformed the life of an entire nation through rock music, stretch pants, custom cars, stock car races, and demolition derbies. Most social observers, he noted, still assumed that the new emerged from higher social orders and in traditional cultural forms, from an educated group in control of the media that relied on "an ancient, aristocratic aesthetic." What they missed was the emergence in the material culture of what he both admired and disdained, "these rancid people" such as stock car racers, custom car designers, rock musicians, Las Vegas entrepreneurs who still seemed "beneath serious consideration," even though they were "creating new styles all the time and changing the life of the whole country in ways that nobody even seems to bother to record, much less analyze." The Los Angeles world of custom cars, like the Las Vegas world of neon signs, revealed creativity of "America's first unconscious avant-garde! . . . Artists for the new age, sculptors for the new style and new money of . . . Yah! lower orders. The new sensibility . . . the new world, submerged so long, invisible, and now arising, slippy, shiny, electric—Super Scuba-man!-out of the vinyl deeps."[20]

In the essay on custom cars, Wolfe excitedly focused on Los Angeles. He found the world of working-class youths both fascinating and gritty. He remained more compelled by styles that came from below than by what he saw as high society's increasingly hollow mores. What he reported was one of many signs in the 1960s that California was becoming the nation's cultural pacesetter. West Coast innovators were "absolutely untouched by the big amoeba god

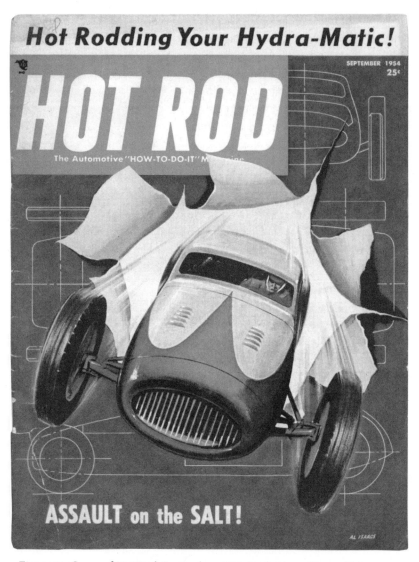

Figure 11. Cover of *Hot Rod*, September 1954. In that year Jürgen Habermas celebrated drivers of hot rods as exhilarated by "fantasy, sensibility, individual willfulness, and desire to be a medium for mechanical excitations." Nine years later Tom Wolfe expressed admiration for the way white working- and lower-middle-class young men created new, expressive forms of commercial culture in California body shops.

of Anglo-European sophistication that gets you in the East." Teenage car stylists, Wolfe remarked, were "maniacal about form," lavishing great attention on the surface elements that transformed a production model into a custom one. Again and again, he compared these stylists with high culture's artists, juxtaposing a custom car designer with "Tiepolo emerging from the studios of Venice" and the resulting automobile with a sculpture by Brancusi. A designer who returned home with a trophy for the hot rod he developed was like Ezra Pound "going back to Hamilton, New York, with his Bollingen plaque." If another joined a design team at General Motors or Ford, that would be comparable to "René Magritte . . . going on the payroll of Continental Can to do great ideas of Western man," a reference to a contemporary series of artful corporate advertisements.[21]

To Wolfe, hot-rod designers were creating objects of great symbolic value, which had "to do with the gods and the spirit and a lot of mystic stuff in the community." Throughout the essay Wolfe described the tension between the rebellious creativity of working-class kids and the desire of the auto industry to copy their designs and co-opt their talents, which had grown out of their innate awareness of what teen culture demanded. Wolfe admired their outsider status ("buried netherworld of teen-age-Californians") but remained aware that Detroit might well succeed in "bringing the whole field into a nice, safe, vinyl-glamorous marketable ball of polyethylene." The cars, he insisted, had highly symbolic value: "they are freedom, style, sex, power, motion, color."[22]

In "Kandy-Kolored" Wolfe displayed many of the distinctive elements of his style, what one critic called "machine-gun rococo" and another his "hypermaniac jitters." He developed a new way of writing that now seems familiar to us: words invented, traditional forms broken, and exaggerated sensibilities expressed. Wolfe's language met the challenge of developing an approach suitable to describing the power and dynamics of pop culture. This was clearest in the final paragraph of his introduction to *Kandy-Kolored*, which captured the flamboyance of customized cars and Las Vegas signs, as well as his own preference for commercial culture over high. "Free form! Marvelous!" he wrote of a designer of Las Vegas signs. "No hung-up old art history words for these guys. America's first unconscious avant-garde! The hell with Mondrian, whoever the hell he is."[23]

With the essays in *Kandy-Kolored*, as a contrarian critic Wolfe articulated many of the key elements in a new understanding of consumer culture. Unlike Theodor Adorno, Wolfe saw new cultural forms emerging from nonelites. "Now," he wrote, "high styles come from low places, from people who have no power, who slink away from it, in fact, who are marginal, who carve out worlds for themselves in the nether depths." He continually blurred the lines between high and low, insisting that the cultures surging from below were comparable in power to what cultural critics had long admired. He asserted that the "aesthetic, psychological and cultural insights" of Bugsy Siegel, the mobster who helped transform Las Vegas, were "like Cézanne's, Freud's, Weber's." He explored how people used the symbols of consumer culture to communicate about social status. Wolfe was chronicling an emerging culture based not on a religious or communal morality of restraint but on one of pleasure that elevated the self to a position of prominence. Above all, he was showing how in the postwar years money and cultural norms of formerly marginalized people were transforming America and in the process upsetting the social order based on hierarchies of taste and class.[24]

In his writings, Wolfe focused primarily on the cultural forms developed by white, lower-class young men. He usually cast women as either their camp followers or as society matrons who desperately clung to an older, decaying order. He saw wealthy Americans as either unbearably stuffy and old-fashioned or, as in the case of Warhol's sidekick Baby Jane Holzer or the pop art collector Robert Scull, as people who reveled in their connection with the cult of the new. Even more telling were his racial politics. At a time when African American expressive culture, in music and in the civil rights movement, was transforming the larger society, Wolfe focused instead on the creativity of whites. So when he talked about the Beatles and the Rolling Stones, he paid no attention to how significantly they drew on earlier traditions of African American music. Moreover, his most extended consideration of race in *Kandy-Kolored* came in his essay on the heavyweight boxer Cassius Clay, which appeared in *Esquire* in October 1963, less than six months before Clay revealed that he was a member of the Nation of Islam and changed his name to Muhammad Ali. Wolfe captured the subtleties of the interaction between Clay and white Southern good old boys who insisted on calling Clay "Boy." He noted that "Cassius treats the fact of color—but not race—casually." Yet Wolfe referred to young African American men as "colored boys" at a time in the fall of 1963 when civil rights activists and others were engaged in a heated debate, not over whether to use 'Colored' or 'Negro,' which had been long decided in the latter's favor, but whether to use "Negro" or "African American." This reminds us that Wolfe was very much a conservative, white Southern gentleman, part of the migration of Southern writers to the North, some of whom brought with them their regional heritage on race issues, in this case a conservative one that underscored his white racial privilege.[25]

Wolfe in the World

Not surprisingly, Dwight Macdonald found Wolfe's book objectionable. He called Wolfe's New Journalism "a bastard form, . . . exploiting the factual authority of journalism and the atmospheric license of fiction." As kitsch, he continued, it promised a false sense of intimacy directed to "a class-mass audience." The book's dramatic sales were explicable "by two *kultur*-neuroses prevalent among adult, educated Americans today: a masochistic deference to the Young" and the new as well as "a guilt-feeling about class" that made readers wonder whether they really deserved their status and claims to sophistication, something intensified when Wolfe told them that young working-class kids had created a style they had not noticed or, if they had, thought vulgar.[26]

In 1973, Wolfe laid bare his concerns with class and status in writing of Macdonald's response. The New Journalism had challenged the hierarchies that had long dominated the world of letters, until then "a stable and apparently eternal status structure": novelists as the upper class; men of letters like Macdonald as the middle class; journalists as members of the lower class, seen as "day laborers who dug up slags of raw information for writers of higher 'sensibility' to make better use of"; and writers for popular magazines and Sunday supplements as the "lumpenproles." In the mid-1960s lumpenproles like himself used the techniques of the novelists, the insights of men of letters, and reportorial skills of hustlers, thus countering century-old "literary class lines." Among the things they were combating was what Wolfe later called the "dreadful solemnity and High Seriousness" of abstract expressionism that pop art and the New Journalism challenged. As Wolfe later said of Macdonald, "the urge to bring morality into writing . . . has become the greatest cop-out among writers." Wolfe might have responded to Macdonald by quoting from his own Ph.D. dissertation, where he stated that "the most important literary critics themselves came from within the New York cliques," with their judgments reflecting "the influence of the status community as a whole and of their particular cliques." As a graduate student, Wolfe recognized that "a favorable social position within the literary community would tend to afford a writer a more favorable fate at the hands of reviewers, other factors being equal."[27]

Writing from Britain in *Encounter* in the summer of 1966, Richard Hoggart also found Wolfe's book problematic, especially in terms of its literary style. He spoke of Wolfe as "a painstaking and tireless leech of a reporter" who felt the compulsion "to be hep, to be souped up, less dullness supervene." He wrote that Wolfe used vivid metaphors "to inflate the experience, grossly," with his "hectic knowingness" becoming "a parody even of itself." Wolfe, "less fussy about accuracy than about making sure that his prose is always swinging," did "violence to his material and his human subjects." Yet if Hoggart found Wolfe's writing style seriously worrisome, he was more appreciative, albeit still critical, about what he took to be Wolfe's central contribution: his exploration of "poise" or style among the young. Now at the Birmingham Center and working with Stuart Hall, Hoggart was beginning to reconsider the attitude to young people's embrace of popular culture that he had viewed so unfavorably in *The Uses of Literacy*. Hoggart appreciated what Wolfe now understood: that poise was "the impulse behind much in the behaviour of young people in commercial mass-societies, the urge to find a stance before all the free-floating and un-ordered offerings, a stance which . . . rejects the call of the old, goal-oriented world." Drawing on Marshall McLuhan, Hoggart argued that Wolfe's "medium, his stylistic poise, is more important than his message." He ended his essay by placing the discussion of youth and popular culture in a Cold War context. The authorities in Russia, he wrote, worked to prevent "the multitudinous play of messages in a 'free' consumers' society." If McLuhan was right, which Wolfe's popularity seemed to confirm, then Soviet officials were wrong. "The best way to keep their people from seeking alternative goals," he concluded, "would be to flood them with 'data,' to offer them the chance to become anxious only about 'form,' so that they came to believe that goals are out and poise is in. Then they might keep on playing roles endlessly, and harmlessly—with no political effect. But by God they'd have style!"[28]

Hoggart's discussion of Wolfe's book looked backward and forward. It recalled David Riesman's 1951 "The Nylon War," in which Riesman wittily told the story of an American "all-out bombing of the Soviet Union with consumers' goods" to tempt the Russian people to stop tolerating "masters who gave them tanks and spies instead of vacuum cleaners and beauty parlors." Yet Hoggart's essay also pointed forward to the ways Stuart Hall, Dick Hebdige, and others saw the style of the disenfranchised young as the seedbed of resistance that relied on a positive use of consumer culture. His essay also underscored how the author *The Uses of Literacy* still saw the adoption of style by young people, here captured by Wolfe's breathless descriptions, as a political copout.[29]

Wolfe's book also bears comparison with Sontag's 1964 "Notes on 'Camp'" and with the kind of art Lawrence Alloway selected for the 1963 Guggenheim exhibit. Like Sontag and pop artists, Wolfe presented a world where surface was central in the process of using commercial iconography to create symbolic power. As one reviewer noted under the title "Popcult Orgy," Wolfe was "the darling of the campy set." Like Hall, Wolfe located creativity within the insurgent, but not political, popular culture created by the lower-class youth.

Like Gans, Wolfe insisted that working-class Americans (whom he did not call working class nor did he acknowledge any ethnic markers) were active consumers who talked back to those in powerful corporations who shaped popular culture, in this case with men who spoke back to Detroit automakers by transforming production vehicles into individually created works of art. Wolfe fully embraced popular culture, a phrase that Matthew Arnold, in Wolfe's words, would have seen as "a contradiction in terms (and worse)." If Theodor Adorno and Max Horkheimer had located the saving remnant of an avant-garde among the most sophisticated developers of high culture and Sontag had found the new avant-garde in Manhattan lofts among artists in their thirties, Wolfe discovered what he called "America's first unconscious avant-garde" in Los Angeles garages among young men in their teens and twenties. Above all, the publication of *Kandy-Kolored* marked Wolfe's arrival as a major writer. As one reviewer said, with rhetorical flourish, evoking what Ralph Waldo Emerson had said to Walt Whitman, "I greet you at the beginning of a great career." No longer would he face daily deadlines for short pieces. Now he was free to develop his style in articles and books.[30]

Herbert Gans: Class and the Sociology of Consumption

If Wolfe was the New Journalist who focused on the lives of ordinary Americans, Herbert J. Gans was the sociologist who did the same. During the 1960s Gans pictured ordinary Americans as people fully capable of reshaping the popular culture they encountered, especially from television. Throughout his adult life, although he paid some attention to gender and more to race and ethnicity, class was his central focus. That, combined with his experience as refugee, fostered in him a sustained and at times adversarial fascination with his adopted land. Gans, like Wolfe, played a key role in undercutting socially and culturally elitist views of popular culture by emphasizing the ways working- and lower-middle-class consumers resisted what the mass media offered. He demonstrated how putting social class first opened the way toward a greater embrace of popular culture.

Growing Up in Cologne and Chicago

Born May 7 1927, Gans spent his first twelve years as a bookish boy in a middle-class Jewish family in Cologne, Germany, with parents who were not only "nonreligious, acculturated, and unconnected" to the local Jewish communities but also disconnected from German high and popular culture as well. Nazi laws forced him into the Jewish educational system, initially secular and then, at his parents' insistence, into an Orthodox gymnasium where he learned English. The family migrated to England in 1939 and then to Chicago a year later. Initially they lived in Woodlawn, a mostly Irish, working-class area close to the University of Chicago. His parents' drive, along with wartime employment opportunities, helped them overcome their initial downward social mobility. With what he later called "an immigrant's initial curiosity about America," Gans quickly discovered American popular culture, reading comics that the landlady left in the basement, listening to comedians like Jack Benny and serials like *Captain Midnight* on the radio, watching westerns at the movie theater, and following professional sports teams in Chicago.[31]

As a young teenager, compared with his working-class peers Gans himself was such an accomplished reader and writer, and so fluent in English, that he became editor of his school newspaper in the eighth grade. This encouraged him to think of a career in journalism, a path he pursued as a writer in high school, college, and the military. In Hyde Park High School on the South Side of Chicago, he developed a skeptical stance toward mass media, as a sophomore writing long critical essays and urging his fellow students to follow him in developing an appreciation for classical music. As a teen, he lived in the world of secular Jews, searching for what he called in 1947 "a rational Jewish religion for myself." During two summers in the early 1940s, Gans went to Jewish camps that, relying on what he later called "labor or democratic socialist Zionism" indebted to the *kibbutzim* in Palestine, contributed to the war effort by assisting truck farmers in harvesting their crops. A series of negative experiences—with rabbis in Germany and Chicago, with school authorities in America, and with his bosses on the farms—fostered in him what in his twenties he understood as an "antiexpert position," opposing those who exercised "absolute and autocratic authority." Like Walter Benjamin, Stuart Hall, and C. L. R. James, Gans had the outsider's fresh perspective.[32]

Coming of Age at the University of Chicago

Gans entered the University of Chicago and slowly found his intellectual bearings and his career. Fourteen months of military service interrupted his education, he became a citizen in October 1945, and with the help of the G.I. Bill he earned a bachelor's degree in 1947 and a master's three years later. At the university he initially felt intensely marginal: provincial, socially immature, intellectually untutored, and politically naive. The passionate political milieu of the immediate postwar period, fueled by assertive, highly politicized veterans including Stalinists and Trotskyites, presented him with a wide range of options, especially on the left. In 1948 he voted for the Socialist Norman Thomas and from his college days on, his politics remained what he later called "social democratic or left liberal." As Gans wrote to Granville Hicks in the early 1950s, since liberals had to avoid alliances with Stalinists, he was trying to avoid the polarization that offered no alternative to "an ideologically black white world." Active in the liberal Americans for Democratic Action (ADA) and the social democratic League for Industrial Democracy (LID), Gans worked to pressure both groups from the left, eventually resigning from LID over its support of the war in Vietnam.[33]

Gans took his master's in sociology, in good measure because it built on his interest in feature journalism, social policy, and approaches to scholarship that were not excessively theoretical. As a master's student, he discovered cultural relativism and, from reading Karl Mannheim, an awareness of relationism, the notion, as he later put it, that "knowledge was a function of the knower's perspective." Reading and studying with Lloyd Warner, he learned about the class dimensions of the social system, how different social groups had distinct perspectives on society that they experienced through symbol systems. He took a course on communications with Bernard Berelson and read widely in sociology, including the works of Robert Park. Studying with Everett Hughes trained him in fieldwork as a participant-observer, which he first carried out in a mostly Jewish Chicago census tract and soon after in suburban Park Forest. From reading Robert Merton, Gans could see, he later reported, that "cultural patterns disliked by one group can be functional for another." As a graduate student, he paid attention to the sociology of communications, with work in political science on how citizens communicated with officials prompting him to think about "audience-feedback processes in mass-media organizations."[34]

By 1950 Gans was developing the concepts that he elaborated for much of the rest of his career. Committed to the serious study of popular culture, he embraced cultural relativism and understood how groups fought over cultural taste. Interested in audience feedback, he explored the relationship between cultural production and consumption. All of this made him skeptical of the claims that elite culture was preferable to a mass culture that supposedly debased taste and lulled common people into passivity. He later remarked that what shaped his perspective was how his "own acculturation as a first-generation ethnic of Jewish origin" spurred his interest in popular culture and how "changes and inconsistencies in class and status," coming from his experience as a refugee, underwrote his commitment to cultural relativism and egalitarianism.[35]

More immediately, what he studied formed the bases for his emerging perspectives. Reading Russell Lynes's 1949 classic essay "Highbrow, Lowbrow, Middlebrow" crystallized "a lot of disconnected thinking" he had been doing "about culture, class, and symbol systems," even though he turned away from Lynes's caustic judgments while he combined his analysis with Warner's emphasis on class hierarchies. Lynes began by making clear his own affiliation with an elite. He argued that cultural positioning based on taste had replaced social class based on money or family where "highbrows are the elite, the middlebrows are the bourgeoisie, and the lowbrows are *hoi polloi*." The highbrows, for whom Clement Greenberg was his prime example, were cultured humanists. Some of them enjoyed and respected lowbrow art, such as jazz, and felt no threat from lowbrows. The lowbrow demanded little of the world, just wanting "to be comfortable and to enjoy himself without having to worry whether he has good taste or not." In contrast were middlebrows, whom highbrows detested because of their tastelessness and cultural aggressiveness, "a dreadful mass of insensible back-slappers, given to sentimentality as a prime virtue, the willing victims of slogans and whims of the bosses, both political and economic."[36]

In contrast to what Lynes stood for, Gans had learned to respect and take seriously a variety of cultural productions, including popular culture. In addition, Gans connected social class and taste cultures. Gans also opposed Lynes's anti-intellectualism and assumption that an intellectual elite could only be condescending. Above all, it was his work and friendship with Riesman that most spurred both Gans's dissent from what Lynes had written and his own interest in popular culture. In the late 1940s Riesman, who had taught Gans at Chicago, let his student read drafts of *The Lonely Crowd* and talked frequently about popular culture with Gans, who served as an informant for his mentor. What mattered to Gans was Riesman's elevation of popular culture as a legitimate topic for serious analysis, something we now take for granted but was unusual at the time when German and American traditions cast a skeptical eye on the field. Although perhaps Gans did not fully realize it in 1950, what came to animate his writing over a long period of time and stood in such strong opposition to what Lynes had written was both a belief in distinctive taste cultures each deserving of respect and a regret that elites looked down on hardworking, respectable members of the middle class.

All this became clear in the first half of 1950 when Gans took a course with Riesman and Elihu Katz, whom Gans had known earlier as president of a Zionist Organization of America youth group. In that course, Gans completed a seminar paper, although it would be years before he published the results of what he was thinking. Titled "The Metaphysics of Popular Culture," the paper explored the problems Gans had with the "moral scorn and social disapproval" that elites displayed. He attacked those who looked down on popular culture from multiple perspectives: aristocratic, humanistic, and sociological. He objected to how Robert K. Merton emphasized the "narcotizing dysfunction of media." Some of what he wrote, he recalled retrospectively, was in response to the prominence of humanists as cultural critics, a situation that kept sociologists out of the game. Though he included among cultural critics such conservatives as Russell Kirk and Ortega y Gasset, what especially bothered him were people like Dwight Macdonald, socialists who "were culturally as elitist as the conservatives." These literary critics on the left and right, he later recalled, reminded him of "the autocratic expert who defended universal standards that fed particularist self-interests," such as "the high-school officials, rabbis, and student Stalinists" he had earlier encountered. Indeed, he later remarked that the urban redevelopers who tore down the apartments where urban villagers lived and the critics who emphasized the conformity of life in Levittown were all authoritative experts who felt a sense of superiority about their own choices and acted accordingly.[37]

In his 1950 paper Gans challenged the hierarchical assumptions of such positions. Relying on what he called "a quite relativistic interpretation," Gans envisioned a "number of leisure cultures, coexisting in a number of ways, with relationships and conflicts on various levels." Yet despite Gans's embrace of a relativistic or pluralistic perspective, again and again he fell into judgments similar to those made by elitist critics. If as a social scientist he accepted the "complete equality" of cultural choices, he nonetheless hesitated. In a footnote to the paper, he confessed that he thought the songs of Frank Sinatra were "trash, but as a researcher I am beginning to realize that they are unsatisfactory only for me, and that I have no right to *force*" anyone "to participate in what I think is good, or to give up what I consider bad." Returning to the theme of how social position influenced taste, he wrote that critics and intellectuals "are especially narrow-minded and snobbish, perhaps more so than the 'low-brows' who consider high-brow activities dull and uninteresting." Although in this 1950 paper Gans did not write explicitly or extensively about the relationships between audience and creators of popular culture, he did articulate themes to which he would return repeatedly: how classes conflicted over choices in what they consumed, how social scientists might challenge humanists in the study of popular culture, and how to think about taste cultures in a democratic or pluralistic manner.[38]

In his graduate work, Gans pursued issues surrounding life in American suburbs and conflicts over leisure. For his master's thesis, under the direction of Martin Meyerson, he wrote on political participation in Park Forest, a new suburb outside Chicago. After completing that degree in 1950, Gans worked as a city planner before beginning his Ph.D. at Penn, which he completed in 1957 with a dissertation on leisure planning. Titled "Recreation Planning for Leisure Behavior: A Goal-Oriented Approach," his doctoral dissertation revealed the powerful issues that over the long term undergirded his view of popular culture, if not yet the accessible style that would characterize his later work.[39]

Although the 739-page-long work was at times plodding and full of social science jargon, Gans made his larger argument powerfully clear, the implications of which became even more apparent in the ensuing decades. For Gans the long struggle in the United States over recreation and leisure involved a battle between suppliers and users of facilities, a battle he cast in terms of values, class, and ethnicity. On one side stood representatives of storied elites, along with reformers and professionals who, as purveyors of Riesman's inner-directed values, saw recreation in terms of culture, civilization, self-control, higher values, and uplift. The forces arrayed against pleasure-seeking users were thus considerable. Wealthy leaders and representatives of the old middle class in the late nineteenth century had launched "a missionary movement" in response to immigration of European peasantry into cities, efforts that had their mid-twentieth-century correlative in the efforts of experts to solve urban problems by many means including "slum clearance." Groups privileged by wealth or expertise emphasized the way formal recreational and cultural facilities promoted values of productivity, democratic citizenship, individualistic self-expression, purification, and responsibility. These groups had an imperfect idea, Gans showed, of how users actually participated in the activities that people with class standing and expertise planned. By blocking users from low-status commercial forms such as drink, gambling, and violence, providers tried to socialize young immigrants to middle-class values. The middle and upper classes thus promoted preindustrial values in an effort to restore the good old days or at least the values they represented.[40]

In contrast stood entrepreneurs, who offered commercial pleasures, and consumers, usually working class and ethnic, who pursued excitement, danger, and fantasy. Here Gans revealed his debt to Riesman, who in *The Lonely Crowd* and later had emphasized the importance of fantasy in play. Gans also developed the notion that users of recreation facilities challenged and overturned but mostly avoided what high-minded suppliers offered. Gans focused his attention on recreational facilities that reformers ignored or demeaned such as streets, amusement parks, taverns, burlesque houses, and gambling dens. The poor, the working class, and immigrants pursued intense pleasures that puritanical elites and reformers opposed because they involved debased emotions.

These included what Gans described as "fantasy that aroused aggressiveness, and especially erotic excitement." Commercial recreational facilities offered people, especially teens, "excitement," opportunities for spontaneity, glamour, and group sociability. They provided as well "vicarious role playing" that revolved "around sexual and romantic situations, both of which are tabooed by the recreation movement" which held popular cultural heroes in such low esteem. "Spontaneous excitement," Gans asserted, came "from playing in illegal or forbidden territory, or from taking risks in the presence of peers." At the end of the thesis, Gans expressed cautious optimism as he pondered the role of the social scientist in improving the situation he had described. He called for social scientists to work with recreation planners on more rational and orderly planning processes to provide facilities that were more user-oriented. He offered this argument even though he also realized the full implications of his dissertation's recognition that every group had it own views and values.[41]

The major arguments Gans articulated in his dissertation helped provide the building blocks of his analysis of popular culture that emerged more fully, and to a wider audience, in the 1960s. In his 1957 thesis Gans revealed his distrust of experts, class-blinded groups who used recreation as instruments of social control through which they tried to teach the poor middle-class values. He was developing a notion that competing taste communities came into conflict. He was working out the contours of the reciprocal relationship between suppliers and users of cultural resources, in this case recreational facilities and later on of popular culture.

Groundwork

In the years surrounding the completion of his thesis but before the publication of his first two books, on urban and then suburban villagers, Gans continued to develop his analysis of popular culture in articles. In 1952, when he was a city planner, he wrote on the relationship between media and political apathy, the initial impetus but not the final focus of *The Lonely Crowd*. People, Gans wrote, were politically disengaged because they saw no connection between themselves and politics, not, as left critics of popular culture argued, because the media anesthetized them. Gans saw the media in a positive light, providing as it did "magic carpets that transport people away from the everyday to the comical, the mysterious, the dramatic and the thrilling." In 1953, with "The 'Yinglish' Music of Mickey Katz," he sympathetically treated one taste culture: the Yiddish English that emerged from the interaction of audience and comedians. At the end of his article Gans noted that "in so far as Katz's songs are foolish, even buffoonish versions of Hit Parade favorites, they contain some criticism of the mass media culture," which "may be their major significance." Then in 1956 he delivered a paper titled "The Creator-Audience Relationship in the Mass Media: An Analysis of Movie Making." Here Gans laid out for the first time in print his ideas about multiple audiences ("innumerable publics" he called them) and their reciprocal relationship to culture's creators, themselves composed of many groups, even among those working in one medium. He explored the complicated feedback processes by which movie makers and their audiences, each group in turn composed of many subgroups, interacted with each other. The commercial success and vast popularity of American movies, he asserted, was due to this reciprocal feedback process "which literally permits the audience to follow the creators into the studio" and, vice versa, the creators into the theater.[42]

In 1958, two years after the initial publication of "Creator-Audience Relationship," Gans extended his argument. In *Dissent* he reacted to a screed by Harold Rosenberg, who in turn was responding to Rosenberg and White's *Mass Culture: The Popular Arts in America*. Using the Yiddish word for dirt or excrement, Rosenberg called for a halt to serious discussions of popular culture because there was "already too much talent and intellect in America steadily draining into the *dreck* of the mass media!" Writers who discovered the "'significance' of Li'l Abner or Mickey Spillane" were helping "to destroy the distinction between kitsch and art" that Rosenberg had so long tried to maintain as a prominent art critic and advocate of abstract expressionism. "The intellectualization of kitsch," he argued, made the "popular media into such a tremendous social force against the individual in this country, as in the Soviet Union." Rosenberg also criticized "certain social scientists" for putting "into practice the notion that a bad work cleverly interpreted according to some obscure Method is more rewarding to the mind than a masterpiece wrapped in silence."[43]

Gans accurately saw Rosenberg's essay as "an angry denial of significance in popular culture." For Gans, a social scientist who opposed the control of cultural criticism by humanists, serious study of mass media involved reducing the gap between Rosenberg's dichotomy of kitsch and art. Especially dismayed, again, that this critique came from "among those who call themselves socialist writers," Gans insisted on the importance of studying the products of popular culture "*as these are responded to by their audiences*." Gans did not believe that studying popular culture necessarily justified it intellectually, asserting that an important objective was to "develop some criteria to distinguish between better and worse art." Yet he also insisted that both "'the masterpiece wrapped in silence'" and popular culture were worthy of serious study.[44]

In 1962, the same year in which *Urban Villagers* appeared, Gans offered a probing analysis of the importance of American popular culture in Britain. As members of the Independent Group would have appreciated, Gans argued that because British movies were so shaped by and for the upper middle class, Hollywood films had broad appeal on the other side of the Atlantic in part because they emerged from working-class, immigrant cultures. The key features of American films ("the star, the lavish settings, the slickness, the approach to reality distortion and the emphasis on 'action'") appealed to adolescents from the British working class precisely because they portrayed "people with working class traits" but middle-class aspirations without relying on middle-class propriety, status, and rationalism. Focusing on western, mystery, and adventure films, Gans asserted that the emphasis in American films on how heroes achieved their goals appealed to "such working class techniques as courage, strength, cunning, physical charm, fate and luck." Gans felt American popular culture would "remain one or two steps ahead of other popular cultures" because it was built on a high standard of living and the demand of audiences that "encourages, and even forces, an endless search for new ideas or new variations on old themes." Several aspects of this study are notable, among them his emphasis on class conflict over cultural productions, the way audience members transformed what the media offered, and the importance of an adversarial teen culture. On this last issue, so important during the 1960s in British cultural studies, Gans was prescient. British working-class teens, he noted, because they sought "extreme styles by which to express their independence from adult culture," were "naturally drawn to the patterns of a country which has traditionally been conceived as extreme by British standards—especially in relation to its teenagers."[45]

Significantly, Gans had carried out the research for this study in the summer of 1957, just after the publication of Hoggart's *The Uses of Literacy*, with its hostility to American popular culture and British youth culture. As Gans noted, without mentioning Hoggart, British critics worried that "postwar prosperity and the continuing breakdown of parental authority" were increasing a teen culture based on spending and expressiveness. Soon after the publication of Hoggart's book, Gans carefully transcribed a number of passages from it: including what Hoggart wrote about the pre–World War II working class having "a mild hedonism, one informed by a more deeply-rooted sense—that the big and long-distance rewards are not for them"; how their values of pride and ambition were "a good deal more healthy than the commercial values"; and how postwar magazines had abandoned earlier moral codes. Yet if Gans absorbed some of what Hoggart wrote, the two also differed. If Hoggart saw declension, Gans painted a more complex picture, one that pointed forward to the work of the Birmingham Center of the 1960s and 1970s: of pleasure-seeking working-class adolescents who were simultaneously enjoying American popular culture and remaining loyal to working-class British culture.[46]

Among the issues that separated Gans from both Rosenberg and Hoggart was whether social scientists or humanists did the best work in the debates over popular culture. Humanists had long defended literature and the fine arts against the encroachments of mass media, which they saw as driven (from the right) by ignorant masses or (from the left) by greedy corporations, in both cases threatening to overwhelm Culture. Increasingly in the post–World War II period, social scientists did groundbreaking investigations that explored how Americans responded to mass media. The commanding work on this subject, one that influenced Gans, was *Personal Influence: The Part Played by People in the Flow of Mass Communications* (1955) by Elihu Katz and Paul F. Lazarsfeld. Working against the notion that all-powerful media controlled public opinion, Katz and Lazarsfeld offered a complicated picture in which opinion leaders, peer kinship groups, and individual predispositions shaped the response to media more than did powerful external forces. In the mid-1960s, Gans relied on the insights of Katz and Lazarsfeld and on what he learned from studying working-class Italian Americans in Boston and predominantly lower-middle-class suburbanites in New Jersey to suggest that popular culture and elite culture, the latter not necessarily better than the former, were simply two versions of distinctive taste communities.[47]

The Urban Villagers (1962)

Gans's first book was *The Urban Villagers: Group and Class in the Life of Italian-Americans*, which appeared in 1962 when he was a researcher at the Institute for Urban Studies at the University of Pennsylvania. Gans pictured second-generation Italian Americans as fatalistic "about deprivation inflicted by the outside world" but held together by "the vitality of peer group life" that made it possible for them to resist mass culture. In this classic community study, Gans drew on what he had learned as a participant-observer from October 1957 to May 1958 in Boston's West End, on the eve of the neighborhood's urban redevelopment that transformed it from an officially declared slum (despite the vitality of its communal and street life) into the site of sterile office and luxury apartment buildings. The National Institutes of Mental Health supported Gans's work. He carried out his research while he lived with his first wife in an apartment in the West End, interviewing five hundred people who were experiencing the loss of their neighborhood. His book was an important contribution to the debate over urban renewal, a federal program that had begun in 1949 and accelerated over time. Gans's book shared much with Jane Jacobs's *The Death and Life of Great American Cities* (1961), which also celebrated the vibrancy of dense urban neighborhoods and criticized urban renewal. In some ways, his book extended what Gans had written in his dissertation about how planners plowed ahead, too little aware of how those whose lives they were trying to improve actually used the physical and cultural resources surrounding them. "Orthodox city planning," he wrote in a review of Jacobs's book, "deserves considerable criticism for its anti-urban bias and for trying to transform ways of living before even examining," as he had done in his thesis and would do with *The Urban Villagers*, "how people live or want to live." The book was part of the rediscovery of the city and of poverty that marked the 1960s, shifting attention away from the suburbs and the middle class.[48]

Acutely aware of the danger of offering a picture of "a charming neighborhood of 'noble peasants' living in an exotic fashion, resisting the mass-produced homogeneity of American culture and overflowing with a cohesive sense of community," in a nuanced manner Gans emphasized the sharp limits on the ability of mass culture to dominate the lives of the people among whom he lived. At a time when many sociologists avoided acknowledging class and many others celebrated the nation's distinctiveness by emphasizing the power of individualism and the weakness of community, Gans stressed the persistence of class and the vibrancy of community. Arguing against those such as the historian Oscar Handlin who emphasized assimilation and ethnicity, Gans instead stressed the power of class and continuity across generations. Here he relied on Hoggart's *The Uses of Literacy* and on Michael Young and Peter Willmott's *Family and Kinship in East London* (1957), which emphasized how the persistence of peer groups and families enabled the working class to resist inroads of mass culture, especially television.[49]

Skeptical of outside forces and strengthened by their loyalty to their peers, Gans's urban villagers carefully accepted from the mass media what affirmed their own values and filtered out what did not. In drawing this picture, Gans took on those cultural critics (whom he did not name) who saw Americans as "powerless to resist" the temptations of mass society. Too poor to be self-indulgent, to make purchases on the installment plan, or to be the objects of the campaigns of mass marketers, they sustained a detachment from the media's

Figure 12. The sociologist Herbert J. Gans emphasized how in the 1950s American families (more ethnic and lower middle class than the one pictured here from the period) did not passively watch television. Instead, he argued, Italian Americans in Boston's West End and people living in modest suburbs like Levittown talked back to their televisions. Courtesy of Photofest.

messages, which, given that they were part of the outside world, they did not trust. When they adopted elements the media offered, they did so "freely and with considerable enthusiasm" in order to enhance their cherished and vibrant peer culture. Thus, they talked back to television, which remained on in their homes for hours on end. For example, having attentively watched an advertisement on TV, they "then bombarded [it] with satirical comments which question exaggerated or dishonest claims and meaningless statements." Though they purchased goods and services in the marketplace, they did not embrace the largely middle-class "social arrangements and ideas" that came along with them. For Gans and for his subjects, commercial goods were thus "culturally neutral," ready to be shaped by the distinctive class and ethnic orientations of those who purchased them. Those purchasers infused goods with their own meanings, displaying their sense of themselves through food, automobiles, and

clothing with an emphatic and bright aesthetic that underscored their commitment to "a careful exuberance." The outside force that significantly shaped
their lives was not television but the way government and developers destroyed
their neighborhood.[50]

Gans offered a rich analysis of his subjects' distinctive style of consumption, one that emphasized how the Italian Americans he studied used their
experiences in the marketplace to find symbolic expression of their commitments. They purchased the latest kitchen appliances and television sets but kept
the same living room and bedroom furniture they purchased when they first
married. They ate typically American food but laced it with Italian spices and
side dishes. Men preferred powerful cars and clothes that were bright, informal, and "jaunty." As an "extension of self," these enabled a man to "express
his toughness." Women preferred furniture that had "bright, cheerful colors,
strong textures, and enough 'body' to provide comfort" rather than the Danish
modern style so in favor among academics. Their aesthetic was one of "exuberance," something that found expression in the religious objects that filled their
apartments.[51]

When it came to media, some preferences were gender specific. Women
chose romantic or family dramas. In contrast, men opted for expressions of
male strength and working-class culture. They disliked Sergeant Friday of *Drag-
net* for his haughtiness toward people like themselves and preferred instead the
hero of *Meet McGraw* because he did not respect the police and used working-
class people to help him solve crimes. The performer they most worshipped was
Frank Sinatra, for whose music Gans had earlier expressed a dislike. Sinatra
had not, the men in Gans's study felt, turned his back on his past as an Italian
American member of the working class but had sustained a rebellious stance
and rejected norms of middle-class respectability. Thus, like their preferences
for food, household goods, clothing, and cars, their choices among mass media
enabled them to "interpret" what they consumed in order to protect themselves
from the outside world and to accept only messages they wished to believe in.[52]

The Urban Villagers earned Gans a reputation as a skillful participant-
observer and writer, someone who combined sympathetic understanding of
his subjects and useful policy recommendations. Over the years it sold more
than 180,000 copies. Two critiques written at the time deserve note. One came
from Joseph Caruso, author of *The Priest* (1956), a friend of Gans and a careful observer of the scene in the West End. Although Caruso admired Gans
for his empathy and jargon-free prose, he found his study too complacent. He
contrasted Gans's belief in "social theories which are sensible and based on the
American tradition of 'fair play'" with his own more cynical judgments. What

was happening to the West Enders only strengthened his hatred "for the capitalist system, makes me a little more vehement and pushes me a little further
left." Gans made clear how different were his goals and position. In March 1960
he wrote to Caruso that he desired to demonstrate that the neighborhood "was
not a hotbed of pathological types, or knife-carrying hoodlums, or a mélange
of happy opera loving Italians. I also wanted to show the people who would
read my manuscript the way that people like West Enders live," in order to
help middle-class people understand the lives of people unlike themselves. In a
response in 1961 to a draft of Gans's manuscript on the West End, Denise Scott
Brown, whom Gans had taught at Penn, was critical from a different perspective. She felt his "usual and clear cool" approach "warms" and "Everything fits
so well into place, + is so logically +, apparently effortlessly, built up." Scott
Brown acknowledged that Gans's sympathy for and understanding of those
he wrote about was abundantly clear but remarked that "snatches" he gave of
"local conversation," though enchanting, were "as incongruous in your cool
prose as paprika in water-ice." Driving home her point, she wondered whether
he was overdoing "this defensiveness" toward his "middle-class audience."[53]

If Caruso and Scott Brown prodded Gans, major sociologists applauded
him. Nathan Glazer called the book a "vivid and compelling picture of a culture and a way of life." Howard S. Becker hailed the book as "a magnificent
achievement, . . . informed by a passionate defense of the underdogs of urban
society against their exploiters" and showing that "such a passion can be put
to worthy scientific use." With its combination of an ethnography of the lives
of residents and critique of urban removal, Gans had produced a compelling
and timely book. Appearing the same year as Michael Harrington's *The Other
America*, *The Urban Villagers* (and Gans himself) played an important role in
discussions of poverty and the Great Society. For our purposes, whether or not
contemporaries recognized this, what Gans accomplished was to help readers
understand how consumers responded to popular culture on their own terms,
terms shaped by their class position.[54]

The Levittowners (1967)

The New Jersey suburbanites to whom Gans next turned his attention differed
significantly from his Boston city dwellers, but the two groups shared a skeptical attitude toward popular culture. In 1956 the real estate developer William
Levitt began to plan a new town in New Jersey. Gans purchased a house and
beginning in October 1958 did three years of fieldwork there. The result was
his 1967 book, *The Levittowners: Ways of Life and Politics in a New Suburban*

Community, which appeared soon after he had left the University of Pennsylvania and joined the faculty at Columbia University. Here Gans offered a study of working- and lower-middle-class inhabitants among whom he had lived. If with *The Urban Villagers* he focused on the impact of people being forced out of their urban neighborhoods, with the new book he explored how the move to the suburbs, usually more voluntary than forced, affected behavior. At least since his days as a graduate student studying Park Forest, Gans had been interested in what happened when planners or developers created suburban towns and urban villagers moved to them. With *The Levittowners* Gans entered into the debate over American suburbs, criticizing those who looked down on the members of the middle class who inhabited them and the scholars and social commentators who assumed that in moving, those who once dwelled in cities passively had their lives transformed. As he said much later, he used data to "debunk the stereotypes that demonized the new post war suburbs." Levittown, he continued, "was not a sterile, conformity ridden and homogeneous aggregation of unhappy young urbanites forced by government to move to the suburbs."[55]

Once again emphasizing the resilience characteristic of the lives of ordinary people, he countered the argument so many writers offered, that the move to the suburbs dramatically changed people's lives. Here he cast a doubtful eye on the "upper middle class ethnocentrism" of unnamed critics who saw suburbanites as "an uneducated, gullible, petty 'mass' which rejects the culture that would make it fully human." Some of them saw in suburbia a "rootlessness and absence of community" that might make Americans, as they had earlier made Germans and Russians, "subject to demagoguery that can incite mass hysteria and mob action." When they viewed suburban America, these cosmopolitans were tourists, disappointed that they did not find in suburbs the exotic, stimulating, varied, pleasure-filled life they associated with cities. Gans criticized their picture of suburbanites as indulging in "hyperactive visiting to counteract boredom and loneliness brought on by the lack of urbanity in their communities." Others, less fearful of the larger consequences of mass society, nonetheless emphasized boredom, loneliness, and apathy.[56]

Gans was not as sympathetic to his Levittown subjects as to his Boston ones: the former were less exuberant and more concerned with being respectable; their children especially (but to some extent the parents as well) more susceptible to pressure from outside forces. Yet Gans was casting a skeptical eye on the work of nonacademic social critics, implicitly but clearly Vance Packard, John Keats, A. C. Spectorsky, and William H. Whyte Jr., writers who in 1961 Gans criticized for exaggerating the homogenization of American life because he felt they paid too little attention to class. In contrast, Gans's judgment of life in Levittown was positive. Accepting its residents' self-descriptions as genuine, perhaps at times too unskeptically, Gans saw them as genuinely happy and hardly homogeneous people who found in their new communities comfortable and convenient ways of life centered on local and family concerns. Rather than being passive, mindless, conformist, gullible, and numbingly inactive, they participated in a vital community life. Their encounters with popular culture hardly proved that the mass media dominated their lives. Although the television was continually on in their homes, its messages came to them "filtered through a variety of personal predispositions so that not many messages reach the receiver intact." They used television for practical and selective purposes, as a topic of conversation in awkward social situations, as a babysitter for their children between play time and dinner, or as a provider of functional information. Like their West End counterparts, the suburbanites talked back to TV, criticizing "anachronisms in the plots" and expressing skepticism toward the claims of advertising.[57]

To the extent that Gans identified trouble in suburbs like Levittown, he located it among women and teens. Writing several years after the publication of Betty Friedan's *The Feminine Mystique* in 1963, but never acknowledging her book, Gans spoke of how many women, differentially across class lines, felt stuck in suburbia. Countering the image of a suburban matriarchy, he painted a complex but at times disturbing picture of women in suburbia. In middle-class families, and even in some working-class ones, husbands and wives developed more common interests and divided household chores more equitably. Yet he also noted what he called "female malaise." He located this among young mothers who had recently worked for pay and now felt trapped by tedious housework, those who had just moved from Philadelphia, some Jewish women, and some women with problematic marriages whose husbands spent long hours on the road. Teenagers, for whom Levittown was "Endsville," were the other group who found suburban life alienating. With their relationships with their parents "fraught with tension" and with "no place to go and nothing to do after school," teens lived in an angry and hostile but pre-political subculture, participating in "an undeclared and subconscious war" with their parents, "as pervasive as the class struggle."[58]

The responses to *The Levittowners* were varied but mostly positive. Like *The Urban Villagers*, this book became a classic community study. To be sure, criticism was forthcoming, with one British observer calling the book "an apologia for the suburbs of America." From other quarters came positive assessments. Writing in the *American Journal of Sociology*, Robert Boguslaw hailed Gans as not only "a highly sensitive participant observer with a well-developed talent for describing the world from the perspective of his subjects" but also "a remarkably insightful planning analyst and planner." Tom Wolfe wrote that although he had stopped reading what "literary intellectuals" wrote on suburbs with such disdain, he was relieved when he read the book because Gans had focused on how suburbanites "actually" lived. Robert Merton, one of the nation's most distinguished sociologists, wrote to Gans, "Everything about it gives me pleasure—your choice of subjects, your human stance (at once involved and detached), your below-the-surface observations, your straightforward writing, the texture of the analysis." Finally, even though he was known for the generosity of his evaluations, came a positive assessment from Riesman, who remarked that "it's really a marvelous book and extremely stimulating."[59]

"Popular Culture in America" (1966)

In 1966 Gans made more explicit some of the larger implications of his two community studies for understanding mass media when he published an extended essay titled "Popular Culture in America: Social Problem in a Mass Society or Social Asset in a Pluralist Society?" The project had a long history, beginning in the 1950 seminar taught by Riesman and Katz and ending in a 1974 book that Gans dedicated to Riesman. In the 1966 essay Gans took on the critics of mass culture, especially T. S. Eliot, Dwight Macdonald, Clement Greenberg, and Theodor Adorno. He emphasized that the contrast between an individualized high culture and a homogenized popular one was suspect, given the segmentation of markets for mass culture. And he asserted that creators of elite and popular culture operated from a variety of quite mixed motives. Gans also took on what Greenberg and Macdonald had said of the negative effects of popular culture, exploring the reciprocal rather than the one-way borrowings that occurred. "Undoubtedly, high-culture creators suffer when they see their work changed," he noted with a sense of irony, "but so do popular-culture creators, even though only the former call it debasement." Gans referenced empirical studies to cast a skeptical eye on the notion of Americans "as brutalized, narcotized, atomized, escapist, or unable to cope with reality," as Macdonald asserted they were. He also emphasized how consumers carefully selected content in accordance with their commitments to the values of their families and communities. Somewhat like Riesman, Gans offered a sociological analysis of the left-wing critics of popular culture. He did this by drawing parallels with the British socialist critics like Hoggart who were "trying to resolve a personal conflict of loyalties between the working-class culture in which they were born and the elite culture by which they earn their living." When Riesman, who was now growing more conservative, read this essay by Gans, he wrote that his former student had offered "a highly distorted presentation of his opponents' views" and then continued by noting that Susan Sontag's "Notes on 'Camp'" made clear that "taste tends to develop very unevenly."[60]

At moments Gans made clear his own preference for high cultures, which he found "superior to the lower ones because they can provide greater, more intense, and perhaps even more lasting aesthetic gratification."[61] His fieldwork among those without the benefit of middle-class culture had caused him to qualify his earlier relativism. However, the overall thrust of his argument still revealed a commitment to a variety of taste cultures that deserved respect. He asserted that advocates of high culture were just another self-interested group, in this case an elitist one engaged in a power struggle over the fate of competing class interests. He adopted a relativistic view in which the existence of a wide range of class-based "*taste subcultures*" competed with one another. This underscored what he called the "pluralism and democracy in American society." He rejected the distinction between high and low culture, along with the assumption that the former represented aesthetic standards the latter did not possess. Skeptical about the claims that high culture was distinctive, he instead saw a situation where borrowings occurred across permeable boundaries. Distinguishing between a "creator-oriented" high culture and a "*consumer-oriented*" popular one (without gendering the distinction), Gans wanted to shift attention from the content of popular culture on which advocates of high culture focused to the effects, on which his two community studies had concentrated.[62]

Conclusions

Couched in sociological language but reaching a considerable audience, these writings that Gans offered between 1962 and 1967 moved on several fronts to recast the debate over popular culture. His two community studies revealed the nuanced and complicated ways in which ordinary Americans absorbed, reshaped, and resisted what they consumed. More generally, Gans criticized the critics of mass culture for failing to understand the ethnocentric and class-based nature of their analysis. His approach to taste cultures chipped away at a clear distinction between high and low. By shifting the focus from cultural products such as advertisements and television shows to their reception, he not only insisted on paying attention to effects but also placed the consumer in a powerful position, distinct from the producer. Gans both drew on and reshaped what his mentor David Riesman had written. Gans focused not, as

Riesman had, on the middle and upper middle classes but on the working class or lower middle class. He drew on Riesman's emphasis on the power of peer culture and criticism of critics of popular culture. Yet compared with Riesman, Gans developed more fully some key themes: how ordinary people drew on their own traditions to resist the intrusion of popular culture and how popular culture had its own creativity and integrity.

Together during the 1960s, in influential books Wolfe and Gans helped legitimate discussion of the popular culture that members of the working class and lower middle class produced and consumed. They bucked a long tradition (represented by, among others, Adorno and McLuhan) that had linked commercial culture with femininity and high culture with masculinity. Race played relatively small roles in their discussions, something especially striking for Wolfe, given his background. Gans was often writing about white ethnics, even as he focused on the class position of those he studied. In contrast, for Wolfe ethnicity remained unmarked. Yet for both of them social class remained the main category of social analysis. And by shifting attention away from elite or avant-garde leadership in shaping American culture, they made possible an endorsement of popular culture.

Chapter 9

Sexuality and a New Sensibility

In the early to mid-1960s Tom Wolfe and Herbert J. Gans explored the class dimensions of consumer culture in ways that emphasized pleasure, resistance, reciprocity, creativity from below, social class, and symbolic communication. At the same time, Susan Sontag challenged well-worn approaches as she reconsidered the relationship between passionate sexuality and some elements of consumer culture. In 1964, Sontag, a thirty-one-year-old novelist and cultural critic, published "Notes on 'Camp.'" This was a daring essay: she was trying to establish herself as a serious cultural critic at the same time that she ventured into dangerous territory in her treatment of the intersections of culture, gender, and sexuality. Writing in *Partisan Review*, the temple of New York intellectuals, she critiqued their commitment to cultural hierarchies, their sacralization of the modernist literary canon, and their avoidance of emergent forms of cultural expression. As a writer and a person Sontag did not indulge in consumer culture as that term is usually understood. Yet at a time when intellectuals scoffed at consumer culture as not worthy of serious consideration, the maverick Sontag rejected mass culture while at the same time acknowledging the vitality of some of the more provocative types of commercial goods and entertainments that she identified with camp. Moreover, she revealed how an embrace of a new avant-garde, one connected to popular culture, provided a source of resistance to commercialism. Above all, what makes her work so important is that she wrote about sexuality as a central aspect in the development of new perspectives on consumer culture. Many of the writers who had looked down on consumer culture did so because they linked it with unacceptable sexual expressions, even while some of them argued that sexual liberation was possible only in a more ideal and less commercialized world. Though Sontag hardly embraced most forms of consumer culture, she linked sexual expressiveness with the pleasure of commercial goods such as Tiffany lamps and comic books. Establishing this connection played a key role in supporting new and more favorable attitudes to consumer culture. In the hands of others, the linkages she made in such complicated ways between sexuality and commercial goods made way for a basic rethinking of consumer culture.[1]

Growing Up Precocious

Sontag's life story is the stuff of legend, one that begins with a childhood of rootlessness, melancholy, and tremendous intellectual engagement at a young age. She was born in New York as Susan Lee Rosenblatt to Jewish parents who were fur traders in China. Her mother came to the United States to give birth to Susan and then placed her with relatives so she could return to China. Her father died of tuberculosis in China when Susan was just five years old. Seeking a climate that would help alleviate Susan's asthma, her mother returned to the United States and then moved with her two daughters, first to Miami and then to Tucson, where Susan started her formal education in the third grade, beginning a pattern of skipping grades. In 1945 her mother married Captain Nathan Sontag, whom Susan Sontag later described as a "bemedalled and beshrapnelled" Army Air Force flier. Both Susan and her younger sister Judith took his name although their stepfather never adopted either of them. In 1946 the family moved to Canoga Park, California, in the San Fernando Valley.[2]

Sontag felt she was a "resident alien" confined by "that long prison sentence, my childhood," in a household with a distant stepfather and violent mother. Neither her mother nor her stepfather knew what to do with such an intellectual, intense, unusually moody child. Doing her best to "ward off" what she called the "jovial claptrap" offered by teachers and students at school and "the maddening bromides" at home, she had already become "a demon reader" and a writer of short stories, poems, plays, and journal entries. Starting at age nine, she began to read serious books—Victor Hugo's *Les Misérables* and Edgar Allan Poe's stories—and soon after she explored distant worlds through Richard Halliburton's *Complete Book of Marvels*. She also devoured Louisa May Alcott's *Little Women*, Jack London's *Martin Eden*, and Eve Curie's *Madame Curie*, through which she learned about the lives of writers and of women with careers. In January 1949 Sontag graduated from North Hollywood High School just before she turned sixteen.[3]

What she wrote as a high school student reveals her as precocious, serious, and deeply engaged. In unpublished poems and essays she focused on World War II, the Soviet Union, refugees, Jewishness, fascism, and concentration camps. She pondered what it meant to be a democratic socialist who wanted to sever the connection Cold Warriors made between democracy and capitalism. Her poems, in which she focused on memory, experience, identity, and death, were serious, ambitious, and often dark. At age fifteen in the fall of 1948, she did an independent study with one of her teachers, focusing on Sigmund Freud's *Civilization and Its Discontents* (1930). Compelled by most of what Freud wrote, she paraphrased his work. "Our bodies are part of nature," she wrote, "and will always contain the 'seeds of dissolution.'" She believed that Freud was "logically erecting a structure which, when completed, can only be identified as a belief that it is impossible for the human animal to achieve an affirmative happiness while bound by the inevitable repression of civilization." The only problem with Freud was his "persistent coupling of masculinity with activity and femininity with passivity," an issue with which she continued to wrestle well beyond her adolescence.[4]

As a high school journalist she continued her campaign of self-education. She wrote about popular movies and aligned herself with Henry Wallace's 1948 presidential campaign and opponents of anti-Communism. By her teens she had already begun to engage European modernism, reading André Gide and learning what it meant to experience intensely a wide range of arts. She watched foreign movies and listened to music by John Cage and the émigré musicians living in Los Angeles. In a legendary story, she told of how as a fifteen-year-old girl, still in high school, at a newsstand in Hollywood she read an essay by Lionel Trilling. "I just began to tremble with excitement," she remembered. "And from then on, my dream was to grow up, move to New York and write for *Partisan Review*."[5]

Self-Fashioning

Before proceeding, some words about sources. From an early age, Sontag made frequent entries into diaries and notebooks. They are especially full and rich for the years beginning in 1948, although in the early years of her marriage in 1950 there are few entries. Her remarks vary considerably in style and tone, ranging from humdrum descriptions of daily activities, to lists of the cultural events she attended, to recordings of intimate experiences, to intense considerations of ideas. Her diaries reveal a young woman playing with gender identities in ways that were common in queer culture at the time. The mood swings she recorded were not that different from what other teens experienced; what was unusual was her ability to intellectualize or articulate what she was experiencing. To help us understand her journals, we can turn to her early 1960s essays. Sontag spoke of the "rawness of the journal form" through which "we encounter the ego behind the masks of ego in an author's work." In modern times, journals are compelling because "the artist (replacing the saint) is the exemplary sufferer." They contain "a long series of self-assessments and self-interrogations." In a journal, she noted elsewhere as she revealed how self-conscious were these writings, an author "builds up, piece by piece, the identity of a writer to himself." These comments by Sontag reveal her portrayal of herself as an "exemplary sufferer" and her awareness of the relationship of public and private selves.[6]

Reading her diaries also confirms what her son David Rieff points us to: that her essays on Walter Benjamin and Elias Canetti, published respectively in 1980 and 1978, provide us with "as close to a sally into autobiography as she would ever make." Writing in ways that were both self-explorations and discussions of another, Sontag saw Benjamin as having a "Saturnine temperament." "Convinced that the will is weak," he made "extravagant efforts to develop it," with the resulting "hypertrophy of will" taking "the form of a compulsive devotion to work." To reading, "the delirium of the child," over time was added "writing, the obsession of the adult." His melancholic disposition infused everything he did. For Benjamin, but just as true for herself, "the self is a project, something to be built." Those consumed by melancholy were secretive, their relationships with others marked by "feelings of superiority, of inadequacy," responses "masked by friendliness, or the most scrupulous manipulation." Similarly, her essay on Canetti, like Benjamin a cosmopolitan, wandering Jew, captures key aspects of his sense of self, including his geographical and intellectual restlessness that followed, as it did for Sontag, "a childhood rich in displacements." Here she talked of Canetti's "intellectual insatiability" as well as of "the purity of moral position and intransigence" that he aspired to. He was "extremely self-involved in a characteristically impersonal way," someone who feared "not being insolent or ambitious enough," impatient "with the merely impersonal" who as a "witness to the age, ... set the largest, most *edifying* standards of despair." Just as she had seen the melancholic Benjamin "haunted by death," the entire body of Canetti's work, Sontag wrote five years after she was first diagnosed with cancer, "aims at a refutation of death."[7]

Berkeley Interlude

In early 1949 Sontag went to University of California at Berkeley for a momentous single semester. Her private writings of the late 1940s and early 1950s reveal the struggles of a teenage girl, intellectually precocious but on an emotional roller-coaster and trying to shape a sense of herself: a brilliant writer struggling with issues of creativity, identity, and sexuality; someone at once judgmental, anxious, ambitious, and earnest. Her attempt to figure out what it meant to be a writer and an intellectual that had begun much earlier now intensified.

Although later she opposed interpretation, here she was always interpreting. However she celebrated passion and pleasure elsewhere, in private she continually distanced herself from her feelings even while she filled the journals with stories of self-destructive, painful affairs. While after she emerged as a public intellectual she refused to talk about her ambition and self-promotion, in her private writings ambition and self-fashioning compelled her. Figuring out that she wanted to be a freelance cultural critic and not a professor was a frequent theme.[8]

Above all, although she rarely made explicit reference to herself as a Jew or even to Jewish topics in what she published before 1966 and even well after that, in her diary for the years up to 1964 she often pondered what it meant to be a Jew or at least made clear how aware she was of Jewish history, religion, and culture. Although she was not religious, the experience of Jewish history weighed heavily on her. In her diaries, she often focused on many of the topics central to the experience of twentieth-century Jews. Several times, she returned to the Holocaust. In 1957 she wondered about the possibility of reforming Judaism in order to "break the stranglehold of men." Among the scores of lists she composed were those that included Hebrew words and their English equivalents. Strikingly, at one moment she noted the "impress of Judaism on my character, my tastes, my intellectual persuasions, the very posture of my personality." To be sure there was an ambivalence in her considerations of her own Jewishness, as there was with how she approached so many facets of her life. "I am proud of being Jewish," she wrote in November 1958, before adding, "Of *what*?"[9]

More central to her brief time at Berkeley were struggles to define her sexuality. Just before she moved there, she admitted to herself with some reluctance that she had "lesbian tendencies," a phrase that suggests how she was thinking about what it means to experience feelings that went against heterosexual norms. At Berkeley in the spring of 1949 she fell in love with Irene Lyons. At the same time she wanted to feel physically attracted to a man to "prove, at least, that I am bisexual," but she continued by noting, "nothing but humiliation and degradation at the thought of physical relations with a man." Rejected by Irene and unable to love a man, in late March she met an experienced lesbian, Harriet Sohmers. Sontag was now ready to transform tendencies into action. Sohmers worked in a bookstore and when Sontag wandered in, Sohmers noticed how striking she was. Urged on by several gay co-workers, she approached Sontag and used a familiar lesbian pickup line, asking her if she had read Djuana Barnes's *Nightwood* (1936), in which lesbianism and bisexuality figured so prominently.[10]

Sontag responded affirmatively and in the ensuing weeks Sohmers introduced her to both the San Francisco queer world and lesbian sex. Helped by alcohol, Sontag overcame her awkwardness and inexperience, enjoying Sohmers's initiation into making love with another woman. In late May, as she considered how her passionate sexuality was prompting her to challenge the expectations society had for teenage girls, she wrote movingly about how the experience had transformed her. "My concept of sexuality is so altered—Thank god!—bisexuality as the expression of fullness of an individual—and an honest rejection of the—yes—perversion which limits sexual experience, attempts to de-physicalize it, in such concepts as the idealization of chastity until the 'right person' comes along—the whole ban on pure physical sensation without love, *on promiscuity*." She now linked same-sex sexuality with intense pleasure in ways that would influence her writings more than ten years later. "I shall anticipate pleasure everywhere and find it, too, for it *is* everywhere!" Pondering her relationship with Sohmers a few weeks later she wrote in ways that reflected her fascination with sadomasochistic sex, "I want to err on the side of violence and excess." Moreover, for Sontag, there was an important connection between her sexuality and her self-display. As she remarked in a revealing journal entry, she was "more and more sure of the link between homosexuality + narcissism—at least in my case." In addition, she connected her awakening to same sex-passion with not "letting myself slide into the academic life." Intense sexual pleasure, same-sex passion, narcissism, excess, and a academic career for which males professors were not gatekeepers—all these came together for a sixteen-year-old Sontag.[11]

University of Chicago

Late in the summer of 1949 Sontag left Los Angeles for the University of Chicago. In some ways, she was fortunate to have had her first sexual experience with another woman in the Bay Area, for more than any other place in the United States, that city had a vibrant (if nonetheless often harassed) public and private queer scene. Like other intellectually ambitious women in the late 1940s and early 1950s who lived in worlds that lacked above-ground feminist or queer social movements, Sontag had to struggle against conventional expectations that their most important mission was to marry and have children. In that sense, the move to Chicago was highly problematic.[12]

Yet the two years at the University of Chicago were important both personally and intellectually. At Chicago she focused on literature and philosophy and earned her B.A. in 1951 at age eighteen. While in high school she had read in *Collier's* about the university's fabled core curriculum and intense intellectuality. With its emphasis on the close reading of texts, classroom performance in intense discussions, and comparative and nonhistorical juxtapositions of key ideas, Chicago provided a superb education. The broader cultural world around the university was also important to Sontag, not, as in the case of Berkeley, for offering the queer world of the city but as an environment that offered the combination of left-wing politics and avant-garde films.[13]

During her first months in Chicago her personal life was quite unsettled. She was wondering about the implications of her sexual awakening in Berkeley, whether she could recapture the experience of passion but this time with men, at the same time that she was wondering about the relationship between promiscuity and commitment. Neither her sexual identity nor her career aspirations were fixed and she knew that both would come up against powerful social forces, including those that reigned at a male-dominated university. Soon after arriving she had a series of sexual encounters with men, having "surmounted," she wrote, "both psychological and physical obstacles." Shortly after she noted, "*I want* the totality of sensual pleasure, of companionship and affection more than anything else in the world—It's just that it seems too unattainable! And I'm so lonely." Her sexual relationships with men, which in one instance she called "cheap," at times made her feel less fearful about the issues of what she called her "sexual normality." In March Sontag talked of "weary, futile loneliness." In the same month she learned that her mother was penniless and remarked to herself that she was "goal-less, formless, ridiculously, adolescently despondent." When in New York on a vacation she resumed her relationship with Sohmers but now felt humiliated by her. Expressing suicidal thoughts, sensing how rootless her life was, and thinking often of death, Sontag was deeply depressed.[14]

In the fall of 1950 she seemed on a somewhat more even keel, though personal problems were never far from her consciousness. The quality of her academic work improved, most visibly so when the distinguished literary critic and University of Chicago professor Kenneth Burke called her paper on *Nightwood*, which she completed in May 1950, a "stunner." And indeed it was. "The Dialectic of Decay" was a brilliant essay in which she explored many elements of the novel, including the parallels between personal and social disintegration, the relationship of three women in a love triangle, and the novel's emphasis on sensuousness. Here she saw how the book's representation of sexual possibilities rebuked conventional limits. Given the constraints she might presume that her professorial audience imposed, she nonetheless offered a complicated and not entirely unambiguous meditation on what she called sexual "perversion." She mentioned "the inversion theme" of weak men and strong women. She wrote how in the novel "all perverse, illegal, decadent, counterfeit behaviour may be considered as normality turned backwards." She explored the "many ways in which perverse sex is directly ennobled," including "not only inversion, but the whole spectrum of frigidities in heterosexual relations: late birth, near impotence, grotesque devices for restoring 'normal' sex relations." What Sontag was trying to do was to pose an argument counter to one that equated perversion only with homosexuality. She was pondering the issue of her sexual normality at a time when society considered her sexual passions so problematic. Yet despite the achievement her thesis and B.A. represented, her worries persisted. She continued to dwell on the issues of vocation and money, noting in her final year at Chicago that experience was ridding her of "aspirations toward proletarian living."[15]

Marriage

All of Sontag's concerns, her worries about vocation and money, unresolved issues of sexual identity, the longing to overcome her loneliness, and the yearning for intellectual fulfillment, provide the background to the dramatic turn her life took when in December 1950 she met and then a few days later married Philip Rieff. In light of the longer trajectory of her life, this is not the easiest decision to understand. The son of Lithuanian Jewish parents who came to the United States in 1921, Rieff grew up poor in Chicago, compelled in his teens both by political radicalism and by reading. His early career centered on the University of Chicago, where he earned his B.A., M.A., and Ph.D. and taught beginning in 1947. In Sontag's journals, their meeting and marriage seem to come out of nowhere. She arrived in his classroom just as he was turning his attention to Sigmund Freud. Her dramatic entrance and striking presence caught his eye, and as she went to leave the classroom, in a possessive act he grabbed her arm and asked her out for lunch. After knowing him for only ten days, Sontag, age seventeen, married Rieff, eleven years her senior. On December 2, 1950, she wrote in her diary, "Last night, or was it early this (Sat.) morning?—I am engaged to Philip Rieff." Soon after she noted, "I marry Philip with full consciousness + fear of my will toward self-destructiveness." Having long yearned to travel to Europe but not having enough funds to do so, and with the Korean War on the horizon, she wrote, "The war is so close. We have reservations on the *Queen Elizabeth* for June 22nd." In the short term, marrying Rieff may have resolved problems about loneliness, sexuality, and finances, but in the long term it only exacerbated her situation. Her feelings were conflicted but for the moment she chose to enter the intellectual life by marrying an academic man with whom she shared so many interests.[16]

Cambridge, Mass.

Rieff and Sontag moved to the Boston area in 1951, where he took a job at Brandeis. They had one child, David, born September 28, 1952, who later went on to a distinguished career as an editor and writer. A year later, Sontag began her graduate education, first at the University of Connecticut in 1953–54 and then at Harvard/Radcliffe, earning an M.A. in philosophy in 1957. As a graduate student at Harvard, Sontag was emotionally unsettled and intellectually engaged, appreciating being taken seriously but unsure of where her commitments would lead. Writing came with difficulty. "I have diarrhea of the mouth and constipation of the typewriter," she wrote in early 1957. Moreover, although she was pursuing a Ph.D., Sontag still cast a skeptical eye on academic life. In September 1956, she wrote, "College instruction is a brand of popular culture; the universities are poorly-run mass media." Several months later she imagined a "story in the manner of Kafka" to understand what an "Academic awaiting a promotion" faced.[17]

Yet her graduate school papers reveal that she was intensely and successfully involved in her study of major philosophical texts. Her professors lauded her work, though not without at least an occasional note of condescension. In response to one paper, Perry Miller wrote to "my dear girl," saying that her paper was "a pure joy to read." One essay in particular deserves notice, "Plato's Theory of Pleasure," written for a course with Raphael Demos in the fall of 1955. Her straw figure was the assumption that there was "little in common between the turbulent passions—like sensuality, anger, hunger, despair—and the disinterested enjoyments of intellectual and aesthetic satisfactions." In contrast, Sontag argued that all kinds of pleasures, the emotional and the intellectual, were connected. "For Plato," she wrote, "pleasure is indeed such a 'polymorphous concept.'"[18]

Once settled in Cambridge, Rieff completed his dissertation and then turned it into *Freud: The Mind of the Moralist* (1959). In this largely admiring book, which marked his arrival as a major American intellectual, Rieff joined others at the time, such as Herbert Marcuse and Norman O. Brown, who saw Freud as not just a founder of a school of psychoanalysis but a major cultural, political, and social theorist. Rieff focused on the tension in Freud's writings between repression and instinct. In a world where Western religions had lost their power, he wrote, psychoanalysts and patients could work on personal conflicts and expect modest results with no hope of achieving ultimate salvation or even anything approaching full happiness.[19]

In understanding how the connections between Rieff and Sontag were not just personal but also intellectual, it is useful to compare the thesis, dated June

1954, when they had been married for more than three years, with the book, published in 1959 but completed in the summer of 1958, when divorce was not far off. Sontag had some role in shaping Rieff's thesis but a more major one in his writing the book on Freud, but as part of their divorce agreement it appeared as his alone. The available evidence makes it difficult to separate what Sontag contributed from what appeared under his name. "Co-authorship," Rieff had written in his dissertation as he referred to Freud's work with Josef Breuer, "is always a difficult art." In the preface to the book on Freud, written in June of 1958 long after they left Chicago and when Sontag knew better than Rieff that their marriage was in jeopardy, Rieff used conventional terms of the time to offer "special thanks" to "My wife, Susan Rieff" who "devoted herself unstintingly to this book." Yet in the thesis, Rieff had drawn on Freud to write that "there is an inevitable inequality even in the happiest marriages," with the "love of man for woman" apparently developing "into a relation of obedience and authority." Here Rieff both asserted male authority and acknowledged the problems that he believed affected even happy marriages.[20]

From thesis to book the treatment of issues of sexuality and gender changed considerably. In the thesis most of what Rieff wrote on these topics appeared in a sixteen-page section titled "The Sexuality of Politics." Here he characterized Freud's "misogyny" as "an integral part of his psychology." Moreover, he ascribed to Freud the view that the difference between the sexes was "not a biological but a psychological one." He explored what he saw as Freud's contrasting view of male and female: the former representing culture, rationality, progress, and the woman standing for the demonic, primal, static, and instinctual. "Freud combined a rationalist faith with a particular romantic image of women," he wrote, "and to the degree he admired intellect, to that same degree woman became the scapegoat of his rationalism—the mysterious, anti-cultural *hausfrau*." In the battle between men and women, Rieff argued when he treated bisexuality in the thesis, "the war of the sexes was never conclusively won, for women began with a heavy advantage: the 'original bisexuality in every individual.'" With "feminine irrationality" for Freud corrupting "male reason," full freedom would always remain elusive.[21]

In contrast, the book more fully embraced cultural analysis, articulated feminist explanations, and explored sexual experimentation. The key section appeared in a thirty-eight-page chapter titled "Sexuality and Domination," a title that underscored the relationship between gender, sexuality, and power. Now the critique of Freud was more fundamental and wide-ranging. The book pictured Freud as a man deeply imbedded in a misogynistic culture. "In the final analysis," Rieff observed, Freud's "personal intuitions mastered him, and cultural causes were slighted in favor of the biological differential and an 'innate' inferiority." "I have overstated the consistency of Freud's deprecation of women," Rieff noted. He then went on to hail how Freud took "women down from the Victorian pedestal of chastity and pure feeling." On the other hand, he insisted that what Freud substituted "is an even less disguised hostility."[22]

The book emphasized both the liberatory and constricting aspects of Freud's view of sexuality, in the process paying attention to divergent sexual experience and identities. It criticized Freud's restricted view of sexual pleasure. Rieff applauded Freud for "liberating" sex by not focusing exclusively on its connection to reproduction, in the process removing the "moral horror that now attaches to the perversions." Yet the book saw Freud's view of sex as focused too exclusively on heterosexual intercourse. Freud viewed "forepleasure" as a mere preliminary "to the serious business at hand." The book talked of Freud's "suppression of earlier erotic zones," including ones sadomasochists used, "so that the genital zone has predominance." The book also explored bisexuality. Although children had, in Freud's words, "'freedom to range equally over male and female objects'" the book ascribed to Freud the regressive nature of "sexual indeterminacy" about adult male and female identities and practices. In the chapter's final paragraph, Rieff focused on Freud's emphasis on an original bisexuality characteristic of all individuals. This, the book noted, "does not alter the pejorative import of the differentiation which Freud sees as proceeding from the period of infantile sexuality" which cast men as rational and women as emotional. In the end, Freud's "polite and profound misogyny" and criticism of bisexuality led to the triumph of the masculine, of control, rationality. and sexual containment.[23]

Although it is impossible to know for sure what in the key chapter Rieff and Sontag each contributed, it is likely that the book reflected Sontag's commitment to a woman's perspective and to sexual experimentation just as it encapsulated Rieff's more constrained and heterosexist views. Beyond these specific remarks on gender and sexuality stood a more fundamental difference. At the most basic level Rieff's book on Freud was a complicated appreciation of one of the modernist masters. To be sure, Rieff rejected any notion of master narratives, but he did insist on the importance of striving for rationalism and self-control. In contrast, Sontag was providing what Alice Kaplan called a "gateway" to postmodernism, someone who would come to reject (if in 1958 she had not already done so), the Freud/Rieff commitment to rationality and instinctual control. Rieff and Sontag both had powerful intellects and wills, but by the late 1950s and early 1960s they were separated not just as husband and wife but also as modernist and emerging postmodernist.[24]

The real drama of the years in the Boston area came in Sontag's marriage to Rieff, which was problematic at best. Living in Cambridge, they inhabited lofty academic circles, socializing with major figures from Brandeis, MIT, and Harvard, including Herbert Marcuse, Walt Rostow, and Jerome Bruner. Yet moving in such circles may have done more to exacerbate than alleviate the problems a young woman faced in the academic world of the mid-1950s. At the time, being a male academic carried with it well-understood roles; being a women with intellectual ambitions, in a world where many academic couples had a clear sense of gender divisions, involved social expectations that were tremendously difficult to navigate let alone resolve. To complicate matters, Rieff had his Ph.D. and an assistant professorship and was moving toward publication of his book on Freud, while Sontag was a graduate student unsure of her future vocation. [25]

They also had dramatically different understandings of marriage and family. Sontag and Rieff fought over how to raise their son. Fashioning himself as a formal gentleman, Rieff wanted what he later called a "traditional" family, with the man in charge. Sontag was more labile and unconventional, restless for something different. Early on she read Simone de Beauvoir's *The Second Sex* (1949; American edition 1953), a book that cast a skeptical eye on marriage and traditional gender roles. By 1956 if not earlier, bitter entries about the marriage began to fill Sontag's notebooks. "Whoever invented marriage," she wrote in early September 1956, "was an ingenious tormentor. It is an institution *committed* to the dulling of the feelings. The whole point of marriage is repetition. The best it aims for is the creation of strong, mutual dependencies." "The sense of not being free," she commented in early January 1957, "has never left me these six years." Two months later, bringing together the personal and political, she remarked that "Philip is an emotional totalitarian. 'The family' is his mystery." [26]

The situation came to a head in the spring of 1957. Leaving David with Philip's parents, in late August Sontag and Rieff parted company without fully acknowledging that the separation would be for good. Philip headed for a year at the Center for Advanced Study in the Behavioral Sciences in Palo Alto, and Sontag, with a dissertation fellowship from the American Association of University Women, in early September left for Europe. For Sontag, the stakes were high. Using words that echoed what Sylvia Plath and Betty Friedan also felt at the time, words that underscored the performative nature of domesticity as she wondered if she could be more than a wife and a mother, in early 1957 Sontag wrote that if she received the fellowship to study abroad, "Then at least I'll know if I am anything outside the domestic stage, the feathered nest." Sontag went first to St. Anne's College, Oxford, and then beginning in late December to the salons, theaters, and cafes of Paris and to the Sorbonne, where expatriate Americans (including members of the beat generation) shaped her social world.[27]

Oxford, Then Paris

Sontag's move from Oxford to Paris in late December 1957, when Sontag and Rieff were making the final changes to the manuscript, was momentous, both intellectually and personally. To Sontag Oxford had the suffocating combination of arid academic work and a powerful, masculine culture among students and faculty, what she called an "elegant malice." As she noted in an unpublished fictionalized rendering soon after she arrived in Paris, the time in Oxford was "a lonely exhilarating term . . . the atmosphere was too much like the one she'd known in America—the tense careerism of the academic world, the talkativeness of it. She felt sick of talk, of books, of intellectual industry, of the inhibited gate of the professor." For the ten or so years until the move to Paris, by and large she had focused on literature and philosophy that was canonical, mainly British and German. In contrast, although she lived in an English-speaking world in Paris, her diaries show how intensely she was concentrating on learning how to speak and read French. She was beginning to shift her attention to French intellectuals and artists such as André Breton, Georges Bataille, Robert Bresson, Jean Genet, Jean-Luc Godard, and Alain Robbe-Grillet. In Paris she also focused not just on written works but on visual ones as well, especially movies. Paris opened up sexual and bohemian possibilities that Cambridge and Oxford did not.[28]

For Sontag as a writer, the French experience provided a series of models of what it meant to be an aesthete and a politically engaged leftist sympathetic to Communist governments and to anticolonialism, even though in her diaries she paid remarkably little attention to France's domestic and international problems. She began to gain perspectives that would soon enable her to develop arguments that saw high and low culture in complicated relationships with one another. She was learning to transform her interest in philosophy, literature, cultural criticism, performance, and self-performance into a powerful amalgam. If one of her teenage idols, Lionel Trilling, had focused on modernist literature, she both broadened the range of texts to consider and begin to shift away from a commitment to modernism. The period in Paris enabled Sontag to embrace a set of new moral perspectives. Soon after her arrival in the city, in an entry that went against the grain of what Trilling would have written, she wrote, "It's corrupting to write with intent to moralize, to elevate people's moral standards." Or as she noted in September 1962 when she was in New

York, in ways that countered Rieff's outlook, "All Freud's heroes are heroes of repression." Freud "was a tremendous champion of the self-mutilating 'heroic' will. The psychoanalysis he created [is] a science of condescension toward the body, the instincts, the natural life—at best."[29]

Again, as was true in Berkeley, same-sex sexuality was central to her sense of herself in Paris and to her attempt, only partially successful, to place passion at the center of a worldview. Increasingly determined to end a marriage she considered suffocating, she returned to where she left off when she met Rieff in December 1950, to an exploration of the broader possibilities she had closed off by marrying Rieff. Sontag and Sohmers renewed their relationship in Paris for about eight months beginning in late December 1957, a time when Sohmers was also romantically involved with Cuban American playwright María Irene Fornés. Sontag's and Sohmers's diary entries for this period capture the tumultuous nature of the love triangle involving the three of them. Sontag was on an emotional roller-coaster ride, with more lows than highs and one which Sohmers's relationship with Fornes haunted. At one moment Sontag could de-clare that Sohmers is "beautiful, relaxed, affectionate. I—dizzy with passion and need for her, and happy . . . good god, I *am* happy!" Soon thereafter Sontag recorded the "total collapse of my affair with H." Not surprisingly, Sontag ex-perienced her relationship with Sohmers through the lens of the memories of her marriage to Rieff. Yet despite the parallels, she had learned in Paris that she craved the attention and love of women. As she noted in early January, when a woman made a pass at her, "it was so good to be home, as it were—to have women, instead of men, interested in me."[30]

By early January 1958 Sontag's new life in Paris had convinced her to seek a divorce from Rieff; it became final later that year. Early in the new year, she wrote a fictionalized version of her decision, in which her female lover is turned into a man. The news in February that Rieff had secured a job at Berkeley made her decision easier. Sontag returned to New York on January 1, 1959, with two suitcases, six-year-old David, and less than one hundred dollars. There she began to establish herself as a major cultural critic.[31]

She Took Manhattan

When Sontag started living in Manhattan, the city was in the midst of a cul-tural boom. As Tom Wolfe wrote later, postwar affluence finally opened up the city so that when he arrived in the early 1960s, it was "pandemonium with a big grin on." The city was "an amazing spectacle" and "a hulking carnival" that Wolfe "saw bubbling and screaming right there in front of my wandering eyes."

Broadway was enjoying a series of good seasons. Robert Moses was leading a major effort at urban renewal. Lincoln Center was soon to take shape, providing new homes for the New York Philharmonic and Metropolitan Opera. However, for Sontag, although she was working uptown, it was the emergence of a powerful, edgy avant-garde in lower Manhattan that proved so compelling. Here was a part of the city that was intellectually and racially diverse, where cosmopolitanism was so evident. Though in many ways abstract expressionism was past its peak, Jackson Pollock (who had died in 1956) had provided a model of the commercially successful, misunderstood artist. The Living Theatre offered a model for experimental drama. The pop artists Andy Warhol, Robert Rauschenberg, Claes Oldenburg, and Jasper Johns commanded attention as figures who melded high and low. Oldenburg's 1962 *The Store* used sculptured items of consumer culture to offer a probing, witty exploration of commodity culture. In the late 1940s and early 1950s, the composer John Cage explored the application of new technologies in his experimental work in music and dance. Art movie houses showed the latest French, German, and Swedish imports.[32]

Although in the late 1950s and into the 1960s Sontag taught at Sarah Lawrence College, City College of New York, and Columbia University, it was experimental culture that compelled her. The happening typified the new experimentalism. Allan Kaprow's "Eighteen Happenings in Six Parts," his first major work, opened in October 1959. As the *New York Times* recorded later, his "early events were scripted assemblages of movement, sound, scent and light, with instructions given to performers and viewers alike." The art historian Judith Rodenbeck has noted that his happenings "were compiled from sources as disparate as Baudelaire, Mallarmé's *Un Coup de dès*, Ginsberg's *Howl*, advertising, motivational speeches, newspapers, and Kaprow's own writing, itself an ironic pastiche of all of the above." Like other emerging forms that owed much to dada and surrealism, happenings involved improvisation, a dynamic relationship between artist and audience, an exploration of the connections between high and low, and expressions concerning the nature of the self as performer. As Sontag said of herself in a diary entry in the 1960s that captured her sense of self as well as the dynamics of happenings, "I live my life as a spectacle for myself, for my own edification. I live my life but I don't live *in* it."[33]

Although the vibrant cultural scene in Manhattan was essential to Sontag's development as an observer and writer, equally important were her intimate relationships. In the very late 1950s and early 1960s, Sontag had a series of romantic and sexual relationships, some with men but principally with women. She continued her entanglement in the triangle of Sontag/Sohmers/Fornes, eventually breaking with Sohmers and connecting with Fornes. In the ensuing several years, as both Sontag and Fornes began to emerge as writers, their relationship continued, albeit on rocky grounds. Struggling to write and unable to achieve a decent balance of love and sex in their relationship, Sontag and Fornes experienced tempestuousness and constant drama.[34]

For Sontag, in New York in 1959, sexuality was once again connected to exhilarating feelings of creativity. In Berkeley in 1949, sexual experimentation and intellectual creativity had come together. The move to Chicago, the marriage to Rieff, and then motherhood had placed her on a different path. In Paris, the frustrations of her involvement with Sohmers, among other issues, had made this period, intellectually, one of learning and absorbing rather than of productive writing. In November 1959, as she had done in Berkeley, Sontag now connected writing with her sexuality. "The orgasm focuses. I lust to write. The coming of the orgasm is not the salvation but, more, the birth of my ego," she confided to her diary. "To write is to spend oneself, to gamble oneself. . . . The writer is in love with himself . . . and makes his books out of that meeting and that violence."[35]

Repeatedly in the late 1950s and early 1960s Sontag linked writing, the performative self, narcissism, violence, passion, being an outlaw to sexual norms, and creativity, noting in 1964 that "intellectual 'wanting' [is] like sexual wanting." In her journal, she wrote, "I *create* myself," and then she went on to give a sense of the fluidity of her own identity and of her relationships with others. She looked around for female writers she would model herself on or react against, including de Beauvoir, Lillian Hellman, and Mary McCarthy. She returned again and again to what writing meant to her, remarking that it was important "mainly, out of egotism. I suppose. Because I want to be that *persona*, a writer, and not because there is something I must say." She also acknowledged that "being queer," as she said of herself in late 1959, made her feel guilty and vulnerable, as when she remarked that her "desire to write is connected with my homosexuality. I need the identity as a weapon, to match the weapon that society has against me." Her sexual identity, she remarked, "increases my wish to hide, to be invisible—which I've always felt anyway." To some extent her concern about her sexuality becoming public was connected to fights over custody of David. "I connect my fear and my sense of guilt with Philip," she wrote while linking her sexuality and vulnerability, "with his publicizing it to everyone all over the world, with the prospect of another custody suit" in which her battle to retain custody of David came up against Rieff's charge that a lesbian mother provided an unsuitable environment in which to raise a young child. In addition, she was still involved in a long process of self-fashioning that included keeping her sexuality a secret from the wider world. "We celebrate our changes of character by altering our personal appearance," she noted in September of 1961 as she was beginning to emerge in print as a writer.[36]

Susan Sontag, Essayist

Sontag quickly began to establish herself in the world of New York writers, an achievement that undercut Wolfe's claim about the emerging cultural scene in New York that "as a writer I had it practically all to myself." In 1959 the twenty-six-year-old Sontag asked William Phillips how she could write for *Partisan Review*, for which he was a founding co-editor. "One asks," he answered, to which she responded, "O.K., I'm asking." In 1962 Sontag published the first of many pieces in *Partisan Review* and in 1963 another in the inaugural issue of the *New York Review of Books*. These publications, plus her brief stint as an editor of *Commentary* in 1959, placed her close to the center of New York intellectual life. In the 1950s and early 1960s *Partisan Review* was an immensely influential magazine whose modest circulation was matched by an immodest cachet. It played a central role in the world of the New York intellectuals, the group of people Norman Podhoretz called family, Jewish writers who had started out in the 1930s. The *Partisan Review* crowd, hostile to both Popular Front realism and to what they saw as the poor taste of the American middle class, embraced the adversarial position of an avant-garde heralded by intellectuals who in sharply written essays served as the nation's cultural critics. Over time, notoriety and success brought them to embrace the United States. The very title of *Partisan Review*'s 1952 symposium, "Our Country and Our Culture," by repeating the word "our," signaled this turn.[37]

Though she had access initially through her marriage to Rieff and then through her own essays and commanding presence, Sontag was clearly an interloper in the world of New York intellectuals. Important female writers, Diana Trilling, Gertrude Himmelfarb, and Midge Decter among them, were married to key male figures. They were what David Laskin called the members of the "last generation of women before feminism." Fiercely intellectual, they "gloried in their domestic control." In crucial ways, they were negative role models for Sontag. Although combative and brilliant like her, to Sontag they had made too many compromises in their careers and personal lives. In 1958 Sontag was a divorced woman, beautiful and flirtatious, and a closeted sexual outlaw, conditions that marked her as different from and perhaps threatening to the other women in the group. As she wrote in a journal, among her "Dangerous vices" was that "I flirt, or seem to be friendlier, with men, than I mean to be. As if I were unaware that my 'friendliness,' might be interpreted as a come-on."[38]

In temperament and outlook, Sontag and the New York intellectuals were on opposite sides of a chasm. To be sure, as was theirs, her métier was the critical essay, though she tried her hand at fiction writing. Yet her sense of what it meant to be a literary and cultural critic and to be in the avant-garde differed dramatically from that of most New York intellectuals. Her heroes were both European modernists and Continental postmodernists such as Roland Barthes, along with experimental New York artists such as Jonas Mekas. If *Partisan Review*'s authors were sophisticated, cultivated modernists, then some of Sontag's favored artists created art that was more erotic and edgy. If New York intellectuals focused on interpretation, intellect, and depth, Sontag stood against interpretation and for feelings and for surface features. As the historian Liam Kennedy has noted, the New York intellectuals were "not a little inhospitable to the emergence of a prodigal daughter," with her relationship to them "a complexly volatile one of affiliation and repudiation."[39]

Writing in 1967, Podhoretz explained Sontag's emergence in nasty, gendered, and generational terms. He noted that her talent explained her rise "but the *rapidity* with which it was accomplished must be attributed to the coincidental availability of a vacant position" of the "Dark Lady of American Letters," previously occupied by Mary McCarthy, who had been elevated "to the more dignified status of *Grande Dame*." Her successor, he continued, "would have to be, like her, clever, learned, good-looking, capable of writing family-type criticism as well as fiction with a strong trace of naughtiness. But," he continued, "the ante on naughtiness having gone up by the 1960's, . . . hints of perversion and orgies" had to be present.[40]

Against Interpretation (1966)

Sontag's essay on camp appeared first in *Partisan Review* in 1964 and then in *Against Interpretation*, a 1966 collection of essays originally published from 1961 to 1965. If the combination of a swirling scene of sexualities and insurgent art forms was the cultural background that shaped her early writing, she also drew on rich sources for what she called in a November 24, 1965, diary entry her "intellectual formation." Here she offered the following list: Modern Library books, her professors at the University of Chicago and Harvard, the world of *Partisan Review*, Jewish refugees from Nazi Germany, modernist German writers and postmodernist French ones, contemporaries from the New York art scene such as Jasper Johns and John Cage—the final result of which was, she remarked, herself as a "Franco-Jewish Cageian." Thus the essays in *Against Interpretation*, though they testify to her continued engagement with modernist classics she had been reading at least since her adolescence, also underscore the decisive shift she had made to French and Continental culture and multiple art forms in ways that moved beyond where her attention was on the eve of her move to Paris in late 1957. In this book Sontag introduced American readers to Antonin Artaud, Georges Bataille, Roland Barthes, Walter Benjamin, Robert Bresson, André Breton, Jean-Luc Godard, Eugene Ionèsco, Cesare Pavese, Alain Resnais, Nathalie Sarraute, Jean Paul Sartre, Claude Lévi-Strauss, and George Lukács.[41]

In her essays in *Against Interpretation*, including the one on camp, without naming names Sontag was distancing herself from the New York intellectuals whose writings since the late 1930s had dominated not only the pages of *Partisan Review* but also the fields of literary analysis and cultural criticism. She had come to believe that writers such as Lionel Trilling, Clement Greenberg, and Dwight Macdonald had placed Culture, especially the canon of modernist literature, in an unassailable position as they admired the works it contained for their seriousness, aesthetic purity, and political detachment. They focused almost exclusively on literary texts, were too committed to the notion that the avant-garde was at a dead end, and were too enamored of a sense of the value of Culture. New York intellectuals had either rejected or failed to acknowledge new forms of cultural expression, many of them visual and aural rather than written: the experimental works of Cage, Rauschenberg, Godard, Mekas, Edward Albee, and Kaprow. Sontag saw the experimental arts as innovative, playful, passionate, and potentially liberating. For her, what was emerging was a "new sensibility . . . defiantly pluralistic; it is dedicated both to an excruciating seriousness and to fun and wit and nostalgia." Or as Phillip Lopate noted in 2009 of Sontag in the early 1960s: "If she was a true revolutionary anywhere, then, it was in the area of sexuality. From the start she was looking for a radical politics that would merge justice with sexiness and sensuality."[42]

The essays in *Against Interpretation* reveal how bold and capacious was Sontag's engagement with new perspectives and cultural forms. As she wrote in the opening essay, carrying the same title as the book, in American culture there was "the hypertrophy of the intellect at the expense of energy and sensual capability," making interpretation "the revenge of the intellect upon art." "In place of a hermeneutics we need an erotics of art," she wrote in what was perhaps the most famous statement in the book. Her elevation of form over content enabled her to emphasize how experiencing the arts engaged a full range of the senses and feelings, in sensuous, erotic, and even violent ways. As she would write in a 1982 essay on Barthes, "The aesthete sustains standards that make it possible to be pleased with the largest number of things; annexing new, unconventional, even illicit sources of pleasure." Thus in her 1961 essay on Norman O. Brown's *Life Against Death* she joined Brown in going far beyond either Freud or Philip Rieff's recovery of Freud. She noted that Brown critiqued Freud's emphasis on the division between lower (sexuality) and higher (artistic). With apparent approbation, she noted that Brown saw humans "unalterably, in the unconscious, in revolt against sexual differentiation, and genital organization. The core of human neurosis," she reported Brown as saying, "is man's incapacity to live in the body—to live (that is, to be sexual) and to die."[43]

With surrealism serving as a model in so many ways, Sontag worked to break down the binaries modernist critics in the United States had relied upon: moral and immoral, high culture and low, producer and audience, art and technology. In her 1962 article on happenings, she talked of surrealism as "a mode of sensibility which cuts across all the arts in the 20th century," all "united by the idea of destroying conventional meanings, and creating new meanings or counter-meanings through radical juxtaposition." Sontag used language that captured her larger project, complete with its challenge to unnamed literary modernists. The French playwright and author Artaud, she wrote, "envisages nothing less than a complete repudiation of the modern Western theater, with its cult of masterpieces, its primary emphasis on the written text (the word), its tame emotional range."[44]

As she turned to the contemporary scene, she cast a skeptical eye on the value of censorious moral judgments. In a review of Jack Smith's experimental movie *Flaming Creatures* (1963), with its portrayal of sexualities including transvestism, hermaphrodism, and homosexuality, Sontag wrote of the film's "depiction of nakedness and various sexual embraces (with the notable omission of straight screwing)." She went on to assert that the movie embodied "pop art's gaiety, its ingenuousness, its exhilarating freedom from moralism." Her focus on science fiction, experimental movies, happenings, and camp enabled her to redefine the avant-garde, away from novels and poems judged on the basis on whether they were worthy of inclusion in a canon that would preserve high art, as Matthew Arnold had established. In contrast, Sontag criticized Arnold, broadened cultural texts to include the visual and the mundane, and looked at the present instead of trying to preserve the past. She was seeing the avant-garde not as part of a great tradition of high culture that stood in a transcendent relationship to popular culture but as a vital, living set of expressions that were closely linked to contemporary media. She welcomed the work of artists who incorporated "new materials and methods drawn from the world of 'non-art,'" such as technology and commercial culture.[45]

Sontag's consideration of popular culture is emblematic of her larger vision. Opposed to rigid binaries, she explored how creative artists wove together the high and the popular. In doing so, she later noted, she remembered that "early modernists like Rimbaud, Stravinsky, Apollinaire, Joyce, and Eliot had showed how 'high culture' could assimilate shards of 'low culture.'" To be sure, she was not embracing materialism and mainstream popular culture. "Ours in a culture based on excess, on overproduction," she wrote in 1964, when such statements were common among social and cultural critics. "The result is a steady loss of sharpness in our sensory experience." Moreover, she shared with New York intellectuals an elitist stance toward the popular and commercial. As she said in a 1965 piece in *Mademoiselle*, "The most interesting and creative art of our time is *not* open to the generally educated; it demands special effort; it speaks a specialized language."[46]

What made her essays important was her emphasis on the sensual pleasure one could derive from ordinary, commercial objects, despite her aversion to conventional commercialism. As she wrote in a 1965 diary entry, style was "the manner in which things appear to us as designed for *pleasure*." Underscoring her antipathy to binaries, in happenings she saw the elimination of "the distance between spectators and performers," though she also acknowledged how much the director controlled the audience. She believed that pop art and other forms of visual expression demonstrated how shallow were distinctions between high and low or mass and popular. In her 1965 "One Culture and the New Sensibility," without naming names other than that of Arnold, she made clear that "virtually all literary intellectuals" in Britain and the United States, "blinded by their personal investment in the perpetuation of the older notion of culture," ignored the new avant-garde, found especially in nonliterary texts. Consequently, they focused on both interpreting content and making moral judgments. Rather than seeing literature involved in the "propounding of moral, social, and political ideas," those with her aesthetic stance were committed to "the new sensibility," to understand "art as the extension of life." For Sontag, "a great work of art is never simply (or even mainly) a vehicle of ideas or of moral sentiments. It is, first of all, an object modifying our consciousness and sensibility." This was why "sensations," "pleasure," and sensuousness were so critical when engaging with the arts. Although she acknowledged ways in which contemporary arts were anti-hedonist, drawing on Norman O. Brown and Herbert Marcuse, she insisted that "the purpose of art is always, ultimately, to give pleasure." The ways younger artists felt about popular arts, she wrote, citing an appreciation of "the singing style of Dionne Warwick," "the personalities and music of the Beatles," and the "brio and elegance" of the 1960 gangster movie *The Rise and Fall of Legs Diamond*, did not reveal an abandonment of standards but the embrace of more pluralistic sensibility, one "dedicated both to an excruciating seriousness and to fun and wit and nostalgia."[47]

"Notes on 'Camp'" (1964)

More than anything else in *Against Interpretation*, it was Sontag's essay on camp, published when she was thirty-one, that launched her career, placed her in the prestigious company she had dreamed of joining since her adolescence, and made it possible for her to devote herself more fully to reading and writing. This essay appeared in the fall 1964 issue of *Partisan Review*, along with writing by such widely respected authors as Robert Lowell, Muriel Spark, Daniel Bell, William Phillips, and Philip Rahv. In other words, Sontag had arrived, and at a very young age. Her essay on camp offered one of the most influential commentaries on the period's culture, brilliantly capturing vantage points that in retrospect seem so salient. Long before she wrote it, she had been aware of camp, especially its usage in homosexual circles. Thus in the summer of 1949, between her semester at Berkeley and her departure for Chicago, in an entry she titled "gay slang," she wrote in her journal "to camp" and then on the next line "campy." This entry came right after she discussed a "gay marriage" officiated by a gay priest and then went on to discuss anal sex engaged in by male homosexuals.[48]

With her 1964 essay on camp, Sontag was taking significant risk by opening up the possibility that critics would dismiss her and what she wrote as somehow contaminated by a new sensibility. She wrote that camp, along with high culture (which was "basically moralistic") and the avant-garde (which "gains power by a tension between moral and aesthetic passion"), was one of three "creative sensibilities" available in contemporary culture. Sontag saw camp as a "sensibility (as distinct from an idea)," whose essential quality was "its love of the unnatural: of artifice and exaggeration." Camp was, she noted, "esoteric—something of a private code, a badge of identity even, among small urban cliques." Her own attitude to what she described was explicitly ambivalent, given that though she was "strongly drawn" to it, she was "almost as strongly offended by it." Indeed, what may have bothered her about camp was that, like pop art and the writings of Marshall McLuhan, whom she at the time considered an "apolitical" critic, it participated in an aesthetics of indifference. Sontag understood that camp was possible "only in affluent societies, in societies or circles capable of experiencing the psychopathology of affluence," among people trying to avoid boredom. Her experimental style of writing was appropriate to what she described, composed as her essay was of fragments, a series

Figure 13. Along with Tiffany lamps, *Flash Gordon* comics, and feather boas, in "Notes on 'Camp'" (1964) Susan Sontag listed the 1933 movie *King Kong* as one of the artifacts that challenged widely accepted views of high culture. In contrast, Sontag appreciated the exaggeration and sexual suggestiveness of ordinary images, what she called the "good taste of bad taste."

of lists and points, "the form of jottings, rather than an essay (with its claim to a linear, consecutive argument)" necessary to explore "this particular fugitive sensibility."[49]

Pointing to lamps by Tiffany, drawings by Aubrey Beardsley, operas by Vincenzo Bellini and Richard Strauss, the ballet *Swan Lake*, popular music, comic books, feather boas, and tabloid newspapers, she characterized camp as relying on artifice, textured surface, theatricality, naiveté, vulgarity, and extravagance. "Emphasizing texture, sensuous surface, and style at the expense of content," she paid particular attention to representations of the body, such as those in Pre-Raphaelite paintings or art nouveau design. Style had utmost importance; the content of items of campy culture mattered hardly at all. Moreover, camp was "disengaged, depoliticized—or at least apolitical." She asserted the people cheated themselves if they respected only "the style of high culture." With the "failed seriousness" of camp came the pursuit of pleasure, enjoyment, and appreciation rather than judgment. "Camp is a solvent of morality," Sontag remarked. "It neutralizes moral indignation, sponsors playfulness."[50]

Camp, with its rejection of "the good-bad axis of ordinary aesthetic judgment," also involved a collapse of the distinctions among high, low, and popular culture. Connoisseurs of camp, she argued, found satisfaction "in the coarsest, commonest pleasures, in the arts of the masses." Sontag pointed out that the usual yardsticks for high culture—seriousness, dignity, and moral uplift—did not apply to some canonical works (such as those of Franz Kafka or Hieronymous Bosch) whose goal was "not that of creating harmonies but of overstraining the medium and introducing more and more violent, and unresolvable, subject-matter." She knew that modernist critics would consider what she admired to be kitsch, but she also underscored that some of what was campy merited serious appreciation. Because "the sensibility of high culture has no monopoly upon refinement," she noted, camp represents the "good taste of bad taste."[51]

Camp, both snobbish and democratic, was a consumer culture of the elite and of marginalized residents of cosmopolitan cities. It both relied on and appropriated commercial culture. It was not, however, the same as the mass culture found on television and in suburbs and shopping centers. As Liam Kennedy has argued, Sontag's take on camp was "an aesthetic lens through which to view mass culture, and a highly discriminating lens at that." Although her analysis of camp reconfigured the debate between high and mass culture, it nonetheless enabled her to sustain a critical and potentially elitist perspective, one for which camp provided both fascination and concern. Indeed, writing in *Partisan Review* in 1967, Sontag made clear her hostility to mass culture. In the context of an impassioned stand against America's role in Vietnam, she remarked that "the quality of American life is an insult to the possibilities of human growth; and the pollution of American space, with gadgetry and cars and TV and box architecture, brutalizes the senses, making grey neurotics of most of us, and perverse spiritual athletes and strident self-transcenders of the best of us."[52]

Sontag understood that sexuality, especially homosexuality, was central. She dedicated the essay to Oscar Wilde, noting that camp represented "how to be a dandy in the age of mass culture." She underscored that campy taste depended on the truth that "the most refined form of sexual attractiveness (as well as the most refined form of sexual pleasure) consists in going against the grain of one's sex," what we would call resistance to rigid gender binaries. "What is most beautiful in virile men," she noted, "is something feminine; what is most beautiful in feminine women is something masculine." Above all, she emphasized that though camp was not the same as homosexual taste (by which she seemed to mean that of male homosexuals), there was a "peculiar affinity and overlap" between the two, with homosexuals in the "vanguard" of camp. Although in preparing to write the essay she jotted down that "some Negroes have very camp taste (sex, clothes)," in the published version, as in much of her writing, race was excised. In the end she focused principally on gay men, noting that homosexuals were "an improvised self-elected class, . . . who constitute themselves as aristocrats of taste."[53]

The combination of "parody and self-parody" Sontag used to describe camp drew on what she had learned from Barthes's analysis of the performative qualities in wrestling, to say nothing of his (as well as hers and camp's) emphasis on artifice, surface, theatricality. Indeed when Sontag wrote of Barthes, including her 1980 eulogy for him, she used phrases to describe his outlook that also illuminated something of her own practice and her own take on camp: the emphasis on the pleasurable and ludic, including the embrace of "new, unconventional, even illicit sources of pleasure"; a "euphoric sense of how meaning proliferates"; the antagonism to "moralistic antitheses"; a world in which "there are neither depths nor heights; . . . only various kinds of surface, of spectacle"; intellectual work that is "genuinely subversive, liberating—playful"; and an "ideal of detachment [that] . . . allows for avowals of passionate, obsessed involvement." Writing of Barthes in 1982, Sontag said that the French critic "assimilates intellectual practice itself to the erotic," something she had worked to achieve in her own life. Echoing what she wrote in her diary in the late 1950s and early 1960s as she wrestled with what it means to be an author, she now spoke of Barthes as engaged in exploring "the self as vocation, life as a reading of the self."[54]

Celebrity and Sexuality:
A New Kind of New York Intellectual

Sontag's essay on camp and the publication of *Against Interpretation* two years later, on her thirty-third birthday, transformed her into a celebrity. Although "Notes on 'Camp'" was published in a literary magazine whose readers, however influential, numbered only in the thousands, Sontag's expectations were high. Just before the essay's appearance, she told a writer better known than she, "I've just written a piece that is going to *put me over*." Shortly thereafter, ever on the lookout to recognize and cast a skeptical eye on the latest cultural fashion, *Time* hailed Sontag as "one of Manhattan's brightest young intellectuals." The author of the *Time* essay focused, much more than had Sontag, on the relationship between camp and sexuality, noting that homosexuals had a self-interest that led them to "neutralize moral indignation." In March 1965, writing in the *New York Times*, Thomas Meehan hailed Sontag as "the Sir Isaac Newton of Camp," as "the person who discovered and defined the already existing phenomenon." The result, he noted, was that "immediately both the intellectual and not so intellectual world was suddenly abuzz" about what she had named. In January 1966 a reviewer in *Life* called her "the most serious young writer we have in America today." With characteristic language, he talked of her as "the Natalie Wood of the U.S. avant-garde—because she is an uncommonly good-looking girl" whose audience was located principally between Greenwich Village and Columbia University.[55]

Over time the rush of publicity and exposure was problematic for Sontag. To be sure, in some ways she brought this on herself. Early on, perhaps for financial reasons, she had published a serious essay in *Mademoiselle*, which appeared above an advertisement for "the Jiffy Jump Suit." Although self-fashioning mattered to her, emerging as a celebrity-commodity was distasteful. She may have feared that overidentification of her with the outré would jeopardize her reputation with an admiring audience, including the men among New York intellectuals she both courted and needed. She grew tired of being best known as the author of an article on camp, in part because by 1966 she wanted to speak out against the war in Vietnam and not for camp. Above all, she wanted to be taken seriously as someone challenging arbiters of cultural taste rather than being pigeonholed because of a singular sexual identity.[56]

Yet as a harbinger of the cultural divide that would come to characterize the 1960s, it was precisely Sontag's rethinking of cultural hierarchy, the supremacy of style over content, the relationship between art and mass culture in an age of mechanical reproduction, and the sexual dimensions of culture that both made her essay important and her critics enraged. Certainly some of what doubtlessly concerned her in the response to her essay had to do with protecting her privacy, including her sexuality. Elisabeth Stevens, writing in the *New Republic* about "Miss Camp Herself," saw Sontag engaged in "effete, but only seemingly harmless literary adventures," someone who "burns for 'style' and 'sensibility' while consigning content" and morality "to the fire." Stevens found especially offensive Sontag's championing of the "unnatural" in matters sexual, which she saw "at the root of her distaste for evaluations of meaning or morality in art and life and her concomitant over-emphasis on mannered styles and delicate, seductive forms." In a letter to *Partisan Review*, the cultural critic John Simon excoriated Sontag for what he saw as her overly sympathetic embrace of the connection between homosexuality and campy style. He pointed to one dictionary definition of "camp" as a noun meaning "effeminate, esp. homosexual mannerisms of speech and gestures" and an adjective connoting "homosexual, Lesbian." As camp spread, he warned, "the heterosexual Smiths will be induced, through the mediation of the androgynous 'fashion world,' to keep up with the homosexual Joneses." In response, pointing to Simon's reference to dictionary definitions and underscoring her decision to stand for a larger sexual vision, Sontag accused him of dragging in "the red herring of homosexuality." She went on to say that "the connection" he drew "between homosexuality and Camp taste . . . is part of the phenomenon, not an argument against it." In 1966 Herbert Gans recognized some of what Sontag had accomplished. He illustrated what he called "consumer-oriented high-culture" by pointing to Susan Sontag's article on camp, which he defined as a "new subfaction—and fashion—in avant-garde high culture, and especially among its sizeable and influential homosexual public."[57]

These comments remind us that understanding gay and lesbian life in New York is critical to placing Sontag and her work in context. Making the connection between camp and homosexuality visible without being an advocate, she was offering an expansive alternative to the constraints that heterosexuality and the ruling intellectual conventions imposed. In the late 1950s and early 1960s, the city had a small but vibrant gay and lesbian culture. As the historian John D'Emilio has made clear about the queer scene in New York and elsewhere, in the early 1960s—precisely when Sontag was emerging and wrote "Notes on 'Camp'"—gay and lesbian activists were increasingly militant well before Stonewall. Camp played a special role in this world and many critics have seen Sontag's perspective as compromised. An art historian remarked that in 1966 Vivian Gornick said Sontag was bringing camp out of the closet but had adopted a "biting and judgmental tone toward Camp—and toward homosexuality." This was because Sontag saw this aesthetic as self-hatred, saw camp as degraded homosexual taste that was based on feminized bad taste and threatened the standards of high culture. More recently, Moe Meyer remarked that Sontag's essay, "with its homosexual connotations downplayed, sanitized, and made safe for public consumption," had erased "homosexuality from the subject of Camp" and "encouraged the public's embrace" of the style. What Sontag missed, writes Cynthia Merrill, was "the possibility that Camp might be a discursive mode which enables homosexuals to adapt to the condition of heterosexual homophobia."[58]

Conclusions

Understanding both the origins of "Notes on 'Camp'" and Sontag's distancing herself from it underscores the importance of the connection between her sexuality and her ideology. In journal entries she wrote, especially during the semester at Berkeley and then again in the late 1950s and early 1960s after she settled in Manhattan, Sontag connected sexuality, sensuousness, and erotic pleasure. These were values she celebrated in *Against Interpretation*, including the essay on camp, with one exception, lesbian sexuality. From an early age Sontag worked at self-presentation, increasingly coming to use a potent combination of braininess, beauty, and sexuality to promote herself, although she consistently ducked questions as to whether she had done this strategically and self-consciously. Her formula was successful with both male intellectuals and a broader public. At least publicly, neither group hinted that that what underlay her perspective was her sexuality. Many members of the queer community in New York, after Stonewall but especially toward the end of the twentieth century, expressed concern about Sontag hiding in the closet. However, she continued to do so to her wider public.[59]

Tellingly, Sontag took considerable efforts to separate herself from her reputation as the author of the essay on camp. This was part of her larger regret about having participated, unwittingly, in the challenge to high culture and the promotion of popular culture. "To laud work condescended to as 'popular' culture," she wrote when she looked back at *Against Interpretation* decades later, was not the same as conspiring "in the repudiation of high culture and its complexities." Even earlier she attempted to distance herself from her essay. In

1966 she talked of how unhappy she was with the strong identification others made between her and the essay. "I did, as I said in the 'Notes,'" she insisted, "have mixed feelings about Camp. Now I'm 100 per cent revolted." It is not too much of an exaggeration to argue that Sontag's distancing herself from her article on camp involved an attempt to keep from an admiring public both her own sexuality and her critique of male homosexual life, and to avoid being pigeonholed.[60]

In the end what was important about the essay and about Sontag from the late 1940s into the 1960s was the link she made between sexuality and the pleasure derived from material goods even as she stood in opposition to most conventional forms of mass culture. Gans and Wolfe in their discussions of social class had paved one avenue that led to fuller, albeit equivocal embrace of popular culture. Sontag, in focusing on the connection between sexuality and commercial goods, had, more unwittingly, made way for another avenue to acceptance, if not celebration, of consumer culture.

Chapter 10

Learning from Consumer Culture

If there were two sites that most horrified critics of mass culture in the 1950s, they were Las Vegas and Los Angeles, the symbols for many observers of gaudiness, poor taste, and moral compromise in the postwar world. In 1972 a leading design theorist labeled the Nevada city "the most brutal, degrading, and corrupt [city] that consumer society has ever created." Similarly, in 1968 a distinguished British journalist called Los Angeles "the nosiest, the smelliest, the most uncomfortable, and most uncivilized major city in the United States." In *The Kandy-Kolored Tangerine-Flake Streamline Baby* (1965), Tom Wolfe went against the grain of the usual reactions when he offered a different response. The world of custom cars in Los Angeles fascinated him, as did the hot-rodders in the California desert. Created by young men of lower-class origins, custom cars seemed filled with vitality and artistic creativity. He also appreciated Las Vegas, which he called "the Versailles of America," a planned city created by mobsters who were "the first uneducated, prole-petty-burgher Americans to have enough money to build a monument to their style of life." He recognized that in the postwar period Las Vegas pioneered in the development of a new aesthetic, with its "forms and symbols," found most prominently in gigantic neon signs that would mark the American landscape for generations to come. "They are the new landmarks of America, the new guideposts, the new way Americans get their bearings." Yet, he added, no one knew anything about the new worlds created in what was emerging as the gambling capital of the United States. In 1968 Wolfe returned to Los Angeles and, in an article titled "I Drove Around Los Angeles and Its Crazy! The Art World Is Upside Down," remarked that "commercial artists in America are now at least 10 years ahead of serious artists in almost every field, including architecture." Then in 1991 Robert Venturi remarked that "for people of culture and taste, Los Angeles didn't exist before Reyner Banham."[1]

In the early 1970s two landmark books appeared that, inspired by and redolent of what Wolfe had suggested, appreciated Las Vegas and Los Angeles in fresh ways: Reyner Banham's *Los Angeles: The Architecture of the Four Ecologies* (1971) and Denise Scott Brown and Robert Venturi's *Learning from Las Vegas* (1972). The work of the members of London's Independent Group influenced both books. Banham was one of the IG's most influential participants. Scott Brown learned from their discussions when she was in England in the early 1950s. Both books had long lives and immense influence: Banham's was one of the most richly suggestive books written on Los Angeles and a book that by its capacious inclusiveness and emphasis on ecologies represented a major break-through in architectural history. With its challenge to an increasingly static international style, the book on Las Vegas quickly and justifiably achieved cult status, especially among students of architecture and cultural geography. Chal-lenging the conventions academics used in writing about architecture, these books helped break open the notion of what urban landscapes involved by shift-ing the focus from cities on the Eastern seaboard to those in the West. What Mike Davis said of Banham's book can be applied to *Learning from Las Vegas* as well: that it "became a turning point in the valuation of the city by the inter-national intelligentsia." If Venturi and Scott Brown mixed irony and fascina-tion in their approach to commercial culture, Banham offered an unrestrained embrace. All three authors explored the symbolic meanings new cultural forms in western cities conveyed, saw creativity coming from common commercial objects, challenged the division between high and low, and implicitly deployed an anthropological approach. Together their books helped reimagine how to think about urban landscapes in holistic ways.[2]

Reyner Banham and the Reimagining of Los Angeles

When Reyner Banham reviewed Wolfe's *Kandy-Kolored* in 1965, he was re-sponding to criticisms of Wolfe's book by what he called "high-minded" Brit-ish and American observers. In contrast, although Banham found some of the book's essays the equivalent of "toilet paper," he asserted that the essays on Las Vegas and custom cars were "full of affirmation and belief." Wolfe, he com-mented, was "not an off-shore moralist, and he consciously rejects the role of New England pundit to which his Yale doctorate presumably entitles him." In-stead, he was, Banham wrote as a visitor from Britain, "the Kandy Kolored Kulture's most *inside* Kikerone." He heaped praise especially on the chapter on customizing, calling it "a model essay in the anthropology of affluence" that effectively argued "that *every* cultural minority should defend itself as aggres-sively as Mrs Leavis." The creation of distinctive autos, Banham held, was more creative than what "any pop painter has done with comic strips or even James Joyce did with commercial prose in parts of *Finnegan's Wake*."[3]

Lifelong experiences prepared Banham to fall in love with American popular culture and with Los Angeles. Born in 1922 in Norwich, England, into a family that had more cultural capital than economic resources, in 1939 Banham entered Bristol Technical College as a scholarship boy, where he focused on mechanical engineering, a training that would fundamentally shape his later writings. During World War II he worked as an engine fitter at an airplane factory, a job which a medical condition forced him to leave. He married Mary Mullett in 1946, with whom he had two children. In 1949 he began studying twentieth-century architecture at the Courtauld Institute of Art, from which he earned his B.A. in 1952. In the same year, he started to participate in discussions of the IG, began working as an editor at *Architectural Review,* and commenced on his doctorate under Nikolaus Pevsner, which he finished in 1958 and published two years later as *Theory and Design in the First Machine Age.* Banham shifted from editorial to academic work in 1964 when he accepted a teaching position at Bartlett School of Architecture at University College London. In 1976 he moved to the United States to join the faculty at the State University of New York at Buffalo, from there going to the University of California at Santa Cruz in 1980. He accepted a position at New York University in 1987, though his death in 1988 prevented him from filling it. Throughout his career he wrote prolifically, producing over a dozen books and more than seven hundred articles on a wide range of subjects, but especially architecture, urbanism, and popular culture.[4]

Banham first came to the United States in 1961 and to Los Angeles later in the decade. However, his encounters with American commercial culture began in his youth when he read pulp magazines and watched Hollywood movies. As he wrote in 1964, as a youngster he did not engage in "a working-class culture à la Hoggart." Rather, he immersed himself in "American pulps, . . . *Mechanix Illustrated,* and the comic books . . . and the penny pictures on Saturday mornings," especially those starring Charlie Chaplin and Buster Keaton. His engagement with American popular culture continued with the discussions at the IG in which he connected what he learned at the Courtauld about iconography to what he gleaned about popular culture across the Atlantic from imported objects and publications. These discussions provided much of the seed bed from which his treatment of Los Angeles would later grow. Members of the IG, including Banham, emphasized the symbolic power of commercial culture, saw high and low culture aligned along a continuum rather than in a hierarchy, developed a fascination for an economy built on obsolescence, and explored the relationship between technology and culture. As Banham had written in 1955, the American automobile was "a thick ripe stream of loaded symbols" that designers used to convey meaning, including "power, brutalism, luxury, snob-appeal, exoticism, and plain common-or-garden sex." Style, he remarked, was a "means of saying something of breathless, but unverbalizable, consequence to the live culture of the Technological Century." His fascination with technology and contemporary American popular culture underwrote a larger vision, in which he criticized twentieth-century modernism's commitment to "the monumental, timeless," the eternal, abstract, pure, and clean. Rather, Banham preferred the superficial, expendable, "the deliberate exposure of technical means," the "glitter, technical bravura, sophistication and lack of reticence," objects like an American Buick "with high immediate signal strength." From his discussions at meetings of the Independent Group, he would bring into his book on Los Angeles what one observer called his "naive techno-optimism."[5]

Banham came to write his book on Los Angeles after a sustained engagement with issues of the relationship of technology, architecture, popular culture, and aesthetics, elements, sans popular culture, he had explored in *Theory and Design in the First Machine Age* and in *The Architecture of the Well-Tempered Environment* (1969). Several themes marked his books and essays. He admired futurist architecture for its boldness and energy. He celebrated what he saw as honest and forceful design, such as Tennessee Valley Authority dams, California mission architecture, and sleek commercial products. He looked favorably on technology's transformative power, at times coming close to embracing technological utopianism. Appreciative of architectural modernism, he wanted to rescue it from practitioners and critics who conceived of its canon narrowly, in terms, he remarked in a 1959 essay on New York's Lever House, of a purist, "respectable" commitment to "a discipline of pure reason." Emphasizing the work of engineers, contractors, artists, and urban planners, he criticized "the architect's claim to be the absolute master of the visual environment." These commitments came together in his writings on "the New Brutalism," an architectural style Denise Scott Brown said was named partly as a joke. Fellow IG members Alison Smithson and Peter Smithson first developed it in the early 1950s, represented by their Hunstanton School, completed in 1954. Banham saw the New Brutalism emerging in reaction to several contemporary styles: the picturesque buildings designed by those who followed in the tradition of William Morris, principally Communist architects who worked for the London County Council; examples of classicism; and the severe creations of the international style. The New Brutalism lacked polished detail and offered no claims to transcendent beauty. It used materials as they were found but not transformed and exposed electrical and plumbing materials, in contrast to the crisper work of Mies van der Rohe or Louis Kahn. Banham listed "Memorability as an image; . . . Clear Exhibition of Structure" with materials "'as found'; . . . and valuation of Materialism" as the main characteristics of the style. Above all what struck Banham about the New Brutalism was precisely its raw brutality—its "bloody-mindedness."[6]

When Banham wrote his book on Los Angeles, he had very much on his mind the skepticism British and American critics held regarding the city. Many critics paid attention to Los Angeles, Reyner Banham noted, but it was "like the attention that Sodom and Gomorrah have received, primarily a reflection of other peoples' bad consciences." In his 1971 book Banham undertook to challenge these responses to Los Angeles, common among intellectuals on the East Coast and in Western Europe. His previous experiences, especially his focus on technology and his work with the Independent Group, prepared him to see Los Angeles as an example of a technologically based utopia.[7]

Before the publication of his 1971 book, Banham reported extensively on Los Angeles in a series of 1968 talks aired on the BBC and later published in the *Listener*. When he first arrived in the city, he was "terrified." Looking out of a bus while riding along the freeways, he found the city "totally incomprehensible." Within twenty-four hours, however, feeling "perfectly at home" in the city, he was no longer suffering from "culture-shock and topographical dismay." Two things put him at ease: he realized that Los Angeles was familiar to him from movies he had watched since his childhood and that Los Angeles, like London, was a series of discrete villages brought together in "illogical and haphazard" ways. Yet despite such similarities, Los Angeles remained "disturbingly different," especially since it offered "radical alternatives" to virtually every commonly accepted notion of what a city should be. Even more than in his subsequent book, he dismissed the problem of smog. Angelenos objected to it, he wrote, because they were unable to stand "anything less than perfection." In addition, he speculated that smog had as much to do with the water used in gardening as with the excessive use of cars. He also wondered whether the negative reaction to it resulted from the bad consciences of those who, having escaped "the Protestant ethic and hard winters of the Bible-punching Middle West," felt they hardly deserved "to have so much fun zooming around in cars in the pleasant sunshine." Indeed, he celebrated the freeways as wonderful feats of engineering that provided him with exciting experiences of spatial transformation. Banham's Los Angeles was a place where people pursued fun-filled pleasures that turned Angelenos into "*the* privileged class of popular culture today," which he saw evident in the custom car culture Wolfe had celebrated and in the

Figure 14. This undated aerial view of a Los Angeles freeway interchange
evokes the combination of technology, vernacular architecture, and
sculpture that Reyner Banham highlighted in *Los Angeles* (1971). Freeway
design exemplified how seemingly prosaic objects embodied cultural
creativity and pleasure. Courtesy of the Security Pacific National Bank
Collection, Los Angeles Public Library.

world of ocean surfers. For Banham, the cult of doing your own thing perfectly
expressed the worldview of those who lived in Los Angeles. "The promise of
this affluent, permissive and free-swinging culture," he insisted as he pointed
to Simon Rodia's Watts Tower, "is that every man, in his own lifetime and to his
own complete satisfaction, shall do exactly what he wants to do."[8]

Yet despite the largely positive impression Banham gained from his 1968
trip, he found some cause for concern. He decried the "exercise in Victorian
rapacity" that led Anglos to wrest control of the land from Latinos, actions

that he asserted were the root of "this jungle of divisiveness" that he witnessed all around him. Though he found attractive the region's "free-swinging libertarian ethic," he criticized the absence of a public sense that extended beyond the range of specific communities. He saw this evidenced in the propensity of citizens of wealthy communities like Beverly Hills and San Marino to wall themselves off from less privileged members of society. Yet he also found the African American community of Watts an example of how groups fragmented themselves into a series of "social monocultures."[9]

Los Angeles: The Architecture of the Four Ecologies (1971)

Banham approached Los Angeles, where he often visited but never lived, as a cultural critic and an architectural historian, but one with a distinctive approach to the city. Against architectural revivals, he favored the modern, the vernacular, and the technological. He focused not on great, permanent buildings as if they were free-standing monuments but on the multiple contexts in which architecture existed and could be understood. In addition to discussing a range of buildings and the design of the transportation system, Banham focused on the four ecologies in the subtitle of Los Angeles: "Surfurbia," the coastal towns from Malibu to Balboa where surfers developed new art forms and a distinctive culture; the Foothills, where wealthy people lived on twisting roads and in houses whose placement often defied nature; "The Plains of Id," the flat land in the valleys inhabited by the poor, the middle class, and businesses that serviced the vast metropolitan area; and "Autopia," the vast network of freeways, built according to networks laid out by previous transportation systems and over which people now traveled distances unimaginable to most Americans and perhaps to Banham himself. Indeed in 1964 he had bragged that he provided an example of "The Atavism of the Short-Distance Mini-Cyclist" as he rode around London on his bicycle. Banham wrote Los Angeles with optimism, naiveté, and an excited sense of discovery, but apparently without a sense of irony. Driving home his point by placing on the book's cover a 1968 painting by the West Coast pop artist David Hockney of a swimming pool and a modern home, palm trees in the distance, with more gusto than precision Banham traced the lineage of the "dream of a good life outside the squalors" of European cities back to the country houses of America's founding fathers and even further to Palladian villas in Italy.[10]

For twenty years, Banham had waited for this moment, finally finding in Los Angeles a subject that allowed him to soar with the excitement he first sensed in the discussions of the IG. Here after all was a quintessentially nonhierarchical, heterogeneous site, filled with possibilities for fulfillment, all its components of seemingly equal value and laden with symbolic richness. As befitting its subject, *Los Angeles* was a nonlinear book, flowing in ways that gave the reader a series of continuous experiences, not unlike what tourists experienced as they traveled from site to site.

Banham scattered examples of architectural monuments throughout the book, ones that more traditional architectural historians would have scoffed at but that he found compelling. The freeway stack, where two or more highways came together, their interchanges creating a complicated mid-air sculpture, was for Banham "a work of art, both as a pattern on the map, as a monument against the sky, and as a kinetic experience as one sweeps through it." He also appreciated the richly decorative commercial signs and buildings that un- ashamedly hawked their products. The Jack in the Box sign that loomed over the ordinarily shaped restaurant paralleled the "assemblage of functional and symbolic elements" of the "fantastic hamburger" spread across a plate with its components presented separately. More tellingly, the 1925 Aztec Hotel in Mon- rovia or the 1965 Tahitian Village restaurant in Bellflower, both with elaborate signage barely hiding a relatively plain building, suggested to Banham a pro- found realization about American life. They represented what happened "when traditional cultural and social restraints have been overthrown and replaced by the preferences of a mobile, affluent, consumer-oriented society, in which 'cul- tural values' and ancient symbols are handled primarily as methods of claim- ing or establishing status."[11]

For Banham, Los Angeles opened a world where commercial culture, not at all morally problematic, provided a system of symbols that conveyed key val- ues, with "freedom of movement" as the city's "prime symbolic attribute." Hav- ing learned to drive an automobile so he could study Los Angeles, as he set out on his voyage he remarked that "the city will never be fully understood by those who cannot move fluently through its diffuse urban texture, cannot go with the flow of its unprecedented life." If critics offered LA as a place where "visual pollution" reigned, Banham instead asserted that the commercialization in the region was what made it distinctive. Calling up a series of images that leveled the cultural playing field, Banham remarked that to eliminate advertising signs from Los Angeles "would be like depriving San Gimignano of its towers or the City of London of its Wren steeples." Again and again, he interpreted what oth- ers might see as materialistic in nonmaterial terms, as when he talked of beach culture as involving an egalitarian "symbolic rejection of the values of the con- sumer society, a place where a man needs to own only what he stands up in— usually a pair of frayed shorts and sun-glasses." Not unlike the decorated cars that Wolfe wrote about, surfboards provided one example of the transcendent qualities of material objects. "Leaning on the sea-wall or stuck in the sand like plastic megaliths," he noted appreciatively, "they concentrate practically the whole capacity of Los Angeles to create stylishly decorative imagery, and to fix those images with all the panoply of modern visual and material techniques."[12]

For Banham, Hollywood provided the source of dreams in Los Angeles, the fantasy factory that produced "the most extravagant myths of private gratification and self-realization, institutionalized now in the doctrine of 'doing your own thing.'" Expressions of this were everywhere, in the decorative elements that cloaked otherwise ordinary houses, factories, or office buildings; in the back lots of studios; in the amusement parks that drew inspiration from movies. Watts Tower was his favorite fantasy realized concretely, a piece of folk art Simon Rodia had fashioned from the industrial and commercial debris others had discarded. Working alone and with simple tools, Rodia assembled a series of towers (with the highest reaching ninety-nine feet) from bent steel rebar, wire mesh, concrete, sea shells, discarded soda cans, shards of pottery, pieces of baling wire. Like the surfer's board and the hot-rodder's customized car, Watts Towers was for Banham the result of "an ingenious and technically proficient cult of private and harmless gratifications" that characterized California. He admired Rodia's "uninhibited ingenuity in exploiting the by-products of an affluent technology," his ability to do his own thing, and then his willingness to walk away from it when finished. Banham appreciated all these examples of the creativity of Southern Californians because, in combining commerce and art, they provided public artifacts that dealt "in symbolic meanings the populace at large can read."[13]

With his book, Banham offered an interpretation of Los Angeles (and, by extension, of much that was new in American culture) that, by avoiding the usual tropes of moral condemnation, richly suggested how to think about commercial culture in symbolic and nonhierarchical terms. Yet what he wrote was not unproblematic. For him, any criticism of Los Angeles too easily became the product of "timid souls who cannot bear to go with the flow of Angeleno life." His love affair with American automobiles, which intensified when he saw a Chevrolet in London in 1952, led him to an unquestioning embrace of Autopia. The freeway became for him the place where drivers "spend the two calmest and most rewarding hours of their daily lives," a remark more convincing in 1971 than decades later. Similarly, he asserted that "the extreme concentration required" of freeway drivers seemed "to bring on a state of heightened awareness that some locals find mystical."[14]

Some reviewers took note of how Banham imaginatively challenged widely accepted views of Los Angeles. Yet others called attention to the book's limitations. Tom Hines, an architectural historian recently arrived at UCLA, underscored Banham's avoidance of pollution and traffic jams, which, if he had to experience them as a resident (not just as an occasional visitor), would have eroded his optimism. John Donat insisted that Banham glossed "too lightly over the social consequences of mandatory mobility, of pollution, poverty, race, and politics." The artist and art critic Peter Plagens found that the book, filled with "garish pop deliriums," overlooked the region's serious social problems.[15]

As a participant in the IG discussions in the mid-1950s, Banham had grown fascinated by the tension between his celebration of American popular culture and his left-wing politics. Yet it was one thing to laud American automobiles and advertisements with the Allied victory fresh in memory and rationing still in effect in postwar Britain. It was something else to sing the praises of a pleasure-seeking Los Angeles in 1971, with the war in Vietnam ongoing and Earth Day fresh in the memory of many. Nothing more tellingly reveals the limitations of Banham's vision than his inattention to the Watts riot, which occurred in 1965. In his 1968 articles he wrote more extensively about race, smog, and rapacious Anglo land grabbers than he did in his book three years later. Banham included "Burn, Baby, burn!" as a "Slogan of the Watts rioters" among many epigraphs he placed at the beginning of the book. Elsewhere in the book he offered vague hints of trouble in paradise, referring to Watts as the site of "only sporadic flares of violence." This illuminates how his enthusiasm for America and for Los Angeles (and his desire to write a book with dramatic exaggeration) prevented him from talking about the more problematic aspects of life in Los Angeles. Indeed, a reading of Banham's book on LA begins to suggest the limitations of symbolic analyses of commercial culture that avoided issues of ecological degradation, economic power, and racial justice. Paradoxically and problematically, Banham's celebration of Los Angeles freeways and automobiles appeared exactly when the environmental movement was calling into question the ecological damage car culture inflicted on the United States. His emphasis on the utopian possibilities of new technologies was both transformative and problematic.[16]

Las Vegas as a Site of Commercial Symbolism

In *Learning from Las Vegas: The Forgotten Symbolism of Architectural Form*, Denise Scott Brown and Robert Venturi did for the gambling capital what Banham had done for the City of Angeles: offer an analysis of the symbolic power of an emerging built environment by focusing on the relationship between commercial culture and buildings. Members of the IG had explored the connection between popular culture and architecture, and in 1952 the Smithsons proposed a housing project that incorporated images of Marilyn Monroe and Joe DiMaggio. Seven years later, Lawrence Alloway pointed to "attempts . . . now being made to bring within architectural reach much of the pop art that has thrived without being architecture in the qualitative sense of the work." And then in 1962 Banham called for the elimination of "the *cordon sanitaire* between architecture and Pop-Art." Soon after the publication of *Learning from Las Vegas*, Banham, sympathetic to what its authors had written (unlike the book's critics, who saw "Las Vegas as the total surrender of all social and moral standards to the false glamour of naked commercial competition"), observed that Scott Brown and Venturi offered the "image of the Strip as a working exemplar of a more flexible and less absolutist style of urbanism" than European theorists imagined. Indeed, Banham had anticipated the work of Scott Brown and Venturi in a 1967 essay that hailed Wolfe's celebration of the way the Nevada city heralded a culture "based on free-form self-fulfilment."[17]

In their lives and work, beginning in 1960 Scott Brown and Venturi collaborated, but they came to common projects from distinctive experiences and perspectives. As architects they designed sites that playfully combined commercial and historic imagery. As critics and writers, they offered richly suggestive and immensely influential works that played a major role in the reaction against the severity and seriousness of modernist architecture. In *Learning from Las Vegas*, arguably the most important work of architectural criticism written in the last half of the twentieth century, they presented a provocative and transformative exploration of the relationships between buildings, their sites, and the ways commercial culture communicates symbolic meanings. Before and after that book's publication, they wrote extensively about how to understand the interaction between cities, architecture, social conditions, and popular culture in complex and nuanced ways. If Banham's work in the IG resulted in an unabashed embrace of commercial culture, then what Scott Brown took from the IG and more generally what she and Venturi derived from numerous sources was a combination of fascination, irony, and social conscience in their approach. Indeed some of their writings more fully incorporated an engagement with commercial culture than did the buildings they designed.

Scott Brown's preparation for her work on Las Vegas began with her childhood in Africa. Born into a Jewish family in 'Nkana, a copper town in Northern Rhodesia (now Zambia), where her father was a merchant, Denise Lakofski grew up in a Johannesburg suburb in one of South Africa's first modernist houses, with a father who earned a handsome living, some of which he gained by distributing Hollywood movies, and a mother who had longed to be an architect. As a child she developed a passion for architecture, which she thought of as work appropriate for a woman. When she was about ten, an art teacher suggested that she keep her eyes open to the world around her, which prompted her to pay attention to popular culture and vernacular architecture. Coming of age where she did, Scott Brown much later commented, she learned about "multi-culturalism, about signs, . . . about artistic impurity."[18]

Growing up in South Africa in an elite, cosmopolitan, émigré-filled world also made her aware, she later asserted, of what it meant to live in a multiracial but racist society that had a complex relationship to the cultural power of England, not unlike that of Las Vegas to New York or Philadelphia. After attending the University of Witwatersrand, where she studied architecture and in 1951 helped develop the exhibition Man-Made Johannesburg, in 1952 she left for Europe, where she worked in a London architectural office and continued her education at the Architectural Association, from which she graduated in 1955. Her teachers in London opened her eyes to the social functions of architecture and to an appreciation of the unseen beauty of vernacular buildings, advertising, and technology. From 1955 to 1958 she and fellow South African Robert Scott Brown, whom she had married in 1955 and to whom the Las Vegas book was dedicated, worked in architectural offices in Europe and South Africa and traveled around Europe taking pictures of mannerist architecture, ordinary street signs, and storefronts, like the ones IG member Richard Hamilton was shooting at the same time. Seeing American pop art in Venice in 1958 intensified her interest in American popular culture.[19]

More than Venturi, Scott Brown advocated an appreciation of American popular culture, although she shared with him an interest in ordinary landscapes. She drew inspiration from her involvement with the work of the IG during her years in London, commenting later that the interest of members of the IG "in pop imagery, urban communications and advertising, their recognition of the design implications of car culture" became vitally important to her. Although their closed meetings were unknown to her, she participated in the discussions swirling around the group. While in architecture school in London, with some friends she developed an interest in commercial architecture, popular culture, street life, and vernacular landscapes.[20]

Among those connected with IG, she was especially familiar with the work of the architects Alison Smithson and Peter Smithson, whom she first met in 1953. What was important to Scott Brown was that they insisted on the relationship between architecture and social conditions, preferred the early modernists to the later and more austere ones, and embraced the ugly and ordinary in contemporary buildings. In 1956 they had written that the "technical virtuosity" of advertisements was "almost magical." The Smithsons "decried the gap," Denise Scott Brown noted, "between the sentimentalism of British architecture's domesticated Modernism and the facts ('brutal' and ordinary) of urban experience." Scott Brown learned a number of lessons from the Smithsons, including what it meant for a married couple to work together as professional architects. She appreciated their commitment to "looking intensely at what was immediately around them—popular culture, the industrial and commercial vernacular, and neighborhood street life." They emphasized "active socio-plastics," the process of learning from the street life of working-class Londoners living in the East End and then developing an architecture in which, as she later remarked, beauty emerged from what many considered ugly objects, prompting the "designing and building . . . for community life as it is and not for some sentimentalized version of how it should be."[21]

Denise Scott Brown came to the United States in 1958 with her husband Robert Scott Brown to study with Louis Kahn at the University of Pennsylvania's Graduate School of Fine Arts, but upon arrival they learned that Kahn taught in the architecture program and they were enrolled in the city planning one. In 1959 her husband was killed in an auto accident while Denise sat next to him as a passenger. This was a transformative event, for she lost someone she deeply loved and over time was liberated from the conventions of 1950s womanhood. In her first semester at Penn she studied with Herbert Gans just as he was completing his work on Boston's West End and was moving to Levittown as a participant-observer. She earned her master's degree in city planning in 1960 and her master's of architecture five years later and taught at Penn from 1960 to 1965, including in courses she and Venturi collaborated on. During her years at Penn, when Philadelphia was undergoing major urban renewal, the university's planning program brought together city planners and social scientists who engaged in momentous discussions over urban redevelopment, poverty, race, and class.[22]

In 1965, with her degree in architecture now in hand, she left Philadelphia to teach a term at Berkeley and then went to UCLA for two years. In 1965, for the first time, she saw Las Vegas, a site her parents had visited and appreciated in the 1930s, and shortly thereafter she invited Venturi to visit the desert gambling capital with her. "The Pop artists and Herb Gans," she said of herself and Venturi, "led us to Las Vegas," though she also acknowledged the influence of others, including Charles Seeger, Sigfried Giedion, J. B. Jackson, and Vincent Scully. Scott Brown and Venturi fell in love on their November 1966 trip to Las Vegas. She later reported that as they drove around Las Vegas, "both loving and

hating what we saw, we were jolted clear out of our aesthetic skins," a response
she had prefigured in a 1965 essay when she discussed the disorienting nature
of "urban agnosia," the inability to recognize shapes or objects. As Venturi later
remarked (and as Marshall McLuhan would have said in 1951 in a different context), Las Vegas "horrified *and* fascinated" them. In 1967 Scott Brown and Venturi married, and she joined the architectural firm he had earlier established
with others.[23]

Robert Venturi was born in Philadelphia into an Italian American family. His father was a wholesale produce merchant who had developed a passion for architecture as a child. His mother was a Norman Thomas socialist, a
Quaker, and a self-educated woman. Venturi earned his B.A. and M.F.A. from
Princeton in 1947 and 1950 respectively. An early childhood interest in material
culture and historic buildings intensified at Princeton where the architectural
historian Donald Drew Egbert and the Beaux Arts–trained architect Jean La-
batut influenced him. He wrote his master's thesis, a gentle critique of international style for its quest for purity, on the relationship of architecture to its
environment. Against the notion of seeing a building in isolation, he asserted
that "its setting gives a building expression; its content is what gives a building
its meaning."[24]

Like Scott Brown, Venturi appreciated the richness and decorative qualities
of premodern architecture, something he learned especially during his two-
year fellowship at the American Academy in Rome in 1954–56. Also like Scott
Brown, in the 1950s Venturi was influenced by the work of Louis Kahn and by
the ferment in urban planning in Philadelphia and at the University of Pennsylvania. He worked in a series of architectural firms (including those of Eero
Saarinen and Louis Kahn) from 1950 to 1958 and with others started his own
firm in 1958. He taught at Penn from 1957 until 1965; while at the same time,
for about twenty years after his father's death in 1953, he ran the family produce business located just south of the city's center. As an architect, already by
the early 1960s Venturi was experimenting with the incorporation into architecture of large-scale graphics and iconography that drew on commercial and
industrial design.[25]

In 1962 Venturi wrote *Complexity and Contradiction in Architecture* (1966),
which emerged out of a course that he and Scott Brown taught. This book was a
pathbreaking critique of the sterility of much of modern architecture. Here he
developed his critique of moralism and his celebration of both the popular and
the symbolic that would emerge full-blown a decade later. Venturi drew heavily
on contemporary literary critics, including T. S. Eliot, William Empson, Kenneth Burke, and Cleanth Brooks, in order to support his own insistence on

the importance of ambiguity and tension in artistic productions. Calling on architects to stop being "intimidated by the puritanically moral language of orthodox Modern" design, he celebrated the hybrid, impure, distorted, perverse, compromising, redundant, inconsistent, and sensuous over the pure, the clean, and the simple; in sum, the "messy vitality over obvious unity." He explored the contradictions and complexities of both/and, inside/outside, and top/bottom. He contrasted such modernist monuments as the Seagram Building in Manhattan with European buildings in the early modernist, mannerist, baroque, or rococo style, as well as with American examples ranging from the vernacular to those by Frank Furness and Louis Sullivan.[26]

The vernacular and popular held a special fascination for him. He denounced architects and planners who promoted "elaborate methods for abolishing or disguising honky-tonk elements in the existing landscape." He cited Times Square as among his preferred American landscapes with its "vitality" coming from "the jarring inconsistencies of buildings and billboards . . . contained within the consistent order of the space itself." At the end of the book Venturi explored the tensions between elite and popular arts, between Roman palaces and Main Street stores. Venturi drove home his points with his typical wit, ambiguity, playfulness, complexity, and contradiction, what Vincent Scully in the introduction to the book called Venturi's "own ironic disclaimers." Were not Main Street and Route 66's commercial strip "almost all right?" Venturi asked and then continued on to wonder "what slight twists of context will make them all right?" The "seemingly chaotic juxtapositions of honky-tonk elements" his book offered "express an intriguing kind of vitality and validity." He hoped that "Pop Art, involving contradictions of scale and context," might awaken "architects from prim dreams of pure order" so visible in the compromised modern architecture used in urban renewal. In the book's last sentence he wondered whether "from the everyday landscape, vulgar and disdained" it would be possible to "draw the complex and contradictory order that is valid and vital for our architecture as an urbanistic whole."[27]

Scott Brown and Venturi settled in Philadelphia as a married professional couple in 1967. Their only child, Jimmy, was born in 1971 and a year later they moved to an art nouveau house in Mt. Airy, a neighborhood in that city. Their firm, in which over time Scott Brown assumed a more central position, struggled. It did not earn a series of major commissions until the mid-1970s, with the addition to Oberlin College's Allen Memorial Art Museum (1973–77) as a turning point. This was despite some of the firm's early, symbolically playful commissions such as the Vanna Venturi House (1959–64) and Guild House (1961–66), both in Philadelphia, and Fire Station No. 4 (1966–68) in Columbus,

Indiana. Both as critics and as architects they worked so collaboratively that it was usually impossible to separate their contributions. Scott Brown "has been so long intertwined in our joint development," Venturi remarked, "that it is impossible to define where her thought leaves off and mine begins, except to say that the social basis of our architectural argument comes more from her and the historical more from me; we combine around popular culture and Pop Art." Throughout her career, Scott Brown was intensely aware of the sexist reaction to her and her work. Book reviewers, colleagues, and clients continually recognized Venturi's achievements but overlooked hers. This painful situation came to a head in 1991 when he alone won the prestigious Pritzker Prize in architecture.[28]

If their work as architects and writers was central to their lives, also formative were their political and social commitments. Both were on the left, interested in the intersections of architecture and city planning with the politics of class and race in contemporary cities. Nowhere was this clearer than when in the late 1960s and early 1970s Scott Brown played a major role in the fights over urban redevelopment in Philadelphia. Beginning in 1968 Scott Brown worked with the Citizens Committee to Preserve and Develop the Crosstown Community. Asked by what she described as "a primarily black citizens' group," the committee successfully prevented the building of a highway through an area that included the headquarters of the Venturi family business and served as the "center of African American life and commerce." Had it been built, the highway would have destroyed vernacular buildings and separated African American from modest white neighborhoods. Scott Brown's activity, plus Venturi's involvement in his family's business, gave them firsthand experience with the working people in Philadelphia, something that helped shape their book on Las Vegas.[29]

Learning from Las Vegas (1972)

Their 1972 book emerged from a fall 1968 studio project, which Scott Brown had originally conceived, at Yale's School of Art and Architecture. Venturi and Scott Brown both taught there, he from 1966 to 1970, she from 1967 to 1970. The year 1968 saw tumultuous events, among them the Tet offensive, the assassinations of Martin Luther King Jr. and Bobby Kennedy, and LBJ's withdrawal from the presidential race. Yale was hardly an ivory tower when Scott Brown and Venturi were there; the trial of members of the Black Panther Party took place in a New Haven courthouse in 1969–70, a few blocks from the university. At a time when they were associated with two universities caught in the mael-

Figure 15. With Robert Venturi driving and Denise Scott Brown in the passenger seat, we look out the front window at this 1968 scene of the Las Vegas Strip, replete with the neon signs that were dramatically more vivid at night. Four years later, in *Learning from Las Vegas* (1972), Venturi and Scott Brown explored the symbolic richness of vernacular architecture in the Nevada gambling capital, how it challenged the dryness of contemporary modern architecture and offered an example of the creativity of commercial culture. Courtesy VSBA.

stroms of protests against the war in Vietnam and serious challenges to those concerned about race relations and the future of American cities, Scott Brown and Venturi developed a series of studios, including one on Las Vegas and the other on Levittown, in both of which race was notable for its absence. With their studios, they expanded the boundaries of traditional architecture education, with mass media, pop art, and the social sciences among the tools the studio drew on. Beginning in 1968 they reported the results in essays that were the heart of the Las Vegas book. Four years later came the first edition of the book. A second revised and more widely circulated edition appeared in 1977.[30]

Learning from Las Vegas was a landmark, transformative book on architecture, planning, urban landscape, and commercial culture. It appeared at a time when modernist architecture, most typically expressed in metal and glass skyscrapers designed by major practitioners and firms such as I. M. Pei, Edward Durrell Stone, and Skidmore, Owings and Merrill, was coming to dominate the skylines of major American cities. Scott Brown and Venturi appreciated the early modernism of the 1920s and 1930s represented by works of Frank Lloyd Wright, Le Corbusier, and Mies van der Rohe. But they rejected modernism's later, more sterile examples, what they called "the irrelevant and distorted prolongation of that old revolution today" seen in contemporary "striving and bombastic buildings" that were dull and boring. To them, contemporary modernists had sacralized space and form. As a consequence contemporaries rejected the symbolic possibilities that would come from integrating architecture with painting, graphics, and sculpture. If proponents of the international style asserted, as Mies van der Rohe remarked, that "Less Is More," then Venturi countered with "Less Is a Bore."[31]

To illustrate what this meant, Scott Brown and Venturi contrasted two types of vernacular architecture: the duck and the decorated shed. The duck, which they had seen when Peter Blake had featured it in his 1964 *God's Own Junkyard*, was named for a drive-in store on Long Island built in the early 1930s in the shape of the bird after which it was named. In contrast, the decorated shed was a building, usually simple in form but marked by a sign that was physically independent of it. For them the duck, a building that was in itself a symbolic form, found its contemporary expression in modern buildings that architects designed as entities that in themselves conveyed their symbolic meaning. With a decorated shed, such as boxlike casinos in Las Vegas heralded by a dramatic sign, the contrast was between a conventional building and a dramatic symbol that defined its meaning. Modernists rejected the use of commercial symbolism in architecture or design as debased, not even worthy of consideration. To Scott Brown and Venturi, this meant that contemporary modernist architects had turned their backs on a historic tradition in which architects had integrated symbolic decorative elements into their buildings. The distinction between duck and decorated shed underscored Scott Brown and Venturi's commitment to a symbolically rich architecture, not only what their firm designed but also what Las Vegas offered. "Architecture depends in its perception and creation," they wrote, "on past experience and emotional association" even though or precisely because such "symbolic and representational elements may be contradictory to the form, structure, and program with which they combine in the same building." For them the choice was between modernist architecture, which its partisans heralded as "heroic and original" (but they found stale and boring), and "the ugly and ordinary," a phrase Gordon Bunshaft used against their work but that for them had the advantage of suggesting "concrete meanings" and historic associations.[32]

Thus, just as Banham had appreciated the boxlike building of the Jack in the Box with its dramatic signage or the decorative elements added to the

Aztec Hotel or the Tahitian Village restaurant, so Scott Brown and Venturi admired the plain, boxlike hotels of Las Vegas with their elaborate, expressive neon signs. Just as they had admired the decorative elements of premodern European architecture, so now they looked appreciatively at Las Vegas signs as elaborate, expressive communication systems. They rejected the heroic, monumental buildings then in fashion and celebrated instead architecture that resonated with the tastes of ordinary people expressed through popular culture. With its rejection of the severity of much of modern architecture and its preference for decorative elements, including ones that incorporated popular culture, their book was critical in breaking the hold of modernism and heralding postmodern architecture.[33]

Although their focus was on architecture, like others who were recasting discussions of consumer culture in the 1960s and 1970s, Scott Brown and Venturi reconsidered the relationships among folk, commercial, and high culture. They emphasized playfulness and found pleasure in commercial culture. They replaced moral judgments with apparently nonjudgmental perspectives. Less so than Banham but still significantly so, they viewed expressive culture in nonhierarchical terms. They insisted on the validity of juxtaposing what they saw in Las Vegas with canonical buildings and landscapes in ancient Greece and Rome, medieval towns, and the Renaissance, mannerist, and neoclassical landscapes that they had seen during their European travels. They understood that creativity came from below and above. Thus they reported that their students in 1968, "as the spirit of Las Vegas got to them," changed the subtitle of their project from "Learning from Las Vegas: Form Analysis as Design Research" to "The Great Proletarian Cultural Locomotive." Working in urban universities and aware of Tom Wolfe's characterization of Las Vegas as the creation of proletariat mobsters, Scott Brown and Venturi (as well as their students) worked on the project at a time when issues of urbanism, class, race, and sexuality were never far from their consciousness. On the book's cover was a billboard advertising "Tan Hawaiian with Tanya," a nearly nude and heavily oiled women writ large. The sensuous, erotic, and pleasure-filled iconography of Las Vegas never seemed far from the authors' imaginations.[34]

In *Learning from Las Vegas*, Scott Brown and Venturi relied on the work of Herbert Gans in several ways, especially by appreciating the culture of working-class and lower-middle-class whites and by using the example of Levittown to critique the way elitist designers looked down their noses at the aspirations of ordinary people. Scott Brown and Venturi accused architects of allowing "commercial hucksterism" to prevent them from understanding the relationship between form and symbolism in suburban designs. Pointing to the preference of real estate developers for colonial homes and their occupants for rococo decoration, they asserted that to many architects "the symbolic decoration of the split-level suburban sheds represents the debased, materialistic values of a consumer economy." People were so "brainwashed by mass marketing" that they inhabited "ticky-tacky" homes which went against the aesthetics that demanded respect for material and for visual purity. As a result, they insisted, critics threw "out the variety with the vulgarity." In a sharp linking of national politics with architectural design, they argued that elitist architects rejected places like Levittown because they associated them with the white silent majority. In the original, 1972 edition they called such an approach "this Nixon-silent-majority critique." In the revised, 1977 edition their language was stronger. In a new passage they insisted that "one does not have to agree with hard-hat politics to support the rights of the middle-middle class to their own architectural aesthetics."[35]

Despite such statements, Scott Brown and Venturi continually insisted that their attitude was nonjudgmental, something that many readers assumed was true about their attitude to commercial culture. In a 1969 article Scott Brown explored the emergence of an approach that acknowledged what people wanted even though critics found their taste choices problematic. She located the most persuasive expressions of such a view in Le Corbusier's love of grain elevators, Gans's discussion of Levittown, Wolfe's development of a writing style that effectively described Las Vegas, and Ruscha's photos of Los Angeles. When they initially established the aims for the studio at Yale in 1968, Scott Brown and Venturi said that their approach would be "open-minded and nonjudgmental." Later on, using an analogy that placed cultural products on a level playing field, they playfully wrote that "just as an analysis of the structure of the Gothic cathedral need not include a debate on the morality of medieval religion, so Las Vegas's values are not questioned here." Pointing to the way in which Italians joined the fine and the lowly arts, they asserted, again with humor, that "naked children have never played in *our* fountains, and I. M. Pei will never be happy on Route 66." Again and again, they called for an architecture that was playful, ironic, and subversive.[36]

Among the influences they acknowledged as shaping their vision was American pop art. They equated contemporary modernist architects with abstract expressionist painters, considering both of them overly concerned with the monumental and heroic and not sufficiently engaged with the ordinary. They credited pop artists of the early 1960s with prompting some architects, like themselves, to incorporate iconography in their designs. With its three-dimensionality and playful embrace of commercial culture, the art of Ed Ruscha and Claes Oldenburg, pop artists whose work did not make its way into the Guggenheim's 1963 show, influenced their outlook. Their understanding of pop art led them to insist that as architects and architectural critics they did not cravenly worship at the altar of commerce. "If the commercial persuasions that flash on the strip are materialistic manipulation and vapid subcommunication," they insisted, "which cleverly appeal to our deeper drives but send them only superficial messages," it did not follow that architects who drew on such imagery "must reproduce the content or the superficiality of their messages." Thus if Roy Lichtenstein borrowed from popular culture to "convey satire, sorrow, and irony," so too did the architect use symbolism to convey a range of human emotions without endorsing "the necessity to buy soap or the possibility of an orgy."[37]

Above all, what *Learning from Las Vegas* offered was a richly textured analysis of what it meant to think of the emerging commercial landscape in America in ways that emphasized how commercial forms communicated symbolic values. Scott Brown and Venturi celebrated what they called "the symbolism of the ugly and ordinary." In a book laden with maps, photographs, drawings, and diagrams, they taught their readers to understand Las Vegas in visual terms. They fostered an understanding of what it meant to think of a new urban formation created in the midst of the desert. They explored the difference between the Strip and the downtown. They lavished attention on the dramatic signs that created the skyline of Las Vegas, playfully analyzing the relationship between them and their surroundings. They pointed to the complicated roadways, the carefully delineated parking lots, and the relatively plain sheds/casinos for which the signs were the decoration. They dwelled on the relationship of different kinds of spaces: public and private, indoor and outdoor, gambling and residential, wet and dry. In the process, they celebrated the symbolic power of the newly emerging landscape. There is, they wrote, "no reason why the methods of commercial persuasion and the skyline of signs analyzed here should not serve the purpose of civic and cultural enhancement." They hailed what they saw in Las Vegas as "an architecture of communication over space" and part of an effort to use architecture for "commercial persuasion." Just as Venturi had written about complexity and contradiction, so too did the Las Vegas book reveal how in combination the buildings and the signs "embrace continuity *and* discontinuity, going *and* stopping, clarity *and* ambiguity, cooperation *and* competition, the community *and* rugged individualism." Highway signs, they wrote, "make verbal and symbolic connections through space, communicating a complexity of meanings through hundreds of associations." Yet if Banham had emphasized the way the symbolism of Los Angeles communicated the core value of mobility, Scott Brown and Venturi were vague as to exactly what the symbolism of Las Vegas conveyed. Moreover, compared to Banham they distanced themselves from an unalloyed embrace of what they studied. "This is a study of method, not content," they had remarked at the outset.[38]

The most important response of critics to the book paralleled what skeptics had said of the writing of members of the IG, the sociology of Gans, and the work of pop artists: that Scott Brown and Venturi too uncritically accepted a consumer culture that capitalism greedily produced and that purchasers mindlessly bought. Ada Louise Huxtable, arguably the nation's most respected architectural critic, offered a mild and in many ways appreciative version of this response. She found their book "original, brilliant" yet admitted that she had "nagging doubts" as to whether the "products of the fast-buck operators have such social and aesthetic validity." Making "schlock the standard-setter," she insisted, "is a dangerous game." In an article published in 1976, Scott Brown summarized the arguments others made against what they had written. First, she wrote, the critics of the work on Las Vegas alleged that she and Venturi heaped praise on Las Vegas, a key component of the consumer society that was, in the words of one critic, "'rammed down'" people's "'throats by the unscrupulous power structure,'" and that *Learning from Las Vegas* arrogantly praised. Second, architects who praised "'this capitalist environment'" had to be "'Nixonites'" who "'were probably in favor of America's intervention in Vietnam.'" In contrast, their opponents asserted, "'We other architects must fight for what we believe in and against the social ills of our society. Social progress is often achieved as an imposition, against the popular will.'" The argument that with *Learning from Las Vegas* Scott Brown and Venturi had cravenly celebrated the degraded gambling capital with all its poor taste and rampant commercialism reflected major currents in American intellectual and political life. Among them were the reconsideration of popular culture and the class and ethnic dynamics set in motion by events of the late 1960s. Scott Brown and Venturi, like Gans before them, aligned themselves with the white working and lower-middle classes rather than, as limousine liberals did, with African Americans.[39]

Scott Brown took the lead in responding to critics. In a 1969 article she wrote, "The best thing an architect or urban designer can offer a new society, apart from a good heart, is his own skill, used *for* the society, to develop a respectful understanding of its cultural artifacts and a loving strategy for their development to suit the felt needs and way of life of its people." In 1976 she published a more extensive defense, one that reiterated her concerns with the social responsibility of architects and social planners who grappled with the relationship between formal aesthetics and urban design, especially as they confronted the challenges of urban decay and renewal. Here she relied on the works of Gans, Wolfe, and pop artists. From pop artists she drew out the notion that it was possible to work with popular culture playfully and ironically without endorsing the capitalist system that produced the commercialism in the first place. From Wolfe she borrowed the concept of radical chic, explaining how upper-middle-class architects enjoyed the fruits of their success yet used the language of revolution to describe, inaccurately she thought, the social impact of their work. From Gans she derived a sympathy for the pleasures and aspirations of ordinary Americans and an understanding of the relationship between social class and taste communities. From both Wolfe and Gans she drew out an appreciation of the white silent majority on whom many academic liberals and modernist architects heaped such disdain. The criticism of *Learning from Las Vegas*, she concluded, was not really about consumer culture, capitalism, or suburbia but about "class prejudice against white, lower middle class Americans, on the part of American architects who wouldn't dream of expressing anti-Black feelings and consider themselves liberal."[40]

The controversy over *Learning from Las Vegas* highlights a number of issues. One is the role of judgment in response to consumer and popular culture. It was one thing for Banham to fall in love with Los Angeles and quite another for Scott Brown and Venturi to take a more nuanced and pedagogical stance by learning from Las Vegas. Yet many readers often missed the irony, skepticism, ambivalence, and ambiguity with which Scott Brown and Venturi threaded their book. This caused some to assume that the authors naively embraced capitalist-driven commercialism. In their publications, however, a careful reader did not have to read between the lines to uncover their mixed feelings. In 1971 Scott Brown pointed to the "agony in our acceptance of pop." "Mannerist we are," she continued, "we are part of a high art, not a folk or popular art, tradition." In correspondence, Scott Brown and Venturi made their positions even clearer. They acknowledged the importance of making judgments but not ones that were too restrictive. They told correspondents that they embraced skeptical attitudes and that it was important to understand what lay behind what some saw as their expressionless responses.[41]

Scott Brown and Venturi chose Las Vegas as the subject of their work not because they loved it but because few other sites offered such rich resources for understanding the relationships between architecture, planning, and consumer culture. Moreover, in the most exaggerated and powerful way, the Strip highlighted the ways in which commercialism was transforming the American landscape and architecture. They also selected it for the Yale studio because they felt the way to engage students was to focus on something fascinating to which they would instinctively stand in opposition. Nonetheless, choosing to focus on signs, symbolism, and Las Vegas was not without its problems. After all, as a Las Vegas architect wrote in 1970, "while the nation still quakes from riots and crime, Las Vegas remains the friendliest, most hospitable city in our country, where children can play safely and where adults are secure when out and about after dark." Indeed, given Scott Brown's consciousness of growing up in a multiracial but racist South Africa and living, when working on the Las Vegas book, near or in two urban universities struggling with the problems of race in troubled cities, one can still wonder how the choice of Las Vegas as a subject and the focus on symbolism rather than social structure and power shaped the book in fundamental ways. What Scott Brown said of the Smithsons could be applied to what she and Venturi wrote in *Learning from Las Vegas*. "Seen from the United States," she remarked in early 1968, "their notions of urbanism appear peripheral to the main issues here of urban unrest, the re- lation of planning especially in ghetto areas to social needs and democratic processes."[42]

Yet the left-liberal and social justice bona fides of Scott Brown and Venturi were undeniable. Perhaps Scott Brown put it best in 1995 when she remarked, "A heritage of Socialism and Quakerism in Bob's family and my African social and racial concerns, tied in with movements for social justice in America of the 1960s, have caused us to try in our practice to join social concern with design and to remain committed as architects to achieving social justice." Moreover, she could have pointed out their sustained political commitments, especially to a socially concerned architecture and city planning that had its origins in her experiences in Johannesburg, in the "active socio-plastics" she learned from the Smithsons, in her education in the classroom at Penn (especially from Gans), and in their engagement with social and political issues in Philadelphia starting in the late 1950s. In 1971 Scott Brown, drawing on Gans and on her experience protesting the building of a Philadelphia highway that would displace and di- vide African Americans and whites, responded forcefully. "One can be totally committed to civil rights, social progress, and the needs of the poor without having to hate the lower middle classes who face injustice too. But," she contin- ued pointedly, "the concept of a hard-hat majority to be scorned will legitimize and expose a lot of now repressed upper-middle-class prejudice."[43]

Yet in the end what is striking is how Scott Brown and Venturi's book on Las Vegas invoked and recapitulated the responses of contemporaries. Scott Brown called herself "a wandering Jew" and together with Venturi she explored the roles of technology and commerce in the late twentieth-century equiva- lent of Walter Benjamin's nineteenth-century Parisian arcades. Though by no means steeped in semiotics, nonetheless like Umberto Eco and Roland Barthes they explored the meaning of commercial symbolism. Like Jürgen Habermas, they lamented the decline of the public sphere over time and with the rise of new cities; as Scott Brown remarked, Las Vegas illustrated the way "the public sector is dwarfed by the private sector." Like David Riesman and Marshall McLuhan, they responded with reluctant fascination. Moreover, the work of Wolfe, Gans, and the IG inspired them. As it had for others, the embrace of the working class, sensuousness, and cultural inclusiveness fundamentally shaped their view of consumer culture. They well understood, if they did not always fully embrace, the pleasures of consumer culture and its power to communicate symbolic meaning.[44]

And this is where Scott Brown and Venturi differed from Banham. His response to consumer culture seemed unbridled, even naive; theirs, more complicated and ironic. To be sure, they shared a good deal in common, including debt to the Independent Group and a capacious, integrated understanding of the changing American landscape. All three writers played a major role in the shift from seeing consumer culture as dangerous to understanding it as a source of pleasure and symbolic communication. Yet Banham's book on Los Angeles represents an important end point in the evolution of attitudes to consumer culture.

Conclusion

The World of Pleasure and Symbolic Exchange

With the books by Denise Scott Brown, Robert Venturi, and Reyner Banham, we reach a key turning point in how American and European intellectuals developed imaginative ways of understanding consumer culture. Before then, on the Continent, Roland Barthes, Umberto Eco, and to a lesser extent Jürgen Habermas had provided pathbreaking analyses of commercial culture. However, their influence, as well as that of C. L. R. James, was delayed by issues of translation. In North America, David Riesman and Marshall McLuhan reluctantly moved to new, more suggestive formulations. In Britain, members of the Independent Group, Richard Hoggart, Paddy Whannel, and Stuart Hall had broken fresh ground in understanding the popular arts. In the United States, Tom Wolfe and Herbert Gans shifted attention to the working and lower middle classes, thereby helping to undermine the elitism that put high culture on a pedestal and kept low, commercially infused culture at bay. By linking the pleasures of diverse sexual expression and materialism, Susan Sontag helped break the hold of puritanical attitudes to goods and experiences. In their books on the allure of cities in the American west, Reyner Banham, Denise Scott Brown, and Robert Venturi played crucial roles in the story of emergence of new views of consumer culture that emphasized pleasure and symbolic communication.

Challenging cultural hierarchies, all of these writers helped undermine the distinction between high culture and low. They increasingly saw consumer culture as less dangerous and more pleasurable. They emphasized the ways in which commercial culture made it possible for individuals and societies to communicate symbolic meanings. Over time the power of literary analysis waned as that of the social sciences grew. Reciprocity between producers and consumers, and even resistance by consumers, replaced a belief in the top-down power of producers. Cultural critics had come to appreciate if not embrace the richness of popular culture, albeit almost always with hesitation or qualification.

By the early 1970s, these writers had made a number of contributions that in the hands of others would continue, in even more thoroughgoing ways, to shift the nature of the debates. What cultural observers had accomplished by the early 1970s became even more fully delineated, and in some cases transformed, in the ensuing years. To be sure, some writers continued in and updated the warnings about how morally problematic consumer culture was, and they did so in powerful, influential ways. A wide range of observers asserted that we were living in a society where everything was commodified—religion, politics, and family life included. Yet a new vision, built on the writings of those discussed in this book, had also developed, although it hardly dominated intellectual life. In place of memories of Stalinism, anti-Stalinism, the Popular Front, Nazism, and literary modernism, the experiences with the social movements of the 1960s and early 1970s emerged as formative influences.[1]

The most notable changes in the decades after the early 1970s came from the work of cultural theorists and feminists, as well as those whose focus expanded beyond American and Western Europe to the world at large. If literary theory dominated discussions in the late 1950s, semiotics, sociology, and anthropology pervaded forty years later.[2] Some feminists in the 1960s argued that capitalism turned women into passive objects of an oppressive consumer culture, but others soon transformed women into active agents who derived pleasure from what they consumed.[3] Finally, social scientists eventually envisioned a global world of consumer goods and experiences, one in which the developed nations no longer necessarily stood at the center.[4]

The results of these new perspectives were momentous, at times going beyond what scholars had written by 1972. Debates over the relationships between high, middle, low, and folk cultures virtually disappeared. Writers cast a skeptical eye on moral condemnation in ways that emphasized pleasure, which in turn relied on and shaped new attitudes toward class, sexuality, and gender. Viewing consumer culture as a means of individual and social communication increasingly involved a belief that the meanings derived from commercial goods and experiences were fractured, multiple, constantly shifting. In its most radical formulation this view involved the separation of meaning from objects, thus enabling the development of a view of fragmented identities playfully exploring multiple meanings through commercial culture. Writers emphasized agency, meaning, and culture, as well as the relationships between identity and social structure. The new vision focused less on a mass, undifferentiated middle class and more on subordinate groups such as youth, racial minorities, homosexuals, and women. Contemporaries challenged the binary of producers and consumers and instead emphasized reciprocity and resistance. Indeed, common to the ideology of writers in the last third of the twentieth century was the notion that through consumer culture insurgent individuals and social groups

resisted the forces the powerful arrayed against them. Some saw this as heralding a utopian moment if not a utopian world. A new politics of consumption
emerged, one that moved beyond moral condemnation to advocate the agency
of consumers in the public sphere. Working out the implications of feminism,
cultural theory, and globalism, writers carried the trajectory even further than
had the writers of the early 1970s. Much happened after the early 1970s, but by
then the diverse groups I have discussed in this book had paved the way.[5]

Abbreviations

AE	*Adult Education*
AQ	*American Quarterly*
AHR	*American Historical Review*
AJS	*American Journal of Sociology*
ArN	*Art News*
ASR	*American Sociological Review*
CLRJ-CU	C.L.R. James Papers, Rare Book and Manuscript Library, Butler Library, Columbia University, New York, N.Y.
Co	*Commentary*
DR-HU	David Riesman Papers, Harvard University Archives, Harvard University, Cambridge, Mass.
FAZ	*Frankfurter Allgemeine Zeitung*
Han	*Handelsblatt*
Hi	*Highway*
HJG-CU	Herbert J. Gans Papers, Columbia University Archives, Rare Book and Manuscript Library, Butler Library, Columbia University, New York, N.Y.
IJCS	*International Journal of Cultural Studies*
JAH	*Journal of American History*
JMH	*Journal of Modern History*
LA-GMA	Lawrence Alloway Papers, Guggenheim Museum Archives, New York, N.Y.
LA-GRI	Lawrence Alloway Papers, Getty Research Institute, Los Angeles, Calif.
MF-VT	Marshall Fishwick papers, Special Collections, Newman Library, Virginia Polytechnic Institute and State University, Blacksburg, Va.
MM-AC	Marshall McLuhan Papers, Library and Archives Canada/Bibliotheque et Archives Canada, Ottawa, Canada
NGC	*New German Critique*
NH-Tate	Nigel Henderson Papers, Research Center, Tate Britain, London, United Kingdom
NLR	*New Left Review*
NYRB	*New York Review of Books*
NYT	*New York Times*
NYTBR	*New York Times Book Review*
NYTM	*New York Times Magazine*
PR	*Partisan Review*

PW-NU Paddy Whannel Papers, Northwestern University Archives, Northwestern University, Evanston, Ill.

RH-Hull Richard Hoggart Papers, U-ADU/1/270–2, Records of the Department of Adult Education of the University of Hull, Hull History Center, Worship Street, Hull, United Kingdom

RH-S Richard Hoggart Papers, Special Collections, University of Sheffield Library, Western Bank, Sheffield, United Kingdom

ShR *Shenandoah Review*

SS-UCLA Susan Sontag Collection, Department of Special Collections, Charles E. Young Research Library, UCLA, Los Angeles, Calif.

SwR *Sewanee Review*

TB *Tutors' Bulletin of Adult Education*

Te *The Teacher*

TLS *Times Literary Supplement*

TW-NYPL Tom Wolfe Papers, Farrar, Straus and Giroux Collection, New York Public Library, New York, N.Y.

ULR *Universities and Left Review*

VSB-Penn Papers of Venturi Scott Brown, Architectural Archives, University of Pennsylvania, Philadelphia, Pa.

WAG Whitechapel Art Gallery, London, United Kingdom

WP *Washington Post*

Notes

Preface

1. Andrew Kopkind, *Thirty Years' War: Dispatches and Diversions of a Radical Journalist, 1965–1994* (London: Verso, 1995), xix. Sheridan (1893–1979) had a distinguished career, during which she pioneered in the teaching of film in high school, which I cannot remember her doing in any class in which I was enrolled. For information on her, see Sharon Hamilton-Wieler, "Marion Sheridan: Tapping the Imagination," paper presented at the Annual Meeting of the National Council of Teachers of English, 1990, http://www.eric.ed.gov/PDFS/ED325855.pdf (accessed February 11, 2011).

2. Marion C. Sheridan, "Rescuing Civilization through Motion Pictures," *Journal of Educational Psychology* 11 (November 1937): 174. I also came across Marion C. Sheridan, "The Menace of Communism," *English Journal* 43 (February 1954): 87, in which she talked about a high school essay contest she developed about two years before I emerged as the American Legion Connecticut State Champion Orator by delivering a speech on the virtues of the United States Constitution.

3. (Baltimore: Johns Hopkins University Press, 1985) and (Amherst: University of Massachusetts Press, 2004).

Introduction

1. For a discussion of parallel changes in Japan, see Marilyn Ivy, "Formations of Mass Culture," in *Postwar Japan as History*, ed. Andrew Gordon (Berkeley: University of California Press, 1993), 255. For an extensive discussion of consumer culture in postwar East Asia, see the essays in Sheldon Garon and Patricia Maclachlan, eds., *The Ambivalent Consumer: Questioning Consumption in East Asia and the West* (Ithaca, N.Y.: Cornell University Press, 2006). For the spread of American advertising into Latin America, see James P. Woodard, "Marketing Modernity: The J. Walter Thompson Company and North American Advertising in Brazil, 1929–1939," *Hispanic American Historical Review* 82 (May 2002): 257–90. For the positive impact of popular music in Brazil, see Bryan McCann, *Hello, Hello, Brazil: Popular Music in the Making of Modern Brazil* (Durham, N.C.: Duke University Press, 2004). A less positive view emerges in Antônio Pedro Tota, *The Seduction of Brazil: The Americanization of Brazil during World War II*, trans. Lorena B. Ellis (Austin: University of Texas Press, 2009).

A standout among the many discussions of major changes in the scholarship on consumer culture is Roberta Sassatelli, *Consumer Culture: History, Theory and Politics* (London: Sage Publications, 2007). Another treatment of the sociology of consumption is Robert Bocock, *Consumption* (London: Routledge, 1993). Daniel Miller, ed., *Consumption: Critical Concepts in the Social Sciences*, 4 vols. (London: Routledge, 2001), brings together many of the key texts.

For the increasingly positive views of consumer culture in Western Europe, see Adam Arvidsson, *Marketing Modernity: Italian Advertising from Fascism to Postmodernity* (New York: Routledge, 2003), 133. On the shift in Italy from a focus on domination and condemnation to resistance and an appreciation of the complexities of responses, see John Foot, *Milan since the Miracle: City, Culture, and Identity* (Oxford: Berg, 2001), 20, 23, and 36; David Forgacs, "Cultural Consumption, 1940s to 1960s," in *Italian Cultural Studies: An Introduction*, ed. David Forgacs and Robert Lumley (Oxford: Oxford University Press, 1996), 273–90; Alessandro Portelli, *The Battle of Valle Giulia: Oral History and the Art of Dialogue* (Madison: University of Wisconsin Press, 1997). On parallel changes in Germany, see Kaspar Maase, *Grenzenloses Vergnügen: Der Aufstieg der Massenkultur, 1850–1970* (Frankfurt am Main: Fischer Taschenbuch, 1997), 274–75, quoted in Volker R. Berghahn, *America and the Intellectual Cold Wars in Europe: Shepard Stone between Philanthropy, Academy, and Diplomacy* (Princeton, N.J.: Princeton University Press, 2001), 293. Similarly for France, one scholar has noted a shift in the works on mass culture from a theory of declension to a position where the audience has become communal, democratic, resisting; this involves, he writes, an "insistence on authentic communities rising out of the consumption of mass culture": Gregory Shaya, "The Flâneur, the Badaud, and the Making of a Mass Public in France, circa 1860–1910," *AHR* 109 (February 2004): 44.

2. For a discussion of changing terms, see Michael Denning, "The End of Mass Culture," *International Labor and Working-Class History* 37 (Spring 1990): 4–18; Lawrence Glickman, *Buying Power: A History of Consumer Activism in America* (Chicago: University of Chicago Press, 2009), 202, 264–65, and 294–97; Lawrence Glickman, email to author, January 26, 2011, copy in author's possession. The first use of the term "consumer culture" in the *New York Times* was by Erich Fromm: see Natalie Jaffe, "Psychiatry Urged to Shift Emphasis," *NYT*, April 14, 1966, 30; the first use of the term in a book title is Stuart Ewen, *Captains of Consciousness: Advertising and the Social Roots of the Consumer Culture* (New York: McGraw-Hill, 1976). For some examples of scholarship that emphasize the pleasure of consuming, see Erika D. Rappaport, *Shopping for Pleasure: Women in the Making of London's West End* (Princeton, N.J.: Princeton University Press, 2000); Daniel Miller, *A Theory of Shopping* (Ithaca, N.Y.: Cornell University Press, 1998).

3. Elizabeth Fraterrigo, *"Playboy" and the Making of the Good Life in Modern America* (New York: Oxford University Press, 2009), introduction and chap. 2, explores the emergence of an ethic of pleasure in post-1945 America; John D'Emilio and Estelle B. Freedman, *Intimate Matters: A History of Sexuality in America* (New York: Harper and Row, 1988), 278–79 and 305–6, explore the close connections between sexual liberation and a pleasure-infused consumption.

4. Richard Dyer, "In Defence of Disco," *Gay Left* 8 (Summer 1979): 21; Dennis Altman, *The Homosexualization of America; The Americanization of the Homosexual* (New York: St. Martin's, 1982), 20–21. On the commercialization of gay culture beginning in the 1970s, see Daniel Harris, *The Rise and Fall of Gay Culture* (New York: Hyperion, 1997). For an

even broader discussion of the historical dimensions of these issues, see John D'Emilio, "Capitalism and Gay Identity," in *Powers of Desire: The Politics of Sexuality*, ed. Ann Snitow, Christine Stansell, and Sharon Thompson (New York: Monthly Review Press, 1983), 100–113. Surrealism—visible in the writings of Benjamin, members of the Independent Group, Barthes, and Sontag—was central to the embrace of playfulness and the integration of shards of popular culture into symbolically rich cultural productions.

5. For early suggestions of a more nuanced position, see Richard Hoggart, *The Uses of Literacy: Aspects of Working-Class Life with Special Reference to Publications and Entertainments* (London: Chatto and Windus, 1957).

6. Robert S. Lynd and Helen M. Lynd, *Middletown: A Study in American Culture* (New York: Harcourt, Brace, 1929). On some dimensions of this shift to the cultural, see James W. Cook and Lawrence B. Glickman, "Twelve Propositions for a History of U.S. Cultural History," in *The Cultural Turn in U.S. History: Past, Present, and Future*, ed. James W. Cook, Lawrence B. Glickman, and Michael O'Malley (Chicago: University of Chicago Press, 2008), 3–57; Norman Yetman, "Introduction to 'American Studies: From Culture Concept to Cultural Studies,'" *American Studies* 38 (Summer 1997): 5–6; Barry Shank, "The Continuing Embarrassment of Culture: From the Culture Concept to Cultural Studies," *American Studies* 38 (Summer 1977): 95–116; and *AHR Forum*: "Geoff Eley's *A Crooked Line*," *AHR* 113 (April 2008): 391–437.

7. See the elitist position in Q. D. Leavis, *Fiction and the Reading Public* (London: Chatto and Windus, 1932).

8. Later on, others, such as Dick Hebdige, envisioned subversive avant-gardes emerging from within the realm of popular culture: see Dick Hebdige, *Subculture: The Meaning of Style* (London: Methuen, 1979).

9. Eugene Lunn, "Beyond 'Mass Culture': The Lonely Crowd, the Uses of Literacy, and the Postwar Era," *Theory and Society* 19 (February 1990): 63.

10. Bernard Rosenberg and David Manning White, eds., *Mass Culture: The Popular Arts in America* (Glencoe, Ill.: Free Press, 1957).

11. Paul Gorman, *Left Intellectuals and Popular Culture in Twentieth-Century America* (Chapel Hill: University of North Carolina Press, 1996).

12. I am indebted to Daphne Lamothe, Kevin Rozario, and Ken Warren for helping me find my way to and through the works of Ellison and Bakara. On the cultural criticism of Ellison and Baraka, see John Gennari, *Blowin' Hot and Cool: Jazz and Its Critics* (Chicago: University of Chicago Press, 2006), 155–62 and 264–89. On Ellison, see the following essays in Ralph Ellison, *The Collected Essays of Ralph Ellison*, ed. John F. Callahan (New York: Modern Library, 1995): "Richard Wright's Blues [1945]," 128–44, "The World and the Jug, Part II [1964]," 168–88, "Living with Music [1955]," 227–36, "On Bird, Bird-Watching and Jazz [1962]," 256–65, "Blues People [1964]," 278–87; Robert G. O'Meally, "Introduction: Jazz Shapes," in Ralph Ellison, *Living with Music: Ralph Ellison's Jazz Writings*, ed. Robert G. O'Meally (New York: Modern Library, 2001), ix–xxxv. For Baraka, see LeRoi Jones, *Blues People: Negro Music in White America* (New York: W. Morrow, 1963). In contrast to what Ellison and Baraka wrote, E. Franklin Frazier, *Black Bourgeoisie* (Glencoe, Ill.: Free Press, 1957), analyzed the combination of racial exclusion and class inequality

in ways that led him to a harsh denunciation of commodity consumption that stood in opposition to respectability.

13. See Andreas Huyssen, "Mass Culture as Woman: Modernism's Other," in *Studies in Entertainment: Critical Approaches to Mass Culture*, ed. Tania Modleski (Blooming-ton: Indiana University Press, 1986), 44–58, for an important exploration of the gendering of mass culture debate.

14. Howard Brick, *Transcending Capitalism: Visions of a New Society in Modern American Thought* (Ithaca, N.Y.: Cornell University Press, 2006), 235–36.

15. Shannan W. Clark, "'White Collar Workers Organize': Class Consciousness and the Transformation of the Culture Industries of the United States, 1925–55" (Ph.D. diss., Columbia University, 2006), and the revised version, *The Creative Class: White-Collar Workers and the Making of America's Culture of Consumer Capitalism* (forthcoming, Ox-ford University Press, draft manuscript, copy in author's possession), esp. 204–74; Michael Denning, *The Cultural Front: The Laboring of American Culture in the Twentieth Cen-tury* (London: Verso, 1996), 454. More generally this summary relies on Joyce Appleby, "Consumption in Early Modern Social Thought [1993]," in *Consumer Society in American History: A Reader*, ed. Lawrence Glickman (Ithaca, N.Y.: Cornell University Press, 1999), 130–44; James Livingston, *Pragmatism and the Political Economy of Cultural Revolution, 1850–1940* (Chapel Hill: University of North Carolina Press, 1994); Nancy Bentley, *Frantic Panoramas: American Literature and Mass Culture, 1870–1920* (Philadelphia: University of Pennsylvania Press, 2009); Gilbert Seldes, *The Seven Lively Arts* (New York: Harper, 1924); Anzia Yezierska, *Salome of the Tenements* (New York: Boni and Liveright, 1923).

16. Alexis McCrossen, "Drawing Boundaries between Markets, Nations, and Peoples, 1650–1940," in *Land of Necessity: Consumer Culture in the United States–Mexico Border-lands*, ed. Alexis McCrossen (Durham, N.C.: Duke University Press, 2009), 26. For the emphasis on "the politics of pleasure" among consumer activists well before 1950, see Glickman, *Buying Power*, 272.

17. On Jackson, the best place to begin is John Brinkerhoff Jackson, *Landscape in Sight: Looking at America*, ed. Helen Lefkowitz Horowitz (New Haven, Conn.: Yale Uni-versity Press, 1997).

18. Thomas Bender, *A Nation Among Nations: America's Place in World History* (New York: Hill and Wang, 2006), 7. For general discussions of transnational and/or global history, see Gary Reichard and Ted Dickson, eds., *America on the World Stage: A Global Approach to U.S. History* (Urbana: University of Illinois Press, 2008); Daniel T. Rodgers, *Atlantic Crossings: Social Politics in a Progressive Age* (Cambridge, Mass.: Harvard Uni-versity Press, 1998), 1–7; Ian Tyrrell, "American Exceptionalism in an Age of International History," *AHR* 96 (October 1991): 1031–55; Michael McGerr, "The Price of the 'New Trans-national History,'" *AHR* 96 (October 1991): 1056–67; David Thelen, "Making History and Making the United States," *Journal of American Studies* 32 (December 1998): 373–97. On transnational aspects of the history of consumer culture, start with Victoria de Grazia, *Irresistible Empire: America's Advance through Twentieth-Century Europe* (Cambridge, Mass.: Harvard University Press, 2005); see also Arjun Appadurai, ed., *The Social Life of Things: Commodities in Cultural Perspective* (Cambridge: Cambridge University Press,

1986). On other aspects of the history of consumerism, see Martin Daunton and Matthew Hilton, eds., *The Politics of Consumption: Material Culture and Citizenship and Europe* (Oxford: Oxford University Press, 2001); Matthew Hilton, *Consumerism in Twentieth-Century Britain* (Cambridge: Cambridge University Press, 2002); Lizabeth Cohen, *A Consumers' Republic: The Politics of Mass Consumption in Postwar America* (New York: Alfred A. Knopf, 2003). For a probing consideration of how cultural influences work in reciprocal ways, see Richard Pells, *Modernist America: Art, Music, Movies and the Globalization of American Culture* (New Haven, Conn.: Yale University Press, 2011).

19. James T. Kloppenberg, *Uncertain Victory: Social Democracy and Progressivism in European and American Thought, 1870–1920* (New York: Oxford University Press, 1986), 3. On the concept of a "discourse community," see David A. Hollinger, "Historians and the Discourse of Intellectuals," in *New Directions in American Intellectual History*, ed. John Higham and Paul K. Conkin (Baltimore: Johns Hopkins University Press, 1979), 42–63.

20. The literature of the international response to American popular culture, and to the United States more generally, is vast, but among the places to begin (including for their footnotes) are two forums. First, "Historical Perspectives on Anti-Americanism," *AHR* 111 (October 2006): 1041–1129; see esp. Jessica C. E. Gienow-Hecht, "Always Blame the Americans: Anti-Americanism in Europe in the Twentieth Century," 1067–91, which provides a nuanced, multinational discussion that emphasizes the dialectic of anti- and philo-Americanism. Second, Rob Kroes, "European Anti-Americanism: What's New?" *JAH* 93 (September 2006): 417–31, and the responses, 432–51. Much of the best work on cultural relationships across the Atlantic emphasizes the dynamics of reciprocal exchanges: see, for example, Richard Pells, *Not like Us: How Europeans Have Loved, Hated, and Transformed American Culture since World War II* (New York: Basic Books, 1997); Rob Kroes, *If You've Seen One, You've Seen the Mall: Europeans and American Mass Culture* (Urbana: University of Illinois Press, 1996). For collections of recent essays, see Alexander Stephan, ed., *The Americanization of Europe: Culture, Diplomacy, and Anti-Americanism after 1945* (New York: Berghahn, 2006); Andrew Ross and Kristin Ross, eds., *Anti-Americanism* (New York: New York University Press, 2004). Jessica Gienow-Hecht, "Shame on US? Cultural Transfer, Academics, and the Cold War—A Critical Review," *Diplomatic History* 24 (Summer 2000): 465–94, analyzes a shift among scholars, beginning in the late 1980s, from an emphasis on American cultural imperialism to one of local adaptation. See also Greg Castillo, *Cold War on the Home Front: The Soft Power of Midcentury Design* (Minneapolis: University of Minnesota Press, 2010), xiv.

21. The summary in this and the following paragraph draws on Tony Judt, *Postwar: A History of Europe since 1945* (New York: Penguin, 2005), 220–37, 324–53, 377–80, with the quote from p. 13.

22. On the development of postmodernism in the 1950s, see Kevin Rozario, *The Culture of Calamity: Disaster and the Making of Modern America* (Chicago: University of Chicago Press, 2007), 166–67. Robert Genter, *Late Modernism: Art, Culture, and Politics in Cold War America* (Philadelphia: University of Pennsylvania Press, 2010), esp. 1–17, sees both romantic modernism and late modernism as providing the missing links in the transition from high modernism to postmodernism; in important ways, his discussion of late

modernism, which came to my attention after the development of the main lineaments of my argument, parallels some of what this book covers. The literature of postmodernism is immense, but among the places to start are Perry Anderson, *The Origins of Postmodernity* (London: Verso, 1998); David Harvey, *The Condition of Postmodernity: An Enquiry into the Origins of Cultural Change* (Oxford: Blackwell, 1989); Fredric Jameson, *Postmodernism, or, The Cultural Logic of Late Capitalism* (Durham, N.C.: Duke University Press, 1991); Jean-François Lyotard, *The Postmodern Condition: A Report on Knowledge*, trans. Geoff Bennington and Brian Massumi (Minneapolis: University of Minnesota Press, 1984). Among the sources that link postmodernism and consumer culture are Andreas Huyssen, *After the Great Divide: Modernism, Mass Culture, Postmodernism* (Bloomington: Indiana University Press, 1986); Don Slater, *Consumer Culture and Modernity* (Oxford: Polity Press, 1997); Fredric Jameson, "Postmodernism and Consumer Society," in *The Anti-Aesthetic: Essays on Postmodern Culture*, ed. Hal Foster (Port Townsend, Wash.: Bay, 1983), 111–25; and Jonathan Clark, *Our Shadowed Present: Modernism, Postmodernism, and History* (London: Atlantic, 2003). For a probing discussion of the two phenomena mentioned in the book's title, see Mike Featherstone, *Consumer Culture and Modernism*, 2nd ed. (Los Angeles: Sage Publications, 2007). In most of the chapters that follow, the notes will reveal the connection between the authors and postmodernism, but for now one example suffices: Stjepan Meštrovic, "Recontextualizing David Riesman's *The Lonely Crowd*," in *Postemotional Society* (London: Sage Publications, 1997), 43, counts Riesman's book as among those that prefigured postmodernism.

    23. Over the years, a number of scholars, whose work I admire and draw on, have explored the history of changing ideas about mass media and consumer culture. Daniel Czitrom led the way as he explored the tension between domination and liberation in writings on mass communications from the 1830s until the 1960s: Daniel J. Czitrom, *Media and the American Mind from Morse to McLuhan* (Chapel Hill: University of North Carolina Press, 1982). A year later, reaching back to ancient Greece and Rome and then going forward into the 1960s, Patrick Brantlinger published a book that focused on what he called the "negative classicism" that excoriated mass culture and then contrasted it with a more positive vision that he saw emerging in the 1970s in the debate over a postindustrial society: Patrick Brantlinger, *Bread and Circuses: Theories of Mass Culture as Social Decay* (Ithaca, N.Y.: Cornell University Press, 1983), 9. In a less well-known book, *Ideology and Art: Theories of Mass Culture from Walter Benjamin to Umberto Eco* (New York: Peter Lang, 1984), Robin Ridless focused on Walter Benjamin, Bertold Brecht, Theodor Adorno, Umberto Eco, and Roland Barthes. With *Left Intellectuals*, Paul Gorman traced a left tradition from the 1890s until what he sees as its culmination in the essays of Dwight Macdonald from the 1930s to the 1950s, which then came under attack from a new generation of progressive writers in the last third of the twentieth century. In his wide-ranging and richly suggestive *American Culture, American Tastes: Social Change and the Twentieth Century* (New York: Alfred A. Knopf, 1999), Michael G. Kammen explored the shifting terms of the debates over taste, leisure, and popular culture from the late nineteenth century until nearly the end of the twentieth. In *An All-Consuming Century: Why Commercialism Won in Modern America* (New York: Columbia University Press, 2000),

Gary S. Cross offered a thoughtful and sweeping history of the triumph of commercial culture in twentieth-century America; he seems to see the changes I am charting coming later than I do: see p. 11. This list only begins to cover all the books available. For example, see also John Storey, *An Introduction to Cultural Theory and Popular Culture*, 2nd ed. (New York: Harvester/Wheatsheaf, 1997), a book intended for classroom use that covers many of the texts my book focuses on. John S. Gilkeson, *Anthropologists and the Rediscovery of America, 1865–1965* (New York: Cambridge University Press, 2010), explores some of the terrain of this book—including the emergence of class analysis and the shift from cultural anthropology to cultural studies.

In addition to books that offer broad coverage of the history of responses to commercial culture, there is an abundant literature on the changing views of mass culture that covers more than one of the figures whose works I explore. See Lunn, "Beyond 'Mass Culture'"; James B. Gilbert, *A Cycle of Outrage: America's Reaction to the Juvenile Delinquent in the 1950s* (New York: Oxford University Press, 1986), 109–26; Donald Lazere, "Mass Culture, Political Consciousness, and English Studies," *College English* 38 (April 1977): 751–67; and David Gross, "Lowenthal, Adorno, Barthes: Three Perspectives on Popular Culture," *Telos* 45 (Fall 1980): 122–40.

Most of the writers this book covers have commanded the attention of scholars in a wide range of fields—history, cultural studies, women's studies, literary theory, and sociology among them. In some instances there are enough books and articles to fill shelf upon shelf, with scholars having paid abundant attention to the works and lives of many of the authors under consideration here. In other cases there is a vast literature but little of it from historically minded scholars. In still other instances there is relatively little scholarship available from any but the most specific quarters and sometimes not even that.

24. For essays that review the results of the increasing attention scholars have paid to popular culture and in the process cover some of the ground the present book goes over, see Michael Schudson, "The New Validation of Popular Culture: Sense and Sentimentality in Academia," *Critical Studies in Mass Communication* 4 (March 1987): 51–68; Chandra Mukerji and Michael Schudson, "Popular Culture," *Annual Review of Sociology* 12 (1986): 47–86; and Chandra Mukerji and Michael Schudson, "Rethinking Popular Culture," in *Rethinking Popular Culture: Contemporary Perspectives in Cultural Studies*, ed. Chandra Mukerji and Michael Schudson (Berkeley: University of California Press, 1991), 1–61. Slater, *Consumer Culture*, explores the changing definitions of key concepts. The shift my book charts can be also seen in the writings of historians of consumer culture. The work of Jackson Lears reveals a change from seeing consumer culture as morally problematic to a more positive vision: contrast T. J. Jackson Lears, *No Place of Grace: Antimodernism and the Transformation of American Culture, 1880–1920* (New York: Pantheon Books, 1981), with T. J. Jackson Lears, *Fables of Abundance: A Cultural History of Advertising in America* (New York: Basic Books, 1994). In between his two books, but with his position closer to what he expressed in *Fables*, Lears engaged in a spirited debate with Lawrence Levine, who had insisted on questioning the dichotomies between producer/consumer, folk/popular, formulaic/original, escapist/real, derivative/avant-garde, functional/aesthetic: Lawrence Levine, "The Folklore of Industrial Society: Popular Culture and Its Au-

diences," *AHR* 97 (December 1992): 1369–99; Lears's response ("Making Fun of Popular Culture"), 1417–26; and Levine's reply ("Levine Responds"), 1427–30. David Steigerwald, "All Hail the Republic of Choice: Consumer History as Contemporary Thought," *JAH* 93 (September 2006): 385–403, captures the tension in historical writings on consumer culture between manipulation and emancipation but does not see how historians have changed their views over time. Elsewhere in the scholarship, one can witness the same, relatively new emphasis on pleasure and symbolic communication: Appleby, "Consumption," 130–44; T. H. Breen, *The Marketplace of Revolution: How Consumer Politics Shaped American Independence* (New York: Oxford University Press, 2004), 150 and 331; William Leach, *Land of Desire: Merchants, Power, and the Rise of a New American Culture* (New York: Pantheon, 1993), xiii, xv, and 149; Nan Enstad, *Ladies of Labor, Girls of Adventure: Working Women, Popular Culture, and Labor Politics at the Turn of the Twentieth Century* (New York: Columbia University Press, 1999), 10, 51, and 207; Ted Ownby, *American Dreams in Mississippi: Consumers, Poverty, and Culture, 1830–1998* (Chapel Hill: University of North Carolina Press, 1999), 3; Thaddeus Russell, *A Renegade History of the United States* (New York: Free Press, 2010), esp. 207–28, offers the fullest synthesis of a pro-consumer pleasure argument. Louis A. Pérez Jr., *On Becoming Cuban: Identity, Nationality, and Culture* (Chapel Hill: University of North Carolina Press, 1999), 161–62. In addition, Peter Stearns, "Stages of Consumerism: Recent Work on the Issues of Periodization," *JMH* 69 (March 1997): 105, discusses issues of desire, identity, and meaning in the historiography. Similarly, for a review essay of books by Richard Ohmann, Ellen Garvey, and Jennifer Scanlon that explores similar themes, see R. F. Bogardus, "The Reorientation of Paradise: Modern Mass Media and Narratives of Desire in the Making of American Consumer Culture," *American Literary History* 10 (Autumn 1998): 508–23. In *The Industrious Revolution: Consumer Behavior and the Household Economy, 1650 to the Present* (Cambridge: Cambridge University Press, 2008), Jan deVries places in a central position not the self-fashioning individual but the active, empowered, desiring household as the engine of the consumer society and emphasizes as well the importance of how consumer goods communicate meaning. These works of history that articulate a more sympathetic vision of consumption relied on a number of pathbreaking works in the humanities and social sciences: from the 1920s and 1930s, writings by Marcel Mauss, Walter Benjamin, Johan Huizinga, Antonio Gramsci, and Georges Bataille; and from the 1940s and 1950s, the utopian strain in the critical theory of the Frankfurt School. They also drew on works of social scientists and humanists from the 1960s on, esp. works of Jean Baudrillard, Judith Butler, Colin Campbell, Mary Douglas and Baron Isherwood, Lewis Hyde, William Leiss, Grant McCracken, Susan Sontag, and Michael Taussig. In important ways, Cohen, *Consumers' Republic*, is an attempt to shift the discussion of postwar consumer culture away from charged moral terms. Warren I. Susman, *Culture as History: The Transformation of American Society in the Twentieth Century* (New York: Pantheon, 1984), is among the many influential works by historians that evidenced a commitment to treat popular culture seriously. Moreover, Susman's discussion of the relationship of intellectuals to pleasure and abundance marks a crucial turn toward fresh perspectives: although heralded in some of the earlier essays in this volume, his transformative arguments emerge most clearly in Warren Susman, "Introduction: Toward a History of the Culture of Abundance: Some Hypotheses," in Susman, *Culture as History*, xix–xxx, which he seems to have composed in the early 1980s for his 1984 book.

25. For the argument that appreciation might cross the border to complicity, see Thomas Frank, *The Conquest of Cool: Business Culture, Counterculture, and the Rise of Hip Consumerism* (Chicago: University of Chicago Press, 1997); Thomas Frank and Matt Weiland, eds., *Commodify Your Dissent: Salvos from "The Baffler"* (New York: Norton, 1997); Thomas Frank, *New Consensus for Old: Cultural Studies from Left to Right* (Chicago: Prickly Paradigm Press, 2002).

Chapter 1

1. Edward Shils, "Daydreams and Nightmares: Reflections on the Criticism of Mass Culture," *SwR* 65 (Autumn 1957): 587.

2. Bernard Rosenberg and David Manning White, eds., *Mass Culture: The Popular Arts in America* (Glencoe, Ill.: Free Press, 1957); Daniel Bell, "America as a Mass Society: A Critique," in Daniel Bell, *The End of Ideology: On the Exhaustion of Political Ideas in the Fifties* (1960; rev. ed., New York: Free Press, 1962), 21; Michael G. Kammen, *The Lively Arts: Gilbert Seldes and the Transformation of Cultural Criticism in the United States* (New York: Oxford University Press, 1996), 335; Theodor Adorno, *Introduction to the Sociology of Music* [1962], trans. E. B. Ashton (New York: Seabury, 1967), 132. Though designed as a reader for university courses, the book nonetheless provoked passionate responses: see a review from *The Nation*, quoted on back cover of 1964 paperback edition (copy in author's possession); Harold Rosenberg, "Popular Culture and Kitsch Criticism," *Dissent* 5 (Winter 1958): 14–17; Shils, "Daydreams," 587–608; Edward Shils, "Mass Society and Its Culture," *Daedalus* 89 (Spring 1960): 288–314. Norman Jacobs, ed., *Culture for the Millions? Mass Media in Modern Society* (Princeton, N.J.: Van Nostrand, 1961), was a more focused and less influential collection of essays than the Rosenberg and White volume. James Gilbert, *A Cycle of Outrage: America's Reaction to the Juvenile Delinquent in the 1950s* (New York: Oxford University Press, 1986), 109–126, discusses the Rosenberg and White volume, placing it in the larger context of debates over mass culture in the postwar world. On important aspects of the history of distinctions among levels of culture, see Lawrence W. Levine, *Highbrow/Lowbrow: The Emergence of Cultural Hierarchy in America* (Cambridge, Mass.: Harvard University Press, 1988).

3. S. I. Hayakawa, "Popular Songs vs. the Facts of Life [1955]," in Rosenberg and White, eds., *Mass*, 393; Bernard Rosenberg, "Mass Culture in America," in Rosenberg and White, eds., *Mass*, 3–4. In the other essay in the book on jazz, the author was more interested in how the form became popular among white intellectuals than in jazz itself: Morroe Berger, "The New Popularity of Jazz [1946]," 404–7.

4. On the issue of race and ethnicity, the most notable exception is Bernard Berelson and Patricia J. Salter, "Majority and Minority Americans: An Analysis of Magazine Fiction [1946]," in Rosenberg and White, eds., *Mass*, 235–50. With gender, the main exception is Martha Wolfenstein and Nathan Leites, "The Good-Bad Girl [1950]," in Rosenberg and White, eds., *Mass*, 294–307. The essay that came closest to offering a class analysis but was

nonetheless equivocal on the value of popular culture was Leslie A. Fiedler, "The Middle against Both Ends [1955]," esp. 546. I am grateful to Herbert J. Gans for helping me think about the relationships of Jews to popular culture, even though we did not always agree: emails between author and Gans, July 7 and 16, 2009, copies in author's possession. See Andrew R. Heinz, *Jews and the American Soul: Human Nature in the Twentieth Century* (Princeton, N.J.: Princeton University Press, 2004), 273–74, for a discussion of the concern among Jews about mass society.

5. James Gilbert, *Men in the Middle: Searching for Masculinity in the 1950s* (Chicago: University of Chicago Press, 2005), 189–214, with the quote on 191; Rosenberg, "Mass Culture," 7; Paul F. Lazarsfeld and Robert K. Merton, "Mass Communication, Popular Taste and Organized Social Action [1948]," in Rosenberg and White, eds., *Mass*, 466. In a 1944 essay not included in the book, Adorno and Max Horkheimer asserted that mass culture "cannot renounce the threat of castration": Horkheimer and Adorno, *Dialectic of Enlightenment* [1944], trans. John Cumming (New York: Seabury, 1972), 141. For a different take on the relationship between gender and popular culture, see Dwight Macdonald, notebooks and loose pages, 1935–36, quoted in Michael Wreszin, *A Rebel in Defense of Tradition: The Life and Politics of Dwight Macdonald* (New York: Basic Books, 1994), 39.

6. T. W. Adorno, "Television and the Patterns of Mass Culture [1954]," in Rosenberg and White, eds., *Mass*, 486.

7. Bernard Rosenberg and David Manning White, "Preface," *Mass*, v.

8. Daniel Horowitz, *The Morality of Spending: Attitudes toward the Consumer Society in America, 1875–1940* (Baltimore: Johns Hopkins University Press, 1985), xviii–xix and 166–68; the "open society" quote is from Melvin Tumin, "Popular Culture and the Open Society," in Rosenberg and White, eds., *Mass*, 551; compare Clement Greenberg, "Avant-Garde and Kitsch," *PR* 6 (Fall 1939): 34–49, with Clement Greenberg, "Avant-Garde and Kitsch," in Rosenberg and White, eds., *Mass*, 98–107. See also Paul R. Gorman, *Left Intellectuals and Popular Culture in Twentieth-Century America* (Chapel Hill: University of North Carolina Press, 1996), 144.

9. Bernard Rosenberg, "Mass Culture," 5, 7, 9, and 10.

10. Ibid., 8 and 9.

11. David Manning White, "Mass Culture in America: Another Point of View," in Rosenberg and White, eds., *Mass*, 14 and 21, n 1.

12. Ibid., 16 and 17.

13. Ibid., 14. See Rosenberg, "Mass Culture," 10, and White, "Another Point," 13, for references to McLuhan's 1951 book.

14. Leo Lowenthal, "Historical Perspectives of Popular Culture [1950]," in Rosenberg and White, eds., *Mass*, 49 and 51; Ernest van den Haag, "Of Happiness and of Despair We Have No Measure," in Rosenberg and White, eds., *Mass*, 524. Rosenberg's and White's framing essays did not make explicit the two methodological issues that pervaded the book—first, the focus on "effects" that swirled around the question of whether popular culture causes criminal activity, and second, content analysis, a careful, sociological study of the language and plots offered in the media. On the first, see for a few of many examples, Rosenberg and White, eds., *Mass*, 124, 187, 190, 204, 212, 342, 345, 408,

and 458. On the second, for an example, see Lyle W. Shannon, "The Opinions of Little Orphan Annie and Her Friends [1954]," in Rosenberg and White, eds., *Mass*, 212–17. For a full statement of content analysis, see Patricke Johns-Heine and Hans H. Gerth, "Values in Mass Periodical Fiction, 1921–1940 [1949]," in Rosenberg and White, eds., *Mass*, 226–27

15. Charles J. Rolo, "Simenon and Spillane: The Metaphysics of Murder for the Millions [1952]," in Rosenberg and White, eds., *Mass*, 165–75; Arthur J. Brodbeck and David M. White, "How to Read 'Li'l Abner' Intelligently," in Rosenberg and White, eds., *Mass*, 218 and 223. There is some evidence of fresh approaches, ones that would become more prominent later, in Leo Bogart, "Comic Strips and Their Adult Readers," in Rosenberg and White, eds., *Mass*, 189–98.

16. David Riesman, "Listening to Popular Music [1950]," in Rosenberg and White, eds., *Mass*, 409; Herbert J. Gans, "The Creator-Audience Relationship in the Mass Media: An Analysis of Movie Making," in Rosenberg and White, eds., *Mass*, 315.

17. Henry Rabassiere [Henry Pachter], "In Defense of Television [1956]," in Rosenberg and White, eds., *Mass*, 372 and 374; Marshall McLuhan, "Sight, Sound, and the Fury [1954]," in Rosenberg and White, eds., *Mass*, 489, 493, and 495.

18. Gilbert Seldes, "The People and the Arts [1951]," in Rosenberg and White, eds., *Mass*, 74, 75, 79, 75, and 80–81. See also Gilbert Seldes, *The Seven Lively Arts* (New York: Harper and Brothers, 1924). In writing on Seldes, I benefited from and drew on Kammen, *Lively*, which contains an extensive and nuanced discussion of how Seldes's view of popular culture changed after 1945 (315–51); for the controversy between Seldes and Macdonald, see Kammen, *Lively*, 326–28.

19. Seldes, "People," 74; Gilbert Seldes, "The Public Arts," in Rosenberg and White, eds., *Mass*, 558; Seldes, "People," 97.

20. Greenberg, "Kitsch," 98–107; Dwight Macdonald, "A Theory of Mass Culture," in Rosenberg and White, eds., *Mass*, 59–73, originally in *Diogenes* 2 (Summer 1953): 1–17. For an earlier version of Macdonald's essay, see Dwight Macdonald, "A Theory of Popular Culture," *Politics* 1 (February 1944): 20–23. Macdonald published an even later version: Dwight Macdonald, "Masscult and Midcult," *PR* (Spring-Summer 1960), later republished in Dwight Macdonald, *Against the American Grain* (New York: Random House, 1962). For a fuller discussion of Greenberg, Macdonald, and the Frankfurt School, see Gorman, *Left Intellectuals*, 137–85. Macdonald both contributed to and reviewed the book: Dwight Macdonald, "'A Corrupt Brightness,'" *Encounter* 8 (June 1957): 75–82. On these changes, see Eugene Lunn, "Beyond 'Mass Culture': The Lonely Crowd, the Uses of Literacy and the Postwar Era," *Theory and Society* 19 (February 1990): 63. For a discussion of kitsch as a concept, see Matei Calinescu, *Five Faces of Modernity: Modernism, Avant-Garde, Decadence, Kitsch, Postmodernism* (1977; rev. ed., Durham, N.C.: Duke University Press, 1987), 223–62.

21. Greenberg, "Kitsch," in Rosenberg and White, eds., *Mass.*, 102. Gorman, *Left Intellectuals*, 150–57, explores the debate between Macdonald and Greenberg; for an important discussion of how New York intellectuals viewed popular culture, see Andrew Ross, *No Respect: Intellectuals and Popular Culture* (New York: Routledge, 1989), esp. 42–64.

22. Macdonald, "Theory," 60, 63, 72, and 61. Gorman, *Left Intellectuals*, 158–85 examines Macdonald's arguments, including how versions of his essays changed over time.

23. Lowenthal, "Perspectives," 52–57, offers a critique of the focus on effects; the more important essay is Leo Lowenthal, "Biographies in Popular Magazines [1944]," in *Mass Communication and American Social Thought: Key Texts, 1919–1968*, ed. John D. Peters and Peter Simonson (Lanham, Md.: Rowman and Littlefield, 2004), 188–205; Günther Anders, "The Phantom World of TV [1956]," in Rosenberg and White, eds., *Mass*, 359.

24. Adorno, "Television," 480; Eugene Lunn, *Marxism and Modernism: A Historical Study of Lukács, Brecht, Benjamin and Adorno* (Berkeley: University of California Press, 1982), 213. The literature on Adorno is immense, but in addition to what is cited elsewhere, there are two recent biographies: Stefan Müller-Doohm, *Adorno: A Biography*, trans. Rodney Livingstone (Cambridge: Polity, 2005), and Detlev Claussen, *Theodor W. Adorno: One Last Genius*, trans. Rodney Livingstone (Cambridge, Mass.: Harvard University Press, 2008). For a discussion of exiles from Weimar Germany living in the Los Angeles area, see Ehrhard Bahr, *Weimar on the Pacific: German Exile Culture in Los Angeles and the Crisis of Modernism* (Berkeley: University of California Press, 2007); for its treatment of Horkheimer and Adorno, *Dialectic*, see 30–68. While in the United States, though he found much to dislike about the country's popular culture and more broadly its culture industry, Adorno developed a thorough, often firsthand knowledge of both its techniques and products: see David Jenemann, *Adorno in America* (Minneapolis: University of Minnesota Press, 2007), xxv. Thomas Wheatland, *The Frankfurt School in Exile* (Minneapolis: University of Minnesota Press, 2009), explores the exchanges between members of the Frankfurt School and Americans, including (pp. 140–88) New York intellectuals. Martin Jay, "Adorno in America," *NGC* 31 (Winter 1984): 160–65, cogently warns against overemphasizing the negative impact on Adorno of his experience in the United States.

25. Adorno, "Television," 475–76.

26. Ibid., 474–75. For a discussion of the distinctions among levels of art, see Robin Ridless, *Ideology and Art: Theories of Mass Culture from Walter Benjamin to Umberto Eco* (New York: Peter Lang, 1984), x–xi.

27. Adorno, "Television," 479, 474, and 487.

28. Rosenberg and White failed to include two key social science approaches: anthropology, represented by the Lynds' *Middletown* studies, and communications theory represented by Paul Lazarsfeld and Elihu Katz's *Personal Influence: The Part Played by People in the Flow of Mass Communications* (Glencoe, Ill.: Free Press, 1955). This book countered the pessimists by emphasizing the agency of consumers, the complicated nature of audience, and the importance of intermediaries between powerful capitalist producers and supposedly anomic, individualized consumers. Herbert Marcuse, *Eros and Civilization: A Philosophical Inquiry into Freud* (Boston: Beacon Press, 1955). My discussion of David Riesman later in the book includes a consideration of Fromm's contributions

29. Jenemann, *Adorno*, xviii, shows that Adorno's papers contain materials, both by him and that he collected, that would have revealed for the radio project how fully

Adorno understood the dialectical relationship between producers and their audiences; see also Jenemann, *Adorno*, 194, n. 23.

30. Horkheimer and Adorno, *Dialectic*, 149; see also xi. Bahr, *Weimar*, 65, explores the importance of the Chaplin reference. Adorno and Horkheimer, as well as other advocates of European high culture, gave serious, even perhaps appreciative attention to some key aspects of American popular culture, especially movies by Chaplin, the Marx Brothers, and Disney: John MacKay, ed. and trans., "Chaplin Times Two," *Yale Journal of Criticism* 9 (Spring 1996): 57–61; Horkheimer and Adorno, *Dialectic*, 137–38.

31. Horkheimer and Adorno, *Dialectic*, 137. For a discussion of the Frankfurt School's (and Adorno's) treatment of mass culture, see Martin Jay, *The Dialectical Imagination: A History of the Frankfurt School and the Institute of Social Research, 1923–1950* (Boston: Little, Brown, 1973), 173–218.

32. Horkheimer and Adorno, *Dialectic*, 138, 139, 142, and 167.

33. Jay, "Adorno in America," 162; Eugene Lunn, "The Frankfurt School in the Development of the Mass-Culture Debate," *Journal of Comparative Literature and Aesthetics* 11 (1988): 4; Theodor Adorno to Walter Benjamin, March 18, 1936, in Theodor Adorno et al., *Aesthetics and Politics* (London: New Left Books, 1977), 123; Horkheimer and Adorno, *Dialectic*, xv. For a useful corrective to linking members of the Frankfurt School with conservatives, see Jay, "Adorno in America," 157–82.

34. Uta G. Poiger, *Jazz, Rock, and Rebels: Cold War Politics and American Culture in a Divided Germany* (Berkeley: University of California Press, 2000), 145; see also John Gennari, *Blowin' Hot and Cool: Jazz and Its Critics* (Chicago: University of Chicago Press, 2006), 87–88. For some of Adorno's writings on jazz, see Theodor Adorno, "On Jazz [1936]," in Theodor Adorno, *Essays on Music*, ed. Richard Leppert and trans. Susan H. Gillespie (Berkeley: University of California Press, 2002), 470–92; Jay, *Dialectical*, 186; Theodor Adorno, "The Perennial Fashion—Jazz [1953]," in Theodor W. Adorno, *Prisms*, trans. Samuel Weber and Shierry Weber (London: Spearman, 1967), 212–32. Leppert's work offers a more positive view of Adorno's take on jazz than the usual, more critical attitude. With these, as with many of his writings on jazz, it is important to distinguish between authentic African American jazz and its more commercialized forms as performed by both African Americans and whites. For a nuanced discussion of Adorno's essays on jazz, including the 1936 one, see Catherine G. Kodat, "Conversing with Ourselves: Canon, Freedom, Jazz," *AQ* 55 (March 2003): 1–28.

35. George Orwell, "Raffles and Miss Blandish [1944]," in Rosenberg and White, eds., *Mass.*, 154–64. To be sure, at least one essay in the volume, by Siegfried Kracauer, had an international and comparative dimension: Siegfried Kracauer, "National Types as Hollywood Presents Them [1949]," in Rosenberg and White, eds., *Mass*, 257–77.

36. Patrick Brantlinger, *Bread and Circuses: Theories of Mass Culture as Social Decay* (Ithaca, N.Y.: Cornell University Press, 1983), 185. For a discussion of the culture and society tradition, see Raymond Williams, *Culture and Society, 1780–1950* (London: Chatto and Windus, 1958). In *Mass Culture* there were some, but remarkably few, mentions of Arnold and Eliot; none of Richards or the Leavises.

37. Matthew Arnold, *Culture and Anarchy: An Essay in Political and Social Criticism*, ed. Ian Gregor (Indianapolis: Bobbs-Merrill, 1971), 5–6, 42, and 56 (this volume reproduces the third edition, from 1882). This discussion of *Culture and Anarchy* relies on Helen Lefkowitz Horowitz, *Culture and the City: Cultural Philanthropy in Chicago from the 1880s to 1917* (Lexington: University Press of Kentucky, 1976), esp. 18–19; on the response to Arnold by Americans, and a discussion of Arnold's ideas, see Daniel J. Czitrom, *Media and the American Mind: From Morse to McLuhan* (Chapel Hill: University of North Carolina Press, 1982), 31–34.

38. Seldes, "People," 82; T. S. Eliot, *Christianity and Culture* (New York: Harcourt, Brace, 1960), 104. On his appreciation of a British music hall performer, see T. S. Eliot, "London Letter," November 1922, http://world.std.com/~raparker/exploring/books/london_letter_1922_12.html (accessed February 12, 2011). A good place to begin to understand Eliot's literary criticism is Timothy Materer, "T. S. Eliot's Critical Program," in *The Cambridge Companion to T. S. Eliot*, ed. Anthony David Moody (Cambridge: Cambridge University Press, 1994), 48–59. On Eliot's social and cultural criticism, see Peter Dales Scott, "The Social Critic and His Discontents," in Moody, ed., *Eliot*, 60–76. For a comparison of Arnold and Eliot, see Adam Kirsch, "Matthew Arnold and T. S. Eliot," *American Scholar* 67 (Summer 1998): 65–73. On the limitations of his vision, see Brantlinger, *Bread*, 204–5; Stuart Hall and Paddy Whannel, *The Popular Arts* (London: Hutchinson Educational, 1964), 56–58.

39. T. S. Eliot, *After Strange Gods: A Primer of Modern Heresy* (London: Faber and Faber, 1934), 19–20 and 15; Eliot, *Christianity*, 51. This discussion draws on *Christianity and Culture*, which in turn contains *The Idea of a Christian Society* (1939) (pp. 1–77) and *Notes towards the Definition of Culture* (1948) (pp. 79–202).

40. Eliot, *Christianity*, 184; T. S. Eliot, "On the Place and Function of the Clerisy," quoted in Scott, "Social Critic," 73; Eliot, *Christianity*, 36–37, 114–15, and 177.

41. Eliot, *Christianity*, 17 and 83; see also Eliot, *Christianity*, 185.

42. These terms appear in chapter titles and in the text: see I. A Richards, *Practical Criticism: A Study of Literary Judgment* (New York: Harcourt, Brace, 1929), xi–xii. This section relies on Richards, *Practical* and John Paul Russo, *I. A. Richards: His Life and Work* (Baltimore: Johns Hopkins University Press, 1989), esp. 294–316.

43. Richards, *Practical*, 248 and 320; I. A. Richards, *Principles of Literary Criticism* (New York: Harcourt, Brace, 1928), 202–4.

44. Richards, *Practical,* 320; Richard Hoggart, "Introduction to the Transaction Edition," in I. A. Richards, *Practical Criticism: A Study of Literary Judgment* (New Brunswick, N.J.: Transaction, 2004), xiv–xv.

45. For the relationships between Richards and F. R. Leavis, see Russo, *Richards*, 534–38.

46. In writing on Leavis and his circle, I am relying on F. R. Leavis, *Mass Civilisation and Minority Culture* (Cambridge: Minority Press, 1930); F. R. Leavis and Denys Thompson, *Culture and Environment: The Training of Critical Awareness* (London: Chatto and Windus, 1933). On his life, see Ian MacKillop, *F. R. Leavis: A Life in Criticism* (London:

Allen Lane, 1995); Stefan Collini, "Richard Hoggart: Literary Criticism and Cultural Decline in Twentieth-Century Britain," in *Richard Hoggart and Cultural Studies*, ed. Sue
Owen (Houndmills: Palgrave Macmillan, 2008), 36. On the contrast between the tremendous influence of Leavis in Britain and his relatively scant impact on American literary criticism, see Paul Alpers, "Leavis Today," in *Under Criticism: Essays for William H.
Pritchard*, ed. David Sofield and Herbert F. Tucker (Athens: Ohio University Press, 1998),
182–96. On the long-term impact of Leavis, see Grant Farred, "Leavisite Cool: The Organic Links between Cultural Studies and *Scrutiny*," *Dispositio/n* 21 (1999): 1–19; Gary
Day, *Re-Reading Leavis: "Culture" and Literary Criticism* (New York: St. Martin's Press,
1996).

47. Leavis and Thompson, *Environment*, 1; Leavis, *Mass Civilisation*, 6; Leavis and
Thompson, *Environment*, 99; Leavis, *Mass Civilisation*, 10; Leavis and Thompson, *Environment*, 102.

48. Leavis, *Mass Civilisation*, 3 and 5; Hall and Whannel, *Popular*, 377. This discussion
draws on Dennis L. Dworkin, *Cultural Marxism in Postwar Britain: History, the New Left,
and the Origins of Cultural Studies* (Durham, N.C.: Duke University Press, 1997), 80–83.

49. Q. D. Leavis, *Fiction and the Reading Public* (London: Chatto and Windus, 1932),
212, and 270. On the influence of Richards on Q. D. Leavis, see Russo, *Richards*, 539–40,
and Leavis, *Fiction*, xiv–xv.

50. Leavis and Thompson, *Environment*, 42, 6, 48, 51, and 58.

51. Francis Mulhern, *The Moment of "Scrutiny"* (London: New Left Books, 1979), 95;
Dworkin, *Cultural*, 82.

Chapter 2

1. Walter Benjamin, "The Work of Art in the Age of Mechanical Reproduction," in
Hannah Arendt, ed., *Illuminations*, trans. Harry Zohn (New York: Harcourt Brace Jova-
novich, 1968), 217–51.

2. This summary of German attitudes toward the United States relies on Uta G. Poiger, *Jazz, Rock, and Rebels: Cold War Politics and American Culture in a Divided Germany*
(Berkeley: University of California Press, 2000), 20–21; Volker R. Berghahn, *America and
the Intellectual Cold Wars in Europe: Shepard Stone between Philanthropy, Academy, and
Diplomacy* (Princeton, N.J.: Princeton University Press, 2001), xiii, 77–107, and 284–95.
The quote is from Hans Siemsen, "Jazz Band" (1921), quoted in Peter Jelavich, *Berlin Cab-
aret* (Cambridge, Mass.: Harvard University Press, 1993), 170. Among the other useful
discussions of German-American cultural relations are Alexander Stephan, "A Special
German Case of Cultural Americanization," in *The Americanization of Europe: Culture, Diplomacy, and Anti-Americanism after 1945*, ed. Alexander Stephan (New York:
Berghahn, 2006), 69–88; Alexander Stephan, ed., *Americanization and Anti-American-
ization: The German Encounter after 1945* (New York: Berghahn, 2005).

3. Ludwig Erhard, *Prosperity through Competition*, trans. Edith Temple Rogers and
Robert B. Wood (New York: Frederick A. Praeger, 1958), 68, 169, 171, 172, and 173. For a discussion of Erhard that explores competing German visions of a new consumer economy,

that of East Germany and West Germany, between the CDU on the right and the SDP on the left, see Greg Castillo, *Cold War on the Home Front: The Soft Power of Midcentury Design* (Minneapolis: University of Minnesota Press, 2010), esp. 16.

4. Poiger, *Jazz*, 4.

5. Jürgen Habermas, "Political Experience and the Renewal of Marxist Theory [1979]," in Jürgen Habermas, *Autonomy and Solidarity: Interviews with Jürgen Habermas*, ed. Peter Dews (London: Verso, 1992), 78; Tony Judt, *Postwar: A History of Europe since 1945* (New York: Penguin, 2005), 276. In my discussion of Habermas, I am relying on Martin Matušík, *Jürgen Habermas: A Philosophical-Political Profile* (Lanham, Md.: Rowman and Littlefield, 2001); Andrew Edgar, *The Philosophy of Habermas* (Montreal: McGill-Queen's University Press, 2005), 1–55; James Gordon Finlayson, *Habermas: A Very Short Introduction* (Oxford: Oxford University Press, 2005), esp. xi–xvii and 1–19; David Ingram, *Habermas: Introduction and Analysis* (Ithaca, N.Y.: Cornell University Press, 2010); Martin Jay, *Marxism and Totality: The Adventures of a Concept from Lukács to Habermas* (Berkeley: University of California Press, 1984), 462–509; Thomas A. McCarthy, *The Critical Theory of Jürgen Habermas* (Cambridge, Mass.: MIT Press, 1978); William Outhwaite, *Habermas: Critical Introduction* (Stanford, Calif.: Stanford University Press, 1994), 1–13; Matthew G. Specter, *Habermas: An Intellectual Biography* (New York: Cambridge University Press, 2010); Chris Thornhill, *Political Theory in Modern Germany: An Introduction* (Cambridge: Polity Press, 2000), 130–73; Rolf Wiggershaus, *The Frankfurt School: Its History, Theories, and Political Significance*, trans. Michael Robertson (Cambridge, Mass.: MIT Press, 1994), 537–66. For a collection of interviews, see Habermas, *Autonomy*, especially 44–47, 77–83, 95–99, 147–48, and 187–88. A complete list of his writings can be found at http://www.habermasforum.dk/index.php?type=bibliografi2 (accessed February 13, 2011) or http://www.springerlink.com/content/gh80687305243730/ (accessed February 13, 2011). For a printed bibliography of his works, see René Görtzen and Frederik van Gelder, "Jürgen Habermas: The Complete Oeuvre: A Bibliography of Primary Literature, Translations, and Reviews," *Human Studies* 2 (October 1979): 285–300. For the story of how German writers came to terms with recent history, see A. Dirk Moses, *German Intellectuals and the Nazi Past* (Cambridge: Cambridge University Press, 2007).

6. Jürgen Habermas, "Life-Forms, Morality and the Task of the Philosopher [1984]," in Habermas, *Autonomy*, 188; Jürgen Habermas, "The Dialectics of Rationalization [1981]," in Habermas, *Autonomy*, 98.

7. Max Horkheimer to Theodore Adorno, September 27, 1958, quoted in Wiggershaus, *Frankfurt*, 555; Gadamer's record during the Nazi period, though hardly like that of Heidegger, was not unambiguous.

8. Around 1954, Habermas began to read works of industrial sociology, including American and French ones, which would soon influence his writings on work and leisure: Jürgen Habermas, "A Philosophico-Political Profile [1984]," in Habermas, *Autonomy*, 148. In the vast scholarship on Habermas in English, I cannot find much beyond the mention of his journalistic essays of the 1950s and relatively little on his early philosophical essays published between 1954 and 1958. This is especially true of his journalistic pieces on consumer culture. Moses, *Intellectuals*, 141–45, discusses his journalistic essays on

universities. Outhwaite, *Habermas*, 6, states that in his 1950s journalism Habermas offered "a 'left' alternative to the technological determinism" prevalent among many German intellectuals. Most scholars whose work is available in English go from Habermas's 1954 "Dialectics of Rationalization" to the essays that appeared in *Theory and Practice* and *Structural Transformation*, without much if any attention to other mid-1950s essays Habermas wrote on consumer culture: see, for example, Jay, *Totality*, 465–67; Edgar, *Habermas*, 4–5. The Habermas scholar David Ingram has pointed out how, over a long period of time, Habermas's ideas about technology, work, and aesthetics changed: David Ingram, email to author, November 9, 2010, copy in author's possession. As far as I can determine, even among scholars writing in German there is virtually no attention paid to these early journalistic pieces: note, for example, their absence from Wolfgang Kraushaar, ed., *Frankfurter Schule und Studentenbewegung: Von der Flaschenpost zum Molotowcocktail, 1946–1995* ([1998]; Hamburg: Hamburger Digital Edition, 2003). My uncovering of these early journalistic essays by Habermas is now beginning to turn the attention of scholars to their importance: see, as the only example thus far, David Ingram, "The Moloch and the Arts: Habermas and Feenberg on Technology, Modernity, and Aesthetic Rationality," esp. 10–13, unpublished paper, March 17, 2011, copy in author's possession.

9. Jürgen Habermas, "Für und Wider—Der Mensch Zwischen den Apparaten," *Süddeutsche Zeitung*, September 6–7, 1958, 48 (masking of powerful forces); Jürgen Habermas, "Können Konsumenten spielen?" *FAZ*, April 13, 1957, Feuilleton 1 ("amusement apparatuses" through "consumption-compulsion"); Jürgen Habermas, "Des Hörspiels Mangel ist seine Chance," *FAZ*, September 15, 1952, 4 (differences between media); Jürgen Habermas, "Der Moloch und die Künste: Gedanken zur Entlarvung der Legende von der technischen Zweckmäßigkeit," *FAZ*, May 30, 1953, 20 ("bigotry"); Jürgen Habermas, "Auto Fahren: Der Mensch am Lenkrad," *FAZ*, November 27, 1954, 29–30 (on automobiles); Jürgen Habermas, "Man möchte sich mitreißen lassen: Feste und Feiern in dieser Zeit," *Han*, February 17, 1956, Feuilleton, 4 ("recreate"). For other sources where Habermas comes to terms with the implications of contemporary culture, see Jürgen Habermas, "Ornament und Maschine," *FAZ*, December 31, 1954, 23; Jürgen Habermas, "Die Letzte Phase der Mechanisierung," *FAZ*, January 8, 1955, 29. Feuilleton is a special section tucked in the middle of the paper.

10. Jürgen Habermas, "Die Masse – das sind wir: Bildung und soziale Stellung kein Schutz gegen den Kollektivismus? – Das Gift der Menschenverachtung," *Han*, Feuilleton, October 29, 1954, 4 ("Hitler"); Habermas, "Für und Wider," 48 (new ways of organizing work); Habermas, "Konsumenten," 1 ("secret correlation"); Jürgen Habermas, "'Stil' auch für den Alltag – Die 'Industrieformung' nutzt und hilft dem Konsumenten," *Han*, September 23, 1955, 4 ("fantasy and initiative"); Habermas, "Hörspiels," 4. In many of these essays and elsewhere Habermas was vague, even convoluted when it came to exploring remedies for such a situation.

11. Habermas, "Moloch," 20 ("thing character"); Habermas, "Fahren" 29–30 (on automobiles); Habermas, "Man möchte," 4 (public celebrations); Habermas, "Man möchte," 4 ("mistrust"). Habermas was referring to hot-rodders in California, near Muroc Lake: see Conor McNally email to author, June 29, 2010, copy in author's possession; in his discus-

sion of hot-rodders, Habermas relied on Robert Jungk, *Brighter than a Thousand Suns: A Personal History of the Atomic Scientists* (New York: Harcourt Brace, 1958), a book about the development of the atomic bomb in the United States and Germany.

12. On the timing of the engagement by Habermas with the work of his mentors, see Specter, *Habermas*. On the issue of existential worries, as on other issues, I am indebted to Conor McNally.

13. I have been unable to find much written in English on this essay; but exceptions are Edgar, *Habermas*, 4–6; Wiggershaus, *Frankfurt*, 540–41; and Paul Gottfried, "The Habermasian Moment," *Journal of Libertarian Studies* 19 (Spring 2005): 52.

14. Jürgen Habermas, "Die Dialektik der Rationalisierung: Vom Pauperismus in Produktion und Konsum [1954]," in Jürgen Habermas, *Arbeit, Freizeit, Konsum: frühe Aufsätze* (The Hague, Netherlands: von Eversdijk, 1973), 10 and 12. I am grateful to Herwig Friedl for translating this essay as a summary and to Katharina Motyl for providing a more detailed translation; this paragraph is a summary of Habermas, "Dialektik," 3–26.

15. Jürgen Habermas, "Soziologische Notizien zum Verhältnis von Arbeit und Freizeit [1958]," 77 and 79, in Habermas, *Arbeit*, 63–79.

16. To see how he mediated between extremes, compare Habermas, "Für und Wider," 48, with Habermas "Letzte"; or see, for both sides of the dialectic, Jürgen Habermas, "Der Geist geht zu Fuß . . . eine Tagung zum Thema Kulturkonsum," *Han*, October 28, 1955, 4.

17. Specter, *Habermas*, 35; see also Thornhill, *Theory*, 130–45. Matušík, *Habermas*, xxx–xxxii and 1–33, provides a thoughtful and thorough discussion of the events that shaped Habermas.

18. Jürgen Habermas, *Structural Transformation of the Public Sphere: An Inquiry into a Category of Bourgeois Society*, trans. Thomas Burger and Frederick Lawrence (1962; Cambridge, Mass.: MIT Press, 1989), 175, 188, and 192; Habermas, *Structural*, 175. John Durham Peters, "Distrust of Representation: Habermas on the Public Sphere," *Media, Culture and Society* 15 (October 1993): 541–71, offers a probing analysis of the way Habermas, in *Structural Transformation* and in his later work, less than fully worked against Adorno and Horkheimer's negative views of mass media. A number of scholars have correctly noted that in this and other works of the period, Habermas also drew on conservative writers: see, for example, Thornhill, *Theory*, 135; Wiggershaus, *Frankfurt*, 538–40.

19. Habermas, *Structural*, 215, 179, 217, 169, and 161.

20. Wiggershaus, *Frankfurt*, 560; Habermas, *Structural*, 234–35 and 250. Around 1960, Habermas also began to publish a series of essays brought together in Jürgen Habermas, *Theory and Practice* [1963], trans. John Viertel (Boston: Beacon Press, 1973), in which he addressed many of the issues he discussed in *Structural Transformation*. Especially important on issues of work and leisure is chap. 6, "Between Philosophy and Science: Marxism as Critique," originally published around 1963. The footnotes for the 1973 English translation contain many references to works published between 1963 and the early 1970s, which makes it likely that the essay in translation was also revised. For this reason I have not relied on it for evidence of positions Habermas took in the early 1960s. For a summary of some of these essays, see Edgar, *Habermas*, 5.

21. Lizabeth Cohen, *A Consumer's Republic: The Politics of Mass Consumption in Postwar America* (New York: Alfred A. Knopf, 2003), 8–9.

22. Jürgen Habermas, "Consciousness-Raising or Redemptive Criticism: The Contemporaneity of Walter Benjamin [1972]," *NGC* 17 (Spring 1979): 41.

23. Roland Barthes, *Mythologies*, trans. Annette Lavers (1957; New York: Hill and Wang, 1972), and Roland Barthes, *The Eiffel Tower and Other Mythologies,* trans. Richard Howard (New York: Hill and Wang, 1997). From the vast literature on Barthes, I have benefited from reading Louis-Jean Calvet, *Roland Barthes: A Biography*, trans. Sarah Wykes (Bloomington: Indiana University Press, 1995); Jonathan Culler, *Roland Barthes* (New York: Oxford University Press, 1983); Michael Moriarty, *Roland Barthes* (Stanford, Calif.: Stanford University Press, 1991); George R. Wasserman, *Roland Barthes* (Boston: Twayne, 1981). Mike Gane and Nicholas Gane, eds., *Roland Barthes* (London: Sage, 2004), is a three-volume collection of essays on Barthes; vol. 2, pp. 45–144, offers essays that comment on *Mythologies*: especially useful are those by Peter Fitting, Steven Ungar, and Marianne DeKoven (who discusses Barthes in relationship to postmodernism). For a history of Paris in the immediate postwar period, one that mentions neither Barthes nor Sontag, see Rosemary Wakeman, *The Heroic City: Paris, 1945–1958* (Chicago: University of Chicago Press, 2009). For a later book on how the text provides erotic pleasure, see Roland Barthes, *The Pleasure of the Text*, trans. Richard Miller (1973; New York: Noonday Press, 1975).

24. Susan Sontag, preface to Roland Barthes, *Writing Degree Zero* (New York: Hill and Wang, 1968), vii; Barthes, quoted in Culler, *Barthes*, 22.

25. Barthes, *Mythologies*, 109, 113, 116, and 125; Roland Barthes, preface to the 1970 edition, in Barthes, *Mythologies*, 9 (emphasis in original). Barthes first read Saussure in the late 1940s or early 1950s: Calvet, *Barthes*, 94–95.

26. Barthes, *Mythologies*, 16. His essay on wrestling was published in *Esprit*, October 1952, and "The Writer on Holiday" in *France-Observateur*, September 1954. On French intellectuals responding to modernization, see Kristin Ross, *Fast Cars, Clean Bodies: Decolonization and the Reordering of French Culture* (Cambridge, Mass.: MIT Press, 1995), 4–7.

27. Barthes, *Mythologies*, 15.

28. Ibid., 31, 56, 15, and 84–85.

29. Ibid., 88 and 97; Dick Hebdige, "Object as Image: The Italian Scooter Cycle [1988]," in *The Consumer Society Reader*, ed. Douglas B. Holt and Juliet B. Schor (New York: New Press, 2000), 117.

30. Barthes, *Mythologies*, 38; Victoria de Grazia, *Irresistible Empire: America's Advance through Twentieth-Century Europe* (Cambridge, Mass.: Harvard University Press, 2005), 420.

31. Barthes, *Mythologies*, 59, 58, 61, 116, 140, 141, and 140 (emphasis in original). On the link between the colonization of everyday life and the decolonization of Algeria, see Ross, *Fast Cars*, 7.

32. Barthes, *Mythologies*, 11, 100–101, 75, and 123 (emphasis in original).

33. Ibid., 125 and 146; Roland Barthes, "Maîtres et esclaves," *Lettres nouvelles* (March

1953): 108, quoted in Culler, *Barthes*, 40. Among the reviews was one by Edward Said, *NYTBR*, July 30, 1972, 5. For a discussion of Barthes's politics, see Calvet, *Barthes*, 118–20. For the French reception, see Calvet, *Barthes*, 126–27.

34. Calvet, *Barthes*, 128 (on his trip to New York); Barthes, *Eiffel Tower*, 39–45 and 63–66 (on essays on American subjects in later edition). I am grateful to Judith Surkis for the suggestion that French writers assume problems came from elsewhere. Among the many works on French anti-Americanism, see Philippe Roger, *The American Enemy: A Story of French Anti-Americanism*, trans. Sharon Bowman (Chicago: University of Chicago Press, 2005); Ross, *Fast Cars*; Jean-Philippe Mathy, *Extrême Occident: French Intellectuals and America* (Chicago: University of Chicago Press, 1993); Richard F. Kuisel, *Seducing the French: The Dilemma of Americanization* (Berkeley: University of California Press, 1993); Denis Lacorne, Jacques Rupnik, and Marie-France Toinet, eds., *The Rise and Fall of Anti-Americanism: A Century of French Perception*, trans. Gerald Turner (Houndmills: Macmillan, 1990). Michel Winock, "The Cold War," 74–75, in Lacorne, Rupnik, and Toinet, eds., *Rise and Fall*, 74–75, discusses how positive the French response was to the American model.

35. Barthes, *Eiffel Tower*, 149, 151, and 152.

36. Roland Barthes, *Roland Barthes*, trans. Richard Howard (Berkeley: University of California Press, 1994), 45 (emphasis in original). Barthes wrote the entries in this book between August 8, 1973, and September 3, 1974.

37. Barthes, *Barthes*, 63 and 164 (emphasis in original); D. A. Miller, *Bringing Out Roland Barthes* (Berkeley: University of California Press, 1992), 6 and 31; Sontag, preface to Barthes, *Writing Degree Zero*, viii; Habermas, "Consciousness-Raising," 57. On Barthes's discretion about his sexuality, see, for example, Calvet, *Barthes*, 89 and 97. For some discussions of the relationships between Barthes's sexuality and his writings, see Graham Allen, *Roland Barthes* (London: Routledge, 2003), 98–99 and 106–7; Miller, *Bringing Out*; Harold Beaver, "Homosexual Signs (In Memory of Roland Barthes)," *Critical Inquiry* 8 (Autumn 1981): 99–119; Robert K. Martin, "Roland Barthes: Toward an 'Écriture Gaie,'" in *Camp Grounds: Style and Homosexuality*, ed. David Bergman (Amherst: University of Massachusetts Press, 1993), 282–98. For posthumous publications that were more revealing than what he wrote during his life, see Allen, *Barthes*, 149

38. Georges Perec, *Things: A Story of the Sixties*, trans. David Bellos (London: Collins Harvill, 1990), 42. On the relationship between Barthes and Perec, see David Bellos, *Georges Perec: A Life in Words* (London: Harvill, 1993), 95. Calvet, *Barthes*, 140–43, discusses the impact of *Mythologies*. On the acquisition of luxury goods as a mark of distinction, see Rosalind H. Williams, *Dream Worlds: Mass Consumption in Late Nineteenth-Century France* (Berkeley: University of California Press, 1982) and Debora Silverman, *Art Nouveau in Fin-de-Siècle France: Politics, Psychology, and Style* (Berkeley: University of California Press, 1989).

39. Perec, *Things*, 39; David Bellos, introduction to Perec, *Things*, 9 and 10. For the biography, see Bellos, *Perec*, esp. 315.

40. This summary of Barthes's relationship to Publicis relies on Cavet, *Barthes*, 141–43.

41. Umberto Eco, preface to *Misreadings*, trans. William Weaver (San Diego: Har-

court Brace, 1993), 1; Umberto Eco, "The Socratic Strip [1960]," in Eco, *Misreadings*, 28, 30, and 31. As was true with *Mythologies*, not all of the essays in the untranslated edition appeared in the translated one: compare Eco, *Misreadings*, with Umberto Eco, *Diario minimo* (Milan: Arnoldo Mondadori, 1963). In addition, although the 1963 book reproduces essays from *Il Verri* published between 1959 and 1963, *Misreadings* includes some of those, as well as essays published between 1964 and 1972.

    42. For biographical information on Umberto Eco, see http://www.themodernword. com/eco/eco_biography.html (accessed February 14, 2011). Peter Bondanella, *Umberto Eco and the Open Text: Semiotics, Fiction, Popular Culture* (Cambridge: Cambridge University Press, 1997), includes biographical information and offers a useful analysis in English of Eco's work, on which I have relied. Bondanella's book also contains a discussion of Eco as a postmodernist (xiii). Among the other useful commentators on Eco are Robert Lumley, introduction to Umberto Eco, *Apocalypse Postponed*, ed. Robert Lumley (Bloomington: Indiana University Press, 1994), 1–14; Norma Bouchard, "Eco and Popular Culture," in *New Essays on Umberto Eco*, ed. Peter Bondanella (Cambridge: Cambridge University Press, 2009), 1–16. Eco was one of the original members of Gruppo 63. The scholarship in English on Eco is not very extensive but often helpful: see, for example, David Robey, "Umberto Eco: Theory and Practice in the Analysis of the Media," in *Culture and Conflict in Postwar Italy: Essays on Mass and Popular Culture*, ed. Zygmunt G. Baranski and Robert Lumley (Houndmills: Macmillan, 1990), 160–77; David Robey, "Umberto Eco," in *Writers and Society in Contemporary Italy: A Collection of Essays*, ed. Michael Caesar and Peter Hainsworth (Leamington Spa: Berg, 1984), 63–87; Gary P. Radford, *On Eco* (Belmont, Calif.: Thompson/Wadsworth, 2003), esp. 39–43; Christine Ann Evans, "Eco's Fifth Column: The Critic of Culture within the Precincts of the Popular," in *Umberto Eco's Alternative: The Politics of Culture and the Ambiguities of Interpretation*, ed. Norma Bouchard and Veronica Pravadelli (New York: Peter Lang, 1998), 241–56. For a bibliography in Italian of Eco's works, see Patrizia Magli, Giovanni Manetti, and Patrizia Violi, *Semiotica: Storia, teoria, interpretazione* (Milan: Bompiani, 1992), 445–65. In English, see Bondanella, *Eco*, 200–212; Bondanella, ed., *New Essays*, 171–84, contains bibliographies of Eco's primary works and scholarship on him. Writing about Eco poses a series of challenges, among them the relative lack of secondary works on him in English; the fact that translations are often partial and in the case of his early writings on popular culture nonexistent; and Eco's own penchant for continually revising what he wrote, thus producing unstable texts. For a discussion of some of these issues, see Bondanella, *Eco*, xi–xvi. Although it is not clear how Eco's family responded to fascism, it is nonetheless useful to look at the experience of others of a somewhat older generation: see the essays on "The Fascist Past of Italian Intellectuals," *Telos* 139 (Summer 2007): 45–108.

    43. Umberto Eco, preface to *The Aesthetics of Thomas Aquinas*, trans. Hugh Bredin (Cambridge, Mass.: Harvard University Press, 1988), ix; the dating of this statement is uncertain, although it seems to appear for the first time in English in this 1988 preface. For one of Eco's discussions of his move away from fixed truths, see Eco, preface to *Aesthetics*, vii.

    44. Adam Arvidsson, *Marketing Modernity: Italian Advertising from Fascism to Post-*

modernity (London: Routledge, 2003), provides a discussion of the worlds in which Eco's writings took place. Michael Caesar and Peter Hainsworth, "The Transformation of Post-War Italy," in Caesar and Hainsworth, eds., *Writers*, 1–34, provides a useful discussion of the relationship between postwar economic changes and intellectual life.

45. Arvidsson, *Marketing*, esp. 67–89, discusses these changes. In English, the best discussion of both Milan's centrality in the new economy and the debates over the impact of consumer culture is John Foot, *Milan since the Miracle: City, Culture and Identity* (Oxford: Berg, 2001), esp. 1–3 and 19–36. Foot discusses the debates over the impact of popular culture on the working class, in full swing in the early 1970s, influenced particularly by the writings of Pier Paolo Pasolini and by empirical studies. He places Eco's discussion of apocalyptic opponents of mass culture in that context: Foot, *Milan*, 22, n. 9.

46. Francesco Alberoni, *Consumi e società* (Bologna: Il Mulino, 1964), 39, quoted in Arvidsson, *Marketing*, 108; Gerardo Ragone, "I consumi in Italia tra 'novità', 'distinzione', e qualità,'" in Aa. Vv., *La moda italiana: Dal antimoda allo stilismo* (Milan: Electa, 1987), quoted in Arvidsson, *Marketing*, 133.

47. In discussing the development of Eco's ideas, I am relying on Bondanella, *Eco*, 1–18; for a brief discussion of his 1954 essay that linked interest in detective stories and culture, see Peter Bondanella, "Eco and the Tradition of the Detective Story," in Bondanella, ed., *New Essays*, 91.

48. On Eco's pre-1956 publications concerning media, see Umberto Eco, "Problemi estetici del fatto televisivo," *Atti del III congresso internazionale di estetica* (Turin: Edizioni della Rivista di Estetixca, 1956). On the history of his engagement with popular culture, see Umberto Eco, "The Reactions of the Author: Now (1974 and 1977) [1977]," in Eco, *Apocalypse*, 51–57. On how other cultural critics responded to Americanization, see Lumley, introduction to Eco, *Apocalypse*, 2; Bondanella, "Detective Story," 91. On how writers incorporated popular culture, see Umberto Eco, "Reactions of Apocalyptic and Integrated Intellectuals: Then (1964) [1977]," in Eco, *Apocalypse*, 46. Although it is not always easy to date these essays with full confidence or to be sure that the English translations are the same as the original Italian version, I rely on the following texts: the essays in Eco, *Diario minimo*; Umberto Eco, "The Myth of Superman [1962]," first English publication in *Diacritics* 2 (Spring 1972): 14–22, and then printed, with some minor changes, in Umberto Eco, *The Role of the Reader: Explorations in the Semiotics of Texts* (Bloomington: Indiana University Press, 1979), 107–24; Umberto Eco, "Rhetoric and Ideology in Sue's *Les Mystères de Paris* [1965]," first published in English as "Rhetoric and Ideology in Sue's *Les Mystères de Paris*," *International Social Sciences Journal* 14 (1967): 551–69, and in a revised version in Eco, *Role*, 125–43; Umberto Eco, "Narrative Structures in Fleming [1965]," first published in English in Oreste del Buono and Umberto Eco, *The Bond Affair* (London: Macdonald, 1966), 35–75, and then published, with revisions, in Eco, *Role*, 144–72; Umberto Eco, "A Reading of Steve Canyon," published in Italian in Umberto Eco, *Apocalittici e integrati: Comunicazioni di massa e teorie della cultura di massa* (Milan: Bompiani, 1964), and first published in English in *Twentieth Century Studies* 15/16 (December 1976): 18–33; Umberto Eco, "The Structure of Bad Taste," published in *Apocalittici e integrati* and then in Umberto Eco, *The Open Work*, trans. Anna Cancogni (Cambridge, Mass.: Harvard University Press, 1989), 180–216; Umberto Eco, "Apocalyptic and Integrated intellectuals

[1964]," originally published in *Apocalittici e integrati* and then appearing in Eco, *Apocalypse*, 17–35; Umberto Eco, "The World of Charlie Brown [1963]," originally published as the introduction to the first volume of "Peanuts" cartoons, *Arriva Charlie Brown!*, and then in English in Eco, *Apocalypse*, 36–44. For his more theoretical works, I am relying on Umberto Eco, *Opera aperta: Forma e indeterminazione nelle poetiche contemporanee* (Milan: Bompiani, 1962), essays which appear in Eco, *Open Work*; and Eco, *Role*.

49. Eco, "Industry and Sexual Repression [1962]," in Eco, *Misreadings*, 71, 89, and 90.

50. Ibid., 90, 91, and 92–93.

51. Eco, "The End Is at Hand [1963]," in Eco, *Misreadings*, 111, 113, and 95–97 (emphasis in original).

52. Umberto Eco, "Apocalyptic and Integrated Intellectuals: Mass Communications and Theories of Mass Culture [1964]," in Eco, *Apocalypse*, 17–35. On Eco and McLuhan, see Eco, "Reactions of the Author: Now (1974 and 1977)," 55. It is unlikely that Eco had read this book of McLuhan's when he published *Apocalittici* in 1964; there is no evidence that Eco read McLuhan's *Mechanical Bride* (1951), a book in which McLuhan's position was more apocalyptic than integrated.

53. Eco, "Apocalyptic and Integrated," 18, 34, 25, 29, and 30.

54. Ibid., 18, 24, 22, 18, 23, 22, 30, 31, and 32 (emphasis in original).

55. Ibid., 27, 25–26, and 32.

56. Umberto Eco, "Verso una civiltà della visione," *Pirelli: Rivista e informazione* 1 (January 1961), quoted in Lumley, "Introduction," 2 ("revision"); Umberto Eco, "Form as Social Commitment," in Eco, *Open Work*, 131–32. Here Eco was summarizing a passage from a novel by Elemire Zolla, an influential Italian writer who opposed popular culture from a traditionalist position; what Zolla described as problematic, the erotic connection between a car and a person, Eco embraced.

57. Eco, "Commitment," 136, 150, and 156.

58. Umberto Eco, "Openness, Information, Communication," in Eco, *Open Work*, 51.

59. Umberto Eco, "The Poetics of the Open Work," in Eco, *Open Work*, 9 ("stances"); Umberto Eco, "Analysis of Poetic Language," in Eco, *Open Work*, 39 ("shifting" and "aesthetic"); Eco, "Openness, Information, Communication," 83 ("unable" and "liberating").

60. Eco, "Charlie Brown," 38, 39, and 36.

61. Umberto Eco, "The Phenomenology of Mike Bongiorno [1961]," in Eco, *Misreadings*, 156–64, with the quote on 158.

62. Umberto Eco, "Chance and Plot: Television and Aesthetics," in Eco, *Open Work*, 116 and 122.

63. Eco, "Socratic," 27 ("codified"); Eco, "Superman," 15 ("renders"); ibid., 20 and 21 ("scheme" and "circular"); ibid., 22 ("plot" and "concept"; emphasis in original). The contents page of Eco, *Role*, listed the essays on *Superman*, Fleming's novels, and Sue's stories as "closed": Eco, *Role*, v.

64. Eco, "Fleming," 58 ("foregone" and "geared") and 75 ("poetic").

65. Eco, "Fleming," 60 ("racialist"); Eco, "Fleming," 60 ("demand"); ibid., 62 ("modes"); ibid., 75 ("product"); Eco, "Superman," 14 ("satisfy"); ibid., 15 ("mediocre").

66. Umberto Eco, preface to *Art and Beauty in the Middle Ages* (New Haven, Conn.:

Yale University Press, 1986), x ("arguable"); Umberto Eco, "The Structure of Bad Taste," in Eco, *Open Work*, 194 ("intellectual") and 195 ("fetish"). Eco, "The Structure of Bad Taste," appeared in *Apocalittici e integrati*, published in Italian in 1964. However, the copyright page of *Open Work*, where the essay appears in translation, offers a more ambiguous dating (1962 or 1964): Eco, *Open Work*, iv. Eco shared some of Macdonald's concerns about midcult: Eco, "Structure of Bad Taste," 194.

67. Eco, "Structure of Bad Taste,"187 ("renewing"); 188–89 ("borrow"); 215 ("museum"); 216 ("mercenary").

68. Eco, "Superman," 16–18 (on Sartre and others) and ibid., 19 ("diffuse"); Eco, "Canyon," 26 and 32 ("conventional" and "intrinsic") and ibid., 30, 31, and 32–33 ("autonomous," "syntax," and "rules," emphasis in original). For a version of Eco's own relationship to consumer culture, in which he explores the contradiction between his opposition to war and his looking forward to buying toy guns for his son, see Umberto Eco, "Letter to My Son [1964]," in Eco, *Misreadings*, 117–25.

69. Eco, "Canyon," 32 ("legend"); Eco, "Charlie Brown," 38 ("Birch Society"); Bondanella, *Eco*, 56; Eco, "Superman," 21. This summary of Eco's politics emerges more clearly in David Robey, introduction to Eco, *Open Work*, xvi–xvii, than it does in Eco's own words.

70. On the 1969 volume, see Arvidsson, *Marketing*, 117; Romano Luperini, *Il Novecento: Apparati ideologici, ceto intelletuale, sistemi formali nella letteratura italiana contemporanea* (Turin: Loescher, 1981), 722 (for mentions of Eco in this book, see 724, 737, 877, 881, 885, and 896. I am grateful to Jim Hicks for translating this passage). Caesar and Hainsworth, "Transformation," 24, discuss Luperini's treatment of cultural critics. On Eco's discussion of advertisements, see Robey, "Umberto Eco: Theory and Practice," 172.

71. Umberto Eco, "The Death of Gruppo 63 [1969]," in Eco, *Open Work*, 247 and 237. In Italian the first version appeared in the periodical *Quindici*. The first English version appeared in *Twentieth Century Studies* 5 (September 1971): 60–71.

Chapter 3

1. In thinking about border crossing, I have benefited from reading a number of works, the most recent of which is Claudia Sadowski-Smith, *Border Fictions: Globalization, Empire, and Writing at the Boundaries of the United States* (Charlottesville: University of Virginia Press, 2008).

2. In terms of title, contents, and publication, this essay has a complicated history. In my discussion I have relied on the second version of Walter Benjamin, "The Work of Art in the Age of Its Technological Reproducibility," in Walter Benjamin, *The Work of Art in the Age of Its Technological Reproducibility and Other Writings on Media*, ed. Michael W. Jennings, Brigid Doherty, and Thomas Y. Levin; trans. Edmund Jephcott, Rodney Livingstone, Howard Eiland, and others (Cambridge, Mass.: Harvard University Press, 2008). This splendidly edited book makes it possible to understand the origin and nature of the ideas in Benjamin's "Work of Art" essay. Benjamin considered this the "master version": Michael W. Jennings, "The Production, Reproduction, and Reception of the Work of Art," in Benjamin, *Work of Art*, 17, n. 1. Benjamin wrote the first version in Paris in the

fall of 1935 and it was first published in May 1936. For the pressure that Max Horkheimer put on Benjamin to eliminate from this essay discussions of historical materialism and fascism, see Rolf Wiggershaus, *The Frankfurt School: Its History, Theories, and Political Significance*, trans. Michael Robertson (Cambridge: Polity Press, 1994), 210–12. For information on the fate of the essay, see editor's note at the end of Benjamin, "Work of Art," second version, in Benjamin, *Work of Art*, 42–43, and Hannah Arendt, "Introduction," in Walter Benjamin, *Illuminations*, ed. Hannah Arendt and trans. Harry Zohn (New York: Schocken Books, 1968), 52–53, n. 7.

3. The literature by and about Benjamin, even in English, is extensive. For my purposes, the most important writings by Benjamin are Walter Benjamin, *The Arcades Project*, trans. Howard Eiland and Kevin McLaughlin, prepared on the basis of the German volume edited by Rolf Tiedemann (Cambridge, Mass.: Harvard University Press, 1999), and Benjamin, *Work of Art*. Among the secondary works on which I have relied, in addition to the notes and introductions to the two volumes mentioned above, are Eugene Lunn, *Marxism and Modernism: A Historical Study of Lukács, Brecht, Benjamin, and Adorno* (Berkeley: University of California Press, 1982); http://www.wbenjamin.org/walterbenjamin.html (accessed February 14, 2011), a site that contains, among other things, a chronology of Benjamin's life and a bibliography of his works; http://www.iwbg.uni-duesseldorf. de/Wer_wir_sind_english (accessed February 14, 2011); David S. Ferris, ed., *The Cambridge Companion to Walter Benjamin* (Cambridge: Cambridge University Press, 2004), which includes (xi–xiv) a useful chronology of Benjamin's life; Bernd Witte, *Walter Benjamin: An Intellectual Biography*, trans. James Rolleston (Detroit: Wayne State University Press, 1991); Esther Leslie, *Walter Benjamin* (London: Reaktion, 2007). Vanessa Schwartz, "Walter Benjamin for Historians," *AHR* 106 (December 2001): 1721–43, is an invaluable essay, on which I have draw considerably. Hannah Arendt's introduction to *Illuminations* is a probing and insightful if not always dispassionate discussion of Benjamin's life and thought. On the history of Benjamin's relationship to the Frankfurt School, see Wiggershaus, *Frankfurt School*, 81–89, 161–64, 189–97, 201–18, and 310–12. On the Frankfurt School, including Benjamin's relationship to it, see Martin Jay, *The Dialectical Imagination: A History of the Frankfurt School and the Institute of Social Research, 1923–1950* (Boston: Little, Brown, 1973), 173–218. Among the many discussions of the relationship between Adorno and Benjamin is Susan Buck-Morss, *The Origin of Negative Dialectics: Theodor W. Adorno, Walter Benjamin, and the Frankfurt Institute* (New York: Free Press, 1977), 136–84.

4. Susan Sontag, "Under the Sign of Saturn [1978]," in Susan Sontag, *Under the Sign of Saturn* (New York: Farrar, Straus and Giroux, 1980), 111, with the quote from Walter Benjamin on his Berlin childhood on the same page; Arendt, "Introduction," 7. The collected works in English have begun to appear: Walter Benjamin, *Selected Writings*, ed. Marcus Bullock and Michael W. Jennings (Cambridge, Mass.: Harvard University Press, 1996–). For the debates over Benjamin's fate, and the memorialization of his life, see Leslie, *Benjamin*, 216–33.

5. Jürgen Habermas, "Consciousness-Raising or Redemptive Criticism—the Contemporaneity of Walter Benjamin [1972]," *NGC* 17 (Spring 1979): 30.

6. Walter Benjamin to Gershom Scholem, in Walter Benjamin, *Briefe*, ed. Theodor

W. Adorno and Gershom Scholem (Frankfurt: Suhrkamp, 1966), 373, quoted in Witte, *Benjamin*, 87.

7. Lunn, *Marxism*, 173; Arendt, "Introduction," 4 and 27. On Benjamin's radio programs, see Jeffrey Mehlman, *Walter Benjamin for Children: An Essay on His Radio Years* (Chicago: University of Chicago Press, 1993), and Susan Buck-Morss, *The Dialectics of Seeing: Walter Benjamin and the Arcades Project* (Cambridge, Mass.: MIT Press, 1989), 34–35. Before he departed from Paris in 1940, Benjamin left some of his work in his apartment (where the Gestapo confiscated it) and entrusted some of it, including material for *The Arcades Project*, to his friend Bataille, who worked at the Bibliothèque Nationale, where he kept the material secure. In 1947 Adorno obtained Benjamin's manuscripts for *The Arcades Project* but, unable to make sense of them, turned them over to his student Rolf Tiedemann, who edited and then brought them out in German in 1982.

8. Benjamin, *Arcades*, 171. On how Benjamin envisioned what he saw, see Michael W. Jennings, "Photography," in Benjamin, *Work of Art*, 265. In addition to works cited more generally, on *The Arcades Project* the best places to start are Benjamin, *Arcades*; Buck-Morss, *Dialectics of Seeing*; and Margaret Cohen, "Benjamin's Phantasmagoria: The Arcades Project," in Ferris, ed., *Benjamin*, 198–220.

9. Buck-Morss, *Dialectics of Seeing*, 39 (emphasis in original); Benjamin, *Arcades*, 464.

10. Arendt, "Introduction," 3; Walter Benjamin, 1930 letter, quoted in Howard Eiland and Kevin McLaughlin, "Translators' Foreword," in Benjamin, *Arcades*, x; Walter Benjamin, "Paris, Capital of the Nineteenth Century: Exposé," in Benjamin, *Arcades*, 14.

11. Benjamin, *Arcades*, 460 ("inventory"); Cohen, "Phantasmagoria," 210 ("fused"); Walter Benjamin, *The Correspondence of Walter Benjamin, 1910–1940*, ed. Gershom Scholem and Theodor W. Adorno, trans. Manfred R. Jacobson and Evelyn M. Jacobson (Chicago: University of Chicago Press, 1994), 509, quoted in a modified translation in Michael Jennings, Brigid Doherty, and Thomas Y. Levin, "Editors' Introduction," in Benjamin, *Work of Art*, 6 ("penetrated"; emphasis in original); Walter Benjamin, "Theses on the Philosophy of History," 1940, quoted in Howard Caygill, "Walter Benjamin's Concept of Cultural History," in Ferris, ed., *Benjamin*, 73 ("barbarism").

12. Arendt, "Introduction," 21; Benjamin, quoted in Arendt, "Introduction," 42; original is Walter Benjamin, *Gesammelte Schriften*, ed. Rolf Tiedemann and Herman Schweppenhauser (Frankfurt: Suhrkamp, 1972–89), 1: 416.

13. Sontag, "Saturn," 121; Schwartz, "Benjamin," 1727; Walter Benjamin, quoted in Rolf Tiedemann, "Dialectics at a Standstill: Approaches to the *Passagen-Werk*," in Benjamin, *Arcades*, 938. For Benjamin's use of Giedion, especially his *Building in France, Building in Iron, Building in Reinforced Concrete*, see Wiggershaus, *Frankfurt*, 203. On his use of commodity fetishism, see Benjamin, *Arcades*, 181.

14. Benjamin, *Arcades*, 80. I assume Benjamin's focus on the erotic was influenced to some degree by the work of his friend Georges Bataille.

15. Ibid., 61, including a quote from Baudelaire, *"My Heart Laid Bare" and Other Prose Writings*, trans. Norman Cameron (1950; New York: Haskell House, 1975), 156 ("intoxication"); Schwartz, "Benjamin," 1728 ("capitalism" and "potential"); Benjamin, *Arcades*, 460 ("expression"); Buck-Morss, *Dialectics of Seeing*, 23. Especially important in his mak-

ing a connection between surrealism and the pleasure of commerce is Walter Benjamin, "Dream Kitsch: Gloss on Surrealism," in Benjamin, *Work of Art*, 236–39, and Brigid Doherty, "Painting and Graphics," in Benjamin, *Work of Art*, 202.

16. Walter Benjamin, quoted in Jay, *Dialectical*, 200; original is Benjamin, *Briefe*, 2: 524 ("theological"); Moritz Goldstein, "Deutsch-jüdischer Parsnass" (German-Jewish Parnassus), in *Der Kunstwart*, 1912, quoted in Arendt, "Introduction," 31 ("unrequited"); ibid., 32 ("denial"); Goldstein, "Deutsch," 283, quoted in Anson Rabinbach, "Between Enlightenment and Apocalypse: Benjamin, Bloch and Modern German Jewish Messianism," *NGC* 34 (Winter 1985): 92 ("denies"), 78–124 ("Messianism"), and 121 ("Messianic"). For another take on Benjamin's outlook, including the influence of Jewish messianism, see Michael Löwy, *Redemption and Utopia: Jewish Libertarian Thought in Central Europe: A Study in Elective Affinity*, trans. Hope Heaney (1988; Stanford, Calif.: Stanford University Press, 1992), 95–126.

17. Walter Benjamin, "Reflections on Broadcasting," in Benjamin, *Schriften*, 2: 1506, 638 ff., quoted in Witte, *Benjamin*, 121.

18. Benjamin, "Work of Art," 22 and 23. On how Benjamin and Adorno wrestled with the concept of authenticity, see Martin Jay, "Taking on the Stigma of Inauthenticity: Adorno's Critique of Genuineness," *NGC* 97 (Winter 2006): 15–30.

19. Benjamin, "Work of Art," 24, 21, and 22 (emphasis in original).

20. Ibid., 31, 28, 26, and 45, n. 11 (emphases in original).

21. Ibid., 34.

22. Ibid., 33–34, 36, 40, and 37 (emphasis in original).

23. Ibid., 33–34.

24. Ibid., 22, 33, and 34.

25. The quotes are from ibid., 20 (emphasis in original). The discussion of the politics of Benjamin and the Institute comes from Jay, *Dialectical*, 211. On the debates between Benjamin and Adorno, see Buck-Morss, *Negative Dialectics*, 146–50. What Adorno found especially problematic about Benjamin's 1935 essay was his discussion of aura: Adorno saw art for art's sake or autonomous art as standing in opposition to mass culture and fascism, while Benjamin asserted that the destruction of the aura undermined the notion of pure art and made way for an antifascist mass culture. On Benjamin's response to the Soviet Union, see Walter Benjamin, *Moscow Diary*, ed. Gary Smith, trans. Richard Sieburth (Cambridge, Mass.: Harvard University Press, 1986).

26. Benjamin, "Work of Art," 31 and 38 (emphasis in original). Thomas Y. Levin, "Film," in Benjamin, *Work of Art*, 315–22, offers a suggestive analysis of Benjamin's discussion of cinema.

27. Benjamin, "Work of Art," 38 ("sadistic," "laughter," and "release"; emphasis in original); Madame de Duras, quoted at the head of ibid., 19 ("false"); Benjamin, *Arcades*, 395. See also Walter Benjamin, "Mickey Mouse [1931]," in Benjamin, *Work of Art*, 338–39.

28. Benjamin, "Work of Art," 42; Jay, *Dialectical*, 205. Leslie, *Benjamin*, 166, discusses some of the changes Horkheimer persuaded a reluctant but financially dependent Benjamin to accept.

29. C. L. R. James, *Beyond a Boundary* (1963; New York: Pantheon, 1983); Paul Gilroy,

The Black Atlantic: Modernity and Double Consciousness (Cambridge, Mass.: Harvard University Press, 1993).

30. "C. L. R." stood for "Cyril Robert Lionel." Among what I have found most useful in the vast literature on James are Kent Worcester, *C. L. R. James: A Political Biography* (Albany: State University of New York Press, 1996); Anna Grimshaw, ed., *The C. L. R. James Reader* (Oxford: Blackwell, 1992), including the introduction ("C. L. R. James: A Revolutionary Vision for the Twentieth Century," 1–22) and bibliography (426–44); Paul Buhle, *C. L. R. James: The Artist as Revolutionary* (London: Verso, 1988); Paul Buhle, introduction to C. L. R. James, *State Capitalism and World Revolution*, written in collaboration with Raya Dunayevskaya and Grace Lee (Chicago: Charles H. Kerr, 1986), xi–xxii; Richard H. King, *Race, Culture, and the Intellectuals, 1940–1970* (Washington, D.C.: Woodrow Wilson Center Press, 2004), 199–200 and 215–38; Justin Jackson, paper on C. L. R. James and Stuart Hall, history seminar, University of Massachusetts, Amherst, Spring 2006, copy in author's possession; Brian Alleyne, "Cultural Politics and Globalized Infomedia: C. L. R. James, Theodor Adorno and Mass Culture Criticism," *Interventions: International Journal of Postcolonial Studies* 1 (1999): 361–72; Grant Farred, ed., *Rethinking C. L. R. James* (Cambridge, Mass.: Blackwell, 1996); Darrell E. Levi, "C. L. R. James: A Radical West Indian Vision of American Studies," *AQ* 43 (September 1991): 486–501; Scott McLemee and Paul Le Blanc, eds., *C. L. R. James and Revolutionary Marxism: Selected Writings of C. L. R. James, 1939–1949* (Atlantic Highlands, N.J.: Humanities Press, 1994); Aldon Lynn Nielsen, *C. L. R. James: A Critical Introduction* (Jackson: University Press of Mississippi, 1997); Stuart Hall, "A Conversation with C. L. R. James," in Farred, ed., *Rethinking*, 14–44; Stuart Hall, "C. L. R. James: A Portrait," in *C. L. R. James's Caribbean*, ed. Paget Henry and Paul Buhle (Durham, N.C.: Duke University Press, 1992), 3–16; Michelle Ann Stephens, *Black Empire: The Masculine Global Imaginary of Caribbean Intellectuals in the United States, 1914–1962* (Durham, N.C.: Duke University Press, 2005), 205–40; Grant Farred, *What's My Name? Black Vernacular Intellectuals* (Minneapolis: University of Minnesota Press, 2003), 95–148. Farrukh Dhondy, *CLR James* (London: Weidenfeld and Nicolson, 2001), contains a good deal of information (much of it about James's personal life) and documentation not available elsewhere but suffers from inadequate evidence about the sources on which it relies. For some of what James wrote on popular culture after *American Civilization*, see C. L. R. James, ["Superman and the A Bomb]," c. 1955, folder titled "Superman and the A Bomb," box 9, CLRJ-CU; C. L. R. James, *The Nobbie Stories for Children and Adults*, ed. Anna Grimshaw (Lincoln: University of Nebraska Press, 2006), 17–19.

31. On the alternate title, see Anthony Bogues, *Caliban's Freedom: The Early Political Thought of C. L. R. James* (Chicago: Pluto Press, 1997), 134. In addition to the discussions of *American Civilization* in the sources on James cited above, several essays are notably helpful in understanding its importance: Andrew Ross, "Civilization in One Country? The American James," in Farred, *Rethinking*, 75–84; Neil Larsen, "Negativities of the Popular: C. L. R. James and the Limits of 'Cultural Studies,'" in Farred, ed., *Rethinking*, 85–102; Anna Grimshaw and Keith Hard, "*American Civilization*: An Introduction," in C. L. R. James, *American Civilization* [1950], ed. Anna Grimshaw and Keith Hart (Cam-

bridge, Mass.: Blackwell, 1993), 1–25; Robert A. Hill, "Literary Executor's Afterword," in James, *American Civilization*, 293–366.

32. The quote is from Levi, "James," 487. On his choice of the team to join, see James, *Boundary*, 55–59. C. L. R. James, *Cricket*, ed. Anna Grimshaw (London: Allison and Busby, 1986), contains many of the articles on the sport that he wrote for newspapers. See also Neil Lazarus, "Cricket and National Culture in the Writings of C. L. R. James," in *C. L. R. James's Caribbean*, ed. Paget Henry and Paul Buhle (Durham, N.C.: Duke University Press, 1992), 92–110. While still in Trinidad, James made a decision that he regarded as momentous, joining a cricket club whose members were brown skinned and middle class rather than one whose members were from the black lower middle class, while not even thinking of joining one whose members were even lower in the social order: Grant Farred, "The Maple Man: How Cricket Made a Postcolonial Intellectual," in Farred, ed., *Rethinking*, 166–86.

33. Hall, "C. L. R. James: A Portrait," 5; James, *Boundary*, 71.

34. C. L. R. James, *Minty Alley* (London: Secker and Warburg, 1936); C. L. R. James, *The Life of Captain Cipriani: An Account of British Government in the West Indies* (Nelson: Coulton, 1932).

35. C. L. R. James, *The Black Jacobins: Toussaint L'Ouverture and the San Domingo Revolution* (London: Secker and Warburg, 1938).

36. James, "A Conversation with C. L. R. James," 28 ("complete"); C. L. R. James, "Fraternity," *Workers Party Internal Bulletin*, November 12, 1940, 2, quoted in Worcester, *James*, 66 ("songbird"). In December 1939, he asked Constance Webb to "drop me a line c/o Dwight MacD": C. L. R. James to Constance Webb, December 12, 1939, in *Special Delivery: The Letters of C. L. R. James to Constance Webb, 1939–1948*, ed. Anna Grimshaw (Cambridge, Mass.: Blackwell, 1996), 62. For a sketch of the relationship between James and Macdonald, see Grimshaw, ed., *Special Delivery*, 386.

37. "Johnson" was the pseudonym for James and "Forest" for Raya Dunayevskaya. Grace Lee, another key member of the Tendency, discovered Marx's 1844 writings when she read Herbert Marcuse's *Reason and Revolution: Hegel and the Rise of Social Theory* (New York: Oxford University Press, 1941): Hill, "Literary Executor's," 313. For a picture of the Tendency and how fully it involved participation by workers in discussion of philosophical issues, see Grace Lee Boggs, "Thinking and Acting Dialectically: C. L. R. James, the American Years," *Monthly Review* 45 (October 1993): 38–46. Lee is critical of James for what she saw as his self-centeredness after 1952. For a discussion of James's theories of state capitalism, within the larger context of Marxist thought, see Christopher Phelps, "C. L. R. James and the Theory of State Capitalism," in *American Capitalism: Social Thought and Political Economy in the Twentieth Century*, ed. Nelson Lichtenstein (Philadelphia: University of Pennsylvania Press, 2006), 157–90.

38. C. L. R. James, "The Revolutionary Answer to the Negro Problem in the U.S. [1948]," in *C. L. R. James on the "Negro Question,"* ed. Scott McLemee (Jackson: University Press of Mississippi, 1996), 138–47, with the quote on 139. More orthodox Trotskyists did not accept the idea that the Russian Revolution had gone fundamentally wrong as

Communism devolved into a state capitalism; rather, they believed that the USSR was a degenerated workers' state.

39. On the marriage to Webb, see Worcester, *James*, 70. Grimshaw, introduction to *Special Delivery*, 17, notes that James treated the women in his life, including those he worked closely with in politics and writing, "as colleagues and collaborators (though he always sought to incorporate them into *his* vision of the world); at worst, he used them as domestic servants." Dennis Dworkin, "C. L. R. James in Nevada," *History Workshop Journal* 63 (Spring 2007): 90–112, provides a picture of James in 1948 that includes a discussion of his difficulties with intimacy.

40. Hall, "C. L. R. James: A Portrait," 15; Grimshaw, introduction, in Grimshaw, ed., *C. L. R. James Reader*, 12; C. L. R. James to [Daniel] Bell, June 1953, in Grimshaw, ed., *C. L. R. James Reader*, 220. For the Bell-James letter, the specific date is June 22, 1953: for the original, see C. L. R. James to [Daniel] Bell, June 22, 1953, folder 21, box 1, CLRJ-CU. James paid no attention to television in *American Civilization* but by 1953 was watching it avidly: James to Bell, 228–29. Unless otherwise noted, the references to this letter are to the shorter, published version. In mostly minor ways, Grimshaw edited the letter, without indicating where she made changes. Although James had often written of the enduring power of the puritanism he learned as a child, there is remarkably little of it in *American Civilization*; in his memoir, he defined puritanism not as moralism but in terms of self-restraint and an adherence to the rules: James, *Beyond*, 17, 35, 47, and 51.

41. James to Bell, 228; Anna Grimshaw, introduction to Grimshaw, ed., *Special Delivery*, 12; C. L. R. James to Constance Webb, [undated] 1944, in Grimshaw, ed., *Reader*, 138 (emphasis in original).

42. C. L. R. James to Constance Webb, September 1, 1943, in Grimshaw, ed., *Special Delivery*, 73 and 129; C. L. R. James to Constance Webb, [undated] 1943, in Grimshaw, ed., *Reader*, 131 (emphases in original).

43. James, *American Civilization*, 27, 40, and 44.

44. Ibid., 85; see also 156. In his discussion of antebellum writers, James was relying on F. O. Matthiessen, *American Renaissance: Art and Expression in the Age of Emerson and Whitman* (New York: Oxford University Press, 1941).

45. James, *American Civilization*, 166 ("horses"); James, *State Capitalism*, 41–42 ("pensions," "realm," and "weapon"); C. L. R. James, "Lenin on Agriculture and the Negro Question [1947]," in McLemee, ed., *C. L. R. James*, 133.

46. James, *American Civilization*, 116.

47. Ibid., 256 and 229–30. Elsewhere James remarked in 1947 on the bankruptcy of bourgeois "intellectuals who run to and fro squealing like hens in a barnyard when a plane passes overhead": C. L. R. James, "Dialectical Materialism and the Fate of Humanity [1947]," in Grimshaw, ed., *Reader*, 153.

48. James, quoted in Stephens, *Black Empire*, 226 (emphasis in original).

49. James, *American Civilization*, 210–11.

50. Ibid., 213, 221, and 215. In addition to his discussion of feminism, James also focused on homosexuality and intimacy among men: see ibid., 223–24.

51. Ibid., 81; see also 132–36 and 143. The index of the book, for which James was hardly responsible, contained no reference to the Marx Brothers; however, the index listing of "Marx, Karl" in one instance leads to a mention of the Marx Brothers: see 135 and 381.

52. Ibid., 119.

53. Ibid., 121; Ross, "Civilization," 78; James, *American Civilization*, 144. See also Michael Denning, *The Cultural Front: The Laboring of American Culture in the Twentieth Century* (London: Verso, 1996), 460–62.

54. James, *American Civilization*, 138.

55. Ibid., 127, 129, 146, 147, and 142. For his definition of the masses, see 136.

56. Ibid., 123, 122, 137, and 130. There were moments when James saw reciprocity operating most powerfully in the period before art became commercialized: for example, he talked of jazz as a form in which "a sensitive leader *caught the rhythm for the evening from the dancers*" (emphasis in original): see 137.

57. Ibid., 28; James to Bell, 228. In 1952, while he was detained on Ellis Island and facing deportation, James began writing a book on Herman Melville. It was published in 1953 and James sent copies to all members of Congress: C. L. R. James, *Mariners, Renegades and Castaways: The Story of Herman Melville and the World We Live In* (1953; Hanover, N.H.: University Press of New England, 2001). In this book, James protested state power over him and others and identified with the crew in Melville's novel: for a probing discussion of the book, see Donald E. Pease, introduction to James, *Mariners*, vii–xxxiii.

58. James to Bell, 222–23. In James to Bell, archival version, 6, he made clear that he supported public protests against the movie, a statement that the editor did not include in the published version.

59. Larsen, "Negativities of the Popular," 89; see also Worcester, *James*, 66–67.

60. James to Bell, 225, 226, 221, and 229. The quote about Armstrong's greatness appears in the archival version (p. 13) but not in the published one.

61. C. L. R. James, "Popular Art and the Cultural Tradition [1954]," in Grimshaw, ed., *Reader*, 247. Worcester, *James*, 134–37, is especially astute in discussing this essay. Nielson, *James*, 146, discusses James's skepticism that those who sponsored the conference, despite their promises to do so, would publish the essay.

62. For discussions of similarities between James and Benjamin, see Hill, "Literary Executor's," 358–40; Nielsen, *James*, 146–47; Ross, "Civilization," 78.

Chapter 4

1. Howard Brick, *Transcending Capitalism: Visions of a New Society in Modern American Thought* (Ithaca, N.Y.: Cornell University Press, 2006), 172. Riesman wrote the book, as the title page indicated, "in collaboration with" Reuel Denney and Nathan Glazer. Following widely accepted convention, I speak of Riesman as the author. For one of his many reconsiderations of what he tried to convey in the original edition, see David Riesman, preface to *The Lonely Crowd: A Study of the Changing American Character*, abridged ed. (New Haven, Conn.: Yale University Press, 1961), xi–xlviii. The original edition (cited in this chapter unless otherwise noted) is David Riesman, *The Lonely Crowd: A Study of*

the Changing American Character (New Haven, Conn.: Yale University Press, 1950). Well before Riesman did so, the anthropologist Franz Boas had appeared on the cover of *Time* in 1936.

2. Riesman wrote several autobiographical essays: David Riesman, "Becoming an Academic Man," in *Authors of Their Own Lives*, ed. Bennett M. Berger (Berkeley: University of California Press, 1990), 22–74; David Riesman, "A Personal Memoir: My Political Journey," in *Conflict and Consensus: A Festschrift in Honor of Lewis A. Coser*, ed. Walter W. Powell and Richard Robbins (New York: Free Press, 1984), 327–64; David Riesman, "On Discovering and Teaching Sociology," *Annual Review of Sociology* 14 (1988): 1–24. Among the secondary works I have drawn on are Neil McLaughlin, "Critical Theory Meets America: Riesman, Fromm, and *The Lonely Crowd*," *American Sociologist* 32 (Spring 2001): 5–26; Eugene Lunn, "Beyond 'Mass Culture': The Lonely Crowd, the Uses of Literacy, and the Postwar Era," *Theory and Society* 19 (February 1990): 63–86; Robert Genter, *Late Modernism: Art, Culture, and Politics in Cold War America* (Philadelphia: University of Pennsylvania Press, 2010), 73–89; Joseph Galbo, "From *The Lonely Crowd* to *The Cultural Contradictions of Capitalism* and Beyond: The Shifting Ground of Liberal Narratives," *Journal of the History of the Behavioral Sciences* 40 (Winter 2004): 47–76; and the following works by Wilfred M. McClay: "Fifty Years of *The Lonely Crowd*," *Wilson Quarterly* 22 (Summer 1998): 34–42; "The Strange Career of *The Lonely Crowd*: or, The Antinomies of Autonomy," in *The Culture of the Market: Historical Essays*, ed. Thomas L. Haskell and Richard F. Teichgraeber III (New York: Cambridge University Press, 1993), 397–440; "Where Have We Come since the 1950s? Thoughts on Materialism and American Social Character," in *Rethinking Materialism: Perspectives on the Spiritual Dimension of Economic Behavior*, ed. Robert Wuthnow (Grand Rapids, Mich.: William B. Eerdmans, 1995), 25–71; *The Masterless: Self and Society in Modern America* (Chapel Hill: University of North Carolina Press, 1994), esp. 233–61. For a bibliography of Riesman's work, see Herbert Gans et al., eds., *On the Making of Americans: Essays in Honor of David Riesman* (Philadelphia: University of Pennsylvania Press, 1979), 319–46. For essays on Riesman's work, see Seymour Martin Lipset and Leo Lowenthal, eds., *Culture and Social Character: The Work of David Riesman Revisited* (New York: Free Press, 1961), esp. Eric Larrabee, "David Riesman and His Readers," 404–16, and David Riesman, with the collaboration of Nathan Glazer, "*The Lonely Crowd*: A Reconsideration in 1960," 419–58. For a probing analysis, based on archival research, of how Riesman's work on *The Lonely Crowd* developed, see James Gilbert, *Men in the Middle: Searching for Masculinity in the 1950s* (Chicago: University of Chicago Press, 2005), 34–61; Rupert Wilkinson, "'The Lonely Crowd,' at 60, Is Still Timely," *Chronicle Review, Chronicle of Higher Education*, September 15, 2010. Rupert Wilkinson has in his possession (and has deposited in Riesman's papers at the Harvard archives) a summary of interviews and correspondence with Riesman from 1988 that is exceptionally rich, especially on the issue of Riesman's identity as a Jew, which the interview reveals as more significant than Riesman usually acknowledged.

3. Riesman, "Memoir," 357 ("sentiment"); ibid., 328 ("aesthete"); David Riesman to Marshall McLuhan, October 9, 1959, folder 71, box 34, MM-AC; David Riesman, "Culture: Popular and Unpopular," in David Riesman, *Individualism Reconsidered and Other*

Essays (Glencoe, Ill.: Free Press, 1954), 180 ("donnish"); Riesman, "Becoming," 66, fn. 7 ("Socialists"); Riesman, "Memoir," 335 ("debutante").

4. McClay, "Fifty," 39. For information on his clerkship with Brandeis, see Samuel J. Konefsky, unpublished interview notes with David Riesman, September 12, 1951, original in possession of Professor Alfred S. Konefsky, University of Buffalo Law School.

5. Leo Lowenthal, "The Triumph of Mass Idols [1943]," in Leo Lowenthal, *Literature, Popular Culture, and Society* (Englewood Cliffs, N.J.: Prentice Hall, 1961), 115, 129, 116, and 136. Among others who influenced Riesman were Hannah Arendt, Robert Merton, Paul Lazarsfeld, Paul and Percival Goodman, Martha Wolfenstein, Nathan Leites, and, of course, Karl Marx and Sigmund Freud. For discussions between Riesman and Arendt for four years beginning in 1947, on the topic of totalitarianism, see Peter Baehr, *Hannah Arendt, Totalitarianism, and the Social Sciences* (Stanford, Calif.: Stanford University Press, 2010), 35–61.

6. Erich Fromm, *Escape from Freedom* (New York: Holt, Rinehart and Winston, 1941), 67, 62, 68, 73, 134, and 258 (emphasis in original); Erich Fromm, *Man for Himself: An Inquiry into the Psychology of Ethics* (New York: Holt, Rinehart and Winston, 1947), 82; see also 84. On the influence of this book, see Genter, *Late Modernism*, 57–61. For the importance of Fromm's ideas to Riesman, see David Riesman, "From Morality to Morale," in *Personality and Political Crisis: New Perspectives from Social Science and Psychiatry for the Study of War and Politics*, ed. Alfred H. Stanton and Stewart E. Perry (Glencoe, Ill.: Free Press, 1951), 88; David Riesman, "The Saving Remnant: An Examination of Character Structure [1949]," in Riesman, *Individualism*, 99 and 117; McLaughlin, "Critical," 9. On Fromm as an émigré intellectual concerned with mass culture, see Andrew R. Heinze, *Jews and the American Soul: Human Nature in the Twentieth Century* (Princeton, N.J.: Princeton University Press, 2004), 272–73 and 278–84. More generally, for the influence of émigré intellectuals on Riesman, see McClay, *Masterless*, esp. 253–57. On Riesman's relationship with Fromm, see McLaughlin, "Critical," 5–26. Lawrence Friedman is working on a biography of Fromm that will explore, among other topics, Riesman's relationship with Fromm. As an undergraduate, Riesman developed a close relationship with another émigré, the historically oriented political scientist Carl Joachim Friedrich; eventually they bought a Vermont farm together.

7. McLaughlin, "Critical," 8, makes the point on how Riesman combined traditions.

8. Larrabee, "Readers," 406.

9. Lunn, "'Mass Culture,'" 66; McClay, "Fifty," 428–29; David Riesman to Cushing Strout, January 14, 1964, folder "TLC" [first of three so labeled], box 39, series 99.16, DR-HU.

10. Riesman, *Lonely*, 26 (emphasis in original).

11. McClay, "Fifty," 40, on how contemporaries read the book as "a great secular jeremiad *against* other-direction" (emphasis in original).

12. Ibid., 40; Riesman, *Lonely*, 35 and 350–51.

13. Riesman, *Lonely*, 174 ("snobbery"), 78 ("self-righteous"); Lunn, "'Mass Culture,'" 66, David Riesman, *Thorstein Veblen: A Critical Interpretation* (New York: Charles Scribner's Sons, 1953), 170, and McClay, "Where Have We," 44 (all three on aestheticism); David

Riesman, "The Themes of Work and Play in the Structure of Freud's Thought [1950]," in Riesman, *Individualism*, 328 and 332 ("sinful").

14. Riesman, *Lonely*, 341 (n. 9), 357, and 158–59.

15. Ibid., 359, 79–80; see also 85, 99, 101, and 111.

16. Ibid., 326–27, 341, 345, and 302–3; see also 348; McClay, "Fifty," 40; McClay, "Where Have We," 45 and 48. For a later statement of some of these themes, see Reuel Denney and David Riesman, "Roundtable: Leisure and Human Values in Industrial America," in *Creating an Industrial Civilization: A Report on the Corning Conference*, ed. Eugene Staley (New York: Harper and Brothers, 1952), 278–79.

17. Riesman, *Lonely*, 153–55 and 303.

18. Ibid., 156, 332, and 303.

19. David Riesman, statement in "Our Country and Our Culture," *PR* 19 (May–June 1952), 311–13. There is at least one relevant but oblique passage and accompanying footnote in which Riesman hinted at the reciprocal relationship between the media and its audiences and then mentioned Macdonald and Greenberg in the footnote: Riesman, *Lonely*, 99 and fn. 6. See also David Riesman, "Culture: Popular and Unpopular," in Riesman, *Individualism*, 180–81; David Riesman, "The Ethics of 'We Happy Few' [1947]," in Riesman, *Individualism*, 41.

20. Riesman, "Country," 311 ("constitute," "manipulated," and "meanings"; emphasis in original); David Riesman, "Listening to Popular Music," *AQ* 2 (Winter 1950): 361 ("purposes). In David Riesman and Evelyn T. Riesman, "Movies and Audiences," *AQ* 4 (Autumn 1952): 195–202, Riesman (and here his wife) struck the themes of reciprocity and critical resistance, as they identified the youthfulness of movie audiences. See also Riesman, "Roundtable," in Staley, ed., *Creating*, 59, 67, and 88; Riesman and Glazer, "Reconsideration," 454 and 458.

21. Riesman, "Music," 359; characteristically, a reader would not know from reading this article that Riesman was critiquing Adorno; T. W. Adorno, "A Social Critique of Radio Music [1945]," in *Reader in Public Opinion and Communication*, ed. Bernard Berelson and Morris Janowitz, enlarged ed. (Glencoe, Ill.: Free Press, 1953), 311 and 315. Riesman and Riesman, "Movies," 195–202; and Riesman, "Music," 359–71. In *Faces in the Crowd: Individual Studies in Character and Politics* (New Haven, Conn.: Yale University Press, 1952), written in collaboration with Nathan Glazer, Riesman presented and analyzed much of the material on which he had drawn in *The Lonely Crowd*. Many of these themes appear in the essays reprinted in Riesman, *Individualism Reconsidered*. Not normally given to humor in his writing, Riesman's hilarious spoof concerning how the dropping of nylon stockings on the Soviet Union might ease Cold War tensions still makes for compelling reading: David Riesman, "The Nylon War," *Common Cause* 4 (February 1951): 279–85.

22. Riesman, *Faces*, 81–269.

23. For his tendency to blur the lines between groups, see Riesman, *Lonely*, 13, 32, and 113; Brick, *Transcending*, 172

24. Riesman, *Lonely*, 303, 309, 331, 326 and 332–33; see also 302–3 and 330–34.

25. Betty Friedan, *The Feminine Mystique* (New York: W. W. Norton, 1963), 180; Bar-

bara Ehrenreich, *The Hearts of Men: American Dreams and the Flight from Commitment* (New York: Anchor Books, 1983), 32–35; Riesman, *Lonely*, 131. This discussion also draws on Jennifer Kalish, "Spouse-Devouring Black Widows and Their Neutered Mates: Postwar Suburbanization—A Battle over Domestic Space," *UCLA Historical Journal* 14 (1994): 128–54; K. A. Cuordileone, *Manhood and American Political Culture in the Cold War* (New York: Routledge, 2005), 105–10 and 118–21; Gilbert, *Middle*, 34–61.

26. Ehrenreich, *Hearts*, 35; Kalish, "Spouse," 129; Cuordileone, *Manhood*, 120–21; Gilbert, *Middle*, 37, 51, and 54. My own sense, from knowing Riesman in the mid to late 1960s, is that he was inner-directed in his ambition and other-directed in his possession of traits associated with the feminine, caring for others and with a finely tuned radar screen.

27. Riesman, *Crowd*, 36 and 112; Elizabeth Hardwick, "Riesman Considered," *PR* 21 (September–October 1954): 548–49. When he was working on the book, the four Riesman children, born between 1938 and 1943, were pre-teens.

28. This discussion of Riesman's politics relies on Riesman, "Memoir" and "Becoming." For his engagement with nuclear war, see, for example, David Riesman, "Individualism and Its Context," in Riesman, *Individualism*, 16. For a brief discussion of the roots of his ideas in the writings of Edmund Burke, see Riesman, *Faces*, 39, fn. 6.

29. Russell Kirk, "Return to Principle in Politics: Conservatives and Liberals Take Thought," *Southwest Review* 41 (Spring 1956): 149–51; Norman Mailer, "David Riesman Reconsidered," *Dissent* 1 (Autumn 1954): 349–50; Herbert Aptheker, "The Cadillac Credo of David Riesman [1955]," in *History and Reality* (New York: Cameron Associates, 1955), 76. Kirk's book is Russell Kirk, *The Conservative Mind in America, from Burke to Santayana* (Chicago: H. Regnery, 1953). Gentler than these reviews was the one by the social democrat Irving Howe, who, writing in the *Nation* in 1950, praised much of what Riesman wrote but criticized his view of the United States as a socially fluid and politically open society and cast a skeptical eye on his praise for the nation's popular culture: Irving Howe, review of *The Lonely Crowd*, *Nation*, December 2, 1950, 510–11. It must have pleased Riesman that Fromm found *The Lonely Crowd* "a significant book full of ideas, stimulating, and brilliantly written. . . . I am very glad about it," he continued, "in terms of what it means as a milestone in your own development. Looking back as both of us can, I hope you are just as pleased": Erich Fromm to David Riesman, December 8, 1950, folder "Lonely Crowd Correspondence" [third in a sequence so labeled], box 40, series 99.16, DR-HU.

30. Marshall McLuhan, *The Mechanical Bride: Folklore of Industrial Man* (New York: Viking Press, 1951), vi; Robert Fulford, "Meet France's Marshall McLuhan," *Toronto Star*, June 17, 1978, in *Letters of Marshall McLuhan*, ed. Matie Molinaro, Corrine McLuhan, and William Toye (Toronto: Oxford University Press, 1987), 539. On the meeting of Barthes and McLuhan in Paris in 1973, and discussion of a collaborative project, see Gary Genosko, "The Paradoxical Effects of *Macluhanisme*: Cazeneuve, Baudrillard, and Barthes [1994]," in *Marshall McLuhan: Critical Evaluations in Cultural Theory*, ed. Gary Genosko (London: Routledge, 2005), 241–52. On a comparison of Barthes and McLuhan, see Janine Marchessault, *Marshall McLuhan: Cosmic Media* (London: Sage, 2005), 48–55.

For his later books, see Marshall McLuhan *The Gutenberg Galaxy: The Making of Typographic Man* (Toronto: University of Toronto Press, 1962); Marshall McLuhan, *Un-*

derstanding Media: The Extensions of Man (New York: McGraw-Hill, 1964); and Marshall McLuhan and Quentin Fiore, *The Medium Is the Massage: An Inventory of Effects* (New York: Random House, 1967). In understanding McLuhan, I have benefited from reading two biographies: W. Terrence Gordon, *Marshall McLuhan, Escape into Understanding: A Biography* (New York: Basic Books, 1997), and Philip Marchand, *Marshall McLuhan: The Medium and the Messenger* (New York: Ticknor and Fields, 1998). Donald F. Theall, *The Virtual Marshall McLuhan* (Montreal: McGill-Queens's University Press, 2001), based on scholarship and personal experience, provides an especially probing treatment. Douglas Coupland, *Marshall McLuhan: You Know Nothing of My Work!* (New York: Atlas, 2010), is an idiosyncratic but suggestive book. For two collections of essays that appeared when McLuhan's influence was just past its highest point, see Raymond B. Rosenthal, ed., *McLuhan: Pro and Con* (New York: Funk and Wagnalls, 1968), and Gerald E. Stearn, ed., *McLuhan: Hot and Cool: A Primer for the Understanding of and a Critical Symposium, with a Rebuttal by McLuhan* (New York: Dial Press, 1967). For a later collection, see the three volumes of Genosko, ed., *McLuhan*. For a helpful work that relies on a thorough examination of McLuhan's papers (but pays little attention to *The Mechanical Bride*), see Andrew B. Chrystall, "The New American Vortex: Explorations of McLuhan," Ph.D. diss., Massey University, New Zealand, 2007. Among those who have written on McLuhan, there is a good deal of disagreement on his shifts in attitude to capitalism and popular culture: compare Marchand, *McLuhan*, 49, 69, 113, and 115; Jonathan Miller, *Marshall McLuhan* (New York: Viking Press, 1971); and Neil Compton, "The Paradox of Marshall McLuhan [1968]," in Rosenthal, ed., *McLuhan*, 106–24. For discussions of McLuhan's attitude to popular culture, see Patrick Brantlinger, *Bread and Circuses: Theories of Mass Culture as Social Decay* (Ithaca, N.Y.: Cornell University Press, 1983), 263–74; Judith Stamps, *Unthinking Modernity: Innes, McLuhan, and the Frankfurt School* (Montreal: McGill-Queen's University Press, 1995), esp. ix–xv and 97–121; Marchessault, *McLuhan*, esp. 45–72. See also Daniel J. Czitrom, *Media and the American Mind from Morse to McLuhan* (Chapel Hill: University of North Carolina Press, 1982), 147–82, including his probing reading of *The Mechanical Bride*.

31. Marchand, *McLuhan*, 28. For biographical information, I am relying on the Marchand biography and Molinaro, McLuhan, and Toye, eds., *Letters*.

32. Marshall McLuhan, diary entry, October 19, 1935, quoted in Molinaro, McLuhan, and Toye, eds., *Letters*, 7. For his statement of the importance of Leavis, Eliot, Pound, and Richards to his examination of media, see Marshall Mcluhan, foreword to *The Interior Landscape: The Literary Criticism of Marshall McLuhan, 1943–1963*, ed. Eugene McNamara (New York: McGraw-Hill, 1969), xiii–xiv. For an important letter on his conversion, one that contains some hints of the relationship between his Catholicism and his cultural criticism, see Marshall McLuhan to Elsie McLuhan (his mother), September 5, 1935, in Molinaro, McLuhan, and Toye, eds., *Letters*, 72–76. Throughout this section on McLuhan, as he does, I use the term "America" to refer to the United States. For the influence of Lewis Mumford's *Technics and Civilization* (1934), see Marchand, *McLuhan*, 77.

33. Marshall McLuhan to Corinne Lewis [January 21, 1939], in Molinaro, McLuhan,

and Toye, eds., *Letters*, 102–3 (emphases in original). On his money-making schemes, see Marchand, *McLuhan*, 92–110.

34. Czitrom, *Media*, 167; Marchand, *McLuhan*, 33. On his sense of threats to family life in the late 1930s, see Marchand, *McLuhan*, 55.

35. Marshall McLuhan, "G. K. Chesterton: A Practical Mystic," *Dalhousie Review* 15 (January 1936): 456 ("agriculture"); H. Marshall McLuhan, "Education of Free Men in Democracy: The Liberal Arts," *St. Louis University Studies in Honor of St. Thomas Aquinas* 1 (1943): 47 (on St. Thomas); Herbert Marshall McLuhan, "The Southern Quality of Life," *SwR* 55 (Summer 1947): 374, 383, and 382. For Chesterton's position on women and imperialism, see *What's Wrong with the World* (London: Cassell, 1910).

36. Marshall McLuhan, "Dagwood's America," *Columbia*, January 1944, quoted in Marchand, *McLuhan*, 74; Marchand, *McLuhan*, 86. On his college romance, see Marchand, *McLuhan*, 32. See also Ehrenreich, *Hearts*, 42–51

37. Marshall McLuhan, "Book Four: Sixty Million Mama Boys or Typhon," 33, folder 7, box 64, MM-AC. On his larger project, see W. Terrence Gordon, *McLuhan: A Guide for the Perplexed* (New York: Continuum, 2010), 70–83; Marchessault, *McLuhan*, 45–72; Chrystall, "McLuhan." MM-AC, box 63, contains material on "New American Vortex" and box 64 on "Typhon." Another title he used for the project was "Sixty Million Mama Boys": see McLuhan, "Book Four," 1. For the *Esquire* proposal, see Marchand, *McLuhan*, 74. On his proposal for formal education in media, see Marshall McLuhan, "A Strategy for an English School," no date, but probably late 1940s, folder 41, box 63, MM-AC; this was a response to F. R. Leavis, *Sketch for an English School* (London: Chatto and Windus, 1943).

38. McLuhan, "Southern Quality," 1–9 (on the bomb); McLuhan, "Know-How or Daedalus," in "Typhon," 48 ("Know-How"). This discussion draws on the following material by McLuhan in MM-AC: "The Southern Quality," folder 38, box 63, and on the contents of three folders which contain one version of the manuscript of "Typhon in America": folders 5, 6, and 7, box 64. In the notes I call these documents successively "Typhon" ("Typhon, or Guide to Chaos" in folder 5); "Atomic Power" and "Book Three" ("Book Three: Jitterbugs of the Absolute or Dionysus" in folder 6); "Book Four" ("Book Four: Sixty Million Mama Boys or Typhon" in folder 7). MM-AC, boxes 65–70, contain the materials and notes with which McLuhan built *The Mechanical Bride*, with many of his comments more biting and sarcastic than what he offered in the book; see, for example, materials in folder 7, box 66; folder 8, box 66; folder 31, box 70.

39. McLuhan, "Book Four," 62 ("subvert"; emphasis in original); ibid., 82 ("pursuits"); McLuhan, "Strategy for an English School," 1c ("zombies"). On the attempt to get published in leading New York periodicals, Felix Giovanelli to Marshall McLuhan, September 8 1948, folder 72, box 24, MM-AC. On McLuhan's ambitions for media education, see especially McLuhan, introduction to "Typhon," 1–6.

40. Marshall McLuhan, diary entry, March 26, 1930, quoted in Molinaro, McLuhan, and Hoye, eds., *Letters*, 3.

41. Ibid. ("generation" [ellipses in edited version, perhaps also in original]); Mar-

shall McLuhan, interview with Gerald Emanuel Stearn, *Encounter* 28 (June 1967): 50 ("approach").

42. On the influence of the Leavises on McLuhan, see McLuhan, Stearn interview, 51; Marchand, *McLuhan*, 41. For McLuhan's criticism of F. R. Leavis for what he saw as a failure to really look at ordinary aspects of contemporary culture, see Marshall McLuhan to Walter J. Ong and Clement J. McNaspy, December 23, 1944, in Molinaro, McLuhan, and Toye, eds., *Letters*, 166.

43. McLuhan, Stearn interview, 51 ("environment"); Wyndham Lewis, *Time and Western Man* (New York: Harcourt, Brace, 1928), 11 and 13. In *The Doom of Youth* (New York: Robert McBride, 1932), 145–241, Wyndham Lewis presented advertisements that illustrated the battle between the young and their elders; because of copyright restrictions, which McLuhan inexplicably bypassed, Lewis did not present either visual material or even full reproductions of print material. In *Hitler* (London: Chatto and Windus, 1931) Lewis hailed the German leader as a man of peace, a favorable view he retracted later in *The Hitler Cult* (London: Dent, 1939) and *The Jews, Are They Human?* (London: G. Allen and Unwin, 1939). On Lewis, see Andrea Freud Loewenstein, *Loathsome Jews and Engulfing Women: Metaphors of Projection in the Works of Wyndham Lewis, Charles Williams, and Graham Greene* (New York: New York University Press, 1993), 119–87.

44. Lewis, *Doom*, 206–11, with the quotes ("dependent") on 210–11; H. Marshall McLuhan, "Wyndham Lewis: Lemuel in Lilliput," in *St. Louis University Studies in Honor of St. Thomas Aquinas* 2 (1944): 71, n. 35 ("homosexuality"); Wyndham Lewis, *Doom*, 145–97.

45. McLuhan, "Lewis: Lemuel," 60, 63, 68, and 70.

46. Marshall McLuhan to J. Stanley Murphy, March 9, 1944, in Molinaro, McLuhan, and Toye, eds., *Letters*, 157 (on the focus on his course) ; McLuhan to Ong and McNaspy, December 23, 1944, 166 ("daily"); Marshall McLuhan to Ezra Pound, June 30, 1948, in Molinaro, McLuhan, and Toye, eds., *Letters*, 194 (on slide shows); editors, in Molinaro, McLuhan, and Toye, eds., *Letters*, 214, n. 1 ("restrained"); Marshall McLuhan to Ezra Pound, January 5, 1951, in Molinaro, McLuhan, and Toye, eds., *Letters*, 217.

47. Susan Sontag, preface to Roland Barthes, *Writing Degree Zero* (1953; New York: Hill and Wang, 1968), vii; McLuhan, *Mechanical*, vi. For a review of *Understanding Media* that includes a brief discussion of *The Mechanical Bride*, see Harold Rosenberg, "Philosophy in a Pop Key," *New Yorker*, February 27, 1965, 129–36.

48. McLuhan, *Mechanical*, 98–99.

49. Ibid., vi ("intelligible"); Marshall McLuhan to Felix Giovanelli, January 12, 1949, in Molinaro, McLuhan, and Toye, eds., *Letters*, 209 ("point"); McLuhan, *Mechanical*, v (Poe); Herbert Marshall McLuhan, "American Advertising," *Horizon* 93–94 (October 1947): 134–36 (in this essay, McLuhan was more critical of Madison Avenue than he was in *The Mechanical Bride*; for example, he pointed to the "totalitarian techniques of American market research": 136). On the attempt to get McLuhan published in *Commentary*, see Felix Giovanelli to Marshall McLuhan, September 8, 1948, folder 72, box 24, MM-AC. Giovanelli and McLuhan were discussing Harold Rosenberg, "The Herd of Independent Minds: Has the Avant-Garde Its Own Mass Culture?" *Co* 7 (September 1948): 244–52.

50. McLuhan, *Mechanical*, 59 and 66.

51. Ibid., 21–22 and 11.

52. Ibid., 115 and 117.

53. Ibid., v–vi, 10, 11, 21, 24, and 13.

54. Ibid., 3, 4, 34, 50, and 97. My interpretation of *The Mechanical Bride* both draws on and differs from that offered by Jonathan Miller, who sees more evidence than I of McLuhan's development of a full and complicated argument on how modern advertisements offered methods of resisting what they promoted: see, for example, Miller, *McLuhan*, 68–69. For an analysis of McLuhan's relation to modernism and postmodernism, see Glenn Willmott, *McLuhan, or Modernism in Reverse* (Toronto: University of Toronto Press, 1996); for his analysis of *The Mechanical Bride*, see 76–91 and 94–100.

55. McLuhan, *Mechanical*, v; David L. Cohn, review of *The Mechanical Bride*, *NYT*, October 21, 1951, 26; Rudolph E. Morris, review of *The Mechanical Bride*, *Renascence* (Spring 1952), reprinted in Stearn, ed., *McLuhan*, 78–82, with quote on 82. For more reviews, see folder 10, box 71, MM-AC. For review of a later book by McLuhan, which stated that he lacked "moralistic nattering," see Benjamin DeMott, review of Stuart Hall and Paddy Whannel, *The Popular Arts*, *Reporter*, October 21, 1965, 55.

56. McLuhan, *Mechanical*, 68 ("wedlock"); Compton, "Paradox," 112 ("Victorian"); McLuhan, *Mechanical*, 113 ("harmonious"), 134 ("push"), 21 ("noncommercial"), and 144 ("habits"); Howard Brick, *Age of Contradictions: American Thought and Culture in the 1960s* (New York: Twayne, 1998), 63.

57. Walter J. Ong, review of *The Mechanical Bride*, *Social Order* 2 (February 1952): 82–83. On McLuhan's relationship to Ong, see Marchand, *McLuhan*, 67, 116, 166, and 242. On how difficult it is to decipher his politics, see, for example, the passage that begins with "overlooks the fact that" and ends with "points the way to health": McLuhan, *Mechanical*, 22. On his antimodernism, see Mark Krupnick, "Marshall McLuhan Revisited: Media Guru as Catholic Modernist," *Modernism/Modernity* 5 (September 1998): 110.

58. Moira Roth, "The Aesthetics of Indifference," *Artforum* 16 (November 1977): 47; Compton, "Paradox," 107; Brick, *Contradictions*, 63. On the influence of Catholicism on McLuhan, see Marchessault, *McLuhan*, 5–6 and 35–39; Theall, *McLuhan*, 33; Marchand, *McLuhan*, 44–49.

59. McLuhan, "Lewis: Lemuel," 58 ("crave"); Marshall McLuhan to W. J. Ong, December 15, 1945, folder 22, box 33, MM-AC ("confront" and "front"). Here Kroker is relying on Marshall McLuhan, "Joyce, Aquinas, and the Poetic Process," *Renascence* 4 (Autumn 1951): 3–7. On the prejudice against Catholics in higher education, see John T. McGreevy, "Catholics, Catholicism, and the Humanities since World War II," in *The Humanities and the Dynamics of Inclusion since World War II*, ed. David Hollinger (Baltimore: Johns Hopkins University Press, 2006), 196 and 198. For the difference between his Catholicism in public and private, see Marchand, *McLuhan*, 51. Arthur Kroker, *Technology and the American Mind: Innis/McLuhan/Grant* (Montreal: New World Perspectives, 1984), 62, cogently makes the point about McLuhan's reliance on reason, citing the maelstrom metaphor that McLuhan used in *The Mechanical Bride*; Kroker's analysis, though quite ahistorical, is nonetheless penetrating. On the impact of Chesterton on McLuhan, see Marchand, *McLuhan*, 30. On the Catholic dimensions of McLuhan's approach, see also

Kroker, *Technology*, 85–86. Stamps, *Unthinking*, 98–99, discusses McLuhan's decision to suppress his religious identity and shows that indeed in the late 1960s and 1970s critics attacked him on religious grounds. For a later article on Lewis, see Herbert Marshall McLuhan, "Wyndham Lewis: His Theory of Art and Communication," *ShR* 4 (Summer–Autumn, 1953): 77–88. For his discussion of how he "deliberately" hid his religion, see Marshall McLuhan to Edward T. Hall, July 23, 1969, in Molinaro, McLuhan, and Toye, eds., *Letters*, 384.

60. Hugh Kenner to Marshall McLuhan, June 24, 1946, folder 1, box 28, MM-AC; Ong, review, 82; McLuhan, *Mechanical*, 97. This discussion of the impact of Catholicism on McLuhan relies heavily on Jeet Heer, "Catholicism, Mass Culture, Technology and Literary Modernism: The Intellectual Parameters of the McLuhan Circle," M.A. thesis, copy in author's possession, with the quote on p. 44. This probing and original essay explores a number of issues, including McLuhan's relationships with Walter Ong, Hugh Kenner, the Southern Agrarians, and the New York intellectuals. Some of this essay appears in http://www.jeetheer.com/culture/ong.htm (accessed February 11, 2011). As Heer makes clear, although Ong was McLuhan's student, in his work on popular culture in the immediate postwar world, McLuhan was also drawing on Ong's writings on popular culture. See also Jeet Heer, "Divine Inspiration: How Catholicism made Marshall McLuhan one of the twentieth century's freest and finest thinkers," *Walrus*, July/August 2011, http://www.walrusmagazine.com/articles/2011.07–media-divine-inspiration/1/ (accessed June 24 2011). See also Marshall McLuhan, *The Medium and the Light: Reflections on Religion and the Media*, ed. Eric McLuhan and Jacek Szlkarek (Eugene, Ore.: Wipf and Stock, 2010).There is an abundant literature on the history of Roman Catholicism in North America, but little of it sheds any but the most indirect light on how McLuhan responded to popular culture. Among the good places to begin are John T. McGreevy, *Catholicism and American Freedom: A History* (New York: W. W. Norton, 2003), 189–215, and Gerald A. McCool, S.J., *From Unity to Pluralism: The Internal Evolution of Thomism* (New York: Fordham University Press, 1989). On the more general link between antimodernism and modernity, see T. J. Jackson Lears, *No Place of Grace: Antimodernism and the Transformation of American Culture, 1880–1920* (New York: Pantheon, 1981), xiv–xvii.

61. John Kenneth Galbraith, quoted in Studs Terkel, *"The Good War": An Oral History of World War Two* (New York: Pantheon, 1984), 323. The discussion of consumer culture in Canada relies on Joy Parr, *Domestic Goods: The Material, the Moral, and the Economic in the Postwar Years* (Toronto: University of Toronto Press, 1999), 22–39, 64, and 270; Doug Owram, *Born at the Right Time: A History of the Baby-Boom Generation* (Toronto: University of Toronto Press, 1996), 88. In *Becoming Myself: A Memoir* (Toronto: Stoddart, 1996), 24, Maria Tippett reveals how compelling she found the popular culture of the United States when she was a teen and young adult (43 and 73); how bland she found Canadian culture (77); and how European culture remained something she sought (89–90). Viv Nelles has helped me understand Canadian politics and intellectual traditions: Viv Nelles, email to Daniel Horowitz, August 14, 2006, copy in author's possession. For a discussion of how being a Canadian affected McLuhan's work, see Marchessault, *McLuhan*, esp. 4–6. The relationship between the work of McLuhan and Harold Innis is important.

Daniel Czitrom has McLuhan reading Innis earlier than he actually did: Czitrom, *Media*, 147, 166, and 173. On McLuhan and Innis, see Alexander John Watson, *Marginal Man: The Dark Vision of Harold Innis* (Toronto: University of Toronto Press, 2006), 405; Graeme H. Patterson, *History and Communications: Harold Innis, Marshall McLuhan, the Interpretation of History* (Toronto: University of Toronto Press, 1990), 29.

62. Peter Jackson and Nigel Thrift, "Geographies of Consumption," in *Acknowledging Consumption*, ed. Daniel Miller (London: Routledge, 1995), 230, quoted in Parr, *Domestic*, 267. On some dimensions of Canadian anti-Americanism, see Joseph Barber, *Good Fences Make Good Neighbors: Why the United States Provokes Canadians* (Indianapolis: Bobbs-Merrill, 1958), 36–37, 72–73, and 82–83; J. L. Granatstein, *Yankee Go Home? Canadians and Anti-Americanism* (Toronto: HarperCollins, 1996).

63. See, for example, Tom Dilworth, "McLuhan as Medium," in *At the Speed of Light There Is Only Illumination: A Reappraisal of Marshall McLuhan*, ed. John Moss and Linda M. Morra (Ottawa: University of Ottawa Press, 2004), 38–39; Kroker, *Technology*, 7–8. Kroker, *Technology*, 82, argues (mostly in reference to the 1960s) that McLuhan looked southward to the United States "with no sign of disaffection." For an exploration of American-Canadian relations, one that focuses on trade and diplomacy but has some astute observations about popular culture, see Miriam Chapin, *Contemporary Canada* (New York: Oxford University Press, 1959), esp. 3, 170–73, 267, and 301–2.

64. Donald Creighton, *Canada's First Century, 1867–1967* (Toronto: Macmillan of Canada, 1970), 269; see also 285 and 352–53. For other relevant works, see Donald Creighton, *The Forked Road: Canada 1939–1957* (Toronto: McClelland and Stewart, 1976), 126 and 260; John Farthing, *Freedom Wears a Crown* (Toronto: Kingswood House, 1957), 8–9; W. L. Morton, *The Canadian Identity* (Madison: University of Wisconsin Press, 1961), vii, 58, 80–87, and 108–114; Daniel Drache, "Harold Innis: A Canadian Nationalist," *Journal of Canadian Studies* 4 (May 1969): 7–12. For the economic background, see Parr, *Domestic*, 76. See also Donald Wright, "Reflections on Donald Creighton and the Appeal of Biography," *Journal of Historical Biography* 1 (Spring 2007): 15–26.

65. Royal Commission on National Development in the Arts, Letters and Sciences, *Report*, 19 and 40–41, quoted in Carl Berger, *The Writing of Canadian History: Aspects of English-Canadian Historical Writing, 1900–1970* (Toronto: Oxford University Press, 1976), 179; this commission was known as the Massey Commission after its chair, Vincent Massey. Berger, *Writing*, 180, links this report to McLuhan's *The Mechanical Bride* as criticisms of popular culture. Czitrom, *Media*, 222, n. 19, mentions how antipathy to the impact of American communications on Canada was a major theme in the Massey report. For an exploration of the differences between American and Canadian values, see Robert Babe, *Canadian Communication Thought: Ten Foundational Writers* (Toronto: University of Toronto Press, 2000), 23–30. George Grant offered the strongest arguments along these lines, but well after the publication of *The Mechanical Bride*. See George Grant, *Lament for a Nation: The Defeat of Canadian Nationalism* (Princeton, N.J.: D. Van Nostrand, 1965), 4, 9, 54, 76, 90, and 97. For a discussion of Grant's importance, see Ramsay Clark, *The Maple Leaf Forever: Essays on Nationalism and Politics in Canada*, rev. ed. (Toronto: Macmillan of Canada, 1977), 45–66.

66. Herbert Marshall McLuhan, review of W. J. Cash, *The Mind of the South*, *ShR* 5 (Summer 1957): 83.

67. Marshall McLuhan, "The *Playboy* Interview with Marshall McLuhan," *Playboy*, March 1969, 74; Marchand, *McLuhan*, 119. For a rich, suggestive, and nonmoralistic essay, see Marshall McLuhan, "The Age of Advertising," *Commonweal* 58 (September 11, 1953): 555–57.

68. This summary relies on McLuhan, *Gutenberg Galaxy*; McLuhan, *Understanding Media*; and McLuhan and Fiore, *The Medium Is the Massage*. Many scholars now see more consistency than change in McLuhan's outlook over time as they have cast doubt on whether his later work was more celebratory than critical: Marchessault, *McLuhan*, 68.

69. McLuhan, *Gutenberg*, 250.

70. Ibid., 269, 276, and 277. From 1953 to 1959, McLuhan co-edited *Explorations*, whose subscribers included Roland Barthes and Susan Sontag, and Riesman among its contributors: Babe, *Communications*, 269.

71. McLuhan, *Medium*, 150 ("amusement"), and McLuhan, *Mechanical*, v ("whirl"); Richard Hoggart, "Marshall McLuhan and Making Choices [1964]," in *Speaking to Each Other: Essays by Richard Hoggart*, ed. Richard Hoggart (New York: Oxford University Press, 1970), 1: 115–16 (emphasis in original).

72. McLuhan, *Mechanical*, 22. On McLuhan's involvement with commercial promotions of his ideas, see Miller, *McLuhan*, 69; Gordon, *McLuhan: Escape*, 168–71, 207–9, 215–17, 225–27, 241, and 268–89; Marchand, *McLuhan*, 3, 109–10, 149, 161, 182–83, 185, 195, and 209–10.

73. Tom Wolfe, "Suppose He Is What He Sounds Like, the Most Important Thinker since Newton, Darwin, Freud, Einstein, and Pavlov, What If He Is Right?" *New York Herald Tribune*, 1965, www.digitallantern.net/mcluhan/course/spring96/wolfe.html (accessed February 15, 2011).

74. Wolfe, "Suppose" (emphasis in original).

75. Ibid. (emphasis in original); Czitrom, *Media*, 182 (emphasis in original). For McLuhan's response, see Marshall McLuhan, "Sheep in Wolfe's Clothing," *Culture Is Our Business* (New York: McGraw-Hill, 1970), 212–13. In 1996, Wolfe wrote, narrated, and hosted a six-part television series called *The Video McLuhan* (Toronto: McLuhan Productions, 1996), six videocassettes. In tape 1, Wolfe talked of McLuhan's *The Mechanical Bride*.

76. Marianne DeKoven, "Modern Mass to Postmodern Popular in Barthes's Mythologies," *Raritan* 18 (1998), quoted in *Roland Barthes*, ed. Mike Gane and Nicolas Gane (London: Sage, 2004), 116.

77. Susan Sontag, "Remembering Barthes [1980]," in *Under the Sign of Saturn* (New York: Farrar, Straus and Giroux, 1980), 173.

78. Bernard Rosenberg, "Mass Culture Revisited [1968]," in *Mass Culture Revisited*, ed. Bernard Rosenberg and David Manning White (New York: Van Nostrand Reinhold, 1971), 3–4; Thomas C. Frank, *The Conquest of Cool: Business Culture, Counterculture, and the Rise of Hip Consumerism* (Chicago: University of Chicago Press, 1997). In *McLuhan*, 47, Marchessault calls *The Mechanical Bride* "an early cultural studies text."

79. Marshall McLuhan, "Sight, Sound, and the Fury [1954]," 495, in *Mass Culture*, ed. Rosenberg and White.

Chapter 5

1. Richard Hoggart, *The Uses of Literacy: Aspects of Working-Class Life with Special Reference to Publications and Entertainments* (London: Chatto and Windus, 1957); unless otherwise noted, pages cited are from this edition. The first American edition is Richard Hoggart, *The Uses of Literacy: Changing Patterns in English Mass Culture* (Fair Lawn, N.J.: Essential Books, 1957). Among the writings on Hoggart on which I have drawn are Ellen McClure, "Beyond Gramsci: Richard Hoggart's Neglected Contributions to the British New Left," *Disposito/n* 21 (1996): 21–30; Eugene Lunn, "Beyond 'Mass Culture': The Lonely Crowd, the Uses of Literacy, and the Postwar Era," *Theory and Society* 19 (February 1990): 63–86; Melissa Gregg, "A Neglected History: Richard Hoggart's Discourse of Empathy," *Rethinking History* 7 (November 2003): 285–306; Andrew Goodwin, "Introduction to the Transaction Edition: The Uses and Abuses of In-Discipline," in Andrew Goodwin, *The Uses of Literacy* (New Brunswick, N.J.: Transaction, 1998), xiii–xxxix; John Corner and Richard Hoggart, "Postscript: Studying Culture—Reflections and Assessments: An Interview with Richard Hoggart," in *Uses*, Transaction edition, 269–84; Susan M. Brook, *Literature and Cultural Criticism in the 1950s: The Feeling Male Body* (Houndmills: Palgrave Macmillan, 2007), 22–27. In April 2006, the University of Sheffield hosted an international conference on Hoggart's work. Some of the papers appeared in the Sue Owen and John Hartley, eds., special issue of *IJCS* 10 (March 2007); in addition, see Sue Owen, ed., *Richard Hoggart and Cultural Studies* (London: Palgrave Macmillan, 2008), and Sue Owen, ed., *Re-Reading Richard Hoggart: Life, Literature, Language, Education* (Newcastle: Cambridge Scholars, 2008). The three volumes of Hoggart's autobiography are brought together in Richard Hoggart, *A Measured Life: The Times and Places of an Orphaned Intellectual* (New Brunswick, N.J.: Transaction, 1994), as follows: *A Local Habitation: 1918–1940* (London: Chatto and Windus, 1988); *A Sort of Clowning: 1940–1959* (London: Chatto and Windus, 1990); *An Imagined Life: 1959–1991* (London: Chatto and Windus, 1992). For a discussion of the changes the lawyers for the publisher, fearing a libel case, forced Hoggart to make (including dropping the original title of "The Abuse of Literacy"), see Sue Owen, "*The Abuse of Literacy* and the Feeling Heart: The Trials of Richard Hoggart," *Cambridge Quarterly* 34 (2005): 147–76. For his classic statement on the special qualities of fine literature and the importance of applying literary analysis to a variety of texts, see Richard Hoggart, "Literature and Society," *American Scholar* 35 (Spring 1966): 277–89. As early as 1961, Hoggart used the phrase "cultural studies" to characterize the work he was doing: Richard Hoggart to [Terrence] Spencer, May 16 [1961], 4/2/54, RH-S. On postwar Britain, in addition, to sources cited elsewhere in this chapter, see Robert Hewison, *In Anger: British Culture in the Cold War, 1945–60* (New York: Oxford University Press, 1981), and Stefan Collini, *Absent Minds: Intellectuals in Britain* (Oxford: Oxford University Press, 2006). On the broader historical background, see John Benson, *The Rise of Consumer Society in Britain, 1880–1980* (London: Longman, 1994).

2. For contrasting assessments of the relationship between Hoggart and the Leavis-ite tradition, see Stuart Hall, "Richard Hoggart: *The Uses of Literacy* and the Cultural Turn," *IJCS* 10 (March 2007): 42; Stefan Collini, "Richard Hoggart: Literary Criticism and Cultural Decline in Twentieth-Century Britain," in Owen, ed., *Cultural Studies*, 33–56; Grant Farred, "Leavisite Cool: The Organic Links Between Cultural Studies and *Scru-tiny*," *Dispositio/n* 21 (1999): 1–19.

3. Dominic Sandbrook, *Never Had It So Good: A History of Britain from Suez to the Beatles* (London: Little, Brown, 2005), 106; Tony Judt, *Postwar: A History of Europe since 1945* (New York: Penguin, 2005), 300. For an extended discussion of Britain as an affluent society in this period, see Sandbrook, *Never*, 28, 97–136, 173–74, and 210–11; on how, during World War II, younger and less educated citizens welcomed American consumer culture, see David Reynolds, *Rich Relations: The American Occupation of Britain, 1942–1945* (New York: Random House, 1995), 437.

4. Dick Hebdige, "Towards a Cartography of Taste, 1935–1962 [1983]," in Dick Heb-dige, *Hiding in the Light: On Images and Things* (London: Routledge, 1988), 47, 52–55, and 58; Lunn, "'Mass Culture,'" 71; Alan O'Shea, "English Subjects of Modernity," in *Modern Times: Reflections on a Century of English Modernity*, ed. Mica Nava and Alan O'Shea (London: Routledge, 1996), 30; Dominic Strinati, "The Taste of America: Americaniza-tion and Popular Culture in Britain," in *Come on Down? Popular Media Culture in Post-War Britain*, ed. Dominic Strinati and Stephen Wagg (London: Routledge, 1992), 46–81; Herbert J. Gans, "Hollywood Films on British Screens: An Analysis of the Functions of American Popular Culture Abroad," *Social Problems* 9 (Spring 1962): 325.

5. On the background events, see Hewison, *Anger*, 127–30 and 162. Williams and Thompson developed their positions before the discovery of Antonio Gramsci. On Thompson, see Harvey J. Kaye, *The British Marxist Historians: An Introductory Analysis* (1984; New York: St. Martin's Press, 1995), esp. 168–71; Perry Anderson, *Arguments within English Marxism* (London: New Left Books, 1980); Bryan D. Palmer, *The Making of E. P. Thompson: Marxism, Humanism, and History* (Toronto: New Hogtown Press, 1981). For their key books in the period, see E. P. Thompson, *The Making of the English Working Class* (London: Gollancz, 1963); Raymond Williams, *Culture and Society, 1780–1950* (Lon-don: Chatto and Windus, 1958), and *The Long Revolution* (London: Chatto and Windus, 1961). For discussions of the development of cultural studies, the events of 1956, Hoggart's work, and the shift from Old to New Left, see Dennis L. Dworkin, *Cultural Marxism in Postwar Britain: History, the New Left and the Origins of Cultural Studies* (Durham, N.C.: Duke University Press, 1997); Grant Farred, "Introduction," *Disposito/n* 21 (1996): v–xx; Hewison, *Anger*, 162.

6. Hoggart, *Clowning*, 142.

7. Hoggart, *Habitation*, 23, 160, 130, and 179. For essays on Hoggart's politics that focus mainly on the years after the publication of *Uses*, see Charlie Ellis, "Relativism and Re-action: Richard Hoggart and Conservatism," and Bill Hughes, "The Uses and Values of Literacy: Richard Hoggart, Aesthetic Standards, and the Commodification of Working-Class Culture," in Owen, ed., *Cultural Studies*, 198–212 and 213–26.

8. Hoggart, *Habitation*, 182. Their first child was Simon Hoggart, who later emerged as a leading British journalist.

9. Tom Steele, "Questions of Taste and Class: Richard Hoggart and Bonamy Dobrée," in Owen, ed., *Re-Reading*, 148. For Hoggart's impression of his teacher, see Richard Hoggart, "Bonamy Dobrée: Teacher and Patron of Young Men," in *Of Books and Humankind: Essays and Poems Presented to Bonamy Dobrée*, ed. John Butt (London: Routledge and Kegan Paul, 1964), 195–208. On Mass-Observation, a British organization that carried out social research on the lives of ordinary citizens, see Tony Kushner, *We Europeans? Mass-Observation, "Race" and British Identity in the Twentieth Century* (Aldershop: Ashgate, 2004); Nick Hubble, *Mass-Observation and Everyday Life: Culture, History, Theory* (Houndmills: Palgrave Macmillan, 2006). The two books from Mass-Observation are *The Pub and the People: A Worktown Study* (London: Victor Gollancz, 1943) and *Puzzled People: A Study in Popular Attitudes to Religion, Ethics, Progress and Politics in a London Borough* (London: Victor Gollancz 1947). For Hoggart's early essays, see H. R. H., "An Answer to Mr. Hull," *Gryphon* (February 1937): 173–74; H. R. H., "Kingship and Anarchy," *Gryphon* (March 1939): 231; H. R. H., "Neglected Legacy," *Gryphon* (February 1940): 130.

10. Hoggart, *Clowning*, 51. On the ABCA, see Roger Fieldhouse, "The Ideology of Adult Education for HM Forces during the Second World War," in *The Political Education of Servants of the State*, ed. Roger Fieldhouse (Manchester: Manchester University Press, 1988), 100–116; S. P. Mackenzie, *Politics and Military Morale: Current Affairs and Citizenship Education in the British Army, 1914–1950* (Oxford: Oxford University Press, 1992); Martin Lawn, "The British Way and Purpose: The Spirit of the Age in Curriculum History," *Journal of Curriculum Studies* 21 (March–April 1989): 113–28; Penelope Summerfield, "Education and Politics in the British Armed Forces in the Second World War," *International Review of Social History* 26 (1981): 133–58; Hoggart, *Clowning*, 59–62.

11. Hoggart, *Clowning*, 61–62. For an essay he wrote while temporarily back in England between stays in Italy, see Richard Hoggart, "GOODBYE TO ENGLAND: A Letter to a Lot of Englishmen," August 1945, 2/3/5, RH-S.

12. Hoggart, *Clowning*, 81 and 84.

13. Richard Hoggart, "Report on Activities," probably October or November 1946, U-ADU/1/271, RH-Hull ("respectable"); Richard Hoggart, "Some Notes on Aim and Method in University Tutorial Classes," *AE* 20 (June 1948): 187–94, reproduced in John McIlroy and Sallie Westwood, eds., *Border Country: Raymond Williams in Adult Education* (Leicester: National Institute of Adult Continuing Education, 1993), 137 ("steelworks"); Richard Hoggart, "Prolegomena to the Second Session," *TB* (November 1947): 7 ("deep"; emphasis in original); Richard Hoggart, "Report for March 1948," U-ADU/1/271, RH-Hull ("blackout"; emphasis in original); Richard Hoggart, "Report for January," probably 1947 or 1948, U-ADU/1/271, RH-Hull. This discussion relies on Richard Hoggart, "The Working Tutor," in Richard Hoggart, *Teaching Literature* (London: National Institute of Adult Education, 1963), 32–62. For more material on his teaching, including responses from his students, see notebook titled "Scarborough W.E.A. Literature Class Log," 4/1/3, RH-S. On the nature of WEA students more generally, see Stephen K. Roberts, "The Centenary of

the WEA," *History Today* 53 (February 2003): 28; Tom Steele, *The Emergence of Cultural Studies: Adult Education, Cultural Politics and the "English" Question* (London: Lawrence and Wishart, 1997), 30; John McIlroy, "Border Country: Raymond Williams in Adult Education," in McIlroy and Westwood, eds., *Border Country*, 274–76.

14. Hoggart, "Working Tutor," 35 and 58. On the reaction of one of his peers, see C. Joad, "I Pontificate," *TB* (April 1952): 5, quoted in McIlroy, "Border Country," 276. See Hoggart, *Clowning*, 118, for his retrospective story of a female student he encountered early in his teaching who was feisty and direct. More generally, this discussion relies on Hoggart, "Working Tutor"; these are "Class Reports" he submitted between 1949 and 1958.

15. Hoggart, "Working Tutor," 37, 46–47, 43, and 47. For a study of the clerical group, see David Lockwood, *The Blackcoated Worker: A Study in Class Consciousness* (London: Allen and Unwin, 1958).

16. Richard Hoggart, "Introduction to the Transaction Edition," in I. A. Richards, *Practical Criticism: A Study of Literary Judgment* (New Brunswick, N.J.: Transaction, 2004), xiv; Hoggart, "Working Tutor," 42, 61, 40, 41–42, 45, 49, and 55.

17. For Hoggart's laments about the administrative burdens of adult education, see Richard Hoggart, "Some Questions on the Work of Full-Time Tutors in University Extra-Mural Departments," *TB* (July 1952): 24, quoted in McIlroy, "Border Country," 284. The films listed above are among those Hoggart mentions in *Clowning*, 91. In *Clowning*, he discusses the challenges of adult education; see especially 94–96 and 122–35.

18. On adult education in Britain, I have drawn on Richard Taylor, Kathleen Rockhill, and Roger Fieldhouse, *University Adult Education in England and the USA: A Reappraisal of the Liberal Tradition* (London: Croom Helm, 1985); Roger T. Fieldhouse, *Adult Education and the Cold War: Liberal Values under Siege, 1946–1951* (Leeds: Leeds Studies in Adult and Continuing Education, 1985), esp. 5–28; Roger Fieldhouse, "The Problems of Objectivity, Social Purpose and Ideological Commitment in English University Adult Education," in Taylor, Rockhill, and Fieldhouse, *University*, 29–51; Lawrence Goldman, "Education as Politics: University Adult Education in England since 1870," *Oxford Review of Education* 25 (January 1999): 89–101. Steele, *Emergence*, is the indispensable book that explores the relationship between adult education and cultural studies; it includes a chapter on Hoggart (118–43) that is similarly indispensable in understanding the centrality of Hoggart's experience in adult education. For a key article by Hoggart's good friend, see Roy Shaw, "Objectivity, Ideologies, and the Present Political Situation," *Hi* 42 (1950–51): 105–7. Hoggart dedicated *Clowning* to Gwen and Roy Shaw. On the perspective of another tutor, see E. P. Thompson, "Against University Standards," *Adult Education Papers*, 1: 4, University of Leeds, Department of Extramural Studies, 1950; Thompson was a member of that department from 1947 to 1965.

19. Steele, *Emergence*, 17. For another important statement, see Raymond Williams, "Some Experiments in Literature Teaching," *Rewley House Papers* 2 (1949): 15, quoted in McIlroy, "Border Country," 289.

20. Hoggart, *Clowning*, 134, 129, 135, and 130. On influence of Orwell and Lewis, see also Hoggart, *Imagined*, 94.

21. Hoggart, "Aim and Method," 140. For a helpful collection of essays and docu-

ments on Raymond Williams in adult education, see McIlroy and Westwood, eds., *Border Country*: this book reinforces a number of parallels between the work of Hoggart and Williams in adult education: including the importance of the work of F. R. Leavis and the *Scrutiny* group, along with the determination to connect it to a Marxist critique; the nonproletarian nature of the students taught; the need to justify the teaching of literature; and the central importance of reading. Much more so than Hoggart, Williams worked to incorporate sociology and social history and to understand what it meant to develop a disciplined study of popular culture: see esp. Raymond Williams, "Books for Teaching 'Culture and Environment,'" *The Use of English* 1 (1950): 134–40, reproduced in McIlroy and Westwood, eds., *Border Country*, 174–80. For a careful exploration of the nature of Williams's work in adult education, in organizational, pedagogical, and intellectual terms, see McIlroy, "Border Country," 269–323.

22. John Harrison, Richard Hoggart, and Roy Shaw, "What Are We Doing?" *TB* (Autumn 1948): 9–10 ("serious-minded" and "emancipation"); Hoggart, "Writer and Society," 20 ("authoritarian"); Richard Hoggart, "What Shall the W.E.A. Do?" *Hi* 44 (November 1952): 47 ("indivisible"; emphasis in original). On the contending forces within adult education, see Steele, *Emergence*, 4. For a statement of a leading culturalist, see Roy Shaw, "On Objective Ideologies," *Hi* (1950–51): 106–7; on Hoggart's close relationship with Shaw, see Hoggart, *Clowning*, 92 and 135; on his own position on these issues, see Richard Hoggart, *Auden: An Introductory Essay* (London: Chatto and Windus, 1951), 113. For his relationship with Eliot's work, see Richard Hoggart, "The Writer and Society," *Hi* 40 (November 1948): 20.

23. Hoggart, "Aim and Method," 139; Richard Hoggart, "The Literature Tutor and the Cultural Renascence," *Hi* 38 (July 1947): 198 ("surface"); Raymond Williams, "A Note on Mr Hoggart's Appendices," *AE* 21 (1948): 96–98, reproduced in McIlroy and Westwood, eds., *Border Country*, 144. On how Williams and Hoggart were blind to reactionary, anti-Marxist aspects of F. R. Leavis' work, see Steele, *Emergence*, 186–87. This discussion also draws on Richard Hoggart, "Poetry and Adult Classes [1952]," reprinted in *Richard Hoggart, Speaking to Each Other: Essays by Richard Hoggart,* vol. 2: *About Literature* (New York: Oxford University Press, 1970), 232.

24. Hoggart, "English Studies," 222 and 230 ("flatness"); Hoggart, "Prolegomena to the Second Session," 7 ("remnant"). On how his relationship to students was different from what obtained in more traditional settings, see Hoggart, *Clowning*, 127. There was a strong streak of anticommercialism among adult education tutors: see McIlroy, "Border Country," 291, summarizing E. P. Thompson "The Condition of the Arts," *Hi* (April 1949): 138. For essays from a Communist Party conference, see *The American Threat to British Culture* (London: Arena Publication, 1952), including E. P. Thompson's "William Morris and the Moral Issues of To-day," 25–30. This paragraph also draws on Hoggart, "Writer and Society," 19–20; Hoggart, "Poetry and Adult Classes," 226–27; Hoggart, "Some Notes," 136–37; Richard Hoggart, "English Studies in Extramural Education," *Universities Quarterly* (May 1951), reprinted in *To Each Other*, 2: 221–22; Hoggart, "Introduction to the Transaction Edition," xiii–xv; Steele, *Emergence*, 120 and 121. For his retrospective, and critical, view of pre-1957 essays on adult education, see Hoggart, *Clowning*, 126–27. For a

response to Hoggart's position, see Williams, "A Note on Mr Hoggart's Appendices," 143. Robert Colls, *Identity of England* (Oxford: Oxford University Press, 2002), 364, discusses the impact of F. R. Leavis on Hoggart. Hoggart dissented from the way Eliot and Leavis wanted to use literary studies to create a clerisy that would lead the nation away from the brink of cultural and social degradation: Hoggart, "Some Notes," 137.

25. Hoggart, "Some Notes," 141 ("hurt"); Hoggart, "English Studies," 218–19 ("confused"). This discussion also relies on Harrison, Hoggart, and Shaw, "What Are We Doing?" 8; Hoggart, "Some Notes," 136. To compare Hoggart's experience with that of Thompson, see Steele, *Emergence*, 152–55; Thompson "Against 'University' Standards," 36. For a discussion of Thompson's hostility to American popular culture, see Steele, *Emergence*, 163–64; Thompson, "William Morris." For Thompson's report on his teaching in 1948–49, see Peter Searby et al., "Edward Thompson as Teacher: Yorkshire and Warwick," in *Protest and Survival: The Historical Experience, Essays for E. P. Thompson*, ed. John Rule and Robert Malcomson (London: Merlin Press, 1993), 1–17.

26. David Lodge, *Changing Places: A Tale of Two Campuses* (1975; London: Penguin, 1978), 17. On these issues, see Steele, *Emergence*, 119 and 122.

27. Richard Hoggart to Bonamy Dobrée, February 10, 1948, 2/2/59, RH-S; Steele, *Emergence*, 16. For Hoggart's anti-Marxism, see Thompson, "Politics of Theory," 397. See also Hoggart, *Clowning*, 142; Steele, *Emergence*, 123.

28. Hoggart, *Auden*, 137. See also Hoggart, *Auden*, 111; W. H. Auden, quoted in Benjamin Appel, in "The Exiled Writers," *Saturday Review of Literature*, October 19, 1940, quoted in turn in Hoggart, *Auden*, 137. Hoggart's first published analysis of poetry, a 1947 essay on Sydney Keyes, revealed his literary critical approach that would become fully clear in the book on Auden: Richard Hoggart, "The Journey of Sydney Keyes," *Poetry Review* 38 (January–February 1947): 31–32. On Hoggart's response to Auden, especially his emphasis on the poet's status as an outsider, see Sue Owen, "Richard Hoggart and Literature," in Owen, ed., *Re-Reading*, 71–74.

29. Hoggart, *Auden*, 9, 13, and 9.

30. Ibid., 113, 115, and 116. At another point, Hoggart, speaking of Auden in his later years, remarked that he "is no longer a near-Marxist, but he retains a great admiration for Marx's insistence on the importance of social life and the need for co-operation, and for his analysis of the economic forces of society": Ibid., 156. Auden's "Lay Your Sleeping Head, My Love" provided one opportunity to discuss the connection between Auden's poetry and his sexuality: Richard R. Bozorth, *Auden's Game of Knowledge: Poetry and the Meanings of Homosexuality* (New York: Columbia University Press, 2001), 191. The word "homosexual" does not appear in the index to Hoggart's book; moreover, in his discussion of the theme of love in Auden's poetry, Hoggart treats the topic in an abstract manner: Hoggart, *Auden*, 129–34. It is likely, however, that Hoggart knew that Auden was gay: see Richard Bozorth to author, email, September 6, 2008; Sue Owen to author, email, September 8, 2008, both in author's possession. For evidence on Hoggart's awareness of the relationship between a homosexual and his writings, in this case E. M. Forster, see Richard Hoggart to Professor [G. E. T.] Mayfield, Sunday, probably late August or early September 1948, U-ADU/1/272, RH-Hull.

31. Hoggart, *Auden*, 136 ("crowd"); 14 ("echoes"); 37 ("moralist"). For his sober view of the 1930s, see ibid., 112. For additional evidence of Hoggart's familiarity with Riesman's book, see Richard Hoggart, in panel discussion with Raymond Williams, *NLR* 1 (January 1960): 26–30, reproduced in McIlroy and Westwood, eds., *Border Country*, 117.

32. Richard Hoggart, "The Bookstall," *Tribune*, October 29, 1948, 23. For the parallel and in some cases identical discussion, see Hoggart, *Uses*, 212–13 and 217–20. The comparison is between similar passages in "Bookstall" and *Uses*, 220. One inspiration for this piece was George Orwell, "Boys' Weeklies," 1940: http://orwell.ru/library/essays/boys/english/e_boys (accessed February 16, 2011).

33. Richard Hoggart, review of Thomas Brackley, *From This Foundation*, *Hi* 41 (March 1950): 116–17.

34. Richard Hoggart, "Reflections on *Life*," *Hi* 39 (June 1948): 176–77 (emphasis in original). Despite the criticism of the culture of the United States that Hoggart made in the 1940s and 1950s, he offered a more balanced view when he was living in Rochester, apparently influenced by his appreciation for things American while there: Arthur Deutch, "Briton Describes Long Look at U.S.," probably in a Rochester, N.Y., newspaper, early 1957, 4/1/5, RH-S; Richard Hoggart, "A Matter of Rhetoric? American Writers and British Readers," *Nation*, April 27, 1957, 361–64; Richard Hoggart, "The American Small Town," *New Republic*, March 24, 1958, 17–18.

35. Hoggart, *Clowning*, 141 and 96; see also Owen, introduction to Owen, ed., *Cultural Studies*, 1–2; Hoggart, *Clowning*, 135. For a probing essay on Hoggart's book as ethnography, see Jean-Claude Passeron, "Introduction to the French Edition of *The Uses of Literacy* (1971)," in *CCCS Selected Working Papers*, ed. Ann Gray et al. (London: Routledge, 2007), 2: 25–34.

36. Melvin Maddocks, review of *The Uses of Literacy*, *Christian Science Monitor*, September 12, 1957, 7. For a discussion of the reviews, see Hoggart, *Imagined*, 4–9. Hoggart's papers in Sheffield contain many reviews; for a summary by his publisher, see "Extracts from Reviews of THE USES OF LITERACY . . . as at 7th , March, 1957," 3/11/6, RH-S. To sample the reviews, see those in 3/11/96–210, RH-S. For an essay on Hoggart's book by Hall, see Stuart Hall, "USES OF LITERACY, History and Class," November 13, 1970, 3/11/375, RH-S.

37. Hoggart, *Uses*, 11, 24, and 239. For an example of the impact of Hoggart's discussion of the "Scholarship Boy," see Richard Rodriguez, *The Hunger of Memory: The Education of Richard Rodriguez: An Autobiography* (Boston: David R. Godine, 1982), 43–73.

38. E. P. Thompson, "Commitment in Politics," *ULR* 6 (Spring 1959): 53. Thompson offered additional critiques of the book—a lack of conflict portrayed in the interwar period, inattention to the labor movement and to workplace struggles, and the unexamined distinction between what the media portrayed and what people actually experienced. On how Hoggart's work prefigured postmodernism, see Gregg, "Neglected History," 286–87.

39. Alexis de Tocqueville, *Democracy in America*, quoted in Hoggart, *Uses*, 141; Hoggart, *Uses*, 45 and 78; Matthew Arnold, *Culture and Anarchy*, quoted in Hoggart, *Uses*, 171; Hoggart, *Uses*, 195 and 219. Although some scholars have argued that Hoggart offered a sense of the reciprocal relationship between major writers and popular ones, more

typically he used the former to criticize the latter. Susan Brook has asserted that Hoggart's book "revalues working-class cultural practices, arguing that the everyday speech and popular culture of working-class people reveals similar values and qualities to those of 'high culture': irony, criticism, compassion, and responsibility": Brook, *Literature*, 22.

40. On the importance of *The Mechanical Bride* to Hoggart, see Hoggart, *Uses*, 312; Richard Hoggart to Marshall McLuhan, October 20, 1966, folder 48, box 26, MM-LC.

41. Hoggart did not mention F. R. Leavis in the text but listed *Culture and Environment* by Leavis and Thompson in the bibliography: Hoggart, *Uses*, 312. To catch the dimensions of the more general response to Leavis, see W. John Morgan and Peter Preston, eds., *Raymond Williams, Politics and Letters: Interviews with "New Left Review"* (London: NLB, 1979), 66 and 176–77; Hewison, *Anger*, 45–47. For a critical assessment of the consequences of Hoggart's reliance on the Leavises, see Malcolm Pittock, "Richard Hoggart and the Leavises," *Essays in Criticism* 60 (January 2010): 51–69.

42. Hoggart, *Uses*, 33, 113, 118, and 123.

43. Ibid., 171, 23, and 142.

44. Ibid., 144, 277, 24, and 145. On Hoggart's relationship to the work of D. H. Lawrence, see Sean Matthews, "The Uses of D. H. Lawrence," in Owen, ed., *Re-Reading*, 84–101.

45. Hoggart, *Uses*, 195 and 174.

46. Ibid., 23–24.

47. Ibid., 15, 25, 41, and 83–84; Richard Hoggart, "A Sense of Occasion [1959]," in Richard Hoggart, *Speaking to Each Other: Essays by Richard Hoggart*, vol. 1: *About Society* (New York: Oxford University Press, 1970), 28 and 30 ("Blandness"). In this essay, more so than in his 1957 book a year earlier, Hoggart acknowledged the changes in the condition of the working class in Britain, especially the physical and emotional movement from older urban areas and the spur of consumer culture to upward social mobility: 29 and 30. On the issue of class relations in postwar Britain, see Dworkin, *Cultural*, 83 and 97; Hoggart, in Goodwin, "Introduction," xxix.

48. Hoggart, *Uses*, 202 ("Juke-Box"); 238 ("Scholarship"); 185 ("equipment"). On his late acquisition of a television set, see Hoggart, quoted in interview in Corner, "Postscript," 275; the book appeared early in 1957 and Hoggart purchased a set later in the year. David Fowler, "From Jukebox Boys to Revolting Students: Richard Hoggart and the Study of British Youth Culture," *IJCS* 10 (March 2007): 73–75, sees Hoggart, especially in work he did after *The Uses of Literacy*, as pointing forward to the work of Hebdige and Hall on youth culture. For a discussion of one genre to which *The Uses of Literacy* belongs, see Katie Wales, "The Anxiety of Influence: Hoggart, Liminality, and Melvyn Bragg's *Crossing the Lines*," in Owen, ed., *Re-Reading*, 102–17.

49. Judt, *Postwar*, 347; Hoggart, *Uses*, 204. On popular music in postwar Britain, see Robert J. C. Young. "'Them' and 'Us,'" *IJCS* 10 (March 2007): 51–62.

50. Hoggart, *Uses*, 160, 203, and 205. David Fowler, *Youth Culture in Modern Britain, c. 1920–c. 1970* (Houndmills: Palgrave Macmillan, 2008), 251 n. 13, identifies Goole as the place where Hoggart saw jukebox boys.

51. Hoggart, *Uses*, 195, 202, 277, 163, 260, 282, and 276; see also Lunn, "'Mass Culture,'" 74.

52. Fowler, "Jukebox Boys," 74; 74–82 offers a probing examination of the changing nature of Hoggart's views of youth culture. For his more extended examination, see Fowler, *Youth Culture*. Adrian Horn, *Juke Box Britain: Americanization and Youth Culture, 1945–60* (Manchester: Manchester University Press, 2009), 3, notes, as scholars have for other nations, that critics of Americanization were "a vociferous minority that overshadowed a massive popular acceptance."

53. Hall, "Richard Hoggart, *The Use of Literacy* and the Cultural Turn," 41; Richard Hoggart, interview, in John Comer, "Studying Culture—Reflections and Assessments: An Interview with Richard Hoggart [1991]," 271, in Hoggart, *Uses*, ed. Andrew Goodwin. For his acknowledgment of his debt to Leavis in the book's second half, see Hoggart, *Imagined*, 5. For a cogent analysis of Hoggart's debt to Leavis and to even older moral and pessimistic laments about the impact of commercialism, seen in his book's second half, see Collini, "Hoggart," 40–41; see also Colls, *Identity of England*, 363–64. Among those who have pointed out the ways in which the writings of F. R. Leavis profoundly shaped Hoggart's perspectives on postwar Americanization and popular culture is Steele, *Emergence*, 119. On the left-Leavisite tradition, see Steele, *Emergence*, 24; Francis Mulhern, *The Moment of "Scrutiny"* (London: NLB, 1979), 63–71.

54. Richard Hoggart, "The Quality of Cultural Life in Mass Society," lecture given at Congress of Cultural Freedom conference, Paris, June 16–22, 1960, 6–8, 3/180/1, RH-S; see also Hoggart, *Imagined*, 9.

55. Dwight Macdonald, "'A Corrupt Brightness,'" *Encounter* 8 (June 1957): 75–82; J. F. C. Harrison, review of *The Uses of Literacy*, *New Statesman and Nation*, March 2, 1957, 284; F. R. Leavis, letter to the editor, *New Statesman and Nation*, March 9, 1957, 309–10. For the review of Hoggart's book by Amis, see Kingsley Amis, review of *Uses of Literary*, *Spectator*, March 1, 1957, 285; for the response by one of the authors of *The Lonely Crowd*, see Reuel Denney, review of *Uses of Literacy*, *New Republic*, December 2, 1957, 16–17. For Hoggart's discussion of the reaction to the book, see Hoggart, *Clowning*, 142–43.

56. Raymond Williams, review of *Uses of Literacy*, in *Essays in Criticism* 7 (October 1957): 422–23, 425, 426, 428, and 425. Williams touched on some of these same issues in Raymond Williams, "Working Class Culture," *ULR* 1 (Summer 1957): 29–32. This essay was one of four in a series of essays on Hoggart's book, including Alan Lovell, "Scholarship Boy," 33–34; John McLeish, "Variant Reading," 32–33; and Gwyn Lewis, "Candy Flossing the Celtic Fringe," 34 and 39–40. For an affectionate, probing discussion between Hoggart and Williams, one in which they make clear they had not met until then, see Richard Hoggart and Raymond Williams, "Working Class Attitudes," *NLR* 1 (January–February 1960): 26–30.

57. Hoggart, interview with John Comer, "Studying Culture," 271. For a discussion of Hoggart's treatment of women as protofeminist, rather than, as many feminists argued, unfeminist, see Sue Owen, "Hoggart and Women," in Owen, ed., *Cultural Studies*, 227–42. The summary of other critiques of Hoggart relies on Goodwin, "Introduction," xiii–xxxiv; Colls, *Identity*, 364–65; and the articles in *IJCS*, including those by Fowler, Lee, Owen, Hall, and Young.

58. Hoggart, *Uses*, 174, 118, 144, and 141. Lunn, "'Mass Culture,'" 76, writes that

with Hoggart's book "in the multiple exchanges between working-class and 'mass culture' . . . adaptations and manipulations occurred on both sides." On the distinctive nature of working-class style in the United States in the 1950s, see Shelley Nickles, "More Is Better: Mass Consumption, Gender, and Class Identity in Postwar America," *AQ* 54 (December 2002): 581–622.

59. On these issues, see Lunn, "'Mass Culture,'" 76; Steele, *Emergence*, 5; Richard E. Lee, "Cultural Studies, Complexity Studies and the Transformation of the Structures on Knowledge," *IJCS* 10 (March 2007): 16; Sue Owen, "Richard Hoggart as Literary Critic," *IJCS* 10 (March 2007): 85–87; Hall, "Richard Hoggart: *The Uses of Literacy* and the Cultural Turn," 42; Young, "'Them,'" 51–62.

60. In his inaugural address at Birmingham, Hoggart set out his ideas for the Center's program: Hoggart, "Schools of English," esp. 254–59. For Hoggart's later, and largely negative, views of popular culture and consumerism, see Richard Hoggart, *The Way We Live Now* (London: Chatto and Windus, 1995), esp. 97–113.

Interlude

1. Eugene Lunn, "Beyond 'Mass Culture': The Lonely Crowd, the Uses of Literacy, and the Postwar Era," *Theory and Society* 19 (February 1990): 72.

2. John G. Cawelti, "Beatles, Batman, and the New Aesthetic," *Midway* 9 (Autumn 1968): 54–55; at a number of points my remarks draw on Cawelti's essay.

Chapter 6

1. David Lodge, "Richard Hoggart: A Personal Appreciation," *IJCS* 10 (2007): 31.

2. On the Independent Group, see Anne Massey, *The Independent Group: Modernism and Mass Culture in Britain, 1945–59* (Manchester: Manchester University Press, 1995); Lawrence Alloway, "The Development of British Pop," in *Pop Art*, ed. Lucy Lippard (London: Thames and Hudson, 1966), 27–66; Lynne Cooke, "The Independent Group: British and American Pop Art: A 'Palimpcestuous' Legacy," in *Modern Art and Popular Culture: Readings in High and Low*, ed. Kirk Varnedoe and Adam Gopnik (New York: Harry Abrams, 1990), 192–215; David Brauer et al., *Pop Art: U.S./U.K. Connections, 1956–1966* (New York: Hatje Cantz, 2001); Kristine Stiles, "Material Culture and Everyday Life," in *Theories and Documents of Contemporary Art: A Sourcebook of Artists' Writings*, ed. Kristine Stiles and Peter Selz (Berkeley: University of California Press, 1996), 282–95; David Robbins, ed., *The Independent Group: Postwar Britain and the Aesthetics of Plenty* (Cambridge, Mass.: MIT Press, 1990); Lawrence Alloway et al., *Modern Dreams: The Rise and Fall and Rise of Pop* (Cambridge, Mass.: MIT Press, 1988); Dick Hebdige, "Toward a Cartography of Taste, 1935–1962," *Block* 4 (1982): 39–56; Dick Hebdige, "In Poor Taste: Notes on Pop," *Block* 8 (1983): 54–68. See also the especially helpful websites: www.independentgroup.org.uk (accessed February 16, 2011) and http://www.thisistomorrow2.com/pages_gb/1956gb.html (accessed February 16, 2011). David Robbins, "The Independent Group: Forerunners of Postmodernism?" in Robbins, ed., *Independent Group*, 239, suggests that the IG's use of a tack-board for one part of the 1956 exhibition was an early exploration of semiotics; more generally, in this piece Robbins makes a case for the IG as postmodern-

ists. James Hyman, *The Battle for Realism: Figurative Art in Britain during the Cold War, 1945–1960* (New Haven, Conn.: Yale University Press, 2001), provides a useful corrective to the attention scholars have paid to the IG. On March 30, 2011, the Tate Britain held a conference, "Lawrence Alloway Reconsidered"; especially suggestive is Eric Stryker, "Parallel Systems: Eduardo Paolozzi and Lawrence Alloway," copy in author's possession.

3. Lawrence Alloway, "The Long Front of Culture [1959]," in *Pop Art Redefined*, ed. John Russell and Suzi Goblik (New York: Frederick A. Praeger, 1969), 42. Richard Hamilton to Peter Smithson and Alison Smithson, January 16, 1957, in Richard Hamilton, *Collected Words, 1953–1982* (London: Thames and Hudson, 1982), 28. The most widely accepted claim about the first use of the phrase "pop art" gives credit to Alloway in a February 1958 article. Yet in that publication (Lawrence Alloway, "The Arts and the Mass Media," in *Pop Art: A Critical History*, ed. Stephen H. Madoff [Berkeley: University of California Press, 1997], 7–9), Alloway in fact did not use the phrase "pop art" but rather "popular arts," "popular art," "mass media," "mass arts," and "mass produced arts" to refer to products of commercial culture such as movies, mass market paperbacks, advertisements. As far as I can determine, an even earlier use of the phrase "pop art" to refer to products of mass media and commercial culture appears a full year before Alloway's use, in the January 16, 1957, letter from Richard Hamilton to the Smithsons (cited above). John McHale's son claims an even earlier use by his father: John McHale (son of John McHale), email to author, August 29, 2007, copy in author's possession. Surprisingly, in the extensive collection of letters from Alloway to Sleigh during the years of the IG's discussions, he rarely commented on the conversations at the IG, and when he did so, what he said was on occasion negative: Alloway to Sleigh, November 13, 1953, folder 2, box 5, LA-GRI.

4. Clement Greenberg, "How Art Writing Earns Its Bad Name [1962]," in *Clement Greenberg: The Collected Essays and Criticism: Modernism with a Vengeance, 1957–1969*, ed. John O'Brian (Chicago: University of Chicago Press, 1993), 137; Alloway, "Development," 31–32.

5. Brian Wallis, "Tomorrow and Tomorrow and Tomorrow: The Independent Group and Popular Culture," in Alloway et al., *Modern Dreams*, 9; Roger Hilton, quoted from a 1956 gathering, quoted in turn by Colin St. John Wilson in Jeremy Millar, "This Is Tomorrow," *Whitechapel Art Gallery Centenary Review*, March 10, 2001, 68.

6. David Lodge, *Changing Places: A Tale of Two Campuses* (1975; London: Penguin, 1978), 22; Reyner Banham, quoted in revised draft script of *Fathers of Pop*, in turn quoted in Massey, *Independent*, 84; see also Hebdige, "Poor Taste," 60. Banham used Peter as his first name.

7. Nigel Henderson, diary entry, August 8, 1947, TGA 9211/1/1/9, NH-Tate.

8. Ibid.; Roger Fry, quoted in Alloway, "Development," 33; David Riesman, "Some Observations on Changes in Leisure Attitudes [1952]," in David Riesman, *Individualism Reconsidered and Other Essays* (Glencoe, Ill.: Free Press, 1954), 205.

9. For biographical information on Henderson, see his resume in TGA 9211/15/1, NH-Tate; on the Smithsons, see Elain Harwood, "Peter Smithson" and "Alison Smithson," *Oxford Dictionary of National Biography*, www.oxforddnb.com/view/printable/89834 (accessed February 16, 2011).

10. Lyall Sutherland, "Reyner Banham," *Oxford Dictionary of National Biography*, www.oxforddnb.com/view/printable/39982 (accessed February 16, 2011); see also S. C. Maharaj, "Richard Hamilton," www.oxfordartonline.com.subscriber./article/grove/art/T)36398 (accessed February 16, 2011); Hamilton, *Collected*, 8; Richard Hamilton, *Richard Hamilton*, ed. Hal Foster with Alex Bacon (Cambridge, Mass.: MIT Press, 2010). Some of this information on the IG comes from *This Is Tomorrow* (London: Whitechapel Art Gallery, 1956), [23]. In the copy I am relying on, reproduced from a copy at the Getty Research Institute, I can see no page numbers, therefore I placed page numbers for my copy in brackets.

11. For biographical information, I am relying on Richard Kalina, "Imagining the Present: Context, Content, and the Role of the Critic," in *Imagining the Present: Context, Content, and the Role of the Critic*, ed. Richard Kalina (London: Routledge, 2006), 1–30; Amy Ingrid Schlegel, curator, *An Unnerving Romanticism: The Art of Sylvia Sleigh and Lawrence Alloway* (Philadelphia: Philadelphia Art Alliance, 2001); obituary for Lawrence Alloway, *Art in America* 78 (February 1990): 196; [David Robbins], "Lawrence Alloway," in Robbins, ed., *Independent*, 163; Grace Glueck, "Lawrence Alloway Is Dead at 63; Art Historian, Curator and Critic," *NYT*, January 3, 1990, D19; "Lawrence Alloway," Contemporary Authors Online, Gale, 2002 (accessed July 8, 2011); *Marquis Who's Who*, 2004; Alex Seago, *Burning the Box of Beautiful Things: The Development of a Postmodern Sensibility* (Oxford: Oxford University Press, 1995), 114–15; Lawrence Alloway, "An Interview with Lawrence Alloway," by James L. Reinish, *Studio International* 186 (September 1973): 62; Lawrence Alloway, resume, folder "Curator: Lawrence Alloway, 1962–64," box 691755, LA-GMA. Information on some aspects of Alloway's life is sketchy: The *New York Times* obituary mentions the WEA but not the location of his courses for that program. The *New York Times* says Alloway was director of the ICA from 1954 to 1957; Contemporary Authors Online and *Marquis Who's Who* name him as deputy director, 1957–60; Alloway, in "Development," 200, n. 9, says he worked at ICA 1956–60 "as assistant, deputy, and programme director"; Alloway's resume at the Guggenheim archives has him working at the ICA in 1956 and 1957. I accepted Kalina's dates when available; his is a very useful essay on Alloway's criticism. On Alloway's life I am also relying on Sylvia Sleigh, interview with Daniel Horowitz, January 18, 2010, New York, N.Y. Sleigh married Alloway in 1954 and emerged as an important feminist artist in the 1970s. On Sleigh, and her relationship with Alloway, see Schlegel, curator, *An Unnerving Romanticism*.

12. Reyner Banham, "The Atavism of the Short-Distance Mini-Cyclist," *Living Arts* 3 (1964): 96; Lawrence Alloway, quoted in Ray Thorburn, "An Interview with Lawrence Alloway," August 1974, 192, in turn quoted in Kalina, "Imagining the Present," 11. This interview is part of Thorburn's master's thesis at Ohio State University, available on audiotape from the university's Department of Art Education; there was also a copy of the interview in possession of Alloway's widow, Sylvia Sleigh, in Manhattan. This discussion of their social location relies on Massey, *Independent*, 33–38.

13. Reyner Banham, "Vehicles of Desire [1955]," in Alloway et al., *Modern Dreams*, 69 ("symbolic"); Alloway, "Arts and the Mass Media," 8 ("perpetual"); on IG and Banham, see David Robbins, "American Ads," in Robbins, ed., *Independent*, 59; Reyner Banham,

"Towards a Million-Volt Light and Sound Culture," *Architectural Review* 141 (May 1967): 331. I am grateful to Anne Massey for helping me understand the relationship between Lewis and members of IG. On the importance of Fuller, Loewy, and Eames, see Nigel Henderson, notebook, TGA/9211/3/2, NH-Tate. For the impact of the work of Wiener and the Center, see Sylvia Harrison, *Pop Art and the Origins of Post-Modernism* (Cambridge: Cambridge University Press, 2001), 44–45. On Malraux, see Nigel Henderson, untitled, handwritten essay, TGA/9211/5/1/9, NH-Tate. To catch the flavor of their optimism about technology, see Reyner Banham, *Theory and Design in the First Machine Age* (London: Architectural Press, 1960), 9–12. See also Reyner Banham, "Machine Aesthetic," *Architectural Review* 117 (April 1955): 227; Massey, *Independent*, 89. For a later criticism of McLuhan by an IG member, see Lawrence Alloway, "The Cult of Media—Mottos for All Occasions," *Art Voices* 5 (Summer 1966): 107. For the importance of the book by McLuhan, see also John McHale to Marshall McLuhan, May 1, 1959, file 34, box 31, MM-LC.

14. Nigel Henderson, undated entry in notebook, but well after the event itself, TGA/9211/3/7, NH-Tate. For information on and a partial recreation of this lecture, see Eduardo Paolozzi's early 1960s film *History of Nothing*, screened in December 2009 at the Tate Modern. On the notebooks, see Nigel Henderson, scrapbooks, TGA 9211/13/37 and TGA 9211/13/4, NH-Tate.

15. Alloway, "Arts and the Mass Media," 8 ("values"); Banham, "Vehicles," 69 ("expendability"); Alloway, "Arts and the Mass Media," 8 ("intense"). For a discussion of their views on technology, see Massey, *Independent*, 45 and 73–93. In London Paolozzi had purchased reams of clippings from popular magazines and in 1956 McHale brought back from the United States a suitcase filled with similar material: Millar, "Tomorrow," 70, and Jacquelynn Baas, "John McHale," in Robbins, ed., *Independent*, 87.

16. Alloway, "Arts and the Mass Media," 8 ("lust"); Banham, "Vehicles," 69 ("stylists"). This discussion relies on Banham, "Vehicles," 65–69; Banham, "Atavism," 91–97; Richard Hamilton, "Persuading Image [1960]," in Alloway et al., *Modern Dreams*, 57–63; Richard Hamilton, "Letter to Peter and Alison Smithson," in Madoff, ed., *Pop Art*, 5–6; Alison Smithson and Peter Smithson, "But Today We Collect Ads [1956]," in Madoff, ed., *Pop Art*, 3–4; Alloway, "Arts and the Mass Media," 7–9; Lawrence Alloway, "Notes on Abstract Art and the Mass Media," *Art News and Review*, February 27–March 12, 1960, 3 and 12; John McHale, "The Fine Arts in the Mass Media [1959]," in Madoff, ed., *Pop Art*, 43–47; Richard Hamilton, "Popular Culture and Personal Responsibility [1960]," in Hamilton, *Collected*, 151–56; Alloway, "Long Front," 41–43. There are two good summaries of the IG's ideology: Massey, *Independent*, 72–93; Nigel Whiteley, *Reyner Banham: Historian of the Immediate Future* (Cambridge, Mass.: MIT Press, 2002), 96–112. The papers of Nigel Henderson contain material that explores the relationships of art, sciences, and technology: see, for example, material on the 1953 exhibit "Parallel of Life and Art": memorandum, March 27 1953, TGA 9211/5/1/1, NH-Tate and notebook entry, October 1, 1951, TGA 9211/3/1, NH-Tate.

17. Reyner Banham, "Coronation Street, Hoggartsborough," *New Statesman*, February 9, 1962, 200; Alloway, "Development of British Pop," 40; Hamilton, "Personal Responsibility," 155. For later references to Hoggart, see Alloway, "Development," 40; Reyner Banham, "Design by Choice," *Architectural Review* 130 (July 1961): 44.

18. Alloway, "Arts and the Mass Media," 7; Banham, "Atavism," 94, 95, and 97; see also Hale, "Fine Arts," 44.

19. Hamilton, "Personal Responsibility," 154 ("humour"); Alloway, "Arts and the Mass Media," 7–8 ("fatally" and "layers"); Alloway, "Long Front," 41 ("sensitiveness"); McHale, "Fine Arts," 45 and 47.

20. Lawrence Alloway, "Personal Statement [1957]," in Kalina, ed., *Imagining*, 51–53; Banham, "Atavism," 92 and 97. See also Wallis, "Tomorrow," 17

21. Hamilton, "Persuading Image," 60; Alloway, "Long Front," 41–42; Banham, "Vehicles," 66. Massey, *Independent*, 72–93, contextualizes and summarizes these debates.

22. David Mellor, "A 'Glorious Techniculture' in Nineteen-Fifties Britain: The Many Cultural Contexts of the Independent Group," in Robbins, *Independent*, 229, 232, and 229 (emphasis in original).

23. Wallis, "Tomorrow," 9; Lawrence Alloway, "The Robot and the Arts," *Art News and Review*, September 1, 1956, press clippings, WAG; Lawrence Alloway, "Robot Opens Exhibition of Design in the Future," undated press release, probably early August 1956, WAG/EXH/2/45/2, WAG. For the catalog, see *This Is Tomorrow* (London: Whitechapel Art Gallery, 1956). For a retrospective discussion of the show, see Millar, "Tomorrow," 67–70.

24. Lawrence Alloway, "Progress Report," undated but probably late August 1956, WAG/EXH/2/45/1, WAG (crowds); "Where Highbrow Art Makes Lowbrow Fun," *Northern Echo*, August 9 1956, press clippings, WAG; "1,000 a Day at Exhibition," *East London Advertiser*, September 7, 1956, press clippings, WAG; Wallis, "Tomorrow," in Alloway et al., *Modern Dreams*, 9 ("hang"); Eric Newton, "Tomorrow and Tomorrow and Tomorrow," *Time and Tide*, August 18, 1956, press clippings, WAG ("target"); "A Shaft from Apollo's Bow: This Is To-morrow—or Is It?" *Apollo* 64 (September 1956): 89; Basil Taylor, "Dada," *Spectator*, August 24, 1956, press clippings, WAG; John Stillman and John Eastwick-Field, "This Was Yesterday," *Architecture and Building* (September 1956): 329, press clippings, WAG. For another essay on the show in which Taylor characterized it as looking more to the past than to the future, see Basil Taylor, "Yesterday, Certainly; Tomorrow, Perhaps," *Spectator*, August 17, 1956, 234.

25. "Shaft," 89 ("silly"); JM [presumably John McHale], in "Are They Cultured?" *This Is Tomorrow*, [22] ("sensory"); Lawrence Alloway, "Design as a Human Activity," *This Is Tomorrow*, [2] ("whole"); Geoffrey Holroyd, Toni del Renzio, and Lawrence Alloway, diagram, *This Is Tomorrow*, [91] ("destination"). See Stuart Hall, "Encoding/Decoding," in *Culture, Media, Language: Working Papers in Cultural Studies, 1972–79*, ed. Stuart Hall et al. (London: Hutchinson, 1908), 128–38.

26. In extensive correspondence, John McHale has helped me understand the references; the younger McHale says the design of the collage was his father's, and Hamilton assembled it: John McHale to author, email, August 27, 2007; this and other emails in author's possession.

27. For one of their essays on New Brutalism, see Alison Smithson and Peter Smithson, "Thoughts in Progress: The New Brutalism," *Architectural Design* 27 (April 1957): 111–12.

28. Banham, "Million Volt," 331 (on the accusation); M. Neufeld, *NLR* 6 (1960): 71, quoted in Massey, *Independent*, 129 ("vulgar"); Alloway, "Personal Statement," 52–53 ("taste" and "freed"); Banham, "Atavism," 92 ("curious"). Only later would members of the IG learn that in the 1950s the Central Intelligence Agency used the ICA as a host for shows and talks that played an important role in Cold War cultural battles, especially ones that celebrated the high modernism of the abstract expressionists: Massey, *Independent*, 62–71. For the way in which the Cold War shaped British debates about advertising, see Stefan Schwarzkopf, "They Do It with Mirrors: Advertising and British Cold War Consumer Politics," *Contemporary British History* 19 (June 2005): 133–50.

29. Roland Barthes, "That Old Thing, Art . . . [1980]," reprinted, with translation by Richard Howard, in Paul Taylor, ed., *Post-Pop Art* (Cambridge, Mass.: MIT Press, 1989), 21. In September 1962 there had been a show, "The New Painting of Common Objects," at the Pasadena Art Museum; in April 1963, there were also shows of pop art at the Atkins Museum in Kansas City, the Contemporary Art Museum in Houston, and the Washington Gallery of Modern Art.

30. For a bibliography of his works, see Kalina, ed., *Imagining*, 257–94. For the fullest development of Alloway's position on popular culture and mass media, see Alloway, "Long Front," 41–43. For other essays that cover the topics Alloway explored, see Alloway, "Notes on Abstract Art," 3 and 12; Lawrence Alloway, "Pop Art: The Words [1969]," in Mahsun, ed., *Pop Art*, 175–79. For an earlier collection of Alloway's essays, with a focus on the period from 1963 to the early 1970s, see Lawrence Alloway, *Topics in American Art since 1945* (New York: W. W. Norton, 1975). For an assessment of Alloway as an art critic, see Hyman, *Battle for Realism*, 193. All of this is not to minimize his appreciation of abstract expressionism: Alloway, "Personal Statement," 52. For his early appreciation of painters like Mark Rothko, Willem de Kooning, and Barnett Newman, see Lawrence Alloway, "The New American Painting," *Art International* 3 (1959): 21–27. For Alloway's appreciation of Jackson Pollock, whose work he placed in both American traditions and in the context of the long stretch of European art, see Lawrence Alloway, *Jackson Pollock: Paintings, Drawings, and Watercolours from the Collection of Lee Krasner Pollock* (London: Marlboro Fine Art, 1961).

31. Lawrence Alloway, "From Mickey to Magoo," *Living Cinema*, March 3, 1957, 146 (Kalina, ed., *Imagining*, 287, lists this as a 1967 article, yet both the copy of the article in Alloway's papers at the Getty Research Institute and WorldCat's database make it clear that the article appeared in 1957: copy of article, folder 8, box 14, LA-GRI); Lawrence Alloway, "Artists as Consumers [1961]," in Kalina, ed., *Imagining*, 72. In another essay, Alloway called Hilton Kramer "the professionally grouchy American critic": Alloway, "Junk Culture [1961]," in Kalina, ed., *Imagining*," 79; Alloway, "Personal Statement," 53. This paragraph also relies on Lawrence Alloway, "Dada 1956 [1958]," in Robbins, ed., *Independent*, 164; Lawrence Alloway, "Technology and Sex in Science Fiction: A Note on Cover Art [1956]," in Kalina, ed., *Imagining*, 43; Kalina, "Imagining the Present," 14; Alloway, "Long Front," 25–26, 41, and 43; Alloway, "Human Activity," [1]–[2]; Lawrence Alloway, "Quick Symbols," *Encounter* 6 (March 1956): 93; Alloway, "Arts and the Mass Media," 7 and 8; Clement Greenberg, "Avant-Garde and Kitsch," quoted in Alloway, "Develop-

ment of British Pop," 36. For a discussion of Alloway's attitude toward what Greenberg wrote, both appreciative and critical, see Kalina, "Imagining the Present," 3–4 and 13–14. For other examples of his movie criticism, see Lawrence Alloway, "Lawrence Alloway on the Iconography of the Movies," *Movie* 7 (February 1963): 4–6; Lawrence Alloway, talk at Seminar on Public Communications, Columbia University, May 8, 1964, folder 8, box 14, LA-GRI.

32. Lawrence Alloway, "City Notes [1959]," in Kalina, ed., *Imagining*, 61; Alloway, "Human Activity," [2]. This summary also draws on Alloway, "Long Front," 42; Alloway, "Artists as Consumers," 72. In one of his most important essays on popular culture and mass media, Alloway talked of the influence Riesman's 1950 book had on him: Alloway, "Arts and the Mass Media," 8. Harrison, *Pop Art*, 47–48, explores the parallels between Alloway and Riesman.

33. Alloway, "London: Beyond Painting and Sculpture," *ArN* 55 (September 1956): 64 ("play"); Alloway, "Quick Symbols," 94 ("habits"); 93 ("rabble" and "symbols"). This summary also relies on Alloway, "Artists as Consumers," 72; Alloway, "Personal Statement," 51–53; Alloway, "Arts and the Mass Media," 9.

34. Alloway, "Technology and Sex," 44 ("riotous"); Alloway, "City Notes," 66 ("configuration"); Alloway, "City Notes," 67 ("neon"); Alloway, "City Notes," 68 ("jumbly"). See also Lawrence Alloway, "Technology and Sex," 43–46.

35. Alloway, "Personal Statement," 52 ("decadent"); Lawrence Alloway to Sylvia Sleigh, June 2, 1958, quoted in Anne Massey and Amy Ingrid Schlegel, "Life in the U.K.: The Creative Partnership of Sylvia Sleigh and Lawrence Alloway," in Schlegel, curator, *Unnerving Romanticism*," 19 ("sold"); Alloway to Sleigh, May 17, 1958, folder 7, box 7, LA-GRI ("Mies"). This section also relies on Richard Kalina, telephone conversation with author, February 3, 2009; Lawrence Alloway, "'Pop Art' since 1949 [1962]," in Kalina, ed., *Imagining*, 87. For evidence of his opposition to British anti-Americanism, see Lawrence Alloway, "Sic, Sic, Sic," *Art News and Review*, April 11, 1958, 5 and 8, folder 8, box 29, LA-GRI. On his experience during his first visit to the United States, see these 1958 letters from Alloway to Sleigh in LA-GRI: May 5, folder 8, box 7; May 10, folder 8, box 7; June 2, folder 9, box 7; June 4 (postmark), folder 9, box 7.

36. The image with the peep hole that I have been able to locate bears a somewhat different title: "I Can See the Whole Room! . . . And There's Nobody in It!"

37. Barbara Rose, "Pop Art at the Guggenheim [1963]," in Madoff, ed., *Pop Art*, 82.

38. For the proposal, see L[awrence] A[lloway] to [H. H.] Arnason and [Thomas] Messer, "Memorandum RE: Proposed Pop Artists Exhibition," August 28, 1962, folder "Exhibition Planning, undated 1962, 1963," box 148-T, LA-GMA. In this memo Alloway emphasized the historical precedents for representations of the popular in art. For his emphasis on paintings over objects, see Lawrence Alloway, "Six Painters," [3], in Lawrence Alloway, *Six Painters and the Object* (New York: Solomon R. Guggenheim Foundation, 1963). This catalog is unpaginated and the references are to pages on my marked copy, with [1] as the page of the introduction by Thomas M. Messer.

39. Sir Joshua Reynolds, from Robert R. Wark, ed., *Sir Joshua Reynolds, Discourses on*

Art (San Marino, Calif.: Huntington Library, 1959), 107, quoted in Lawrence Alloway, "Six Painters and the Object," in Alloway, *Six Painters*, [6]; Alloway, "Six Painters," [6] and [13].

40. Alloway, "Six Painters," [15], [3], [4], and [6].

41. John Ashbery, untitled essay, 1962, in *New Realists*, [2]; Pierre Restany, "A Metamorphosis in Nature," 1962, in *New Realists*, inside cover; S. J. [Sidney Janis], "On the Theme of the Exhibition," *New Realists*, [5] and [6]. For the works in the show, see exhibition catalog, *The New Realists* ([New York: Sidney Janis Gallery, 1962]).

42. "Pop Goes the Easel," *Newsweek*, April 1, 1963, 80; Thomas M. Messer, introduction to Lawrence Alloway, *Six Painters*, [1].

43. Hilla Rebay, "The Power of Spiritual Rhythm," in *Art of Tomorrow: Fifth Catalogue of the Solomon R. Guggenheim Collection of Non-Objective Paintings . . . Opening June 1st, 1939* (New York: Solomon R. Guggenheim Museum, [1939]), 5. Sleigh, interview, noted the way, among other factors, Messer's eagerness to please members of the Guggenheim family caused tension between Messer and Alloway.

44. Oral history interview with Thomas M. Messer, October 1994–January 1995, Archives of American Art, Smithsonian Institution, conducted by Andrew Decker. The quotes in this section come from that interview. On Messer, I am also relying on Contemporary Authors Online (Gale, 2002); http://www.radio.cz/en/article/103926 (accessed February 16, 2011). The former gives Messer's birth year as 1920 and the latter as 1919.

45. Messer, oral history.

46. Grace Glueck, "Not Exactly Trying to Please," *NYT*, June 19, 1966, 108, including quotes from Alloway; see also Glueck, "Alloway."

47. For discussions of the debates on pop art, on which what follows relies, see Carol Anne Mahsun, *Pop Art and the Critics* (Ann Arbor, Mich.: UMI Research Press, 1987), and two collections of essays—Madoff, ed., *Pop Art* and Carol Anne Mahsun, ed., *Pop Art: The Critical Dialogue* (Ann Arbor, Mich.: UMI Research Press, 1989). Cécile Whiting, *A Taste for Pop: Pop Art, Gender, and Consumer Culture* (Cambridge: Cambridge University Press, 1997), offers a penetrating analysis of the debate in historical and gendered terms. For some of the important scholarship on the relationship between pop artists and the media, see Michael Lobel, *Image Duplicator: Roy Lichtenstein and the Emergence of Pop Art* (New Haven, Conn.: Yale University Press, 2002); Joseph Branden, "'A Duplication Containing Duplications,'" *October* 95 (Winter 2001): 3–27. There is a huge literature on pop art, including William C. Seitz, *Art in the Age of Aquarius, 1955–1970* (Washington, D.C.: Smithsonian Institution Press, 1992); Sidra Stich, *Made in U.S.A.: An Americanization in Modern Art, the '50s and '60s* (Berkeley: University of California Press, 1987); Christin J. Mamiya, *Pop Art and Consumer Culture: American Super Market* (Austin: University of Texas Press, 1992); Russell Ferguson, ed., *Hand-Painted Pop; American Art in Transition, 1955–62* (Los Angeles: Museum of Contemporary Art, 1992). Heinz Beck, *Pop-sammlung Beck* (Dusseldorf: Rheinland-Verlag, 1990), contains a comprehensive list of critical reaction to pop art.

48. Paul Berg. "About-Face from the Abstract," *St. Louis Post-Dispatch: Sunday Pictures*, December 31, 1961, 10–11. The summary in this paragraph draws on Whiting, *Taste for Pop*, 4.

49. Leo Steinberg, comments at symposium on pop art, Museum of Modern Art, December 13, 1962, reprinted in Madoff, ed., *Pop Art* , 73; John Coplans, "Pop Art, USA [1963]," in Madoff, ed., *Pop Art*, 98.

50. Clement Greenberg, "After Abstract Expressionism [1962]," in Henry Geldzahler, *New York Painting and Sculpture: 1940–1970* (New York: E. P. Dutton, 1969), 371; Clement Greenberg, introduction to *Post Painterly Abstraction* ([Los Angeles]: [Los Angeles County Museum of Art and Contemporary Arts Council], 1964), [5]; Harold Rosenberg, "The Art Establishment," *Esquire*, January 1965, 46; Stanley Kunitz, comments at symposium on pop art, Museum of Modern Art, December 13, 1962, reprinted in Madoff, ed., *Pop Art* , 74–75 ("genius").

51. John Canaday, "Pop Art Sells On and On—Why?" *NYTM*, May 31, 1964, 7 ff, reprinted in Madoff, ed., *Pop Art*, 121; Peter Selz, "The Flaccid Art [1963]," in Madoff, ed., *Pop Art*, 86; Alan R. Solomon, "The New Art [1963]," in Madoff, ed., *Pop Art*, 92; "Pop Art—Cult of the Commonplace," *Time*, May 3, 1963, 69 (nouveau); Max Kozloff, "Pop Culture, Metaphysical Disgust and the New Vulgarians [1962]," in Mahsun, ed., *Pop Art*, 22; Herbert Read, "Disintegration of Form in Modern Art [1965]," in Mahsun, ed., *Pop Art*, 90. Read did not mention any specific artists but instead illustrated his article with pieces by Dine, Oldenburg, Rauschenberg, Johns, Lichtenstein, and Warhol.

52. Thomas Hess, "Mixed Media for a Soft Revolution [1960]," in Mahsun, ed., *Pop Art*, 8; Henry Geldzahler, comments at December 13, 1962, symposium at Museum of Modern Art, reprinted in Madoff, ed., *Pop Art*, 66 (emphasis in original); Brian O'Doherty, "Art: Avant-Garde Revolt," *NYT*, October 31, 1962, quoted in Madoff, ed., *Pop Art*, 41.

53. Susan Sontag, "Against Interpretation [1964]," in Susan Sontag, *Against Interpretation, and Other Essays* (New York: Farrar, Straus and Giroux, 1966), 10; Susan Sontag, "Happenings: An Art of Radical Juxtaposition [1962]," in Sontag, *Against Interpretation*, 269 and 267–69; Sontag, "Notes on 'Camp' [1964]," in Sontag, *Against Interpretation*, 292. Harold Rosenberg said that McLuhan's *Mechanical Bride* was "'a kind of pop art'": Rosenberg, quoted in Arnold Rockman, "McLuhanism: The Natural History of an Intellectual Fashion," *Encounter* 31 (November 1968): 28.

54. Susan Sontag, "Jack Smith's *Flaming Creatures* [1964]," in Sontag, *Against Interpretation*, 226 and 229–30. Sontag's view of pop art—its reception rather than the art itself—soon changed dramatically. She linked her opposition to the escalation of the war in Vietnam with the way she believed promoters of pop art celebrated the American way of life: Susan Sontag, "Non-Writing and the Art Scene [1965]," in *The New Art: A Critical Anthology*, ed. Gregory Battcock (New York: E. P. Dutton, 1966), 152–54 and 156.

55. Jim Dine, in "What Is Pop Art: Interviews with G. R. Swenson," part 1, *ArN* 62 (November 1963): 62; Roy Lichtenstein, in "What Is Pop Art," part 1, 25. See also Stich, *Made in the U.S.A*, 17 and 19.

56. Andy Warhol, in "What Is Pop Art," 26; James Rosenquist, in "What Is Pop Art: Interviews with G. R. Swenson," part 2, *ArN* 62 (February 1964): 63; Jasper Johns, in "What Is Pop Art," part 2, 43 and 66. For a later, more political response, see James Rosenquist, interview with G. R. Swenson, *PR* 32 (Autumn 1965): 589–601.

57. Jean Baudrillard, "Pop—An Art of Consumption? [1970]" in Taylor, ed., *Post-Pop Art*, 44 (emphasis in original); Max Kozloff, "American Painting during the Cold War," *Artforum* 11 (May 1973): 52; Donald Kuspit, "Pop Art: A Reactionary Realism [1976]," in Madoff, ed., *Pop Art*, 203–5; Moira Roth, "The Aesthetics of Indifference," *Artforum* 16 (November 1977): 53. For an example of how to complicate the debate over complicity and criticism, see Hal Foster, *Return of the Real: The Avant-Garde at the End of the Century* (Cambridge, Mass.: MIT, 1996).

58. Hebdige, "Poor Taste," 59, 60, and 67. An example of another critic is Fred Orton, *Figuring Jasper Johns* (Cambridge, Mass.: Harvard University Press, 1994), 51, 129–30, and 145–46. For a critique of Hebdige's essay that also contains useful information on the IG, see Anne Massey and Penny Sparke, "The Myth of the Independent Group," *Block* 10 (1985): 48–56.

59. Kenneth E. Silver, "Modes of Disclosure: The Construction of Gay Identity and the Rise of Pop Art," in Ferguson, ed., *Hand-Painted*, 179–203.

60. Greenberg, "After Abstract Expressionism" 363; Whiting, *Taste for Pop*, xi; see also 1–7, 65, 78, 80–81, and 109–10.

61. All of these appear in Lawrence Alloway, *American Pop Art* (New York: Collier, 1974).

62. Alloway, "Pop Art: The Words," 176–79; Robert Venturi, *Complexity and Contradiction in Architecture* (New York: Museum of Modern Art, 1966), 52, partly quoted in Alloway, "Pop Art: The Words," 149. For a hardly defensive position on pop, see Alloway, "Development," 27–66. At crucial points in "Pop Art: The Words" Alloway seemed confused. Much of the art displayed at the Guggenheim in 1963 was produced before 1961 and was thus part of the first, expansive phrase. Yet if I am correct in reading the document in autobiographical terms, as an acknowledgment of the context in which he developed the Guggenheim exhibition, then the notion of expansion and narrowing helps us explain his perspective on his own work. In addition, a key paragraph, the one that begins "During 1965–66," seems to indicate that Alloway saw explosive, not constrictive elements in the second period. However, overall the thrust of the article is that a second, narrowing period (1961–64) followed an expansive, capacious one. For other places where he repeated much of what he said in "Pop Art: The Words," see Lawrence Alloway, "Popular Culture and Pop Art," *Studio International* 178 (July 1969): 16–21; Alloway, *American Pop Art*, 3–23. This book appeared in conjunction with an exhibition he curated at the Whitney Museum of American Art in the spring of 1974.

63. Seago, *Burning the Box*, 3; Harrison, *Pop Art*, 1–8 and 37–67, with the quote on 37. Seago, *Burning the Box*, 114–22, explores the transformative contribution of Alloway's work. See also Kalina, "Imagining the Present," 4, where he sees Alloway as "an early voice for the broadened view of postmodernism; for his work is a brief for complexity, competing messages, multiple readings, antagonistic cooperation, and ambiguity." In 1981 Alloway gave a talk on the subject of postmodernism in which he resisted the use of the term and its application to his work: Lawrence Alloway, in Lawrence Alloway et al., *The Idea of the Post-Modern: Who Is Teaching It?* (Seattle: Henry Art Gallery, University of Washington, 1981), 7–12.

Chapter 7

1. Among the places to enter the voluminous literature on the Center are Lawrence Grossberg, "The Formation of Cultural Studies: An American in Birmingham," *Strategies* 2 (1989): 114–49 and http://www.gseis.ucla.edu/faculty/kellner/papers/CSETHIC.htm (accessed February 17, 2011); Stuart Hall, "Cultural Studies and the Centre: Some Problematics and Problems," in *Culture, Media, Language*, ed. Stuart Hall (London: Routledge, 1980), 15–47. Frank Webster, "Cultural Studies and Sociology at, and after, the Closure of the Birmingham School," *Cultural Studies* 18 (November 2004): 847–62, offers a history of cultural studies at the university. Ann Gray et al., eds., *CCCS Selected Working Papers* (London: Routledge, 2007), has collected many of the most important essays in two volumes. For discussions of the development of cultural studies, the events of 1956, and the shift from Old to New Left, the best place to begin is Dennis Dworkin, *Cultural Marxism in Postwar Britain: History, the New Left, and the Origins of Cultural Studies* (Durham, N.C.: Duke University Press, 1997); see also Grant Farred, "Introduction," *Disposito/n* 21 (1996): v–xx, and some of the secondary literature cited below. For one of Hall's discussions of cultural studies, where he emphasizes the difference between the late 1950s paradigm that grew out of the work of Hoggart and Williams and the paradigm that began to develop in the late 1960s following the works of Antonio Gramsci, Claude Lévi-Strauss, Louis Althusser, and others, see Stuart Hall, "Cultural Studies: Two Paradigms," *Media, Culture and Society* 2 (1981): 57–72. On the history of the New Left, including its development of clubs and coffeehouses, as well as its connection to the Free Cinema movement, see David R. Holden, "The First New Left in Britain, 1956–1962" (Ph.D. diss., University of Wisconsin, Madison, 1976); Lin Zhun, *The British New Left* (Edinburgh: Edinburgh University Press, 1993). For a bibliography of Hall's writings, see "A Working Bibliography: The Writings of Stuart Hall," in *Stuart Hall: Critical Dialogues in Cultural Studies*, ed. David Morley and Kuan-Hsing Chen (London: Routledge, 1996), 504–14. Grant Farred, *What's My Name: Black Vernacular Intellectuals* (Minneapolis: University of Minnesota Press, 2003), 151, 154, and 179–94, remarks that Hall began to write about race in his published writings beginning in 1970. As noted in my text and notes, beginning as an editor of and writer in *Universities and Left Review* and continuing with *The Young Englanders* (London: National Committee for Commonwealth Immigrants, 1967), Hall focused on race earlier than Farred suggests. Yet Farred is correct that in his writing Hall did not turn to a full engagement with race and with West Indians in Britain until relatively late in his career. Farred is even more perceptive in his discussion of how it was not until the late 1980s that Hall revealed the role race played in his family's life when he was growing up in Jamaica.

2. Stuart Hall and Paddy Whannel, *The Popular Arts* (London: Hutchinson Educational, 1964). The evidence is that Hall and Whannel were coauthors, although who is responsible for what is impossible to determine; what complicates this situation is that Hall is more famous than Whannel and there is more information on Hall than there is on Whannel.

3. Grant Farred, "'The First Shall Be Last': Locating *The Popular Arts* in the Stuart Hall *Ouevre*," in Brian Meeks, *Culture, Politics, Race and Disapora: The Thought of Stuart*

Hall (Kingston: Ian Randle, 2007), 91; for Farred's perceptive discussion of the Hall and Whannel book, to which I came after writing this chapter, see 85–97.

4. For information on Whannel I am relying on the finding aid to his papers at the University Archives, Northwestern University: http://www.library.northwestern.edu/archives/findingaids/paddy_whannel.pdf (accessed February 17, 2011). On Whannel's work at the BFI, I am relying on Laura Mulvey and Peter Wollen, with Lee Grieveson, "From Cinephilia to Film Studies," in *Inventing Film Studies*, ed. Lee Grieveson and Haidee Wasson (Durham, N.C.: Duke University Press, 2008), 217–32, and Terry Bolas, *Screen Education: From Film Appreciation to Media Studies* (Bristol: Intellect, 2009), esp. 6, 58, 84–85, 90–93, 110, 123–25, 138–47, 152–53, 163–69, 172–80, and 182–86. Neither piece pays adequate attention to the origin of Whannel's film work in his experience as a teacher in secondary schools. The work by Bolas, otherwise thorough in locating sources, does not focus on what Whannel wrote as Albert Casey. For other material on film, see Paddy Whannel, "Where Do We Go from Here?" *Screen Education* 7 (March–April 1961): 7–9.

5. For confirmation of his authorship, see Whannel's c.v., folder 1, box 1, PW-NU. My discussion of Whannel's early writings draws on his articles published in the *Teacher* up to and including the one in which he talked about *The Popular Arts*. For the writings of others on teaching mass media, see, for example, a six-part series that begins with Donald Leach, "We Are Responsible," *Te*, March 1, 1963, 13.

6. Albert Casey, "Background to Debate," *Te*, March 5, 1965, 8. The second quote on Macdonald comes from Albert Casey, "Two Sides of a Coin," *Te,* July 12, 1963, 10.

7. Paddy Whannel, "Artist, Critic and Teacher," *ULR* 4 (Summer 1958): 34, including a quotation ("aristocratic") from a writer in *Times Educational Supplement*. See also Brian Groombridge and Paddy Whannel, "Something Rotten in Denmark Street Popular Art," *NLR* 1 (January–February 1960): 53

8. Paddy Whannel, "Towards a Positive Criticism of the Mass Media," *Film Teacher*, May 17, 1959, 30 ("cinema"); Albert Casey, "Are These the Corrupters?" *Te*, April 12, 1963, 16 ("communication"); Albert Casey, "Newsom, Sex and the Cinema," *Te*, November 8, 1963, 14 ("indignation"); Groombridge and Whannel, "Rotten," 52 ("scratch"). See also Albert Casey, "Do We Care?" *Te*, December 13, 1963, 8; Albert Casey, "Two Sides of a Coin," *Te*, July 12, 1963, 10. For a list of books on which he drew, see Whannel, "Towards," 29–30. On his debt to Leavis, see Paddy Whannel and Peter Harcourt, "Introduction," in Paddy Whannel and Peter Harcourt, eds., *Studies in the Teaching of Film within Formal Education: Four Courses Described* (London: British Film Institute, 1968), 7.

9. Whannel and Harcourt, "Introduction," 7 ("whole"; I date this as 1964, since the editors made clear that there were few changes made to the first, 1964 edition: Whannel and Harcourt, "Note to the Second Edition," *Studies in the Teaching,* 9); Whannel and Harcourt, "Introduction," 5 ("bring"); Casey, "Corrupters," 16 ("comparable," "modest," and "pure"). For other iterations on these themes, see Albert Casey, "On the Same Side," *Te*, June 14, 1963, 10; Albert Casey, "Blood without Thunder," *Screen Education* (September–October 1962): 25–26; Albert Casey, "When the Masterpieces Aren't Around," *Te*, February 14, 1964, 18.

10. Casey, "Same Side," 10. See also Albert Casey, "Worth Encouraging," *Te*, February 15, 1963, 16; Whannel and Harcourt, "Introduction," 6–8.

11. Albert Casey, "Christmas Revelation," *Te*, January 18, 1963, 10 ("sickening" "Chandler"); Albert Casey, "The Last of the Movies," *Te*, October 11, 1963, 16 ("submerged"). See also Albert Casey, "Rich Man's Spillane," *Te*, November 6, 1964, 14.

12. Albert Casey, "About England," *Te*, April 17, 1964, 16.

13. Albert Casey, "A Bleak Christmas for Pop Art," *Te*, January 10, 1964, 14.

14. Albert Casey, "A Question of Values," *Te*, August 16, 1963, 3.

15. Albert Casey, "The Popular Arts on 625," *Te*, July 3, 1964, 12 ("lovable"); Casey, "Corrupters?" 16 ("raw"). There is at least one mention, somewhat in passing, of race and colonialism in Britain: Casey, "Newsom," 14. I did not locate much in the way of discussion of homosexuality. In one instance Whannel focused on a film, *The Leather Boy*, which told the story of a "relationship where there is no sexual tension" between a "boy who happens to be a homosexual" and a friend dealing with an unhappy marriage: Casey, "Masterpieces," 18. The one example I could find of his treatment of same-sex love among women seemed to reflect a homophobia not present in his discussion of male-male relations: he found the film version of *Goldfinger* "less perverted" than the novel because it had eliminated the "Lesbianism of Pussy Galore and Tilly Masterman": Casey, "Spillane," 14 (Whannel misspelled the name of Tilly Masterson). For a favorable review of Francis Newton's *The Jazz Scene*, see Paddy Whannel, "Jazz and Its Publics," *ULR* 7 (Autumn 1959): 69–70; on how Hall and Whannel handled jazz, see George McKay, *Circular Breathing: The Cultural Politics of Jazz in Britain* (Durham, N.C.: Duke University Press, 2005), 30 and 36. Francis Newton, the pseudonym of Eric Hobsbawm, was the author of an important book on jazz that he published as he was about to emerge as an influential Marxist historian: Francis Newton, *The Jazz Scene* (1959; New York: Monthly Review Press, 1960). On the place of this book in the history of jazz criticism, see John Gennari, *Blowin' Hot and Cool: Jazz and Its Critics* (Chicago: University of Chicago Press, 2006), 61–63 and 94–95; McKay, *Circular Breathing*, 309, n 1.

16. Whannel and Harcourt, "Introduction," 5 ("vehicle"); Albert Casey, "Critics and Sociologists," *Te*, December 4, 1964, 10 ("ourselves"); Paddy Whannel, "Receiving the Message," *Definition* 3 (1960): 15 ("viewer").

17. Groombridge and Whannel, "Rotten," 53 ("non-conformism") and 54 ("boxes"); Paddy Whannel, "Room at the Top," *ULR* 6 (Spring 1959): 24 ("peep-show"); Casey, "Corrupters," 16 ("picture"); see also Casey, "Newsom," 14. For his discussion of how media reinforced already existing beliefs rather than imposed new ones, see Albert Casey, "Facts and Prejudices," *Te*, March 13, 1964, 16. See also Casey, "Corrupters," 116. For his review of a report on the influence of television on children, see Paddy Whannel, "Television and the Child," *ULR* 6 (Spring 1959): 69–71. For Whannel's skepticism about the work of sociologists and appreciation of the Q. D. Leavis and the Birmingham Center, see Albert Casey, "Prejudices," 16; Albert Casey, "Sociologists," 10.

18. Casey, "Corrupters," 16 ("leisure"); Albert Casey, "Celluloid Beatles," *Te*, August 7, 1964, 8 ("sour"); Groombridge and Whannel, "Rotten," 54 ("nourish"); on Ella, see Casey, "Corrupters," 16, and Groombridge and Whannel, "Rotten," 54. In another article Whan-

nel paid some attention to working-class and middle-class youth, but principally in the context of a consideration of the lives of middle-class adults: Casey, "About England," 18.

19. Stuart Hall, in Maya Jaggi, "Prophet at the Margins," http://www.guardian.co.uk/ books/2000/jul/08/society (accessed February 18, 2011). Chris Rojek, *Stuart Hall* (Cambridge: Polity, 2003), 49–63, offers a careful, sophisticated, and probing analysis of Hall's situations in Jamaica and Britain and their relationships to his ideas. Hall was right in thinking of his parents' position as anachronistic, especially given that brown, middle-class men played such a prominent role in the nationalist movement that began in the late 1930s. Though advocating political independence from Britain, in most other ways his parents relied on Britain for the social, cultural, and political norms: Rojek, *Hall*, 52. For Hall's assertion that he never heard the word "black" spoken while in Jamaica before he left for Oxford, see Stuart Hall, "Negotiating Caribbean Identities [1995]," in *New Caribbean Thought: A Reader*, ed. Brian Meeks and Folke Lindahl (Kingston: University of West Indies Press, 2001), 30.

In addition to works cited elsewhere, for information on Hall I am relying on Stuart Hall, interview with Tim Adams, *Observer*, September 23, 2007, http://www.guardian. co.uk/society/2007/sep/23/communities.politicsphilosophyandsociety (accessed February 18, 2011); Stuart Hall, "The 'First' New Left," in Robin Archer et al., *Out of Apathy: Voices of the New Left Thirty Years On* (London: Verso, 1989), 13–38; Jaggi, "Prophet"; Stuart Hall, "The Formation of a Diasporic Intellectual: An Interview with Stuart Hall by Kuan-Hsing Chen," in Morley and Chen, ed., *Stuart Hall*, 484–503; Stuart Hall, "Minimal Selves," in *Black British Cultural Studies: A Reader*, ed. Houston A. Baker Jr., Manthia Diawara, and Ruth A. Lindeborg (Chicago: University of Chicago Press, 1996), 114–19; Stuart Hall, "Cultural Studies and Its Theoretical Legacies," in *Cultural Studies*, ed. Lawrence Grossberg, Cary Nelson, and Paula A. Treichler (New York: Routledge, 1992), 277–93; Helen Davis, *Understanding Stuart Hall* (London: Sage, 2004); Stuart Hall, interview with Caryl Phillips, *Bomb: A Quarterly Arts and Culture Magazine* 58 (Winter 1997), http://www.bombsite.com/issues/58/articles/2030 (accessed February 18, 2011); Stuart Hall, "Old and New Identities, Old and New Ethnicities," in *Culture, Globalization and the World-System: Contemporary Conditions for the Representation of Identity*, ed. Anthony D. King (Minneapolis: University of Minnesota Press, 1997), 41–68; Stuart Hall, "Interview with Professor Stuart Hall (by Roger Bromley) [1992]," in *A Cultural Studies Reader: History, Theory, Practice*, ed. Jessica Munns and Gita Rajan (London: Longman, 1995), 658–73; Stuart Hall, "Negotiating," 3–14; Stuart Hall, "Epilogue: Through the Prism on an Intellectual Life," in Meeks, ed., *Culture, Politics, Race and Diaspora*, 269–91; James Procter, *Stuart Hall* (London: Routledge, 2004); Rojek, *Hall*; Grant Farred, "You Can Go Home Again, You Just Can't Stay: Stuart Hall and the Caribbean Diaspora," *Research in African Literatures* 27 (Winter 1996): 28–48; Harry Stecopoulos, "Stuart Hall," *Dictionary of Literary Biography* (Detroit: Gale, 2001), 242: 199–208; Dworkin, *Cultural*, esp. 118–20. For a critical assessment of Hall's ideas from a more orthodox Marxist perspective, see three essays by Colin Sparks: "Experience, Ideology, and Articulation: Stuart Hall and the Development of Culture," *Journal of Communication Inquiry* 13 (July 1989): 79–87; "Stuart Hall, Cultural Studies and Marxism," in Morley and Chen, eds., *Stuart Hall*, 71–101;

"Abuses of Literacy," *Working Papers in Cultural Studies* 6 (November–December 1974): 7–23.

20. Hall, in Jaggi, "Prophet" ("brown"); Hall, "Minimal," 116 ("family").

21. Hall, "'First,'" 16; see also Hall, "Interview with Professor Stuart Hall," 660.

22. Hall, "Interview with Professor Stuart Hall," 663 ("seriously"; emphasis in original); Stuart Hall, interview with Dai Smith, 1990, in Dai Smith, *Raymond Williams: A Warrior's Tale* (Cardigan: Parthian, 2008), 398–99 ("Henries"). Only beginning in the later 1960s, when translations of Louis Althusser, Walter Benjamin, and Georg Lukács became available, was Hall able to understand Marxism in new ways: Hall, "Interview with Professor Stuart Hall," 668.

23. Hall, "'First,'" 17–18. He also listed John Strachey, *The End of Empire*, which did not appear until 1959; perhaps he meant John Strachey, *Contemporary Capitalism* (1956).

24. Hall, "Interview with Professor Stuart Hall," 663–64. On the impact of these events, see Stuart Hall, "Political Commitment," in *The Committed Church*, ed. Laurence Bright and Simon Clements (London: Darton, Longman and Todd, 1966), 13.

25. Rojek, *Hall*, 58 speculates on the ways in which the writings of James were important to Hall.

26. On the emergence of the New Left in Britain, see Robert Hewison, *In Anger: British Culture in the Cold War, 1945–1960* (New York: Oxford University Press, 1981), 163–65.

27. Dworkin, *Cultural*, 3. On the dichotomies, see editorial, *ULR* 1 (Spring 1957): i.

28. Stuart Hall, "Absolute Beginnings," *ULR* 7 (Autumn 1959): 17 ("affronted"); Hall, *Young Englanders*, 3 ("stealing"). In *Young Englanders* Hall discussed teen culture, race, and resilience more fully than in previous works; page 15 provides some biographical information.

29. "The Habit of Violence," *ULR* 5 (Autumn 1958): 4–5. Notwithstanding this editorial, although it was unsigned, Farred, *Name*, 190–91, somewhat exaggerates Hall's silence on race and riots in the late 1950s, even as he acknowledges Hall's bravery in escorting black students to safety at the time of the riots. Yet is it puzzling that *ULR*, in reproducing the testimonials of white teenage girls, as well as in other ways, paid more attention to the alienation and grievances of white youth than black youth.

30. [Stuart Hall], "ULR to New Left Review," *ULR* 7 (Autumn 1959): 2. Of American writers, Mills was most important to those at *ULR*: there were eighteen references to him; five to Galbraith, and six to Riesman. For his discussion of the transformative nature of CND, see Hall, "Commitment," 25. For his retrospective view of CND, see Hall, "'First,'" 32.

31. On his secondary school teaching, see Hall, "Interview with Professor Stuart Hall," 665. For Hall's discussions of the Birmingham Center, including the hostility it experienced from departments of English and sociology, as well as how it discharged its debt to F. R. Leavis and Antonio Gramsci, see Stuart Hall, "The Emergence of Cultural Studies and the Crisis of the Humanities," *October* 53 (Summer 1990): 11–23. For a discussion of Hall as a postmodernist, see Stuart Hall, interview with Lawrence Grossberg, "On Postmodernism and Articulation [1986]," in Morley and Chen, eds., *Stuart Hall*, 131–50. For a discussion of Hall (and others in the New Left) as a bridge between modernism and postmodernism, see Susan M. Brook, *Literature and Cultural Criticism in the 1950s: The*

Feeling Male Body (Houndmills: Palgrave Macmillan, 2007), 1, 16, 19, and 20. For one of Hoggart's discussions of the history of the Center, see Richard Hoggart, *An Imagined Life* (London: Chatto and Windus, 1992), 90–100.

32. Stuart Hall and Norm Fruchter, "Notes on the Cuban Dilemma," *NLR* 9 (May–June 1961): 2 ("system"), 6 ("flair"), and 9 ("abuse"); Stuart Hall and Perry Anderson, "Politics of the Common Market," *NLR* 10 (July–August 1961): 14 ("radical"). In addition to works already cited, this discussion of Hall's ideas draws on the following articles: "The New Conservatism and the Old," *ULR* 1 (Spring 1957): 21–24; "In the No Man's Land," *ULR* 3 (Winter 1958): 86–87. For a slightly later essay, in which he made clear how youth, race, and anticolonialism upset the usual political calculations, see Hall, "Commitment," 3–25.

33. "Editorial," *NLR* 1 (January–February 1960): 1 ("future"); Stuart Hall, "Crosland Territory," *NLR* 2 (March–April 1960): 4 ("needs").

34. "Editorial," *NLR* 1 (January–February 1960): 1; see also Hall, "No Man's Land," 86. Although the editorial is unsigned, I assume that Hall played a key role in its composition.

35. Hall, "A Sense of Classlessness," *ULR* 5 (Autumn 1958): 28 and 30. As well as this essay, the key writings that reveal his reading of American writers include Stuart Hall, "The Big Swipe," *ULR* 7 (Autumn 1959): 50–52; and Stuart Hall, "The Supply of Demand," in *Out of Apathy*, ed. E. P. Thompson (London: New Left Books, 1960), 56–97. In addition, there are hints in Hall's writing of the influence of William H. Whyte Jr.'s *The Organization Man* (1956) and Vance Packard's *The Status Seekers* (1959), the former more acknowledged than the latter. Hall has written that a key turning point came when Taylor returned from Paris with a French version of the early writings of Marx, which were soon translated into English: Hall, "'First,'" 27–28. In addition, he would have had access to some of Marx's early writings, especially on alienation, which appeared in Karl Marx, *Selected Writings in Sociology and Social Philosophy*, ed. T. B. Bottomore and Maximilien Rubel, trans. T. B. Bottomore (London: Watts, 1956), esp. 167–73, 177, and 243–46. The French connection was important in the shaping of the British New Left, through the explorations of common interests with the *nouvelle gauche*: Dworkin, *Cultural*, 55.

36. Hall, "Supply," 74–75.

37. Ibid., 95 ("telly"; emphasis in original); Hall, "Classlessness," 29 ("alienation," emphasis in original); ibid., 82 ("demanded" and "prosperity") and 81 ("Dorchester"). For another reference to Jamaicans, this time in London, see Stuart Hall, "Liberal Studies," in Whannel and Harcourt, *Film Teaching*, 15. See also Hall, "Classlessness," 31, Hall, "Supply," 65 and 71, Hall, "Crosland," 3. For Hall's complex view of sex, see Stuart Hall, "The Novel and Its Relationship to Lawrence's Work," *NLR* 6 (November–December 1960): 32–35. If "Classlessness" represented his boldest effort to reorient social analysis, in "Supply," published two years later in 1960, he offered a more hard-edged critique of capitalism. The difference, I suspect, came from Hall's having to respond to the criticisms of the first piece.

38. Hall, "Classlessness," 28 ("shops"; emphasis in original) and 40 ("competitiveness"); Hall, "Supply," 71 ("bland") and 90 ("envy").

39. Hall, "Classlessness," 31 ("styles"; emphasis in original); Hall, "Supply," 63 ("faults").

40. Editorial, *ULR* 4 (Summer 1958), 1 ("community"); Hall, "Classlessness," 27 ("vulgar") and 31 ("peripheral"). On Hall's rethinking of the relationship between base and superstructure, see Procter, *Hall*, 16–18.

41. C. Wright Mills, "Letter to the New Left," *NLR* 5 (September–October 1960): 22; Hall, "Absolute," 20, 18, and 19. For an important discussion of Mills as a part of the global New Left, see Daniel Geary, "'Becoming International Again': C. Wright Mills and the Emergence of a Global New Left, 1956–1962," *JAH* 95 (December 2008): 710–36. The editors of *ULR* made clear that a key element of their audience was young people: editorial, *ULR* 4 (Summer 1958): 3. For articles that focused on youth, see, for example, Michael Kullman, "The Face of Youth: The Anti-Culture Born of Despair," *ULR* 4 (Summer 1958): 51; Derek Allcorn, "The Unnoticed Generation," *URL* 4 (Summer 1958): 54; Greta Duncan and Roy Wilkie, "Glasgow Adolescents," *ULR* 5 (Autumn 1958): 24–25.

42. Hall, "Absolute," 20 and 21.

43. Ibid., 25. For his analysis of the political implications of youthful rebellion in the wake of the riots at Notting Hill, see Stuart Hall, "Politics of Adolescence?" *ULR* 6 (Spring 1959): 2–4. Here he focused on the difficulty the Labour Party had in holding the allegiance of working-class youth, their "instinctive" radicalism (p. 2), the strength of their feeling combined with their lack of a language to express what they felt. On the discovery of youth culture in the late 1950s and early 1960s, see Dominic Sandbrook, *Never Had It So Good: A History of Britain from Suez to the Beatles* (London: Little, Brown, 2005), 407–12 and 417–19.

44. Hall, "No Man's Land," 87; Brook, *Literature*, 16; for her more extended argument, on which I am drawing in important ways, see Brook, *Literature*, 1–43. See also Raymond Williams, "Film and the Dramatic Tradition," in Raymond Williams and Michael Orrom, *Preface to Film* (London: Film Drama, 1954), 21–22.

45. Hall, "Adolescence," 3 ("conciliatory"); Hall, "No Man's Land," 86 ("moral") and 87 ("novel"); F. R. Leavis quoted on 87.

46. Hall, "Adolescence," 3. Hall clearly knew of Mailer's essay, which Clancy Sigal had written about in *ULR*: Clancy Sigal, "Nihilism's Organization Man," *ULR* 4 (Summer 1958): 59–65.

47. Stuart Hall, "Inside the Whale Again?" *ULR* 4 (Summer 1958): 15 ("meaning"); Stuart Hall, "Commitment Dilemma," *NLR* 10 (July–August 1961): 68 ("treatises"); Stuart Hall, "Mr Raymond and the Dead Souls," *ULR* 4 (Summer 1958): 82 ("depth"). For a discussion of the relationship between advertising, capitalism, and status systems, see Robert Cassen, compiler, "I Dreamed I Stopped the Traffic . . . ," *ULR* 5 (Autumn 1958): 75–78.

48. E. P. Thompson, "Commitment in Politics," *ULR* 6 (Spring 1959): 50–51.

49. Stuart Hall, "Swipe,"50. Another critique appeared in Ralph Samuel, "Class and Classlessness," *ULR* 6 (1959): 44–50. Among other things, Samuel criticized Hall for applying the analysis of Riesman and Whyte, developed to explain the world of the American upper middle class to the British working class. For a discussion of this controversy, see Michael Kenny, *The First New Left: British Intellectuals after Stalin* (London: Lawrence and Wishart, 1995), 54–66. On the changes in the New Left in the early 1960s, see Bryan

D. Palmer, *The Making of E. P. Thompson: Marxism, Humanism, and History* (Toronto: New Hogtown, 1981), 55–64.

50. S. W. Exworthy, opening comments, in NUT, National Union of Teachers, *Popular Culture and Personal Responsibility: A Conference of Those Engaged in Education . . . to Examine the Impact of the Media of Mass Communications on Present-Day Moral and Cultural Standards* (London: National Union of Teachers, 1960), 1. For a discussion of the conference, see Stuart Laing, *Representations of Working-Class Life, 1957–1964* (Houndmills: Macmillan, 1986), 193–217. Tony Judt, *Postwar: A History of Europe since 1945* (New York: Penguin, 2005), 230, emphasizes the persistence of traditional cultural authority well into the postwar period.

51. Whannel, comments in NUT, *Responsibility*, 94–96 and 317.

52. Hall, comments in NUT, *Responsibility*, 327–28.

53. Hamilton, in NUT, *Responsibility*, 138, 139, and 150; resolution from 1960 National Union of Teachers Annual Conference, quoted in Hall and Whannel, *Popular*, 23. For their own discussion of the shoals the teacher had to navigate, see 391–92.

54. Hall and Whannel, *Popular*, 47. For a full statement of Hall's approach to teaching film, see Hall, "Liberal Studies," 10–27. For their list of projects, see Hall and Whannel, *Popular*, 402–68. Among the discussions of the book are Dworkin, *Cultural*, 117–20; John Storey, *An Introductory Guide to Cultural Theory and Popular Culture* (New York: Harvester/Wheatsheaf, 1993), 60–67; Procter, *Hall*, 19–25; Farred, *Name*, 163–65; Graeme Turner, *British Cultural Studies: An Introduction* (Boston: Unwin Hyman, 1990), 73–74.

55. Hall and Whannel, *Popular*, 13 and 37.

56. McLuhan, *Mechanical Bride*, quoted in Hall and Whannel, *Popular*, 401; Hall and Whannel, *Popular*, 37 and 51.

57. Hall and Whannel, *Popular*, 29, 53, 39 (and Q. D. Leavis, quoted on 39), 90, 72, 72, 90, 307, and 108. For further discussion of communication between performer and audience, see 229 and 232–33.

58. Ibid., 64–65.

59. Hall, "Liberal Studies," 10 and 19; Hall and Whannel, *Popular*, 31. See also Hall and Whannel, *Popular*, 32, 38, 45, 64, 191–95, 196–97, and 203–4. In *The Popular Arts*, Hall and Whannel made clear that they drew on Williams's discussion of structure of feeling in his *Preface to Film*: see p. 45.

60. Hall and Whannel, *Popular*, 47, 329, 15, and 47 (emphasis in original); see also ibid., 42–44 and plates 2 and 3.

61. Raymond Williams, "The Magic System [1960]," quoted in Hall and Whannel, *Popular*, 314 and 319; Hall and Whannel, *Popular*, 336.

62. Hall and Whannel, *Popular*, 322, 319, and 336. For the Vaseline ad, see 322–24 and photo insert, number 15.

63. Ibid., 316 and 336.

64. Ibid., 273, 269–70, 276, and 190. Inspired by the Leavisite tradition of analyzing popular culture, in the early 1950s Hoggart had begun to write a textbook on mass culture but instead produced *The Uses of Literacy*: John Corner and Richard Hoggart, "Postscript:

Studying Culture—Reflections and Assessments: An Interview with Richard Hoggart [1991]," in Richard Hoggart, *The Uses of Literacy* (New Brunswick, N.J.: Transaction Publishers, 1998), 271.

65. Hall and Whannel, *Popular*, 281, 311, 312, 276, 32, and plate 1. For their discussion of the Twist, see 302.

66. Ibid., 296. The reviews of *The Popular Arts* were not terribly positive, in part because many reviewers felt the book paled in comparison with Marshall McLuhan's *Understanding Media*, and in one case Umberto Eco's *Apocalittici e integrati*, both of which also appeared in 1964: Eli M. Oboler, review of *The Popular Arts*, *Library Journal* 90 (July 1965): 3062; the joint review of works by Hall/Whannel and Eco appeared in *TLS*, December 17, 1964, 1137–38. For a favorable review that played Hall/Whannel off both McLuhan and Hoggart, see DeMott, review of Hall/Whannel, *The Popular Arts*, *Reporter*, October 21, 1965, 55–57. Davis, *Hall*, 20–23, provides a careful evaluation of the book, its reception, and influence.

67. Hall and Whannel, *Popular*, 302, 305, 282, and 287. See also Dworkin, *Cultural*, 119. At the last minute, Hall and Whannel added a more appreciative postscript on the Beatles' *A Hard Day's Night*, which premiered in London on July 6, 1964: Hall and Whannel, *Popular*, 312. Whannel found it difficult to come to terms with the Beatles, Ornette Coleman, and newer expressions of R and B: Chuck Kleinhaus, email to author, October 21, 2009, copy in author's possession.

68. Farred, "Locating," 92, offers an explanation of why Hall and Whannel could not offer a racialized discussion of popular culture in contemporary Britain.

69. Hall, Phillips interview, http://bombsite.com/issues/58/articles/2030 (accessed February 20, 2011). In this section, I draw on Stuart Hall, "A Conversation with C. L. R. James," in *Rethinking C. L. R. James*, ed. Grant Farred (Cambridge, Mass.: Blackwell, 1996), 15–44; Stuart Hall, "C. L. R. James: A Portrait," in *C. L. R. James's Caribbean*, ed. Henry Paget and Paul Buhle (Durham, N.C.: Duke University Press, 1992), 3–16; Stuart Hall, interview with Phillips; Stuart Hall interviewed by Bill Schwarz, "Breaking Bread with History: C. L. R. James and *The Black Jacobins*," *History Workshop Journal* 47 (Autumn 1998): 17–31. I have also benefited from reading Farred, *Name*, especially the chapters on Hall and James.

70. On his views of the United Sates, see Hall, "C. L. R. James: A Portrait," 11.

71. Hall and Whannel, *Popular*, 78; Dworkin, *Cultural*, 120. On Hall and gender, I draw on Brook, *Literature*, 41.

72. DeMott, review, 55 ("nattering"); Storey, *Introductory*, 66 (emphasis in original). On how *The Popular Arts* broke fresh ground and pointed toward Hall's future work in cultural studies, see Farred, "Locating," 92–96. Scholars have put ample focus on the origins of cultural studies in adult education but have paid relatively little attention to the origins of cultural studies in a new generation's engagement with secondary school education. Indeed, most scholars when they deal with Hall move from work he did at *ULR* and *NLR* directly to his role at the Birmingham Center, skipping over the book he wrote with Whannel.

Chapter 8

1. Tom Wolfe, quoted in Michael Dean, "Pop Writer of the Period—Tom Wolfe Talks to Michael Dean," *Listener*, February 19, 1970, 250. For biographical information and some interpretative issues, I am relying on www.tomwolfe.com (accessed February 20, 2011); Marc Weingarten, *The Gang That Wouldn't Write Straight: Wolfe, Thompson, Didion, and the New Journalism Revolution* (New York: Crown, 2006), esp. 1–101; and William McKeen, *Tom Wolfe* (New York: Twayne, 1995). See also Dorothy M. Scura, ed., *Conversations with Tom Wolfe* (Jackson: University Press of Mississippi, 1990); Martin L. Gross, interview with Tom Wolfe, "Conversation with an Author: Tom Wolfe," *Book Digest*, March 1980, 19–29; Tom Wolfe, interview, Academy of Achievement, 2006, http://www.achievement.org/autodoc/page/woloint-1 (accessed February 21, 2011).

2. Wolfe, interview, Academy of Achievement, 1. On Wolfe and race, see Tony Schwartz, "Tom Wolfe: The Great Gadfly," *NYTM*, December 20, 1981, 22 ff; Howard Fast, "The Wolfe Isn't at Our Door," *NYT*, February 21, 1988, 23. In 1948 Dabney won the Pulitzer Prize for his editorials. In 1943 Dabney had responded to the threat of a march on Washington by warning that "a small group of Negro agitators and another small group of white rabble-rousers are pushing this country closer to an interracial explosion" of unprecedented proportions: Virginius Dabney, "Nearer and Nearer the Precipice," *Atlantic*, January 1943, 94. For responses by prominent African Americans, see J. Saunders Redding, "A Negro Speaks for His People," *Atlantic*, March 1943, 58–53, and Charles H. Thompson, "Mr. Dabney and the 'Precipice,'" *Journal of Negro Education* 12 (Spring 1943): 141–43. On race in Richmond, see Lewis A. Randolph and Gayle T. Tate, *Rights for a Season: The Politics on Race, Class, and Gender in Richmond, Virginia* (Knoxville: University of Tennessee Press, 2003), 119–36; Megan Taylor Shockley, *"We, Too, Are Americans": African American Women in Detroit and Richmond, 1940–54* (Urbana: University of Illinois Press, 2004), 170–204; Megan Taylor Shockley, email to author, September 6, 2007, copy in author's possession. For race relations in an earlier period of Richmond's history, see Elsa Barkley Brown and Gregg D. Kimball, "Mapping the Terrain of Black Richmond," in *New African American Urban History*, ed. Kenneth W. Goings and Raymond Mohl (Thousand Oaks, Calif.: Sage, 1996), 66–115.

3. On W&L, see Mame Warren, *Come Cheer for Washington and Lee: The University at 250 Years* (Lexington, Va.: Washington and Lee University, 1998), and Washington and Lee University, *Catalog*, 1950–51. The student newspaper mixed stories of parties with those of national and international events: see the following items in *The Ring-Tum Phi*: "Needed—A Reaction," December 12, 1950, 2; "The Editor's Mirror," October 27, 1950, 2; "Professor E. C. Griffith, Law Student Discuss University and Non-Communist Oaths," November 7, 1950, 1; "Cross Burned on Campus at University of Texas; Paper Attacks KKK Action," November 14, 1950, 5. For a parody of life in the USSR, see "Moscow Diary," *Southern Collegian* (Spring 1951): 6. In describing the presence of African Americans in the town and on the campus, I am relying on Professor Ted DeLaney, interview with Daniel Horowitz, Lexington, Va., November 1, 2008.

4. Bill Hoffman, quoted in Marshall Fishwick, talk introducing Tom Wolfe as a

speaker at Virginia Tech, November 1, 1998, MF-VT (The Wolfe-related material in the Fishwick papers is in three folders in box 18); Tekay Wolfe, "Thirty-Yard Shot by Trundle Averts Shutout for Generals," *The Ring-Tum Phi*, October 7, 1949, 3. On W&L's ambitions to become a football powerhouse, see Warren, *Cheer*, 46. For Wolfe's hailing this effort, see T. K. Wolfe, "W. and L. at the Crossroads," *Southern Collegian*, openings 1950, 6–7. On the 1954 cheating scandal involving football players, see Warren, *Cheer*, 46–47. Fishwick, November 1, 1988, talk introducing Tom Wolfe, remarked that already as an undergraduate Wolfe dressed with a stylistic flair that became his signature, flouting "the Sacred Cow of the dress code with styles that were both hyper-English and Hollywood tough-guy." In contrast, and to me more believable, a classmate of Wolfe's remarked that a shy and retiring Wolfe dressed like his peers: Sol Wachtler, telephone interview with author, January 29, 2009.

5. T. K. Wolfe Jr., "Shattered," *ShR* 1 (Spring 1950): 13–26; T. K. Wolfe Jr., "The Ace of Spades is Black," *ShR* 1 (Summer 1950): 22–37.

6. T. K. Wolfe Jr., "A Zoo Full of Zebras: Anti-Intellectualism in the United States," term paper for Marshall Fishwick's Humanities 253, spring 1951, MF-VT, and Marshall Fishwick, "Introduction" [to issue on Tom Wolfe], *Journal of American Culture* 14 (Fall 1991): 2–3. The only version of the paper I could locate is in the Fishwick papers but is not a complete copy. I have in my possession a scattered twenty-eight pages. It is likely, given the more polished passages that Fishwick quotes, that some of it is in draft stage. The source of the quotes is as follows: "abortions," "threadbare," "pristine" from Fishwick without quotation marks, which would indicate that the words are directly from Wolfe; "animal materialism," Wolfe, quoted in Fishwick, "Introduction," 2; "spiritual movement," Wolfe "Zoo," [11], "Nazism," Wolfe, "Zoo," [10]. Generally speaking, when Fishwick summarized and reproduced some of Wolfe's paper, he omitted the favorable references to Communism. On Wolfe's Yale years, see Tom Wolfe, interview, *Yale Bulletin and Calendar*, October 20, 2000. For his discussion of the paper, see Fishwick, "Introduction," 1–5. It is possible that another copy is elsewhere in the Fishwick papers, perhaps in a folder he created when he was writing the article for *Journal of American Culture*. The numbering of the pages on the copy I have in my possession is erratic or nonexistent; in making citations, I have relied on a pagination that I entered on my own copy. To reconstruct the paper, it is necessary to draw on Fishwick, "Introduction."

7. The source of the quotes is as follows: "Goodguys," "fetish," and "spray," Wolfe, quoted in Fishwick, "Introduction," 2; "hypnotized," Wolfe, from Fishwick without quotation marks, which would indicate that the words are directly from Wolfe "Zoo," [25]; Fishwick, comments, on Wolfe, "Zoo," [21]. Fishwick, "Introduction," draws a number of parallels, stylistically and in terms of content, between Wolfe's 1951 paper and what he wrote later; see also Marshall Fishwick to Tom Wolfe, September 21, 1990, MF-VT.

8. William Robertson Coe to Charles Seymour, May 25, 1950; William Robertson Coe to Lawrence B. Tighe, January 2, 1951, both in A. Whitney Griswold Records, Yale University Library, quoted in Liza Nicolas, "Wyoming as America: Celebrations, A Museum,

and Yale," *AQ* 54 (September 2002): 452; Wolfe to Fishwick, probably spring of 1953 or 1954 (on Pearson). On the ways Yale and Coe negotiated the terms of the gift, see Sigmund Diamond, "The American Studies Program at Yale: Lux, Veritas, et Pecunia," *Prospects* 16 (1991): 41–44; Michael Holzman, "The Ideological Origins of American Studies at Yale," *American Studies* 40 (Summer 1999): 71–99. The thesis had its origins in a course taught by Ralph Henry Gabriel: Wolfe to Fishwick, spring 1953 or 1954, MF-VT. For his discussion of his sources, especially his reliance on published testimony before congressional committees, see Thomas Kennerly Wolfe Jr., "The League of American Writers: Communist Organizational Activity among American Writers, 1929–1942," Ph.D. dissertation, Yale University, 1956, 340–55. At the time Wolfe had no access to the League's papers, which since 1966 have been at the Bancroft Library at the University of California at Berkeley. When Wolfe listed studies of the Soviet Union and international Communism, he included C. L. R. James, *World Revolution, 1917–1936: The Rise and Fall of the Communist International* (New York: Pioneer, 1937): Wolfe, "League," 343. See Franklin Folsom, *Days of Anger, Days of Hope: A Memoir of the League of American Writers, 1937–1942* (Boulder: University Press of Colorado, 1994), for an insider's favorable view of the League. In writing on Pearson, I am drawing on my personal familiarity with him; Norman Holmes Pearson, "The Nazi-Soviet Pact and the End of a Dream," in *America in Crisis*, ed. Daniel Aaron (New York: Alfred A. Knopf, 1952), 327–63; Holzman, "Ideological," 71–99. On Wolfe's expression of gratitude to Pearson for providing him with crucial material, see Wolfe, "League," 355. The date on the thesis is 1956 but Wolfe received the degree in 1957. On his introduction to the concept of social status, see Wolfe, Yale interview; for the influence of sociology, see Tom Wolfe, "Do I Dare?" foreword to Marshall Fishwick, *Popular Culture in a New Age* (New York: Haworth, 2002), xv. Early in his time at Yale, David Potter, also a transplanted white Southerner, was Wolfe's academic adviser: T. K. Wolfe to Marshall Fishwick, probably spring of 1953 or 1954, MF-VT.

9. Wolfe, "League," 20; see also Wolfe, "League," "Summary" page, preceding p. 1, and 203. Wolfe drew on Philip Selznick's *The Organizational Weapon: A Study of Bolshevik Strategy and Tactics* (Santa Monica, Calif.: Rand, 1952), about which its author said "this volume may be used as an advanced-training manual for anti-communist forces": Selznick, *Organizational*, 16. Wolfe drew on Selznick's discussion of the way an elite cadre of Communist infiltrators, with their "strong emphasis on the power of disciplined minorities," relied on the "combat party" to achieve the goal of influencing a population that could be easily manipulated: Selznick, *Organizational*, 1 and 114–15. Selznick's discussion of the transition from informal networks into disciplined organizations dovetailed with Max Weber's emphasis on the change from an informal community to more formal society. Wolfe also cited the work of Yale professor Frederick C. Barghoorn, even though an examination of the essay of he cited (Frederick C. Barghoorn, "The Ideological Weapon in Soviet Strategy," in *The Threat of Soviet Imperialism*, ed. C. Grove Haines [Baltimore: Johns Hopkins University Press, 1954], 82–97) reveals that the emphasis of its author was on ideology not organization.

10. Wolfe, "League," 15, 249, 252–53, and 288; see also 192. Wolfe's interest in how

cocktails functioned politically pointed forward to Tom Wolfe, "Radical Chic [1971]" in Tom Wolfe, *Radical Chic and Mau-Mauing the Flak Catchers* (New York: Farrar, Straus and Giroux, 1971), 63.

11. Wolfe, "League," 16.

12. Wolfe, "League," 91 and 154; see also 51–52. The thesis also points forward to his later opposition to political correctness. For some of my judgments about Wolfe's thesis, I am drawing on Arthur Casciato, telephone conversation with author, February 13, 2009. On the League and more broadly on the literary left, see Daniel Aaron, *Writers on the Left* (New York: Harcourt, Brace and World, 1961); James B. Gilbert, *Writers and Partisans: A History of Literary Radicalism in America* (New York: John Wiley, 1968); Richard H. Pells, *Radical Visions and American Dreams: Culture and Social Thought in the Depression Years* (New York: Harper and Row, 1973); Michael Denning, *The Cultural Front: The Laboring of American Culture in the Twentieth Century* (London: Verso, 1996). The most recent work on the League, one that stands in sharp contrast to Wolfe's treatment, is Arthur D. Casciato, "Citizen Writers: A History of the League of American Writers, 1935–1942," Ph.D. diss., University of Virginia, 1986; for his critique of Wolfe's thesis, see p. 9. For his essay on one figure active in the League, see Arthur D. Casciato, "The Bricklayer as Bricoleur: Pietro de Donato and the Cultural Politics of the Popular Front," *Voices in Italian Americana* 2 (Fall 1991): 67–75. Most of this scholarship predates the fall of the Soviet Union, and work based on post-1989 material from the Soviet archives, though not uncontested, emphasizes the extent of Comintern control of the left in the United States.

13. Yevgeny Zamyatin, "On Literature, Revolution, Entropy, and Other Matters [1923]," in *A Soviet Heretic: Essays by Yevgeny Zamyatin*, ed. and trans. Mirra Ginsburg (Chicago: University of Chicago Press, 1970), 110, quoted in Yevgeny Zamyatin, *We* (New York: Modern Library, 2006), xvi. For the influence of Russian experimental writers on Wolfe, see Elaine Dundy, "Tom Wolfe . . . But Exactly, Yes! [1966]" in Scura, ed., *Conversations*, 10.

14. Thomas Wolfe, "10-Block Parade Gives Watchers 5-Hour Thrill," *WP*, May 14, 1961, B1. Without Wolfe's help, and possibly not even then, what he wrote for the *Union* would be hard to track down: the articles then had no bylines and the successor paper, the Springfield *Republican*, has no files for Wolfe: Jim Gleason, email to author, February 27, 2009. On Wolfe's writing at the *Washington Post,* see James Rosen, "In the Post's Clip Files Blossoms Tom Wolfe," *Seattle Times*, July 17, 2006, available at http://community.seattletimes.nwsource.com/archive/?date=20060717&slug=wolfestyle17 (accessed February 21, 2011).

15. Thomas Wolfe, byline to "Gen'l Lee, Suh, Was Almighty," *WP*, April 17, 1960, E7; see also Thomas Wolfe, "Poles Still Refuse to Bow to Masters," *WP*, August 2, 1959, A14. On relatively rare occasions, Wolfe paid explicit attention to issues of race and civil rights: see, for example, Thomas Wolfe, "Negro Writers View Lag in Their Literature," *WP*, March 19, 1960, A9.

16. Thomas Wolfe, "Hidden Group Directs Rule," *WP*, June 29, 1960, A1 and A23; Thomas Wolfe, review of C. Wright Mills, *Listen, Yankee: The Revolution in Cuba, WP*, November 27, 1960, C18. For the articles that picked up on themes from his doctorate,

see Thomas Wolfe, "Newsmen Split on Role of Reds in Castro Rule," *WP*, April 22, 1960, A19; Thomas Wolfe, "Foes of Revolution Are Cut Off as Cuba Cleanses 'Impurities,'" *WP*, June 30, 1960, A1; Thomas Wolfe, "'Social Justice' is Law in Cuba, Middle Class Mentality Its Target," *WP*, July 1, 1960, A1; Thomas Wolfe, review of Leo Huberman and Paul M. Sweezy, *Anatomy of a Revolution*, *WP*, August 7, 1960, E6; Thomas Wolfe, "Lower-Income Cuban Put in Reach of Country Club Life," *WP*, July 3, 1960, A6; Thomas Wolfe, "Students Really Rate in Revolutionary Cuba," *WP*, July 4, 1960, A1.

17. Thomas Wolfe, "Sales Sharks Ruin Arts, Poet Kunitz Remarks," *WP*, March 22, 1960, B7; Thomas Wolfe, "Nothing's Tabu to GOP Dior-to-Dior Workers," *WP*, April 5, 1960, C1; Thomas Wolfe, "Supermarket Sirens Are Hip," *WP*, March 18, 1962, F1; William McKeen, quoted in Rosen, "Post Clip Files." Although at times he covered local aspects of the civil rights movement and the failures of Communism in Cuba, China, and the USSR, many of the articles he wrote were on local zoning disputes, scientific advances, freakish weather, and train wrecks. Indeed, his final story, dated March 29, 1962, appeared on page one under the headline "Ill Pupil Sent to Lie Down for Rest Found at Night by Cleaning Woman." For other themes in his articles, see Thomas Wolfe, "Area Tobacconists Hurt, Saddened by Decline in Smokers' Taste," *WP*, July 19, 1959, C9; Thomas Wolfe, "Arab Drums Sound along the Potomac," *WP*, October 19, 1957, A1; Thomas Wolfe, "It Is the Illustrious Who Are Rated at a Mere Dime a Dozen in Washington," *WP*, December 23, 1959, A6; Thomas Wolfe, "Cars with Brains and Girls Featured at New Auto Show," *WP*, January 14, 1960, B5; Thomas Wolfe, "Reporter (Stripped-Down Version) Has His Style Ramped by Nudists," *WP*, August 6, 1960, A1; Thomas Wolfe, "Pate de Foie Gras Goose Was Cooked by U.S. Act," *WP*, December 2, 1960, A1; Thomas Wolfe, "Writer Sees Need for 'Culture Snobs,'" *WP*, March 21, 1961, B2.

18. Tom Wolfe, "Like a Novel [1972]," in *The New Journalism*, ed. Tom Wolfe and E. W. Johnson (New York: Harper and Row, 1973), 10–11. For a vivid picture of the life of reporters and writers at the *Tribune*, as well as his own emergence as a writer, see Tom Wolfe, "The Feature Game [1972]," and Wolfe, "Like a Novel," in Wolfe and Johnson, eds., *New Journalism,* 3–9 and 10–22.

19. Wolfe, "Like a Novel," 15 ("emotionally"); Tom Wolfe, *The Kandy-Kolored Tangerine-Flake Streamline Baby* (New York: Farrar, Straus and Giroux, 1965), x ("nutballs"); Tom Wolfe, "Introduction," in Wolfe, *Kandy*, xi ("vulgar"; emphasis in original); Wolfe, "Introduction," in Wolfe, *Kandy*, xii ("maniac"). The original version of the title essay was Tom Wolfe, "There Goes [Varoom! Varoom!] That Kandy-Kolored Tangerine-Flake Streamline Baby," *Esquire*, November 1963, 114–15, 118, 155, 158, 160, 162, 164, 166, and 168, and in the book as "The Kandy-Kolored Tangerine-Flake Streamline Baby," 76–107. For quotations I am drawing on the book. Among the many scholarly sources on hot-rod culture is H. F. Moorhouse, "The 'Work' Ethic and 'Leisure' Activity: The Hot Rod in Post-War America [1987]," in *Consumer Society in American History: A Reader*, ed. Lawrence Glickman (Ithaca, N.Y.: Cornell University Press, 1999), 277–97.

20. Jürgen Habermas, "Ornament und Maschine," *FAZ*, December 31, 1954, 23; Wolfe, "Introduction," in Wolfe, *Kandy*, xiii, xiv, and xvii.

21. Wolfe, "Kandy-Kolored," 82, 78, 82, and 96–97.

22. Ibid., 86, 105, and 79.

23. Joseph Epstein, review of Wolfe, *Kandy-Kolored*, in *New Republic*, July 24, 1965, 27; William Barrett, "The Hyperthyroid Journalist," *Atlantic*, July 1965, 140; Wolfe, "Introduction," in Wolfe, *Kandy*, xvii.

24. Tom Wolfe, "The Girl of the Year [1964]," in Wolfe, *Kandy*, 212; Tom Wolfe, "Las Vegas (What?) [1964]," in Wolfe, *Kandy*, 11. Weber, "Happiness Explosion," is especially effective in capturing the emergence of a culture based on pleasure. For a later expression of the ways advocates of pleasure and restraint were engaged in a fight, see Tom Wolfe, *The Pump House Gang* (New York: Farrar, Straus and Giroux, 1968), 13. For a later statement on the theme of consumption and status, see Tom Wolfe, "Seizing the Power [1972]," in Wolfe and Johnson, eds., *New Journalism*, 32. See Ronald Weber, "Tom Wolfe's Happiness Explosion," *Journal of Popular Culture* 8 (Summer 1974): 71–78, on the importance of postwar culture emerging from below.

25. Tom Wolfe, "The Marvelous Mouth [1963]," in Wolfe, *Kandy*, 118 and 124. The literature on the impact of Southerners on American culture in the postwar period is considerable, though the emphasis is usually more on the movement to the North of liberal white writers than of conservative white good old boys: see, most recently, James N. Gregory, *The Southern Diaspora: How the Great Migrations of Black and White Southerners Transformed America* (Chapel Hill: University of North Carolina Press, 2005), 183–92 and 283–320.

26. Dwight Macdonald, review of Wolfe, *Kandy-Kolored*, *NYRB*, August 26, 1965, 3 and 4. For the story of the dispute between Macdonald and Wolfe, which was in part due to an article Wolfe wrote on the *New Yorker*, see Wolfe, "Seizing," in Wolfe and Johnson, eds., *New Journalism*, 24–25; Weingarten, *Gang*, 1–6.

27. Wolfe, "Seizing," in Wolfe and Johnson, eds., *New Journalism*, 25; Tom Wolfe, *Painted*, 77; Wolfe, in Dean, "Pop Writer," 251; Wolfe, "League," 28–29.

28. Richard Hoggart, "The Dance of the Long-Legged Fly: On Tom Wolfe's Poise," *Encounter* 27 (August 1966): 64, 63, 70, and 71.

29. David Riesman, "The Nylon War [1951]," in David Riesman, *Abundance for What? And Other Essays* (Garden City, N.Y.: Doubleday, 1964), 67.

30. C. H. Simonds, "Popcult Orgy," review of Wolfe, *Kandy-Kolored*, *National Review*, November 2, 1965, 990; Tom Wolfe, "Preface," 5 (perhaps in an earlier version than the one that appeared, without the words "a contradiction in terms (and worse)," in Marshall Fishwick, *Probing Popular Culture: On and Off the Internet* (New York: Haworth Press, 2004), xv–xvi; Wolfe, "Introduction," in Wolfe, *Kandy*, xvii; William James Smith, review of Wolfe, *Kandy-Kolored*, *Commonweal*, September 17, 1965, 672. Wolfe's editor thought this was the review that most fully captured what Wolfe had accomplished: Henry Robbins to William James Smith, September 15, 1965, box 396, TW-NYPL. The book was greatly successful. It went into a fourth printing within a month: Doug Shomette, introduction to Doug Shomette, ed., *The Critical Response to Tom Wolfe* (Westport, Conn.: Greenwood Press, 1992), xiv. For some of the reviews, see Shomette, *Wolfe*, 3–10; Wallace Markfield, "Alas and Alack for the Merry Men Bit," *Bookweek*, June 27, 1965, 5. The papers of his publisher concerning Wolfe's *Kandy-Kolored* are not especially rich, though they do

contain some correspondence, from the fall of 1966, about how offended Wolfe was about the cover of the original paperback edition by Pocket Books. Much of the correspondence concerns reviews and promotional efforts; especially interesting are letters from Walt Kelly, Jessamyn West, and Seymour Krim. See Farrar, Straus and Giroux Collection, folders on *Kandy-Kolored*, box 397, TW-NYPL.

31. Herbert J. Gans, "Relativism, Equality, and Popular Culture," in *Authors of Their Own Lives: Intellectual Autobiographies by Twenty American Sociologists*, ed. Bennett M. Berger (Berkeley: University of California Press, 1990), 434 ("unconnected"); Herbert J. Gans, "Working in Six Research Areas: A Multi-Field Sociological Career," mimeograph copy in author's possession (2008; later published in *Annual Review of Sociology* 35 [August 2009]: 5). For biographical information, I am relying on Gans, "Relativism"; Gans, "Working." For a discussion of Gans's critique of critics of mass culture, see Eugene Lunn, "Beyond 'Mass Culture': The Lonely Crowd, the Uses of Literacy, and the Postwar Era," *Theory and Society* 19 (February 1990): fn. 7, pp. 81–82; fn. 23, p. 82; and fn. 55, p. 85. For a bibliography of works by Gans, see Léon Deben and Johannes van der Weiden, *Sociologie en gebouwde omgeving* (Deventer: Van Loghum Slaterus, 1982), 181–200. Gans married and divorced Iris Lezak and in 1967 married Louise Gruner: Gans, "Relativism," 451.

32. Gans, 1947 autobiography, quoted in Gans, "Relativism," 437 ("religion"); Gans, "Working," 9 ("Zionism"); Gans, "Relativism," 440 ("authority"). On his early interest in thinking about popular culture, see Herbert J. Gans, *Popular Culture and High Culture: An Analysis and Evaluation of Taste* (New York: Basic Books, 1974), xi. To some extent, Gans's early antipathy to the perspective of culture users continued: writing in a newspaper while in the army, he decried the way soldiers whistled at onscreen events while watching a movie: Herbert J. Gans, interview with author, New York, N.Y, November 12, 2008.

33. Gans, "Working," 15; Herbert J. Gans to Granville Hicks, May 27 [probably 1951], "Misc. Corresp. 1950s (early to mid)" folder, box 14, HJG-CU. For Gans's insistence on his loyalty as an American citizen in the context of the witch hunts of the late 1940s, see Herbert J. Gans, affidavit for case of former Private Seymour Smidt, September 25, 1955, "Misc. Corresp. 1950s (early to mid)" folder, box 14, HJG-CU.

34. Gans, "Relativism," 439–40. For information on what Gans read and studied, see folders in box 1, HJG-CU.

35. Gans, "Relativism," 433. In an email to the author, August 27, 2004, Gans made clear that he was a refugee, not an immigrant. He explores his early interest in taste in Gans, "Relativism," 432–51.

36. Gans, "Relativism," 441; Russell Lynes, "Highbrow, Lowbrow, Middlebrow," *Harper's Magazine*, February 1949, 19, 25, and 27. On Lynes, see Richard Severo, obituary for Russell Lynes, *NYT*, September 16, 1991, http://query.nytimes.com/gst/fullpage.html?res=9D0CE5DC103EF935A2575AC0A967958260 (accessed February 21, 2011).

37. Herbert Gans, "The Metaphysics of Popular Culture," seminar paper for Riesman/Katz class, June 15, 1950, 2, folder on late 1950s article in *Dissent*, box 12, HJG-CU, 5 ("scorn"), 2 ("dysfunction"); Gans, "Relativism," 442 (on cultural critics and Stalinists). On his reaction to urban redevelopers, see Gans, "Relativism," 444. On his studying with

Katz, see Gans, interview with author. This same antipathy to sectarianism and authoritarians may have shaped Gans's response to the New Left: Herbert J. Gans, "The New Radicalism: Sect or Action Movement?" *Studies on the Left* 5 (Summer 1965): 126–31; Herbert J. Gans, "Rational Approach to Radicalism," *Studies on the Left* 6 (January–February 1966): 37–46.

38. Gans, "Metaphysics," 9, 14, 3, 13, and 15, fn. 1 (emphasis in original). Excerpts from this paper appear in Gans, "Relativism," 442. Gans wrote the paper soon after he did some fieldwork in Park Forest. He gives somewhat varying titles and dates for this paper. In a recent autobiographical essay he located it in 1949 and gives the title of "Popular Culture and High Culture": Gans, "Working," 18. In an email responding to my location of a 1950 paper titled "The Metaphysics of Popular Culture," Gans said this may have been the term paper and he may have written it in 1950.

39. Herbert J. Gans, "Recreation Planning for Leisure Behavior: A Goal-Oriented Approach," Ph.D. diss., University of Pennsylvania, 1957. While still in Chicago, from 1950 to 1953, Gans worked in city planning, including for a local firm planning mining towns in the upper Midwest. Beginning in 1953 Gans worked as a researcher in planning, mostly at Penn; he moved to Teachers College at Columbia in 1964, to MIT in 1969, and to Columbia in sociology in 1971, becoming emeritus in 2007. At the University of Chicago, Gans knew Susan Sontag: Gans, interview.

40. Gans, "Recreation," 78; see also 9 and 129.

41. Ibid., 129, 312–13, and 558; see also 6.

42. Herbert J. Gans, "Political Participation and Apathy," *Phylon* 13 (third quarter 1952): 186 ("thrilling"); Herbert J. Gans, "The 'Yinglish' Music of Mickey Katz," *AQ* 5 (Fall 1953): 218. Herbert J. Gans, "The Creator-Audience Relationship in the Mass Media: An Analysis of Movie Making [1956]," in *Mass Culture: The Popular Arts in America*, ed. Bernard Rosenberg and David Manning White (New York: Free Press, 1957), 316. Gans explored the notion of how feedback from audiences affected those who created popular culture, as well as ideas about pluralistic taste cultures, in Herbert J. Gans, "The Rise of the Problem-Film: An Analysis of Changes in Hollywood Films and the American Audience," *Social Problems* 11 (Spring 1964): 327–36; Herbert J. Gans, "The Relationship between the Movies and the Public, and Some Implications for Movie Criticism and Movie-Making," paper read at Annenberg School of Communications Lecture Course, "The Mass Media Today," University of Pennsylvania, February 18, 1960, copy in folder 10, box 14, LA-GRI. For another, later article on Jewish popular culture, in this case with appeal to non-Jews, see Herbert J. Gans, "Alan Sherman's Sociologist Presents . . . ," *Reconstructionist*, May 3, 1963, 25–31. Early on Gans studied the lives of Jews in Park Forest: Herbert J. Gans, "Park Forest: Birth of a Jewish Community," *Co* 11 (April 1951): 330–39. For Gans's broader discussion of the lives of American Jews, see Herbert J. Gans, "American Jewry: Present and Future," *Co* 21, "Part I: Present" (May 1956): 422–30, and "Part II: The Future of American Jewry" (June 1956): 555–63. Nathan Glazer, who had worked with Riesman on *The Lonely Crowd*, was an editor at *Commentary* who encouraged Gans to publish there.

43. Harold Rosenberg, "Pop Culture and Kitsch Criticism," *Dissent* 5 (Winter 1958): 14–15.

44. Herbert J. Gans, "Popular Culture and High Culture Critics," *Dissent* 5 (Spring 1958): 185–87 (emphasis in original).

45. Herbert J. Gans, "Hollywood Films on British Screens: An Analysis of the Functions of American Popular Culture Abroad," *Social Problems* 9 (Spring 1962): 325 and 328; Herbert J. Gans, "American Films and Television Programs on British Screens: A Study of the Functions of American Popular Culture Abroad," Institute of Urban Studies, University of Pennsylvania, 1959, 173, copy 1, HJG-CU 174. The published essay drew on Gans, "American Films." Decades later, British scholars would come to a somewhat similar conclusion about the class dimensions of the reception of American films in Britain: see, for example, Alan O'Shea, "English Subjects of Modernity," in *Modern Times: Reflections on a Century of English Modernity*, ed. Mica Nava and Alan O'Shea (London: Routledge, 1996), 30–32.

46. Herbert J. Gans, "Hoggart-UL," reading notes from *The Uses of Literacy*, probably 1956 or 1957, folder titled "Related Materials," box 2, HJG-CU; the references were to Richard Hoggart, *The Uses of Literacy* (London: Chatto and Windus, 1956), 99 and 127. Herbert J. Gans, "America's New Sexual Idols," *20th Century* 173 (Autumn 1964): 86–92, focused on the emergence in Britain of a new image "in which Englishmen appear as potent sexual idols, armed with unusual energy and vitality, and given to public declarations of skepticism and satire": Gans, "Sexual Idols," 87.

47. Elihu Katz and Paul F. Lazarsfeld, *Personal Influence: The Part Played by People in the Flow of Mass Communications* (Glencoe, Ill.: Free Press, 1955), xiii–xiv. Gans mentioned the book's influence in Gans, interview. In *Media and the American Mind: From Morse to McLuhan* (Chapel Hill: University of North Carolina Press, 1982), 137–38, Daniel J. Czitrom explores how in the late 1950s empirical communications research undercut key elements of mass culture theory, including the contrast between a passive, atomized audience and powerful producers.

48. Herbert Gans, *The Urban Villagers: Group and Class in the Life of Italian-Americans* (New York: Free Press, 1962), 73; Herbert J. Gans, "City Planning and Urban Realities," *Co* 33 (February 1962): 175. See also Hoggart, *Uses*; Michael Young and Peter Willmott, *Family and Kinship in East London* (London: Routledge and Kegan Paul, 1957). For an analysis of a distinctive working-class style of consumption in the postwar period, see Shelley Nickles, "More Is Better: Mass Consumption, Gender, and Class Identity in Postwar America," *AQ* 54 (December 2002): 581–622.

49. Gans, *Villagers*, 16. For another critique of urban renewal, see Herbert J. Gans, "The Failure of Urban Renewal: A Critique and Some Proposals," *Co* 39 (April 1965): 29–37. For his reliance on these books, see Gans, *Villagers*, bibliography and index. For placing Gans in the debate over ethnicity and assimilation, see Michael Parenti, review of *The Urban Villagers*, *Co* 35 (June 1963): 544–47. In 1967 Stuart Hall and Richard Hoggart tried unsuccessfully to persuade Gans to come to Birmingham to be at the Center: Herbert J. Gans to Richard Hoggart, May 4, 1967, folder "Misc Corr 1967 1 of 2," box 16, HJG-CU.

50. Gans, *Villagers*, 181, 182, 181, 194, 182, 183, and 186. In "Relativism," 442, Gans named names (Dwight Macdonald, Ortega y Gasset, and Russell Kirk) and discussed his tendency not to reveal the identity of the "anonymous member of an unspecified elite I called the literary critic" in a paper he wrote in 1950.

51. Gans, *Villagers*, 185–86.

52. Ibid., 193 and 195. In his major works, Gans focused relatively little attention on race: for his favorable response to the Moynihan Report, see Herbert Gans, "The Negro Family: Reflections on the Moynihan Report," *Commonweal*, October 15, 1965, 47–51. For a satirical piece on the politics of race relations, see Herbert J. Gans, "The White Problem," *Dissent* 66 (September–October 1966): 538–39.

53. Joe Caruso to Herbert J. Gans, March 30, 1960, folder "[illegible] with Wenders," box 2, HJG-CU; Joe Caruso to Herbert J. Gans, January 14, 1958, folder "[illegible] with Wenders," box 2, HJG-CU; Herbert J. Gans to Joe Caruso, March 27 [1960], folder "[illegible] with Wenders," box 2, HJG-CU; "D" to Herbert J. Gans, [August 1961], folder "W E book corr," box 2, HJG-CU. On the top of this letter Gans wrote "Denise Ag. 61." The sales figure comes from Gans, "Working," 9.

54. Nathan Glazer, typescript review of *Urban Villagers*, folder of reviews, box 2, HJG-CU; Howard S. Becker, review of *Urban Villagers*, *Sociological Quarterly* 5 (Winter 1964): 95. For a highly favorable review that places the book in these contexts, see S. M. Miller, review of *The Urban Villagers*, *ASR* 28 (June 1963): 476. For other reviews, see a folder in box 2, HJG-CU. For his discussion of his role as speaker and consultant on these issues, see Gans, "Working," 10–14.

55. Gans, "Working," 8. Scott Donaldson, *The Suburban Myth* (New York: Columbia University Press, 1969), explores the accepted assumptions and he honors (108–9) Gans for challenging them. For an article that is a bridge between his Park Forest and his Levittown studies, see Herbert J. Gans, "The Sociology of New Towns; Opportunities for Research," *Sociology and Social Research* 40 (March–April 1956): 231–39.

56. Herbert Gans, *The Levittowners: Ways of Life and Politics in a New Suburban Community* (New York: Alfred A. Knopf, 1967), vi, 185, and 164. In emphasizing cosmopolitans, Gans was drawing on Robert K. Merton, "Patterns of Influence: Local and Cosmopolitan Influentials," in *Social Theory and Social Structure* (New York: Free Press, 1957), 387–420. See also on these themes, Herbert J. Gans, "Suburbs and Planners," *Landscape* 11 (Autumn 1961): 23–24.

57. Gans, *Levittowners*, 190–91. For his critique of the critics of suburbs, see Herbert Gans, "Diversity Is Not Dead: A Report on Our Widening Diversity and Range of Choice," *New Republic*, April 3, 1961, 11–15. For Gans's critique Packard's *A Nation of Strangers* (1972), see Daniel Horowitz, *Vance Packard and American Social Criticism* (Chapel Hill: University of North Carolina Press, 1994), 246–48.

58. Gans, *Levittowners*, 225, 206, and 213.

59. "Apologia for Suburbs," *TLS*, December 7, 1967, 1194; Robert Boguslaw, review of *Levittowners*, *AJS* 73 (November 1967): 357; Tom Wolfe to Mr. Hall, January 29, [1966 or 1967], folder "Correspondence Levittown," box 4, HJG-CU; Robert Merton to Herbert J. Gans, February 25, [probably 1968], folder "Correspondence Levittown," box 4, HJG-

CU; David Riesman to Herbert J. Gans, December 13 1967, folder "Correspondence Levittown," box 4, HJG-CU.

60. Herbert J. Gans, "Popular Culture in America: Social Problem in a Mass Society or Social Asset in a Pluralist Society?" in *Social Problems: A Modern Approach*, ed. Howard S. Becker (New York: John Wiley and Sons, 1966), 561; Peter Marris, personal communication to Herbert Gans, quoted in Gans, "Popular Culture," fn. 56, 575; David Riesman to Herbert J. Gans, November 30, 1964, folder on late 1950s article in *Dissent*, box 12, HJG-CU. Gans later published this 1966 essay, somewhat modified and updated, as Gans, *Popular Culture and High Culture*. Gans focused on this subject in a short 1961 article on "pluralist aesthetics" that appeared in a journal with very limited circulation and then in the essay on British films that he published in 1962: Herbert J. Gans, "Pluralist Aesthetics and Subcultural Programming: A Proposal for Cultural Democracy in the Mass Media," *Studies in Public Communication* 3 (Summer 1961): 27–35. See also Gans, "American Films." In his discussion of class and intellectuals there was no mention here of Hoggart, but the connection was clear. Gans noted that most of the American socialists he was discussing, Macdonald and Greenberg among them, were middle class in origin.

61. Gans, "Popular Culture," 601.

62. Ibid., 601, 550–51, 578 (emphasis in original); see also Gans, "Relativism," 443. Here Gans was amplifying Riesman's notion of distinctive consumption communities: Andrew Ross, *No Respect: Intellectuals and Popular Culture* (New York: Routledge, 1989), 53. This notion of multiple communities of consumers stands in opposition to Daniel Boorstin's more flattened view: Daniel J. Boorstin, *The Americans: The Democratic Experience* (New York: Random House, 1973), 89–164. Gans also offered an analysis of gender dynamics here: he wrote that "working-class society practices sexual segregation in social life: male and female roles are sharply differentiated, and there is relatively little social contact between men and women, even within the family. . . . There are male and female types of content [in movies and television], rarely shared by both sexes": Gans, "Popular Culture," 591.

Chapter 9

1. Howard Brick points to Sontag's essay when he discusses the 1960s penchant for the tension between authenticity and artifice: Howard Brick, *Age of Contradiction: American Thought and Culture in the 1960s* (New York: Twayne, 1998), 66–67. For how William Phillips, editor of *Partisan Review*, later viewed Sontag's essay, see George Cotkin, "The Democratization of Cultural Criticism," *Chronicle of Higher Education*, July 2, 2004, B9. For discussions of Sontag's career and ideas, see Sohnya Sayres, *Susan Sontag: The Elegiac Modernist* (New York: Routledge, 1990); Liam Kennedy, *Susan Sontag: Mind as Passion* (Manchester: Manchester University Press, 1995); Carl Rollyson, *Reading Susan Sontag: A Critical Introduction to Her Work* (Chicago: Ivan R. Dee, 2001); Carl Rollyson and Lisa Paddock, *Susan Sontag: The Making of an Icon* (New York: W. W. Norton, 2000); Joan Acocella, "The Hunger Artist [2000]," in Joan Acocella, *Twenty-Eight Artists and Two Saints* (New York: Pantheon, 2007), 437–57; Barbara Ching and Jennifer A. Wagner-Lawlor, eds., *The Scandal of Susan Sontag* (New York: Columbia University Press, 2009);

Phillip Lopate, *Notes on Sontag* (Princeton, N.J.: Princeton University Press, 2009). For a fully annotated bibliography, see Leland Poague and Kathy A. Parsons, comps., *Susan Sontag: An Annotated bibliography, 1948–1992* (New York: Garland, 2000). As I was finishing my manuscript, I benefited from reading a prepublication version of Alice Kaplan, *Dreaming in French: The Parisian Years of Jacqueline Kennedy, Susan Sontag, and Angela Davis* (forthcoming, University of Chicago Press, 2012).

2. Susan Sontag, "Pilgrimage," *New Yorker*, December 21, 1987, 38. In this memoir Sontag focused on a visit she and some classmates made to Thomas Mann when they were still in high school. Sontag dated the visit to December 1947, but her diary suggests that the date was most likely December 28, 1949: Susan Sontag, diary entry, December 28, 1949, "Notebook # 24," folder 8, box 123, SS-UCLA.

3. Sontag, "Pilgrimage," 38. For a description of her family as "sub-nuclear," see Susan Sontag, response to questionnaire on women's liberation 1972, 34, folder 26, box 75, SS-UCLA. For more on her childhood, see Susan Sontag, interview with Marithelma Costa and Adelaida López, 1985, in *Conversations with Susan Sontag*, ed. Leland Poague (Jackson: University Press of Mississippi, 1995), 228. On her childhood, see material in folders 1, 2, 8, 11, and 12, box 146, SS-UCLA.

4. Susan Sontag, essays on Freud's *Civilization and Its Discontents*, October 20, 1948, 1 and 2, and October 22, 1948, 3, folder 12, box 146, SS-UCLA.

5. Susan Sontag, quoted in Roger Copeland, "The Habits of Consciousness," *Commonweal*, February 13, 1981, 87. On her early engagement with European modernism, see Sontag, "Pilgrimage," 41.

6. Susan Sontag, "The Artist as Exemplary Sufferer [1962]," in Susan Sontag, *Against Interpretation and Other Essays* (New York: Farrar, Straus and Giroux, 1966), 41, 42, and 44; Susan Sontag, "Camus' Notebooks [1963]," in Sontag, *Against Interpretation*, 59. On Sontag's work on her own image, see Carl Rollyson, *Female Icons: Marilyn Monroe to Susan Sontag* (New York: iUniverse, 2005), 1–7 and 94–150. I use the word "queer" advisedly to refer to the world she often inhabited without suggesting that this is a term she might consistently use to describe herself. Sontag's journal entries for the Berkeley/San Francisco period reveal the existence of (and her consciousness of) what a later generation would call queer culture. My generalization about her combination of emotional lability and intellectual acuity rests on readings of her diaries offered by students in a spring 2010 history seminar at Smith College.

7. David Rieff, "Preface," in Susan Sontag, *Reborn: Journals and Notebooks, 1947–1963*, ed. David Rieff (New York: Farrar, Straus and Giroux, 2008), xi–xii; Susan Sontag, "Under the Sign of Saturn [1979]," in Susan Sontag, *Under the Sign of Saturn* (New York: Farrar, Straus and Giroux, 1980), 117, 126, 125, 117, and 118; Susan Sontag, "Mind as Passion [1980]," in Sontag, *Saturn*, 183, 181, 182, 183, and 185 (emphasis in original); Sontag, "Saturn," 119; Sontag, "Mind as Passion," 192.

8. On her moods and emotional turmoil, see Susan Sontag, "Coming out of 4A Lecture," March 1, 1949, folder 2, box 123, SS-UCLA. For a rich analysis of the sexual and social experience of women at colleges, see Babette Faehmel, "Before the Second Wave:

College Women, Cultural Literacy, Sexuality, and Identity, 1940–1965" (Ph.D. diss., University of Massachusetts, 2008). Faehmel located more than a dozen diaries and letter collections by collegiate women for these years, none of them by women who experienced lesbian sexuality.

9. Sontag, entry of January 5, 1957, *Reborn*, 100 ("stranglehold"); Sontag, entry, probably fall 1959, *Reborn*, 214 ("personality"); Sontag, entry of November 4, 1957, *Reborn*, 158 ("proud"; emphasis in original). On the ways a Catholic nurse influenced her as a child, see Sontag, interview, Costa and López, 109–26. On a moment when she realized the patriarchal nature of Judaism, see Sontag, interview, Costa and López, 228; Sontag, entry of September 25, 1957, leather notebook "Notebook 1956–1957," folder 10, box 123, SS-UCLA. On her response to the Holocaust, see Sontag, entry, probably for late February 1957, *Reborn*, 138; on the impact of seeing pictures of concentration camps when she was twelve, see Susan Sontag, *On Photography* (New York: Farrar, Straus and Giroux, 1977), 20. For one of many examples of her list making, see Sontag, entry, probably fall 1959, Sontag, *Reborn*, 213–25.

10. Sontag, entry of December 25, 1948, *Reborn*, 11 ("tendencies"); Sontag, entry of April 6, 1949, *Reborn*, 15 ("bisexual"). The Sohmers-Sontag story is from Harriet Sohmers Zwerling, introductory note to "Memories of Sontag: From an Ex-Pat's Diary," http://www.brooklynrail.org/2006/11/express/memories-of-sontag, (accessed February 21, 2011). For an astute analysis of the impact of Burke and *Nightwood* on Sontag, see Kaplan, *Dreaming*. For Sontag's descriptions of gay and lesbian life in San Francisco, which the edited volume captures only partially, see "Notebook # 22," folder 6, box 123, SS-UCLA, and spiral notebook, folder 5, box 123, SS-UCLA. For the worlds of gays and lesbians in the Bay Area in the late 1940s, see Susan Stryker and Jim Van Buskirk, *Gay by the Bay: A History of Queer Culture in the San Francisco Bay Area* (San Francisco: Chronicle, 1996), esp. 29–67; Nan Alamilla Boyd, *Wide Open Town: A History of Queer San Francisco to 1965* (Berkeley: University of California Press, 2003), esp. 68–101. For a diary of a lesbian of Sontag's generation, albeit of a different social background, see Marge McDonald, "From the Diary of Marge McDonald," in *Persistent Desire: A Femme-Butch Reader*, ed. Joan Nestle (Boston: Alyson, 1992), 124–27. Judith Butler, "Imitation and Gender Subordination," in *Inside/Out: Lesbian Theories, Gay Theories*, ed. Diana Fuss (New York: Routledge, 1991), 13–31, provides some theoretical perspectives to understand issues of identity, sexuality, performance, and concealment in Sontag's life and writing. On the situation of young, heterosexual women in the 1950s, see Wini Breines, *Young, White, and Miserable: Growing Up Female in the Fifties* (Boston: Beacon Press, 1992).

11. Sontag, entry of May 23, 1949, *Reborn*, 28 ("pure physical" "everywhere"); Sontag, entry of June 15, 1949, *Reborn*, 37 ("excess"); Sontag, entry of January 26, 1950, "Notebook # 24," folder 8, box 123, SS-UCLA ("case"); Sontag, entry of May 26, 1949, *Reborn*, 30 ("academic") (emphases in original). Sontag connected same-sex sexuality and narcissism earlier, in an entry published in the edited book, although here the link with her own sense of self was not as clear: Sontag, entry of September 15, 1949, *Reborn*, 48.

12. Among the useful sources on the situation lesbians faced in this period and more

specifically on the connection between lesbian sexuality and creativity is Marilyn Schuster, *Passionate Communities: Reading Lesbian Resistance in Jane Rule's Fiction* (New York: New York University Press, 1999).

13. On her Chicago years, see Susan Sontag, "A Gluttonous Reader," in *An Unsentimental Education: Writers and Chicago*, ed. Molly McQuade (Chicago: University of Chicago Press, 1995), 160–68. See also material in an envelope with playbills and fliers, folder 7, box 123, SS-UCLA, including her engagement with films by Kenneth Anger, Fritz Lang, and Joseph Von Sternberg.

14. Sontag, entry of January 15, 1950, "Notebook # 24," folder 8, box 123, SS-UCLA ("surmounted"); Sontag, entry of January 21, 1950, "Notebook # 24," folder 8, box 123, SS-UCLA ("lonely"); Sontag, entries of April 13, 1950, and April 26, 1950, "Notebook # 24," folder 8, box 123, SS-UCLA ("cheap"); Sontag, entry of March 8, 1950, "Notebook # 24," folder 8, box 123, SS-UCLA ("loneliness"); Sontag, entry of March 23, 1950, "Notebook # 24," folder 8, box 23, SS-UCLA ("despondent"). See also Sontag, entries of March 23, 1950, and April 3, 1950, "Notebook # 24," folder 8, box 123, SS-UCLA; Sontag, entries of April 4, 1950, and April 22, 1950, "Notebook # 24," folder 8, box 123, SS-UCLA. In these years, Sontag was encountering powerful and prevalent antilesbian sentiment, something exacerbated in the late 1940s and into the 1950s by the scapegoating of gays and lesbians in the quest to root out national security risks. On the animus against lesbians, see Lillian Faderman, *Odd Girls and Twilight Lovers: A History of Lesbian Life in Twentieth-Century America* (New York: Columbia University Press, 1991), esp. 37–61 (on early sexologists), 118–58 (on the 1940s and 1950s), and 130–34 (discussion of the connection between unhappiness, lesbianism, and mental illness). Moreover, it is important to note that both Adrienne Rich and Audre Lorde were two other women in Sontag's generation who got married and then later developed different views of their sexual orientation.

15. Kenneth Burke, quoted in Sontag, entry of November 12, 1950, in Sontag, *Reborn*, 69; Susan Sontag, "The Dialectic of Decay," B.A. thesis, University of Chicago, May 15, 1950, 2, 21, and 22, folder 5, box 147, SS-UCLA; Sontag, entry of October 21, 1950, "Notebook # 24," folder 8, box 123, SS-UCLA. My best judgment is that Sontag, at the time or soon after, labeled this paper as her "B.A. Thesis," even though it is more correctly an honors paper written in lieu of an exam: in figuring this out, I am grateful to Alice Kaplan, emails of December 22, 2010. Sontag, *Reborn*, 54–55, incorrectly dates this entry as October 21, 1949; the notebook in which it appears begins with an entry of December 28, 1949.

16. Sontag, entry of December 2, 1950, *Reborn*, 56; Sontag, entry of January 3, 1951, *Reborn*, 62; Sontag, entry of February 13, 1951, *Reborn*, 65. In her diary she first mentioned Rieff in an entry dated November 21, 1950: *Reborn*, 56 (in the published diary this date is misdated as 1949). Although in the end she used the name of the man her mother married, at the time she debated the alternatives: the name of her biological father, of her husband (a choice she used in a story she wrote on the naming problem), and even, following Philip's suggestion, solving the problem by using a historical or fictional last name: Susan Rieff, story titled "Decisions," 1952, folder 7, box 146, SS-UCLA.

17. Sontag, entry of January 6, 1957, *Reborn*, 102; Sontag, entry of September 4, 1956, *Reborn*, 81; Sontag, entry of January 6, 1957, *Reborn*, 103. At Harvard and later in New York, the Judaic studies scholar Jacob Taubes and his wife Susan Taubes were among the important influences on Sontag.

18. Perry Miller, comment on Susan Sontag, "Some Notes on the Repudiation of Intellect in 19th Century American Literature," January 25, 1955, folder 8, box 152, SS-UCLA; Susan Sontag, "Plato's Philosophy of Pleasure," written for Philosophy 102, fall 1955, folder 6, box 149, SS-UCLA, 2 and 3. The material on her graduate work at Harvard is in boxes 149–52, SS-UCLA.

19. On Rieff, see Philip Rieff, *The Feeling Intellect: Selected Writings*, ed. Jonathan B. Imber (Chicago: University of Chicago Press, 1990); Kenneth S. Piver, "Philip Rieff: The Critic of Psychoanalysis as Cultural Theorist," in *Discovering the History of Psychiatry*, ed. Mark S. Micale and Roy Porter (New York: Oxford University Press, 1994), 191–215; Antonius A. W. Zondervan, *Sociology and the Sacred: An Introduction to Philip Rieff's Theory of Culture* (Toronto: University of Toronto Press, 2005). Jonathan B. Imber, "Philip Rieff: A Personal Remembrance," *Society* 44 (November–December 2006): 72–79, is a probing essay that contains, among other contributions, some information on Rieff's relationship to Sontag.

20. Philip Rieff, "Freud's Contribution to Political Philosophy," Ph.D. diss., University of Chicago, 1954, 40 ("difficult"); Philip Rieff, *Freud: The Mind of the Moralist* (New York: Viking, 1959), xvi ("unstintingly"; unless otherwise noted, references are to this edition); Rieff, "Contribution," 254 ("obedience"). For information on the collaboration between Rieff and Sontag, see James Toback, "Whatever You'd Like Susan Sontag to Think, She Doesn't" *Esquire*, July 1968, 60. For Rieff's later views of Sontag, see Philip Rieff, *Fellow Teachers* (New York: Harper and Row, 1973), 16; Philip Rieff, *Fellow Teachers*, quoted in Susan Sontag, 1975 interview with Robert Boyers and Maxine Bernstein, *Salmagundi* 31–32 (Fall–Winter 1976): 29–48, reproduced in *A Susan Sontag Reader*, ed. Elizabeth Hardwick (New York: Farrar, Straus and Giroux, 1982), 342–43. For how he acknowledged her not long after their marriage ended, see Philip Rieff, "Preface to the Second Edition," in *Freud: The Mind of the Moralist*, 3rd ed. (Chicago: University of Chicago Press, 1979), xxi. On the divorce agreement, see editor's note, Sontag, *Reborn*, 144.

21. Rieff, "Contribution," 114, 106, 109, and 115–16, and Sigmund Freud, quoted from *Psychopathology of Everyday Life*.

22. Rieff, *Freud*, 181–82.

23. Ibid., 156–57 and 184–85.

24. Alice Kaplan, phone conversation with author, November 3, 2010.

25. Lopate, *Sontag*, 49, and Acocella, "Hunger Artist," 447, say that for a year Herbert Marcuse lived with Sontag and Rieff. The best guess by Marcuse's son, conveyed to me by the grandson, is that Marcuse lived with Sontag and Rieff in 1954: Harold Marcuse to author, December 13, 2010, copy in author's possession. For a fictional story of a marriage that has autobiographical aspects, see Susan Sontag, untitled story, probably 1957, folder 1, box 271, SS-UCLA. To date this story I am relying on another about people she called Lee and Martin, dated January 1957, in folder 3, box 124, SS-UCLA. This is a story about

a marriage told from the woman's perspective and focusing on emotional turmoil, sex, the woman's role in shaping her husband's writings, as well as on the limitations that marriage and motherhood imposed on the wife's ambitions. The story also focuses on an abortion followed by fights over a pregnancy.

26. Philip Rieff, quoted from *Esquire*, in Rollyson and Paddock, *Sontag*, 41; Sontag, entry of September 4, 1956, *Reborn*, 81 ("dependencies"; emphasis in original); Sontag, entry of January 3, 1957, *Reborn*, 98–99 ("six years"); Sontag, entry of March 27, 1957, *Reborn*, 140 ("mystery").

27. Sontag, entry of January 15, 1957, *Reborn*, 128.

28. Sontag, entry of January 29, 1960, *Reborn*, 234 ("malice"); Sontag, entry of January 2, 1957, *Reborn*, 171 ("inhibit"). Her tutor at Oxford was Stuart Hampshire, a moral philosopher and literary critic. Among the authors whose works she read were Jeremy Bentham, Joseph Conrad, Feodor Dostoyevsky, André Gide, Johann Goethe, Herman Hesse, Henry James, Franz Kafka, Søren Kierkegaard, Gerard Manley Hopkins, Thomas Mann, Friedrich Nietzsche, and Leo Tolstoy.

29. Sontag, entry of December 31, 1957, *Reborn*, 165; Sontag, entry of September 7, 1962, *Reborn*. On her political and artistic engagement in Paris, see Rollyson, *Reading*, 10–11; Rollyson and Paddock, *Sontag*, 48–50; Sontag, entries for 1958, *Reborn*, 167–208.

30. Sontag, entry of January 12, 1958, *Reborn*, 182 (ellipses and emphasis in original); Sontag, entry of February 8, 1958, *Reborn*, 184–85; Sontag, entry of January 12, 1958, 183. For one version of the relationship between Sontag and Sohmers, see Sohmers Zwerling, "Memories," entries of December 22, 1957, February 25, 1958, March 15, 1958, and April 3, 1958. For another version, see these entries in Sontag, *Reborn*: December 30, 1957, 163; December 31, 1957, 165; January 6, 1958, 177; January 7, 1958, 180; February 8, 1958, 184–85; February 20, 1958, 189; July 14, 1958, 204. On how the memory of her relationship with Rieff shaped her new experiences, see Sontag, entry of July 14, 1958, *Reborn*, 204–5; Sontag, entry of July 16, 1958, *Reborn*, 207. For a discussion of Sontag's relationships with members of her circle—including Sohmers, Fornes, and Alfred Chester—see Edward Field, *The Man Who Would Marry Susan Sontag and Other Intimate Literary Portraits of the Bohemian Era* (Madison: University of Wisconsin Press, 2005), esp. xiii and 160–69.

31. Sontag, entry of early 1958, *Reborn*, 168–72; Sontag, entry of February 25, 1958, *Reborn*, 193; Zoe Heller, "The Life of a Head Girl," September 20, 1992, *Independent* http://www.independent.co.uk/arts-entertainment/the-life-of-a-head-girl-1552506.html (accessed February 22, 2011).

32. Tom Wolfe, "Seize the Power [1972]," in *The New Journalism*, ed. Tom Wolfe and E. W. Johnson (New York: Harper and Row, 1973), 30.

33. Obituary for Allan Kaprow, *NYT*, April 10, 2006, B7; Judith Rodenbeck, "Madness and Method: Before Theatricality," *Grey Room* 13 (Fall 2003): 68; Susan Sontag, undated entry from the 1960s, folder 8, box 125, SS-UCLA (emphasis in original). For a brief but suggestive picture of Sontag as a figure at Columbia, see Lopate, *Sontag*, 37–38. For a picture of Sontag later in her life, see Sigrid Nunez, *Sempre Susan: A Memoir of Susan Sontag* (New York: Atlas, 2011). In Sontag's papers there is relatively little material on her time at Oxford or Columbia.

34. Harriet Sohmers Zwerling, *Notes of a Nude Model and Other Pieces* (New York: Spuyten Duyvil, 2003), 61; the following entries in Sontag, *Reborn*: undated entry but probably late January 1960, 230–31; February 19, 1960, 241–42; March 14, 1960, 259; August 23, 1961, 281–82; September 15, 1962, 305; October 16, 1962, 309; and March 26, 1963, 314. Fornes wrote a play, *The Successful Life of 3*, first produced in 1965 and dedicated to Sontag, that focused on a love triangle, sexual rivalry, issues of faithfulness and sexual preference, and a divorce from an unhappy marriage: Irene Fornés, *A Successful Life of 3*, in María Irene Fornés, *Promenade and Other Plays* (New York: Winter House, 1971), 161–206.

35. Sontag, entry of November 19, 1959, 218 (second ellipsis in original).

36. Sontag, entry of November 17, 1964, "On Self: From the Notebooks and Diaries of Susan Sontag, 1958–67," *NYTM*, September 10, 2006, 56; Sontag, entry of December 31, 1958, *NYTM*, 53 (emphasis in original); Sontag, entry of December 24, 1959, *NYTM*, 54; Sontag, entry of December 24 1959, 221; Sontag, entry of September 19, 1961, *Reborn*, 292. See also Sontag, entry of December 9, 1961, *NYTM*, 55, and Sontag, entry of November 19, 1959, *Reborn*, 218.

37. Wolfe, "Seize," 30; William Phillips, "Radical Style," *PR* 36 (1969): 389. For a different version of how Sontag came to write for *Partisan Review*, see Rollyson and Paddock, *Sontag*, 66. For the symposium, see "Our Country and Our Culture," *PR* 19 (May–June 1952). This discussion of *Partisan Review*, and more generally of the world of New York intellectuals, draws on Richard H. Pells, *Radical Visions and American Dreams: Culture and Social Thought in the Depression Years* (New York: Harper and Row, 1973), 334–46; Alan H. Wald, *The New York Intellectuals: The Rise and Decline of the Anti-Stalinist Left from the 1930s to the 1980s* (Chapel Hill: University of North Carolina Press, 1987), 75–97 and 139–47; Alexander Bloom, *Prodigal Sons: The New York Intellectuals and Their World* (New York: Oxford University Press, 1986), 60–140, 177–78, and 198–203; Neil Jumonville, *Critical Crossings: The New York Intellectuals in Postwar America* (Berkeley: University of California Press, 1991); and James B. Gilbert, *Writers and Partisans: A History of Literary Radicalism in America* (New York: John Wiley and Sons, 1968). *Commentary*, founded by the American Jewish Committee in 1945, was edited by Norman Podhoretz from 1960 until 1995. Sontag's brief stint there came around the time of the death of its editor Elliot Cohen.

38. David Laskin, *Partisans: Marriage, Politics, and Betrayal among the New York Intellectuals* (New York: Simon and Schuster, 2000), 16 and 17; Sontag, undated entry, sometime between 1960 and 1969, bluish notebook, folder 8, box 125, SS-UCLA.

39. Kennedy, *Sontag*, 7. On her relationship to Barthes, see Sontag, preface to Roland Barthes, *Writing Degree Zero*, trans. Annette Lavers and Colin Smith (New York: Hill and Wang, 1968), vii–xx. Soon after his death, Sontag wrote two essays on Barthes: Susan Sontag, "Remembering Barthes [1980]," 169–77, and Susan Sontag, "Writing Itself: On Roland Barthes [1981]," in Sontag, *Sontag Reader*, 425–46. For other examples of her attention to the work of Roland Barthes, see Susan Sontag, ed., *A Barthes Reader* (New York: Hill and Wang, 1982).

40. Norman Podhoretz, *Making It* (New York: Random House, 1957), 115 (emphasis in original). Sontag's ambition was a prominent theme in critiques of her: Podhoretz twice raised the issue but then denied that there was any calculation behind her rapid rise.

41. Susan Sontag, entry of November 24, 1965, *NYTM*, 57.

42. Susan Sontag, "One Culture and the New Sensibility [1965]," in Sontag, *Against Interpretation*, 304; Lopate, *Sontag*, 50. See also Eliot Weinberger, "Notes on Susan," *NYRB*, August 16, 2007, 27.

43. Susan Sontag, "Against Interpretation [1964]," in Sontag, *Against Interpretation*, 7 and 14; Sontag, "Writing Itself," 439; Susan Sontag, "Psychoanalysis and Norman O. Brown's *Life Against Death* [1961]," in Sontag, *Against Interpretation*, 259.

44. Susan Sontag, "Happenings: An Art of Radical Juxtaposition [1962]," in Sontag, *Against Interpretation*, 269 and 272.

45. Sontag, "Jack Smith's *Flaming Creatures* [1964]," in Sontag, *Against Interpretation*, 227 and 229; see also, on the Arnoldian tradition, Sontag, "New Sensibility," 296.

46. Sontag, Boyers and Bernstein, interview, 337 ("modernists"); Sontag, "Against Interpretation," 13 ("sensory"); Susan Sontag," Opinion, Please from New York," *Mademoiselle*, April 1965, 58 ("language"; emphasis in original).

47. Susan Sontag, entry of January 16, 1965, in spiral notebook labeled "Nov. 1965—," folder 2, box 125, SS-UCLA ("appear"; emphasis in original); Sontag, "Happenings," 274 ("performers"); Sontag, "New Sensibility," 298, 300, 303, and 304. For the influence of Brown and Marcuse on Sontag, see Craig J. Peariso, "The 'Counterculture' in Quotation Marks: Sontag and Marcuse on the Work of Revolution," in Ching and Wagner-Lawlor, eds., *Sontag*, 168, fn. 2. For an exploration of the philosophical aspects of Sontag's analysis of pop art, see Sylvia Harrison, *Pop Art and the Origins of Post-Modernism* (Cambridge: Cambridge University Press, 2001), 171–207. For her later critique of Anglo-American critics for undercutting the importance of experimental modernists and turning away entirely from French postmodernists, see Sontag, preface to Barthes, *Writing Degree Zero*, vii and ix. See also Sontag, "Happenings," 271, where she followed the surrealists and Simone de Beauvoir in adopting a playful fascination with material culture.

48. Susan Sontag, undated entry titled "Gay Slang," which appears right after August 3, 1949, entry, Notebook 22a, folder 7, box 123, SS-UCLA. The connection here between gay culture and Sontag's mention of "camp" and "campy" is important, but some caution is in order: "camp" and "campy" are written in green ink and not, as is the discussion of gay slang, in pencil. In addition, the handwriting is different in the two sections. It is possible that at a point later than 1949 Sontag added the words "camp" and "campy" to this section. For a later discussion of expressions of camp, see Andrew Ross, *No Respect: Intellectuals and Popular Culture* (New York: Routledge, 1989), 135–70. For a recent discussion on the camp essay, see Peariso, "The 'Counterculture' in Quotation Marks," 164–68.

49. Susan Sontag, "Notes on 'Camp, [1964]'" in *Against Interpretation*, 287, 275, and 276; Susan Sontag, "The Literary Criticism of Georg Lukács [1965]," in Sontag, *Against Interpretation*, 90 ("apolitical"); Sontag, "Notes," 289 and 276–77. The essay originally appeared as Susan Sontag, "Notes on 'Camp,'" *PR* 31(Fall 1964): 515–30. For perceptive remarks on this essay, see Brick, *Age of Contradiction*, 82–83. Sontag developed some of these same points in "New Sensibility," 293–304.

50. Sontag, "Notes," 277, 278, 287, and 290.

51. Ibid., 286, 289, 287, and 291.

52. Kennedy, *Sontag*, 33; Susan Sontag, contribution to a symposium of American life titled "What's Happening to America," *PR* 34 (Winter 1967): 51.

53. Sontag, "Notes," 288, 279, and 290; Sontag, notes on a yellow piece of paper, folder 23, box 33, SS-UCLA. Sontag linked Jews and homosexuals as "the outstanding creative minorities in contemporary culture," representing respectively "moral seriousness" and "aestheticism and irony": Sontag, "Notes," 290.

54. Sontag, "Writing Itself," 437, 439, 440, 442, xxii and xxxiii. See also Sontag, "Notes," 282.

55. Susan Sontag, comment to unidentified person, quoted in Lopate, *Sontag*, 37 (emphasis Lopate's); "'Camp,'" *Time*, December 11, 1964, 75; Thomas Meehan, "Not Good Taste, Not Bad Taste—It's 'Camp,'" *NYTM*, March 21, 1965, 30; Robert Phelps, review of *Against Interpretation*, *Life*, January 21, 1966, 8. For a summary of reviews of the book, see Rollyson, *Reading*, 70–77. For other important comments on Sontag in this period, see Mary Ellmann, "The Sensational Susan Sontag," *Atlantic*, September 1966, 59; Albert Goldman, review of *Against Interpretation*, *Vogue*, April 1966, 110; "Sontag & Son," *Vogue*, June 1966, 96–97; Julian Moynahan, review of Sontag, *Against Interpretation*, *Observer*, n.d., probably 1966, folder 3, box 95, SS-UCLA; Benjamin DeMott, review of *Against Interpretation*, *NYTRB*, January 23, 1966, 5 and 32, and Jonathan Baumbach, "A Plea for Art Unexplicated," *Saturday Review*, February 12, 1966, 33. For a critical review that focused on the contradictions between Sontag's theory and her practice, see Thomas Samuels, review of *Against Interpretation*, *Nation*, February 21, 1966. 219–21. For an extended analysis of Sontag's career, one that fully captures the range of responses, especially from "middle-aged liberals" and "loudmouthed moral conservationists" in 1969, see Phillips, "Radical Styles," 388–400.

56. Sontag, "Opinion, Please," 58–59. On her distaste for celebrity status, see Phelps, review, 8; Toback, "Sontag," 59, 60, and 119. On courting New York intellectuals, see Toback, "Sontag," 115. On her turning away from a reputation as the author of the article on camp, see "The Role of the Writer as Critic," *Publishers Weekly*, March 28, 1966, 36.

57. Elisabeth Stevens, "Miss Camp Herself," *New Republic*, February 19, 1966, 24; John Simon, letter to editors, *PR* 32 (Winter 1965): 156 (the dictionary quote is from Eric Partridge's *Dictionary of Slang*); Susan Sontag, letter to editors, *PR* 32 (Winter 1965): 157–58; Herbert J. Gans, "Popular Culture in America: Social Problem in a Mass Society or Social Asset in a Pluralist Society?" in *Social Problems: A Modern Approach*, ed. Howard S. Becker (New York: John Wiley and Sons, 1966), 586–87, including fn. 68 on 587. Alicia Ostriker, review of *Against Interpretation*, *Co* 41 (June 1966): 83, used somewhat more coded language than Simon, denouncing Sontag for having "respect for the unconventional, the immoral, the extreme sensation, be it sensuous justification or madness." For a trenchant critique of Sontag from a democratic socialist, see Irving Howe, "The New York Intellectuals [1968], " in Irving Howe, *Decline of the New* (New York: Harcourt, Brace and World, 1970), 227, 257, 259, and 260. For her critique of the New Left for letting its bourgeois commitments undermine its radicalism, see Susan Sontag, "Some Thoughts on the Right Way (for Us) to Love the Cuban Revolution," *Ramparts*, April 1969, 6, 10, 14, 16, and 18–19. For critiques of her from conservative New York intellectuals, see Norman

Podhoretz, *Breaking Ranks: A Political Memoir* (New York: Harper and Row, 1979), 268; Hilton Kramer, quoted from *Commentary*, 1979, in Podhoretz, *Breaking Ranks*, 268 and 270. For the mixed feelings Phillips had about the role he unwittingly played in making her famous, see Phillips, "Radical Style," 389, and William Phillips, *A Partisan View: Five Decades of the Literary Life* (New York: Stern and Day, 1983), 256. For Kenneth Burke's assessment of the book, see Kenneth Burke to Susan Sontag Rieff, January 15, 1966, folder 47, box 82, SS-UCLA.

58. Cécile Whiting, *A Taste for Pop: Pop Art, Gender, and Consumer Culture* (Cambridge: Cambridge University Press, 1997), 178 (the reference was to Vivian Gornick, "It's a Queer Hand Stoking the Campfire," *Village Voice*, April 7, 1966, 20–21); Moe Meyer, "Introduction: Reclaiming the Discourse of Camp," in *The Politics and Poetics of Camp*, ed. Moe Meyer (London: Routledge, 1994), 7; Cynthia Merrill, "Revamping the Gay Sensibility: Queer Camp and *dyke noir*," in Meyer, ed., *Politics and Poetics*, 118. See also John D'Emilio, *Sexual Politics, Sexual Communities: The Making of a Homosexual Minority in the United States, 1940–1970* (Chicago: University of Chicago Press, 1983), 150, 158–60, 164, 170, and 173. Along lines similar to what Merrill and others have written, see Chuck Kleinhaus, "Taking Out the Trash: Camp and the Politics of Parody," in Meyer, ed., *Politics and Poetics*, 195. For continuing discussion of Sontag's attitude to homosexuality, see Lopate, *Sontag*, 36; Weinberger, "Notes on Susan," and the response by Suzanne Jill Levine, letter to editor, *NYRB*, September 27, 2007, 106; Barbara Ching and Jennifer A. Wagner-Lawlor, "Unextinguished: Susan Sontag's Work in Progress," in Ching and Wagner-Lawlor, eds., *Sontag*, 10 and 13–15; Terry Castle, "Some Notes on 'Notes on Camp,'" in Ching and Wagner-Lawlor, eds., *Sontag*, 23 and 29. For an important essay on Sontag written after her death, one that includes a consideration of her attitudes to her sexuality, see Terry Castle, "Desperately Seeking Susan," *London Review of Books*, March 17, 2005, 17–20. For the importance of camp to both gays and lesbians, see Esther Newton, *Cherry Grove, Fire Island: Sixty Years in America's First Gay and Lesbian Town* (Boston: Beacon Press, 1993), esp. chaps. 5–9; Fabio Cleto, ed., *Camp: Queer Aesthetics and the Performing Subject: A Reader* (Ann Arbor: University of Michigan Press, 1999). On the lives of gays and lesbians in New York in this period, see also Joan Nestle, *A Restricted Country* (Ithaca, N.Y.: Firebrand, 1987). For a theoretical consideration of lesbian sexuality, see Teresa de Lauretis, *The Practice of Love: Lesbian Sexuality and Perverse Desire* (Bloomington: Indiana University Press, 1994). For a discussion of the politics and ethics of sexual shame, see Michael Warner, *The Trouble with Normal: Sex, Politics, and the Ethics of Queer Life* (Cambridge, Mass.: Harvard University Press, 1999), 1–40.

59. See Rollyson and Paddock, *Sontag*, 74, 92–93, 152, 205, 250–52, and 266–78, for discussion of these issues.

60. Susan Sontag, "Thirty Years Later," in Susan Sontag, *Against Interpretation, and Other Essays*, rev. ed. (New York: Farrar, Straus and Giroux, 2001), 312; Sontag, quoted in Dick Schaap, "Breaking Camp," *Book Week*, March 13, 1966, 6. Parallels between Sontag and W. H. Auden and Oscar Wilde are worth noting. See W. H. Auden, review of Oscar Wilde's letters, *New Yorker*, March 9, 1963, quoted in Rollyson and Paddock, *Sontag*, 83. Field says that the origin of Sontag's essay on camp was her discussions with him about

an article by W. H. Auden on Oscar Wilde that had recently appeared in the *New Yorker*: Field, *Would Marry*, 164, and Rollyson and Paddock, *Sontag*, 47–48.

Chapter 10

1. Tomás Maldonado, *Design, Nature, and Revolution: Towards a Critical Ecology*, trans. Mario Domandi (New York: Harper and Row, 1972), 60; Adam Raphael, from the July 22, 1968, issue of *Guardian*, quoted in Reyner Banham, *Los Angeles: The Architecture of the Four Ecologies* (New York: Harper and Row, 1971) 16; Tom Wolfe, "Introduction," to *The Kandy-Kolored Tangerine-Flake Streamline Baby* (New York: Farrar, Straus and Giroux, 1965), xv–xvi; Tom Wolfe, "I Drove Around Los Angeles and Its Crazy! The Art World Is Upside Down," *Los Angeles Times*, December 1, 1968, Q18–19 ("Its" in original); Robert Venturi, March 21, 1991 comment at Pacific Design Center in West Hollywood, quoted in Joe Day, "Foreword to the 2009 Edition: After *Ecologies*," in Banham, *Los Angeles*, xv. Tom Wolfe, "Las Vegas (What?) Las Vegas (Can't hear you! Too noisy) Las Vegas !!!!" in Wolfe, *Kandy*, 3–22, played a key role in turning the attention of Venturi and Scott Brown to the importance of signs, symbols, and architecture in Las Vegas. For another essay along these lines, see Tom Wolfe, "Electro-Graphic Architecture," *Architecture Canada* 45 (October 1969): 41–47.

2. Mike Davis, *City of Quartz: Excavating the Future of Los Angeles* (New York: Vintage Books, 1992), 74. The books are Banham, *Los Angeles*, and Robert Venturi, Denise Scott Brown, and Steven Izenour, *Learning from Las Vegas* (Cambridge, Mass.: MIT Press, 1972). Izenour was one of the book's authors. The convention is to talk of the book as one by Scott Brown and Venturi. For a cogent discussion of the similarities and differences between the two books, see Nigel Whiteley, "Learning from Vas Vegas . . . and from Los Angeles and Reyner Banham," in *Relearning from Las Vegas*, ed. Aron Vinegar and Michael J. Golec (Minneapolis: University of Minnesota Press, 2009), 195–210. For a thoughtful treatment of the relationship between the two books and the work of a Los Angeles artist, see Alexandra Schwartz, *Ed Ruscha's Los Angeles* (Cambridge, Mass.: MIT Press, 2010), 130–62. A comparison of Banham's 1971 book with his 1972 video, *Reyner Banham Loves Los Angeles* (http://video.google.com/videoplay?docid=1524953392810656786#, accessed February 25, 2011), reveals that in the video he paid somewhat more attention to the Watts riots, offered more criticism of privatized communities, and remained equally skeptical about smog. Moreover, although in the video he reveals considerable wit and humor, there is no irony in his celebration of Los Angeles. On the place of Banham's book in the reconfiguration of architectural history, see Anthony Vidler, *Histories of the Immediate Present: Inventing Architectural Modernism* (Cambridge, Mass.: MIT Press, 2008), 107–55.

3. Reyner Benham, review of *Kandy-Kolored*, *New Society*, August 19, 1965, 25–26 (emphases in original).

4. Reyner Banham, *Theory and Design in the First Machine Age* (London: Architectural Press, 1960). For biographical information I am relying on Nigel Whiteley, *Reyner Banham: Historian of the Immediate Future* (Cambridge, Mass.: MIT Press, 2002), esp. 4–29. I have drawn on this book on a number of points, not least his discussion of the Los

Angeles book: Whiteley, *Banham*, 228–41. For an indispensable collection of Banham's essays, see Mary Banham et al., eds., *A Critic Writes: Essays by Reyner Banham* (Berkeley: University of California Press, 1996), which includes (301–39) a bibliography of works by and about him. The papers of Reyner Banham at the Getty Research Institute contain very little material for the period before 1970 that is not available elsewhere. William A. McClung, *Landscapes of Desire: Anglo Mythologies of Los Angeles* (Berkeley: University of California Press, 2000), explores changing views of Los Angeles and includes a short section (225–27) on Banham's book. Catherine Gudis, *Buyways: Billboards, Automobiles, and the American Landscape* (New York: Routledge, 2004), illuminates many of the issues Banham, Scott Brown, and Venturi considered. On how European intellectuals responded to Los Angeles and Las Vegas, see Richard Pells, *Not Like Us: How Europeans Have Loved, Hated, and Transformed American Culture since World War II* (New York: Basic Books, 1997), 165–68. Kevin Starr is the leading scholar writing about visions of California but none of his many works focuses on the relevant issues in period in which Banham was writing about Los Angeles.

5. Reyner Banham, "The Atavism of the Short-Distance Mini-Cyclist," *Living Arts* 3 (1964): 92; Reyner Banham, "Vehicles of Desire [1955]," in *Modern Dreams: The Rise and Fall and Rise of Pop* (Cambridge, Mass.: MIT Press, 1988), 66 and 69; Reyner Banham, "'Parallel of Art and Life [1953]," in *The Independent Group: Postwar Britain and the Aesthetics of Plenty*, ed. David Robbins (Cambridge, Mass.: MIT Press, 1990), 170; Reyner Banham, "Industrial Design and Popular Art [1960]," in Robbins, ed., *Independent*, 174; Felicity D. Scott, *Architecture or Techno-Utopia: Politics after Modernism* (Cambridge, Mass.: MIT Press, 2007), 5. Whiteley, *Banham*, 28, says Banham first visited Los Angeles in 1965 but Banham dates his first trip there in 1968: Reyner Banham, "Reyner Banham Writes the First of Four Pieces on Los Angeles," *Listener*, August 22, 1968, 235. However, for confirmation that his first visit was in 1965, see George A. Dudley to Robert Venturi, December 2, 1965, 283.22, VSB-Penn.

6. Reyner Banham, "The Glass Paradise [1959]," in Mary Banham et al., eds., *Critic Writes*, 37; Reyner Banham, "Design by Choice [1961]," in Mary Banham et al., eds., *Critic Writes*, 77; Denise Scott Brown, "Learning from Brutalism [1990]," in Robbins, ed., *Independent*, 203; Reyner Banham, "The New Brutalism [1955]," in Mary Banham et al., eds., *Critic Writes*, 11. For his later, more extended analysis, see Reyner Banham, *The New Brutalism: Ethic or Aesthetic?* (London: Architectural Press, 1966). For a discussion of Banham, the Smithsons, and New Brutalism, see Whiteley, *Banham*, 123–39. On his appreciation of futurism, see Reyner Banham, "Primitives of a Mechanized Art [1959]," in Mary Banham et al., eds., *Critic Writes*, 39–45. On his love of compact American design and gadgets, see Reyner Banham, "The Great Gizmo [1965]," in Mary Banham et al., eds., *Critic Writes*, 109–18. For his appreciation of technology, see Banham, *Theory*, 9–12. For his more extended attempt to recast the history of buildings in order to emphasize the importance of people other than architects, see Reyner Banham, *The Architecture of the Well-Tempered Environment* (London: Architectural Press, 1969).

7. Banham, *Los Angeles*, 235.

8. Banham, "Banham Writes," 235–36; Banham, "Roadside," 267–68; Reyner Banham,

"The Art of Doing Your Thing," *Listener*, September 12, 1968, 330 (emphasis in original). See also the following articles by Reyner Banham: "Banham Writes," 235–36; "Roadscape with Rusting Nails," *Listener*, August 29, 1968, 267–68; "Beverly Hills, Too, Is a Ghetto," *Listener*, September 5, 1968, 296–98.

9. Banham, "Beverly Hills," 296–98.

10. Banham, "Atavism," 91; Banham, *Los Angeles*, 238.

11. Banham, *Los Angeles*, 89–90, 111–12, and 124.

12. Ibid., 36, 23, 139, 38–39, and 49.

13. Ibid., 124, 129, and 132.

14. Ibid., 210, 222, and 214–15.

15. Thomas Hines, review of Banham, *Los Angeles*, *Journal of the Society of Architectural Historians* 31 (March 1972): 76; John Donat, review of Banham, *Los Angeles*, *RIBA Journal* 78 (May 1971): 218; Peter Plagens, "Los Angeles: The Ecology of Evil," *Art Forum* 11 (December 1972): 76. For reviews that appreciated how Banham challenged conventional responses to the city, see Richard Schickel, review of Banham, *Los Angeles*, *Co* 52 (November 1971): 97–100; Francis Carney, review of Banham, *Los Angeles*, *NYRB*, January 1, 1972, 26–29. On the response to Banham at the time and over time the growing appreciation for what he accomplished, see Day, "Foreword," xv–xxviii. For appreciations of how Banham's work reconfigured how we think about architecture and cities, see Anthony Vidler, "Foreword to the 2000 Edition: Los Angeles: City of the Immediate Future," xxxiii–xlviii, in Banham, *Los Angeles*, 2009 edition; Vidler, *Histories of the Immediate Present*.

16. Banham, *Los Angeles*, 17 and 25; see also 173 and 248. Whiteley, *Banham*, 237–41, discusses some of the limitations of Banham's book. On African Americans, compare Banham, *Los Angeles*, 173, with Banham, "Beverly Hills," 296–98.

17. Lawrence Alloway, "City Notes [1959]," in *Imagining the Present: Context, Content, and the Role of the Critic*, ed. Richard Kalina (London: Routledge, 2006), 69; Banham "Towards a Pop Architecture [1962]," in Robbins, ed., *Independent*, 175; Reyner Banham, "Mediated Environments, or: You Can't Build There [1975]," in *Superculture: American Popular Culture and Europe*, ed. C. W. E. Bigsby (London: Elek, 1975), 80; Reyner Banham, "Towards a Million-Volt Light and Sound Culture," *Architectural Review* 141 (May 1967): 335. On the Smithsons' incorporation of popular culture, see Richard Kalina, "Imagining the Present: Context, Content, and the Role of the Critic," in Kalina, ed., *Imagining*, 10. For information on Scott Brown and Venturi's careers, including bibliographies, see www.vsba.com (accessed February 23, 2011); David B. Brownlee, David G. DeLong, and Kathryn B. Hiesinger, *Out of the Ordinary: Robert Venturi, Denise Scott Brown, and Associates: Architecture, Urbanism, Design* (Philadelphia: Philadelphia Museum of Art, 2001), esp. the indispensable biographical essay, David B. Brownlee, "Form and Content," 2–89, and Diane L. Minnite, "Chronology," 244–51. For discussions of *Learning from Las Vegas*, see Aron Vinegar and Michael J. Golec, eds., *Relearning from Las Vegas* (Minneapolis: University of Minnesota Press, 2009); Kester Rattenbury and Samantha Hardingham, *Supercrit # 2: Robert Venturi and Denise Scott Brown, Learning from Las Vegas* (Abington: Routledge, 2007); Aron Vinegar, *I Am a Monument: On Learning from Las Vegas* (Cambridge, Mass.: MIT Press, 2008). The subtitle of the Las Vegas book appears in the 1977

edition, and not in the original 1972 edition, which was of a nonstandard and controversial design to which its authors objected. For a history of the city, see Hal Rothman, *Neon Metropolis: How Las Vegas Started the Twenty-First Century* (New York: Routledge, 2002).

18. Scott Brown, in Rattenbury and Hardingham, *Superscrit # 2*, 89; Denise Scott Brown, "Some Ideas and Their History," in Robert Venturi and Denise Scott Brown, *Architecture as Signs and Systems: For a Mannerist Time* (Cambridge, Mass.: Harvard University Press, 2004), 105–19; Scott Brown "Learning from Brutalism," 203–6; "Denise Scott Brown: A Biographical Note," in Denise Scott Brown, *Urban Concepts* (London: Academy Editions, 1990), copyright page; Denise Scott Brown, "Between Three Stools: A Personal View of Urban Design Pedagogy [1982]," in Scott Brown, *Urban Concepts*, 9–20; Denise Scott Brown, "Towards an Active Socioplastics," in Denise Scott Brown, *Having Words* (London: Architectural Association, 2009), 22–54; Andrea Gabor, *Einstein's Wife: Work and Marriage in the Lives of Five Great Twentieth-Century Women* (New York: Viking, 1995), 57–229; Denise Scott Brown, "Learning from Africa: Denise Scott Brown Talks about Her Early Experiences to Evelina Francia," *Zimbabwean Review* (July 1995): 26–29. For a richly suggestive discussion of the sources of the ideas that shaped them both, see Denise Scott Brown, "'A Worm's Eye View of Relevant Architectural History,'" *Architectural Record* 172 (February 1984): 69, 71, 73, 75, 77, 79, and 81; Denise Scott Brown oral history interview, Archives of American Art, October 25, 1990–November 9, 1991. Note to reader: Although I have been able to examine the papers of Robert Venturi, those of Denise Scott Brown, also housed at the University of Pennsylvania's Architectural Archives, were not available for me to examine before I completed work on the manuscript.

19. Denise Scott Brown, interview with Daniel Horowitz, Philadelphia, Pa., November 10, 2008 provides information on the parallel with Hamilton.

20. Scott Brown, "Learning from Brutalism," 205.

21. Alison Smithson and Peter Smithson, "But Today We Collect Ads [1956]," in *Pop Art: A Critical History*, ed. Steven Madoff (Berkeley: University of California Press, 1997), 3; Scott Brown, "Learning from Brutalism" 203. For their later critique of the Smithsons, including of their condescension toward the suburban tradition represented by people who lived in places such as Levittown, see Robert Venturi and Denise Scott Brown, "Learning from Lutyens: Reply to Alison and Peter Smithson [1969]," in Robert Venturi and Denise Scott Brown, *A View from the Campidoglio: Selected Essays, 1953–1984*, ed. Peter Arnell, Ted Bickford, and Catherine Bergart (New York: Harper and Row, 1984), 20–23.

22. See Gabor, *Einstein's Wife*, 182, on Scott Brown's response to the death of her first husband. On the situation at Penn, see Ann L. Strong and George E. Thomas, *The Book of the School: The Graduate School of Fine Arts of the University of Pennsylvania* (Philadelphia: Graduate School of Fine Arts, 1990), 146, and Scott Brown, "Worm's Eye," 69–81. Scott Brown shared with Gans an interest in Michael Young and Peter Willmott, *Family and Kinship in East London* (London: Routledge and Kegan Paul, 1957), a book that lamented the impact of urban redevelopment on urban villagers. Gans, she later wrote, challenged urban planners and architects to look at "social reality": Scott Brown, "Between Three Stools," 10. Scott Brown commented on Gans's book on Boston when it was

still in manuscript: Herbert J. Gans, *The Urban Villagers: Group and Class in the Life of Italian-Americans* (New York: Free Press, 1962), xii.

23. Scott Brown, "Worm's Eye," 77 ("Gans"); Denise Scott Brown, "Denise Scott Brown," in *Particular Passions: Talks with Women Who Have Shaped Our Times*, ed. Lynn Gilbert and Gaylen Moore (New York: Clarkson N. Potter, 1981), 316 ("skins"); Denise Scott Brown, "The Meaningful City," *Journal of the American Institute of Architects* 43 (January 1963): 30 ("agnosia"); Venturi, in Rattenbury and Hardingham, *Supercrit # 2*, 69. For her essay on the relationship between pop art and their work, see Denise Scott Brown, "Learning from Pop," *Casabella* 359–60 (December 1971): 15, 17, and 22–23. For an extended exploration of the impact of the work of Gans on her, see Scott Brown, "Towards an Active Socioplastics," 22–54. On the influence of Jackson, see Denise Scott Brown, "Learning from Brinck," in *Everyday America: Cultural Landscape Studies after J. B. Jackson*, ed. Chris Wilson and Paul Groth (Berkeley: University of California Press, 2003), 49–61. In important ways, Jackson led the way toward a new aesthetic: see his early appreciation of the highway strip (J. B. Jackson, "Other-Directed Houses [1956–57]," in John Brinckerhoff Jackson, *Landscape in Sight: Looking at America*, ed. Helen Lefkowitz Horowitz [New Haven, Conn.: Yale University Press, 1997], 185–97), and of new vernacular architecture: J. B. Jackson, "The Missing Motel," *Landscape* 15 (Winter 1965–66): 4–6 .

24. Robert Venturi, "Context in Architectural Composition," M.A. thesis, Princeton University, 1950, in Robert Venturi, *Iconography and Electronics upon a Generic Architecture: A View from the Drafting Room* (Cambridge, Mass.: MIT Press, 1996), 335. See also Robert Venturi, "An Evolution of Ideas," in Venturi and Scott Brown, *Architecture as Signs and Systems*, 7–11.

25. Brownlee, "Form," 20–29.

26. Robert Venturi, *Complexity and Contradiction in Architecture* (New York: Museum of Modern Art, 1966), 22. For an assessment of Venturi that both pays no attention to Scott Brown's contribution and incorrectly emphasizes the timidity of Venturi's architecture and criticism, see Tom Wolfe, *From Bauhaus to Our House* (New York: Farrar, Straus and Giroux, 1981), 103–43.

27. Venturi, *Complexity*, 52 and 59; Vincent Scully, introduction to Venturi, *Complexity*, 13; Venturi, *Complexity*, 102–3. For an analysis of this book, see Mary McLeod, "Architecture and Politics in the Reagan Era: From Postmodernism to Deconstuctivism [1989]," in *Architecture Theory since 1968*, ed. K. Michael Hays (Cambridge, Mass.: MIT Press, 1998), 684.

28. Robert Venturi, "Postscript," untitled folder, VSB-Penn (there is a somewhat different version of this statement on p. xii of the original edition of *Learning from Las Vegas*). On the sexist response, see Gabor, *Einstein's Wife*, 158–59; Mike Capuzzo, "Plight of the Designing Woman," *Philadelphia Inquirer*, December 10, 1992; Scott Brown, "Denise Scott Brown," in *Passions*, 315. On how to understand their working relationship, see Scott Brown, Horowitz interview.

29. Denise Scott Brown, in "Robert Venturi and Denise Scott Brown," in John W. Cook and Heinrich Klotz, *Conversations with Architects* (New York: Praeger, 1973), 265; Brownlee, "Form," 47–49, with the quote on 47. Scott Brown wrote about this experi-

ence at a number of points, including Denise Scott Brown, "Pop Off: Reply to Kenneth Frampton [1971]," in Scott Brown and Venturi, *Campidoglio*, 36–37. On their role in urban renewal in Philadelphia, see Christopher Klemek, *The Transatlantic Collapse of Urban Renewal: Postwar Urbanism from New York to Berlin* (Chicago: University of Chicago Press, 2011), esp. 96–97, 100, 102, 184–86, 194–99, and 212–16.

30. For an early precursor of the Las Vegas work, see Scott Brown, "Meaningful City," 27–32. On her role in first developing the studio, see Scott Brown, Horowitz interview. With Denise as the more important intellectual force in *Learning from Las Vegas*, they wanted her name first on the title page, a preference MIT Press did not honor: Gabor, *Einstein's Wife*, 195. There are actually several different versions of their work: early articles that ended up in the book; the first edition (Robert Venturi, Denise Scott Brown, and Steven Izenour, *Learning from Las Vegas* [Cambridge, Mass.: MIT Press, 1972]) and the revised edition (Robert Venturi, Denise Scott Brown, and Steven Izenour, *Learning from Las Vegas: The Forgotten Symbolism of Architectural Form* [Cambridge, Mass.: MIT Press, 1977]). Except where noted, I am relying on the 1977 edition because it is the one that has had the widest circulation and is more readily available. Rattenbury and Hardingham, *Supercrit # 2*, 26–48, reproduce some of the material from the often difficult to find first edition. Michael J. Golec, "Format and Layout in *Learning from Las Vegas*," in Vinegar and Golec, eds., *Relearning*, 31–47, examines the differences between the 1972 and 1977 versions. On the earlier studios, see Katherine Smith, "Mobilizing Visions: Representing the American Landscape," in Vinegar and Golec, eds., *Relearning*, 99. The best places to begin focusing on the immense amount of material on the Las Vegas book are Brownlee, "Form," Vinegar, *Monument*, and the essays in Vinegar and Golec, eds., *Relearning*. The essays I found most helpful in that book are Vinegar and Golec, "Provocation," 1–18; Golec, "Format," 31–47; Smith, "Mobilizing Visions," 97–128; John McMorrough, "On Billboards and Other Signs around (*Learning from*) Las Vegas," 129–46; Dell Upton, "Signs Taken for Wonders," 147–62; Aron Vinegar, "The Melodrama of Expression and Inexpression in the Duck and Decorated Shed," 163–93; Nigel Whiteley, "Learning from Las Vegas . . . and Los Angeles and Reyner Banham," 195–210.

31. Ibid., xiii and xvii.

32. Ibid., 87 and 129. Their particular contrast was between two buildings, Paul Rudolph's Crawford Manor in New Haven and their firm's Guild House in Philadelphia. For a full elaboration of the contrasts they were making, see "Table 2. Comparison of Urban Sprawl with Megastructure," Venturi, Scott Brown, and Izenour, *Learning*, 118.

33. For a discussion of postmodern architecture, see Robert M. Collins, *Transforming America: Politics and Culture during the Reagan Years* (New York: Columbia University Press, 2007), 150. The relationship of Scott Brown and Venturi to postmodernism generally is complex. Although many cultural critics have connected them to postmodernism, seeing *Learning from Las Vegas* as a key, even transformative text, Scott Brown and Venturi have distanced themselves from this broader movement: see Scott Brown, in Rattenbury and Hardingham, *Supercrit # 2*, 137, and Robert Venturi, in Rattenbury and Hardingham, *Supercrit # 2*, 141; Aron Vinegar and Michael J. Golec, "Instruction as Provocation," in Vinegar and Golec, eds., *Relearning*, 1.

34. Venturi, Scott Brown, and Izenour, *Learning*, xi. Golec, "Format," 37–38, ascribes this focus more to Scott Brown than Venturi. Denise Scott Brown was intensely aware of the sexist response to the book, which turned it from a collaborative effort into the work of Robert Venturi: Venturi, Scott Brown, and Izenour, *Learning*, xv–xvi; Denise Scott Brown, "Sexism and the Star System in Architecture [1975]," in Scott Brown, *Having Words*, 79–89. In their reviews, both Fred Koetter and Ada Louise Huxtable treated the book as if Venturi were the sole author; Koetter said he did this "in the interests of convenience": Fred Koetter, review of Venturi and Scott Brown, *Learning from Las Vegas*, *Oppositions* 3 (May 1974): 98.

35. Venturi, Scott Brown, and Izenour, *Learning*, 153. For the comparison of the two editions, see Venturi, Scott Brown, and Izenour, *Learning*, 155, with Venturi, Scott Brown, and Izenour, *Learning*, 1972 ed., 106. On Gans's work, see Herbert J. Gans, "Popular Culture in America: Social Problem in a Mass Society or Social Asset in a Pluralist Society," in *Social Problems: A Modern Approach*, ed. Howard S. Becker (New York: John Wiley and Sons, 1966), 549–620. Herbert Gans, *The Levittowners: Ways of Life and Politics in a New Suburban Community* (New York: Alfred A. Knopf, 1967), had appeared before the articles that made their way into Scott Brown and Venturi's book, while Herbert J. Gans, *Popular Culture and High Culture: An Analysis and Evaluation of Taste* (New York: Basic Books, 1974), had appeared between the appearance of the first and the revised editions of the book. In 1970 Venturi, Scott Brown and others developed a project on Levittown: see Denise Scott Brown, "Remedial Housing for Architects Studio," in *Venturi, Scott Brown, and Associates on Houses and Housing*, Architectural Monographs 21 (London: Academy Editions, 1992), 51–57. Scott Brown fully applied the class analysis of Gans's work book to architecture. For her most extensive discussion of the importance of Gans's taste cultures, see Scott Brown, "Architectural Taste," 41–51.

36. Denise Scott Brown, "On Pop Art, Permissiveness, and Planning," *Journal of the American Institute of Planners* 35 (May 1969): 184–86; Venturi, Scott Brown, and Izenour, *Learning*, xi, 6, 53, and 161.

37. Venturi, Scott Brown, and Izenour, *Learning*, 162. This discussion also draws on Venturi, Scott Brown, and Izenour, *Learning*, 104; Smith, "Mobilizing Visions," 101–16.

38. Venturi, Scott Brown, and Izenour, *Learning*, 90, 6, 8, 9, 13, and 6 (emphasis in original).

39. Ada Louise Huxtable, review of Venturi and Scott Brown, *Learning from Las Vegas*, *NYRB*, October 18, 1973, 47; Scott Brown, quoting an unnamed source, in Denise Scott Brown, "On Architectural Formalism and Social Concern: A Discourse for Social Planners and Radical Chic Architects," *Oppositions* 5 (Summer 1976): 102–3. For a list of reviews, see Rattenbury and Hardingham, *Supercrit # 2*, 149. Among the important reviews are Koetter's; Kenneth Frampton, "America, 1960–1970: Notes on Urban Images and Theory," *Casabella* 359–60 (December 1971): 25–35, which was a reply to Scott Brown, "Learning from Pop." For Scott Brown's forceful and compelling response, see Scott Brown, "Pop Off," 34–37. For a discussion of the role of Robert Venturi and Denise Scott Brown in the reaction against modernism, see Alice T. Friedman, *American Glamour and the Evolution of American Architecture* (New Haven, Conn.: Yale University Press, 2010), 225–30.

40. Scott Brown, "On Pop Art," 186 (emphasis in original); Scott Brown, "Architectural Formalism," 104 (the summary draws on the whole essay, 99–122). On Wolfe, besides *Kandy-Kolored*, see Tom Wolfe, *Radical Chic & Mau-Mauing the Flak Catchers* (New York: Farrar, Straus and Giroux, 1970), and Tom Wolfe, *The Painted Word* (New York: Farrar, Straus and Giroux, 1975), which Scott Brown drew on in "Architectural Taste," 44.

41. Scott Brown, "Pop Off," 34 and 37. For discussions of the book and the reaction to it, I am relying on Whiteley, "Learning," 204; Vinegar and Golec, "Provocation," 2; Vinegar, *Monument*, 4–18; Upton, "Signs," 147–59. To sample their private responses, see Mrs. Robert Venturi to Grady [Clay], November 26, 1968, 285.29, VSB-Penn; Robert Venturi to Peter Collins, April 2, 1968, 282.22, VSB-Penn; Robert Venturi to Tom Wolfe, January 16, 1969, 225.II.A.27.6, VSB-Penn; Robert Venturi to Edmund N. Bacon, November 21, 1967, 225.II.A.26.13, VSB-Penn.

42. Robert A. Fielden, "In Defense of the Strip," *AIA Journal* (December 1970): 64; Denise Scott Brown, review of Alison Smithson and Peter Smithson, *Urban Structuring*, *Architectural Design* 38 (January 1968): 7. On the site selection for pedagogical reasons, see Denise Scott Brown, in Rattenbury and Hardingham, *Supercrit # 2*, 113.

43. Denise Scott Brown, "Learning from Africa," 29; Scott Brown, "Pop Off," 35. The sources concerning her education on issues of race, poverty, cities, and social protest are abundant, but to begin, see Scott Brown, review of Alison Smithson and Peter Smithson, *Urban Structuring*, 7; Scott Brown, "Denise Scott Brown," in *Passions*, 311–23; Gabor, *Einstein's Wife*, 201–2. Robert Venturi and Denise Scott Brown, "Learning from Levittown," course description for spring 1970 Yale course, 225.II.A.443.01, VSB-Penn makes clear that central to this course was the lack in the United States of public housing or "social" housing for poor.

44. Scott Brown, "Learning from Africa," 26; Scott Brown, in Rattenbury and Hardingham, *Supercrit # 2*, 87.

Conclusion

1. For the persistence of moralistic positions, see Naomi Klein, *No Logo: Taking Aim at the Brand Bullies* (New York: Picador, 2000); Daniel Horowitz, *The Anxieties of Affluence: Critiques of American Consumer Culture, 1939–1979* (Amherst: University of Massachusetts Press, 2004), 252–54; Allan D. Bloom, *The Closing of the American Mind: How Higher Education Has Failed Democracy and Impoverished the Souls of Today's Students* (New York: Simon and Schuster, 1987). One way to see the changes in the last quarter of the twentieth century is to look at Juliet B. Schor and Douglas B. Holt, eds., *The Consumer Society Reader* (New York: New Press, 2000), which stands as a bookend opposite the book by Bernard Rosenberg and David Manning White. Among the other books that capture the changes are Neva R. Goodwin, Frank Ackerman, and David Kiron, eds., *The Consumer Society* (Washington, D.C.: Island Press, 1997); John Brewer and Roy Porter, eds., *Consumption and the World of Goods* (London: Routledge, 1993); Jennifer Scanlon, ed., *The Gender and Consumer Culture Reader* (New York: New York University Press, 2000); Lawrence B. Glickman, ed., *Consumer Society in American History: A Reader* (Ithaca, N.Y.: Cornell University Press, 1999); Don Slater, *Consumer Culture and Moder-*

nity (Cambridge: Polity, 1997). Eric J. Arnould and Craig J. Thompson, "Consumer Culture Theory (CCT): Twenty Years of Research," *Journal of Consumer Research* 31 (March 2005): 868–82, summarizes work in the professional field, with many themes reflected in the writings under discussion here.

2. In Schor and Holt, *Consumer Society Reader*, the key essays are by Jean Baudrillard, "The Ideological Genesis of Needs [1969]," 58–80, and Pierre Bourdieu, "The Aesthetic Sense as the Sense of Distinction," 205–11. Among other important writers in this vein, who are hardly in agreement, are Mary Douglas and Baron Isherwood, *The World of Goods: Towards an Anthropology of Consumption* (New York: Basic Books, 1979); Marshall Sahlins, *Culture and Practical Reason* (Chicago: University of Chicago Press, 1976); Colin Campbell, *The Romantic Ethic and the Spirit of Modern Consumerism* (Oxford: Blackwell, 1987); Michel de Certeau, *The Practice of Everyday Life*, trans. Steven F. Rendell (Berkeley: University of California Press, 1984); Fredric Jameson, "Post Modernism and Consumer Society," in *The Anti-Aesthetic : Essays in Postmodern Culture*, ed. Hal Foster (Port Townsend, Wash.: Bay Press, 1983); and the work of the anthropologists Daniel Miller and Richard Wilk. Marina Bianchi, ed., *The Active Consumer: Novelty and Surprise in Consumer Choice* (London: Routledge, 1998), contains essays by economists on how to understand the consumer as active, pleasure seeking inspired by novelty, and engaged in symbolic communication. Matthew Hilton, *Consumerism in Twentieth-Century Britain* (Cambridge: Cambridge University Press, 2002), 8–24, provides an excellent discussion of the issues in recent scholarship.

3. The book by Schor and Holt offers a variety of feminist perspectives, from Betty Friedan's emphasis on corporate domination; to intermediate positions of Janice Radway, Elizabeth Wilson, and Susan Bordo; to John Fiske's and Angela McRobie's more liberatory emphasis. The literature of feminism and consumer culture is immense but among the places to begin are Janice Radway, *Reading the Romance: Women, Patriarchy, and Popular Literature* (Chapel Hill: University of North Carolina Press, 1984); Judith Williamson, *Decoding Advertisements: Ideology and Meaning in Advertising* (London: Boyars, 1978); Women's Studies Group, Center for Contemporary Cultural Studies, University of Birmingham, *Women Take Issue: Aspects of Women's Subordination* (London: Hutchinson, 1978); Ellen Willis, *Beginning to See the Light: Pieces of a Decade* (New York: Alfred A. Knopf, 1981); Ann Snitow, Christine Stansell, and Sharon Thompson, eds., *Powers of Desire: The Politics of Sexuality* (New York: Monthly Review Press, 1983); Angela McRobbie, *Feminism and Youth Culture: From "Jackie" to "Just Seventeen"* (Houndmills: Macmillan, 1991).

4. To sample some of the most important late twentieth-century books on the globalization of consumer culture, see Arjun Appadurai, ed., *The Social Life of Things: Commodities in Cultural Perspective* (Cambridge: Cambridge University Press, 1986); Arjun Appadurai, *Modernity at Large: Cultural Dimensions of Globalization* (Minneapolis: University of Minnesota Press, 1996); George Ritzer, *The McDonaldization of Society: An Investigation into the Changing Character of Contemporary Social Life* (Newbury Park, Calif.: Pine Forge Press, 1993); Benjamin Barber, *Jihad vs. McWorld* (New York: Times Books, 1995); Thomas L. Friedman, *The Lexus and the Olive Tree* (New York: Farrar, Straus

and Giroux, 1999). In many ways, in *The Black Atlantic: Modernity and Double Conscious-ness* (Cambridge, Mass.: Harvard University Press, 1993) and other books Paul Gilroy completed the work C. L. R. James and Stuart Hall could not develop.

5. The classic statement on the connection between utopia and mass culture is Fredric Jameson, "Reification and Utopia in Mass Culture," *Social Text* 1 (Winter 1979): 130–48.

Index

Page numbers in italics refer to illustrations.

Abendroth, Wolfgang, 50
Adorno, Theodor: access to writings of, 33; on American popular culture, 378n24, 379n30; on audiences, 99, 109; on authenticity, 393n18; and Benjamin, 88, 95, 101, 102, 392n7, 393n25; on capitalism, 132; on cinema, 379n30; and Frankfurt School, 30–31; on gender, 22; and Habermas, 52, 58, 384n18; on jazz, 35, 379n34; literature on, 378n24; and mass culture debate, 20, 31–33, 84, 102, 376n6, 393n25; radio project of, 378n29; Riesman on, 400n21; in U.S., 90. Works: "The Culture Industry," 33–35, 50, 102; *Dialectic of Enlightenment*, 45, 49, 53, 74; *Mass Culture* contributions, 20, 31; "A Social Critique of Radio Music," 132; "Television and the Patterns of Mass Culture," 31–33, 35–36

adult education, British, 412n18; anticommercialism in, 413n24; contending forces within, 413n22; "culturalists" versus "workerists" in, 171; debates over, 171, 172; elitism in, 174; Hall in, 247, 249; Hoggart's work with, 17, 163, 168–75, 176, 188, 266, 411n13, 412nn14,17

advertising: Barthes on, 58, 68; capitalism and, 434n47; Eco on, 84, 390n70; Hall and Whannel on, 265–66; Hall on, 251; Independent Group on, 162, 205; Italian, 71; in Los Angeles, 342; materialistic, 41; McLuhan on, 142–45, 147–51, 194, 266, 404n49, 405n54; persuasion in, 251; playfulness in, 266; pop art in, 230; resistance to, 150; symbolic meanings of, 45, 137, 265; use of semiotics, 68, 72; Whannel on, 240; Wyndham Lewis on, 143, 404n43

African Americans: enslavement of, 110, 111; of Los Angeles, 341; Riesman on, 133; role

in social movements, 104, 107–8, 112–13. *See also* culture, African American
Agrarians, Southern, 155, 406n60
Alberoni, Francesco: *Consumi e società*, 72
Algeria, 63, 65; decolonization of, 385n31
Ali, Muhammad, 284
Alloway, Lawrence, 7, 16, 200, 227, 420n11; American experiences of, 218–19; on American mass media, 215; anthropological approach of, 216; on anti-Americanism, 424n35; on architecture, 345; as art critic, 216–19, 423n30; on cultural continuum, 216–17; education and career of, 203; at Guggenheim, 218, 219–25, 286, 427n62; in Independent Group, 202, 203–4, 221; with Institute of Contemporary Arts, 420n11; on mass arts, 205, 208; on mass audiences, 209; and Messer, 223–25; movie criticism of, 424n31; pop art exhibitions of, 215, 232; pop art writings, 232–33, 234, 419n3, 427n62; on popular music, 218; on postmodernism, 427n63; Riesman's influence on, 424n32; and This Is Tomorrow exhibit, 210, 217; on urban art, 217–18
Altman, Dennis, 3
Amis, Kingsley: *Lucky Jim*, 188, 241
Anders, Günther: "The Phantom World of TV," 31
Anderson, Perry, 258
anthropology: in cultural studies, 1, 5–6, 196, 216, 235, 378n28; Hall and Whannel on, 268; shift from literary theory to, 196, 362
anti-Americanism: British, 424n35; Canadian, 407n62; of 1950s, 65
anti-Communism: American, 65; James's, 106
anti-Semitism: denial of, 96; T. S. Eliot's, 37, 39; Wyndham Lewis's, 143
anti-Stalinism, 121, 362; of British Left, 178; in *Mass Culture*, 20; modernist sensibility in, 28; and popular culture, 9–10, 12

Index

Acknowledgments

Researching and writing this book has involved abundant pleasure and symbolic (and not-so-symbolic) exchanges. I benefited from the thoughtful responses of friends and colleagues when I presented my work. Early on this happened at the Department of American and Pacific Studies at Tokyo University, the Graduate Program in American Studies at Doshisha University in Kyoto, the Annenberg School for Communication at the University of Pennsylvania, the Five College History Seminar, my inaugural lecture for the Mary Huggins Gamble Professorship in American Studies at Smith College, the German Historical Institute in Washington, D.C., the University at Buffalo Law School, SPUI25 in Amsterdam, a conference on public intellectuals in Cambridge, Mass., and two reading groups in Cambridge, Mass. As I was finishing the manuscript I benefited from the response to my talks at Caltech, Occidental College, the Henry E. Huntington Library, and Scripps College. As the Ray Billington Visiting Professor in U.S. History at Occidental College in 2010–11, I benefited from the presence of colleagues and availability of resources at Occidental and at the Huntington Library, where I held a fellowship.

When I began this book, I imagined one shorter and less intensively researched than the one that resulted. Before long, I found myself compelled by what my research into materials, published and unpublished, revealed. Archives continually yielded wonderful material. Helping me in that process was the unstinting assistance of librarians whose holdings are mentioned in the notes. For nonarchival material I have relied heavily on the libraries of two institutions: Smith College, with its superb collections, supplemented by the interlibrary loan office, where Christina Ryan has been especially helpful; and the almost inexhaustible collections at Harvard, especially Widener's all-too-tempting holdings.

At the outset I had only the slightest inkling that my attention would shift to Western Europe, a move that required me to rely on translators. Jim Hicks and Fernando Fasce each helped me with essays by Umberto Eco. To be able to access material by Jürgen Habermas in German, I needed even more help. I prevailed on my friendship with Herwig Friedl, who generously provided translations and interpretations of some Habermas essays; Katharina Motyl developed fuller renditions. Conor McNally located early essays by Habermas. He then translated them, worked to help me understand them, and then more fully, almost as a coauthor on some key sections, was responsible for making my statements more accurate.

I am grateful to the editors of the *Buffalo Law Review* for granting me permission to incorporate into this book material that originally appeared as Daniel Horowitz, "David Riesman: From Law to Social Criticism," *Buffalo Law Review* 58 (July 2010): 1005–29, and to both the German Historical Institute and Palgrave Macmillan for allowing me to use material in Chapter 2 that will also appear as "Continental Europeans Respond to American Consumer Culture," in *Decoding Modern Consumer Societies*, ed. Hartmut Berghoff and Uwe Spiekermann (New York: Palgrave Macmillan, 2011).

The long list of people who offered suggestions, leads, and clarifications reminds me of the myriad forms in which scholarly exchanges come. At one point or another, and sometimes at multiple points, strangers, colleagues, and friends have pitched in. Though in some cases my notes extend the list, I can mention here only those who helped the most: Roger Abrahams, Paul Alpers, David Hollinger, Jonathan Imber, David Ingram, Alice Kaplan, Ken Marcus, Mena Mitrano, H. Vivian Nelles, Steve Whitfield, Rupert Wilkinson, and Karen Winkler.

I am grateful to colleagues who urged me on in ways that strengthened the book. More than she realized, at a critical moment Judy Coffin helped me see that the book was closer to completion than I imagined. Then in the spring of 2010 I turned to my two best writing buddies, Lynn Dumenil and Helen L. Horowitz, who pushed me to sharpen my argument and focus my prose. The two readers for the press, Howard Brick and Richard King, offered incisive comments, and my responses, which did not always match their recommendations, impelled me to greater precision and clarity. Then there is a group of readers who helped me with individual sections, and did so perceptively and unstintingly: Bob Boyers, Ben Clarke, Dennis Dworkin, Paul Groth, Jeet Heer, Doug Holt, Martin Jay, Alice Kaplan, Anne Massey, Kevin Rozario, Marla Stone, Cheryl Walker, Frazer Ward, Katherine Wheeler, Cécile Whiting, and Sean Wilentz. Other readers who generously read a late draft of the entire manuscript draft not only caught mistakes but also astutely pressed me on a range of issues: Kevin Mattson, Judy Smith, and Alison Isenberg.

My friendship with Peter Agree and Kathy Peiss led me to the University of Pennsylvania Press. From the earliest moment my editor, Bob Lockhart, made a commitment to support what I was trying to do. From start to finish he urged me on in more ways and with more understanding than I could have imagined was possible. Erica Ginsburg skillfully oversaw the transformation of the manuscript into a book.

Two institutions provided support that was important symbolically and materially. A fellowship from the John Simon Guggenheim Memorial Foundation for 2008–9 spurred me on at a crucial moment. I am deeply indebted to my colleagues and students at Smith College for providing me a home that was a continuous source of pleasure and encouragement. President Carol Christ, Provosts Susan Bourque and Marilyn Schuster, and the Committee on Faculty Compensation and Development of Smith College continually offered support that though material in nature was nonetheless important to me in what it communicated about their commitments. MacKenzie Brigham, Rosalie Genova, and Kimberly Probolus ably served as student research assistants. Above all, this book resulted from the transformative power of the American Studies Program at Smith. Thanks to the efforts of many, but especially Mary Maples Dunn and Jack Wilson, Helen L. Horowitz and I arrived at Smith College during the summer of 1988 as the first professors to have an appointment in the program, which was already fifty years old.

In my career I have straddled the intellectual worlds of history and American studies. At Smith if my institutional home was American studies, intellectually I continued to go back and forth between these two fields. I write this book as an intellectual historian. But I also do so as a result of my struggles to come to terms with European and American culture theory during my years at Smith, something intensely experienced with my students in the legendary American Studies 202, Methods in American Studies. Then there is the broadening circle of Smith colleagues in American studies. That circle begins with Helen L. Horowitz, with whom over the decades I have shared the pleasures of scholarship, teaching, and program development—and of course the sustained engagement in love and family. However, the circle of colleagues only begins with her. It expands to include senior colleagues who took on leadership of the program: Bob Averitt, Don Robinson, Rosetta Cohen, Richard Millington, and Michael Thurston. Then it widens further to include a group of younger colleagues. I know that Floyd Cheung, Jennifer Guglielmo, Alex Keller, Kevin Rozario, Steve Waksman, and Frazer Ward think I mentored them successfully, to the point of tenure and beyond. However, they should also appreciate how much they taught me, especially about how a more senior scholar learns from younger peers as he wrestles with new ideas and approaches.